VALENCES OF THE DIALECTIC

VERSO

VALENCES OF THE DIALECTIC

FREDRIC JAMESON

VERSO

First published by Verso 2009
Copyright © Fredric Jameson 2009
All rights reserved

The moral rights of the author have been asserted

1 3 5 7 9 10 8 6 4 2

Verso
UK: 6 Meard Street, London W1F 0EG
USA: 20 Jay Street, Suite 1010, Brooklyn, NY 11201
www.versobooks.com

Verso is the imprint of New Left Books

ISBN-13: 978-1-85984-877-7

British Library Cataloguing in Publication Data
A catalogue record for this book is available from the British Library

Library of Congress Cataloging-in-Publication Data
A catalog record for this book is available from the Library of Congress

Typeset in Garamond by WestKey Ltd, Falmouth, Cornwall
Printed in the United States by Maple Vail

for Roberto Schwarz and Grecia de la Sobera
and
for Perry Anderson

O Wechsel der Zeiten! Du Hoffnung des Volkes!

Contents

V. POLITICS

VI. THE VALENCES OF HISTORY

Part I. Making Time Appear

Part II. Making History Appear

PART I

THE THREE NAMES
OF THE DIALECTIC

Chapter 1

The Three Names of the Dialectic

Innumerable introductions to the dialectic have been written, although the tempo seems to be slowing down today. The sheer number of traditional "presentations," along with the historical changes that have taken place since their flood tide, suggests, that a new attempt might be useful, particularly if it takes into consideration all the new thoughts about thinking that have been pioneered since the critique of representation (Heidegger) and since structuralism. In addition, the Hegel revival, which seems as vigorous today as it will ever be, promises to ensure the inclusion of many indispensable "theological niceties" that a Marxism unschooled in Hegel left out or even censored.

Traditional presentations have tended to stage the dialectic either as a system on the one hand, or as a method on the other—a division that faintly recalls the shift of emphasis from Hegel to Marx. Both alternatives have been seriously discredited by contemporary, and even modern, thought: for while the ideal of the philosophical system has been seriously called into question since Nietzsche—how to go on claiming some unified system when even the self or subject is structurally disunified or dispersed?—that of method is no less disgraced by its obvious instrumentalization and by the radical opposition it necessarily carries within itself between means and ends. If the dialectic is nothing but a means, what can be its ends? If it is a metaphysical system, what possible interest can it claim after the end of metaphysics?

However, we will want to return to these two temptations, which hint at some deeper properties of the dialectic itself; and we will want to add a few more options, such as its relationship to temporality. For did not the dialectic, even in its Hegelian form, set out to inscribe time and change in our concepts themselves, and to show how some all-too-human longing for timelessness obscured the inadequacy of our mental categories and filtered out the glare of contradictions as such (a diagnosis Marx will recapitulate at the level of the everyday with the various doctrines of ideology)? Indeed, the omission of temporality in non-dialectical philosophy may well serve to identify what characterizes the latter as the most "natural" form of the ideology of daily life, and as that common sense which it is the vocation of the dialectic most often to rebuke (Aristotle and Kant then constituting the great summas of common-sense thinking and subject-object empiricism).

This un-naturality of the dialectic, its provocative and perverse challenge to common sense as such, might then itself be generalized into a kind of definition, by way of its natural enemies. For are these not, alongside ordinary, unphilosophical common sense, dogmatism on the one hand and empiricism on the other? The belief in solid concepts, on the one hand, and the certainty of real things, on the other—such are the sources of the most inveterate anti-dialectical positions, and of the various idealisms as well as the various positivisms, which Hegel will combat as so many forms of *Verstand*, while the Marxian diagnosis of reification comes at them from a different yet related direction (neither one presuming that *Verstand*, or common sense, or even reification itself, can ever permanently be dissipated, as though it were a mere illusion of some kind).

Yet have we not here begun to replicate the commonplaces with which we began, and to approximate something like a dialectical system with the suggestion of a content identified with temporality and contradiction, while the formal task of undermining non-dialectical attitudes and philosophies slowly begins to turn into a newer version of dialectical method? In fact, what has inevitably to be said is that this very opposition is itself dialectical: to resolve it one way or another is the non-dialectical temptation; while the deconstruction of each side of this alternative, rather than leading to the self-destruction of the dialectic as such, ought to offer a perspective in which the problem becomes its own solution.

Indeed, this is the perspective in which we might well attempt to turn our own current problem—the presentation of the dialectic—into a solution in its own right, namely, by dwelling on the various words with which we seek ritualistically to identify and to analyze something whose existence we have not yet even demonstrated. For the parts of speech offer so many camera angles from which unsuspected functions and implications might be seized and inspected; if they do not, indeed, bring with them their own metaphysical implications, in the shape of inevitable structural distortion.

So it is that to speak of the dialectic with the definite article cannot but reinforce the more universalistic claims of this philosophy, as well as its unity. At the same time this identification enhances its singularity, after the fashion of a proper name; and indeed, it is rare for the dialectic as such to be evoked in reference to any thinkers other than Hegel and Marx and people seeking to develop lines of thought affiliated with them.

But an indefinite article changes all this; and it is mostly in this form that dialectical moments are discovered and identified in other writers, such as Kant or Deleuze, Wittgenstein or Bergson, that is to say in non- or even anti-dialectical philosophies. Such identifications come before us as the laws of specific or isolated zones, within universes of an altogether different character; and tend retroactively to confirm our impression that the definite article (in the previous acceptation) seeks to convey some unified field theory and to project well-nigh scientific regularities. The indefinite article, however, generally seems to involve the discovery of multiple local patterns, and indeed, as we shall see shortly, of binary oppositions.

Finally there is the adjective "dialectical", which is generally used to clarify moments of non-dialectical perplexity and to rebuke established thought processes (such as an inveterate confidence in the law of non-contradiction). To identify a phenomenon or a formulation as dialectical is implicitly or explicitly to accuse the interlocutor of the lazy habits of common sense, and to startle us into a distinction between at least two kinds of thinking.

These three versions of the word may be enough to organize a more substantial account of the thing itself.

1. The Dialectic

To speak of the dialectic, with a definite article or a capital letter, as you prefer, is to subsume all the varieties of dialectical thinking under a single philosophical system, and probably, in the process, to affirm that this system is the truth, and ultimately the only viable philosophy—something like that "untranscendable horizon of thought" Sartre claimed for Marxism in our time.[1] I sometimes think this too; but nothing is *indépassable* and for the moment I merely want us to be aware of the problems such a position entails.

It first of all presupposes the unassailability of philosophy as such, something already questionable since Nietzsche and certainly exceedingly dubious since the emergence of what we call theory. If Hegel's was the last great traditional philosophy, the last philosophical system (to use one of his favorite words), then the omnipresence only yesterday of attacks on Hegel and of various strident anti-Hegelianisms may had as much to do with a disbelief in philosophy and in system as they did with the dialectic. (They also had much to do with the question of idealism, to which I will return later on.)

---

[1] Jean-Paul Sartre, *Search for a Method*, New York: Knopf, 1963, xxxiv. Hazel E. Barnes translates "indépassable" as "which we cannot go beyond." See "Question de méthode," in *Critique de la raison dialectique*, Paris: Gallimard, 1985, 14. Future references to *Critique de la raison dialectique* are denoted *CRD*.

i.

As for Marxism, there have clearly been any number of attempts to endow it with a philosophy of its own, and those range from positivism to religion, from pragmatism to structuralism, and passing through historicism and existentialism on their way to a Marxian analytic philosophy and a Marxian sociobiology. But the predominant form taken by Marxism as a philosophical system is surely that official philosophy so often in the West referred to as orthodox Marxism or even vulgar Marxism or Stalinism, and which Annette Michelson has aptly termed demotic Marxism; but whose official name, in the old socialist countries, was in fact dialectical materialism.

It will be useful at this point to recall the three fundamental points on which so-called Western Marxism[2] distinguished itself from this ideological relative which had come to power as an official state philosophy in one-third of the world. First of all, the various Western Marxisms reaffirmed themselves as historical materialisms, that is to say, as worldviews which did not posit the dialectical character of science or of nature. Then too, they were willing to embrace psychoanalysis, something to which dialectical materialism had been unremittingly hostile (and in a way, this inclusion of psychoanalysis not only modified and enriched the conceptions of ideology developed by the Western Marxisms, but also underwrote their claim to place culture and the superstructures on a plane of significance and determination as equal to the economic—even though from another perspective their inclination was to denounce and abandon the base/superstructure distinction altogether). Finally, the Western Marxisms voiced healthy doubts about the productive role of Engels in the development of the Marxist tradition, even though they acknowledged his achievements, particularly in his familiarity with the scientific writings of the period as well as with military theory.

I want to emphasize what the first and third points imply about dialectical materialism as such. The notion of the dialectic, with a definite article—of dialectics as a philosophical system, or indeed as the only philosophical system—obviously commits you to the position that the dialectic is applicable to everything and anything, and I use the ugly word "apply" advisedly. In order to qualify as a real philosophy, in other words, this one will also have to have a metaphysics of its own, that is to say, a philosophy of nature, something that necessarily includes an epistemology or, in other

---

[2] Perry Anderson names and crystallizes this tendency in his influential *Considerations on Western Marxism*, London: New Left Books, 1976. The Viconian agnosticism observed by Western Marxism about nature and natural science is, however, vigorously criticized, from a dialectical viewpoint, by John Bellamy Foster, in his pathbreaking *Marx's Ecology: Materialism and Nature*, New York: Monthly Review Press, 2000, which argues for a materialism in the lineage of Epicurus.

words, a dialectical philosophy of science. And here I would like to distinguish between a dialectics of scientific concepts of research and a dialectics of nature itself, the former seeming to me a good deal more plausible than the latter. Western Marxism, indeed, stakes out what may be called a Viconian position, in the spirit of the *verum factum* of the *Scienza Nuova*; we can only understand what we have made, and therefore we are only in a position to claim knowledge of history but not of Nature itself, which is the doing of God.

Ironically, the appropriation of science and nature by dialectical materialism—which was of course pioneered by Engels—can ultimately be traced back to Hegel himself, whose philosophy was never promoted by Soviet state philosophy, despite Lenin's enthusiasm for the *Logic*. Indeed, it can be argued that the very conception of a dialectics of nature is an idealist one, an argument that demands a moment's reflection in its own right, particularly owing to the critiques of Hegel and of idealism mounted in recent times by Althusser and others. It probably will not do to remind ourselves of the recurrently activist politics of so many idealisms from Plato on down; better to take on the problem of idealism from two distinct perspectives, the first of which is that of the philosophical problem of consciousness itself.

It is a problem which must be sharply distinguished from those of the so-called centered self and of personal identity and individuality; as well as from that of the psyche and its structure (the question of psychoanalysis); or indeed from those of self-consciousness or reflexivity (issues relating to the ideology of modernity as such); or finally from the various spiritualisms. The seeming ineradicability of idealism then in this sense results from the fact that human beings are incapable of imagining anything other than this element of consciousness in which we are eternally submerged (even in sleep); incapable therefore of theorizing this phenomenon in the light of what it is not—by virtue of the law that identifies determination with negation (Spinoza). Such agnosticism is not a defense of idealism as a philosophy, but rather an acknowledgement of the limit under which it must necessarily place all philosophy.

But what of that materialism in whose name the critique of idealism is most often waged? This is our second perspective on the problem of idealism, and here the idealists celebrate their conceptual triumphs, making it clear that the idealist position is not a substantive one in its own right, but rather draws its real power and finds its true vocation reactively, as a critique of materialism as such. For as thinkers from Berkeley on have demonstrated, the concept of matter as such is an incoherent one, what Deleuze would call a bad concept: it follows that, however intolerable the idealist position in philosophy may be, the materialist one is an untenable alternative. We might add to this Berkeley's interesting (well-nigh Deleuzian) observation that materialism robs our existential life and our bodily sensations and perceptions of their freshness and intensity by substituting for them just such a formless and non-immediate, sensorily unverifiable substratum as matter itself.[3]

The easiest solution to the problem is clearly the one which identifies the alternative between idealism and materialism as a binary opposition, and which thereby encourages the conclusion that the urge to decide between materialism and idealism is motivated by the "law of non-contradiction" and can therefore itself be ruled undialectical. The fact is that the choice between these alternatives is only imposed on thought which aspires to become a system or a philosophy as such: and with this we turn to the third feature of so-called Western Marxism to be elucidated, not only about Hegel, but also about Marx himself. I want to argue that neither is to be associated with the construction of a philosophy as such. In the case of Marx, this is historically obvious enough: for it was not Marx but Engels who invented Marxism and constructed this system in such a way that it could seem to be a philosophy in its own right or at least to demand completion by this or that philosophy.

ii.

The assertion seems a good deal more perverse when it is a question of a thinker so philosophically voluminous as Hegel, and so obsessively systematic in the construction of his various complementary subfields (logic, science, anthropology, law and politics, history, aesthetics, religion, the history of philosophy itself, and so forth). But in Hegel's case I will merely claim that, after the *Phenomenology*, it is Hegel himself who turns his own thought into a philosophy and a system; in other words, who, with the later collaboration of his disciples, produces something we may call Hegelianism, in contrast to that rich practice of dialectical thinking we find in the first great 1807 masterpiece. Such a distinction will help us understand that virtually all the varied contemporary attacks on Hegel are in reality so many indictments of Hegelianism as a philosophy, or, what amounts to the same thing, as an ideology. Indeed, the suffix "ism" always designates both, besides betraying the operations of what Lacan called the "discourse of the university,"[4] which is to say the irrepressible urge to identify all thoughts with a named source (as when we speak of the Hegelian dialectic or, indeed, of Marxism).

All of which is complicitous with the institutional self-perpetuation of philosophy itself. It is no doubt always amusing to observe the compulsion

[3] George Berkeley, *A Treatise Concerning the Principles of Human Knowledge*, in *The Works of George Berkeley*, eds. A. A. Luce and T. E. Jessop, London: Thomas Nelson, 1949, 27–33, 42, 72–74.

[4] Jacques Lacan, *Le séminaire, Livre XVII: L'envers de la psychanalyse*, Paris: Seuil, 1991.

offered by professional philosophers from Hegel to Althusser or Deleuze to waste their vital energies in the philosophical defense and apologia of philosophy as such. No doubt—and the work of Pierre Bourdieu is there to remind us of it—those of us in other institutional disciplines are driven in much the same way to our own analogous institutional self-justifications; but the emergence of theory in the past years has seemed to offer a space outside the institutions and outside the rehearsal of such compulsory rationalizations, and it is the claims of theory (if not its achieved realities) which allow us to grasp the limits of philosophy as such, very much including dialectical philosophy. I believe that theory is to be grasped as the perpetual and impossible attempt to dereify the language of thought, and to preempt all the systems and ideologies which inevitably result from the establishment of this or that fixed terminology. Deconstruction is thus the very paradigm of a theoretical process of undoing terminologies which, by virtue of the elaboration of the terminology that very process requires, becomes a philosophy and an ideology in its own turn and congeals into the very type of system it sought to undermine. The persistence of the proper name in theory, indeed—as when we identify various texts as Derridean, Althusserian, or Habermassian—only serves to betray the hopelessness of the nonetheless unavoidable aim of theoretical writing to escape the reifications of philosophy as well as the commodifications of the intellectual marketplace today.

Yet theory offers the vantage point from which the commodification of the philosophical system becomes visible and inescapable. This "end of philosophy" may be argued in another way as well, in terms of its aspiration to closure and its exemplification of one of the currently fashionable pop-scientific formulas, the one called Gödel's Law, which is supposed to exclude the possibility for any system to ground itself or to include its own foundation within its own axiomatic. I will in fact argue (in the next section of this book) that Hegel's is not a closed or circular teleological system; and that we are not to take Absolute Spirit as a historical moment, let alone any "end of history," just as we are not to take the ethical individual of civil society and constitutional monarchy as the culmination of social development for Hegel. Hegel is therefore not to be read as projecting a closed system, even though Hegelianism may be: but we also need to refuse the old ideological paradigm of closed versus open systems, a Cold War invention if there ever was one, part and parcel of the equally spurious concept of "totalitarianism."

One may very well welcome the current slogans of anti-foundationalism and anti-essentialism—and reread Marx himself as well as Hegel in the light of the demands they make on us—without ignoring the obvious, namely that these preeminently theoretical slogans and programs have already themselves become thematized and reified—in other words, have themselves begun to turn into foundationalisms and philosophical systems in their own right.

When it comes to philosophical and theoretical critiques of this kind, indeed, I think it is always best to assess their political content and to reevaluate them in terms of the situation for which they were designed. The attacks on Hegel, for example, have a very different significance for the European (Lefts, for which they functioned as critiques of communism and dialectical materialism, than in the United States, where anti-communism is a Cold War theme, and where "Hegel"—along with what we call theory itself in general—has the very different function of an onslaught on the whole Anglo-American tradition of empiricism and common sense. The philosophical attempt to undermine that tradition has of course its own political significance, but it is a radical one and quite different from the anti-communisms of the various European extra-parliamentary Lefts, however one may evaluate the latter.

I've said enough to suggest that it will be unwise to identify the dialectic as a unified philosophical system, and this, not merely because we are unlikely to want to endorse a philosophy of nature at this point in the development of the sciences, but also because we are no longer tempted, in the age of theory, by the traditional rhetoric of philosophy itself and its philosophical self-justifications. It is now time to explore some other possibilities—the notion of a multiplicity of local dialectics on the one hand, and also some conception of the radical break constituted by dialectical thinking as such.

But before moving on to those two other possibilities, it may be worthwhile proposing, not a further description of contemporary theory, nor even a more comprehensive theory of the dialectic as such, but rather some more local characterization of the distinctiveness of both Freud and Marx, psychoanalysis and historical materialism, as specifically differentiated from philosophy as such. I'm not particularly tempted by Alain Badiou's notion of anti-philosophy, a term he deploys for Lacan, as well as for seemingly non-systematic or fragmentary thinkers like Pascal and Nietzsche. One sees what he means, but the formulation tends to restore a certain centrality to that very philosophy of which such thinking was alleged to have been the critique or the negation.

But there exists, at least in the Marxist tradition, an old formula which does not yet propose a new concept even though it stakes out the ways in which both psychoanalysis and Marxism transcend the systematic closures of philosophy. This formulation is that of the unity of theory and practice; and while it does not yet use the word "theory" in a contemporary sense, it conveys rather vividly the way in which, for these two kinds of concept formation, concepts can never exist on their own, autonomously, but must always remain open to the completion of realities external to themselves:

thus the conceptualities of psychoanalysis are ultimately fully meaningful only by way of the analytic situation itself, of the pole of the Other, the analyst, outside individual consciousness: while in Marxism significance is finally only achieved by way of our concrete class situation and the act—individual or collective—within class history itself. These unities of theory and practice are therefore distinct from the implied autonomy of the philosophical concept and cannot in any sense be completed by philosophy but only by praxis.

iii.

As for Marx, and whatever his own responsibility for the transformation of his thinking into a philosophy (or a method) may be, we cannot undialectically abandon the claims of Marxism to be a system in quite so cavalier or relativistic a fashion, which would tend to reduce the quarrels between the dialectic and other philosophies to mere verbal epiphenomena. The rivalry between the various isms opens such debates to ideological analysis, and to the suspicion that each has some relationship to the dynamics of a group and its specific practices. In that case, the self-identification with "Marxism" is clearly a choice of group affiliation and a political act (just as the avoidance of such overt language might also be a political strategy). Just as clearly, the term is to be welcomed as a rallying point and as one of the possible signifiers around which new groups and collectivities might organize, just as the historical associations this word has accumulated might well, in specific national situations, turn people away.

Meanwhile, the organization of this signifier around a proper name is no longer, in consumer society, so peculiar a development as it might once have been: displacing the affiliation of the various isms but now implying commodification rather than *Weltanschauung*. Indeed, the thing called Marxism seems to stand uneasily between these two historical tendencies: it presents the appearance of the named theory (such as Derrideanism or Althusserianism), but at the same time evidently seeks to avoid the implication of the intellectual or quasi-religious sect conveyed by modern aesthetic or theoretical commodification and by the niche fragmentation of the modern consumer publics. Still, the ideological struggles within Marxism itself have generated their own named tendencies (Trotskyism, Maoism), Lukács and Althusser only being the most prominent philosophers to have lent their names to distinct theoretical movements which still claim to represent Marxism as such. Such struggle would seem to recapitulate an older religious schismatics; the complex substitutions of Lacan for Marx in Žižek's thought, meanwhile, also reflect the problem of the big Other or the central charismatic leader in revolutionary politics, and raise questions of collective organization alongside those of ideological content.

In any case, the presence of the proper name in the word "Marxism" may be taken to be the equivalent of the use of the definite article in this first acceptation of the word "dialectic"; and before leaving this first perspective, a final justification of this practice needs to be considered. In effect, this locution stands as a barrier to transcoding as such; to any attempt to restate the essentials in a more palatable vocabulary and in terms less historically and ideologically charged: a barrier, in other words, to any attempt to "pass," and to smuggle the philosophical or political essentials through without attracting attention. Sartre once wisely observed that an analysis is not dialectical unless you say so and identify it as such.[5] On a political level, James Weinstein has pointed out that, however else they differed, the three great moments of the American Left—Debsian socialism before World War I, the Communist Party in the 1930s, the New Left in the 1960s—all shared one fatal characteristic, namely the conviction that you could not talk socialism and revolution openly to the American people; a conviction not exactly calculated to promote either of those things.[6]

On the other hand, as far as words go, it can be argued that the word "socialism" is as historically tainted as the word "democracy" is in capitalism: socialism then bears the weight of everything oppressive or unproductive associated with the Soviet Union (if not, for communists, with all the betrayals of social democracy). To name this word, then, is at once to arouse suspicion and to awaken all the historical objections which it may not be fair to associate with the ideal, but which cannot practically be done away with for all that. This places us squarely in a contradiction in which not to use the word is inevitably to fail politically, while to use the word is to preclude success in advance. Does this not constitute an argument for changing the political and ideological language and substituting another one, effectively transcoding an older Marxism into something new? There is, however, I would argue yet a third possibility, and that is to deploy a language whose inner logic is precisely the suspension of the name and the holding open of the place for possibility, and that is the language of Utopia, which neither rules out the eventual return of the vocabulary of socialism nor offers a positive alternative (such as that of "radical democracy") which might then be appropriated in an altogether different and manipulative way.

---

[5] Sartre, "la connaissance dialectique est en fait connaissance de la dialectique," in *CRD*, 139–140.

[6] James Weinstein, *Ambiguous Legacy: The Left in American Politics*, New York: New Viewpoints, 1974.

iv.

The productive side of the scientific or metaphysical pretensions of "the dialectic" and of "Marxism" lies, however, not in their claim to constitute an absolute philosophical system, but rather in the negative function of both these versions—namely, the insistence on what cannot be omitted from the doctrine without transforming it altogether and losing its originality and its most radical implications. A lower-level example may be given in the case of that still scandalous notion which is the concept of ideology: the attempt in the 1960s and 70s to substitute the more acceptable notion of "practices" can only be evaluated by enumerating what is gained and what is lost in the transfer (and most notably what happens to the idea of social class in the process). Gramsci's substitution of "hegemony" for "ideology" is an even more complicated matter, whose exploration usefully enriches the whole problematic.

As far as "the dialectic" is concerned, it would seem that what is at stake in the most general way in its polemic effects is the belief in common sense or non-dialectical thought: *Verstand*, which in Marxism becomes that far more specialized and limited phenomenon called reification. But in Marxism the range of exclusions is much wider: summed up, no doubt, in phrases like "bourgeois ideology", the identification of the central non- or anti-Marxist themes is a crucial operation, which can pass from the lack of historicity of the classic political economists to the occultation of social class.

Still, neither one is thematized as such in Engels's famous recapitulation of the three laws of the dialectic, which it is now worth quoting in their entirety, for a definition of "dialectical materialism" which is far from outmoded:

> The law of the transformation of quantity into quality and vice versa;
> The law of the interpenetration of opposites;
> The law of the negation of the negation.[7]

To be sure, these laws of Engels are not themselves wholly without content (that is to say, they bear the traces of a situation in which their formation was meant to be a political act). The Hegelian language and conceptuality are designed to include reminiscences of various moments in Marx's economic analyses; that is, they are meant to signal a kind of general applicability of Hegelianism to the economic sphere, as well as to suggest the philosophical credentials and respectability of that Marxism qua philosophy which Engels is promoting here. At the same time, these "laws" are also meant to

---

[7] Friedrich Engels, *The Dialectics of Nature*, New York: International Publishers, 1940, Chapter 2.

suggest an immediate relevance to the science of Engels's time (Helmholtz and others), and thus to add in a formidable pedigree derived from the prestige of science and its applicability to, if not its derivation from, nature itself. As for history and politics, that is the area to which all this is to be applied: a third terrain we are then asked to scan for glimpses of the same regularities at work. And there are many ways of systematizing these "laws" even further[8]: indeed, just as Kant reduced Aristotle's categories to his four groups of triads, so any ambitious philosopher might be expected to demonstrate the unity of these three and to propound an even more general unitary abstraction under which they might fall (actually, we will try to do something like this in the next section).

But it is with the category of "law" that the most serious questions arise, as any careful reading of the relevant sections of Hegel's *Phenomenology* might suggest.[9] Law is predicated on a notion of inner and outer worlds, of a world of appearances or phenomena corresponding to an inner essence which subsumes them. A law notoriously covers a multitude of instances and thus calls for a casuistry (which constitutes legal studies and the legal tradition) which in the "casus"[10] is supposed to adjust the empirical contingency of the facts to the abstract universality of law—something even more problematic when it has to do with psychological or subjective laws, even those of historical decision—the "law of the heart," an inner frenzy having to do with individuality and universality, or worse yet, the ruse of reason, in which the world-historical individual is little more than a pawn in the hands of a suprahistorical Law that seems more like a big Other or transcendental subject. At any rate, Hegel's own analysis would seem to show that the dialectic is out to destroy the concept of law rather than to offer the chance of formulating some new ones. (But then in that case, what is the status of Hegel's own sequence of forms? Does it not betray some lawful regularities in the way in which one of these forms eventually yields to another one?)

At any rate, however practical this checklist of Engels may be philosophically, it is worth noting that it fails to include any of the themes Marxists might want to include in their fundamental definition of Marxism, namely social class, contradiction, or the base/superstructure distinction. To be sure, how people wishing to describe themselves as Marxists formulate what

---

[8] See Bertell Ollman on the various "categories" in terms of which the dialectic has been staged: "for Lukács, it was the concept of totality that played this role; for Mao, it was 'contradiction'; for Raya Dunayevskaya, it was the 'negation of the negation'; for Scott Meikle, it was 'essence'; for the Ollman of *Alienation* it was 'internal relations,' and so on." *Dialectical Investigations*, New York: Routledge, 1993, 26–27.

[9] G. W. F. Hegel, "Force and Understanding," in *Phenomenology of Spirit*, trans. A. V. Mill, Oxford: Oxford University Press, 1977. Future references to this work are denoted *PoS*.

[10] Andre Jolles, "Kasus," in *Einfache Formen*, Tübingen: Niemeyer, 1982, 171–199.

they take to be the core "beliefs" of the doctrine is an indispensable way of sorting out the possible varieties of Marxism (it probably would not any longer include historical inevitability). Would it include revolution (or does the absence of that concept designate revisionism or heresy)? We have already touched on ideology; what about modes of production? And so forth. The enumeration concerns the sine qua non: that without which a political or economic ideology could not really be considered to be Marxist. The rearrangement of all these indispensable themes into a system or a philosophy (or even a coherent system of "beliefs") is another task entirely, one for specialists or ideologists: yet it is on the conviction that such a system exists that the exclusionary moves, the anathemata and excommunications, are necessarily based.

As for the implied projection of a philosophical system in the dialectic, it can be taken as a distorted expression of a rather different dialectical requirement, namely that of totality. In other words, the philosophical claim of unity turns out to be a symptomal transformation of the deeper claim or aspiration to totality itself, about which any number of misconceptions need to be addressed. Right now, it is enough to say that totality is not something one ends with, but something one begins with; and also that it is capitalism as a new global system which is the totality and the unifying force (so that we can also say that the dialectic itself does not become visible historically until capitalism's emergence).

Our unexpected conclusion must therefore be that the notion of the dialectic as system has its uses as well as its disadvantages; and that it would therefore be profoundly undialectical to exclude this patently undialectical description of the dialectic (along with its opposite number, the dialectic as method, as will perhaps be corroborated in the next section) from any truly dialectical account of the dialectic as such.

2. Many Dialectics

The logical sequel to the definite article is the indefinite one: and it is clear enough that when we isolate dialectical moments in the work of non- or anti-dialectical thinkers, such as Nietzsche or Deleuze, Bergson or Wittgenstein, it is of a local dialectic we are speaking. In any case, this makes for multiple dialectics, of whatever dimensions or significance, and it is this plurality which cancels the claim of the dialectic to articulate the laws of a universe governed by some unified field theory or "theory of everything." The analogy with physics is in that case rather to be found in the way in which Newtonian law becomes a mere local system within an Einsteinian cosmos, as a set of properties valid for the human scale of our own everyday perceptual world, but irrelevant for the twin infinities (Pascal) which bound it on either side (the microcosm and the macrocosm). At that point the dialectic, which formerly reigned supreme, is reduced to a local law of this or that corner of the universe, a set of regularities observable here or there, within a cosmos which may well not be dialectical at all, but rather one of sheerest chance, of virtualities, say, or chaos theory, when not some altogether untotalizable and non-theorizable noumenon.[11] In fact, the dialectic itself claimed to do something of this subsuming when (in Hegel) it asserted its more universal superiority to the common sense or *Verstand* (understanding) posited as the local law of our everyday life in a physical world of objects and extension.

The notion of a local dialectic, or of many dialectics, can however take this metaphysical humiliation in stride, and now poses a rather different conceptual problem than the complexities of philosophical unity posed in the last section. For now we will be concerned to abstract a form of thinking sufficiently empty of content to persist throughout the multiple local dialectics we just posited; and to retain a recognizable and identifiable shape through a variety of materials, from the economic to the aesthetic, from the political to the psychoanalytic or even the natural sciences. But we will not want this form to have anything of the content of Engels's three laws, nor even of the Hegelian logical "moments"; indeed, we will want this abstract pattern to be as innocent of philosophical or ideological presuppositions as possible, even though we will eventually have to deal with the way in which its acknowledgement ultimately brings a whole commitment to Marxism with it in its train. The identification of such an empty form will no doubt have to build on the Hegelian groundwork, even though it need no longer struggle with the unrewarding starting point the latter had to navigate in its initial struggles with identity and with being as such.

For it now seems possible to abstract an emptier mechanism from the stages of Hegelian logic, one formalistic enough to claim application to an impressive variety of material and disciplinary, social and ideological, contents. In fact, that was exactly what structuralism achieved with the binary opposition,[12] and this is perhaps the moment to celebrate that breakthrough,

---

[11] The model is that of Newton's laws as a local feature of some vaster Einsteinian cosmos. See Ilya Prigogine and Isabelle Stengers, *Order Out of Chaos: Man's New Dialogue with Nature*, New York: Bantam, 1984, chapters 1 and 2.

[12] See Gilles Deleuze, "A quoi reconnâit-on le structuralisme?" in *L'île déserte et autres textes*, Paris: Minuit, 2002, 238–269; and François Dosse, *Histoire du structuralisme*, Paris: LGF, 1995. But already in his first book Hegel speaks of *Entzweiung* (translated "dichotomy" or "bifurcation"): "Dichotomy is the source of the need of philosophy ... Life eternally forms itself by setting up oppositions, and totality at the highest pitch of living energy is only possible through its own reestablishment out of the deepest fission. What Reason opposes, rather, is just the absolute fixity which the intellect gives to the dichotomy; and it does so all the more if the absolute

with which, in my opinion, and unbeknownst to the structuralists themselves, dialectical thought was able to reinvent itself in our time. To be sure, the seemingly purer formalism of the binary opposition had its own specific content; its linguistic origins in phonology seemed already to mark a fundamental distance from semantics and thus already from that conceptuality to which it was at once "applied." Meanwhile, the anthropological sources in Malinowski's exchange and Mauss's gift, although ambiguously mined for various political and psychological purposes, also retained their appearance as extrapolations after the fact: the various structuralist ideologies developed out of them can by now be omitted.

Even the primal production of meaning as such—which was the burden of Saussure's extraordinary formulation "differences without positive terms"[13] —is easily transferable to problems of the emergence of ideologies and indeed to social constructivism itself. Meanwhile, the doctrine of the binary opposition could serve as a fundamental weapon in the battle of a whole range of modern philosophical tendencies against an older Aristotelian common sense: and in particular against the notion of things and concepts as positive entities, as free-standing autonomous substances, with their own properties or accidents and their own isolated definitions, substances only later inserted into relationships and larger networks and structures. But in process-oriented thought it is the relationships that come first; while in the doctrine of the binary opposition, concepts are necessarily defined against each other, and come in constellations, of which the binary pair is only the simplest and most rudimentary form.

In Hegel, to be sure, this discovery is a historical one; that is, it is calibrated on the development of philosophy and takes place as an event when we pass over from simple externalizing thought (*Verstand*) to the more internal complications of reflection. At that point, identity begins to emerge as something that can only be distinguished from what it is not. It therefore not only signals the looming into view of the fullest constructional function of the negative, but also the appearance of difference as such, as something strangely inseparable from the identity from which it was supposed to be different: "the different is not confronted by *any* other but by *its* other… the

---

opposites themselves originated in Reason." *The Difference between Fichte's and Schelling's System of Philosophy*, Albany: State University of New York Press, 1977, 89, 91. An excellent account of the binarism of structuralism's founder is to be found in Jean-Jacques Nattiez, *Lévi-Strauss musicien*, Arles Paris: Actes Sud, 2008. And see, for a different kind of defense of the heuristic value of binary oppositions, Michael McKeon's dialectical masterwork *Origins of the Novel*, Baltimore: Johns Hopkins University Press, 1987, xiii–xv (and see also his remarks on Lévi-Strauss, 4–8).

[13] Ferdinand de Saussure, *Cours de linguistique générale*, Lausanne Paris: Payot, 1916, 166.

other's *own* other."[14] But this now at once fully dialectical process was already germinal within the binary opposition itself. (Meanwhile, Marx's analysis of the commodity form, in the famous opening chapter of *Capital*, Volume 1, offers a textbook exercise in binary oppositions which is at one and the same time their deconstruction and their critique: a demonstration of the necessary asymmetry of the equation and of equivalence as such, now unmasked as the "objective appearance" of non-identity.)

At this point a cascade of historical forms pours out: the dialectic of good and evil, but also that of subject and object; the dialectic of rich and poor and also that of male and female or black and white; the dialectic of Right and Left, but also of poetry and prose, high culture and mass culture, science and ideology, materialism and idealism, harmony and counterpoint, color and line, self and other, and so on virtually from the beginnings of history to its far future, if it has one (but let's not omit future versus past). We can imagine several ways of dealing with this unwanted empirical profusion of oppositions. They might, for example, all be folded back and assimilated into one great primal binary: that of gender for some feminist philosophers, that of power for Nietzscheans, and so forth. I would myself be tempted to assign this generative role to the ethical binary (good and evil); but it is also necessary that social class not be reduced in this way, no matter how fundamental its mechanism in historical change as such.

Meanwhile, we must also take note of the proposition, which developed rapidly in the period following the first structuralist discoveries, that the binary opposition is the paradigmatic form of all ideology, and that therefore, far from being celebrated as the elementary structure of all meaning, it is rather to be tracked down and eradicated as the fundamental mechanism of all false consciousness and social and political error. The methodological result of this view is, however, to make the binary opposition even more important than it was for the structuralist ideologues, and to encourage an unremitting confrontation with it as the privileged object of philosophical and theoretical study; and this is all we need to secure agreement on at present.

We must, however, now begin to generate the varieties of opposition enabled by this simple form, for it does not always express itself as a dualism, even though metaphysical dualisms (such as some of the ideological oppositions listed above) seem to stand as the strong form if not indeed the inner truth of the binary opposition as such. But dualistic oppositions posit absolute equals or equivalents, turning Hegel's minimal dialectic into an eternal alternation between identical forces which it is finally impossible to adjudicate: turning ceaselessly into one another in such a way that, as with

---

[14] G. W. F. Hegel, *Hegel's Logic: Part One of the Encyclopaedia of the Philosophical Sciences*, trans. William Wallace, Oxford: Clarendon Press, 1975 [1830], 172.

Manichaeanism, the forces of light become indistinguishable from those of darkness or good from evil. The fundamental problem of such mythic dualisms—their secret conceptual and even dialectical weakness, as it were —lies in the implication that each term or force is fully positive, and wholly autonomous in its own right. Yet as each is the opposite of the other one despite everything, it is hard to see where in that case that portion of negativity could come from which is presumably required of each term in order that it also be an opposite in the first place.

What will become apparent is that a variety of distinct oppositions can be identified, depending on the degree of autonomy claimed for each term of the initial opposition. Indeed, even the inaugural dead end of metaphysical dualism may well turn out to generate more productive developments than we have first suspected; while half a dozen other oppositional shapes also offer distinct lines of development in which a given dialectic proves to have far from predictable or stereotypical results for us. Our only rule, in the examples and illustrations that follow, will be a strict avoidance of the old pseudo-Hegelian caricature of the thesis/antithesis/synthesis; while our only presupposition will be the assumption that any opposition can be the starting point for a dialectic in its own right.

i.

We may begin with the inevitable degradation of a sheerly metaphysical dualism or Manichaeanism into the conventional opposition in which one term turns out to be more defective than the other one, or in other words in which that second term radiates a kind of essentiality or plenitude which cannot be ascribed to its alleged opposite. Sun-words and moon-words as the old Arabic grammars have it; and the situation seems to be one in which the moon-term is the opposite of its other, while that other in its autonomy is the opposite of nothing. This then seems to constitute a peculiar opposition in which only one genuine opposite exists: it shares the sorry fate of Evil, which once upon a time, in the original mythic dualism, shone with its own absolute brightness (or darkness, as the case may be); but which is now reduced to mere reflection of its other.

The new form will in any case be an asymmetrical one, in which we can identify a center and a margin, an essential and an inessential term. Here clearly we glimpse the fundamental structure of racisms and xenophobias, of sexism and ethnocentrism, of law and crime. It was probably Sartre who first denounced the structural oppression inherent in all such oppositions, which he so extensively identified in works like *Saint Genet*; but Foucault's subsequent analyses generalized and popularized these diagnoses, which probably extend through the entire range of conventional ideological binaries, from the metaphysical ones, such as good and evil, or subject and object, all the way through to seemingly more innocent conventional ones, such as north and south, up and down, arts and sciences, or First and Third Worlds. Race and gender categories are those which today most often trigger the alarm systems of ideological suspicion; and yet they also seem to return in the more philosophical forms of the opposition of race and gender to class (or to each other). Meanwhile the phenomenological opposition of left and right hands reminds us that something of the ineradicability of such asymmetrical oppositions lies in the biological centrality of the human body and in the existential singularity of its experience of space as such.[15]

Meanwhile, a rather different philosophical problem is raised by the logical objection that the instances we have enumerated are in fact not really binary oppositions at all, inasmuch as the subordinate term ought in principle to be able to be subsumed under the dominant one, thus offering at least a caricature of the pseudo-Hegelian synthesis we have been denouncing. Thus, the Slave is not the opposite of the Master, but rather, along with him, an equally integral component of the larger system called slavery or domination; and it is only with the reintroduction of individual existence that the two "aspects" become individual terms in their own right. This reintroduction is then a political intervention, and only then does the asymmetrical opposition take its place in ideology, as has already been suggested. Its "resolution" then presumably lies in the obliteration of both terms, or in other words the effacement of the opposition as such: this is classically what happens when, for example, Marx shows us that the only way in which class struggle can be eliminated lies in the effacement of the very category of social class as such (and of the system of value which produces it). Yet not only the more notorious "dictatorships of the proletariat" in recent socialist history, but also the interminable political arguments between assimilationists and secessionists in the realms of race, gender, and ethnicity, remind us that such "solutions" are far from being merely logical matters.

These asymmetrical dualisms also raise the issue of the negative and the negativity—a crucial one indeed in contemporary philosophy's critique of the dialectic as such. The Sartrean analysis of subject and other remains a dialectical one; while Foucault's subsumption of both terms under "power" should seem to generate a situation in which power has no opposite (or is its own opposite). I believe that this seeming impasse can at least be clarified by the suggestion that this particular type of opposition is to be grasped as the superposition of at least two binary systems: a purely logical opposition (in other words one in which we merely have to do with two equivalents) on which has been superimposed the quite different form of an opposition between essential and inessential or center and margin. Here the "negation" lies in the differentiation between the initial equivalents,

---

[15] See Rodney Needham, *Right and Left*, Chicago: University of Chicago Press, 1974.

while its ideological investment—the very content of domination itself—derives from the way in which this second opposition reappropriates the first one. The force of negation is then transferred from the latter to the former.

Yet the elimination of the opposition as such is not always desirable in situations in which it is somehow the dissymmetry itself which is productive and which is to be preserved. We may still think of these arrested asymmetrical oppositions as dialectical despite their immobilization, inasmuch as they solicit a puzzlement which alternates between separation and conflation, between the analytic work of the negative and the temptation of synthesis.

In the realm of aesthetics such a perpetual asymmetrical dualism can, for example, be found in Coleridge's opposition between Imagination and Fancy. The two functions can to be sure be read historically or chronologically, in which case "Fancy" designates the decorative work of eighteenth-century rhetoric, while "Imagination" names the new organic and natural powers of Romanticism which are called upon to supplant it. This reading emphasizes the contrast between the way in which Fancy operates through wit and detail, through "fixities and definites," as Coleridge puts it; and that force of Nature expressed in some vision or overall "act of creation," whose function is "to idealize and to unify."[16] At this level, the distinction is very much an implicit Romantic manifesto, which pits a neoclassical sensibility against the new Wordsworthian sublime. And it is this identification of the two modes which also authorizes their larger generalization to historical periods and in particular to the cultural logic of the Enlightenment period as it is denounced by the younger generation of the Romantics themselves. Here not only does the one term eclipse the other, but an ethical and even a political binary makes its firm choices and decisively rejects the poetics of the *ancien régime* in favor of the new and proto-modernist mode.

Leaving aside the explicit identification of Fancy with eighteenth-century association theory and that of Imagination with a far more Germanic tradition of objective idealism, Coleridge himself also often dramatizes his opposition in terms of thought modes, as though the summoning of Imagination were a call to the awakening (or reawakening) of a whole new kind of poetic power, of a type radically distinct from the mechanical shuffling around of Fancy's pre-given "counters," which require no creativity.

Clearly, it is an account framed by the perspective of the Imagination, very much to the detriment of Fancy; and not nearly so even-handed as that Kantian distinction between the beautiful and the sublime to which it is distantly related. Yet it is enough to think of the anti-Romantic positions of

---

[16] Samuel Taylor Coleridge, *Biographia Literaria*, London: J. M. Dent and Company, 1906, 145–146.

the New Criticism on such Fancy-oriented phenomena as wit and paradox to see how this particular bias could be corrected in the other direction.

Still, if these two forces are grasped as corresponding to functions of the mind—Imagination to the architectonics of larger form, say, or plot; Fancy to the execution of the work and its individual detail—then not only will the ratio between them remain permanently in force and determine the bandwidth or vanishing points of that variable scanning process inherent in reading; but the concrete text itself will also now be able to be seen as something of a unique or singular "synthesis" of the two axes. Yet this scarcely yields any permanent solution to the "contradiction," save perhaps for the perpetuation of certain generic stereotypes. Despite its grounding in some properly metaphysical gaps—between unity and multiplicity, or the sublime and the beautiful, between the metaphysical absolute itself, perhaps, and its empirical counterpart in physical time and space—it is hard to see how this opposition could be received in any non- or anti-dialectical way.

A related literary dualism on which I have often insisted has the function, on the contrary, of enlarging the gap between incommensurables and of staging their opposition as something approaching a contradiction. Clearly enough, it is this sense of crisis which the term "incommensurable" itself implies, namely the attempt to unify by way of translation and the coming up short against the absolute impossibility of doing so.[17] The outcome would then be similar to that static or arrested dialectic we have rehearsed above, in which no third term seems to propose itself beyond the unity of the negative opposites; except that here it is a fissure in being itself that seems to bring the process of unification to a halt.

An exemplification of this kind of dialectic might then be the incommensurability of plot and style in the novel, in which neither the macro-level of the narrative nor the micro-level of the language can be reduced to the other. It is an incommensurability which is less visible when, as in the early novel, language seems essentially to stand in the service of storytelling as such; or on the contrary in the modernist period when the narrative function seems to have been effaced by the foregrounding of language and style as such. But practical criticism faces an insurmountable dilemma when these two levels take on equal weight (or when, as with Dickens, a modernist sensibility rediscovers the realistic novelist's style as a value in its own right). This is not to say that critics and readers do not in practice invent solutions to this impossible and insurmountable difficulty: indeed, it is the very vocation of criticism to do just that, and the "solutions" vary from the positing of homologies between style and narrative to the detection of minute or garish

---

[17] Most strongly affirmed in Niels Bohr's theory of complementarity. See Arkady Plotnitsky, *Complementarity: Anti-Epistemology after Bohr and Derrida*, Durham, NC: Duke University Press, 1994.

ways in which they contradict or undermine each other. But these "solutions," which posit the essential organic unity of the work, in reality presuppose the existence of the fundamental dilemma in advance, thereby cutting themselves off from any theoretical or philosophical solution insofar as they already confront two separate entities which can only be reunified in some additive way, or by mechanical homologies.

This kind of dialectic is therefore not so much dualistic as it is revelatory of some ontological rift or gap in the world itself, or, in other words, of incommensurables in Being itself. The opposition then has as its function not the dialectical identification of two seemingly distinct existential items as being in reality the same, so much as the detection, where common sense presumed a continuous field of uninterrupted phenomena in an unproblematic real world, of strange rifts or multiple dimensions, in which different laws and dynamics obtain (as with gravity and electromagnetism).

Approaches to such ontological discontinuities can be found in all the disciplines. Leaving aside the only too well-known case of waves and particles in physics, there would figure prominently the irresolvable tension in social interpretation between history and sociology—or indeed between sociology and psychology (see below)—or event and structure, diachrony and synchrony, as such methodological antagonisms play themselves out in multiple forms and with multiple consequences.

More immediately dramatic, however, and full of lessons for the dialectic as such, will be the theory of the three orders in Lacanian psychoanalysis, which begins with an unabashed dualism, only slowly to evolve into a triad of centers (dramatized by Lacan in his image of the Borromean interlocking rings), and finally disintegrating or drifting apart under the latter's internal pressure. As is well known Lacan's three orders are identified as the Imaginary, the Symbolic, and the Real; yet as Žižek has so often suggested it is less misleading to see Lacan's notions in their historical evolution than to grasp them as a static system.[18] Readers of the first seminars will indeed appreciate the emphasis on the initial theorization of the Imaginary as a semi-autonomous zone of psychic reality, only at once to grasp the way it is called into question and repositioned by a critique in the name of the Symbolic. Yet the Imaginary is a good starting point in our present context, insofar as it is the very element in which dualism itself flourishes: the so-called mirror stage itself situates the Imaginary in the binary opposition between self and other, all the while deeply rooting it in the visual as such. The subsequent discovery of the Symbolic—although riddled with threes (as in the allegories of Irma's Dream and later on of the Purloined Letter)[19] and redolent of the

---

[18] Slavoj Žižek, *The Sublime Object of Ideology*, London: Verso, 1989, 73–75.

[19] Sigmund Freud, *The Interpretation of Dreams* in *The Standard Edition of the Complete Psychological Works of Sigmund Freud*, Vol. 4, London: Hogarth Press, 1958, Chapter

linguistic ideologies of a then dominant structuralism—does not so much constitute the mere addition of a third term as it signals a shift in registers altogether, and a wholly new dynamic.

Yet that dynamic will continue to play itself out dialectically, insofar as its strong form continues to lie in the intersection between the asymmetrical dimensions of the Imaginary and the Symbolic, or in other words in the "critique" of the former (or of the overemphasis of the former) by the latter. When that tension disappears, and the theoretical triumph of the Symbolic threatens to turn into some more orthodox celebration of a structuralist philosophy of language as such, Lacan resists; and this is the moment when his third term, the enigmatic Real, makes its appearance, as what cannot be assimilated to language. From being a shadowy horizon in front of which the older dualism played itself out, this new term now comes to offer a field of investigation in its own right, one which, from Seminar XI on, will tend to displace the other two orders altogether, in its emphasis on drives and part-objects, on "sinthomes" and gender, on knots (the latter then standing as something of a distant and allegorical memory of the system of the three orders with which Lacan had begun his prodigious theoretical journey).

We do not have to pursue the Lacanian adventure any further here (we might also have mentioned the theory of the four discourses as another illustration of Lacan's virtuosity as a thinker of incommensurables and discontinuities[20]); suffice it to underscore the new vocation this trajectory has opened for the dialectic itself. Now we may begin to hazard the guess that something like the dialectic will always begin to appear when thinking approaches the dilemma of incommensurability, in whatever form; and that the dialectic henceforth seems to be the shift of thinking on to a new and unaccustomed plane in an effort to deal with the fact of distinct and autonomous realities that seem to offer no contact with each other.

But this particular opposition (and others like it) is clearly not to be "solved" by a mere identification of the unity of such opposites: indeed, it is probably not to be solved at all, but rather approached in a different way, which remains dialectical but which illustrates another face of the dialectic altogether from the one just described. Indeed, these two versions of the dialectic (of "a dialectic of ...") may well be considered as the two extremes of binary possibility: on the one hand the identification of the opposites with each other, and on the other their greatest possible dissociation from each

2. See also Jacques Lacan, *Le séminaire, Livre II*, Paris: Seuil, 1978, chapters 13–14. For a comprehensive discussion of the range of interpretations of this, the object of Freud's first dream analysis, see Mladen Dolar's essay in *Maska*, Vol. 16, Nums. 1–2, Winter 2001, 58–65.

[20] Lacan, *Le séminaire, Livre XVII*, 99–135.

other while remaining within some minimal relationship which makes it possible to speak of both together as participating in an opposition in the first place.

The incommensurability thesis thus holds that each pole of the specific dualism posited by this version of the dialectic is governed by distinct laws and dynamics, which cannot be made to apply to or to govern the opposite term. Yet here again we must invoke the methodological caution already hinted at above, which draws the consequences from Hegel's distinction between "difference" and "diversity" as categories. The two distinctions might indeed be said to presuppose that proposed by Sartre (and following him by Bertell Ollman) between internal and external negations.[21] In other words, if the relationship between the two constitutive terms of the binary opposition breaks down into a mere external negation between two radically different items, the opposition passes over into an inert multiplicity of various things, all different from each other but entertaining no particular relationship.

It is clear enough that the formulation of the (internal) dialectic strongly emphasizes the interrelationship of the two phenomena, thus avoiding the problem of heterogeneous multiplicity, only to be confronted by a second danger, namely the possibility that difference might vanish altogether in some premature identity. In the case of the dialectic of incommensurables, however, the problem is the reverse: radical difference is certainly very strongly underscored in the concept of incommensurability but with the risk that the two phenomena thus contrasted may simply drift away from each other into the teeming variety of inert multiples. Here, then, powerful reasons must be invoked for positing any kind of relationship between the incommensurables, which is to say that some form of internal negation between the two must be theorized (something which also implies that while external negation can be relatively simply defined, internal negation will take a bewilderingly dialectical variety of forms).

It remained for Derrida to propose a temporalization of this non- or anti-dialectic—this blocking of the dialectic by incommensurability or the limitation of internal negation by external negation—or in other words a reincorporation of the dialectically inassimilable back into some new and enlarged dialectic as such:

> In the end everything we have said about the system comes down to a question of the "third." This third term can be taken as the mediator that permits synthesis, reconciliation, participation; in which case that which is neither this nor that

---

21 Sartre, "Critique de l'expérience critique," in *CRD*, 159–180. Bertell Ollman, *Alienation: Marx's Conception of Man in Capitalist Society*, New York: Cambridge University Press, 1976.

permits the synthesis of this and that. But this function is not limited to the form it has taken in Hegelian dialectic, and the third of neither-this-nor-that and this-and-that can indeed also be interpreted as that whose absolute heterogeneity resists all integration, participation and system, thus designating the place where the system does not close. It is, at the same time, the place where the system constitutes itself, and where this constitution is threatened by the heterogeneous, and by a fiction no longer at the service of truth. What particularly interests me here is that which participates in participation and non-participation.[22]

Yet what is suggestive is precisely the formulation of a closing and an opening, a participation and a non-participation. For we might equally well argue that the dialectic is, on the contrary, that the very moment in which the system confirms its structure as a closure—or in other words, it reidentifies itself as a philosophy (and thus necessarily a closed system)—it also reopens itself and begins all over again.

As philosophy or system, the dialectic—"the conventional one, of totalization, reconciliation and reappropriation through the work of the negative, etc."—is closed and indicted by the very opposition or irreducibility and heterogeneity which lies outside it and is inassimilable to it. Yet this excess or inassimilability itself constitutes a dialectic—"between the non-dialectizable and the dialectizable"—which potentially renews the dynamics of the process and opens up the possibility of a new and enlarged dialectic in its turn, the clock of dialectical temporality once again beginning to tick.[23]

The interpretation of Derrida's insight may also shed fresh light on the differences between deconstruction and the dialectic, at the same time that it (as a consequence) reconfirms their family likeness, that is to say that kinship which allows the differences to be articulated and perceptible in the first place.

For it is as though the dialectic moves jerkily from moment to moment like a slide show, where deconstruction dizzily fast-forwards like a film by Dziga Vertov. I intend both of these comparisons to carry their negative or critical note, which marks the inevitable debility of all thinking.

The dialectic proceeds by standing outside a specific thought—that is to say a conceptual conclusion about a problem (which might range from object to subject, from ethics or politics to philosophy, from the pragmatic to the epistemological, art to science, etc., etc.)—in order to show that the alleged conclusions in fact harbor the workings of unstable categorical oppositions. The paradoxes, antinomies, and ultimately contradictions which then historicize the previous moment of "conclusion" and enable a new

---

[22] Jacques Derrida and Maurizio Ferraris, *A Taste for the Secret*, Cambridge: Polity, 2001, 5.

[23] Ibid., 33.

dialectical "solution" then in some sense reincorporate this last back into "philosophy" or "system" and come as a new—more properly dialectical—conclusion in their own right.

So far, dialectics and deconstruction are consonant with each other: both work to bring up into the light the structural incoherences of the "idea" or conceptual "positions" or interpretations which are their object of critique. But where the dialectic pauses, waiting for the new "dialectical" solution to freeze over in its turn and become an idea or an ideology to which the dialectic can again be "applied" (as it were from the outside of the newly reformed system), deconstruction races forward, undoing the very incoherence it has just been denouncing and showing that seeming analytic result to be itself a new incoherence and a new "contradiction" to be unraveled in its turn. Whence the sense that deconstruction is a kind of nihilism (see the attacks on Paul de Man), that like Foucauldian madness, *elle ne compose pas*, it results in no result, no tangible outcome, but simply devours its own tail, and thus itself in the process. One of the outcomes thus devoured and unraveled is of course the dialectic itself, which paused too long, and became another ideology in its own right, yet another object of deconstruction.

ii.

The next of our logical possibilities will significantly put this first one in perspective, for it brings before us a binary opposition which cannot be considered asymmetrical to the degree that both of its terms are what can be considered negative ones, privative phenomena, and, in contrast to the fully positive forces of mythic dualism and of incommensurables alike, neither can assume a central or dominant role. Here it is not a matter of restoring the marginal term to wholeness, or of incorporating it in the positive or central term in which it was the flaw or crack, but rather of disclosing an equal fissure in its opposite, the hitherto positive term. Indeed, the language (and opposition) of positivity and negation is here subjected to a good deal of logical and metaphysical stress, to the degree to which it seems difficult to retain the qualification of negation in a situation in which there is nothing positive for the alleged negative to negate. Yet it is perhaps this very paradox which is expressed in that originary Saussurean paradox of a pure relationship "without positive terms," and in which identity or meaning are both defined by sheer difference.

It seems more appropriate at this point to insist on the diagnostic function of this kind of opposition, whose dialectic is certainly present in various places in Marx, but which does not know its full polemic deployment until we get to Lenin. For in this first set of examples the "unity of opposites" will be a classification of polemic targets, of the political strategies of those opponents which Lenin considers to be seriously flawed and ineffective.

Nonetheless, the argument, in *What Is to Be Done?* (1902), is startling and paradoxical. For here Lenin sends economism and terrorism off back to back, as it were, and mounts a powerful critique which envelops a gradualist social democracy (and a workerism based on the trade unions) as well as the "extraparliamentary" activities of extreme-left activists; both of them characterized by what he calls a "subservience to spontaneity":

> At first sight, our assertion may appear paradoxical, for the difference between these two appears to be so enormous: one stresses the "drab every-day struggle" and the other calls for the most self-sacrificing struggle of individuals. But this is not a paradox. The Economists and terrorists merely bow to different poles of spontaneity: the Economists bow to the spontaneity of the "pure and simple" labor movement, while the terrorists bow to the spontaneity of the passionate indignation of the intellectuals, who are either incapable of linking up the revolutionary struggle with the labor movement, or lack the opportunity to do so.[24]

It should be said that the polemic is not to be grasped as a dismissal of the content of either group. Lenin did not underestimate the significance of workplace issues or union organizing, any more than he dismissed the heroism of the dramatic acts of the students and intellectuals (his own brother, it will be recalled, was executed for planning the assassination of Czar Alexander III). But it is the extrapolation of both these social dynamics into a politics and a political strategy which he here stigmatizes as a union of bad opposites. We may see this dialectical procedure as the diagnosis of two distinct symptoms united in a single cause, namely "spontaneity"; or, following the Aristotelian method, we can see these two political flaws or deviations as the two extremes which can be avoided by adhering to that golden mean which is here the Leninist conception of the party (uniting intellectuals and the working class). The former, to be sure, has a greater resemblance to that moment of synthesis posited by the old thesis-antithesis-synthesis model, while the Aristotelian procedure is no less tired and stereo-typical. What is more seriously dialectical in these analyses remains the "paradoxical" proposition that the two positions under indictment are somehow "the same." But this is not only a union of opposites but also a union of negative terms.

We may observe another version of this same local dialectic in Louis Althusser's analysis of modern socialist history. Althusser also focuses on what is ostensibly a crucial opposition within left history, namely that between Socialists and Communists, and one which has taken the form, at various junctures, of a seeming incompatibility between Social Democracy

---

[24] V. I. Lenin, *Essential Works of Lenin*, ed. Henry M. Christman, New York: Bantam, 1966, 109.

and Stalinism (or, in ideological terms, between humanism and dogmatism[25]). These two poles, like Lenin, he sends off back to back as unacceptable sides of the same coin, on the grounds that both are secretly nourished by the ideological conviction of gradualism (or of what Walter Benjamin called progress). Social Democracy, in its pre–World War I heyday, believed in a gradual and peaceful transition from capitalism to socialism on the basis of the voting strength of its party; and later on, in the possibility of a gradual reform of capitalism from the inside and its transformation into a welfare state which would more or less constitute socialism. Stalin meanwhile believed in a continuous progress, via heavy industrialization, in which socialism could be achieved incrementally. For Althusser, both these positions, and the politics they project, are politically and intellectually pernicious owing to a single great flaw they share, namely the omission of class struggle. And although he seems to have had misgivings about the term, we may say that it is class struggle that restores a dialectical reading of history insofar as it necessarily proceeds by breaks and discontinuities, and not the uninterrupted (or "homogeneous") temporality of progress or inevitability. We may therefore speak of a dialectic of bad opposites here, which is less obviously overcome than in the positive strategy Lenin theorizes in *What Is to Be Done?*, but which can probably be identified in Althusser's situation as the promise of Maoism.

But it is time to give a literary or cultural illustration of this dialectic, which opposes both ideologies and practices (or, at the least, political programs and platforms), and which is thus an already partially superstructural one. Indeed, Georg Lukács's analysis of modernism (in literature) also links faulty ideological convictions with practical failure (in the production of bad books or poor art).[26] What is striking is that modernism is seen as having its own internal dialectic and taking two seemingly antithetical forms, naturalism and *symbolisme*. The historical contemporaneity of these two literary movements lends the analysis an attractive plausibility, and the effect of the identification is once again startling and dialectical. Lukács wishes to stigmatize naturalism as a mechanical aesthetic in which a premium is placed on description and on raw unprocessed data which are offered as objectivity and reality (he goes so far as to include the documentary materials and collage productions of the Dos Passos type in this category).[27] It is worth adding that the political function of this diagnosis lies in its veiled

---

[25] Louis Althusser, *Réponse à John Lewis*, Paris: Maspero, 1973, 85–88.

[26] Georg Lukács, *Realism in Our Time: Literature and the Class Struggle*, New York: Harper and Row, 1971.

[27] But now see Barbara Foley's discussion of Dos Passos in her extraordinary *Telling the Truth: The Theory and Practice of Documentary Fiction*, Ithaca: Cornell University Press, 1986.

attack on Stalinist socialist realism fully as much as in some call to Western radical writers to incorporate the "great bourgeois tradition" in something of a literary popular front (thereby offering the Soviets an alibi in their crackdown on "experimentation").

How is *symbolisme* (and its various later modernist poetic avatars) then to be assimilated to this diagnosis (and leaving aside corroborating evidence such as Mallarmé's admiration for Zola, along with the more obviously symbolic and poetic moments of the latter's production)? The analysis of *symbolisme* indeed makes much clearer what is being objected to in naturalism: for the procedures of symbolism in general result in the endowment of seemingly lifeless object with all kinds of superimposed and "symbolic" meanings. A meaningless object world is here posited which requires the supplement of subjective meaning in order to constitute suitable artistic material. But what Lukács deplores is less to be seen as symbolism's subjectivism than as its very starting point, namely the experience of the external world as somehow dead and meaningless, lifeless and inert, without any internal dynamic of its own.

But it was precisely to have posited this same ideology of the external world that gave naturalism its literary originality: to have embraced this world of lifeless extension and to have reproduced it in the only way possibly, namely the additive process of description and mechanical enumeration. This renewal of the analysis of naturalism, however, now gives us a key to the missing third term of the diagnosis, and to that norm against which Lukács finds both aesthetic movements wanting. It is indeed given in the title of one of the philosopher's most important essays, "Erzählen oder Beschreiben?" ("Narrate or Describe?"[28])—and the recommendation of narration then returns us to that realism with which the name of Lukács seems, for good or ill, indissociable. For the very possibility the "great realists" had of narrating (rather than of describing) is inherent in their view of the outside world as historical process, as a world of tendencies variously working themselves out in such a way that the putative object itself can never be "described" in the textbook sense of the word insofar as it is never static and will not sit for its portrait: it is already an implicit narrative and thereby holds a narrative meaning within itself that does not have to be imposed from the outside by subjective fiat or by symbolist transformation. The external world, however ugly or depressing, can never be inert or meaningless, if only because it has been historically produced and already has its meaning in historical production. Indeed, if seen in this way, Lukács may be said dialectically to rejoin his antagonist Brecht, for whom the very function of the so-called estrangement effect was to show how things considered

---

[28] Georg Lukács, "Narrate or Describe?" in *Writer and Critic and Other Essays*, ed. and trans. Arthur D. Kahn, New York: Grosset and Dunlap, 1970, 110–148.

natural (and thus inevitable or eternal) were in fact the results of human action (and could therefore be changed by other human beings). The presupposition of both aesthetics is the narratability of human action and human production.

At any rate, in Lukács we see something of a replay, on the aesthetic level, of the old polemics against mechanical materialism on the one hand and idealism on the other. The dialectical feature of these polemics lies, not in the fight on two fronts which is characteristic of so many conceptual arguments, but rather in the way in which the bad opposites are identified by way of a single underlying flaw or ideological error which they share. Thus the alleged moment of synthesis, in which the two distinct and dissonant phenomena are somehow reunited, precedes their separation rather than following and triumphantly overcoming it. But it would be equally mistaken to suppose that this local kind of dialectic posits some initial moment of unity which then breaks down into two distinct and seemingly antithetical results (and thus nostalgically posits an earlier unity to which we are encouraged to return): for what is at issue here is a union of negative opposites rather than positive ones, and their reidentification does not give us any new and positive value, but only an enlarged target of critique at a higher and more comprehensive level.

iii.

This is the point, however, at which we must again confront the pseudo-Hegelian triad and ask again, more insistently, whether it is not by way of the allegedly synthesizing third term that both Lenin and Lukács "solve" their problems. In the case of Lenin, it is well known that it is the institution of the revolutionary party which overcomes the collective paralysis of union activity and the individual futility of the anarchist "deeds" alike. And as for Lukács, has it not always been apparent that his doctrine of "realism" was meant to overcome both the mechanical materialism with which naturalism received its object and the narcissistic and solipsistic excess with which symbolism or modernism indulged its subjectivity? Realism then seemed to take the positive elements of both these pathological deformations and to unite them in a new kind of art; just as intellectuals and workers found a more productive combination and synthesis within the form of the Leninist party. The problem with such conventional formulations is that they omit Hegel's famous "labor of the negative," that is to say, they overleap the work of the so-called synthesis itself and the process whereby we reach the "progressive" from the earlier stage diagnosed by both theorists.

The proof is that in both cases the gap is papered over by sheer willpower: Lukács asks his writers to convert to critical realism by adopting the Marxian standpoint on reality, while Lenin, as is well known, relies on his formidable powers of argumentation and polemic, neither one acknowledging the deeper unconscious roots of ideology as the individual subject—writer or militant—sinks and disperses, by way of Freud's navel of the unconscious, into the multiple interrelationships of historical reality itself.

That process will be one, I want to argue, of neutralization,[29] and it will only be by way of a kind of negative work on the negative itself—do we really want to identify this as the famous "negation of the negation"?—that the new forms are to be produced. For Lenin's diagnosis, I will use the example of the Cuban revolution as a clearer small-scale and perhaps more successful process of neutralization.

For in the case of the Cuban revolution, a spatial or geographical "experimental laboratory" will be present which allows us to witness this process at first hand (via the theorization of Debray's *Revolution in the Revolution?*[30]). Indeed, the revolutionary *foco*—the isolated mountain camp from which guerrilla warfare is waged and in which a true revolutionary party is forged—will be a space in which both intellectuals and workers—these two essential components of the revolutionary party according to Lenin—lose their social determinations and become truly classless in the new revolutionary sense. Intellectuals are then physically removed from the specializations of academic work and the ideological temptations of the ivory tower and of purely intellectual labor; while the former factory workers and peasants who join the great movement in the Sierra Maestra will have abandoned factory alienation, the division of labor, and the subordinations of the workplace, the subalternity with respect to management or overseer, the professional habits of obedience and of Taylorism alike. In both cases, a powerful neutralization burns away everything that Lenin has diagnosed in his program-essay; the negative itself, we may say, has reduced all these individuals, not to their most elementary essence as commodity and labor power (as Lukács argued in *History and Class Consciousness*), but precisely to their elemental power as negation and revolutionary refusal, as agency, as a pure form of revolt in which they are all equal and from which new post-revolutionary forms can be expected to emerge.

As for art, it does not seem particularly rewarding to follow Lukács along a path which has not reached the aesthetic realizations he called for in the anti-fascist period (or later in the then socialist countries); and I will therefore limit this demonstration of neutralization in the arts to a unique trajectory within modernism itself. It may well be possible to argue that, from a formal perspective, modernism itself is dialectical to the degree to

---

[29] See for a fuller discussion my *Archaeologies of the Future*, London: Verso, 2005, 170–181.

[30] Régis Debray, *Revolution in the Revolution?*, Harmondsworth, England: Penguin, 1967.

which it is obliged to posit its own formal oppositions and to navigate them by way of invention and differentiation. Still, in that dismantling of convention we call modernism, certain artists have been more keenly aware of the dialectical nature of the process than others, thereby producing what it does not seem abusive to call a properly dialectical aesthetic program, even though it seems preferable to emphasize the role of the historical process in this development, rather than the consciousness of the artist and his or her intention. The issue is not whether Piet Mondrian—preeminent among such dialectical artists—was or was not Hegelian (whatever the verb "to be" might mean in this context), or whether his writings do or do not adequately articulate the philosophical dialectic as such (they do!)—but rather the objective moment in which the process of abstraction has gone far enough to reveal dialectical oppositions at work, and at work in a dynamic rather than a static fashion.

What Mondrian realized[31] was that cubism had stopped halfway in its move towards abstraction and that it had left intact and central a figure, a sculptural object, which continued to function as a representation and a mimesis, no matter how multiple its faces and dimensions. He resolved to dissolve even this figure itself, all the while realizing that the very concept or experience of the figure depended on a fundamental binary opposition, that between figure and ground: it was therefore necessary not merely to eliminate the figure but also to eliminate the ground against which it was perceived, or in other words space itself—a ground still persisting within the frame of the painting as a kind of three-dimensional illusion, a perceptual fiction or mirage. At the same time, Mondrian realized that it was not merely by eliminating the ground, but only by disabling this basic opposition itself that he would be able to do away with the centrality of the figure as well as to abolish the background of space itself, along with its planes.

It is indeed well known that the history of painting has been marked by aesthetic quarrels which were inevitably organized by binary oppositions (that between line and color is only the most famous of these); and it will be clear enough that several distinct positions or choices are logically possible when faced with such an alternative. One can make a stand for one or the other, and invent a practice whose aesthetic theory promotes one of these poles over the other one: Ingres or David versus Delacroix! One can however also attempt to invent a style in which the two are given equal prominence and somehow harmonized: this would be the famous "synthesis" of the pseudo-Hegelian triad. But one can finally also attempt to destroy the

---

[31] Here and in what follows I draw on the extraordinary readings of Yve-Alain Bois in *Painting as Model*, Cambridge, MA: MIT Press, 1991, and in the Mondrian chapters of *Art since 1900: Modernism, Antimodernism, Postmodernism*, New York: Thames and Hudson, 2004.

opposition by neutralizing their tension: this is presumably what Mondrian's deployment of straight lines of color attempts to do.

Even before that, however, we confront, without necessarily realizing it, an opposition between vertical and horizontal: for the human being who contemplates a picture on the wall is vertical and reads it vertically, even when—as in Mondrian—the canvas itself seeks to escape those coordinates and to exist in a world in which verticality and horizontality no longer constitute a meaningful opposition. When Jackson Pollock (whose early genius Mondrian himself was among the first to recognize) lays the canvas out flat on the floor and walks around it, he completes precisely this neutralization of the two-dimensional coordinates Mondrian sought to realize.

Yve-Alain Bois explores a number of such oppositions in Mondrian, whose fundamental doctrine—"all relationship is governed by one prime relationship; that of extreme opposites"[32]—is both profoundly Hegelian and structuralist *avant la lettre*. All of Mondrian's solutions aim to divest the painted surface of any possible optical center, any single place or element on which the eye might dwell for a moment at rest, reestablishing a hierarchy of features and in effect turning a process back into an object in space.

We may think, indeed, of Schoenberg's invention of the twelve-tone system, expressly designed in order to forestall the return of what might correspond in music to centrality and hierarchy, namely tonality as such. The idea was that if one emphasized any single note over the others, however fleetingly, a tonal center would begin to re-form in a kind of local field around it: whence the injunction not to repeat any note of the scale before passing through all the others in the row. Whether this horror of centrality has any equivalents in the philosophical realm is something we will want to consider later on in this discussion.

But this story (as Bois tells it) has an extraordinary twist ending: Mondrian had already gone through several systems in his pursuit of the truly abstract (and I hasten to add that his thinking was not only profoundly stimulated by Hegel, but was also encouraged and justified by the ideological attractions of theosophy and spiritualism). At the end however—and it is a destiny Bois compares to the ultimate fate of Balzac's painter Frenhofer, in *Le chef-d'oeuvre inconnu*—he understands that if one succeeds

---

[32] Piet Mondrian, *The New Art—The New Life: The Collected Writing of Piet Mondrian*, eds. Harry Holtzman and Martin S. James, Boston: Twayne Publishers, 1986, 30. The evolution of Mondrian's theoretical formulations may be described as a gradual realization that his initial language of equilibrium or harmony needed to be supplemented, if not replaced altogether, by a more negative sense of an "annihilation of form" (160), of an "equilibrium that neutralizes" (214). It is this difference between synthesis and neutralization which I have tried to theorize in Part 1, Chapter 11, of *Archaeologies of the Future*, referenced here in note 29 above.

in neutralizing these basic oppositions, one ends up with harmony and with a static equilibrium from which all opposition has disappeared (a path that will be taken by Malevich in the suprematist *Black Square*). One has not succeeded in neutralizing an opposition aesthetically unless one continues to keep that opposition and that tension alive: the very paradox of the aesthetic resolution of contradiction in the first place. So in his final canvas, *Victory Boogie Woogie*, the painter paints and repaints the extraordinary finished work, eliminating his own solutions one after another precisely because they have become solutions and have brought the process to a halt, and leaving the canvas unfinished at his death, as a tragic relic of the insatiability of the dialectic, which here ends up destroying itself.

It is interesting in this context to add that for Mondrian the vertical—the world, external human life—was essentially tragic[33] and that the vocation of the abstract non-dimensional non-space of the painting was very precisely to destroy the tragic in the name of something else. Yet that destruction now seemed to interiorize the tragic within its own seemingly interminable process. The paradox will indeed pose a properly Utopian question for us in the final section of this discussion.

iv.

Yet even dialectics are dialectical, and we cannot escape a fundamental problem in our presentation of the binary opposition and in the primacy of relationship it implies. The content of the binary may well be contradiction, a notion then somewhat attenuated by the formalistic mode in which this presentation has been cast (but to which we will return). Yet the absence of another relational concept normally associated with dialectics is somewhat more surprising: it is the failure of the word (or the concept) "mediation" to appear as such.

Mediation is not only the "black box" through which one state passes, on its mysterious metamorphosis into a radically different one. It also names relationship itself, the very inner link of the binary opposition, the equal sign which can signify either identity or difference, or indeed both at the same time. It is also a logical relationship which can itself be transformed into a temporal one. Meanwhile, as a term it clearly derives from a different philosophical family than the linguistic concepts of structuralism, raising doubts as to whether its baggage of Germanic overtones and undertones (no doubt of a theological nature) can ever sit comfortably with the Franco-Slavic derivations; whether "mediation" itself does not require mediation; whether we do not here confront yet another tension between time and space.

---

[33] Bois, *Painting as Model*, 181.

For it was never clear whether "mediation" designated what was to have been explained or itself constituted the explanation. Did it do away with the need for a third term, or stand itself, as Hegel sometimes seems to imply, as that third term from which the two extremes or opposites derive, as that one which becomes two? Nonetheless (we will return to the problem in Part 3 of this essay), the very history of the concept of mediation—that is, the fact that it already has a history and a past, that it is itself historical—ensures an analytic dissatisfaction with it, and the inevitability of the splitting of its atom by modern logic, which wants to find ever smaller and more elementary constituent parts (the same is true of negation, as Deleuze's work testifies[34]).

Still, we here approach a phenomenon as ultimate and as mysterious as the event itself, as change in time. It is all very well to evoke Engels's dialectic of quantity and to point to the moment when that final feather or speck of dust changes everything: change is not, for all that, explained or even grasped, it is simply named and observed. So also with sheer relationship; when two phenomena are juxtaposed, at what point do they cease to be two separate items and become united in that very unity called juxtaposition? At what point does difference begin to relate, and in the name of what can we deny the right to call the juxtaposition of incommensurables an opposition?

For it is with the incommensurables of modern science and philosophy that we again have to do here, those of nuclear physics and of Lacanian psychoanalysis. The concept of the incommensurable is at the very heart of contemporary philosophies of difference[35]; and we would need to know whether the dialectic is not powerful enough to transform this affirmation of radical difference into a new form of relationship; whether thinking is not dialectical enough to stretch and expand in order to include the unthinkable (Hegel's old reply to Kant, namely, that the setting of a boundary or a limit already exceeds and incorporates it). And we would need to know whether this is a decision we can ourselves somehow make, and in the name of what such a decision could possibly be made.

The binary opposition, meanwhile, is clearly a spatial concept or category, which can to be sure be called upon to take on temporal form and shape. It is also a horizontal one, somehow, and we may now raise the issue of its possible verticalities. What has seemed lacking in the dialectic for modern tastes (let's keep it at first on the aesthetic level) is something extraordinarily paradoxical, namely its negativity. How can one accuse a philosophical system or method of lacking negativity when it is wholly constructed around the negative and negation as such, and ceaselessly sings the latter's praises as the angelic choirs celebrate the godhead? Still, it might not

---

[34] Gilles Deleuze, *Différence et Répétition*, Paris: PUF, 1968.

[35] See above, note 19; and also Jean-François Lyotard, *Le différend*, Paris: Minuit, 1983.

be altogether undialectical to suggest that in some peculiar way the dialectic manages, over and over again, to turn the negative into a positivity (I take it that this is the burden of Deleuze's attack on negation in *Difference and Repetition*). If so, it is a serious matter, indeed, which demands an answer.

The objection is itself a profoundly historical one: and is not only (not even) primarily concerned with refuting the misuses of negativity in relation to absence, say, or to opposition. To be sure, nature (or being) is as full as an egg, there are no absences in it, and no oppositions either; how could nature possibly be dialectical when it does not even include such a thing as the negative? Such was Kant's argument long ago, and Sartre's only yesterday.[36]

But it seems to me that current anti-dialectical arguments have as much to do with positivity as with its opposite (if that is what the negative is), and reflect the obscure feeling that the dialectical conception of negation also makes positivity altogether too positive, and renders reality or being a

---

[36] See on this, for example, Kant's essay on negative quantity ("Versuch, den Begriff der negativen Grössen in die Weltweisheit einzuführen" [1763]) as well as Jean-Paul Sartre, *L'Être et le néant* (Paris: Gallimard, 1943, vi, 30–34). It will be observed that the need for a dialectical dereification would be obviated by avoiding reified terms in the first place; and this is essentially one of the deeper motivations of contemporary critiques of the dialectic. But this is easier said than done, and poses extraordinarily difficult writing problems, which are probably best solved by the multiplication of terms rather than their suppression. Brian Massumi's *Parables for the Virtual: Movement, Affect, Sensation*, Durham, NC: Duke University Press, 2002, is one of the rare examples of such an achievement, and it is predicated on the speed with which each new term is negated and replaced by yet a newer one. He justifies this procedure as follows (in a discussion of the representation of change as such): "It may seem odd to insist that a relation has an ontological status separate from the terms of the relation. But, as the work of Gilles Deleuze repeatedly emphasizes, it is in fact an indispensable step toward conceptualizing change as anything more or other than a negation, deviation, rupture, or subversion. The terms of a relation are normally assumed to precede their interrelating, to be already-constituted. This begs the question of change, because everything is given in advance. The interrelating simply realizes external configurations already implicit as possibilities in the form of the preexisting terms. You can rearrange the furniture, even move it to a new location, but you still have the same old furniture, assuming the precedence of terms in the relation is common to approaches characterized as empirical. Taking pregiven terms, extracting a permutational system of implicit positionings from their form, projecting that system to metaphysical point before the givenness of the terms, and developing the projection as a generative a priori mapping—these moves are common, in varying ways, to phenomenological, structuralist, and many poststructuralist approaches. They back-project a stencil of the already-constituted to explain its constitution, thus setting up a logical time-slip, a vicious hermeneutic circle. What is given the slip, once again, is change" (70).

massive element which is either there or not, and in which there are no degrees or gradations. It does not register, in other words, those qualitative ebbs or flows which an older psychology characterized as a drop in *niveau*, a still too subjective characterization, perhaps, of the waxing and waning of positivity itself. An enlarged conception of reality, it is argued, will be necessary to take account of these fluctuations (in which case the terms "positive" and "empirical" can be restricted to specific modes of appearance of that reality, and not identified with everything that is as such).

It is enough to confront an older dialectic with some of these newer levels or degrees of reality to appreciate the enlargement the dialectic is also called upon to make. From one direction, innumerable theories of virtuality reflect an increasingly informational cosmos and its technologies and at the very least confront a Hegelian tradition with the palpable need for new logical categories beyond those of the possible or the probable. From another level of reality, the peculiar new originalities of an image society pose problems not even Lacan's notion of the Imaginary is capable of solving and tend at their outer limit to substitute themselves for a traditional reality they seem capable of doing altogether without. But how can the simulacrum be said to be negative, and in what way do the seemingly untheorizable temporalities of photography—where the past is still present, even though long dead—offer any kind of handle on the dialectic?

Indeed, as far as time is concerned, a peculiarly contemporary temporal paradox seemed to confront the "teleology" with which the dialectic was always taxed: namely that Freudian *Nachträglichkeit*,[37] in which, "always already," an effect turned out to be its own cause. Very different from all the skeptical paradoxes of ancient sophistry, this one seemed not only to express a permanent present, but to carry the shock of feeling the results of a time become space itself. But in this case—space versus time—the dialectic would presumably still have something to say, as also in that other possibility that this paradox uses the notion of causality to undermine causality itself. In any case, however, such temporal paradoxes have known little attention in the dialectical literature, save perhaps in Althusserian analysis of revolutionary temporality.

Indeed, it is worth wondering to what degree the whole immense Heideggerian problematization of representation has impacted modern dialectical thought; yet surely the question of representation has marked the fundamental break with traditional philosophy, and constituted the source of all the multiple philosophical modernisms (if not, in another way, of the postmodernisms that followed them). Many of these problems and paradoxes were already registered concretely in the analysis of *Capital* and its

---

[37] See Jean Laplanche and J. B. Pontalis, "Après-coup," in *Vocabulaire de la psychanalyse,* Paris: PUF, 1971, 33–36.

causalities and temporalities, its modes of representation and derealization; but they were not thematized in the philosophies of Marxism that followed. We will see, particularly in the paradoxes of objective appearance, that Hegel himself was not altogether innocent of such realities, but the social system that developed after his death made them more unavoidable for us than for him.

V.

I come back, then, to the dialectic of the horizontal and the vertical in dialectics which is most strikingly developed in the doctrine of immanence. Does the success turn into a failure, in other words, as a chronological—that is to say, a horizontal—sequence of opposites; or is it already immanently inscribed as failure in and of itself? Does the opposite have to follow on its own opposite in order to generate the dialectical figures we have been considering; or is it possible that being and its negation may already coexist, may be superimposed, as it were vertically, in such a way that it suffices for us to contemplate a positivity with dialectical intensity for it to turn out to be a negativity under our very gaze? And if so, is this not simply yet another *Gestalt* alternation, or can it correspond to some deeper union of opposites within being itself?

Unexpectedly, the most dramatic illustration of this dialectical ontology is to be found in a literary work whose fuller analysis will be reserved until our final chapter, only its conclusions being noted here. The work itself is, however, one of the most famous in the Western canon, and debates about its literary qualities are only matched by the appropriation of those same qualities in the service of propaganda about the Greco-Roman/Christian "tradition" of Western Europe (a proto-political "value" associated with conservatives like T. S. Eliot). Indeed, the relative indifference of many modern generations to the elegiac mood of Virgil's Tennysonian verse has long been chastened by its standing as a classic, which brooks little levity (one thinks of Pound's joke about the sailor, who, referred to the noble poem's protagonist, Aeneas, exclaims, "Him a hero? Bigob, I t'ought he waz a priest").

David Quint's reading of the *Aeneid*[38] now changes all this, and, in a painstaking review of the ways in which the episodes of the epic pointedly recapitulate the relevant sections of the *Odyssey* (in the search for Rome) and the *Iliad* (in the overcoming of the Italic tribes), demonstrates that such elaborate overtracings are not to be dismissed as archival aestheticism or mere literary allusion, but make a decisive political point which is itself extraordinarily daring in the historical situation of the nascent empire and

---

[38] David Quint, *Epic and Empire*, Princeton: Princeton University Press, 1993.

indeed the presence of Augustus himself over the poet's shoulder. The Homeric poems are indeed "superimposed by a constant process of doubling and surcharge in which the victors of the *Iliad* are also, at one and the same time, the losers of the *Odyssey*, and Aeneas is called upon to assume both roles simultaneously. This simultaneity of victory and defeat also complicates the purely sequential understanding of peripateia; for if on the level of the Trojans' long voyage, the defeat in Troy turns around into the triumphant foundation of the Italian settlement which will eventually and providentially become Rome itself, the victory of the Trojans over the neighboring tribes recapitulates in a ghostly way their own grisly fate at the hand of the triumphant Greeks … the transformation of negative into positive becomes an ambivalent simultaneity, turning from negative to positive and back accordingly as we rotate the episodes in historical space."[39]

The *Aeneid* thereby emerges, not merely as the melodic and complacent epic celebration of the triumph of the last great "world power" and of the empire in all the glory of its own "end of history," tinged with the appropriate melancholy of the Virgilian "tears of things"; it also looms, in a kind of exact double and simulacrum of itself, through the appearance of its triumphalist verses, as the bitter critique of empire itself, as the implicit denunciation of the latter's brutality and carnage, as well as the prophetic warning of retribution to come.

Virgil therefore would seem to offer a quintessential case, not so much of dialectical ambiguity, as rather of the way in which the specification of the dialectic at work here, and the identification of the unity of opposites, allow us to read a subversive message delivered under the emperor's very eyes, and through the elegiac music of Virgil's verse. Now suddenly the poem seems to address its readers as follows: "you Roman victors, never forget that you are also the miserable losers and refugees of defeat and of the loss of your city and country!" It is as though, as in the Roman triumphs, an American writer of great quality had the courage to whisper in the ear of his public: "American warriors and conquerors of empire and business alike, never forget that you are also the cowardly migrants from a tyrannical old regime you preferred to flee rather than to transform!"[40]

---

[39] I here quote myself in advance, see below, 560.

[40] This is essentially Marx's response to Cabet's Icaria, denouncing the emigration of potential revolutionaries: "If those honest people who struggle for a better future leave, they will leave the arena completely open to the obscurants and the rogues … Brothers, stay at the battlefront of Europe. Work and struggle here, because only Europe has all the elements of communal wealth. This type of community will be established here, or nowhere." Quoted in Louis Marin, *Utopics: A Spatial Play*, Atlantic Highlands, NJ: Humanities Press International, 1984, 273–279.

In history, indeed, the negative and the positive seem fatally to assume the form of success and failure, triumph and defeat, as though these categories, above and beyond the superficial, allegedly Hegelian illusions of teleology, offered the only ways in which biological human individuals could imagine the destiny of their collectivities. The dialectical union of these opposites is then a social rebuke as well as a political lesson. It reminds us, not only that "success" was never really in the cards for mortal beings in the first place, but also that history progresses, not by way of victory but by way of defeat: and that if our eyes are trained to see it, we can find this dialectic at work everywhere in the record of our collective existence.[41]

I select, as another and final document in this particular file, Thomas Friedman's popular and starry-eyed celebration of the wonders of globalization, and in particular his truly dialectical narrative of the fate of India in the new dispensation. Friedman is reflecting on the way in which one of the fundamental forces at work in globalization, the informational-technological industries at the very height of their commercial success, suddenly came to a sorry end in the bursting of the so-called dot-com bubble on March 10, 2000. Indeed, a stock-market collapse may well be a better paradigm for defeat today when wars do not seem able to be won or lost. An any rate, the Nasdaq collapse left a good deal of unused expansion behind it, in particular an ambitious fiber-optic system designed to make its investors "endlessly rich in an endlessly expanding digital universe."[42]

The dialectical identity of failure and success here turns on the relationship between America (which can be identified with globalization as such) and India (which in this instance plays the role of a subordinate space of cheap outsourcing). We may already detect the phantom presence of earlier dialectical reversals behind this historical present: for one thing, the inheritance of the English language (positive) from the history of British colonization (negative); for another, the decision of Nehru, with his "preference for pro-Soviet, Socialist economics" (negative), to fund a number of Soviet-style institutes of science and technology (positive). Nonetheless, Nehru's system, according to one native informant, "produced people with quality and by quantity. But many of them rotted on the docks of India like cabbages. Only a relative few could get on ships and get out" (*WiF*, 105), namely to work in America.

---

[41] Although it is not a stylistic matter, I am indebted to Steven Helmling's discovery of this thematics in my own work, in his interesting book *The Success and Failure of Fredric Jameson*, Albany: SUNY Press, 2001.

[42] Thomas L. Friedman, *The World Is Flat: A Brief History of the Twenty-first Century*, New York: Farrar, Straus and Giroux, 2005, 103. Future references to this work are denoted *WiF*.

Suddenly, in a classic dialectical reversal, "the overcapacity in fiber optics … meant that [the Indians] and their American clients got to use all that cable practically for free" (*WiF*, 104), with the legendary result we all know —the development of Bangalore, the outsourcing of American business calls and files of all kinds to unknown locations on the sub-continent, the great leap forward of India into the very center of globalization itself (and of modern capitalism).

Friedman's conclusions on the matter are predictably couched in terms of irony:

> India didn't benefit only from the dot-com boom; it benefited even more from the dot-com bust! That is the real irony. The boom laid the cable that connected India to the world, and the bust made the cost of using it virtually free and also vastly increased the number of American companies that would want to use that fiber-optic cable to outsource knowledge work to India. (*WiF*, 110)

For irony is the way in which a single side of the exchange views the dialectical reversal in which it changes places with its rival—the irony of defeat, the irony of victory: irony is in this sense an incomplete dialectic, and one whose only opposite is the non-ironic, the dumbfounded mesmerization by the empirical state of things, the stubborn belief—against all odds—in that law of non-contradiction which decrees that negative and positive, failure and success, are two distinct dispensations, separated from each other by reality itself, and to be kept that way!

vi.

Is it possible, then, that this distinction between horizontal and vertical oppositions simply leads us back again to the old "incommensurability" between history and sociology, between event and structure, and finally between time and space? The question is probably not so much one of the nature of the object, for events bring out the structure, historical developments necessarily articulate features of the social in time, in the form of antagonism or tension. Rather our leading thread has here been the inquiry into the character of the oppositional relationship—so intimate as to fold it back into unity, so distant or external as to break it apart into two distinct zones or fields, two different objects. We will see in another place what role the Hegelian formulation (embraced by Mao Tse-tung) plays in all this: the One becomes the Two.[43] It is at any rate clear that the ambiguous no-man's-

---

[43] See below, 196; and also *PoS*, 350–351; Mao Zedong, "A Dialectical Approach to Inner-Party Unity," *Selected Works of Mao Zedong*, vol. 5, Peking: Foreign Language Press, 1977, 514–516; Guy Debord, *Society of the Spectacle*, Detroit: Black and Red,

land between them, between internal and external relations, or unity and incommensurability, identity and difference, must be named contradiction if one or the other of these results is not to harden over and become permanent or substantial; equally clear that if contradiction is to be the name we give this problem it will always nudge us in the direction of negation rather than of identification. In fact, to foreground the term "contradiction" is to discover a splendid opportunity to kick the ladder away and to expunge the last traces of that structuralism which offered us a starting point here. For the structuralist perspective always grasps contradiction in the form of the antinomy: that is to say, a logical impasse in which thought is paralyzed and can move neither forward nor back, in which an absolute structural limit is reached, in either thought or reality. This deconcealment of the antinomies at the root of practical or theoretical dilemmas can serve as a powerful instrument of ideological analysis (as in deconstruction), but it should not be confused with that more dynamic and productive act of setting the antinomy itself in motion, that is to say, revealing it to have in reality been the form of a contradiction: for it is the unmasking of antinomy as contradiction which constitutes truly dialectical thinking as such.

But what is contradiction in that case? It is not that which blocks and suspends movement but within which movement itself takes place, as Marx suggests in a luminous passage (he is discussing the structure of commodities):

> The further development of the commodity does not abolish these contradictions, but rather provides the form within which they have room to move. This is, in general, the way in which real contradictions are resolved. For instance, it is a contradiction to depict one body as constantly falling towards another and at the same time consistently flying away from it. The ellipse is a form of motion within which this contradiction is both realized and resolved.[44]

Yet we must now take our vertical oppositions through yet another rehearsal, and replay yet another opposition, the most debatable yet unavoidable one in the traditional Marxian arsenal, which remains unmentioned in Engels's enumeration, and is indeed only articulated once in Marx's entire corpus: I mean the "opposition," if it is one, between base and superstructure. But indeed, what kind of opposition is it? Does not Benjamin tell us, in a formula which he must have taken great satisfaction in proposing, that "the superstructure *expresses* the base"?[45] Is this a contradiction that he is here able

---

1983, Chapter 3; Alain Badiou, *Théorie du sujet*, Paris: Seuil, 1982, 61–62, 131, 228–229.

[44] Karl Marx, *Capital*, Vol. 1, trans. Ben Fowkes, London: Penguin, 1976, 198. Future references to this work are denoted *Cap*.

[45] Walter Benjamin, *The Arcades Project*, trans. Howard Eiland and Kevin McLaughlin, Cambridge, MA: Belknap Press, 1999, 460.

to "express"? Is it any clearer when the Church fathers decree that the super-structure *reflects* the base? And are we not at that point simply back in an opposition of the familiar asymmetrical type, in which we confront a dominant term and a subordinate one? It would be stimulating to attempt a dialectical reversal here, and to argue that, on the contrary, the base reflects the superstructure: something Jacques Attali outrageously posits, in *Bruits*, when he asserts that the music of one era anticipates the economic system of the next one to come.[46] Yet on this scholastic debate, whose 150-year futility has exhausted most of its participants, matters of great significance still depend. Indeed, Marxism would seem to stand or fall with it, for a system in which culture were utterly independent of the economic would spell the end of most Marxisms, while one in which they were undifferentiated from one another would constitute a Foucauldian dystopia, if not a truly archaic life well before even tribal organization or *pensée sauvage*.

The first peculiarity to note about the opposition between base and superstructure is that it already appears within the base itself. This is the distinction between forces of production and relations of production, which has generally been interpreted in the sense of a differentiation between a given technology of production and the labor process that expresses, reflects, or corresponds to it. It is as though, borrowing a Lacanian method, the fraction constituted by inscribing superstructure over base redoubled itself by including yet another fraction in its denominator, namely this earlier or more primordial fraction one gets by writing relations above forces. One hesitates to propose the mathematical solution, however, in which, in one way or another, the second denominator is dialectically flung up into the numerator, thus leaving us with a superstructure now fully tainted by the base if not multiplied by it (what the cultural enemies of Marxism have always accused its conception of culture as being).

I would rather wish to point out analogous but non-symmetrical developments on the other side of the fraction, in the numerator or the place of the superstructure: in which the latter finds itself multiplied into a variety of levels all more or less homologous with one another ("art, ideology, the law, religion, etc."[47]). Not only does this seem to dissolve the state, state power, and the political back into one more epiphenomenal "superstructure" among others (for they can certainly not be assigned to the base), the functional relationship of the opposing forces/relations has here somehow given way to a multiplicity of cultural levels all parallel (and/or homologous) with

---

[46] See Jacques Attali, *Bruits: essai sur l'économie politique de la musique*, Paris: PUF, 1977.

[47] "Morality, religion, metaphysics, and all the rest of ideology as well as the forms of consciousness corresponding to these, thus no longer retain the semblance of independence; they have no history, no development …" etc., Marx and Engels, *The German Ideology*, Moscow: Progress Publishers, 1964, 42.

each other, yet in no particular working relationship to each other at all. The Hegelians might point out, then, at this stage, that we are here dealing with an opposition between relationship and parallelism, or even between opposition and replication: it seems comparable to what obtains when we juxtapose the idea of the dichotomous classes, in a Marxian conception of class struggle, with the idea of social strata in bourgeois sociology.[48] Yet those conceptions are ideologically distinct from one another and belong to different conceptual systems; whereas the oppositions with which we are confronted here are parts of the same concept or system, and form the two separated but related sides of a single theoretical fraction. The problem is therefore dialectical, rather than ideological: and indeed, it reminds us of the very vocation of the dialectic itself to hold two distinct dynamics, two distinct systems of law or well-nigh scientific regularities, together within the unity of a single thought. Yet we named that "single thought" a contradiction, and it is not yet clear that the base-superstructure distinction we have been elaborating here is in fact a contradiction: that is, we have not yet worked our way through to the point at which it can be identified as one, the point at which tension and negativity divide as much as they relate, or relate as much as they divide.

Let's return to the denominator, the "first" opposition between forces of production and relations of production. From one perspective, the opposition would appear to reproduce the old ideological or metaphysical one between body and mind, thereby strengthening an interpretation of the forces/relations distinction as a fundamentally materialist operation. (It is an interpretive temptation reinforced by the far more overt opposition in the first chapter of *Capital*, in which use value is specifically characterized as being material, while the exchange value of the commodity—"objective appearance"—is famously described as spiritual, as having metaphysical or theological overtones.) The forces of production are thus the material technology, that is, the state of the machinery, the tools, the raw material (itself available owing to the development of a certain technology), and so forth. The concept of relations would seem more ambiguous, insofar as it first seems to direct our attention to the relationship of implements and raw material to each other, and only then reveals itself to be the concrete labor process itself, how the tools are used and how the workers need to be positioned in order to do justice to this particular stage of production. (For example, Marx insists on one fundamental historical change in the development of capitalism, namely that from "manufacture," in which the various tools prolong and enhance human labor, to "industry," in which human labor is organized around, and in the service of, the machinery itself.)

---

[48] See the interesting discussion of these two perspectives in Ralf Dahrendorf, *Class and Class Conflict in Industrial Society*, Palo Alto, CA: Stanford University Press, 1959.

Yet these two terms of the opposition—material technology and human agency—stage two distinct perspectives—that of technological determinism and that of humanism—which are each of them clearly unsatisfactory. Given the extensive role played in *Capital* by accounts of machinery and so-called constant capital, it is very hard to ward off impressions of Marx as a technological determinist (and this in spite of his repeated insistence that value comes from human labor and not from machinery). Indeed, it is worth noting that the word "revolution" is used in *Capital* almost exclusively to describe technological change. On the other hand, an emphasis on the centrality of the labor process itself risks encouraging a voluntarism in which the democratic reorganization of the shop floor and the introduction of self-management are in themselves enough to transform the system.

Each of these perspectives—they would be criticized and attacked as materialism ("bad" materialism, of course, mechanical materialism) and idealism respectively, and also as determinism and voluntarism—is evidently an ideology in its own right. What Marx's opposition now does is not only analyze a unified phenomenon (a One) into two distinct dimensions; it also requires each perspective to demystify the other one, and to perform an operation of ideological critique which is internal to the conceptualization itself. Thus, it would be wrong to imagine that the forces/relations distinction only operates in the direction of some materialist critique and regrounding in which we are brought up short against the material history of the various modes of production: the insistence on relations, indeed, precludes that illusion of a purely technological determinism to which we have referred as well, and obliges us to dissolve the seemingly massive and impenetrable materiality of machinery back into its reality as human action (the introduction of new machines as a solution to the power of workers or to economic crisis, the very invention of technology itself, its human meaning as a specific form of exploitation or of discarding of redundant human beings).

Thus this first opposition not only brings into visibility two distinct ways of reading or representing production itself: it posits each as the indispensable correction of the other, in a situation in which neither is the essential term in some asymmetrical opposition and which thereby demands a constant dialectical movement back and forth which must not be allowed to harden into a static sociological model of some kind. The proposal, indeed, casts new light on Karl Korsch's arresting observation that Marxism disposes of two distinct codes—that of production, value, and commodification and that of agency or class struggle—which offer alternate yet finally equally satisfactory ways of describing its objects.[49] The structure of production can, in other words, be translated or transcoded into the language of

---

[49] Karl Korsch, *Karl Marx*, New York: Humanities Press International, 1963.

class struggle, and vice versa. To this proposition we can now add the imperative that the two codes must criticize each other, must systematically be translated back and forth into one another in a ceaseless alternation, which foregrounds what each code cannot say fully as much as what it can.

I will argue that it is this dynamic that is then transferred from that base or infrastructure (whose internal truth it is) to what are called the superstructures and seemed to stand in some indeterminate parallelism to it. In that form, the new and larger opposition clearly reproduces the mind/body, the spirit/matter, opposition on a larger collective and socially more comprehensive scale. And yet we have already seen that the base is not to be considered a purely materialist phenomenon: its relationship to any particular superstructure will then not only be revealed in some materialist correction of the idealistic illusions of the superstructure in question, as when we evoke some economic basis of philosophy or art, or of the law, or of the seemingly autonomous state structure. This is to be sure the standard reading of the base/superstructure relationship, a reading which is then itself the excuse for hand-wringing denunciations of Marxist reductionism and of vulgar-materialist hostility to the autonomous histories and structures of the superstructures in question.

Rather, what is being proposed here is that it is the inner self-correcting dynamic of the base or infrastructure which is transferred to each superstructure, when it is isolated from the social totality in a specific moment of analysis or articulation. That superstructure, then, endowed not only with the material dimension of the base in the form of the "forces of production" level, but also with its interaction with a level of the "relations of production," is then obliged to reconstitute itself into just such a dynamic process in which, having produced itself as a quasi-material object, it is then at once dereified into a complex set of human acts, which are then themselves regrounded in material processes, in a set of linked operations of self-constitution and deconstruction which is potentially interminable.

I will only give a single example of the process, in Althusser's well-known theory of ideology, which clearly deals with an area that has always been considered to be a superstructure in the Marxist tradition.[50] But the two halves of this essay—the first on the ideological state apparatuses—Church, family, school, etc.—and the appended afterthought on "interpellation"—have never been sufficiently interrogated in their disjunction (comparable perhaps in form to the eruption of the theory of the sublime as Kant's supplemental afterthought to his more official theory of beauty). In fact, the two Althusserian theories of institution and subjectivity very precisely replicate the back-and-forth movement of the forces/relations distinction

---

[50] Louis Althusser, "Ideology and Ideological State Apparatuses," in *Lenin and Philosophy,* trans. Ben Brewster, New York: Monthly Review Press, 1971.

we have been presenting here. "Institutions"—the so-called apparatuses— are something like the base or infrastructure of ideology as a superstructure; while the latter—the quasi-Lacanian structure of ideological subjectivity— is the cultural or superstructural form which "expresses" that base, to return to Benjamin's interpretation, and which articulates the material institutions in their social, relational, existential realities.

Two points need to be emphasized in conclusion here: the first is that there can be no static structural or sociological theories or models of base and superstructure. Each analysis is ad hoc and punctual; it sets out from a specific event or text and constitutes an interpretive act rather than a theory of structure. There can thus be no theory of superstructures; and there is therefore no point in objecting, for example, that the state is or is not a superstructure, that it is not sufficiently distinguished from ideological superstructures such as philosophy and art, and so forth.

Indeed, in the spirit of our *Darstellung* in this chapter, we might propose a new and unwieldy modification of the way in which base and superstructure are themselves to be designated. For it is as though the "theory" itself, whether the object of criticism or of promotion, is here still conceptualized in terms of the definite article. It is always *the* base and superstructure, the base, the superstructure, which are discussed: it now seems appropriate to suggest that we rather evoke an indefinite relationship: *a* base and super- structure, or indeed many of them, depending on the circumstances and on the occasion. And in fact, this is the moment to go even further and to observe that our former binary oppositions now seem to have modulated into so many effects: so that, were it felicitous, we might even be tempted to speak of a given phenomenon as "base-and-superstructural" (but see Section 3, below).

8.

We can also speak of such reversals as a changing of the valences on a given phenomenon, where the transformation of value and function in an altered context or system may be said to constitute a changing of its valences, from negative to positive, or the other way round, as the case may be. It is clear that for Marx many of the features of capitalism—the division of labor ("cooperation"), the expansion of firms in the direction of monopoly— constitute what one may characterize as negative, yet potentially positive, phenomena. They are now in this system places of exploitation, yet in the revolutionary change in system they become positive: thus, the division of labor stunts individuals and deforms them in the direction of their own spe- cialization (or in the case of deskilling, the removal of the division of labor does not negate it but makes it worse); and yet in its form as cooperation this tendency replaces the individual with a functioning collective and is the potential source of new social initiatives and new social organization. Much the same can be said for the factory system itself (and, for Lenin, monopoly—in the case of the great banks—was not an evil but rather the possibility of a new step towards popular and collective control of the economy).

We may also think of the change in valences as a form of potentiation, as when a given quantity is squared or generally raised to a higher power: if anything, this is the teleology inherent in Marx's dialectic: things cannot go backwards (at least according to their own inner logic; they can certainly decay or fall apart, cease to be what they were)—there is an inevitable increase in complexity and productivity at work which cannot be reversed. On the other hand, negative potentiation—to follow Hegel's example of imaginary numbers—is not a vision of the collapse of the thing but rather the very space of the imaginary, and thus of the future or, in our sense, of Utopia, as yet unrealized although a conceptualized possibility. This is the sense, finally, in which changing the valences on a given phenomenon can be a visionary act which allows the Utopian imagination to break through, as in my own reading of Walmart as a Utopian phenomenon.[51] This does not mean that Walmart is positive or that anything progressive can come out of it, nor any new system: yet to apprehend it for a moment in positive or progressive terms is to open up the current system in the direction of something else.

3. It's Dialectical!

Despite all these examples, indeed, there would seem to be something fundamentally self-defeating about the presentation of the dialectic in a non-dialectical way. We have already argued that the conception of the dialectic as a system, and indeed as a philosophy as such—along with the very idea of philosophy itself—is undialectical. Yet despite similar warnings about method as an instrumental and non-dialectical idea, the likelihood of the search for binary oppositions turning into a definition, and of the practice of oppositions as such slipping into a version of method (however newfangled and structuralist), seems well-nigh fatal. Perhaps in that case the very effort to remain vigilantly formalistic and to abstract the dialectic from the impurities of content and context was itself a mistake, from which only "method" as such could reemerge.

Meanwhile the accumulation of examples accuses itself from the other side of this practice: for the example is very precisely that bad contingency which is the complement of the bad notion of law denounced in the first

---

[51] "Utopia as Replication," below, Chapter 16.

section of this chapter. Examples are the arbitrary cases that rattle around inside the impossible abstraction called a law; and although it would be amusing to return to this seemingly random lot—politics, aesthetics, big business, history, etc.—and to demonstrate how all this varied content merely articulated a fundamental opposition, subject versus object, say, in the multiplicity of its modes—the exercise might well itself simply demonstrate the deficiencies of the starting point and the one-sidedness of what turned out, not to be a form, but rather a theme in disguise, namely Opposition as such.

Contingency in fact calls up its own opposite in that once popular literary-critical Hegelianism, the concrete universal (something Hegel preferred to call "the thing itself," "die Sache selbst," as we will see in another part of this book): but this is not a place one arrives at by deciding to. Perhaps, if Marxism is to be identified as a unity of theory and practice, the same needs to be said about the dialectic, namely that it will always be its own illustration or example; that any exercise of it will already be its own presentation; that, as Sartre put it, you do not think dialectically without saying so and calling it that: all of which is to say that you have to be grappling with a dialectical reality already in order to be able to show what the dialectic is.

This suggests, not only that our next step needs to replace the noun, singular and plural alike, definite as well as indefinite, with the adjective, but also that we need to attend to "examples" of a somewhat different kind: to those mental events that take place when someone says, rebuking your perplexity before a particularly perverse interpretation or turn of events, "It's dialectical!" This is not only to accuse the worrier of heavy-handed common sense and hidebound conventional logic; it is to propose a startling new perspective from which to rethink the novelty in question, to defamiliarize our ordinary habits of mind and to make us suddenly conscious not only of our own non-dialectical obtuseness but also of the strangeness of reality as such.

I will suggest (here and in the next chapters of this book) that the older common-sense empirical thought overturned in such moments—the law of non-contradiction—is what Hegel called *Verstand* (or Understanding) and what Marx called reification. But for the present it is the contagion of the dialectic, rather than its structure, that we are out to catch a glimpse of: some essential restlessness or negativity that fastens onto our thinking at those moments in which we seem arrested and paralyzed by an antinomy—for, as has been observed above, the relationship between antinomy and dialectic is a crucial one in the contemporary period, where the antinomy has taken the place of the contradiction, expressing intractability rather than energy and construction (or indeed incommensurability rather than relationship).

What happens in moments like these—at least when the dialectic unexpectedly proposes itself, and when it suddenly crosses our minds that "it's dialectical!"—is that the problem itself becomes the solution, and that the opposition in which we are immobilized like a ship in the ice must itself now become the object of our thinking; that to be thus caught in an irresolvable binary opposition is in reality to have been thrown back to the very origins of dialectics itself, a welcome regression which is the very condition of progress itself.

We must therefore shift our perspective from sender to receiver, and approach "the dialectical" from the shock of its effects on reader or listener, in order to appreciate the force of its originality. Here too we will need to accumulate some examples; but this time the contingency of the examples will be proportional to the contingency of our own discoveries rather than to some ontological condition of the world itself; and their discontinuities will ensure us against system and method alike. Still, it will not seem altogether contingent that the contemporary world has thrown up two of the most brilliant dialecticians in the history of philosophy: and it seems only appropriate to scan each one for the dialectical effects with which their pages so often electrify us. Indeed, if we are still intent on oppositions, we may well wish to theorize these two practitioners—T. W. Adorno on the one hand, Slavoj Žižek on the other—as votaries of the tragic and the comic muse, respectively. But just as we previously warned against the temptation of the concepts of irony or antinomy, so here we need to take our precautions against a similar category mistake, namely the identification of their effects as so many paradoxes.

I will therefore preface this discussion with a remark about the paradoxes of Michel Foucault in a hypothetical Foucauldianism. Suppose we observed[52] that one of the extensions of Enlightenment thought is to be found in nature itself, and in particular with an intensification of concern today with animals: it is a concern which goes well beyond the historical programs of vegetarian movements and has now been articulated in the concept of animal rights, an ideal certainly to be welcomed when one thinks of the immemorial suffering of animals at the hands of human beings—a suffering not less great than that inflicted by human beings on each other.

But now we are abruptly called upon to rehearse the classic Foucauldian accounts of "capillary power": the way in which in the modern age power refines and extends its networks through bodies by way of the effects of what Foucault called bio-power: such that the old brutality on bodies was now, beginning with the bourgeois era, transformed into ever more subtle forms

---

[52] I am indebted, for this example, to a paper on animal rights by Laura Hudson, delivered at the summer 2007 conference of the Marxist Literary Group.

of knowledge and control that penetrate ever more unexplored zones of the physical and of natural life.

It is a nightmarish (or dystopian) vision which will now with one stroke suddenly transform our admiration for the animal rights movement itself: for we suddenly grasp the fact that "rights" are a human concept, and that by extending their sway into hitherto uncolonized and untheorized zones of nature and of the animal world, we are preparing an intervention into non-human life and an appropriation of nature by human bio-power far more all-engulfing than anything the planet has hitherto known. "Animal rights" thus becomes the vanguard of bio-power's totalitarian sway over the earth; and hitherto specialized philosophical minutiae such as the problem of whether a given virus should be made utterly extinct by human intervention are now cast in an altogether different and more sinister light.

This hypothetical example is consistent with Foucault's anti-Enlightenment positions, particularly in his books on medicine, insanity, and punishment, where the era of early nineteenth-century bourgeois reform—which traditional histories have narrated in the form of a humane revolution in the treatment of patients and prisoners—is implicitly mocked and ironized as a subtler imperialism of power and control famously epitomized by the "panopticon," the regime of universal surveillance and of a total knowledge identified with total power.

It has indeed already been observed above that Foucault's powerful reinterpretation of these transformations is utterly undialectical, and that the perplexity of readers with the very concept of bio-power—negative or positive? a locus of state domination or a new source of resistance?—can be largely attributed to the fact that in Foucault's thought this term lacks an opposite.

Such a criticism is in my opinion correct, yet we must now pronounce it to be utterly misplaced. The problem with the turn of thought now inextricably linked to and as it were signed by Foucault's name is not that it is non- or anti-dialectical, but rather that it is too dialectical: or better still, that it is a dialectic that has ignored its own name and powers and has, in an excess of dialectical energies, short-circuited itself. For what is left out in the characteristic Foucauldian narrative here is the passage from positive to negative which very precisely characterizes the dialectic as such, or, in other words, the unity of opposites. Foucault attributes the positive valorization of Enlightenment to his deluded bourgeois readers and positions it as an error which the new narrative of paranoia and conspiracy is to correct: whereas from a dialectical perspective both narratives are correct and both narratives are equally in error—and it is this double vision which we find exercised in Adorno's "negative" thinking, which it would probably be better not to reify as a separate species of dialectic, as that "negative dialectic" that stands as the title of one of his most famous books: but which it will also be crucial to rescue from a first impression as misleading as the Foucauldian short-circuit, and which is called, as has already been suggested above, the paradox.

For surely, particularly at Adorno's musically organized beginnings and endings—onsets and final flourishes—his thought tends to embrace the literary and linguistic "simple form" of the paradox. Thus *Aesthetic Theory* (a draft to be sure, published posthumously) begins like this: "It is self-evident that nothing concerning art is self-evident anymore"[53]: a sentence which threatens to undermine the very project of writing an aesthetic before it even gets started. Or perhaps it simply designates philosophy's perpetual problem with beginnings: nothing can be presupposed, not even the idea of presupposition. We are left dangerously in a place in which it may not be possible to say anything (whence Adorno's fascination with Beckett).

Or take the even more famous beginning of *Negative Dialectics*: "Philosophy, which once seemed obsolete, lives on because it missed the moment of its realization."[54] Here, to be sure, the paradox carries another paradox within itself, namely Marx's injunction to philosophy to realize itself, or in other words not only to understand the world but to go on to change it. Still, the very paradox of obsolescence shimmers over this swift orchestral onset: living on as a form of outliving itself, an actuality which is no longer actual, a present that is now past.

In both these cases, what is indicted is the very discipline itself, the field of thinking or consciousness which had evolved historically into a whole autonomous area of culture, before suddenly itself being called into question. The form of the paradox indeed harbors the very play of oppositions we have discussed in our previous moment, and it is that inner antithesis which endows the single word for two opposites—in these instances, "art" or "philosophy"—with its startling and uncanny effect.

A further discussion will then expand this simultaneity into the possession, by the object itself, of two distinct and incompatible attributes. Thus, in *Aesthetic Theory*, Adorno goes on to dwell for a moment on the much celebrated freedoms of the art we call modernism (he might have selected any number of other starting points). At once, however, this freedom—from convention, tradition, perspective, figuration, representation itself—turns around into its opposite: "the process that was unleashed consumed the categories in the name of that for which it [the process] was undertaken. More was constantly pulled into the vortex of the newly taboo" (*AT*, 1). The conquest of aesthetic freedom becomes in a dialectical reversal the invention

---

[53] T. W. Adorno, *Aesthetic Theory*, trans. Robert Hullot-Kentor, Minneapolis: University of Minnesota Press, 1997, 1. Future references to this work are denoted *AT*.

[54] T. W. Adorno, *Negative Dialectics*, trans. E. B. Ashton, New York: Continuum, 1973, 3.

and imposition of ever more stringent prohibitions; and thus that hitherto seemingly unified thing for which we used the single name of art proves to be a dialectical space in which the unity of opposites—freedom and taboo—plays itself out in the most unsettling and destructive fashion, threatening to do away with any common-sense or unified everyday conception of art altogether. (Indeed, I would say that years after this prophetic diagnosis it is just such an explosive disunification which results in the condition of what we used to call art under postmodernity.)

Still, this remains a diagnosis and as such Adorno supplies an explanation: but the explanation is an external one; it stands outside this unity of opposites and indeed outside art altogether. He answers the question of the freedoms of modernism in this way: "absolute freedom in art, always limited to a particular, comes into contradiction with the perennial unfreedom of the whole" (*AT*, 1). In an unfree society, in other words, art cannot itself be truly free: so far this seems to be a sociological analysis. But the unfreedom of society is implied to be the contradiction between the particular and the universal, as well as the impossibility of totality ("the whole," Adorno famously remarked elsewhere, "is the untrue "). So if the explanation is a social one, it is scarcely causal in any vulgar sense, but rather highly mediated. And in any case the lesson is a warning against premature synthesis, against the illusions of unity (and indeed against the very unification glibly suggested by the third term of the pseudo-Hegelian triad).

I now want to illustrate this process in a final example from Adorno, which now begins, not with a single term like "art" or "philosophy" which was assumed to have been unified but turned out to be itself the result of a dialectical opposition. The new illustration will thus begin with that opposition itself, grasped as two fields which ought to be unified but cannot be, namely those of "Sociology and Psychology" (the title of the essay). Here we confront a modern disciplinary form of one of the oldest, most archaic oppositions on the books of human history, namely the opposition between subject and object, mind and body, individual and society, self and other—the permutations of this seemingly incommensurable combination or amalgamation are as multiple as the schools of philosophy itself, each one acknowledging that we have to do with an already unified phenomenon whose unity cannot be grasped by the human mind in any plausible way.

The attempts to unify psychology and sociology (most notably by Talcott Parsons) are then yet another seemingly promising starting point, if not for any unified field theory of the matter, then at least for an account of the reasons it may be impossible. And in a way that account is precisely what

---

[55] T. W. Adorno, *Minima Moralia*, trans. E. F. N. Jephcott, London: New Left Books, 1974, 50.

Adorno offers us, but in the form of a preemptive rejection of the whole project:

> An ideal of conceptual unification taken from the natural sciences cannot, however, be indiscriminately applied to a society whose unity resides in its not being unified. Sociology and psychology, in so far as they function in isolation from one another, often succumb to the temptation to project the intellectual division of labour on to the object of their study. The separation of society and psyche is false consciousness; it perpetuates conceptually the split between the living subject and the objectivity that governs the subjects and yet derives from them. But the basis of this false consciousness cannot be removed by a mere methodological dictum. People are incapable of recognizing themselves in society and society in themselves because they are alienated from each other and the totality. Their reified social relations necessarily appear to them as an "in itself." What compartmentalized disciplines project on to reality merely reflects back what has taken place in reality. False consciousness is also true: inner and outer life are torn apart. Only through the articulation of their difference, not by stretching concepts, can their relation be adequately expressed. The truth of the whole sides with one-sidedness, not pluralistic synthesis: a psychology that turns its back on society and idiosyncratically concentrates on the individual and his archaic heritage says more about the hapless state of society than one which seeks by its "wholistic approach" or an inclusion of social "factors" to join the ranks of a no longer existent *universitas literarum.*[56]

More paradoxes: but this time they are the paradoxes of capitalism itself, whose structural uniqueness in human history lies in the fact that it is a group organized by individuality and separation or atomization rather than by any of the traditional modes of group unification.

What is then the consequence for the two disciplines in question? Their very differentiation—the "separation of society and psyche"—"is false consciousness; it perpetuates conceptually the split between the living subject and the objectivity that governs the subjects and yet derives from them." Why not, then, attempt to overcome this separation by a new interdisciplinary program (as we sometimes call these solutions)? "The basis of this false consciousness cannot be removed by a mere methodological dictum." In other words, contradiction cannot be solved or eliminated by the taking of a thought (the very principle referred to earlier as the unity of theory and practice).

But now we come to the most startling feature of Adorno's dialectic, which seemed to have arrived at the point of unmasking and denouncing false consciousness. Far from it: "The truth of the whole sides with one-

---

[56] T. W. Adorno, "Sociology and Psychology," *New Left Review* Vol. 1, Num. 46, November–December 1967, and Vol. 1, Num. 47, January–February 1968, 69–70.

sidedness," he tells us. "False consciousness is also true: inner and outer life are torn apart." Truth lies in holding to this falsehood, in keeping faith with this contradiction. Yet the formula is less reassuring than it ought to be: for in these situations, Adorno undermines one position on the question, only to turn abruptly and undermine its alternative, thereby leaving us with nothing but the impossibility of concluding anything.

It is evidently this which he chose to call negative dialectics, a movement of negation that can never reach a synthesis, a negativity that ceaselessly undermines all the available positivities until it has only its own destructive energy to promote. It is a process with its own striking family resemblance to that ancient skepticism so important for Hegel himself, in which the key operation—called equipollence—consists in "setting into opposition equally strong propositions or arguments on both sides of an issue that arises and thereby producing an equal balance of justification on both sides of the issue."[57] Or, we might add, producing an equal balance of negativity and the subversion of both alternatives. As with the ancient skeptics, however, the dialectical process is meant to do something to our very sense of reality itself, along with that reality's former truths.

Indeed, Adorno has himself characterized this movement as "mediation" as such, in an extraordinary passage that sheds a whole new light on the problems of this concept as we have staged it above:

> Kant's antithetical poles—form and content, nature and spirit, theory and practice, freedom and necessity, noumenon and phenomenon—have been so completely suffused by reflection that none of these determinations can stand as a final one. Each one, in order to be thought and indeed to exist, requires the production out of itself of that other moment that Kant set in opposition to it. Mediation is therefore in Hegel never—as any number of fateful misunderstandings since Kierkegaard would have it—a midpoint between the extremes; rather mediation takes place within the extremes themselves: and this is the radical feature of Hegel which is irreconcilable with any moderate or intermediate position. What traditional philosophy hoped to achieve as an ontological foundation turns out to be, not distinct ideas set off discretely against each other, but ideas each of which requires its opposite, and the relation of all of them together is process itself.[58]

Now perhaps we can grasp the nature of the dialectical effect—indeed the dialectical shock—more clearly as we follow the process whereby we are led to a critical and negative position, then brutally canceled in a second moment to which we are less likely to lend our absolute credence, having

---

[57] Michael N. Forster, *Hegel and Skepticism*, Cambridge, MA: Harvard University Press, 1989, 10.

[58] T. W. Adorno, *Drei Studien zu Hegel*, Frankfurt: Suhrkamp, 1997, 257.

now learned the experience of the linguistic and conceptual untrustworth-iness of such positions in general. To be sure, this ought to have been a lesson taught by the doctrine of ideology, but the latter still seems to promise a truth ("science"), a final correction, a moment of resolution, or knowledge, for which there is little place in Adorno's implacably negative dialectic.

The latter does not, for all that, leave us in the midst of that postmodern relativism so terrifying to believers of any number of philosophical "old schools." The negative dialectic still seems to retain something of the Absolute that figured so powerfully in the Hegelian version, and even in the Marxian "absolute historicism." But can there be an absolute—or even a truth, or a referent—which is neither linguistic nor conceptual? It is about this possi-bility that Žižek's version of the dialectic will have something to say.

Here too, to be sure, we begin with the denunciation of that stupid old stereotype according to which Hegel works, according to a tripartite and cut-and-dried progression from thesis through antithesis to synthesis. But this is completely erroneous, as there are no real syntheses in Hegel and the dialectical operation is to be seen in an utterly different way (a variety of examples are adduced). Still …that stupid first impression was not alto-gether wrong, there is a tripartite movement in the Hegelian dialectic, and in fact I have just illustrated it: stupid first impression as the appearance; ingenious correction in the name of some underlying reality or "essence"; but finally, after all, a return to the reality of the appearance. It was the appearance that was "true" after all.

What can this possibly have to do with "popular culture"? Let's take a Hollywood product, say, Fritz Lang's *Woman in the Window* (1944). (Well, maybe now Fritz Lang is high culture rather than mass culture, but anyway…) Edward G. Robinson is a mild-mannered professor, who leaving his peaceful club one night gets involved in a desperate web of love and murder. We think we are watching a thriller. At length, he takes refuge in his club again, falls asleep out of exhaustion, and wakes up: it was all a dream. The movie has done the interpretation for us, by way of Lang's capitu-lation to the cheap Hollywood insistence on happy endings (Zhuangzi is not a butterfly after all!). But in reality—which is to say in the true appearance —Edward G. Robinson "is not a quiet, kind, decent, bourgeois professor dreaming that he is a murderer, but a murderer dreaming, in his everyday life, that he is a quiet, kind, decent, bourgeois professor." Hollywood's cen-sorship is therefore not some puritanical, uptight, middle-class mechanism for repressing the obscene, nasty, antisocial, violent underside of life, it is rather the technique for revealing it. The literal first version was true—the dream we first took for reality was real, and not the waking from it.[59]

---

[59] Slavoj Žižek, *Looking Awry*, Cambridge, MA: MIT Press, 1991, 16–17.

We might give a few more examples from other categories. Thus, on some public occasion, Žižek is denounced for frivolously discussing Hitchcock while the Bosnian population, and in particular that in Sarajevo, is suffering through siege and ethnic cleansing. He has indeed often analyzed the West's interest in seeing the Bosnians as victims in that conflict (for if they were not victims, they would at once be transformed into Islamic terrorists, in a classic dialectical reversal). The third position here is the reminder that the Bosnians are not Other to us, but rather the same; that what is astonishing is that during the siege they pursue their daily lives just as we do, and so forth.[60] Thus we go from a first image of daily life as usual (Americans listening to a lecture in peacetime), to an "othered" and melodramatic representation of victims in wartime, back to the first representation which now includes the wartime city and its population itself in the larger picture of daily life as usual. To be sure, this return to the surface, to the stupid first impression, is accompanied by a new knowledge of the errors involved in the second moment, the moment of interpretation; but nonetheless still reaffirms the truth of the starting point.

Another example—which can be as grisly as Stalin's great purge trials or as benign as the Brezhnevite or post-Tito communism of the final years—is that of the three-fold movement of the party's self-justification. In a first moment, the party asserts that many of the old Bolsheviks, the original leaders of the revolution, were in reality traitors and spies for the Nazis. The West, then—for these dialectical transformations most often take the form of dramatic exchanges between subject-positions—interprets such claims as deliberate lies and staged falsehoods, and asks how anyone could believe that figures of this integrity could possibly have betrayed their own revolution, while Stalin's own essential deceitfulness seems only too probable. The West's interpretation is of course correct; but it is also false—third position—insofar as no one believes in the betrayal in the first place; they merely pretend to do so "in order to save the appearance (of the Master's or Leader's omnipotence and knowledge)—to prevent the Master's impotence from becoming visible to all the world."[61] "Saving the appearances," Žižek calls this process, and indeed its philosophical content turns very precisely on Hegel's notion of the objectivity of appearance as such: appearance is not subjective or arbitrary, not to be replaced by some underlying essence, or at the very least the essence must be sought in the appearance itself. The obedient subject does not submit to the omnipotent totalitarian Other, but rather feels sorry for this big Other whose power he then pretends to acknowledge, thereby confirming it.

---

[60] Slavoj Žižek, *The Metastases of Enjoyment*, London: Verso, 1994, 1–2.
[61] Slavoj Žižek, *The Plague of Fantasies*, London: Verso, 1997, 158.

Žižek's interpretive work, from page to page, seems to revel in these paradoxes: but that is only itself some "stupid first impression" (one of his favorite phrases). In reality, the paradox effect is designed to undo that second moment of ingenuity which is that of interpretation (it looks like this to you, but in reality what is going on is this …): the paradox is of the second order; what looked like a paradox was in reality simply a return to the first impression itself.

Or perhaps we might rather say: this is not a paradox, this is perversity. And indeed, the dialectic is just that inveterate, infuriating perversity whereby a common-sense empiricist view of reality is repudiated and undermined: but it is undermined together with its own accompanying interpretations of that reality, which look so much more astute and ingenious than the common-sense empiricist reality itself, until we understand that the interpretations are themselves also part of precisely that "first impression." This is why the dialectic belongs to theory rather than philosophy: the latter is always haunted by the dream of some foolproof, self-sufficient, autonomous system, a set of interlocking concepts which are their own cause. This mirage is of course the afterimage of philosophy as an institution in the world, as a profession complicit with everything else in the status quo, in the fallen ontic realm of "what is." Theory, on the other hand, has no vested interests inasmuch as it never lays claim to an absolute system, a non-ideological formulation of itself and its "truths"; indeed, always itself complicit in the being of current language, it has only the never-ending, never-finished task and vocation of undermining philosophy as such, of unraveling affirmative statements and propositions of all kinds. We have already put this another way by asserting that the two great bodies of post-philosophical thought, marked by the names of Marx and Freud, are better to be characterized as unities of theory and practice, that is to say, that the practical component in them always interrupts the "unity of theory" and prevents it from coming together in some satisfying philosophical system.

Still, what can be the theoretical, if not indeed the philosophical, content of those little interpretive tricks we have enumerated above? Let's first take on that supremely unclassifiable figure who somehow, in ways that remain to be defined, presides over all of Žižek's work. A late seminar of Jacques Lacan, indeed, bears the enigmatic title *Les non-dupes errent*: the joke lies in the homophony of this weird proposition ("the undeceived are mistaken") with the oldest formula in the Lacanian book, namely "le nom du Père," "the name-of-the-Father" or, in other words, the Oedipus complex. However, the later variant has nothing to do with this, but rather with the structure of deception. Indeed, as everyone knows, the truth is itself the best disguise, as when the spy tells his acquaintances, "What do I do in life? Why, I'm a spy!"—a truth invariably greeted with hearty laughter. This peculiarity of truth, to express itself most fully in deception or falsehood, plays a crucial role in analysis, as one might expect. And as one might also expect, it is in that great non- or anti-philosopher Hegel that we find the most elaborate deployment of the dialectic of the necessity of error and that of what he called appearance and essence, the most thoroughgoing affirmation of the objectivity of appearance (one of the deeper subjects of Žižek's work *The Parallax View*). Indeed, that other great modern dialectician Adorno was fond of observing that nowhere was Hegel closer to his heroic contemporary Beethoven than in the great thunderchord of the *Logic*, the assertion that "Essence must appear!"

Yet if essence appears today, it is through the mesmerizing veils of objective appearance, whose tantalizing "error" retains its power even when cognitively dispelled. For an older dialectic, the dispelling of ideology was to lead, not merely to truth, but also to change as such (Marx's final thesis on Feuerbach). To this degree, the Enlightenment belief in pedagogy and persuasion, its faith in demystification and the power of correct analysis, remained intact throughout the modern period. Adorno's desperate attempt to avoid positivities, which he instinctively felt always to be ideological, by embracing a resolutely negative equipollence, is a prophetic but unsatisfying response to our historical situation, which might better be characterized by varying Žižek's famous title to "they know what they are doing (but they do it anyway)." This situation, which is the realm of what has also usefully been termed cynical reason, calls for a reinvention of the dialectic as part and parcel of the reinvention of politics itself (and, clearly enough, of Marxism): while the difference between the "solutions" of Adorno and Žižek might from another perspective be characterized as the distinction between modernist anti-narrative as such (Beckett!) and a kind of non-figurative play with multiple narrative centers (as in more properly postmodern literature).

As if this were not enough, however, a final dilemma must be mentioned which has to do with the dialectic's relationship to Utopia. For the language of error and rectification we have been exercising here retains a fundamental Utopian presupposition within itself like a mirage (an objective mirage, if we may refer back to the previous discussion), insofar as it seems to promise a condition without all error, a life in the truth, which was very precisely the Utopian illusion denounced by Althusser in his proposition that ideology will continue to exist in all societies, no matter how "perfect."

Yet on the face of it, nothing could seem more Utopian than the dialectic, which indicts our everyday consciousness in the reified world of late capitalism and aims at replacing it with a transfigured subjectivity for which the world is a process of construction in which there are no reified or metaphysical "foundations," and from which the old stable essences and essentialisms have disappeared.

Yet it must also be clear from our description that insofar as it is critical, the dialectic is also what must be called reactive thought. That is, it depends for its operation on the normativity of a pre-existing thought mode, to which it is called upon to react: or to use a once popular theoretical expression, it is parasitic on *Verstand* itself, on the externalized thinking of a material world of objects, for its own operations of correction and subversion, of negation and critique.

But this means, from a Utopian perspective, that if the dialectic succeeds, it disappears as such. If dialectical thinking ever fully supercedes undialectical thinking and establishes itself in its place, if everyone then comes to think dialectically, then for all intents and purposes the dialectic will have ceased to exist, and something else, something as yet unidentified, some hitherto unknown species of Utopian consciousness, will have taken its place.

To put all this in a more pedestrian way, it is clear enough that Hegel never expected *Verstand*—the everyday commerce with material objects and identities—ever to disappear: it will always, along with our own bodies, continue to exist and to accompany whatever has been achieved of some dialectically higher consciousness or awareness. As for Marx, it is more probable that with the disappearance of the commodity form, reified consciousness can be expected to disappear; and yet, as Althusser tried to remind us, ideology—as the instinctive cognitive mapping of biological individuals—will always exist in whatever future society can be imagined. Nor can theory today expect to supplant the multitudinous forms of reified thinking and named and commodified thoughts and products on the intellectual market today, but only to wage persistent and local guerilla warfare against their hegemony.

Still, the characteristic anxieties about postmodern relativism, about the status of the referent and the wholesale discrediting of representation and indeed of "truth" as such attributed to this or that postmodernism, intervene here to make this a less than satisfactory solution. In particular, the status of Marxist forms of knowledge and of the Marxian code itself, whether substantive or critical, would seem in this situation to share the fate of the more traditional philosophies, and to find its own specific dialectic following them into optionality and sheerly personal ideological choice (of the free-market variety). The kind of equipollent conceptual critique we have attributed to these dialecticians then becomes very difficult to distinguish from deconstruction, *tout court*.

Indeed, for an older modernism the unrepresentable was still an object to be conquered and subdued, articulated and modeled, expressed and revealed or disclosed, by the invention of wholly new languages, the development of hitherto nonexistent theoretical and representational equipment, the ruthless abandonment of the old traditions and their habits and terminologies, and the confidence in the capacity of innovation and the *Novum* at least asymptotically to approach the Absolute, if not to give it any definitive and universally binding voice. Gramsci's "absolute historicism" promised as much, about a future we could not yet theorize, let alone imagine.

The postmodern, however, seems joyously to have abandoned all these efforts, after a repeated experience of their failures and a disabused conviction as to the ideological nature of all such alleged novelties, inventions, experiments, certainties, and truths new or old. Even "absolute relativism" seems merely to offer a revamped form of absolute skepticism, rather than a squaring of the circle.

This is then the situation in which Žižek's own provisional solution, conveyed in the very title of *The Parallax View*, proposes the possibility of ontological convictions without any accompanying linguistic or philosophical expression: locating the "truth" would then be something like a symptomal operation on the order of the Freudian primal desire which precedes all representation, all translation into the figural codes as such. The formula of a parallax would then compare the process to the determination of a planetary body beyond the capacity of our registering apparatus to record, even though we can approximate its existence hypothetically: and this affirmation of a content beyond all form is clearly very foreign indeed to the spirit of deconstruction and of postmodern relativism in general.

But it is also worth examining the procedures of Marx himself, who was on the face of it never reluctant to denounce the errors of others or to propose his own solutions as self-evident. Yet that those "solutions" were dialectical also becomes apparent. We may leave aside paradoxes which result from the dialectic of whole and part (or the circulation of multiple systems): as in the case of the piece-wage which "has a tendency, while raising the wages of individuals above the average, to lower this average itself" (*Cap*, 697). Rather, it is the deeper paradoxes of modernization itself which need to be translated into the dialectical idiom of contradiction. Thus, one would think that the modernization of agriculture—that is, the draining of the marshes and the reclaiming of unproductive terrain for agriculture—was to be considered a positive development and a benefit for society in general (stupid first impression): "But the inquiry showed the very opposite, namely 'that the same cause which drove away malaria, the conversion of the land from a morass in winter and a scanty pasture in summer into fruitful corn land, created the exceptional death-rate of the infants'" (*Cap*, 521–522).[62] As for modern machinery in general, its historically unparalleled productivity was responsible for a,

---

[62] Quoted from the 1864 Public Health Report.

remarkable phenomenon in the history of modern industry, that machinery sweeps away every moral and natural restriction on the length of the working day … [and results in] the economic paradox that the most powerful instrument for reducing labour-time suffers a dialectical inversion and becomes the most unfailing means for turning the whole lifetime of the worker and his family into labour-time at capital's disposal for its own valorization. (*Cap*, 532)

Yet this is a dialectical "paradox" in which the new interpretation by a vulgar Left (Proudhon, Weitling, etc.) is just as wrong as the obstinacies of bourgeois economists mired in their "stupid first impression" and singing the praises of the new improvements. We are here at the very center of the argument of *Capital*, and of the contradiction at the heart of this system between productivity and the value form. The first casualty of this dialectic is of course any moralizing or ethical approach to the matter (exhibited by the left critics of capitalist exploitation, and implicit in the bourgeois economists' celebration of its benefits for humankind). Marx will frequently attribute some of these "mistakes" to the omission of "the historical element" (*Cap*, 493); but he will also point out the illusions that result from the repression, by the empiricist, of the totality as such, the immense system of circulation of values which constitutes capitalism as a whole. He will also from time to time denounce the attempt to formulate the dynamic of the labor theory of value as a law. "Such a self-destructive contradiction cannot be in any way even enunciated or formulated as a law" (*Cap*, 676)—a proposition which cuts to the very heart of all representation and all philosophical systems.

Yet the fundamental dilemma at the center of such paradoxes, and indeed of the Marxian dialectic as such (if not even the Hegelian one), is the phenomenon of objective appearance to which we have already referred. Marx calls it the *Erscheinungsformen* or "form of appearance," a translation which would seem to minimize or trivialize the grave problem appearance constitutes as such. Thus Marx says, "the general and necessary tendencies of capital must be distinguished from their forms of appearance" (*Cap*, 433). It seems a mild enough epistemological warning, and is indeed followed by some remarks on knowledge and science as such: "a scientific analysis of competition is possible only if we can grasp the inner nature of capital, just as the apparent motions of the heavenly bodies are intelligible only to someone who is acquainted with their real motions, which are not perceptible to the senses" (*Cap*, 433). We are here apparently back in a discourse of external appearances and internal laws, whereas in fact Marx's dialectic is calculated to undermine this opposition altogether.

Consider the following remark: "In the expression 'value of labour,' the concept of value is not only completely extinguished, but inverted, so that it becomes its contrary. It is an expression as imaginary as the value of the earth. These imaginary expressions arise, nevertheless, from the relations of production themselves. They are categories for the forms of appearance of essential relations. That in their appearance things are often presented in an inverted way is something fairly familiar in every science, apart from political economy" (*Cap*, 677). It should be added that the very figure of inversion (to which Marx and Engels frequently returned, particularly in their discussion of ideology as a camera obscura) comes from Hegel's discussion of the "inverted world" of laws, about which it is not clear whether the latter is a philosophical appropriation of the figure in question or on the contrary a critique and a deconstruction of it.

The same is true here, and it is significant that at this point (in the related footnote) Marx recalls his own devastating critique of Proudhon's "tropological" analysis of the evils of capitalism, in whose exploitation of labor "he sees nothing but a grammatical ellipsis. Thus the whole of existing society … is henceforth founded on a poetic license, a figurative expression."[63] At this point the dialectic parts company with a deconstruction based on tropology, and in effect denounces the latter as an illusion derived from the failure to grasp the dialectical "paradox" of objective appearance (it is worth recalling that money itself is one of the most basic forms of just such objective appearance):

> What is true of all forms of appearance and their hidden background is also true of the form of appearance "value and price of labour," or "wages," as contrasted with the essential relation manifested in it, namely the value and price of labour-power. The forms of appearance are reproduced directly and spontaneously, as current and usual modes of thought; the essential relation must first be discovered by science. Classical political economy stumbles approximately onto the true state of affairs, but without consciously formulating it. It is unable to do this as long as it stays within its bourgeois skin. (*Cap*, 682)

This "paradox" is virtually itself constitutive of the dialectic as such, or may at least be seen as the unique situation and dilemma from which the very need to invent such a thing as the dialectic arises in the first place. We may dramatize the problem this way: can a true idea about a false society or a false reality be true? Or is it necessarily false, despite its accuracy? Or do we not confront in this opposition between truth and falsity another one of those binary oppositions which it was the vocation of the dialectic (and its unity of opposites) to overcome and to transcend?

We might also have phrased this dilemma in terms of contradiction: if a concept accurately registers the reality of a contradiction, will it not itself necessarily be contradictory? At any rate, for all the reasons it was the

---

[63] Karl Marx, *The Poverty of Philosophy*, New York: International Publishers, 1963, 54.

purpose of *Capital* to enumerate and to dramatize, capitalism and its law of value are themselves profoundly contradictory; and their reality is a set of false appearances, which are, however, real and objective, and cannot be dissolved by mere analysis (and certainly not by moralizing denunciation). We cannot translate their structure into "laws," all of which remain merely empirical observations, valid for this or that moment in the cycle and themselves invalidated by the inevitable crises and breakdowns in its operations. We might, to be sure, evoke the existential dimension, and argue that our lived experience of a capitalist world remains radically distinct (whatever its own kinds of truth) from the underlying structure or functioning of that world, as distinct as effects from causes. And in a sense, although Marx lacks the whole modern conceptuality of existentialism, this is where his own rhetorical figures tend, as in one of the most famous "bridge-passages" in *Capital*:

> Let us therefore, in company with the owner of money and the owner of labour-power, leave this noisy sphere, where everything takes place on the surface and in full view of everyone, and follow them into the hidden abode of production, on whose threshold there hangs the notice "No admittance except on business." (*Cap*, 279–280)

Elsewhere, and more philosophically, he rehearses the old Hegelian-dialectical opposition between appearance and essence (for example, to distinguish the realm of prices from that of value). But even the Hegelian opposition is misleading to the degree to which it suggests that one can substitute essence for appearance, as one substitutes truth for error, or that one can descend, following Marx, into that true underground realm in which production as such takes place (Wagner's image of the Nibelungen and their clattering forges beneath the earth; or indeed Wells's more carnivorous Morlocks).

Yet the very concept of objective appearance warns us that any such resolution of the contradiction in favor of either essence or appearance, truth or falsehood, is tantamount to doing away with the ambiguous reality itself. The dialectic stands as an imperative to hold the opposites together, and, as it were, to abolish the autonomy of both terms in favor of a pure tension one must necessarily preserve. At this point, perhaps, we leave even the subjective effects of the dialectic behind us, and venture into speculations as to its relevance today: for it is not Marx's description of the "essence" of capitalism which has changed (nor Hegel's of the "determinations of reflection" generally), but rather very precisely that "objective appearance" of the world of global capitalism which seems far enough from the surface life of Marx's Victorian or nascent-modernist period.

4. Towards a Spatial Dialectic

Towards the end of his pathbreaking book, *The Production of Space*, Henry Lefebvre calls for a reconstruction of the dialectic along spatial lines.[64] His recommendation carries even greater weight when we reckon in a theory of postmodernity (which he himself did not accept) for which the dominant of the modern period was an essentially temporal one. The shifting of a temporal center of gravity to a spatial one will then not only involve a transformation of the features of our description here, but also presumably equip this thought mode, and the propositions of both a Hegelian and a Marxian nature which have been associated with it, for greater effectiveness in a contemporary situation characterized by globalization and an essentially spatial economics as well as politics.

Many features of postmodernity speak for the saliency of the spatial in its structure (which we may also designate as late or third-stage capitalism). The displacement of production has not only meant a preponderance of service industries in the so-called advanced countries—that is to say, a restructuration around consumption and a subsequent development of an advertising and image society, or in other words an emergence of commodification as a fundamental social and political issue. Globalization has above all meant the association of space and spatial distance in production itself, whether in terms of outsourcing, of the uneven development of producing and consuming nations, or the migration of labor, as well as the black holes of unemployment, famine, and unspeakable violence into which whole surfaces of the current globe suddenly fall. The dominance of finance capital today is also a spatial phenomenon, in the sense in which its originalities derive from the suppression of more traditional temporalities of transmission and suggest all kinds of new spatial simultaneities. Much the same can be said for the eclipse of national autonomies and the omnipresence within the former national borders of international goods of all kinds, from food to culture. This omnipresence has been described in terms of a net of interdependence from which no single national space can escape and in which no one is any longer self-sustaining: but the nature of the new space this situation produces within the former national borders remains to be theorized, save for isolated symptoms such as tourism (and has mainly been erroneously characterized as the disappearance of the nation-state). The new kinds of cultural production generated by globalization have meanwhile often been enumerated, without attention to their functional role across the world system itself.

However this may be, the list does not yet argue for the necessity of a dialectical approach to the new global historical situation. Yet the rhythms of

---

[64] Henri Lefebvre, *La production de l'espace*, Paris: Anthropos, 1974, 382.

totality, of presence and absence in its effects, may be enough to convey the relevance of the dialectic. We witness today a play of reciprocal influences which go well beyond the old paradox whereby the center sneezes and the periphery catches the flu: for very often now this very relationship finds itself reversed, and storms at the center are generated by breezes on the out-skirts of consumption and affluence. The much repeated dialectic of global and local is certainly just that, a dialectic, even though it has rarely been seri-ously analyzed in those terms, which involve the interrelationship between a totality and a set of empirical particulars. Global capitalism today is clearly not to be thought of in terms of a sum of positivities; and any number of disastrous political strategies and calculations testify to the folly of approaching it in terms of common sense and of empirical facts, even when it is acknowledged that the multiplicity of such facts demands something more complicated than individual reasoning (generally it is the computer which is appealed to in such cases). The permutation schemes of what is so often identified as structuralism have been more successful in this respect, precisely because they are dialectical without knowing it. Finally, the apparently astonishing resurgence of religion as a worldwide political phenomenon demonstrates yet another non-dialectical blind spot; since the invocation of religion is most often a way of designating what we cannot by definition understand in the first place: namely some final "cause" or substance incomprehensible for empiricist thought but which has a long dialectical history as a relational or processual phenomenon.

One does not undertake to summarize or to present a thought mode that does not yet exist, and I will in conclusion only sketch in a few of the issues that seem to me important for its construction. It will, to be sure, be instruc-tive to interrogate traditional dialectical figures—such as Hegel's insistent trope of the returning into itself and the exteriorization of what is interior—for their spatial content; many such figures are to be found in Marx as well (chiasmus!), and in the later dialecticians. Yet that spatiality is perhaps still to be grasped only as a code, and not as some metaphysical proof of the ontological priority of space as such.

Indeed, a more powerful argument for the replacement of temporality could be mounted on the basis of the discussions of *Darstellung* or mode of presentation to be found in both Hegel and Marx. The former observes, of the *Logic*, and indeed against his own historiographic practice, that "the moments, whose result is a further determined form [of the concept], precede it as determinations of the concept in the scientific development of the Idea, but do not come before it as shapes in its temporal development."[65] Marx's versions of the same distinction are resumed in the following

---

[65] G. W. F. Hegel, *Elements of the Philosophy of Right*, ed. Allen W. Wood, trans. Hugh Barr Nisbet, Cambridge: Cambridge University Press, 1991, 61.

warning: "it would be unfeasible and wrong to let the economic categories follow one another in the same sequence as that in which they were historically decisive."[66] Such observations about the form of presentation of the dialectic are then powerful evidence against translating the sequence of topics of categories in both works into any temporal version of narrativity.

They do not, however, yet settle the question; and the language I have proposed, in terms of which time or space is considered a "dominant" in this or that historical chronotope, or spatio-temporal continuum, is obviously meant not to suggest that one dimension somehow replaces the other but rather to convey the fact that their ratios have been modified, or in other words that there has been a shift in the structure of their "form of appearance."

The demonstration of the validity of any new spatial dialectic will then stand or fall not merely with its relevance to contemporary conditions of globalization and postmodernity; but also with the success with which and the extent to which the older temporal categories of Hegelian and Marxist dialectics alike have been able to be translated into the new spatial idiom. What is a spatial contradiction, in other words? What can be the spatial equivalent of the negative or of negation? How do Hegel's "determinations of reflection" fit into a spatial and eventually global scheme? It may be somewhat easier to grasp the complications of the simultaneous Marxian temporalities of production and distribution, of realization and reproduction, of circulations and flows, in terms of the rotations of global space; indeed, this is probably what much of current bourgeois economics has been trying to do without realizing it.

I will limit myself here to a specific problem which seems to me crucial for any such translation process; and that is the role of reflection or self-consciousness in the new system. Much of the scaffolding of traditional philosophy (and also, as I've tried to show elsewhere,[67] of the ideologies of modernism and the "modern") has been built on that equivalence of truth and a reflexivity in which consciousness is at one with itself and with its object. No matter that the philosophical classics, from Plato on, have argued against this notion of a lightning-flash simultaneity of self and world: it persists as an indispensable cornerstone of the various worldviews on which our system rests, and this on all levels, not least of the alibis which justify the privileges modern (or self-conscious, reflexive) peoples have over all the others. But we must here insist that there is no difference between consciousness and self-consciousness and reconstruct a new equality on that basis.

---

[66] Quoted in Christopher J. Arthur, *The New Dialectic and Marx's 'Capital'*, Leiden: Brill, 2004, 4.

[67] See *A Singular Modernity: Essay on the Ontology of the Present*, London: Verso, 2002.

This is to be done, I believe, by insisting on the relationship between the ideologies of self-consciousness or reflection and their temporal thematics: it is as a unique moment of time, or of the suppression of time in a kind of absolute, that the essential vice of the concept of self-consciousness is to be grasped; and any viable proposal for a spatial dialectic will find itself obliged to offer a spatial account of what has traditionally passed for self-consciousness and has validated its uniqueness and its foundational privilege temporally. This is a program which might be executed in various ways: by insisting on the spatiality of the equation of identity itself, for example. Hegel notoriously expressed self-consciousness as the $I = I$, while the role of the equation in Marx's inaugural analysis of value is also well known. We must accustom ourselves to thinking of these equivalencies as temporal operations in which one specific spatial field is appropriated or annexed by another enlarged one. It is space which gives such operations their content, while it was time which encouraged the illusions of simultaneity: in other words, it is space which is the source of difference and time which is that of identity. And should it be argued that in reality this approach simply reinstates time as the very essence of what I have called the operation of equivalence, then I will respond that it has also established space as the secret truth of that time, whose own fundamental internal operation is the error of simultaneity. But it must be kept in mind that these are not ontological propositions but rather representational ones.

However such propositions play themselves out philosophically, I hope it will be more comprehensible to propose a view of that state formerly called self-consciousness as a mode of quasi-spatial enlargement: to the old non-reflexive I or ordinary consciousness there is added something else, which allows us to grasp that former non-reflexive self as itself an object within a larger field. The enlargement of the field of ordinary consciousness itself produces what we call the self or the sense of identity; and it is an operation structurally analogous to the way in which two distinct spatial objects are set

---

[68] To the degree to which this entire first chapter may serve as an introduction to the volume as a whole, it is now best to give a preview of the latter. The chapters on Hegel seek to establish a different case for his actuality than the one normally offered (or rejected). The second of those chapters, and the succeeding ones, examine some of the contemporary philosophical classics from a dialectical perspective (I hope to do something similar for Heidegger at a later date), and also to make a case for the renewed interest of Lukács and Sartre today. A series of shorter discussions then seek to clarify various themes in the Marxian tradition, from cultural revolution to the concept of ideology; followed by a series of political discussions, which, while documenting my personal opinions on topics ranging from the collapse of the Soviet Union to globalization, nonetheless claim to demonstrate the relevance of the dialectic for practical politics. In a long final section, which confronts Ricoeur's

in relationship to each other by perception as such (what I have called "difference relates"). When we add to this list of homologous structures of the spatial expansion implicit in the operations of capitalism, a more complete enumeration of the latter, from the conquest of markets to the spatial aggrandizements of imperialism and now globalization, we may then glimpse some of the advantages to be gained—on philosophical, aesthetic, and economic-political levels—from the substitution of a spatial dialectic for the old temporal ones.[68]

monumental study of history and narrative, I supplement this work by supplying the dialectical and Marxian categories missing from it, without which History today can scarcely be experienced. To be sure, *Valences* is something of a *Hamlet* without the prince, insofar as it lacks the central chapter on Marx and his dialectic which was to have been expected. Two complementary volumes, commentaries on Hegel's *Phenomenology* and Marx's *Capital* (Volume 1), respectively, will therefore complete the project. Meanwhile its unexpected complications could scarcely have been faced without the help of many other people, of whom I can here gratefully name only Sebastian Budgen, Mark Martin, Koonyong Kim, Gopal Balakrishnan, Philip Wegner, and Luka Arsenjuk.

PART II

HEGEL WITHOUT *AUFHEBUNG*

Chapter 2

Hegel and Reification

Hegel was a late developer. He was thirty-seven when the *Phenomenology of Spirit* was published; and his *Science of Logic* followed only when he was forty-two. It was his third book, written in serious professional difficulties. He still had no university position, and was not really suited to the *Gymnasium* directorship he currently occupied. The reception of the *Phenomenology*, on its publication in 1807, was disappointing; indeed, this book will not achieve the centrality it has for us until the work of Dilthey in the late nineteenth century.

It was rather around the *Logic* that what we call Hegelianism began to be organized; it was the *Logic* that underwrote his eventual professorships at Heidelberg (1816) and then Berlin (1818). *The Science of Logic*—the so-called *Greater Logic*—was in fact only the first of Hegel's publications on the subject. A second, smaller version appeared in the three-part *Encyclopedia of the Philosophical Sciences* in 1817. These works were meant to be student handbooks, and to accompany the professor's lectures on the subject: fortunately the modern editions contain many of Hegel's oral commentaries on the individual entries, and offer a more accessible approach to them than the monumental *Greater Logic* itself (in what follows, it will essentially be the *Encyclopedia Logic* that is referenced, in William Wallace's attractive Scottish translation).[1]

Today, however, after the emergence of symbolic logic and all the complexities of modern mathematics (whose emergence with Boole in 1847 Hegel did not live to see), the originality of Hegel's transformation of traditional logic may not be so apparent. Still, the flavor of what happened to

---

[1] The German original is referenced in Volume 8 of the Suhrkamp collected works, Frankfurt, 1986, along with the appropriate paragraph number of Hegel's text. Future references to this work are denoted *EL*. Two translations have been used: the older, more readable one of William Wallace, Oxford: Clarendon Press, 1975; and the more rigorous new translation of T. F. Geraets, W. A. Suchting, and H. S. Harris, Indianapolis: Hackett, 1991. Future references to the Wallace translation are denoted *W*; future references to the Geraets, Suchting, and Harris translation are denoted *GSH*.

Aristotelian logic in the schools may be conveyed by the way in which all the possible forms of the syllogism were given proper names in the Middle Ages; thus, Derit or Cemestres, Featino or Darapti, Patiat, Bocardo, Ferison, and Fesapo, all name specific syllogistic formulas. (One readily imagines the pedagogical practices learning such a list encouraged!)

Hegel hit on the idea of translating the elements of the Aristotelian logical mechanism back into genuine philosophical conceptualities. So successful was this operation indeed that Hegel is scarcely ever mentioned in the history of logic, as though he had somehow suppressed the method and the mechanics which made it "logic" in the first place. These various elements (or aspects, in German, *Momente*) are then lined up in what looks like a sequential or even teleological series. To see what is really at stake here we would have to take into account the issue of "presentation" or *Darstellung*—how to lay all this material out; but also have to come to terms with the concluding term of the "Notion"—the *Begriff* or Absolute Spirit—which is not, I would argue, a temporal idea or a historical stage (the German word *Moment* is ambiguous: when masculine, it has the temporal sense of the English "moment"; but when neuter, it simply means an aspect). What is sequential in Hegel's series of categories is their progressive enlargement, and the degree to which each "moment" cannot stand on its own, but is dependent on another feature or "same" outside itself which has to be factored back into the process of thought. The ultimate Notion or *Begriff* is then a fully self-sufficient concept which is a kind of *causa sui* or "cause of itself": Spinoza's "God or Nature" would be an appropriate analogy, and indeed Hegel thought of himself as a competitor of Spinoza's who attempted to factor subjectivity and consciousness ("system or subject") into the latter's extraordinary vision of totality.

However we wish to see Hegel's progression of forms, the more general outline of both *Logic*s is clear: the three parts—entitled Being, Essence, and the Notion (*Sein, Wesen, Begriff*) in his terminology—designate dimensions of life and thought we might describe as follows. The categories of Being are those of common sense or a daily life among objects, in which the law of non-contradiction holds sway: this is the world of *Verstand* or Understanding (in the philosophical jargon of the day), and it will be more thoroughly dealt with in what follows, inasmuch as it is a thought of extension and objectivity, a reified thought which must reify itself in order to grasp its reified objects.

The realm of Essence is then the way in which categories act and react upon each other within the mind: this is more properly the realm of the dialectic itself, in which we become aware to what degree "definition is negation" (Spinoza again) and each thought is linked to its opposite. This area may be said, in current philosophical language, to be that of reflexivity or self-consciousness.

There remains, finally, the Notion itself, which is divided into two zones: the Syllogism and Life. I propose to translate the first of these Hegelian figures into the language of the Logos, whose movement and dynamism organize the world itself and its time. The idea of Life, then—we are still in a pre-Darwinism context, in which reference to vitalism or the Bergsonian life force would be anachronistic—is I believe Hegel's way of rescuing the world of matter from mechanical materialism and designating the organization of the objective universe (or Nature in its largest sense). The Absolute is then the Deleuzian "fold" between these two parallel dimensions, which in my opinion correspond to what Spinoza called the two "attributes," *cogitatio* (thought) and *extensio* (extension), two coterminous and parallel dimensions or codes into which all realities can be translated back and forth. This seems to me what one might want to call the metaphysics of Hegel, the sense in which he has attempted to give "content" to the abstract form of his thinking: or "meaning" to its grammar and syntax. That he himself knows this may be deduced from his insistence on calling this third section of the *Logic* speculative thought, rather than dialectics: by which he seems to have meant that the affirmation of the identity between thinking and its object could never be proved but only asserted by way of a leap of reason. It is that leap (or its figural content) which we must designate as metaphysical in all its contemporary senses, or even as ideological.

I.

These notes on the *Encyclopedia Logic* need to be prefaced by three observations, on my repeated use of the term "category" to characterize the structures at stake in this text, as well as on my treatment of that temporality traditionally imputed to the way in which those categories, in the *Logic*, are supposed to produce themselves and to generate their own succession in some kind of dialectical time; to which I add a remark on idealism. The first, or terminological, negligence results from my assumption that the *Logic* is Hegel's continuation of the great Kantian insight about the deeper organization of Aristotle's haphazard list of categories. Kant's insight was essentially a spatial one, in which the categories were sorted out in four groups: quantity, quality, relationship, and modality (Hegel deploys the first two groups in the Doctrine of Being, the second two in the Doctrine of Essence). It would be of much interest to examine Kant's arrangement in its own right (its four-fold organization cries out for interpretation). All we can do here is to take note of Hegel's extraordinary modifications in the scheme, which in effect project Kant's spatial groups onto temporality itself (of which more shortly). Although he does not use the term as such, it seems fair to describe the moments of the *Logic*—which range from topics like Being or Necessity to seemingly more minor matters, such as Limit, Reciprocity, Accident, and the like—as a greatly enlarged list of "categories" on the Kantian or Aristotelian mode. In that case, should there not be a category of the Category itself (a popular idea during the structuralist period which Derrida repudiated with some contempt in his essay on Benveniste)? The difficulty perhaps lies in their evolution and transformation in the very course of the *Logic*, such that the initial category of Being—if a category at all—is not meant at all to be the same kind of mental entity as the Notion which concludes the series: thus, to impose this term or classification on the moments from the outset would be to force their development into a rigid and uniform mold. But if these moments cannot be ranged under the classification Category, then what are they exactly?

It is a question which raises even more general questions about the space in which such "categories" develop, questions we did not have to pose for Kant or Aristotle. For the latter, they are simply the various things that can be "said" about a being or a phenomenon. In this way, Aristotle paradoxically rejoins his modern semiotic critics (Benveniste, Eco) who have maintained that his "categories" are merely the projections and hypostases of a local Indo-European grammar. Yet Aristotle did himself already locate them in speech (everything we can say about beings) even if he failed to raise the issue of the epistemological relativity of languages as such.

As for Kant, not yet being a Habermassian or feeling the sway of any structuralist or postmodern doxa about the primacy of language and communication, he sticks to the mind itself and grasps the categories as so many "concepts of the understanding" which operate both judgments and those perceptions understood to be mental "syntheses of representations." Still, he disposes of some fairly recognizable traditional "space"—the mind—in which, as in Aristotle's "speaking," the categories can comfortably be housed and find their field of efficacy. Whatever Hegel thinks about mind or language, those are not the "places" in which his categories evolve: and to call this last Spirit or even Objective Spirit is to beg the question, insofar as it is precisely the space of the categories which will be called on to define Spirit in the first place.

So they seem relatively placeless and disembodied: they are not the thoughts of a Mind, even a transcendental one (since for one thing, they are not yet even thoughts as such): whatever Absolute Spirit may be, or however Hegel's combination of Substance and Subject may be understood, it is not an omniscient and anthropomorphized narrator of some sort. In fact, I tend to think it would be better to imagine the "space" of Hegel's categories in the absence of all such modern container notions of subjectivity or of element, in a kind of spacelessness. This makes the categories in Hegel far more situation- or event-specific; all the while acknowledging the evident fact that whatever "space" or "context" may be invoked, it will always also itself be precisely one of those categories it was alleged to have governed or contained. Thus once again here we confront the well-known paradox of the "class which is a member of itself," something "solved" by the attempt to imagine a state of things—or better still a type of discourse—itself free of such representational homogeneity, and able to accommodate a series of "events" without a frame or background. Add to this the characterization of these moments as somehow related to *pensée sauvage*[2] in that the *Logic* effectuates the construction of local universals out of particulars in a situation in which universals do not yet exist, and we have an even more paradoxical approach to Hegel opening up before us. (Perhaps, to anticipate, one might justify the approach by saying that, even though Hegel emerges long after the coming into being of universals—this is, after all, the very definition of Western philosophy—we may posit a deliberate suspension of universals in his new "speculative" dramatization of the categories themselves.)

But other important questions associated with the notion of the category remain. In particular, there is the Kantian question of their number: can they all not be reduced to four groups of three? If not why not? And in view of Hegel's insistence on the "necessity" of their unfolding (see below), are we to believe that he thinks he has given us a complete list? In other words, one way of philosophically testing (or "falsifying") his program is on the basis of its completeness: can categories be added that he has not thought of? If so, where and why? And to historicize all this even further, can we imagine the historical coming into being of *new* categories which did not exist in Hegel's time; or the disappearance of older ones? And what of *pensée sauvage*? Although Lévi-Strauss is very far from considering this tribal perceptual science as "primitive"—in fact he characterizes it as "structuralist" *avant la lettre*—he certainly argues for its radical difference from our own (Western, bourgeois) thinking, something that entitles us to wonder whether the same list of categories remains in force in tribal times (or in other modes of production). It is the Whorf-Sapir question (our thinking is a projection of the structure of our language) which turns very much on the matter of categories as such, and which is perhaps in the present case exacerbated by what is often enough considered to be Hegel's Eurocentrism.

---

2 Claude Lévi-Strauss, *La Pensée sauvage*, Paris: Plon, 1962: the ambiguous term (mistranslated as "the savage mind," but can also mean "a pansy growing in the wild") names the thinking of tribal peoples, a kind of perceptual science without abstractions. Yet rather than picture-thinking (*Vorstellung*), it would be preferable to describe such thinking as self-referential or allegorical "classes which are classes of themselves." I here consider them to be "categories" analogous to those of Kant, unless it should turn out that the latter are themselves remnants of *pensée sauvage* as such.

2.

Now I come to my second preliminary observation, which has to do with temporality: nor is this simply a matter of organization or *Darstellung* (presentation, staging), according to which Hegel projects the narrative fiction of an unfolding series or sequence in order the more effectively to string the pearls of the categories one after the other. If it were merely a matter of organization, one would expect the account of each category to be a relatively static affair, so that one might open up what is after all called an encyclopedia and consult this or that entry, in case of need extracting the "definition" of "substance", say, or "necessity", or "limit", in order to find out exactly what the meaning is. But we cannot do this, because the temporal sequence of the categories purports to stage the self-production, the self-development, and self-unfolding, of the Notion itself. We would therefore minimally expect any given category to require, for complete discussion, an account of what precedes and what follows it, in what we have seen to be the non-space of the text. This is to say that each conceptual item in effect produces its own context, which it equally well abolishes on its own transformation into something else. The categories are thus all situation- or context-specific, provided we understand that there is no overall situation or context, no overall conceptual landscape, given in advance.

What this means for the reader is that the *Logic* is no traditional piece of philosophical discourse: it does not, turgidly and laboriously, attempt to expound some idea which the reader then attempts, by retracing the steps of the argument, to re-create and thus to grasp or "understand." Or rather, this does seem to happen at specific moments, and we certainly still do struggle to understand what Hegel meant by this or that: but the act of reading the *Logic* is a great deal more complicated than that, and requires, as with a complicated novel, that we dispose of larger units of memory in which to organize the individual episodes. Better still, the *Logic* is like a piece of music, and its text a score, which we must ourselves mentally perform (and even orchestrate). As was so often said about the modernist texts, we can only reread it, and each reading performance brings out new and more subtle interrelationships (thematic repeats, details of the orchestration, harmonic ingenuities) which we had not heard or noticed before. And sometimes the rereadings also make us more receptive to the great climaxes, the melodramatic reversals (Adorno used to say that the great affirmation "Essence must appear!" was like a hammerblow in Beethoven). The analogy does not perhaps fully bear out Greimas' hypothesis that the philosophical text is also, in its deeper structure, a narrative. In any case, the aesthetic set towards the text moves it away from philosophizing and argument, let alone truth, and thereby risks depriving it of its most fundamental driving impulse and passion, indeed, its very justification. So the more we insist on the pleasure of reading the *Logic*, the less are we tempted in the long run to read it in the first place.

3.

So let's now say all this in a very different way by insisting on the failures which constitute the *Logic*'s deeper record; most philosophical discourse claims a certain conceptual success it hopes to record successfully, and even to convey. Hegel's moments are by definition moments of failure: the failure to think, to win through to the concept, to achieve even a limited but complete act of intellection. The task of his writing will therefore be paradoxically self-defeating: to demonstrate (successfully) how completely we must necessarily fail to think this or that category. But in order for it to be meaningful, the failure must be a very basic and fundamental one, it must come as the result of loyally attempting to think, and at the end of a strenuous and absolute assault on the category in question. And it is to be sure a frustrating matter: who can find it in them to commit to a cause lost in advance, an experiment conducted with a view to proving itself impossible? What saves the matter, no doubt, is the simple fact that, however much they may be intellectual or conceptual failures, the categories are the stuff of daily life and daily speech, rehearsed over and over again, and quite impossible to replace with anything better, purer, more Utopian: nor does Hegel try to do so, even though he does seem to posit "philosophizing" as some activity not altogether accessible to the masses.

In any case, we will still need to ward off the impression that all these failures are somehow "the same," just as we will have to guard against the supposition that all the transitions from one category, one failure, to the next, are somehow "the same," let alone the implication that the so-called categories themselves are in their form somehow comparable, if not identical. The terms for all these things fatally reinforce such implications and illusions: if you use the word "category" for a variety of concepts, classifying them all under this particular genus, have you not admitted a fundamental kinship in advance? And if we call Hegel's conceptual movement through the text and its moments dialectical, do we not also imply a certain uniformity, a standard momentum, a repetition of the same transitions, the same metamorphoses? This may be why Hegel uses words like "dialectical," "truth," "rational," "reason," sparingly: whereas the text itself repeatedly characterizes the kinds of errors and illusions described above in this very paragraph: they are the baleful effects of *Verstand*, of "Understanding," of an external and spatial picture-thinking (*Vorstellung*) it is tempting to identify with the more modern (although still no doubt distantly Hegelian) term "reification". *Verstand* is reified, reifying thinking; its domain is that real world of Being, of physical objects, which we meet in Part 1 of the *Logic*. But already we can make a few anticipatory remarks about it.

Verstand, although omnipresent, and the very thinking of daily life itself, is the villain of the piece. We cannot say that throughout the *Logic*, Hegel tracks down the truth like a detective, but we can certainly say that he tracks error, and that error always and everywhere takes the form of *Verstand*. The *Logic* is therefore not a *Bildungsroman*, where the little Notion grows up and learns about the world, and eventually reaches maturity and autonomy: that could be, perhaps, the narrative schema of the *Philosophy of History*, and can still be detected in its alleged teleology. Rather, *Verstand* is the great magician, the Archimago, of the work, the primal source of error itself, and of all the temptations—to persist in one moment, for example, and to make one's home there. Unlike the *Faerie Queene*, however, if there is a villain, there are no heroes: none of the knights, not the Dialectic, not Reason (*Vernunft*), not Truth, nor Speculative Thinking, nor even the Notion itself, goes forth to do battle with this baleful force (although it might perhaps be argued that Philosophy is itself such a heroic contender, a word which, besides meaning Hegel, also means all those other positive things just mentioned). And this may have something to do with the fact that *Verstand* also has its place, as we have suggested, and not only cannot be done away with for good: it would be undesirable to do so, it is the taming and proper use of this mode rather than its eradication, which is wanted. Sin and error in Spenser are no doubt equally difficult to eradicate, or to imagine fully eradicated: but the virtuous or Christian mind continues to wish for such an eventuality and to hope for a realm in which something of the sort might be realized. Whatever the reign of Absolute Spirit might be, it would not seem to presume that; nor could that be the upshot of the notorious "end of history," even assuming there is such a thing in Hegel.

4.

I can be briefer about Hegel's idealism, a reproach relatively unseasonable, insofar as there do not seem to be any idealists anymore in the first place (even though everyone likes to talk about materialism). I suppose there would be some agreement about distinguishing from idealism something called spiritualism, which, despite all kinds of religious revivals, does not seem to me to be particularly extant any longer either. Perhaps, in some more figurative and ideological sense, idealism consists in a drawing away from the body and a consistent sublimation of everything that could be associated with sheer physicality. Here we are on firmer ground, and it is certain that the fundamental movement in Hegelianism consists in a deep suspicion, not only of the perceptual (the "here" and "now" of the opening of the *Phenomenology*), but of the immediate as such. But can there be a mediated materialism, a mediated body which would remain what we still call the body? Yet there are paradoxes to be observed here, and it is important to remember, or to understand in the first place, that Marx's "fetishism of commodities" is not some unmediated materialism either, but on the contrary a tainted kind of unconscious spiritualism in its own right.

As for "idealism" in Hegel's usage in the text, however, its proper translation lies very far from all such considerations, and simply means the quotient of theory in all those discourses claiming to stick to the facts, to eschew metaphysical speculation, and to keep faith with a stubborn empiricism of common sense and everyday life. The argument was renewed in the 1960s by all the varied partisans of theory, who delighted in demonstrating with gusto that all these Anglo-American empirical statements which formed our then hegemonic discourse were deeply if secretly theoretical at their hearts and that plain homespun realistic thinking was rotten to the core with theoretical presuppositions. Such was already Hegel's battle with the scientists and the other "realists": "This ideality of the finite is the chief maxim of philosophy; and for that reason every genuine philosophy is idealism" (*EL*, par. 95; *W*, 140; *GSH*, 203).

The supreme example of such ideality (or theoreticity) active at the very heart of what seems to be sheerly empirical or of the "fact," the external, finite, physical, and the like, is mathematics: "quantity, of course, is a stage of the Idea; and as such it must have its due" (*EL*, par. 99; *W*, 147; *GSH*, 211). Number is the very epitome of such frozen or crystallized theory: emerging from the dialectic between the Continuous and the Discrete, its deployments are supremely philosophical (as Wallace puts it, "all reckoning is therefore making up the tale"—thereby adding his own pun in the German word (*er-zählen*) (*EL*, par. 102; *W*, 150; *GSH*, 215).

This hidden presence of the idealities, the categories, behind our more seemingly external experiences and perceptions, is somehow nonetheless capable of eluding Kantian subjectivism: for it does not seem to push all our "intuitions" back inside the individual mind, to be processed into thoughts and knowledge. Hegel's "idealism" is not subjectivizing in this Kantian sense, insofar as the frame of the individual subject is lacking from his scheme. He benefits from the historical good luck of an absence of individualism which can be judged pre- or post-individualistic alike: the technical reason being, of course, that the individual emerges only at the end of his series, with the Notion, leaving earlier developments relatively innocent of the effects of a subject-object split. Lévi-Strauss's structuralism has famously been termed a "Kantianism without the transcendental subject," and we have counted him also among the philosophers of the "category." With all due qualifications, Hegelian "idealism" might be thought of in a similar way: everything we see and think by definition comes through our minds and consciousnesses, and so even materialists are idealistic in this sense. Yet at the end of the series of categories, "speculative thinking," the thought of the Notion or Concept (*Begriff*) reaffirms the subject-object split anew by asserting the identity between the two; at this point, perhaps, Hegel has again become an idealist in the traditional sense, but not until then.

5.

Now we need to see the whole process at work, by reading or performing the famous opening section of the Doctrine of Being, where, as every schoolchild knows, Being is declared to be "the same" as Nothingness. But this philosophical assertion in fact conceals and expresses a reading problem (which is in fact "the same" as the writing problem with which the *Phenomenology* opens: are not the most basic and immediate things we can say— "here" and "now"—also the emptiest and the poorest?). We want to begin with the realest thing of all, the most fundamental, and, following Descartes, the simplest and most indivisible. Hegel is very clear that it cannot be the Cartesian cogito, however, which is a most complex late product: it can only be Being, something which can be said about everything without exception—and a premise falsifiable to the degree that it is open to anyone to propose something even simpler and more universal.

The reading problem emerges when we try to think Being as such. Clearly enough, it asks to be thought: "it is not to be felt, or perceived by sense, or pictured in imagination: it is only and merely thought" (*EL*, par. 86; *W*, 125; *GSH*, 184). And it has the authority of philosophical history, as the supreme starting point of the Eleatics, who never got beyond it. But what kind of thought is it? The mind remains stalled at the prospect; and one is reminded of Sartre's satiric portrait of the wonderment of vacationers confronted with Nature—"they think nothing about it because they can find nothing to do with it," etc.[3] So it is with Being: an empty thought,

---

[3] Jean-Paul Sartre, *Saint Genet*, New York: Braziller, 1963, 266: "But several times a year the urban communities of honest folk decide in common—taking into account the necessities of economic life—to change their attitude toward the big farming areas. On a given date, town society expands, plays at disintegration; its members betake themselves to the country where, under the ironic eyes of the workers, they are metamorphosed for a while into pure consumers. It is then that Nature appears. What is she? Nothing other than the external world when we cease to have technical relations with things. The producer and the distributor of merchandise have changed into consumers, and the consumers change into meditators. Correlatively, reality changes into a setting; the just man on vacation *is there*, simply there, in the fields, amidst the cattle; reciprocally, the fields and the cattle reveal to him only their simple *being-there*.

which turns out to be nothing, in all the senses of the word. That is to say that the same stunned and empty contemplation occurs when you try to stare into the heart of Nothingness, which in turn has to "be" fully as much as anything we see, think, name, and so forth. The only advantage of this equivalence (which also leads nowhere) is to stimulate the search for a characterization. And it is important that the real search begins only when we have, as here, an opposition or an equivalence, a binary system: Being and Nothingness, Being is the same as Nothingness; but it can't be, as they are absolute opposites, etc. So we reach one of the great moments of this first exposition, in which Hegel identifies the mind in the act of slipping toward a figure:

> If the opposition in thought is stated in this immediacy as Being and Nothing, the shock of its nullity is too great not to stimulate the attempt to fix Being and secure it against the transition into Nothing. With this intent, reflection has recourse to the plan of discovering some fixed predicate for Being, to mark it off from Nothing. Thus we find Being identified with what persists amid all change, with *matter*, susceptible of innumerable determinations … (*EL*, par. 87; *W*, 127; *GSH*, 86)

We may suspect, from what has already been said about Hegel's "idealism," that he is bound to have mixed feelings about the concept of matter, and, in particular, about whether it is any more thinkable, really, when you get right down to it, than Being itself. It is significant that in fact "matter" as such will later on reappear as an official category in its own right, but as a binary term within Essence (*EL*, par. 128), where it cannot provide the basis for a monism. (Still, here too, Hegel nags away at it and works hard to reduce its categorical autonomy, as we shall see later on.)

So we seem to have reached a stalemate, in which only picture-thinking is left: Being as the "bad infinite" of endless plains of sheer matter; or as the somewhat more respectable religious image of sheer light; Nothingness as

---

That is what he calls perceiving life and matter in their absolute reality. A country road between two potato patches is enough to manifest Nature to the city dweller. The road was laid out by engineers, the patches are tilled by peasants. But the city dweller does not see the tilling, which is a kind of work that remains foreign to him. He thinks that he is seeing vegetables in the wild state and mineral matter in a state of freedom. If a farmer goes across the field, he will make a vegetable of him too. Thus, Nature appears at the horizon of the seasonal or weekly variations of our society; it reflects to the just their fictive disintegration, their temporary idleness, in short their paid vacations. They wander through the undergrowth as through the damp, tender soul of the children they once were; they consider the poplars and plane trees planted on the roadside; they find nothing to say about them since they do nothing about them, and they are astonished at the wonderful quality of the silence."

whatever kind of black hole you can imagine. That these concepts are "identical" in the sense in which both utterly lack content of any kind, conceptual or visual, we may perhaps accept. How this "identity" of the two alternating terms might also offer some kind of "unity" seems harder to grasp; and in fact Hegel does not argue it so much as he deploys a kind of introspection: where it turns out that we already have such a concept, and therefore do not need to produce or invent one. Indeed, if it is irreducible (that is, if it cannot be reassimilated to either Being or Nothingness as such), then we can also plausibly assume that it is an original category in its own right. In fact, Hegel offers us two possibilities: Becoming, in the official text of paragraph 88; and in the oral commentary, Beginning. Let us look at the language of the latter:

> If noncomprehension only means that one cannot *represent* the unity of being and nothing, this is really so far from being the case, that on the contrary everyone has an infinite supply of notions [*Vorstellung*] of this unity; saying that one has none can only mean that one does not [re]cognize the present concept in any of those notions, and one does not know them to be examples of it. The readiest example of it is *becoming*. Everyone has a notion of becoming and will also admit moreover that it is *One* notion; and further that, if it is analyzed, the determination of *being*, but also that of *nothing*, the stark Other of being, is found to be contained in it; further, that these two determinations are undivided in this, *One* notion; hence that becoming is the unity of being and nothing.—Another example that is equally ready to hand is the *beginning*; the matter [itself] *is not yet* in its beginning, but the beginning is not merely its *nothing*: on the contrary, its *being* is already there, too. (*EL*, par. 88; *W*, 130; *GSH*, 142–143)

But this is a remarkable turn, and scarcely weakened by Hegel's offhand remark that, indeed, we might have saved ourselves the trouble and begun the *Logic* with Becoming in the first place. For the matter of beginnings and their impossibility is one of the great obsessive leitmotifs of all of Hegel's works, and as unavoidable in the opening pages of each one (save perhaps for the *Philosophy of History* itself) as it is logically unassailable (if we could summarize the content of philosophizing in a page or two, we would not have to do it in the first place). Yet here (in anticipation of some of the cleverest contemporary theory) a beginning is made with the very category of Beginning itself: the text is autoreferential from the outset, a modernist feature which is always a sign of the uncertainty of the institutional and social status of the text in question. One thinks also of what may be called Hegel's ethic of production (and even, if you like, of the production of this particular text, the *Logic*):

The individual who is going to act seems, therefore, to find himself in a circle in which each moment presupposes the other, and thus he seems unable to find a beginning, because he only gets to know his original nature, which must be his End, *from the deed*, while, in order to act, he must have that End beforehand. But for that very reason he has to start immediately, and, whatever the circumstances, without further scruples about beginning, means, or End, proceed to action.[4]

Lenin in April! Indeed, this dialectic of action (whose strongest contemporary influence can be found in Sartre's *Critique of Dialectical Reason*) constitutes the core of Hegel's political theory (far more than accounts of monarchy and constitutions in the *Philosophy of Right*) and may be said to be the closest he ever came to fulfilling his ambition of being the German Machiavelli. So in Hegel to begin with Beginning is no innocent or obvious act, but a whole program, which the *Logic* is very far from realizing, as we shall see.

After this second moment—which turns out in reality to be the initial one—the sequence is far less problematic; providing us with the "determinate being," Wallace's "somewhat," which is not yet really a Thing (as we shall also see later), and raising the issue of determination (quality) and then, since it is one of something, of number and quantity (which conclude the section on Being). I have commented at length elsewhere on the famous opening dialectic of the Essence section[5] (which Lukács called the very heart of Hegel's dialectic): suffice it to say that we observe here a movement from external things to inner relations and determinations which are always binary:

> In Being, the relational form is only [due to] our reflection; in Essence, by contrast, the relation belongs to it as its own determination. When something becomes other (in the sphere of Being) the something has thereby vanished. Not so in Essence: here we do not have a genuine other, but only diversity, relation between the One and *its* other ... In the sphere of Being, relatedness is only *implicit*; in Essence, on the contrary, it is posited. This then is in general what distinguishes the form of Being from that of Essence. In Being, everything is immediate; in Essence, by contrast, everything is relational. (*EL*, par. 111; *W*, 229–230; *GSH*, 173–174)

But at this point I want to tell the story differently, and in particular to examine the structural role of a certain kind of non- or pre-dialectical, maybe even anti-dialectical thinking—*Verstand* or Understanding—in the unfolding of the *Logic*.

---

[4] G. W. F. Hegel, *Phenomenology of Spirit*, trans. A. V. Miller, Oxford: Oxford University Press, 1977, 240.

[5] See my *Brecht and Method*, London: Verso, 1998, 79–81.

6.

But collecting the references to *Verstand* scattered through the *Logic* is more than an exercise in patience: it will in fact reveal a very different narrative structure, and at the same time clarify the nature of this thinking which cannot be a real, abstract thinking and which must be referred to as a thought of externality or of "indifference" (in the period sense). But we must resist the immediate temptation to classify *Verstand* as the thought of the immediate, or of Being itself. In fact the initial discussion of Being says something quite different:

> So when all is said and done, being is the first pure thought; and whatever else may be made the starting point (I = I, absolute Indifference, or God himself) is initially only *something which is represented*, rather than thought. With regard to its thought-content, it is quite simply being. (*EL*, par. 86; *W*, 126–127; *GSH*, 139)

The italics translate from the German "ein Vorgestelltes" ("und nicht ein Gedachtes"), which Wallace renders as "a figure of materialized conception" (*W*, 127). So from the very outset, we find pure thought opposed to representational or picture-thinking, and we find that the movement of the argument turns very much on the process of differentiating these two mental modes from one another. Whether *Vorstellung* is altogether to be identified with *Verstand* as such cannot yet be decided (nor is its relationship to Imagination clarified either). At any rate, in the next paragraph Hegel goes on to show us an even more dramatic substitution of "materialized conception" for the pure thought of Being in his example of the slippage towards "matter," of which more below.

It is not until the discussion of Becoming that we find an explicit onslaught on Understanding as such: specifically it is not only accused of longing for "fixity"—"eine feste Bestimmung"—but also of thereby seeking to avoid confronting contradiction itself.

> The abstracting activity of the understanding is a clinging on to One determinacy by force, an effort to obscure and to remove the consciousness of the other one that is contained in it. (*EL*, par. 89; *W*, 133; *GSH*, 145)

The next sentence explicitly identifies the "consciousness" that would be willing to think the other determination as a consciousness of contradiction as such. We may here therefore in some virtually proto-Freudian movement *avant la lettre* identify a repression of contradiction as one of the driving impulses of *Verstand*, along with a displacement of the contradiction onto the positing of some single stable determination or quality.

It does seem difficult to decide, at this stage, which impulse is the primary one—that of a univocal knowledge which will turn out to be almost visual

in character, or that of an anxiety in the face of contradictions and its insta-
bilities. The two things may of course be one and the same, but they
nonetheless still offer two rather distinct ways of thinking *Verstand* and its
function and motivation, and thereby demand some kind of resolution.
At the same time it becomes clear that these early stages in the evolution of
some concept of Being will constitute privileged traps for thinking and
temptations for a powerful investment by *Verstand*: particularly since the
domain of "quality" is uniquely one in which some "single fixed determination" might successfully and stubbornly block all further development.

But now we get a glimpse of another "property" of *Verstand*, as it emerges
incidentally in a discussion of reality and ideality.

> *Reality* and *ideality* are frequently considered as a pair of determinations that con-
> front one another with equal independence, and therefore people say that apart
> from reality, there is "also" an ideality. But ideality is not something that is given
> outside of and apart from reality … (*EL*, par. 96; *W*, 141; *GSH*, 153)

So it is that "also" comes to be marked negatively, and comes to absorb a
variety of different external compoundings, additions, the uses of "and,"
and so forth: indeed, to the point at which one wonders whether Deleuze's
great exaltation of the form—"et … et"[6]—does not in its fierce anti-
Hegelianism derive specifically from this Hegelian motif.

We will return to it, almost at once, but in a kind of combination with the
previous motifs, and at the very moment when Hegel, arriving at the stage of
Atomism in classical philosophy, confronts the scientists more generally. He
compliments them for the dialectical subtlety of their discovery of the intimate relationship between Attraction and Repulsion, but almost at once
suggests that their well-deserved pride in the discovery is misplaced: for in
substituting molecules for the atoms of the ancients, "science has come
closer to sensuous conception, at the cost of losing the determination
by thought" (*EL*, par. 98; *W*, 143; *GSH*, 155). "Das sinnliche Vorstellen,"
says the German (and unexpectedly Hegel warns us of the greater stakes
involved, since as he points out, this question of the atom and of its forces
is very much a buried metaphor at work in contemporary political theory
as well; he might have added that the matter of its representation is fully as
significant as the theoretical or philosophical content of what gave itself
as some purely physical and non-metaphysical process). This is at any rate
the first moment in which picture-thinking was able to threaten a thought
of opposition, as it were a binary concept: in the process modern science is
itself accused of picture-thinking, while other kinds of modern thinking
(political ideologies) are analyzed as bearing such picture-thinking more

---

[6] Gilles Deleuze and Félix Guattari, *L'Anti-Oedipe*, Paris: Minuit, 1972, 11–12.

deeply and metaphorically within themselves. At this point, Hegel's diagnoses have come very close to ideological analysis itself, and the latter's privileged theme of reification has also begun to rear its head and to be identified as such.

This kind of reification is once again identified with Understanding, at the same time that its conceptual difficulties are underscored.

> It is the abstract understanding that fixes the moment of the many contained in the concept of being-for-itself in the shape of atoms, and sticks to this moment as to something ultimate …

"Abstract" understanding is now pointedly the name for this faculty, which, however, needs picture-thinking to "fix" (*festhalten*) its conceptions. Hegel goes on to add:

> and it is the same abstract understanding which, in the present case, contradicts both unprejudiced perception and genuinely concrete thinking, by considering extensive magnitude to be the one and only form of quantity. (*EL*, par. 103, W, 152; *GSH*, 164)

Perhaps it is no accident that this was the very stumbling block that stopped Pascal's *esprit de finesse* in its tracks: he tells how a highly sophisticated and *mondain* friend (no doubt the chevalier de Méré) was unable to comprehend infinite divisibility. In turn, Pascal's astonishment at this incomprehension of the intensive causes him to elaborate the theory of the opposition between the *esprit de finesse* and that of *géometrie*. If, as Lucien Goldmann thought,[7] Pascal is the great predecessor in dialectical thought, then this coincidence is of the greatest interest, and demonstrates the centrality, for the dialectic, of an account of error fully as much as one of truth.

It is with number that we reach some first notion of the externality of certain forms of thought: it is all the more paradoxical in that what Hegel wants to show about number is precisely its ideality, and the distance of its conceptuality over purely finite, physical, or external realities. But this is precisely the logic of the dialectic: faced with a phenomenon divided against itself, to show the ideality of what was thought to be merely external, and then the externality of that hidden ideality itself. This is a diagnostic mechanism which shows up deep but hidden structural interrelationships, but cannot in itself reunite what is here separated. (To say that such reunification takes place in a later moment is itself paradoxical insofar as the later moment is supposed to be different from this one.) The whole process may be demonstrated by the "end" of the discussion of quantity, which also

---

[7] Lucien Goldmann, *Le dieu caché*, Paris: Gallimard, 1959.

becomes the final moment of the section on Being itself: for Hegel here declares that Measure is the secret telos of number as such:

> Whenever in our study of the objective world we are engaged in quantitative determinations, it is in all cases Measure which we have in view, as the goal of our operations. (*EL*, par. 106; *W*, 157; *GSH*, 169)

Measure is not exactly the "synthesis" of ideality and number as mechanical readings of the Hegelian dialectic would lead us to expect: it is the sheer relationship between numbers as such, a relationship no doubt expressible in number but not itself corresponding to a set of things. With sheer relationship we have touched a certain limit in thinking about the finite, a limit which (as always with Hegelian limits or boundaries) already places us beyond the realm of Being and in that of Essence, where everything is already sheer relationship (the realm of Essence thus corresponds to what is vulgarly thought of as dialectical in general, but also to the whole range of oppositions explored in structuralism, from Lévi-Strauss to Greimas). This is also the passage over from the immediate to mediation: "in Being everything is immediate, in Essence everything is relative" (*EL*, par. 111; *W*, 161; *GSH*, 174: *GSH* translates "relative" as "relational").

This is perhaps the moment to review our description of *Verstand* so far: we found that it often uses the crutch of picture-thinking (*Vorstellung*) although it is not identical with the latter; and that at the same way it wishes to dispel the restlessness or disquiet of "real thinking" (the Notion or the Concept) by nailing things down to specific and unchanging determinations ("fixity"). Meanwhile, it is a thought of separation and externality, a thought somehow wedded to the finite; and it is also the thought of immediacy, and innocent of all complex mediatory processes. We have used the more modern term "reification" to describe Understanding, but as much to enrich our use and conception of reification as to add anything to Hegel (except to underscore his modernity). *Verstand* is thus seemingly the privileged mode of thought for dealing with that realm of externality and "objectivity" which is Being itself, except that in fact we rethink that realm on "higher" levels as we move through the other sections, in the process leaving *Verstand* behind.

Thus, for example, in the section on Being we confront what Wallace in his Scots idiom calls the somewhat. It is what we would normally call the Thing: a specific being with attributes and the like. But *Verstand* does not have the means to think anything philosophically so complex at this stage, having only the "concepts" of being and quality. The somewhat can thus only be characterized as a kind of being with a certain determination (quality). We have to work our way through Being (where the somewhat at least manages to become a One) and into Essence before we meet the Thing as a category (*EL*, par. 125): nor is this a stopping point either, but the superiority of the new version lies in the fact that it constantly foregrounds its own philosophical dilemmas and contradictions, which are those of the very beginning of philosophy manuals as such—is the Thing a container which holds various properties within it, and if so, what is their relationship to each other and can it really have any independent existence as container without the traits contained, etc.? Here the Thing as a category or moment of Essence directs our attention to our internal mental processes and their interrelationship: rather than simply pointing to a whatever which is.

In the final climactic section on the Notion (or Concept itself—the *Begriff*), the former Thing no longer has a name of that kind, it has become any phenomenon which has being and about which we think. But now it is grasped as a "speculative" synthesis, a unity of being and thought. "All things are a judgment," Hegel says (*EL*, par. 167), in his account of the deeper metaphysical sense of traditional logic. In his new language of the Concept, each phenomenon is a union of the Universal, the Specific, and the Individual (*EL*, par. 163); and in fact, we might just as well have said that the former Thing, into which the somewhat once turned, has now become an Individual. Retrospectively then, the realm of Being is that of the singular (qualities), that of Essence, the realm of the Universal (the movement of the categories themselves), and this final world of the Concept is now at last the real world of individualities which are both physical or finite and theoretical or philosophical alike, objective and subjective all at once. What Hegel calls the speculative is precisely this "metaphysical" gamble that the objective and the subjective—what Spinoza called the realm of extension and that of intellect—are one.

But this does not really clarify the status of *Verstand*. It may well be the thought and language of everyday life, without our necessarily agreeing that it is adequate even to that realm (as Kant was willing to do in the first *Critique*). But we cannot say that it constitutes error either, and attempt to do away with it altogether in some absolute and suicidal spiritualization. Were we still in theological allegory, we might call *Verstand* the permanent law of the fallen world, which stands as a perpetual temptation and source of error about which we can only be vigilant. This vigilance is no doubt Hegel's conception of philosophy, as opposed to the intellectual life of ordinary people: a guild or professional self-justification with which we touch the borders of some properly Hegelian ideology.

7.

But let us see how *Verstand* can be handled in the next realm, that of Essence: paragraph 113 gives us some useful precisions:

In Essence, relation-to-self is the form of *identity*, of *inward reflection*. This form has here taken the place of the *immediacy* of being; both are the same abstractions of relation-to-self. The absence of thought in sense-knowledge, which takes everything limited and finite for something that [simply] is, passes over into the stubbornness of the understanding, which grasps everything finite as something-identical-with itself, [and] not inwardly contradicting itself. (*EL*, par. 113; *W*, 165; *GSH*, 178)

It is an explanation which now affords *Verstand* slightly more dignified credentials, insofar as it gets distinguished from *Sinnlichkeit* (Wallace translates the latter simply as "sense" [*W*, 165], which is surely more accurate), which now seems to be little more than the conscious realm of perception and sensation, in which, incidentally, being itself gets left behind. Now we have stubbornness or obstinacy, surely human and personal traits, and we have a sense of identity—the former "fixity"—which takes that word at face value: a stubborn literality that will hear nothing about contradiction. Far more openly than before, therefore, *Verstand* or Understanding is a force that seeks to bar entry on the very threshold of Essence (where internal contradiction will be the law of the land). Perhaps we can now go further than this and suggest that here *Verstand* is able to enlist the support of everyday language as such, which quite agrees with an approach for which identity is one thing and difference something else: but this is an attitude which will continue to have a certain relevance in the realm of Essence as well, where each moment persists in its distinctive identifiability. We can thus here speak of a *reflective understanding*,

> which, while it assumes the differences to possess a footing of their own, and at the same time also expressly affirms their relativity, still combines the two statements, side by side, or one after the other, by an "also," without bringing these thoughts into one, or unifying them into the notion. (*EL*, par. 114; *W*, 166; *GSH*, 179)

Is Understanding then a kind of adaptive chameleon, which modifies its conceptual powers according to its element? Formerly called the abstract understanding, it has now, in the realm of reflection, taken on the latter's properties, without in any way ceasing to be "unequal to the concept" and distinctively insufficient when it comes to thinking the new realities: it becomes reflective in order—"stubbornly"—to avoid the same ontological anxieties on the higher level: temporality ("restlessness"), contradiction, the negative as a force in its own right, and, finally, sheer relationality as such.

The realm of Essence is relational in two distinct ways: one is the familiar binary opposition according to which Identity turns out to be somehow "the same" as Difference, or at least offers the spectacle of a constant metamorphosis of the one into the other. The other fundamental relationality remains binary, but is of a wholly different kind, already foreshadowed by the term "Essence": this is the dialectic of inside and outside, of essence and appearance, of force and expression. In the case of the first of these types of opposition, Understanding, which wants to have one thing *or* the other, one thing alongside the other (and … and), will want to insist on the law of non-contradiction (*EL*, par. 119) as its first line of defense. For the second kind of relationality, an obtuseness centering on the "thing-in-itself" will be more appropriate (and will also offer the occasion for another sideswipe at Kant): here the dialectic of the Thing (described above) will come into play, and it will be clear that Understanding (including common sense) would prefer to arrest it: "If we stick to the 'mere in-itself' of an object, we apprehend it not in its truth, but in the inadequate form of mere abstraction" (*EL*, par. 124; *W*, 181; *GSH*, 194). (It will be remembered that the reproach to Kant was that he stopped with the emergence of an Essence, albeit an unknowable one; whereas Spirit did not stop there.) At this point, then, it becomes a good deal clearer that the insistence of *Verstand* on "fixity" and single determinations is above all a resistance to the temporal process of Hegelian logic.

But in the midst of that discussion of the Thing which we have already anticipated, there occurs an observation about Matter which is crucial for sorting out the question of Hegel's idealism (and of how materialistic it might be thought to be). It will be remembered that Matter first made its appearance as a second-best stand-in for pure Being itself, a kind of degradation of the latter into picture-thought (very much on the order of those Silberer researches into the varied image content of abstractions which so interested the discoverer of the interpretation of dreams).[8] Here, in the realm of essence, matter reappears, but now as a full-fledged category in its own right (*EL*, par. 128), where it is evident enough that the opposition of matter and form will take its place logically enough in the various versions of the dialectic of appearance and essence (the others are Whole and Parts, Force and Expression, Reciprocity and Causality). But Hegel is more than usually insistent on the ephemerality of this category or moment: he cannot exactly repudiate it as contradictory since all his categories are contradictory in that sense, but he does once again identify it with Kant's *Ding-an-sich* (a serious accusation). But here is then the discussion:

> The various matters of which the thing consists are potentially the same as one another. Thus we get one Matter in general to which the difference is expressly attached externally and as a bare form. This theory which holds all things all round to have one and the same matter at bottom, and merely to differ externally

---

8   Sigmund Freud, *The Interpretation of Dreams*, vols. 4 and 5, London: the Hogarth Press, 1953, 344–345.

in respect of form, is much in vogue with the reflective understanding [*sic*!] … Be it noted however that a block of marble can disregard form only relatively … Therefore we say it is an abstraction of the understanding which isolates matter into a certain natural formlessness. For properly speaking the thought of matter includes the principle of form throughout, and no formless matter therefore appears anywhere even in experience [*auch in der Erfahrung*] as existing. (*EL*, par. 128; *W*, 189; *GSH*, 197)

"Even in experience": Hegel's contempt for matter here will no doubt reconfirm that of the materialists for his idealism: although we have already elsewhere noted that Bishop Berkeley's analogous denunciation of the concept of matter was explicitly intended to rescue and to preserve the freshness and uniqueness of the body's sensations and perceptions.

Yet more fundamental errors lie in store for Understanding as it moves up the ladder of Essence: this last is destined—before it opens up into the realm of the Notion itself—to reach its climax in the category of Actuality (and with it of Spinozan Substance), both being later versions of that Ground with which the dialectic of Identity and Difference reached its fulfillment (moving from a binary alternation to that other structure we loosely characterized as an outside and an inside, an appearance and an essence). But even when *Verstand* allows this kind of conceptuality, it necessarily misunderstands it:

It is the customary mistake of reflection to take the essence to be merely the interior. If it be so taken, even this way of looking at it is purely external, and that sort of essence is the empty external abstraction … It ought rather to be said that, if the essence of nature is ever described as the inner part, the person who so describes it only knows its outer shell. (*EL*, par. 140; *W*, 197; *GSH*, 209)

We need to pause at this point and ask ourselves to what degree "reflection" itself—the very movement specific to the new realm of Essence and seemingly sharply distinguished from the external logic of the realm of Being—is itself implicated in these denunciations; or perhaps one should say this lengthy indictment, of *Verstand* or Understanding as such. Hegel has to maintain a delicate and precarious balance here—precisely to avoid some merely binary or ethical opposition between *Verstand* and *Vernunft* as simple evil and good, or negative and positive (error and truth). The thinking of reflection, in other words, constitutes an advance over the pure externalities and fixities—the reifications—perpetuated by the realm of Being: but it brings with it its own characteristic misunderstanding as we approach the thought appropriate to the Notion. (It is probably not helpful to say that the first realm is that of unitary thought, the second of the binary, and the third of the ternary positionings of Universal, Particular, and Individual.) Hegel cannot allow us to remain shackled in the binary system of

Essence either (similarly Tony Smith has identified those misreadings of Marx which result from considering capitalism the realm of the Notion rather than that of Essence),[9] and the above remarks about a purely external understanding of the inside or essence now show the increased dialectical complications (or complexifications) required in order to forestall just such contaminations.

Thus even more elaborate footwork is necessary when we come to put Possibility in its place (as opposed to Actuality) and to make the (fundamentally political and historical) point that Actuality (*Wirklichkeit*) is better than mere Possibility. "Everything," declares Hegel with sweeping sarcasm, "is as impossible as it is possible" (*EL*, par. 143; *W*, 203; *GSH*, 215). But the contamination of analysis and critique of the category betrays the influence and operations of *Verstand* at work:

> Possibility is really the bare abstraction of reflection-into-self—what was formerly called the Inward, only that it is now taken to mean the external inward, lifted out of reality and with the being of a mere supposition, and is thus, sure enough, supposed only as a bare modality, an abstraction which comes short, and, in more concrete terms, belongs only to subjective thought [*W*, 202]. Our picture-thought is at first disposed to see in possibility the richer and more comprehensive, in actuality the poorer and narrower category. Everything, it is said, is possible, but everything which is possible is not on that account actual. In real truth, however, if we deal with them as thoughts, actuality is the more comprehensive, because it is the concrete thought which includes possibility as an abstract element ... Generally speaking, it is the empty understanding which haunts these empty forms: and the business of philosophy in the matter is to show how null and meaningless they are. Whether a thing is possible or impossible depends altogether on the subject-matter: that is, on the sum total of the elements in actuality, which, as it opens itself out, discloses itself to be necessity.

With actuality and necessity—or better still, with actuality as necessity—we arrive at Spinozan substance, where cause and effect are one (*causa sui*), and where the same resistances of *Verstand* are met: "The way understanding bristles up against the idea of substance is equalled by its readiness to use the relation of cause and effect" (*EL*, par. 153; *W*, 216; *GSH*, 229), not grasping the latter as a temporal rather than a static and a spatial matter—"while cause and effect are in their notion identical, the two forms present themselves severed so that, though the cause is also an effect, and the effect also a cause, the cause is not an effect in the same connection as it is a cause," etc. The appearance of the bad (or spatial, additive) infinite here is of course the telltale sign of the limitations of *Verstand*, at the very moment in which we have arrived at the Notion itself as "an infinite form, of boundless activity, as

---

[9] Tony Smith, *The Logic of Marx's 'Capital'*, Albany: SUNY Press, 1990.

it were the *punctum saliens* of all vitality, and thereby self-differentiating" (whereas for the understanding it "stands still in its own immobility") (*EL*, par. 166; *W*, 232; *GSH*, 245).

8.

The structure of the Notion—what gives its name to the project as a whole—is that of traditional logic: the judgment and then the syllogism, whose deeper "philosophical" content is here revealed by Hegel in much the same operation as that by which he revealed the philosophical content of number and mathematics. This is the sense in which the logical judgment is not some mere proposition or statement about things (*EL*, par. 167); it is rather the moment in which it has become clear that "the individual is the universal" (*EL*, par. 166), and the deeper unity of subject with predicate in the judgment means that, in effect, "all things are a judgment" (*EL*, par. 167). The judgment can then be unfolded into its larger form, the syllogism, in which, as has been already noted, universal, particular, and individual are triangulated and identified with each other (the various forms of Aristotelian logic can then be classified according to the various structural combinations formed by the three terms).

Like the judgment, the syllogism is also in the world (and not merely in our heads and our thought). Yet where the judgment is merely a thing in the outside world, it seems more appropriate to grasp the syllogism as an event.

> The several forms of syllogism make themselves constantly felt in our cognition. If any one, when awakening on a winter morning, hears the creaking of the carriages on the street, and is thus led to conclude that it has frozen hard in the night, he has gone through a syllogistic operation—an operation which is every day repeated under the greatest variety of conditions. (*EL*, par. 183; *W*, 247; *GSH*, 260)

In reality, however, it is the very world of this early morning in Berlin so many years ago which has performed a syllogism.

The third moment in the process, the Idea, is then the "infinite judgment" (*EL*, par. 214), which can variously be characterized as "reason … subject-object; the unity of the ideal and the real, of the finite and the infinite, of soul and body; the possibility which has its actuality in its own self; that of which the nature can be thought only as existent," etc. (*EL*, par. 214). (We have already observed that "infinite" is not to be taken in any physical or cosmological or Romantic sense, but rather as what does not belong to the realm of the finite, or, in other words, self-consciousness and ideality.)

I will say later why it seems to me that for modern people this third realm may well seem to be the least interesting part of the *Logic*: but our immediate task here is to understand where Understanding can possibly fit in (or how its operations can be transformed in keeping with the new perspective), not to speak of the errors it may continue to perpetuate even on this supreme level. So it is not without interest that we find the above-cited enumeration followed by this remark: "All these descriptions apply, because the Idea contains all the relations of understanding, but contains them in their infinite self-return and self-identity." So finally all the seemingly new categories of the Notion will already have been grasped and vulgarized; after its fashion, by *Verstand*: all the forms have already passed before our eyes in Being and then again in Essence. To speak allegorically, it is as though the scheme of the levels had been reorganized into a spiral, in such a way that the *Logic* necessarily passes over each point again and again but in some "higher" form. (Nor is the structure of Dante's *Commedia* irrelevant here, whose three realms and canticles correspond rather well to Hegel's scheme.)

But in that sense *Verstand* or Understanding does not exactly correspond to one of the lower levels: it is there as elsewhere always the source of error (it being understood that for Hegel error is always a stage in truth and remains part of the latter). What we now need briefly to examine in conclusion is the form it takes on the level of the Notion and what it is incapable of "understanding" there.

Clearly enough, the first form will be that of traditional logic itself, which Hegel contemptuously refers to as the "syllogism of understanding" (*EL*, par. 182): in other words, the whole elaborate bristling array of propositions which passed for logic for a thousand years and was to be learned by rote.

> The syllogism of existence is a syllogism of understanding merely, at least in so far as it leaves the individual, the particular, and the universal to confront each other abstractly. In this syllogism the notion is at the very height of self-estrangement. (*EL*, par. 183; *W*, 247; *GSH*, 259)

Here, then, *Verstand* operates even more intensively as a function of separation: everything in its place, and according to its own isolated and distinct nature, relationships between these everythings taking place after the fact of their separate existences, in the most external fashion possible. It may be said that here the primary vice of Understanding consists in its effacement of mediation, whose crucial role in the syllogism Hegel thus magnificently describes:

> In this ideality of its dynamic elements, the syllogistic process may be described as essentially involving the negation of the characters through which its course runs, as being a mediative process through the suspension of mediation—as coupling

the subject not with another, but with a suspended other, in one word, with itself. (*EL*, par. 192; *W*, 255; *GSH*, 267)

And elsewhere he characterizes this mediation as a turning movement, whereby each of the three terms becomes the mediation in succession:

> Here we see the particular becoming the mediating mean between the individual and the universal. This gives the fundamental form of the Syllogism, the gradual specification of which, formally considered, consists in the fact that universal and individual also occupy this place of mean. This again paves the way for the passage from subjectivity to objectivity. (*EL*, par. 181; *W*, 245; *GSH*, 257)

Not only can Understanding by definition not grasp processes of this kind, it tends to organize its various separations and externalities into one over-arching dualism which it is the very vocation of the "speculative thinking" of the Notion to refute:

> The Logic of the Understanding … believes thought to be a mere subjective and formal activity, and the objective fact, which confronts thought, to have a separate and permanent being. But this dualism is a half-truth: and there is a want of intelligence in the procedure which at once accepts, without inquiring into their origin, the categories of subjectivity and objectivity. (*EL*, par. 192; *W*, 255; *GSH*, 267)

In fact, Hegel goes on, such separations condemn the logic of Understanding to a form of mechanical relationship which is nothing more than the logical subsumption of the more particular under the more abstract or universal:

> The abstract universal of Understanding … only *subsumes* the particular, and so connects it with itself: but has it not in its own nature. (*EL*, par. 204; *W*, 268; *GSH*, 280)

Yet the subjectivity which we have reached at this point,

> with its functions of notion, judgment, and syllogism; is not like a set of empty compartments which has to get filled from without by separately existing objects. It would be truer to say that it is subjectivity itself, which, as dialectical, breaks through its own barriers and opens out into objectivity by means of the syllogism. (*EL*, par. 192; *W*, 256; *GSH*, 268)

With this vision of the mighty flood of the Notion, it is appropriate to end this discussion of Understanding and its misconceptions. A final summing up of those may, however, not be altogether superfluous:

The understanding, which addresses itself to deal with the Idea, commits a double misunderstanding. It takes *first* the extremes of the Idea … as if they remained abstractions outside of it. It no less mistakes the relation between them … Thus, for example, it overlooks even the nature of the copula in the judgment, which affirms that the individual, or subject, is after all not individual but universal. But in the *second* place, the understanding believes *its* "reflection"—that the self-identical Idea contains its own negative, or contains contradiction—to be an external reflection which does not lie within the Idea itself. But the reflection is really no peculiar cleverness of the understanding. The idea itself is the dialectic which forever divides and distinguishes the self-identical from the differentiated, the subjective from the objective, the finite from the infinite, soul from body …
(*EL*, par. 214; *W*, 277–278; *GSH*, 289)

So it is that both empiricism and Kantian metaphysics are unmasked as distinct moments of *Verstand* as it attempts to adapt, first to the realm of Being, and then to that of Essence.

Hegel's analysis of *Verstand*—so subtle and wide-ranging—thereby proves to be his most fundamental contribution to some more properly Marxian theory of reification. We have indeed had many studies—negative and positive alike—of Marx's Hegelianism; but this particular transmission does not seem to me to bring more grist to a mill still very much in business, however antiquated its technology. I would rather propose for current purposes a more unusual version, namely Hegel's Marxism. This virtually unexplored continent would certainly include the dialectic itself, and it would find encouragement in Lukács's pioneering study of the formative studies of classical political economy in Berne, in *Young Hegel*. It would necessarily attempt to reevaluate the Master/Slave dialectic which Alexandre Kojève famously placed on the agenda. But I like to think that, in the age of consumerism and the world market, reification would also come in for some attention.[10]

What the philosophers rarely offer us, however, is a concept of ideology, despite the suggestiveness of Hegel's insistence on error and its omnipresence (and on the productivity of error as well). If I have characterized the Notion (or Absolute Spirit) and its culmination in the thematic of life as a more properly ideological dimension to Hegel's system, it is because —following Lukács's philosophical analyses in *History and Class Consciousness*[11]

---

[10] For more on what this might mean for practically and politically, see "Actually Existing Marxism," Chapter 15, below. And see also Timothy Bewes, *Reification*, London: Verso, 2002.

[11] The analysis of ideology as a philosophical containment strategy is the achievement of Lukács's central chapter, "Reification and the Consciousness of the Proletariat."

—this final moment must now strike one very much as an ideological "containment strategy," designed to crown and complete a system which seeks to model a historically incomplete or unfinished totality, that of world capitalism. Here too, then, in the spirit of those modernist classics which succeed by failing, Hegel's "aspiration to totality" has prematurely vouchsafed a proffer of his Marxism.

Herbert Marcuse long ago argued for a constitutive relationship between the premature closure of Hegel's system and the incomplete historical situation in which Hegel found himself after Napoleon's defeat.

Chapter 3

Hegel's Contemporary Critics

Now we need briefly to consider external objections to Hegelianism, that is to say, to review the basic positions of the most eminent anti-Hegelians. They too will have much to teach us about our own secret presuppositions and about the longitude and latitude of the *Zeitgeist* itself. I choose three very eminent opponents of the dialectic—Derrida, Deleuze, and Blanchot (if not Foucault)—because it is better to see why the most original philosophers of our time have found the dialectic unproductive for their purposes (which must also, in part, be ours), rather than to parry stray thrusts by camp-followers of current doxa or to think of something to say to Anglo-American complaints about logical inconsistency. The three writers mentioned will then allow us to look again at three crucial problems: that of mediations, that of negativity, and that of exteriority.

I.

Is the dialectic wicked, or just incomprehensible? Theorists who follow the doxa (without realizing to what degree it has been fashioned by the Cold War itself) tend to take the first line, invoking that well-known concept of totality (of which it is precisely well known that it means totalitarianism). The second position seems more awkward, since no one likes to admit they can't understand something, particularly in an age when difficult texts (theoretically difficult ones having apparently taken the place of the literarily difficult) have offered so many Everests for the scaling of the ambitious. You can of course claim that it is the text itself which is unintelligible; but even this raises suspicions. You would have to be able to show that the text failed to deliver, that it was incapable of solving its problems or doing what it claimed it was about to do: something notoriously impossible for literary texts, whose intentions get reconstructed only after the fact, and which in any case never "know what they think till they see what they say." But perhaps philosophy is somewhat different in this regard.

Modern philosophy, in any case, places increasing weight on successful expression, as though it were not enough merely to think something through, one had also to invent the right language or representation for the newly successful thought. Perhaps indeed, as with literature, the difference between the thought and its expression in language has slowly been effaced. Yet some kind of abstract aim is still there, which precedes the thought and the language alike: Husserl wants to think, which is to say, to express and formulate, emergence. So if it can be shown that he failed in doing this, a critique has been achieved.

This is what Derrida set out to do in his 1954 "master's thesis"—*Le problème de la genèse dans la philosophie de Husserl*—only published, with some reluctance it would seem, in 1990. The reluctance stemmed presumably from the way in which the youthful text reflected its moment and its milieu—the heyday of Sartrean existentialism—which is to say of existential Marxism and of the dialectic (as Western Marxism understood it). Derrida's is also a "dialectical" text, which pays due homage to Tran Duc Thao's supremely influential synthesis of Husserl and Marxism,[1] and concludes by wondering why—given the infinite regress in Husserl's successive onslaughts on emergence or origin, each new version only pushing the problem back a little further—he did not have recourse to the most obvious solution: the dialectical instrument called mediation.

In the thirteen years that elapse between this excellent study and Derrida's first published work (again on Husserl), the fifties have been replaced by the sixties, the Sartrean age has come to an end, and the evocation of "the dialectic" has vanished from Derrida's pages. Is it possible that during that period, Derrida slowly came to feel about the Hegelian categories that, like those of Husserl, they were not really forms of thinking but only served notice of the intent to think, without finally doing so? *Glas*[2] is the answer to this question, and a very substantial answer indeed, offering patient and detailed commentaries on a very wide range of Hegel's texts, from the early theological writings to the *Encyclopedia*, from the *Phenomenology* to the *Philosophy of Right*. These commentaries aim to show what really goes on inside the operation called *Aufhebung* (lifting up, preservation and cancellation, sublation, curiously translated by Derrida throughout as *relève*), which is so to speak the strong form of that operation called mediation and which he had recommended to Husserl only a decade earlier. Deconstruction could then here mean a therapeutic working through and dissolution of that, were it not that the texts remain.

To be sure, *Glas* seems to be doing a good many other things as well: its twin columns oppose the conformist and the rebel, Hegel and Genet, the

---

[1] See Tran Duc Thao, *Phénoménologie et matérialisme dialectique*, Paris: Minh-Tan, 1951.

familias and the homosexual, the government functionary and the criminal, philosophy and literature, thought and language—all entwined, as it were, around the twin motifs of flowers and phallic columns, of religion and camp. The texts do not directly reply to one another. Faulkner once combined two rejected story manuscripts into a single volume with alternating chapters; but it is unlikely Derrida faced this particular publishing problem. We have not yet mentioned the central issue: marriage (Genet was a foundling or at least an orphan, Hegel had an illegitimate son alongside two legitimate ones). The Hegel commentary will bear centrally on that section of the *Philosophy of Right* that deals with the family as the antechamber to civil society and, beyond it, the State. It will, in fact, affirm that *Aufhebung* and the family are related, indeed that the former is somehow a "familial" concept. What can this mean, except, in the most general sense, that the two ideas or motifs linked by sublation—the one in the process of being canceled and lifted up into the other—have no more relation to each other than the partners to a marriage (but no less either). They do not magically find themselves transformed, the one into the other; rather they remain linked by the copula, or in other words by copulation (his joke). This is then to say that *Aufhebung* is not really a thought, but at best a word naming a thought that has not been able to happen (and perhaps "family" is such a word as well).

To be sure, *Aufhebung* includes sublimation and spiritualization along with simple mediation; but there is no particular ideological urgency impelling us to denounce as an idealist a philosopher who everywhere openly boasts of his own idealism in the first place. The discussion of the concept of matter is illuminating. Spirit (*Geist*) and matter are not opposites: Spirit is infinite, matter is the unfree and the external, what weighs and falls.

> But there is a law of gravity. If you analyze weight and the dispersal of matter into exteriority, you are obliged to recognize a tendency in this process: a strained effort towards unity and self-reassembling. But as a tendency towards the center and unity, matter is the opposite of spirit only insofar as it resists this tendency, insofar as it opposes its own tendency. But in order to oppose its own tendency, which defines it as matter, matter would have to be spirit in the first place. And if it yields to the same tendency, it is also spirit. It is spirit in either instance, its essence can only be spiritual: All essence is spiritual. (*DG,* 29–30)

It is a magnificent "deconstruction," a demonstration of the way in which matter cannot be thought at all within an idealist system. But one of the disconcerting aspects of Derrida's "method" has always been the way in which,

---

[2] Paris: Galilee, 1974. Unless otherwise noted, all page numbers provided in the text refer to this work. Future references to *Glas* are denoted *DG* in the text. All translations are the author's own.

in his texts, the paraphrase always *precedes* the citation of the original text, rather than following it, as is customarily the case with commentary. Thus, reading on here for another moment, we come across Hegel's original, which says exactly the same things. What we took to be a devastating analysis was not Derrida's deconstruction of Hegel, but rather Hegel's own deconstruction. Of what? Of the concept of matter itself. Are we to conclude that the dialectic is already deconstruction, *avant la lettre*? Or do we have to invoke some infinitesimal, barely perceptible modification by which the dialectic transforms a materialist deconstruction into an idealist sublimation? "Matter tends towards ideality, for in unity it is already ideal," etc. (*DG,* 30). Or is this simply the difference between taking as one's object of analysis a thought (as in Hegel) or a text (as in Derrida)?

So where do we begin with this strange operation called *Aufhebung*? It may well be a spiritualization, but we can evidently not begin with the matter that it transcends/sublimates/spiritualizes, since we have just found that the latter is also already Spirit, albeit secretly. Perhaps we can begin with precisely these three properties of the things: (1) "it is also"—we have to do with the copula or with the affirmation of identity. (2) "Secretly"—we have to do with a hermeneutic process, an appearance which conceals an essence. (3) "Already"—we have to do with an illicit temporality, with precisely those temporal particles (*déjà*—[*DG,* 18]; *zugleich*—[*DG,* 26]) which were the key to Derrida's reading of the philosophies of time.[3]

In fact, *Aufhebung* is not an event but a repetition: "le *Geist* ne peut donc que se répéter" (*DG,* 31). Nothing happens; all *Aufhebungen* are the same. They all seem to involve the transcendence of nature; yet the latter is merely a name for whatever is transcended in any of these processes, it is purely formal, the name of a moment, it has no content in its own right: "Nature is not a determinate essence, a unique moment. It designates all possible forms of the ways in which spirit can be external to itself. It therefore appears— while in the process progressively disappearing as well—at every stage of the becoming of spirit" (*DG,* 45).

Yet on the other hand, these—the crucial moments of transition within the overall dialectic of Hegel's system—the moments at which *Aufhebung* as the crucial transformational mechanism should offer the most dramatic demonstration or *Darstellung*—are singularly muddy not to say undecideable:

> The most general question would now take on the following form: how is the *Aufhebung* of religion into philosophy produced? And on the other hand how is the *Aufhebung* into the structure of civil (bourgeois) society of the family structure produced? Or in other words how, within *Sittlichkeit* itself ... is effectuated the passage from the familial syllogism to that of bourgeois society? (*DG,* 108)

---

[3]   See the opening section of the chapter in this book "From Tragedy to the Dialectic."

Derrida goes on to indicate the crucial text, which for him situates the gap in Hegel, not between the spiritual and the material, but between the spiritual and the political, in what is for him the final transition of the *Phenomenology* (from religion to philosophy, but see his discussion of other versions of this transition on page 244). Unfortunately his faithfulness to Hegel (*DG*, 244–260) is such that the discussion is as dense and as incomprehensible as Hegel's own: I will elsewhere propose a different position, namely that Absolute Spirit is not a concept or a phenomenon one can analyze, let alone understand; but that it is a formal moment that can be grasped only as ideology or as method. If you try to see it as a condition, state, thing, phenomenon, in its own right, you will necessarily produce a religious account, and thus defeat the very purpose of the transition which was to spell out a decisive transformation (*Aufhebung*) between the penultimate chapter of the *Phenomenology* on revealed religion and this one on philosophy itself in everything that distinguishes it from religion. (This would probably be the moment to quote Derrida's discussion of the interesting question of whether one can ever misread Hegel [*DG*, 258–259] …)

But after all, one of the central concerns of Derrida's commentary—which goes back to the early theological texts—is the very traditional one of deciding whether Hegel is not just another religious thinker after all, and whether his dialectic is not simply yet another version of Christianity (that tradition will of course go on to say that Marxism is also in the same sense a "secularized" religion). Derrida, however, gives this traditional strategy (in which Hegel's enemies on the right and on the left can revel) a supplementary twist: for religion is here the Holy Family; and even if we wish to argue that *Aufhebung* and the Hegelian dialectic in general are secular disguises for Christian theology, we are obliged to go on and admit that Christian theology is itself little more than a secularized, or shall we say desexualized and empiricized, disguise for the more general social, public and private, institution of the family and marriage:

> One can no longer rigorously distinguish between a finite and an infinite family. The human family is not *something other* than the divine family. The father-son relationship for man is not *something other* than the father-son relationship in God. Inasmuch as these two relationships cannot be distinguished, and can certainly not be opposed to one another, we cannot feign to take the one as the figure or metaphor for the other. We cannot even compare the one to the other, or pretend to know which of the two can be the term of the comparison. Outside of Christianity, we cannot know what the relationship of the father to his son *is* …
> We cannot even know, and here is the point, what the *is* in general is outside of Christianity. Such is the Hegelian thesis on the spirit of Christianity, which is to say, on rhetoric as such. (*DG,* 76)

It is an extraordinary leap, scarcely disestranged by its attribution to Hegel himself, and forms the core of Derrida's critique of Hegel as an ontologist (he will later in *Specters of Marx* warn against the ontologizing of Marx himself). We can now prematurely summarize:

> Being is *Aufhebung*. *Aufhebung* is being, not as any determinate state nor even as the determinable totality of existents, but as "active" essence, essence productive of being as such. It [the feminine pronoun, which one assumes to refer back to *Aufhebung*] can therefore never be the *object* of any determinate question. We are perpetually referred back to it but this referral never refers to anything determinable. (*DG,* 43)

This is perhaps the strongest statement on the un- or non-intelligibility of *Aufhebung* (and thereby also of mediation): it should be noted, however, that it positions the critique within the logic of Essence rather than the logic of the Notion:

> The spirit of Christianity is … the revelation of that essentiality of essence which in general enables [us] to copulate in *is*, to say *is*. (*DG,* 67)

Even the seemingly primal metaphoricity of the Last Supper ("this *is* my body, this *is* my blood") is beyond all metaphor (Hegel has in fact just compared it to the process of the exteriorization of the interior in language and in the sign as well):

> This whole analogon cannot take form, cannot hold up; cannot be grasped, except by way of the category of categories. It sublates itself all the time. It is an *Aufhebung*. (*DG,* 81)

This is a serious reproach when one recalls Derrida's savage attack on the "category of categories" in his critique of Émile Benveniste; even more serious for us, when we recall the complacent service the "category" was called upon to do here in the previous section. Nor does it stop there: the ideologeme of life (discussed above) is also drawn into the process as yet another conceptual emanation of this undecideable ontological center which is the family (holy or not) and the dialectic itself.

The rest of the analysis is less interesting. Who are the enemies of the dialectic (besides Kant)? The Jews, for as a long paraphrase of Hegel's early Christianity text shows us (*DG,* 46–66), they are the people of *Verstand*, and "when you know life from the inside, you know that it is metaphoricity, living and infinite bond of everything thought through all its parts. The language of the Jews has no access to it" (*DG,* 86, 61). My own account of the baleful effects of *Verstand*, above, is thus little more than an extensive indulgence in unconscious anti-Semitism.

But what is the purpose of the dialectic? What is its motivation, secret or not so secret? It is the "strangling" of singularity: an odd figure, surely derived from Hegel himself somewhere in a place Derrida has neglected to cite, as which the passage from the singular to the universal is over and over again characterized (*DG*, 17, 19, 21, 27, 123, 127–128, 272). I think that this is something a little more than the two standard positions against reason: the classic existential one, in which conceptualization is grasped as a kind of repression of a more authentic lived experience, and that of Bataille, more Nietzschean perhaps, in which hyperconscious intellectuals long to rid themselves of the tyranny of thought and to return to an "acephalic" primitive life. For both of these positions, Hegel is the very symbol of the threat philosophy poses to life itself (and also, for others, to action). It has always seemed to me that Derrida was far less concerned with experience as such than with normality and its oppressions on the one hand, and the internal inconsistencies of thought on the other. Still, the loss of singularity is a fundamental theme in *Glas*, along with the identity and internal lack of articulation of *Aufhebung*, and it is of no little interest to enumerate the kinds of singularities that for Derrida elude the operation of the system.

The brother-sister relationship, for openers: nothing is indeed more moving, in this often arid exegetical context, than the juxtaposition of Hegel's special relationship with his troubled sister, Christiane (who committed suicide a year after his death), and the force of that tragedy exemplary over all others for Hegel which was the *Antigone* of Sophocles, where at the very heart of the *Phenomenology* the demands of the family—and the woman—come into headlong conflict with those of the State. The family—nuclear or holy—can seemingly be *aufgehoben* into "civil society," and both thence into the State itself; yet as Derrida points out, the mechanisms of such *Aufhebungen* are not made clear, and these are among those mysterious transitions which raise questions about change itself, and whether *Aufhebung* is not mere repetition. But in the *Antigone*, even that transition, that peaceful dissolution and absorption, is blocked by the singularity of the brother-sister relationship. This blockage is precisely the *tragic*, for Hegel; although the possibility cannot be excluded that this tragic destruction of two families is also a ruse of reason and of history that wipes the slate clean for the next moment (that of civil society).

Two other features of Derrida's account need to be mentioned here: the first is the seeming imminence and omnipresence of a seething violence one would not have attributed to the philosopher of Absolute Spirit with its universal reconciliations (although, once again, the philosopher of the struggle to the death of Master and Slave to be is certainly a mere plausible opponent for projects like Kant's perpetual peace). The second is a feminist perspective in which the absence of women in these archetypal patriarchal families is precisely denounced and foregrounded by the centrality of Antigone herself, who cannot be absorbed into the system. (There is also a remark in passing about the inassimilability of bastards, although Hegel's illegitimate son, who died as a mercenary in Java in the very year of Hegel's own death, does not come in for any further discussion.)

Along with women, the "powerless, all-powerful arm, woman's inalienable trump card: *irony*" (*DG,* 209). When one realizes that irony is the spiritual private property of Hegel's deadliest enemies, the Romantics and above all Friedrich Schlegel, and when one reads its denunciation in the closing pages of the *Aesthetics*, it is a cruel association, determining an interpretation that can cut both ways. The singularity of women is then part of a more general denunciation of the Schlegels and their doctrine of free love (Schlegel's "scandalous" novel *Lucinde*); or the denunciation of irony is of a piece with some deeper exclusion of the feminine itself. It scarcely matters; the figure of Antigone stands out singularly in either case.

The phenomenon of the fetish (according to Freud, the mother's missing penis) is perhaps also distantly related to these feminist absences, and would determine the peculiar place of Africa as a kind of zero degree of figuration in the *Philosophy of History*: an exclusion which can also mean that "Africa" or the religion of the fetish, which is not yet a religion in Hegelian terms, is also a singularity the system cannot absorb. "A certain undecideability of the fetish leaves us oscillating between a dialectic (of the undecideable and the dialectic) and an undecideability (between the dialectic and the undecideable)" (*DG,* 232). In another place, but more prospectively, Derrida expresses the magnificent speculation that Hegel "could not think or conceptualize the functioning machine as such."[4] Perhaps these two unique blind spots, the fetish and the machine, somehow come together in the point at which Hegel is *aufgehoben* by Marx.

A final singularity is worth mentioning, for it refers us to Derrida's own thought and implicitly to at least its difference from, if not its superiority to, the Hegelian dialectic: this is the thought, if one can call it that, or, better still more neutrally, the phenomenon, of the *trace*, that which is presence and absence altogether, but in some non-dialectical way, and which Absolute Spirit can seemingly not even perceive or register, let alone tolerate (*DG,* 240). But in that sense, in hindsight, we can here glimpse the first spectral glimmerings of *spectrality* itself as that will propose a radically different theory of past and future, and of history, than the dialectical one (see the discussion of *Specters of Marx* in the next chapter).

But we cannot conclude this section without a few remarks on a reading which, however deconstructive, is also from time to time patently interpretative. *Aufhebung* is the place of the familial and of ontology (in the form of

---

[4] Jacques Derrida, *Marges de la philosophie*, Paris: Minuit, 1972, 126; available in English as *Margins of Philosophy*, trans. Alan Bass, Chicago: Chicago University Press, 1983, 107.

the Hegelian essence): in it, the analysis of Christianity, that of the family, that of transition in general and the subsumption of the particular under the universal in particular, are all somehow "the same." *Aufhebung* is also, oddly, the place of castration, we are told at one point (*DG,* 52), and of *refoulement* (Freudian repression) in another (*DG,* 214). But now, clearly, we are dealing not so much with an attack on Hegel (it would be rather crude and unphilosophical to call *Glas* that) as with what is assuredly an attack on Lacan and psychoanalysis (see also "Le facteur de la vérité"[5]). The psychoanalytic hermeneutic is here being assimilated to the Hegelian one, and condemned as dialectical. Circumcision becomes a substitute for castration: and Lacanian castration is notoriously an *Aufhebung,* in which what is lost is really gained. The physical event does not happen as such, but the threat—the *Aufhebung* of physical into spiritual—allows the phallus to come into being as such, and with it the virile function; just as primal repression is the precondition for the psychic system to function in the first place. Derrida wishes to "deconstruct" this novel logic and to show that it is in fact little more than our old friend *Aufhebung* itself:

> To sublate a limit is to preserve it but to preserve (a limit) is here to lose it. To keep what is lost is to lack. The logic of *Aufhebung* turns at every instant around into its absolute other. Absolute appropriation is absolute expropriation. The onto-logical can always be reread or rewritten as a logic of loss or as one of unchecked expense [*dépens sans reserve*]. (*DG,* 188)

It is finally a critique of interpretation which has a distant family likeness to the Deleuze-Guattari denunciation of Freudianism in the *Anti-Oedipus*: you are saying that one thing is really secretly—essentially, to use the Hegelian term which is absolutely relevant here—something else. One thing has an unconscious meaning, which is other than itself. The hermeneutic process—changing the one thing into its more essential meaning—is prepared and indeed imperiously summoned by the very movement of dialectical *Aufhebung* itself, which ensures the preservation of the canceled meaning which is to be revealed by interpretation in the first place. The question of priorities—causes and effects, temporal precedence, ontological superiority, foundational primacy—is less important and indeed need not arise at all, in the kind of indistinct identification in which *Aufhebung* holds its twin distinct, related, and finally indistinguishable forms.

The question to be raised at this point is then the embarrassing one of the status of Derrida's own interpretations: for he makes them too, and it is hard to see why they would not fall under the same strictures. Thus Absolute Spirit is finally the Immaculate Conception:

---

[5] "Le facteur de la vérité," in Jacques Derrida, *La Carte postale,* Paris: Flammarion, 1980.

This determination of sexual difference into opposition, and as an opposition at work in the whole process of opposition (*Entgegensetzung*) in general, and of objectivity (*Gegenständlichkeit*) and of representation (*Vorstellen*), entertains an essential relationship—historical and systematic—with the Immaculate Conception: if not with the dogma concerning Mary's birth, at least with its premise or conclusion, the virginity of the mother. Indispensable to Hegel's whole argument, to the speculative dialectic and to absolute idealism, it commands what we may call the *approach* to Absolute Knowledge. As soon as you transform difference into opposition, you cannot escape the phantasm … of Immaculate Conception: which is to say a phantasm of the infinite mastery of both sides of the oppositional relationship. (*DG,* 250)

The language here would seem to suggest some "causal" priority of the binary opposition as such (something further developed in Deleuze, as we shall see below); but in fact there is no such priority; or rather the "beginning" of the process is itself a kind of mystery of birth and origins (in this case of the birth of philosophy itself):

How to reconcile these two axioms: philosophy only proceeds out of itself and yet she is the daughter of a need or an interest which are not yet themselves philosophy? In its own position, philosophy *presupposes.* It precedes itself and replaces itself in its own thesis. It comes before itself and substitutes itself for itself. (*DG,* 110)

Still, this content of the "philosopheme" cannot be articulated without affirming a certain kind of interpretation. The following passage sums up as well as any other Derrida's fundamental theses about the dialectic:

Ideality, the product of *Aufhebung,* is thus an onto-economic "concept." The *eidos,* philosophy's general form, is properly familial. It produces itself as *oikos*: house, habitation, apartment, room, residence, temple, tomb, hive, possessions, family, race, etc. If there is a common same in all this, it is the guardianship over the "proper": which retains and inhibits, consigns absolute loss or consumes it only the better to watch it return into self, even as the repetition of death. Spirit is the other name of this repetition. (*DG,* 152)

The *propre* is, as is well known, Derrida's term (or one of them) for normativity in general, which seeks to rule everything from thoughts and genres to subjectivities and the State. But such identification is perhaps as Hegelian as the denunciation of Hegelianism itself: everyone complains of the difficulty of breaking with Hegel.

No choice is possible: whenever you try to speak *against* the transcendental, some matrix—striction itself [the strangulation of the concept]—constrains your discourse and forces it to place the non-transcendental, the outside of the transcendental field, what is excluded, in the structuring position. The matrix in question constitutes the excluded as a transcendental of the transcendental itself, as a simili-transcendental, as transcendental contraband. (*DG,* 272)

He goes on to express the hope that this new contraband can be prevented from turning into a dialectical contradiction: it is the hope on which deconstruction itself is founded, yet it is ominous enough that we have to go through the entire Hegelian dialectic to reach it.

2.

That empty repetition with which Derrida seems to tax the dialectic, and which seems to be the object of a kind of psychic horror for him, will on the other hand be welcomed by Deleuze as positive theme, and even as a joyous and life-giving force. It is a repetition that comes from Kierkegaard rather than from Freud: the repetitions of everyday life, the construction and acquisition of habits as those lend existence its charm, its strangeness as well as its familiarity. Yet to this must also be added the joyous and manic repetitions of Nietzsche's Eternal Return; and finally even Freud can be reintegrated here, insofar as he was also the inventor of a specific and unique, incomparable drive (*Trieb*) pushing us to repeat, namely the famous Thanatos or death drive. Needless to say, none of this has anything in common with the otherwise deathly repetitions Derrida attributes to Hegel, but which Deleuze associates with Identity and representation.

Comparing, or even juxtaposing, the two is less a matter of philosophical positions and content—the post-Heideggerian philosopher, for example, contrasted with the neo-Nietzschean—as it does with something I would be tempted to call aesthetics or style, did this last not fatally evoke the sandbox of art and ludic trivialization of thinking itself. Better then to talk about modes of reading (like modes of performance) in which a Stravinsky, say, is contrasted with a Schoenberg, as both, with historical mixed feelings and a vital and creative anxiety of influence, contemplate Beethoven, perhaps.[6] Derrida's replay of long sections of Hegel might well stand comparison with Stravinsky's classical borrowings and deformations; while Deleuze—but now it seems appropriate to compare whole modes of the fine arts themselves, rather than composers as such—deals with each concept as though it were a new kind of color and indeed a new kind of space (indeed, the two philosophers seem to stand to each other as anti-narrative versus a kind of non-figurative play with multiple narrative centers, respectively).

---

[6] The allusion is to Adorno's *Philosophy of Modern Music.*

For such is Deleuze's own idea about how philosophers innovate; and nothing is more profound in him than precisely this modernism which imperiously demands sheer invention of the new, even in the treatment of classical philosophers (we need to deal with them by way of the *collage*, he says, urging us to produce estrangements of the past, "a philosophically bearded Hegel, a philosophically clean-shaven Marx"[7]). Even the most intricate and allusive, scholastic, reasonings of this *doctorus subtilis* are in reality sketches of a whole new space, evoking a kind of cinematographic philosophizing; as opposed to the philosophical cinematography outlined in the film books. So representation as such—"infinite representation" is his term for Hegel's Absolute Spirit—brings a whole new baleful and enveloping magic spell along with it:

> When representation finds the infinite in itself, it appears as orgiastic rather than organic representation: it discovers within itself tumult, disquiet, and passion beneath the apparent calm, the limits of the organized. It rediscovers the monster. At that point it is no longer a matter of that happy instant that would match the entry and exit of determination into the concept in general, a relative minimum or maximum, the puncture proximum and the punctum remotum. On the contrary the eye must be myopic, hypermetropic, in order for the concept to take all the moments upon itself: the concept is now the All, whether it extends its benediction to all the parties or on the contrary grants a sort of absolution to their scission and misery as those are reflected back onto it. The concept thereby follows and unites with determination from one end to another, in all its metamorphoses, and represents it as pure difference by delivering it over to a grounding or foundation [*fondement*] in terms of which henceforth it makes no difference whether we decide we are confronting a relative minimum or maximum, a large or a small, a beginning or an end, since all those pairs coincide in the foundation as one and the same "total" moment which is at one and the same time the swooning away of difference and its production, its disappearance as well as its appearance. (*DR*, 61–62; 42)

Shades of Polanski! This morbid eye of representation into which all the objects of the world are drawn, swollen and elongated, projecting their shapes and shadows against the concave closure of the *Begriff* itself, conveys the "sublime of the infinitely great"(*DR*, 65; 45) in Hegel from the inside, with all that inventive and intelligent sympathy Deleuze brings to philosophers of the past even as he reinvents their very physiognomies. It is a

---

[7] Gilles Deleuze, *Différence et Répétition*, Paris: PUF, 1968, 4; available in English as *Difference and Repetition*, trans. Paul Patton New York: Columbia University Press, 1994. Future references to this work are denoted *DR*, followed by page references to the French and then the English edition, divided by a semicolon. Note that the English translations give here are the author's, not those of the Columbia edition.

problem for him, since this is not a sympathy everywhere desired, and an omnipresent appreciation of texts, works, auteurs, styles, concepts—unique in Deleuze—is incompatible with that combative and aggressive dualism to which he is also committed. Hegel cannot be patiently waited out, and expected to deconstruct himself; he must be classed right away among the apologists of the State rather than the fellow-travelers of the nomads; the flaws in the dialectic are no mere errors, they are dangerous powers and contagions that need to be dispelled and banished by the high purifying wind of the Eternal Return.

Representation, identity, difference—so many themes which one would be tempted to attribute to Deleuze and Derrida alike, along with their mutual loathing of normativity and the Law; both are indeed surely the philosophers of Difference par excellence, whatever the spelling—yet with this fundamental "difference" between them, namely that in the long run Deleuze is an ontologist. His is, to be sure, an ontology of difference rather than identity, but he is certainly willing to celebrate a kind of metaphysic: "It is always the differences that resemble each other, which are analogous, opposed, or identical: difference is behind everything, but behind difference there is nothing" (DR, 80; 57).

In a metaphysical or ontological sense, then, Difference is here Being itself; and when one remembers that for Deleuze repetition is time, the title of his great book modulates into that of *Sein and Zeit* itself, albeit in a Gallic version, inspired by Bergson and Gabriel Tarde far more than by Husserl. It should at any rate be clear enough that nothing is further from the philosophical ethos of Derrida than ontological, let alone metaphysical, assertions or propositions (indeed, his principal objection to "Marxism" later on will be its ontologizing tendencies, that is to say, its temptation to turn itself into Philosophy as such, into a philosophical system).

Thus Deleuze's work marks a convulsive, yet also witty, effort to estrange the conventional meaning of words, wresting "repetition" over and over again away from its normal sense of the boring and the same and conferring on it rather the experience of the singular over against the generality: "repetition is a kind of behavior, but with respect to something unique or singular, which has no likeness or equivalent" (DR, 7; 1), and this is precisely why it escapes the generality or universality of the substitutable, of exchange, of mere likeness, etc. How Time itself then emerges from the "hooked atoms" of repetition is one of the great stories *Difference and Repetition* has to tell.

As for difference, it is somehow the primal monster, the moment of contact with sheer being itself:

> Instead of one thing that distinguishes itself from another thing, let's imagine something which does distinguish itself—and yet what it distinguishes itself *from*

is not distinguished from it. Lightning for example distinguishes itself from the night sky, yet must somehow draw that sky along with it, as though it distinguished itself from something which is not distinct. It is as if the background rises to the surface, without ceasing to be a background. There's something cruel and even monstrous on both sides, in this struggle against an elusive imperceptible adversary, where what is distinct is opposed to something that cannot be distinguished from it and which continues to join with what separates itself from it. Difference is this state of determination as unilateral distinction. (*DR*, 43; 28)

The "monster" of difference reminds one of that shapeless and terrifying Lacanian "Ding" or "chose" that Renata Salecl sees in the broken mirror in Hitchcock's *Wrong Man*[8]: the freshness and horror of the noumenon suddenly tearing through the veils of appearance without warning. Deluzian modernism is then this keeping faith with the freshness and the horror of the New and of sheer difference.

For our purposes, however, what is crucial is the attempt to stage "difference" as a univocal term, without an opposite, and it is the fundamental operation here. Identity must be dethroned as that primary position which it has in all traditional philosophy from Aristotle to Hegel: that which must first be present in order for any difference *from* this identity to emerge. Deleuze credits Spinoza with this fundamental reversal, which posits

that identity is not first, that it does exist as a principle, but only as second principle, as one that is produced [*comme principe devenu*]; that it hovers around the Different, such is the nature of that Copernican revolution that opens up for difference the possibility of having its own concept, rather than maintaining it under the domination of a general concept already posited as identical. (*DR*, 59; 41)

Three other features then join "identity" as what must be avoided if we are to establish and grasp a concept of Difference in its own right: analogy, resemblance, and opposition (*DR*, 44–45; 29–30). It is clearly this last which will be crucial in undermining the dialectic and substituting a radically different logic in its place.

Difference must indeed be prevented at all costs from being "identified" with opposition: it is clear that as soon as we reach the latter, we are in the powerful grip of a Hegelian dialectic that risks taking us the whole way to the end of the *Logic* with it. And in order to avoid the subsumption of some proud and pagan difference under the yoke of a relationship which would turn it back into an identity at the stroke of a magic wand, we must also avoid something else, namely the insidious Hegelian negative, that power of

---

[8]   Renata Salecl, "The Right Man and the Wrong Woman" in *Everything You Always Wanted to Know about Lacan (but Were Afraid to Ask Hitchcock)*, ed. Slavoj Žižek, London: Verso, 1992, 185–194.

negation which is for Hegel the very motor of history—the "labor and suffering of the negative"—and the heart of contradiction itself: Hegel's ontological principle, so to speak, which is the primal force of the world itself. Everything in Deleuze's argument depends on this possibility of quarantining the negative, suspending the energy of the *Logic* in some immense power outage, glimpsing the possibility of what is already here the untouched freshness of the schizophrenic universe.

> For one brief moment we were able to enter this de jure schizophrenia which characterizes thought's highest power, and which opens Being directly onto difference, scornfully bypassing all the mediations and reconciliations of the concept. (*DR*, 82; 58)

It is a standard gambit of the anti-dialectical, anti-Hegelian offensive: there is no negative in Nature, we are told, only sheer being (or beings).[9] Negation is what human reality brings to a seething world of existents: the flaw in the diamond of Being, as Sartre puts it. And obviously any such move sends us back to Kant and disqualifies the whole Hegelian effort, save as a kind of literary exercise or a mystical indulgence.

I'm not sure that the argument can be either acknowledged or refuted at this level. In Hegel, as we have seen, Identity necessarily produces Difference out of itself, and Difference necessarily turns back into Identity the longer we stare at it. Negativity as such emerges from these metamorphoses of the categories themselves, which we witness helplessly as it were. They are not our doing, not merely subjective; and if they are in thought alone, then we need some other word for that as well, a characterization that does not imply individual consciousness. I will try to say in a moment why I think we can just as easily accept this movement of the negative as repudiate it.

But first one must notice the emergence of a supplementary level on which Deleuze wages the argument against the negative, and against opposition. I think we can grant that if this last is successful, the entire dialectic, mediation, and all the rest of it "fall to the ground," as Hegel liked to say, since they all presuppose negation. But at this point, having judiciously measured out what is at stake, and astutely reckoned up the consequences, Deleuze changes the terrain of the argument and shifts to what may be called a narrative mode. This actually is a mode with which he reproached Plato—myth (*DR*, 86; 61), which of course means nothing more than narrative itself anyway, and with which Derrida had already reproached Hegel himself in *Glas*. But in Deleuze this kind of proto-narrative, a sample of which we have already examined in the magic bewitched universe of our very first quote above, and which is the very space of what we have elsewhere

---

[9] The canonical reference here is to Kant's 1763 essay on negative quantities.

called his dualism (see below), brings philosophical credentials with it, and gets baptized with the name of a genuine philosophe, or philosophical theme, and that is Representation. To be sure, with Heidegger, the problem of representation and representational thought became one of the most urgent philosophical issues of modernity, and no one can doubt its significance and relevance. What seems at least more questionable is the association, on which henceforth all of Deleuze's arguments against Hegel will rest, of the categorical and logical issue (does difference really presuppose identity or not?) with representation, as such. For the argument against opposition and the negative is really meant to be an argument against representation, which is finally marked as wedded to mediation (*DR*, 16; 8) and also to unification around a center (*DR*, 79; 56) and finally to the theological (*DR*, 81; 58).

The new "mythic" turn of the argument will depend on this prior identification, which allows it to cast both Identity and Representation in the role of the evil sorcerer, and to shed a properly Nietzschean scorn on the adherents of this dialectic, who like Zarathustra's ass carry the weight of order and ethics on their backs (the very meaning of *Aufheben* [*DR*, 75–76; 53–54]):

> As though Difference were evil and had already become the negative, which can produce affirmation only by expiation, that is to say, by taking up the burden both of what has been negated and of negation itself. Always that old curse that echoes down from the heights of the identity principle: that alone can be saved which is not merely represented but achieves infinite representation as such (the concept or *Begriff*) and which conserves all its power of negation in order finally to deliver over difference to the identical. (*DR*, 76; 53)

Only the Eternal Return can save us from this strange limbo in which the souls of the misguided wander as though they had never even lived:

> Everything negative, everything that denies and negates, all these lukewarm affirmations that carry the negative within themselves, these pale misbegotten Yeses that come out of the No, everything which is incapable of standing the test of the eternal return, all of that is to be negated. Even if the eternal return is a wheel, it must be endowed with a centrifugal power that expels even everything which "can" be negated and which cannot stand the test. Nietzsche spells out a truly light punishment for those who fail to "believe" in the eternal return: they will feel nothing and will have a merely ephemeral life! They will feel themselves and know themselves for what they are: mere epiphenomena; such will be their Absolute Knowledge. (*DR*, 77–78; 55)

Representational thought removes us from the immediacy, indeed the reality of "real life": did not Hegel admit as much when he took immediacy as the very target of his own philosophizing (nor is it an accident that

Deleuze should wish to baptize his counterposition a "hyperempiricism," despite all the misunderstandings to which such a slogan is bound to lead)? Yet Deleuze's position is a little more complicated than the previous existential anti-Hegelianisms we have passed in review: its Nietzscheanism is also a modernism, in which "existential experience" is celebrated, not because it is "lived," nor because it is "authentic," but rather because it is *new*. There is for example an aesthetic satisfaction in this celebration of contemplation (*DR*, 101ff; 70ff) which gives it a different kind of energy and joyousness than more morose existentialisms. Is it "merely" aesthetic? Can it accommodate a properly philosophical position as well (in any traditional sense), and how might its dualistic aggressivity be political as well? A digressive reflection on the tasks of the "philosophy of difference" is revealing in this respect, if not conclusive:

> In general there are two ways of evoking "necessary destructions": that of the poet, who speaks in the name of a creative power capable of overthrowing all the orders and representations in order to affirm Difference as the condition of the permanent revolution of the eternal return: that of the politician, concerned at first to negate what "differs" in order to conserve or prolong an order already established in history or to establish a historical order which already entreats the world for the forms of its representation. (*DR*, 75; 53)

Now that we know the affective charge of these various words, it is clear that the poet carries the day against the statesman and that "philosophies" will have to pick their sides and take their chances.

Still, if representation as a force and a phenomenon turns out to be more deeply akin to the aesthetic than Deleuze might wish, the reproach itself becomes a double-edged sword: perhaps it is not enough to dispel the representational as such, if the non- or anti-representational results (whether in art or philosophy itself) remain aesthetic in their innermost content.

Deleuze has already anticipated other objections in a disarming way: the affirmation of Difference will seem to some a tepid pluralism or liberalism.

> The greatest danger would be to fall into the representations of the "beautiful soul" [Hegel's and Goethe's *schöne Seele*!]: nothing but differences, reconcilable, confederative, far from bloody conflicts ... And the notion of the problem, which we will find linked to that of difference, seems also apt to feed the favorite states of mind of the beautiful soul: only problems and questions count ... (*DR*, 2; xx)

We have already touched on this second theme above: as for the first, one would be tempted to agree that "difference" is not necessarily "diversity" in the liberal pluralist sense. Yet this too has become a political issue today ("is identity politics a politics of difference?") and can perhaps not be dismissed so quickly either.

But my own provisional reaction to Deleuze's powerful critique would be a little different, and it would recall praxis to the scene (perhaps momentarily to replace Deleuze's odd self-characterization in terms of contemplation). In Hegel, and in particular in the *Logic*, the question of the priority of Identity over Difference (or vice versa) does not seem to be as important as the inevitability, once one stares at one of them long enough, of their transformation into each other. Priority is perhaps a metaphysical issue; the Difference hidden away within Identity, the Identity hidden away within Difference, is perhaps something else. What comes of this strange sea-change, along with provisional alternatives—such as sheer "diversity"— that fail to be satisfying for any length of time, is the eruption of Opposition; the way in which at length this restless alternation back and forth is seized and grasped as a new figure in its own right. Deleuze dwells at some length on the attractiveness, for us today, of a chaotic worldview of sheer seething differences, of a dissolution of forms and a rising up to the surface of the formless and indeterminable—

> a distribution we have to call nomadic, a nomadic *nomos*, without property, enclosure or measurement. There, no careful sharing out of what is distributed, but rather the falling out of those who distribute themselves into an open, illimitable space without frontiers. Nothing is the right of anybody or belongs to anybody, everybody is rather strewn about, all over, in order to fill the greatest space possible. Even when we have to do with the gravest things in life, it seems a space of play, a rule of the game, as opposed to sedentary space and sedentary law (*nomos*). (*DR*, 54; 36)

That both these evocations, the depths swimming up to the surface but even more here, the reorientation of the metaphorics around a space to be filled and colonized, are spatial in character will be significant later on.

For the moment, it seems appropriate to say that alongside the evocation of some morose and subjective eye that would reabsorb all this aleatory and joyous randomness into the "sedentary" of an inwardness and a collection (or in Hegel's case a re-collection), other figures are possible; and it may even be possible to return this particular ball to Deleuze himself on the ground that it is he who wanted to stage the matter in terms of contemplation in the first place. But supposing the dialectic were not at all contemplative or subjectivizing in that sense? Supposing that on the contrary the reorganization of identity and difference into opposition were something like an active intervention into the flux and very precisely a kind of praxis in which the cosmological matter were reorganized into great loose forces, in order ultimately to drive them forward into the revolutionary clash of Contradiction itself?

The dualism of a worldview is after all a static matter which reforms itself and returns over and over again without any of the joyousness of the Eternal

Return recommended here. Contradiction on the other hand is a clash in historical time and the seizure of a unique historical instant, whatever its outcome. Finally, the sense of intervention and praxis is more energizing and enabling than a heady Nietzschean euphoria which waxes and wanes.

3.

In a final moment, it may be worthwhile returning to the question of subjectivity and self-consciousness in Hegel. We may already object (mildly) to the constitutive move whereby Hegel insists on the identity of system and subject, and insists on reestablishing his immense processual unities in the framework of something like a subjectivity. That the moments could be reabsorbed by subjectivity, and become rather different kinds of moments —this is not particularly objectionable, and is indeed part and parcel of the speculative gamble of so-called speculative thought itself. But that the Notion finally becomes something like a concrete individual consciousness as its highest form, and that our old friend "bourgeois individuality" here wins the day, or at least spells out the outer limits of this adventurous thought, will strike a post-individualist society as worse than humanist, and as an ideological containment that vitiates the entire dialectic for a generation in thrall to the "death of the subject" and to Foucault's famous "effacement of the human face upon the sands of the sea."

Once again, as always, it is Deleuze who sounds this alarm beat:

> In the great Hegelian synthesis, it is the infinite which is reintroduced into the operation of the finite Ego. You may well wonder about the significance of such changes … Unicity and the identity of the divine substance are [however] in truth the only guarantors of an Ego one and identical, and God remains as long as the Ego remains. A synthetic finite Ego and an analytic divine substance are one and the same. This is why the permutations of Man/God are so disappointing and get us nowhere. Nietzsche seems to have been the first to notice that the death of God only becomes really effective with the dissolution of the Ego. What happens then is a being which is predicated of differences neither in a substance nor in a subject: so many subterranean affirmations. (*DR*, 81; 58)

I think that the crucial feature of all these discussions, however, tends to turn on the nature of self-consciousness, always the lynchpin of any philosophy organized around the subject, and a kind of strange misnomer in its own right, since "consciousness" when it is human and worth talking about—unlike whatever we might want to attribute to animals and plants —is always defined as self-consciousness in the first place.

But what could self-consciousness be consciousness of? Have you not already guaranteed yourself some stability in the self and the ego by even venturing such a slogan which gradually takes on the stability of a name and a reference? I've argued elsewhere[10] that our current malaise with the very idea of self-consciousness (let alone the knee-jerk evocation of "reflexivity" at every turn in which anything like "modernity" needs to be characterized) is the symptom of a representational dilemma which it is best and most convenient to evoke by declaring that subjectivity cannot be represented at all in the first place, and therefore, that its ostensible definitions and descriptions are all so much figural machinery.

Hegel has several machines of this kind: reflection itself, as he often calls what is more loosely termed self-consciousness, is literally described in terms of mirrors and light[11] while the moment of self-consciousness is famously evoked by the clash of two consciousnesses (who will become the Master and the Slave). Neither of these figures has anything particularly mystical about them: they do not even seem to suggest that identificatory indifferentiation with which Derrida taxed *Aufhebung*. Nonetheless the language of interiorization and interiority is everywhere very strong indeed, and would seem to call for some kind of contemporary replacement.

No one has more suggestively projected new possibilities here than Michel Foucault, whose 1966 essay "La Pensée du dehors"[12] (its title and indeed its subject matter indebted to Maurice Blanchot) takes up the challenge of "interiorization" on its own terms and its own terrain by reversing them and proposing the formula of a kind of external thinking, a thought of the outside rather than the inside. Blanchot's own approaches to this new concept are as always provisional and eclectic, and probably indebted to Levinas' notion of the Other: however, as Blanchot's language moves towards *le neutre*—the radically depersonalized—it loses these associations which are now wholly absent from Foucault's theorization. The latter, rather, starts not with thinking but with language, and with the strange floating lack of context of first-person statements which, far from returning us to the warmth of interiority and subjectivity, rather make visible around them a kind of infinite void. Such utterances (in Blanchot they are Nietzsche's fragments) are no longer the meaningful acts and intentions of persons but rather an "étalement du langage en son être brut, pure extériorité déployée" (*DE*, 519). It is this which marks the terrain and the undiscovered continent of a properly modernist literature (not Foucault's language, but certainly Blanchot's object of theorization):

---

[10] In *A Singular Modernity: Essay on the Ontology of the Present*, London: Verso, 2002.

[11] See Hegel, *Encyclopedia Logic*, par. 112, par. 163; and see for a comprehensive history of this doctrine, Rodolphe Gasché, *The Tain of the Mirror*, Cambridge, MA: Harvard University Press, 1986.

[12] Michel Foucault, *Dits et écrits*, Vol. 1, Paris: Gallimard, 1994, 518–539; published in English as "Maurice Blanchot: The Thought from Outside," trans. Brian Massumi, in *Foucault/Blanchot*, New York: Zone, 1987. Future references to this work are denoted *DE*.

> Literature is not language pulling back on itself to the point of a burning manifestation, but rather language as far as possible from itself; and if, in this setting "outside of itself," it unveils its own being, it is a clarity that suddenly reveals a gap rather than a reversion, a dispersal rather than a return of signs upon themselves. (*DE*, 520)

One here certainly recalls Hegel's obsessive counterformulation of the return of the categories on themselves or into themselves, and the generation of their being-for-self as a set of formalized climaxes. Here, to be sure, Foucault has literature in mind, and indeed he recites the great modernist litany, the French modernist canon, for which Blanchot more than anyone else was responsible: Sade (and Hölderlin, naturalized following Laplanche), Mallarmé, Bataille, Klossowski, and of course Blanchot himself (the *Tel quel* group will later on add Lautréamont). The thinkers of exteriority are not enumerated (one assumes Foucault counts himself among them), but their enemies in the "humanist" tradition are: most notably Kant and Hegel, and then the later thinkers of alienation. Yet of the fictional enactments of exteriority, Foucault has this to say:

> Fiction thus consists not in making visible the invisible but in making us see just how invisible that invisibility of the visible really is. Whence its deeper kinship with space as such, which thus grasped is to fiction what the negative is to reflection (it being understood that dialectical negation is linked to the fable of time). (*DE*, 524)

The spatialization of thought: one does not prematurely wish to class Foucault among the postmodernists (his evocations of the dark powers of literature and language in *The Order of Things* are profoundly modernist), but there is certainly something as prophetic and annunciatory in this idea as he himself would have wished.

But are Kant and Hegel quite so old-fashioned as all that? Kant's notion that the subject is unavailable to consciousness, and is in fact a noumenon, a thing-in-itself like the deeper reality of the world or God, would seem very precisely to banish self-consciousness in the hackneyed sense of the doxa, and to impose something closer to a "thought of the outside": a kind of groping blind palpation of the forms of what gets thought inside in order, symptomally, in order to detect what might be its truer external shape. As for Hegel, did not Henri Lefebvre[13] call for a kind of spatial dialectic more suited to our own time and needs than the temporal "fable" as which Foucault characterizes the *Logic*'s great procession of the categories—a true theoria in the etymological sense? But what if the categories of the *Logic*

---

[13] Henri Lefebvre, *La production de l'espace*, Paris: Anthropos, 1974, 382.

were already just this neutral thought of the outside for which Foucault calls? So many strange shapes that appear precisely in the kind of void Foucault evokes for language ... this is then to invoke a related conception of Deleuze, namely that of the "image of thought,"[14] of which we have already seen that it can lodge and express itself in the strange new spaces and colors of the individual concepts. A little like the Lacanian *écoute*, this, an audition of the patient's speech in terms of its rhythms and its pauses, its sonority and timbre, its externality, rather than the conscious ideas the patient thinks he is trying to express. I think we need to entertain the possibility that Hegel's way with the categories is of this kind: a palpation, an audition, of the shape of the individual categories, as it were from the outside, a kind of outer edge in which thought is not expressed but described. This is how one of his listeners characterized his language:

> I can only account for Hegel's cumbersome delivery by the conjecture that he thought in nouns, so that in the contemplation of an object its relationships appeared to him as so many shapes that interacted with each other and whose acts he first had to translate into words. Certain favorite constructions figured notably in this process, such as those imitated from the French ... As a consequence Hegel had to pause occasionally, in order not to write in a grammatically incorrect way. Not that he did not know the rules of grammar, but because he first had to translate the content of his thoughts, so that every utterance must have appeared to him as though in a foreign language.[15]

---

[14] Deleuze, *Différence et Répétition*, Chapter 3.

[15] Karl Rosenkranz, *Georg Wilhelm Friedrich Hegel's Leben*, Darmstadt: Wissenschaftliche Buchhandlung, 1969 (1844), 361, quoted from Professor Sietze.

PART III

COMMENTARIES

Chapter 4

Marx's Purloined Letter

Derrida's book, *Specters of Marx* (1993), is more than an intervention; it wishes to be a provocation, first and foremost of what he calls a new Holy Alliance whose attempt definitively to bury Marx is here answered by a call for a new International. Derrida reminds a younger generation of the complex and constitutive interrelationships between an emergent deconstruction and the Marx-defined debates of the 1950s and 60s in France (he has spoken elsewhere of his personal relationship to Althusser[1]): in this he is only one of a number of significant thinkers of so-called poststructuralism to register a concern with the way in which demarxification in France and elsewhere, having placed the reading of Marx and the themes of a properly Marxian problematic beyond the bounds of respectability and academic tolerance, now threatens to vitiate the activity of philosophizing itself, replacing it with a bland Anglo-American anti-speculative positivism, empiricism, or pragmatism. The book will also speak of the relationship of deconstruction to Marx (as well as of its reservation about the possibility of an implicit or explicit Marxist "philosophy").

Derrida here takes the responsibility of speaking of the world situation, whose novel and catastrophic features he enumerates with all the authority of the world's greatest living philosopher. He reads Marx's texts, in particular offering a remarkable new exegesis of passages from *The German Ideology*. He develops a new concept, that of "spectrality," and does so in a way which also suggests modifications or inflections in the way in which deconstruction handles concepts in general. And he affirms a persistence of that "weak messianic power" that Benjamin called upon us to preserve and sustain within a dark era. It is a wide-ranging performance, and a thrilling one (particularly as it is punctuated by the great shouts and cries of alarm of the opening scenes of *Hamlet* on the battlements). I want to summarize the

---

[1] See E. Ann Kaplan and Michael Sprinker, eds., *The Althusserian Legacy*, London: Verso, 1993.

book more narrowly and then comment in an unsystematic and preliminary way on points I find particularly interesting.

The five chapters of *Specters of Marx* turn variously, as might be expected, around the issue of Marx's afterlife today. *Hamlet* and the ghost of Hamlet's father provide a first occasion for imagining what the apparition of Marx's own ghost might be like for us, who have not even heard the rumor of its reappearances. Some remarkable reflections of Blanchot on Marx,[2] the implied ontology of Hamlet's cry "The time is out of joint," and the structure of the act of conjuring as such—calling forth, allaying, conspiring—now set the stage for what follows in the second chapter, namely, the conspiracy against Marxism, as well as Fukuyama and the ("apocalyptic") end of history, all of which reveal the international (but also US) political forces at work in this new world situation of late capitalism. The latter will then be the object of a direct analysis by Derrida in Chapter 3 ("Usures, tableau d'un monde sans âge") in which ten features of the new globalization are outlined, ranging from unemployment and homelessness to the Mafia, drug wars, and the problem of international law, and passing through the contradictions of the market, the various international forms of the Debt, the arms industry, and so-called ethnic conflict. These characteristics of Fukuyama's global triumph of democracy demand a new International and a transformed resurgence of the "spirit of Marxism" (from which ontology has been expunged, along with Marx's own fear of ghosts). Two final chapters then offer rich readings of passages in Marx specifically related to spectrality. Chapter 4 returns to *The Communist Manifesto* and *The Eighteenth Brumaire*, not least in order to suggest Marx's own ambivalence with respect to spectrality as such; while the last chapter examines Marx's critique of Stirner and effectuates a displacement in the conventional view of commodity fetishism, whose "turning tables" now strongly suggest poltergeists as much as they do items for sale on a shelf somewhere.

One's question—as to whether these are new themes for Derrida—ought to involve a rethinking of the notion of the "theme" in philosophical writing fully as much as a story about periodization. Indeed, changes within deconstruction in recent years have seemed to motivate a variety of descriptions. Despite Heidegger's role in all this, the notion of an affirmative—that is, an "interpretive"—deconstruction[3] has not seemed to impose itself in the form of a *Kehre*, not least because the implicit opposition (to some classical "destructive" or even critical, negative deconstruction) would seem to reintroduce any number of those tedious and conventional binary oppositions

---

[2] Maurice Blanchot, "Les trois paroles de Marx," in *L'Amitié*, Paris: Gallimard, 1971, 115–117.

[3] Jacques Derrida, *Spurs: Nietzsche's Styles/Éperons: Les Styles de Nietzsche*, trans. Barbara Harlow, Chicago: University of Chicago Press, 1979, 36–37.

which it was precisely the merit of deconstruction to have banished from our daily intellectual life in the first place.

Changes in the intellectual situation in which deconstruction has had to make its way have obviously played a fundamental role in its style as well as its strategies. As far as Marx is concerned, for example, the sympathies as well as the philosophical reservations with the Marxist problematic were as evident twenty years ago—in the dialogues entitled *Positions*,[4] much of which are spent warding off the overenthusiastic embraces of his Leninist interviewers—as they are in the present work: in particular the endorsement of materialism is a question to which we will want to return here.

Meanwhile, it can be supposed that the academic respectability a now multi-volumed deconstruction has begun to acquire in US philosophy departments (along with the consecration, in France, of the *collège de philosophie* founded by Mitterrand's socialist government, with Derrida himself as its first head) has inevitably modified the appearance of a corpus long since given over to the care of merely literary intellectuals. On the other hand, you could just as plausibly argue that Derrida has grown more literary over the years, and has been ever more willing to experiment with language and with a variety of smaller discursive genres in ways that call the philosophical vocation of the earlier, more conventional works more strongly back into question, even where the vocation of those earlier works consisted in challenging academic philosophy itself.

Can a change in tone be detectable, since the waning of the older polemics and the gradual implantation of Derridean strictures on various forms of metaphysical thought (presence, identity, self-consciousness, and the like) which from maddening gadfly stings have settled down into the status of doxa in their own right? Heidegger looms ever larger in this work, but is it fair to sense a new complacency in its dealings with this particular ghost, whose hauntings seem particularly inescapable? Is it not rather our own "vulgar" reading of deconstruction as critique (implying that the sequel to the deconstruction of metaphysical concepts will be their replacement by something better, truer, etc.) which is responsible for this or that current astonishment that Heidegger's work continues to demand such respectful attention (even within the present book, as we shall see)? But as an intellectual operation, it was always a crucial necessity for deconstruction to move Heidegger, and in particular Heidegger's view of the history of philosophy, centrally into the canon of philosophical reading, to impose Heidegger's problematic inescapably within contemporary philosophy: if only in order, in a second movement, to be able to draw back from Heidegger's own positions and to criticize the essentially metaphysical tendencies at work in them as well. It cannot really be a question of Derrida's "development" or of the

---

[4] Jacques Derrida, *Positions*, Paris: Minuit, 1972.

"evolution" of deconstruction where the perpetually shifting emphases of this calculated ambivalence are concerned.

If that particular impression harbored the implied reproach that deconstruction has grown less political—less polemic, more mellow—in recent years, a complementary one could be expressed according to which it has grown more political, in the more conventional sense of the word. Indeed, a series of interventions on South Africa[5] (to which we must now add the dedication of the present book to the slain Marxist leader Chris Hani) stands side by side with critiques of the new Europe and seems to prepare the "committed writing" of the present text, whose subtitle significantly reads "the state of the debt, the work of mourning, and the new International"; except that Derrida has always been a political figure, his specific public pronouncements going back at least as far as the controversy over the *loi Habib* in the 1970s (the Pompidou regime's attempt to "exorcize" the spirit of May '68 by dropping the teaching of philosophy from the program of the *lycées*). Some of the confusion stems from the frame itself in which political interventions are necessarily evaluated and have their effectivity: the earlier occasion was a specifically French one, nor has Derrida often felt able to intervene in a US situation in which he has worked for so many years now. But on the new Europe he has found it important to express himself (see below), while virtually the first and most crucial thing he finds to say about Marx himself in the present work is as a thinker of the world market, the world political situation: "no text of the tradition seems as lucid on the current globalization of the political".[6] It is thus globalization itself which sets the stage for a new kind of politics, along with a new kind of political intervention. Many of us will feel deep sympathy with his conception of a new International, as far as radical intellectuals are concerned: for the cybernetic possibilities that enable post-Fordism along with financial speculation, and generate the extraordinary new wealth that constitutes the power of the postmodern business establishment, are also available to intellectuals today on a world scale. It does not seem in the least derisive to foresee networks analogous to those formed by exiles, within a newspaper media situation, in Marx's own time, but on a qualitatively as well as quantitatively modified scale (in both cases, the relationship of the working-class movements to which such intellectuals correspond is a rather different, more problematic development).

---

[5] See "Le dernier mot du racisme" (1983), and "Admiration de Nelson Mandela, ou Les lois de la réflexion" (1986), in Jacques Derrida, *Psyché*, Paris: Galilée, 1987, 353–362, 453–476.

[6] Jacques Derrida, *Spectres de Marx*, Paris: Galilée, 1993, 35. Future references to this work are denoted *SM*.

But now we must also observe that it is precisely this kind of periodization, this kind of storytelling—what has happened to deconstruction? How has it changed over the years? Are these internal concerns consistent with the topics of the earlier writings?—that makes up the deeper subject (or one of the deeper subjects) of the present book on Marx, whose occasion certainly seems to be just such a story or periodizing effect: Marx, who seemed living, is now dead and buried again; what does it mean to affirm this?

In particular, notions of development, influence, conversion, include within themselves oversimplified narratives whose fundamental decisions turn on continuity and discontinuity, on whether to judge a given development as a "break" (radical or not!) with what preceded it, or to read this or that seemingly novel motif as standing in deeper continuity and consonance with earlier preoccupations and procedures. Identity and difference are the poles around which such decisions turn, and the former is as stark and unconceptual as the latter is arbitrary: no wonder narrative along with its ancillary ideologies (historicism, for instance, or teleology) has fallen into such discredit, no wonder Derrida socratically tells us, in *Memoires for Paul de Man*, "I don't know how to tell stories."[7] On the other hand, he also does so; and not surprisingly it is to the Heideggerian story that he is fundamentally committed—"the foundational concepts of substance and cause, with their whole system of connex concepts, are enough whatever their differentiation and their internal problematic, to cure the relay and assure us of the uninterrupted (although strongly differentiated) continuity of all the moments of Metaphysics, Physics, and Logic, with a detour through Ethics."[8] But this immediately poses a problem about Derrida's new work, and not only the question of whether his relationship to Marx is "the same" as it was in the past (he has himself said that his affirmation of a political affiliation to Marxism depended very much on the general intellectual situation and on the place of Marx in current doxa[9]). But there also persists, alongside this uncertainty, the question as to whether the very nature of his theorization or his conceptual-scriptual work has not been modified since the first published texts. And the same question arises for Marxism, both within the works of Marx himself (do they really evolve, is there a "break" as Althusser so famously insisted) and in their uses over time (few thinkers, recalls Derrida, have so strenuously insisted on "their own possible 'ageing' and their intrinsically irreducible historicity … who has ever called for the *transformation* to come of his own theses?" [*SM*, 35]). But the relation of

---

[7] *Memoires for Paul de Man*, rev. ed., New York: Columbia University Press, 1989, 3. Future references to this work are denoted *MPM*.

[8] "Ousia et Grammé," in *Marges de la philosophie*, Paris: Minuit, 1972, 42. Future references to *Marges de la philosophie* are denoted *MP*.

[9] See interview in *Oxford Literary Review*.

Marx to narrative, and to the various possible narratives we might be tempted to invent about his work and the fortunes of his work, is then, if not simplified, at least varied, by the fact that, not having been a philosopher exactly, Marx is to that degree ("not exactly") a part of the history of metaphysics: "answers without questions," says Blanchot; which does not mean that Marx will not be reproached for certain ontological tendencies and temptations, but rather that these "answers" somehow already escape the onto-logo-phallo-centric. Presumably one can at least tell about them the story of their "temptations," which is what Derrida does in part (Marx's fear of ghosts).

It may also be worth suggesting that, along with narrative, goes argument, at least in the sense in which philosophical conservatives have used this rather legal concept to separate sheep from goats and to try to reestablish a notion of philosophizing which Derrida would surely classify as the "proper." It's very interesting, but does he present arguments? Derrida's arguments are his readings, surely, and no one who has worked through some of the great philosophical *explications de texte* can doubt that he is saying something; but my feeling is that the very conception of argument here is not unrelated to that of narrative, in the sense of what we understand to count as "saying something," in the sense of definitions and the clarification of proper names and characters, articulated terminology whose destinies we can then follow through the various conceptual peripeteias and even metamorphoses. Greimas thought one ought to be able to make a narrative analysis of the *Critique of Pure Reason*, and read its arguments as so many stories intertwining and reaching the appropriate narrative climaxes. In that sense, perhaps, Derrida is truly non-Narrative; and readers who follow up his own careful indications ("for more on fetishism, see *Glas*, pp. 51, 149, 231ff, 249ff, 264ff" [*SM*, 264, n. 1]) will surely be disappointed if they imagined they would find definitions in those places, and statements or propositions by Derrida as to the nature of fetishism and the plausibility of its various theorizations, that they could then take back into the present context and introduce as the "meanings" of the words they find there. Rather, it is as though these page numbers indicated so many themes, and documented the movement through Derrida's work of various image-clusters, as they used to be called in a now old-fashioned literary criticism: yet it would presumably be important to avoid the misleading overtones of words like "image" and "theme" (which are thought to be literary only on account of their philosophical uselessness) and to think these procedures in more rigorous ways.

Benjamin's notion of the constellation may well offer one way of doing this, and I invoke it (like a ghost) on the strength of what I am tempted to describe as a primitive accumulation of text in Derrida's own work, which now makes it possible for him (and for us) to mobilize cross-referencing as a kind of philosophical procedure in its own right, which demonstrates something fundamental about a given concept or motif by exhibiting the various contexts in which it has been able to appear, in which its appearance has proved unavoidable. Such mobile constellations are variable, without the rhythms at which they replace or reconfigure each other really proving anything narratively about "development" or "evolution." It is, for example, certain that the constellation we will be concerned with here—centered on the ghost—allows us to reread Derrida's entire corpus and to refocus henceforth classical early texts in utterly new ways (in particular, as we shall see, with reference to phenomenology): but does this mean, as T. S. Eliot might have said, that the "order" of Derrida's work is thereby "modified ever so slightly," or could we not equally well build on a model of latency and "argue" that spectrality was the name of the game all along, even before we or Derrida became aware of it? But the force of the arguments against narrative, historicism, diachrony, telos, and the like, and of concepts like that of the constellation, surely works to deprive such questions of much of their interest or at least of their urgency.

Still, our examination of the new Marx book will not be particularly improved by neglecting the insistent question as to whether the new figurality, the figured concept of the ghost or specter, is not of a somewhat different type than those that began to proliferate in Derrida's earlier work, beginning most famously with "writing" itself and moving through a now familiar spectrum of marked terms like "dissemination" and "hymen", along with the inversion of this practice, which consisted in modifying a letter in a word whose sound thereby remained the same (*différance*). Even beyond the issue of whether philosophy today can produce new concepts (and new terms or names for them), this goes to the whole issue of theoretical discourse today (or yesterday, if theory is really dead, as they tell us, or even if theory is only as dead as Marx, whose answers without questions played some role in its historical elaboration after all): this must first be addressed before we can examine the shape of the constellation mapped by *Specters of Marx*; the supplementary advantage of telling the story of the emergence of such discourse will lie in its analogies with problems of materialism to be considered later on.

At any rate, it seems safe enough to locate the situational origins of such theoretical discourse in the general crisis of Philosophy after Hegel, and in particular in Nietzsche's guerrilla warfare against everything noxious concealed within the "desire called philosophy" as well as in Heidegger's discovery that the philosophical system itself (or worse yet, the "worldview") constitutes what he calls metaphysics (or what another tradition might describe as degraded or reified thought). As far as language is concerned, this means that any affirmation one makes is at least implicitly a philosophical proposition and thereby a component of just such a metaphysical system.

The bad universalism of metaphysics has thereby infected language itself, which cannot but continue to emit and endlessly to regenerate the "metaphysical" or the ontic, and comically to affirm one proposition after another, which outlast their pragmatic uses and know an afterlife as what another tradition might call ideology. One can silence such a production, but at enormous cost (for one thing, the others continue talking; for another, did Wittgenstein really manage to do so?); but other methods seemed to come into view in the era sometimes called poststructuralist.

For if all propositions are ideological, perhaps it is possible to limit the use of language to the denunciation of error, and to renounce its structural impulse to express truth in the first place. That this strategy turns language over to a certain terrorism, the practice of the Althusserians and the *Tel quel* group can historically testify: Derrideanism, which had its family relations with both, was not exempt itself from the impression that when it was merely "specifying" someone else's position, this last was also in the process of being roundly denounced (none of Derrida's qualifications about the difference between deconstruction and critique ever really made much of a dent in this impression). For specifying the other position meant specifying it as ideology (Althusser) or as metaphysics (Heidegger, Derrida): identifications which naturally enough led the unforewarned reader to suppose that truth was about to be put in its place, whereas Althusser taught us that we would never be out of ideology, and Derrida consistently demonstrated the impossibility of avoiding the metaphysical. But both left their own "ideology" or "metaphysics" unidentified, unspecified: and I think it would be possible to show (and this for all so-called poststructuralisms and not merely these two named bodies of theory) how into this void certain motifs emerged which were reified and turned into "theories" and thenceforth into something like old-fashioned philosophies or "worldviews" in their own right. This is the point at which Althusser is supposed to be about overdetermination, and Derrida about writing: it is also the point at which their formal dilemmas seem closest to fundamental contradictions in modernism in general, and most notably to the one Barthes described in *Writing Degree Zero*, as that of avoiding the closure of a finished system of signs. The greatest modern literature, he said, tries to avoid thus becoming an official, public, recognized "institutional" language in its own right; but if it succeeds, it fails, and the private language of Proust or Joyce thereby enters the public sphere (the university, the canon) as just such a "style."[10] Others succeed by remaining fragments: Gramsci, Benjamin; something one cannot particularly decide to do in advance, however.

This is at any rate the situation in which it makes sense to talk about something like an "aesthetic" of the Derridean text: a way of describing the

---

[10] Roland Barthes, *Le degré zéro de l'écriture*, Paris: Seuil, 1953.

philosophical dilemmas it renders as a kind of "form-problem," whose resolution is sought in a certain set of procedures, or rather, in consonance with
all of modern art, in a certain set of taboos.[11] Here the taboos very directly
govern the enunciation of new propositions, the formation of new concepts:
the *Grammatology* seems to be the last text of Derrida's in which the possibility for philosophy to produce new and Utopian concepts is raised,
however it is there dealt with. Indeed, there is still a very strong Marxian
flavor about the conviction that genuinely new concepts will not be possible
until the concrete situation, the system itself, in which they are to be
thought, has been radically modified. It is a conviction which only Manfredo
Tafuri has defended well down into the 1990s (and his own death); the idea
that intellectual innovation—not merely the invention of new solutions
but, even more, the replacement of old problems with new ones (implicit in,
for example, Kuhn's related notion of a system)—seems to wane after that
failure which May '68 is perceived by intellectuals as being in France (where
the Communist Party in the *accords de Matignon* draws back from the
notion that France is in a pre-revolutionary situation). This failure will spell
the end, not merely of 1960s Utopianism in France (an analogous but far
more thoroughgoing change in temperature can be registered in Foucault's
works), but also the beginnings of demarxification and wholesale intellectual anti-communism, the beginning of the end of the hegemonic notion of
the radical or left French intellectual. This has more than a merely formal
importance for Derrida's own work: indeed we will later on want to see in
Specters of Marx the overt expression of a persistent if generally subterranean
Utopianism, which he himself (shunning that word) will prefer to call "a
weak messianic power," following Benjamin. But surely, already in the
1960s, his own solution to the problem of conceptual innovation or philosophical Utopianism (so to speak) has its bearing on the capacity of this
weak messianic power to weather the storm in his own work and not, as in
so many others, to be desiccated and blown away for lack of deeper roots.

There is perhaps no corresponding disappointment and reversal in Derrida,
since from the outset the form itself presupposed that philosophy as a
system and as a vocation for conceptual innovation was at an end. But it presupposed this by means of a form-principle which navigated the problem of
a tired acceptance of the traditional status quo by way of a simple solution:

---

[11] Derrida once privately expressed to me his discomfort with my use of "aesthetic"
here, which probably recalled the once unavoidable dismissal of his work by philosophers, who considered it merely "literary." But I wanted to use "aesthetic" as a noun
—I might have tried to invent the neologism of a "linguistic" as well—to designate
that series of rules which govern the production of acceptable sentences (or here,
propositions) in a given generic system. The word "aesthetic" therefore, which I
retain, is in no way meant to imply that Derrida's texts "belong to" literature rather
than to philosophy, whatever that might mean.

the avoidance of the affirmative sentence as such, of the philosophical proposition. Deconstruction thus "neither affirmeth nor denieth": it does not emit propositions in that sense at all (save, as is inevitable in a work now so voluminous as this one, in the unavoidable moments of the lowered guard and the relaxation of tension, in which a few affirmations slip through or the openly affirmative sentence startles the unprepared reader—as most notably in the late-capitalism section of the present book [Chapter 3] or the great essay in celebration of Nelson Mandela).

The question then necessarily arises how this taboo can actually be put into practice in the writing; and, first and foremost, where content can be generated in an exercise otherwise so seemingly *fruste* and barren as one thus vigilantly policed and patrolled by the intent to avoid saying something. Derrida's own personal aesthetic tastes—not merely the interest in Mallarmé, but above all, and well beyond the admiration for Ponge and Jabès, the fascination with Roger Laporte (of all contemporary writers the most intransigently formalist in the bad sense of writing about nothing but your own process of writing)—document a minimalism which is not quite put into practice in his own ultimately far richer philosophical texts.

What saves the day here is, as has been suggested above, the central formal role of the Heideggerian problematic, which assigns a minimal narrative to the entire project, and thus converts an otherwise random series of philosophical texts and fragments into an implicitly grand history: one of metaphysics within philosophy itself. This is the sense in which one might argue that Rorty's project, which effectively destroys philosophy itself as a history and as a discipline (and leaves its Samson-like destroyer in the self-trivialized role as an aesthete and a belletrist, when not a merely liberal political and cultural critic and commentator), is more radical than Derrida's, which manages to rescue the discipline secretly in this backdoor Heideggerian manner and thereby to invest its own texts with a certain dignity as moves and positions within a larger theoretical project: after which Heidegger himself, as we shall see again shortly, can be thrown to the winds and deconstructed as so much metaphysics in his turn.

This frame now enables the practice of deconstruction to find a consecrated form: that of the commentary or philosophical *explication de texte*, within which it can pursue its own augustly parasitical activity. It need no longer articulate its own presuppositions, nor even the results of its own textual critique of the various thinkers thereby glossed and architectonically undone or undermined: they themselves know it all in advance, these texts deconstruct themselves, as Paul de Man showed in his own indispensable supplement to nascent deconstruction as a "methodology" (indeed, the crucial addition is to be found in his own essay on Derrida himself,[12] and on

---

[12] Paul de Man, *Blindness and Insight: Essays in the Rhetoric of Contemporary Criticism*, Minneapolis: University of Minnesota Press, 1971.

the latter's alleged critique of Rousseau, which is shown to correspond to little more than Rousseau's—or better still, Rousseau's text's—critique of itself). With this, then, the "aesthetic" procedure of deconstruction is complete: it will be a form that posits some prior text on which it claims to be a commentary, appropriating portions—and in particular terminological subsections—from that text provisionally to say something which the text does not exactly say as such in its own voice or language, within a larger context which is the frame of the Heideggerian master-narrative, modified, enlarged, or restricted as one will (later on very much by way of Lacanian-related additions which will come to look relatively feminist, as in the concept of onto-logo-phallo-centrism).

This "aesthetic," or solution, to an historical form-problem is clearly enough a whole philosophical position in its own right and to put it this way is also to understand why the issue of Derrida's literariness is poorly engaged or posed from the outset. For the deconstructive text is also "postmodern" in the sense in which it flees the attempted originality of essayism. Not only does it not wish to generate a new philosophical system in the old sense (as in Ricoeur, or even more so in deliberately traditional/reactionary thinkers like J-L Marion, whose "resistance to" or reaction against theory can above all be measured by their return to and defense of the philosophical institution as such); it does not lay claim to a "distinctive voice" or an "original set of perceptions," as is the case with the tradition of the philosophical essay, in Cioran, for example, or Canetti: originality in that sense being suspect and as Brecht might put it "culinary" or belletristic (something the canonized Blanchot seemed to overstep into theory, or, along with Klossowski, into the novel itself).

On the other hand, we have also suggested in passing, no formalist strategy can ever succeed in any permanent way; and deconstruction is not the only example—but it is a particularly striking one—of the reification of a principle that wished to remain purely formal, its translation back against its own wishes into a philosophical worldview or conceptual thematics it set out to avoid being in the first place. Such are for example the exoteric readings of Derrida's texts as the expressions of a "philosophy" of *écriture* or *différance*, and later on the transformation of "deconstruction" into a full-fledged philosophical system and position in its own right.[13] These degradations and transformations confirm Derrida's emphasis on the *name* (or the *noun*, the substantive: the two words are the same in French [*le nom*]): paleonymy is a clever strategy, but even the filling of old wineskins with new content ends up foregrounding the new emphasis of a term, which can then function in the traditional philosophical manner as the name for a concept.

---

[13] As in Rodolphe Gasché's (admirable) *The Tain of the Mirror: Derrida and the Philosophy of Reflection*, Cambridge, MA: Harvard University Press, 1986.

The question we have in the context of a reading of *Specters of Marx* is whether the new name "spectrality" represents yet another move in this interminable and ultimately necessarily unsuccessful effort to avoid names in the first place, or whether it can be seen as the modification of that strategy and as the attempt to strike out away from the philosophical noun altogether in some new figural direction.

It seems at least plausible that the emergence of what we have characterized as Benjaminian constellations in Derrida's work tends to displace the older framework of the Heideggerian narrative, and thereby to modify the exegetical strategies determined by this last (Marx however being in any case, as has already been observed, scarcely the prototype of the philosophical text or fragment you can deconstruct in this classical way in the first place). In order to verify this proposition, however, we must now look more closely at the nature of the present "constellation," and at the same time return to a starting point which is that of all contemporary theory and post-philosophical discourse, and not merely that of Derrida himself.

For from this perspective the central problem of the constellation called spectrality is that of matter itself, or, better still, of materialism as such, that is to say, as a philosophy or a philosophical position in its own right (*SM*, 1). (This was incidentally the central issue Derrida discussed with "the Marxists" in the 1972 interviews collected in *Positions*.) Or perhaps it might be better to say that it is the absence of the problem of materialism, its occultation or repression, the impossibility of posing it as a problem as such and in its own right, that generates the constellation with which we have to do here: whose specific moments are—the central apparition of spectrality itself (*SM*, 2), and the relationship of this to "spirit" as an ideologeme on the one hand (*SM*, 5) and phenomenology as a philosophical protect in its own right (*SM*, 4); while to both these correspond as it were the semiotic reversals of religion (*SM*, 6) (particularly in its relationship to the fetishism of commodities) and the messianic (*SM*, 7), or if you prefer the political. But this is not merely a semiotic system: it has its ancillary dimensions, and to the repression of materialism as it were on one face of the constellation correspond the four-dimensional depths of its other face, in the twin phenomena of individual mourning and historical temporality as such (*SM*, 3) (both past and future, tradition and revolution). In any case the reason for being of the very concept of a constellation lies in its capacity to resist formalization, just as the multidimensionality of the stars themselves rebukes mythological line drawings in the sky and stands as their secret deconstruction. We will, however, want to move slowly across these various moments as though they were points on the ceiling of some philosophical planetarium.

I.

As for materialism—as it were the black hole these visible stars conceal and designate all at once—it ought to be the place in which theory, deconstruction, and Marxism meet: a privileged place for theory, insofar as the latter emerges from a conviction as to the "materiality" of language; for deconstruction insofar as its vocation has something to do with the destruction of metaphysics; for Marxism (or "historical materialism") insofar as the latter's critique of Hegel turned on the hypostasis of ideal qualities[14] and the need to replace such invisible abstractions by a concrete that included production and economics. It is not an accident that these are all negative ways of evoking materialism: matter as such—the Greek *hyle* (or wood or "stuff," raw material) will later on reappear in the form of Marx's dancing tables in the first chapter of *Capital*—does not seem particularly promising as a starting point. Its sheer immediacy overwhelms anything you might want to do with it or think about it: or perhaps it would be better to say, the other way around, that when you begin to think about matter you have already added something else to it, isolated it, articulated it, abstracted it, and turned it into either an idea or a word, and probably into both. But how are we to understand the expression, a materialist idea? Materialist philosophies attempt to sap or undermine the autonomy of ideas or consciousness, to assign them material origins somewhere in the bodily senses or in the brain cells, to scrape away at the gap and reduce the distance between something like an experience and this or that mechanism (which of course itself remains a representation or an idea): but I think that no one has suggested a differentiation among ideas themselves whereby some may be classified as more material than others. It is a distinction that should not be confused with that between science and ideology (which may of course be equally unfounded), for as far as I know, no one has suggested that scientific ideas feel different and offer a radically different experience of consciousness than ideological ones. One is tempted to conclude that all ideas, all experiences of consciousness, are somehow idealistic: it is a conclusion that would assign "materialism" a rather different and non-systematic, pragmatic or therapeutic task from the philosophical one of constructing a system of truths.

These dilemmas are exacerbated if we think, not in terms of consciousness as the older philosophies did, but in terms of language: where the notion of writing materialist sentences already offers something of a paradox, at least insofar as it suggests that you might also be able to write "idealist" sentences. But probably those philosophically unacceptable sentences are merely sentences whose necessary linguistic materiality we have

---

[14]   Karl Marx, *Critique of Hegel's 'Philosophy of Right,'* trans. Joseph O'Malley, Cambridge: Cambridge University Press, 1970.

forgotten or repressed, imagining them to be somehow pure thought. In that case, "materialism" would simply involve reminding ourselves at every turn that we are using words (rather than thinking pure thoughts or having "experiences" of consciousness): and this is of course what contemporary "theoretical discourse" tries to do. This is the deeper reason why, as has been suggested above, it cannot know allegiance to any truths, but only commitment to the deconcealment and denunciation of error (that is to say, of idealism). But this also marks the moment in which contemporary theory or post-philosophy crosses wires with the modern movement in art, and belatedly reveals itself to be a kind of modernism in its turn (that is, from our current perspective, as a kind of historical style).

In either case, materialism would seem precluded as a philosophy: at best it could be a polemic slogan, designed to organize various anti-idealist campaigns, a procedure of demystification and de-idealization; or else a permanent linguistic reflexivity. This is, among other things, why Marxism has never been a philosophy as such, but rather a "unity of theory and practice" very much like psychoanalysis, and for many of the same reasons. This is not to say that a number of different Marxist philosophies have not been proposed: indeed it has been felt to be compatible with Hegelianism, with positivism, with Catholicism, with various philosophical realisms, with structuralism, and most recently with analytic philosophy. For me, Lukács's *History and Class Consciousness* has always seemed the most ambitious attempt to argue a philosophical ground for Marxian and specifically class epistemology; while Korsch makes the basic case for what has been called Marxism's "absolute historicism," followed in this by what is for many of us the greatest American contribution to a specifically Marxist philosophy, Sidney Hook's early and self-repudiated *Towards the Understanding of Karl Marx*, which in addition boldly attempts a "synthesis" of Marxism and American pragmatism.

What must be concluded from these remarkably discordant affiliations is clearly that Marxism is not a philosophy as such: "answers without questions," we will hear Blanchot describe it, a characterization which allows for the optional coordination with and adjustment to this or that philosophy if we grasp the latter as a specific problematic or system of questions. Is it plausible then to see in *Specters of Marx* the tentative offer to coordinate Marxism with deconstruction (something already argued in a well-known book by Michael Ryan[15])? The question presupposes deconstruction to be a philosophy, something it has been clear I feel to be premature and misleading. But if it is simply a matter of comparing procedures, and in particular positing analogies of situation (which might then account for the family

---

15 *Marxism and Deconstruction: A Critical Articulation*, Baltimore: John Hopkins University Press, 1982.

likeness in the procedures), then this seems to me useful and the beginnings of an historical account (and indeed my remarks above are made in that spirit). If, however, it is a matter of constructing a new philosophical system, like the notorious Freudo-Marxisms of yesteryear, then the idea is perhaps rather to be deplored.

In any case, Derrida's reserves about Marx, and even more strongly about the various Marxisms, all turn very specifically on this point, namely the illicit development of this or that Marxism, or even this or that argument of Marx himself, in the direction of what he calls an ontology, that is to say, a form of the philosophical system (or of metaphysics) specifically oriented around some basic identity of being which can serve as a grounding or foundational reassurance for thought. That this ontological temptation, although encouraged by the peculiar thematics of matter and "materialism," is not limited to physical or spatial areas but finds its exemplification above all in temporal dilemmas we will see shortly (*SM*, 3). But for the moment we can suggest that under what Derrida stigmatizes as ontology are very much to be ranged all possible conceptions of a materialist philosophy as such.

And as a matter of fact any number of Marxist traditions have themselves been alert to the dangers of such a philosophical ambition: alongside the various philosophical projects listed above, therefore (which very specifically include any number of official materialisms, from Engels to Stalin and beyond), we also need to register those important moments in Marxian philosophizing in which materialism is specifically repudiated as a form of bourgeois thought; in particular in the guise of eighteenth-century mechanical materialism: this includes Marx himself, of course (particularly in *The German Ideology*); it also includes the first original attempt to rewrite Marxism in philosophical terms, that of Antonia Labriola and a certain Italian historicism, which will clearly enough culminate in Gramsci's "philosophy of praxis."[16] His euphemistic slogan, which in part we owe to the requirement to outsmart the fascist censorship of his jailers, nonetheless underscores the very different emphasis Gramsci placed on action, construction, and production, as opposed to the relatively passive and epistemological emphases which have often been those of the "materialisms." Korsch has already been mentioned in this same lineage; but it would equally be important to mention Sartre and Breton as two Marx-related thinkers who both waged powerful polemics against materialism as a weird philosophical eccentricity; while it has often been observed that non-materialist currents —whether they be those of Platonism or of Maoism—are often more

---

[16] Antonio Labriola, *Essays on the Materialist Conception of History*, New York: Kerr, 1908; and see on Labriolo the forthcoming work of Roberto Dainotto, *Philosophy of Praxis/Philosophy of History: The Genesis of Theoretical Marxism in Italy from Labriola to Gramsci*.

conducive to activism (when not indeed to outright voluntarism) than the various materialisms have historically been. To go so far, however, is to raise the most appropriate anxieties about some new spiritualist agenda, anxieties which will also have to be dealt with in their "proper" time and place.

2.

Spectrality is not difficult to circumscribe, as what makes the present waver: like the vibrations of a heat wave through which the massiveness of the object world—indeed of matter itself—now shimmers like a mirage. We tend to think that these moments correspond to mere personal or physical weakness—a dizzy spell, for example, a drop in psychic *niveau*, a temporary weakness in our grip on things: on that reality which is supposed to rebuke us by its changelessness, the *en-soi*, being, the other of consciousness, nature, "what is." Ontology would presumably correspond to some different and more acceptable kind of weakening of consciousness in which it seems to fade away in the face of Being itself. This, which we trivialize by calling it a still relatively psychological name like "experience," Heidegger insisted we think of ontology as something other than humanist: here Being is the measure and not "man." Oddly however, the belief in the stability of reality, being, and matter, far from being an exceptional philosophical achievement, is little more than common sense itself. It is this that spectrality challenges and causes to waver visibly, yet invisibly all at once, as when we say "barely perceptible," wanting, by that, to be perceptible and imperceptible all at once. If this sense of tangible certainty and solidity corresponds to ontology, then, as something on which conceptuality can build, something "foundational," how to describe what literally undermines it and shakes our belief? Derrida's mocking answer—hauntology—is a ghostly echo if there ever was one, and serves to underscore the very uncertainties of the spectral itself, which promises nothing tangible in return; on which you cannot build: which cannot even be counted on to materialize when you want it to. Spectrality does not involve the conviction that ghosts exist or that the past (and maybe even the future they offer to prophecy) is still very much alive and at work within the living present: all it says, if it can be thought to speak, is that the living present is scarcely as self-sufficient as it claims to be; that we would do well not to count on its density and solidity, which might under exceptional circumstances betray us.

Derrida's ghosts are these moments in which the present—and above all our current present, the wealthy, sunny, gleaming world of the postmodern and the end of history, of the new world system of late capitalism—unexpectedly betrays us. His are not the truly malevolent ghosts of the modern tradition (perhaps in part because he is also willing to speak for them and to plead their cause). They do not remind us of the archetypal specters of sheer class *ressentiment* in the servants of *The Turn of the Screw*, for example, who are out to subvert the lineage of the masters and bind their children to the land of the dead, of those not merely deprived of wealth and power (or of their own labor power), but even of life itself. In that sense the classic ghost has been an expression of cold fury (most recently in the ghost who takes possession of Jack Nicholson in *The Shining*). Ghosts, as we learned from Homer's land of the dead long ago, envy the living:

> Better, I say, to break sod as a farm hand
> for some poor country man, on iron rations,
> than lord it over all the exhausted dead.[17]

Ressentiment is the primal class passion, and here begins to govern the relations between the living and the dead: for the step from envy to hatred is a short one, and if the truth were told, the ghosts we are able to see hate the living and wish them harm. Such would at least be the only materialist way of thinking about it, from which the most peculiar images begin to emerge, as in Sartre's *The Flies*, or in Brian Aldiss's *Helliconia Spring*, where the dead hang twittering like bats, ever poised and trembling for a raid on anything that moves with life and breath:

> They resembled mummies; their stomachs and eye sockets were hollow, their boney feet dangled; their skins were as coarse as old sacking, yet transparent, allowing a glimpse of luminescent organs beneath ... All these old put-away things were without motion, yet the wandering soul could sense their fury—a fury more intense than any of them could have experienced before obsidian claimed them.[18]

Such ghosts express the fear of modern people that they have not really lived, not yet lived or fulfilled their lives, in a world organized to deprive them of that satisfaction: yet is this suspicion not itself a kind of specter, haunting our lives with its enigmatic doubt that nothing can dispel or exorcize, as with the peculiar quotation with which Derrida's book begins: "I would like finally to learn how to live," reminding us also to make a place for the ghost of Life itself, of vitalism as an ideology, of living and being alive as social and existential categories, in our anatomy of that spectrality to which it is yet another opposite.

Derrida's and Marx's ghosts—the specter of communism, for example—are not as malevolent as these, perhaps at least in part because their primal

---

[17] Homer, *The Odyssey*, trans. Robert Fitzgerald, New York: Doubleday, 1961, 212 (Book 11, lines 462–464.)

[18] Brian Aldiss, *Helliconia Spring*, New York: Ace Books, 1987, 248.

apparition is that of Hamlet's father, an august kingly Renaissance phantom who demands vengeance, no doubt, but also asks for the work of mourning; who would only need to be exorcized should it turn out that mourning—introjection rather than incorporation, as Abraham and Torok have taught us, partially mediated by Derrida himself[19]—cannot be properly completed and sticks in the craw (incorporation), causing us to waste our lives on a vain suspended obsession with the encrypted desire. There is another perspective, to be sure, in which Hamlet's father hates the living and resents their continuing to live—this holds for the murderer, for Claudius, if not for the Queen, whose guilt is undecideable; just as in some more complicated and Oedipal sense it holds for Joyce's reading of *Hamlet*,[20] and of the failure of the paternal function to fulfill itself, since being a father is a mere psychological illusion, and one can only really (yet impossibly) be a son. But Hamlet's father does not appear to the murderers and attempt to haunt them: while the fact of the murder itself rationalizes the irrational hatred the dead have for the living and contains it, by lending it a semblance of motivation and propriety.

Still, we may conjecture that one reply to Derrida's fundamental critique of Marx—to anticipate, it will be that Marx still wants to exorcize ghosts, to get rid of them, to achieve a state of unhaunted, indeed ontological, normality—lies in this particular conjecture: namely that Marx may be more sensitive to the essential malevolence of the past and the dead than anything that can be found in the prototypical situation of mourning and melancholia as Hamlet archetypally configures it. Yet mourning also wants to get rid of the past, to exorcize it albeit under the guise of respectful commemoration, the Torok-Abraham distinction between true mourning (introjection) and an unsuccessful mourning process that ends up fixated on the past, in the form of an incorporated fantasy that cannot be digested, that persists within its crypt as the unconscious of the Unconscious itself—that distinction, and Derrida's prefatory comments on it, went a long way towards suggesting that mourning is in any case impossible and that the past can never be absorbed and forgotten in a "proper" way. To forget the dead altogether is impious in ways that prepare their own retribution, but to remember the dead is neurotic and obsessive and merely feeds a sterile repetition. The fact is that there is no "proper" way of relating to the dead and the past in the first place, only this oscillation between two equally impossible and intolerable conducts (something mourning tries to gloss over

---

[19] See Nicolas Abraham and Maria Torok, *The Wolf Man's Magic Word: A Cryptonymy*, trans. Nicholas Rand, Minneapolis: University of Minnesota Press, 1987; and Derrida's foreword to the book, "Fors," trans. Barbara Johnson. Future references to this work are denoted *WM*.

[20] See episode 9 of *Ulysses* (the library scene, or "Scylla and Charybdis").

by shifting in bewilderment from one to the other, asking itself how much it is grieving now and how much it should be grieving, how much is enough).

In that spirit, I cannot resist quoting Derrida's hint at some constitutive relationship (even though he is only discussing the case of the Wolf Man in particular) between the obsessive and uninternalizable past and the Self: "The Self: a cemetery guard. The crypt is enclosed within the self, but as a foreign place, prohibited, excluded. The self is not the proprietor of what he is guarding. He makes the rounds like a proprietor, but only the rounds. He turns around and around, and in particular he uses all his knowledge of the grounds to turn visitors away. 'He stands there firmly, keeping an eye on the comings and goings of the nearest of kind who claim—under various titles—to have the right to approach the tomb. If he agrees to let in the curious, the injured parties, the detectives, it will only be to serve them with false leads and fake graves'" (*WM*, xxxv). If the individual psychic past is enlarged to include history itself, and the collective past, as well, as begins to happen in Derrida's other great study of mourning, the *Mémoires for Paul de Man*, then some very peculiar institutional and conservational physiognomies begin to emerge here, people who appoint themselves the guardians of this or that past, this or that undead body within the past, who walk a thin line between keeping the corpse safely in its grave and attracting followers by its continuing phosphorescence. Is Marx's corpse of that type? Or de Man's? How exactly do the dead "weigh on the brain of the living like an *Alpendruck*"? Or is there some way of handling the dead and their texts with impunity, filtering a little of their toxic vitality into the present while preserving our own against their mortiferous influence? It is not only the question of the canon and of tradition that is being raised here; but also that of a present without a past, for which history in any of these more archaic, doom- or curse-like forms has ceased to exist. (It seems to me important to add in here the fact that the Wolf Man's problem is only analogously related to mourning; insofar as the memory in question—incestuous in several ways—is a memory of pleasure, and that what is to be repressed is the guilty pleasure itself; which continues to live and throb within the tomb of its oblivion.)

So what we have to do with here is not only the past as such, but rather the repression of the past in full postmodernity or late capitalism: the extinction of Marx is part of that, part of that "end" of something which will shortly, in distinction to the messianic, be identified as the apocalyptic (a world very much ending "not with a bang but a whimper"). To say so is, however, to realize that there is a way not to grapple with this problem, and it is the equivalent here of the bad ontological or humanist solution, namely, the full-throated pathos with which the loss of the past and of tradition is deplored by philosophical and cultural conservatives (of whom Allan Bloom can stand as a distinguished exemplar): as though we could simply go back to some older form of historicity for which even Marx is part of the Western canon of great books and there already exists a coherent philosophical position with which we are free to identify if we choose to do so. But deconstruction repudiates the (ontological) idea that any such coherent philosophical positions exist in the first place; and the interesting problem Derrida will now confront is that of some *tertium datur* between the traditional-humanist and the trendiness of a certain poststructuralism and postmodernism with which it would be too hasty to identify his own thought (although the conservatives themselves inveterately make this identification, in their knee-jerk attacks on deconstruction in Derrida himself as well as in Paul de Man as "nihilistic"). It is not a situation of binary oppositions in which you concoct some "third way," golden mean, synthesis, or whatever: rather, I believe that the way out of this real if false dilemma, this actually existing contradiction whose very terms are nonetheless ideological through and through, lies in an analysis of its figuration. This is the sense in which I also believe, using an older language, that a certain formalism (albeit of an absolute nature, some kind of ultimate Gramscian or Lukácsean formalism) offers the opportunity to change the valences on the problem, to adjust the lens of thought in such a way that suddenly we find ourselves focusing, not on the presumed content of the opposition, but rather on the well-nigh material grain of its arguments, an optical adjustment that leads us in new and wholly unexpected directions.

One of those directions, indeed, will be that of our very topic here, namely the nature of the conceptuality of the spectral, and in particular what that figuration is, and why we require something like it in the first place. Why does the spectral come as a kind of new solution to the false problem of the antithesis between humanism (respect for the past) and nihilism (end of history, disappearance of the past)? And what is meant by characterizing this new "solution" as an allegorical one? "Un présent n'existe pas," Derrida quotes Mallarmé as saying (in the course of the *Mémoires for Paul de Man*):

> The allegation of its supposed "anterior" presence *is* memory and is the origin of all allegories. If a past does not literally exist, nor more does death, only mourning, and that other allegory; including all the figures of death with which we people the "present," which we inscribe (among ourselves, the living) in every trace (otherwise called "survivals"): those figures strained toward the future across a gabled present, figures we inscribe because they can outlast us, beyond the present of their inscription: signs, words, names, letters, this whole text whose legacy-value, as we know "in the present" is trying its luck and advance, *in advance* "in memory of"… (*MPM*, 59)

Here we can observe, emerging on the track as it were of Derrida's earlier footsteps (the very concept or figure of the "trace" or of *écriture*) the later one, *this* one here and now, of "spectrality." In the text on de Man we observe how an extraordinary detour through de Man's reading of Hegel's idea of allegory[21] (an idea which is emphatically not yet or no longer the contemporary one: rather, which is allegory as the archaic, the spirit buried under the massiveness of the pyramid, etc.) brings us up to the post-contemporary notion of allegory as autoreferential par excellence: "the concept of allegory ... constitutes a kind of allegorical trope in the most general sense of the term"(*MPM*, 74). Allegory is an allegory of itself: the very concept of ghostliness produces ghosts, spectralities emerge in the very gap opened within the empirical or the ontic by the ever so slight and "barely perceptible" distance which a trace betrays within its own material constituents: the minute empirical data are reorganized in such a way as to be able to be read as a trace of the past, at that very instant ghostliness along with historicity rise against the mass and weight of what is, of Being, like a kind of shimmering heat wave (in the postmodern we need ghosts that walk in broad daylight and not those who only come in the silence of the "witching hours"). This is therefore the way in which we come full circle: the conceptual need for a figure like that of spectrality springs from an urgent problem or dilemma which that very figure generates or produces in its own right: "you wouldn't look for me if you hadn't already found me," as Pascal says. To deplore the eclipse of the past is already in ways we cannot yet fathom to have recovered that very past whose extinction we register.

It is also the moment in which space gives way to time: for if the problematics of the ontological, of "reality" as an ideological belief, even of the "trace" as the way to open a gap in the bad concept of the present—if all these alternatives smack of the spatial, of the sheer empirical fact of our confrontation with the spread-out inertia of the project-world and of what is (το ον); then it is crucial to register a new kind of possibility, namely that opened up for us when we read just this spatial figure in the direction of time and for example register the critique of the "ontological" in terms of temporality; and in terms of a critique of a "metaphysical conception of "the present" as such.

3.

This is to retrace our steps and to ask ourselves once again why we need some new kind of concept/figure for the "past," let alone for "history": it is also to confront, not merely the ghost of Heidegger (the ghost of Derrida's father?), but also the ghost of Hamlet's father himself: "The time is out of

---

[21] Paul de Man, "Sign and Symbol in Hegel's 'Aesthetics,'" in *Aesthetic Ideology*, Minneapolis: University of Minnesota Press, 1996, 104.

joint." How could the time, the present, be thought in such a way that it could then in a second but simultaneous moment be thought of as being "out of joint"; unequal to itself, unhinged, upside down, etc. (there follows an elaborate discussion of the various French translations of this verse spoken by Hamlet), where the Heideggerian alternative—literally "out of its hinges"—leads directly back to the great essay on Anaximander which is virtually the dead center of all Derrida's meditations on Heidegger and where it is precisely in these terms that Anaximander's own expression is analyzed.

> Whence things have their origin, there they must also pass away according to necessity; for they must pay penalty and be judged for their injustice, according to the ordinance of time ...[22]

For it is very precisely in this same essay on the "proposition" in Anaximander that we find Heidegger's crucial statement as to the mode of experiencing Being and reality among the Pre-Socratics, which is to say, his most direct formulation of everything lost in the "modern," or Western, or metaphysical, repression of Being that followed on that opening (an opening presumably not limited to the pre-modern West, but also detectable in other forms in Japanese Zen, in the Tao, and in the various Indian experiences and language experiments). It is a passage in which, drawing on a seemingly unremarkable speech by Kalchas the soothsayer, in the *Iliad*, Heidegger articulates the difference between the early Greek experience of time and our own.

> He spoke thus and sat down again, and among them stood up
> Kalchas, Thestor's son, far the best of the bird interpreters,
> who knew all things that were, the things to come and the things past.[23]

In this passage the Greek *physis*, so often baldly translated by one of the modern European words signifying Nature, is evoked by Heidegger in order to argue that for the pre-Platonic, pre-philosophical Greeks, presence (*Anwesenheit*) was not limited to the mere present of time (*Gegenwart*) as for us, rather, "the past and future are also forms of presence [*Anwesendes*] but forms outside the realm of deconcealment. The non-present present [an *Anwesendes* not governed by the sheerly temporal present, or in other words non-*Gegenwärtiges*] is the absent. As such it remains relative to the present presence, whether in the sense in which it is about to unfold or be

---

[22] Martin Heidegger, "Der Spruch des Anaximanders," in *Holzwege*, Frankfurt: Klostermann, 1950, 343.

[23] *The Iliad of Homer*, trans. Richard Lattimore, Chicago: University of Chicago Press, 1951, 61, Book 1, lines 68–70.

deconcealed within that temporal present or is moving away from having done so. The absent is also present, and, qua absent, absenting itself from the realm of unfolding, it is present in that very unfolding or deconcealment."[24]

These lines, one of the rare places in which Heidegger is willing directly to evoke a spatio-temporal system radically different from our own, and even willing to make a stab at describing it for his (necessarily) modern readership, are meant to underscore the radical distinction of a Pre-Socratic experience of the world from the one familiar to us, and theorized from Aristotle to Hegel (and no doubt beyond), in which the present is simply an equivalent unit inserted between the homogeneous units of past and future: in which, to use a familiar slogan (which comes to us more directly from McLuhan, I believe, than from the Germans), time is "linear." One wants to add, at once, that this critique of the Western time sense (to reduce it to an altogether different kind of critical and ideological discourse, à la Bergson or Wyndham Lewis) is far from being the only tactic in Heidegger's more ambitious and strategic design, which has to do with Being itself: for recent philosophy indeed (most notably for Rorty), the critique of the classical Western subject-object categories has been even more suggestive and influential (and equally includes the temptation of corrective forms of "Eastern wisdom").

It is clear at once that it must be this side of Heidegger's thought which is necessarily unacceptable to Derrida, or if you prefer, inconsistent with the Derridean "aesthetic" I have described above, for which the "ontic" positing of an ontological realm of difference, the positive description of such a realm, is inadmissible. On the one hand, there is a logical contradiction involved in positing a phenomenon whose fundamental formal trait lies in its radical difference from everything we know, its resistance to all the categories by which we currently think our own world: something that raises the suspicion that it is little more than a subjective or ideological projection from out of our own present. Meanwhile, an even more serious ideological issue is raised by the essential historicism of such views, which posit a series of radically different forms throughout historical time, if not a more simplified binary opposition in which a modern state of things (either degraded or superior) is opposed to some pre-modern equivalent in which all the former's deficiencies are remedied or its advantages annulled. Heidegger's conception of a "history" of metaphysics is there to document the feeling that late nineteenth-century cultural and historical relativism of this historicist type is still very much with us: namely, the idealist notion that, within a general systemic determination by linear time, we can still somehow find it possible to imagine a radically different temporal experience. The implication—and it is above all this which is "idealistic" about such historicism—is

---

[24] Heidegger, *Holzwege*, 318.

that if we are able to imagine temporality of such radical otherness, we ought to be able to bring it into being as a concrete social possibility and thereby to replace the current system altogether.

In this way, an idealism which conceives of the mind as being free enough to range among the possibilities and sovereignly to choose to think a form radically excluded by the dominant system, leads on into a voluntarism that encourages us to attempt to impose that alternative system on the present one by fiat and violence. In Heidegger's case, this fantasy clearly found its fulfillment in the Nazi "revolution," with its promise of radical social regeneration: Heidegger seems to have entertained the hope of becoming the primary theorist of such a revolution and to have withdrawn from active participation as soon as he understood that the new party apparatus was not particularly interested in his philosophical agenda, let alone in philosophy itself.[25] But this idealist voluntarism is equally at work in other (extreme leftist) versions of radical social change, and even, in a different form, in liberal fantasies of the ways in which rational argument and public persuasion might be capable of bringing about systemic modifications in the logic of our social life.

It is significant that (at least on my reading) Derrida does not here specifically isolate historicism as a feature of conventional or traditional Marxism to be questioned and rethought (his principal targets in passing are class, of which more in a moment, and the notion of the Party, which is of course not yet present in its Leninist form in Marx, whose comparable concept is rather that of the International itself). On the contrary, the emphasis of *Of Grammatology* would seem rather to reinforce this Heideggerian sense of a rigorous ("metaphysical") system within which we moderns are somehow caught and imprisoned. Structural or Althusserian Marxism, with its conception of an overlap and coexistence of various systems within a single social present (not to speak of Balibar's idea that in that sense all social formations are somehow already "transitional" and that Marxism is the very theory of such transitionality[26]), offers a reply to this assimilation of Marx's "philosophy of history" to conventional historicism. We will see shortly, however, that for Derrida teleological thought, or the practice of "philosophies of history" (what he will term apocalyptic thinking), lies essentially on the right rather than on the left: while the notion that Heidegger is himself somehow not so secretly historicist is not at all alien to Derrida and perfectly consistent with the various critiques he is willing to make of this particular, already "ambiguous," figure.

---

[25] I plan to deal more extensively with the question of politics and ideology in Heidegger in another place.

[26] Étienne Balibar, *Cinq études du matérialisme historique*, Paris: Maspero, 1974.

What this perspective suggests in our present context, however, is that if one wishes to espouse Heidegger's reservations about Western concepts of time and temporality, one needs to stage it differently from Heidegger himself. It is not merely that Heidegger's strategy depends on a "vision" that must ultimately be documented by poetry or by a pseudo-poetic discourse within philosophy itself; but rather also that philosophical conceptuality as such—"theories" of temporality—will all necessarily revive and regenerate everything they were meant to correct in the first place. This is in fact the way Derrida wraps the matter up in *Marges*: Heidegger's still essentially philosophical argument turns on the reproach that not only Aristotle, but the whole philosophical tradition that necessarily appealed to him, up to and including Kant, Hegel, and even Bergson himself, deployed an essentially "vulgar" concept of time—what we have called the linear one.[27] But this implies that there exists another, better, somehow "non-linear" way of conceiving of time, of producing a concept of time. This supposes, with Bergson (but then in that case, as we shall see, Heidegger's out-trumping of Bergson's "critique" falls back on his own "critique" of Bergson and ends up condemning itself as well), that there is a bad, spatial way of conceiving time: a kind of visual-representational way, one which is subservient to the *gramme* (or "line, stroke in writing"), and for which some other way of conceptualizing time can eventually be substituted. Yet,

> The *gramme* is *grasped* by metaphysics as lying between the point and the circle, between potentiality and act (or presence), etc.; and all the critiques of the spatialization of time, from Aristotle to Bergson, are confined within the limits of this understanding. *Time* would then be merely the limits within which the *gramme* is thus grasped, and, along with the *gramme*, the possibility of the trace in general. *Nothing* else *has ever been* thought under the name and concept of *time*. (*MP*, 69)

This is the sense in which *all* concepts of time are necessarily "vulgar," and every attempt to think temporality by way of linguistic propositions is caught within a contradictory linguistic mechanism in which two irreconcilable versions of time (a part, a whole; a spatial, a non-spatial) are illicitly affirmed as being the same (*MP*, 61). It is an extraordinary demonstration, which, however, at once brings us up short against the seeming impossibility of evoking time, evoking the present, at all in the first place.

Thus now, alongside a certain taboo leveled upon a seemingly spatial conception of ontology conceived as matter, things, physical being, there is gradually set in place its other face as a taboo upon equivalent notions of temporality and of presence, of a "vulgar" temporality which ends up

---

[27] *MP*, 59, 73; also see Chapter 19 below.

including all versions of temporality (including those of the very critics of vulgar temporality). Ontology is hereby temporal fully as much as it is spatial: blocking both in this fashion, however, would seem to end up paralyzing the philosophical impulse itself and generating the urgent need for some other mode of conceptualization than this abstract one. In a sense, to be sure, it was precisely this that was to have been demonstrated: "The time is out of joint". Such is the "other mode of conceptualization" from which will spring a different way of dealing with what used to be called time and the present onto our intellectual horizon: namely, "spectrality" as that apprehension of the being of things and the present of the world in which both those normally calm and massively self-sufficient modes are somehow undermined in their very being and palpably begin to float and to buckle before incredulous eyes.

The emergence of a different kind of thinking would then clearly seem to demand a theorization of allegory as the attempt of the image itself to think, in a situation in which abstract conceptual thought is somehow blocked: that theorization will be reserved for another section (6 below). What it does seem to authorize is a reminder of the historical originality of that situation itself, which Derrida specifically foregrounds as the one in which demarxification is complete and Marx has vanished without a trace along with the rest of certain kinds of related pasts and traditions. I believe that this state of things also implies that the older kind of internal deconstruction is today, under conditions of augmented postmodernization (not, to be sure, a terminology Derrida recognizes), insufficient, and this fully as much owing to the evolution of the situation as to the increasing futility of conceptual thought itself and specifically of its capacity to undermine itself from within, immanently. In other words, if once upon a time, in a somewhat earlier stage of things, the very demonstration that all concepts of time are somehow inescapably and necessarily linear in and of themselves was sufficient to send a shock wave throughout the then prevalent conceptuality, today and for whatever reason this demonstration does not suffice: and apparitions from the past are required in order for us to come to the realization that "the time," and indeed time itself, is "out of joint."

What is also being implied here is perhaps the supplementary realization that the very force of the earlier Heideggerian/Derridean reversal (concepts of time up till now have been linear/all concepts of time are linear!) was an historical and a narrative one, even to the degree to which it overturned history and narrative. In that case, another defining feature of the current situation, another way of explaining the gradual loss of force of that particular reversal, would consist in positing this present as one in which the past and history, along with historiography (grand or not) and narrative itself, have for whatever reason been eclipsed. In such a situation, it is not enough merely to reverse or even to cancel hegemonic or received narratives: the appearance of the ghost is a non-narrative event; we scarcely know whether it has really happened at all in the first place. It calls, to be sure, for a revision of the past, for the setting in place of a new narrative (in which the king was murdered and the present king was in fact his assassin); but it does so by way of a thoroughgoing reinvention of our sense of the past altogether, in a situation in which only mourning and its peculiar failures and dissatisfactions—or perhaps one had better say, in which only melancholia as such—opens a vulnerable space and entry point through which ghosts might make their appearance.

4.

Supposing, however, that the need for some such strange "concept" of spectrality had already been sensed, however obscurely and imperfectly; and a new kind of containment strategy invented whereby the untraditional mode of thinking were somehow respectabilized in advance and pronounced to be consistent with the dignity of a (to be sure, altogether new) philosophical enterprise? There are indications here that for Derrida such an operation can in fact be identified, and that it is none other than phenomenology itself.

The tangled web of Derrida's dealings with Husserl is at least as interesting as, and thematically and formally very comparable to, the better-known complex of his dealings with Heidegger: only the former is proportionally more forbidding and terminologically and conceptually technical and "rigorous" than the latter to the degree to which Heidegger's philosophy has entered a more general culture and its nomenclature has become naturalized. But the form of the engagement is similar in both cases: for it is a question of setting forth from a basic narrative about the history of philosophy which the analysis will end up dismantling as it goes along (one hesitates to use the Hegelian notion of *Aufhebung* to describe this process, for which Baron Münchhausen might offer a more appropriate figure). The point is that in both cases the master narrative is very similar indeed: Husserl's phenomenology as a project aims at

> reconstituting … an originary meaning which was perverted from the very outset, beginning with its very inscription in the tradition [in Plato and Aristotle]. Whether it is a matter of determining the *eidos* or form (in the problematic of formal logic and ontology) as against "platonism" or that of determining *morphe* (in the problematic of transcendental constitution and in its relationship with *hyle* [matter] as over against Aristotle), in both cases the power, the vigilance, the efficacy of the critique remain intra-metaphysical through and through down to their very instruments of analysis. (*MP*, 187–188)

This conception—which Derrida attributes to Husserl—of the perversion or distortion of the philosophical mission from the very outset—along with the project of somehow making a fresh start on it with corrected and revised categories—can now be seen to have been dramatically perverted and distorted, melodramatically misread by Heidegger in his far more exciting account of the same primal fall of philosophy into "Western metaphysics": and it is the family resemblance of these two master narratives which will determine Derrida's relatively impartial interest in both.

Indeed, if in recent years Heidegger seemed to outweigh Husserl in the French philosopher's preoccupations, we can now, with the publication of his thesis, the as it were "pre-Derridean" *Problem of Genesis in Husserl's Philosophy*,[28] right the balance and chart a Husserlian red thread leading equally through all the most significant themes of deconstruction (a task that will not be undertaken here).

Rather, I want more modestly to indicate a few sparse clues which suggest that the new thematics of spectrality also determine something like a wholesale rereading or reinterpretation of Husserl as well, or at least of the deconstructive interpretation of Husserl. I have already observed the way in which Derrida himself has always been careful to nudge us in the right direction in this (and other) explorations of his own specific constellations: long bibliographical notes document the reappearance of this or that theme in other works with a view towards helping us construct multidimensional models of just such image-clusters. In the case of Husserl, those image-clusters have long been dominated by the most traditionally deconstructive themes of all, those having to do with writing as such: thus virtually archetypally, *Voice and Phenomenon* leads us to unmask the privileging of the spoken voice over the written word in the very procedures of phenomenology, while Husserl's version of "meaning"—*Bedeutung*, for which French can only offer the odd but very useful equivalent of *vouloir dire*, in English "to mean" but also, "to wish to say" (English might indeed enlarge and displace all this in the form of "to mean to say")—turns out to include a kind of writing as a mirror image of an already somehow written content or form (see the crucial essay in *Marges*).

Now suddenly *Specters of Marx* directs our attention[29] to a very different passage in *Voice and Phenomenon* in which the cogito itself, or at least its existential clause, is unexpectedly identified with death or at least the posthumous state, as one might characterize the impenetrable afterlife of stubborn ghosts. Indeed, the original text is extraordinary in this respect and worth quoting at some length:

---

[28] *Le problème de la genèse dans la philosophie de Husserl*, Paris: PUF, 1990. Future references to this work are denoted *PGPH*.

[29] See note 1 on page 212 of *SM*.

My death is structurally necessary to the already enunciated pronoun "I." That I happen to be "living" and have the conviction that I am, happens as it were in addition to and above and beyond the meaning [*vouloir dire*] of these words. And this is an active structure, it retains its original efficacy when I say, "I am living" at the very moment when I have a full intuition of that meaning (if such a thing is possible). The *Bedeutung* "I am" or "I am living," or even "my living present is"—these constructions are what they are, and possess the ideal identity appropriate to all *Bedeutungen*, only on condition they do not permit themselves to be undermined by falsity, that is to say if it is possible for me to be dead at the very moment in which they are functioning. Doubtless such enunciations will be different from the *Bedeutung* "I am dead," but not necessarily from the fact that "I am dead." The enunciation "I am living" is accompanied by my being-dead and its possibility requires the possibility that I may be dead, and vice versa. Nor is this one of Poe's extraordinary tales but rather the most ordinary tale of language itself. Earlier we acceded to the "I am mortal" on the basis of the "I am" itself. Now we grasp the "I am" on the basis of the "I am dead."[30]

This extraordinary deduction amplifies the picture of the Self as grave keeper that has already been given, and generalizes it in an unexpected way that draws the very language of the cogito itself into mortality (my possibility of "being" dead). That the self, "consciousness" of the self along with the expression of that consciousness in the time-honored formula "I am," should be logically and structurally dependent on my own death is not merely a peculiar new twist on the Heideggerian "being-unto-death," it tends to make of our own personal identity and sense of self, our very consciousness itself as that is already immediately a reflexive or self-conscious consciousness virtually by definition, ghosts *avant la lettre*: we are thereby already ghosts to ourselves well before the appearance of any official and external specters: something which suddenly draws a whole immense side of reality along with it into spectrality. The occurrence will be less surprising if we remember the degree to which our personal identity itself—although perhaps not yet that punctual event called the cogito or self-consciousness—consists in the rememorization of our various past selves that it combines within itself and in whose very recognition as "mine" it itself consists. This posthumous structure of the "I" then grounds the problematic of mourning even more fundamentally within the philosophical project than any argument based on its centrality in Freud's own works.

This is perhaps also the moment to entertain a rather different impression, namely that the washing of some new "theme" of death back over the earlier thematics of writing can be seen merely as a biographical displacement and as the increasing predominance of preoccupations with death and the dead in Derrida's most recent writings. From this perspective, for

---

[30] *La voix et le phénomène*, Paris: PUF, 1967, 108.

example, it might be argued that the earlier conception of textuality and *différence* allowed for a far more active deconstructive praxis, one energized by the impossible (Utopian) hope that something radically new might appear against all odds were it only possible to denounce these metaphysical survivals with enough force. Yet that is to neglect the other new themes that have accompanied "mourning" and spectrality in the writing of the last decade as well: these include the resurgence of Levinas's notion of the radical difference of the Other and the need to preserve at all costs the very apparition of the other in the omnipresence of the address itself: "*Viens!*" (as compared to interpellation in Althusser, self-repression in the Foucauldian confession, or even Ricoeur's kerygma); and finally the repeated demonstrations of the impossible (as in the analysis of Mauss's *The Gift*[31]) which turn on the necessity and the urgency of keeping the impossible alive, keeping faith with it, making it continue to be somehow possible in its very impossibility. These motifs correspond to what I would myself be tempted to call the Utopian—and what he himself assuredly terms the messianic in this recent thinking; they admonish us to seize the occasion of this most recent and supreme text on Marx to realize that spectrality is here the form of the most radical politization and that, far from being locked into the repetitions of neurosis and obsession, it is energetically future-oriented and active. *Hamlet* also turned in its very narrative structure on a call to praxis, whose contamination with the residual survivals of the revenge-tragedy it needed first and foremost to grapple with.

The other crucial reference to Husserl suggests that the very phenomenological project—about which everything in Derrida tended to reproach its institutional character and its inseparability from "philosophy" as a disciplinary structure—is fundamentally and absolutely (and not merely accidentally or marginally) concerned with spectrality as such: "what else can a phenomenology be but a logic of the *phainesthai* and of the *phantasma*, and thereby of the phantom itself?" (*SM*, 199). Indeed, this deeper motivational affiliation implies that spectrality as such will inevitably give rise to the various philosophical phenomenologies, as official attempts to master the scandalous and unmasterable "phenomenon" and to convert it into a respectable "field of study" and academic discipline, an acknowledged branch of "philosophy" itself if not indeed (as Husserl himself wished) its very foundation. Whatever the bad faith involved in the project, whatever the misrecognition and repression of the spectral from the outset, we are

---

[31] See *Donner le temps, I: La Fausse Monnaie*, Paris: Galilée, 1991, in which it is argued that the "miracle" of the gift, that falls outside the Symbolic Order, is annulled whenever the gift is named and identified as such, the paradox being that the gift always entails reimbursement (whence the reinsertion of the now institutionalized phenomenon in the exchange circuit of the symbolic).

forced to acknowledge its rigor and its intellectual energies, which make of it something like a "science" of spectrality in contradistinction to the latter's "ideology," to be examined in a moment in the next section.

But it is an extraordinary footnote[32] which now projects a whole rethinking and reinterpretation of Husserl's lifework by locating spectrality at its very heart. A single sentence must suffice to convey this astonishing leap: "the radical possibility of all spectrality might be sought for in the direction of what Husserl identifies, surprisingly but strongly, as an intentional but *unreal* component of the phenomenological lived datum, namely the *noema*." And later on this spectral non-reality of the *noema* leads Derrida to ask: "is this not also what inscribes the very possibility of the other and of mourning within the phenomenality of the phenomenon?"

Spectrality can here be seen to open up wholly new and unexpected lines of rereading, which would seem to me susceptible of modifying current uses of Husserl's work. However that may be, such indications also suggest some further thoughts about the position and function of Husserl within Derrida's own, where the founder of phenomenology can be seen as both opposite and complement to his disciple and betrayer. For it is clearly the Heidegger operation which is the more visible and dramatic one, since it involves temporality and can be succinctly summed up by the (most recent) formula: "The time is out of joint!" Heidegger is here used by Derrida as the name for all those temptations (which the German philosopher himself can be seen both as denouncing and as succumbing to all at once) to perpetuate some unmixed conception of time, some notion of a present that has won itself free of past and future and stands, gleaming and self-contained, as a kind of mirage of *parousia*. Certainly the later Heideggerian emphasis on Being allows one to shift the gears of this critique somewhat in the direction of what it is certainly preferable not to call space, but perhaps (with an eye on Husserl) essences, rather than time, becoming, or temporality?

But this very term "essence" underscores the extraordinarily suggestive and useful role Husserl can be called upon to play in this same Derridean crusade: where Heidegger will offer the pretext for an onslaught on illusions of full temporal being, Husserl will provide a rather different set of occasions for tracking down and detecting such illusions when they manifest themselves under the guise of what Derrida's own language now identifies as the "proper" or "presence" (or any number of the other laboriously generated, technical Derridean words and terms). It would be much too loose and unphilosophical to identify this target with what in Adorno is generally stigmatized as identity; and indeed any attempt (like the present one) to characterize the process generally, and not in the specifics of a given conceptual situation, falls back into culture critique, *belles lettres*, history of ideas,

---

[32] See note 2 on page 215 of *SM*.

and other degraded discourses. But I can have no other recourse in an essay like this, and can only try to characterize the object of this Derridean critique very impressionistically myself as what I will call the "unmixed": what is somehow pure and self-sufficient or autonomous, what is able to be disengaged from the general mess of mixed, hybrid phenomena all around it and named with the satisfaction of a single conceptual proper name. This way of thinking about Derrida's work has two advantages: it can first provide a way for speculating as to the ways in which Derrida's own rigorous and local analyses strike a cognate tone with much else at work in current doxa and contemporary or post-contemporary intellectual life, which for whatever reason is also hostile to such pure or solid-color, unmixed concepts, which it (the *Zeitgeist*) identifies as old-fashioned and outworn, the boring conceptuality of yesteryear that is somehow unreflexive and un-self-conscious (to use the vocabulary of yesteryear, however); and that we need to replace today with something infinitely more mixed and incestuous, miscegenated, polyvocal and multivalenced. Current intellectual politics, such as those of queer theory, bring out into the open this particular prejudice for the internally conflicted and the multiple (and suggest local reasons for such a philosophical need), but they are obviously far from being the earliest in this series which goes back at least to the great break between the modern and what followed that in the course of the 1960s, in which the modern and its Utopian dreams of unmixed languages and Utopian concepts came to be obscurely felt as being old-fashioned in the light of more complexly paradoxical intellectual operations, and where even the dialectic, for some of us the very prototype of a reflexive operation that secretly reversed all the pre-existing stereotypes, was itself stigmatized as one more version of the latter's rehearsal (in Derrida, for example, as yet another example of operations pursued within the closure of Western metaphysics). Philosophy, Derrida will say in his earliest written work, the thesis on Husserl, is "the permanent recourse to the originary simplicity of an act or a being, of a conscious conviction [evidence] or a sense-perception [intuition]."[33] In our present context that says it all: and the very vocation of Derrida's philosophical life's work will now be discovered in the tracking down and identifying, denouncing, of just such recourses, of just such nostalgias for some "originary simplicity," for the unmixed in all its forms.

I have felt that it was important to describe this general vocation at this point, however, for yet another reason that now has to do with Marx himself and with Derrida's reservations about him. It can certainly be imagined that

---

[33] *PGPH*, 32. He continues: "en ce sens, il semble que la dialectique ne puisse s'instituer qu' à partir d'instances déjà constituées comme telles par une conscience transcendentale originaire. Une philosophie dialectique n'a par conséquent aucun droit à se proclamer philosophie première." It is true that this early critique of the "dialectic" is directed towards Tran-Duc-Thao rather than Hegel or Marx.

the attempt to do away with ghosts altogether, that the very fear of ghosts that "haunts" the heart of such an attempt, offers a signal exemplification of just such a longing for primary realities, originary simplicities, full presences, and self-sufficient phenomena cleansed of the extraneous or the residual, the new itself, the origin, from which one can begin from scratch. We'll come back to this later on.

But there are two other features of the Marxian heritage which Derrida seems to assimilate to this more questionable side of the Marxian enterprise, the Marxian tradition, and which it is appropriate to deal with in the present ("phenomenological") context: these are use value and class. About use value, surely one of the slipperier concepts in Marx, it can be affirmed that it is "always-already" if anything ever was: the minute values begin to speak (250–251; in *Capital*, Chapter 1) they have already become exchange values. Use value is one of those lateral or marginal concepts which keeps moving to the edge of your field of vision as you displace its center around the field, always a step ahead of you, never susceptible of being fixed or held (like a leprechaun) by this or that determined, intent, and glittering eye. Use value has always already vanished by the time Marxism has begun: yet an uncertainty may well persist as to whether even its residuality betrays a secret ontological longing at the heart of Marxism, or at least at the center of Marx's own writing. We will return to it later on when we come to the "fetishism of commodities" itself.

As for class, however, merely mentioned in passing as one of those traditional features of Marxism (along with the "party") that can be jettisoned en route by any truly post-contemporary Marxism—"this ultimate foundation which is the identity and the identity with itself of a social class" (*SM*, 97)—it seems to me appropriate to take this opportunity to show how this very widespread conception of class is itself a kind of caricature. It is certain that—even among Marxists—the denunciation of the concept of class has become an obligatory gesture today, as though we all knew that race, gender, and ethnicity were more satisfactory concepts or more fundamental, prior, concrete, existential experiences (these two reproaches not being exactly the same): or else that social classes in the old nineteenth-century sense no longer exist as such in the new multinational division of labor, or in the newly autonomated and cybernetic industries of the postmodern (these two objections also not quite being identical with each other). Finally and more empirically, the abandonment of the very category of class, even on the left—perhaps one should rather say, especially on the left—corresponds to the evolution of contemporary politics in which the old class parties are not around any longer, so that intellectuals find themselves forced to identify with groupings whose dynamics and rationale have quite different intellectual bases. I myself also think, as I want to show later on, that there is a fundamental tendency and movement within Marxism itself to be self-conflicted and to distance itself at once from features other people assume to be intrinsically a part of this ideology, which however turns out to come into being at least in part by denouncing itself (as so-called vulgar Marxism). To denounce class, and concepts of "class affiliation," is thus part of this primal self-definition within all the Marxisms themselves, which have always wanted to make sure you did not think they believed anything so simple-minded or orthodoxly reductive.

And this is of course exactly the gesture I will myself reproduce here, by reminding you that class itself is not at all this simple-minded and unmixed concept in the first place, not at all a primary building block of the most obvious and orthodox ontologies, but rather in its concrete moments something a good deal more complex, internally conflicted, and reflexive than any of those stereotypes. Nor is it particularly surprising that society should have a vested interest in distorting the categories whereby we think class and in foregrounding its current rival conceptualities of gender and race, which are far more adaptable to purely liberal ideal solutions (in other words, solutions that satisfy the demands of ideology, it being understood that in concrete social life the problems remain equally intractable).

In this sense, class is, we may suppose, an "ontological" category like "matter" or "materialism" (and, as we shall see later on, like "messianism"): a category which implies and perpetuates the error of substance and substantiality (of truth, presence, etc.): whereas the "truth" of the concept of class (to speak like the Hegelians) lies rather in the operations to which it gives rise: class analysis, like materialist demystification, remains valid and indispensable even in the absence of even the possibility of a coherent concept of "philosophy" of class itself.

Class categories are therefore not at all examples of the proper or of the autonomous and pure, the self-sufficient operations of origins defined by so-called class affiliation: nothing is more complexly allegorical than the play of class connotations across the whole width and breadth of the social field, particularly today; and it would be a great mistake for Marxism to abandon this extraordinarily rich and virtually untouched field of analysis on the grounds that class categories were somehow old-fashioned and Stalinist and need to be renounced shame-facedly in advance before a respectable and streamlined reappearance of the Left can be made in the field of intellectual debate in the new world system.

5.

If phenomenology then identifies one pole of the experience of spectrality as that has been officially contained and sublimated, transformed, into a respectable and indeed an institutional phenomenon (in this case one that can be reidentified with the academic discipline of philosophy itself), it remains to designate the other pole in which spectrality is appropriated by way of ideology as such and is translated into a powerful ideologeme whose structural possibilities can already be detected in the lexical field across which the ghostly apparition plays in all the modern languages.

For the ghost is very precisely a *spirit*, and the German *Geist* marks even more strongly the way in which a ghostly spirit or apparition, and spirit as spirituality itself, including the loftier works of high culture, are deeply and virtually unconsciously identified with each other. You domesticate the ghost from the past by transforming it into an official representation of Spirit itself, or in other words, at least in American English, in what we call Culture, the humanities and the like: the canon, today, and the right-wing polemic about tradition and the great books of cultural history, thus marks the spot at which otherwise disturbing ghosts of a past soaked in violence and blood guilt, a past which is almost exclusively that of class struggle (and in which, as Benjamin says, the monuments of culture are all revealed as documents of barbarism), can be co-opted at the source and transformed into the supplementary privileges of an upper-class education now increasingly sealed off from the masses of ordinary citizens by virtue of cost and privatization and the withdrawal of government support.

Once again, however, the form of the polemics these phenomena have known in a Europe which is officially a good deal more class conscious than we are in the US is confusing when translated into American polemics and public debate; and therefore, particularly in the present instance, it is crucial to grasp the degree to which Derrida's own philosophical moves have to be grasped as ideological or rather anti-ideological tactics, and not merely as the abstract philosophical discussions as which these texts cross the ocean and become translated here. This will be the moment not only to return to the formal issue of "idealism," as opposed to the various materialisms of Marxism, of deconstruction, and even of Paul de Man's version of deconstructive literary procedures; but also to insist on the very different resonance in Europe of such terms as *esprit* and *Geist*—and of their renewed ideological topicality in the new Europe at the end of the Cold War—as over against the more diffused rehearsals of such polemics here (where intellectuals in general are not only by definition "left" intellectuals, busy propagating theory and "political correctness," but are also invested with a symbolic upper-class value qua intellectuals, as over against the ordinary middle-class people). One would have to return to the far more limited class relations of the US university system before World War II, and the immense demographic opening that followed it, in order to get some sense of the openly class function of "spiritual values" as a hegemonic strategy designed to intimidate the other classes (including—need one really say so—the other gender and the other races and ethnicities).

But in this respect one can see virtually all of Derrida's lifework as an analysis and demystification of just such an ideology of the Spiritual and of idealism, as that continued to inform the European tradition: even the relations with postwar existentialism are informed by the sense that its phenomenological presuppositions remain profoundly idealistic. Americans are poorly placed to grasp the degree to which what Derrida follows Heidegger in calling the metaphysical tradition can also be seen very precisely as a kind of official public Idealism which, despite all the changes in philosophical fashion since the beginnings of the bourgeois era (where it can be seen to have been deliberately refashioned as a specific ideologeme), still holds public sway and is available for political manipulation. Indeed, the central critique of Heidegger himself, in an essay pointedly entitled "De l'esprit,"[34] and although crisscrossed by the (related) issues of sexuality and gender, very much turns on the suspicious and symptomatic return, in Heidegger's political writings of the early Nazi period (and most obviously in his inaugural lecture as rector of the University of Freiburg), of a whole language of *Geist* and spirituality which the earlier, more purely philosophical texts had explicitly stigmatized.

It is interesting to note that although Derrida fails to touch on the central figure in the Anglo-American reinvention of a politics of modernism qua spirituality—in the critical as well as the poetic work of T. S. Eliot—he does significantly single out Matthew Arnold.[35] Above all, however, he insistently returns to that French-language figure who was in so many ways the continental equivalent of Eliot (and whom the latter's cultural strategies, above all in his journal, *The Criterion*, aimed at enveloping and as it were introjecting), namely Paul Valéry. Significantly, a major portion of Derrida's polemic warning about the cultural politics of the new Europe—*L'Autre Cap*[36]—is given over to Valéry's symptomatic thoughts about the menaced and vulnerable Europe of the period between the two wars; for it is precisely this high-cultural European strategy, the Roman-Christian European tradition very precisely from Virgil for Valéry, that the current ideological operation of patching together a new pan-European cultural synthesis around figures like Milan Kundera (in the place of Eliot) has imitated and reproduced as in Marx's famous prediction (the second time as farce!). One is tempted to characterize these very openly high-cultural moves as a replay of "*Encounter* culture" (as the most successful attempt to play off a NATO high culture, now led by the US, as over against an allegedly anti-cultural

---

[34] In *Heidegger et la question*, Paris: Flammarion, 1990. Future references to this work are denoted *HQ*.

[35] Ibid., 90–91, note.

[36] Paris: Minuit, 1991; and see also the essay on Valéry, "Qual Quelle: Les sources de Valéry," in *MP*.

Bolshevism), but one today possibly available for intervention in a hegemonic struggle *against* the US competitor.

At any rate, these are the deeper political and class stakes involved in the anti-idealist theoretical and cultural struggles when those are grasped concretely in a European context; and it is very possible that some of these terminological polemics carry very different overtones here in the US. (Naomi Schor has for example suggestively argued, in a pathbreaking reconsideration of the significance of the work of George Sand,[37] that her literary *idealism* was often more politically effective, energizing, and enabling than the "realisms" or even "materialisms" of her literary competitors.)

At that point the question then also returns to our starting point, namely the political and the class value of the slogans of "materialism" as such. Paul de Man for example was always more open in his deployment of materialist positions than Derrida, at least in part because that particular philosophical strategy tended to undercut the high-spiritual apologia of his literary adversaries in the old New Critical establishment; it could also be argued that his own return to "literature" (which he defined as the kind of text that in effect was able to deconstruct itself and thereby virtually in advance to demystify the illusions of an idealist philosophy) stood somewhat in contradiction with this more explicitly anti-aesthetic *prise de position*. Meanwhile, it could also be argued, I believe, that the more open endorsement of materialism as such in de Man's writings tended rightly or wrongly to raise complicating issues of a materialist philosophy or ontology of the kind Derrida has always been careful to elude (both here, in *Specters*, and in the earlier interviews about Marxism in *Positions*).

The polemic foregrounding of "spirit" and spirituality (high culture and tradition, *esprit* and *Geist*), however, now belatedly answers the earlier fears we acknowledged are bound to be aroused by just this palpable reluctance to endorse materialism as a philosophical position. The distancing of philosophical (let alone Stalin's "dialectical") materialism is not likely to lead to a recrudescence of spiritualism under the banner of the concept of spectrality very precisely because such a concept is designed to undermine the very ideology of spirit itself. Ghosts are thus in that sense material; ghosts very precisely resist the strategies of sublimation, let alone those of idealization. This is also the sense in which "Shakespeare" in this text is not the high-cultural signal it tends to be in the Anglo-American tradition: "Shakespeare" on the continent and in Marx's own personal taste is not the mark of the high culture of European classicism, whether that of the French or of

---

[37] Naomi Schor, *George Sand and Idealism*, New York: Columbia University Press, 1993. Jane Tompkins's reestablishment of sentimentality and religion as counterforces in American literary production prolongs this intervention in a different context (see *West of Everything*, Oxford: Oxford University Press, 1993).

Schiller, but rather of a disturbing and volcanic "barbarism." Shakespeare plus Marx does not equal Schiller, let alone Bradley or Eliot's verse dramas, but rather Victor Hugo: whose *Misérables* indeed also makes its brief appearance significantly and symptomatically within Derrida's pages, alongside *The Eighteenth Brumaire* itself.

The motif of "spirit" as high culture represents the appropriation of spectrality as ideology, just as the project of phenomenology revealed a complementary appropriation as science. Now, however, it is time to see how Derrida deals with the issue of ideology, which his reading of the foundational Marxian texts on the subject specifically links with religion as such.

6.

We must therefore at once situate this discussion within the current European high-cultural revival of religion itself, a strategy which has its obvious relationship to the ideological operations of spirit and of the European cultural tradition. The two in effect offer as it were distinct and alternate tracks, optional alternatives, for an endorsement of European late capitalism (as that was consolidated by the various European social democracies and then colonized by the Thatcherite strategies of privatization and the liquidation of social services). This is not the place to paint the whole sorry picture of a simulacrum of religion as that has been sat in place culturally everywhere from Godard's symptomatic *Je vous salue Marie* to Górecki's Third Symphony: the picture would necessarily also include the current aesthetic revival, as that reproduces as it were a simulacrum of the older high-modernist "religions of art." I believe that "religion" is here to be understood as what comes to replace the missing content in contemporary, or rather more precisely in postmodern, works, which survive the end of the modern period as empty formal imperatives. Empty form is here, however, very different from what emerged in the modern period itself, where a crisis in representation drew attention to the very dynamics of representation itself and generated a kind of self-designation at the same time that it was contemporaneous with an immense movement of differentiation in all the secular sciences and disciplines: the most interesting modern works are thus those which simultaneously push an experience of representation and formal crisis to its limit and also, by a spirit of epistemological rivalry, attempt to absorb the empirical (and even the theoretical) richness of the non-aesthetic disciplines. But in postmodernity it is precisely against the sterility of the modernist autoreferential paradigm that the most characteristic cultural production of the day wishes to demonstrate; while in the "sciences" the new moment is on the contrary a space of an enormous "dedifferentiation" in which, as with a white dwarf, all the older scientific or epistemological "levels" are in the process of identifying with each other and collapsing in upon each other, on their way to the status of the proverbial black hole.

When it comes to "content" in the social sense—and in a certain way, since Marx, all content is social in this sense, or better still, the privilege of the Marxian discovery is to mark the moment in which all content is revealed to be social and secular—the triumph of market ideology and the immense movement of demarxification can also be seen as new kinds of epistemological repression in which it is precisely the sociality of all content, its deeper link to political economy as such, which is occulted. The contemporary or post-contemporary problem of content can be thus now approached through the consensus in all the social sciences that the influence of Marx is so profound upon them all that it is no longer particularly relevant to isolate a "Marxist" sociology, economics, political science, as such. In that case, however, demarxification in aesthetics faces a formidable task, of well-nigh global dimensions: as it were to launder the content of contemporary experience and daily life in such a way that the multifarious traces of this deep and omnipresent "Marxism" are tuned out or abstracted from the general spectrum by means of new kinds of representational technology, or at the least (since I will want to posit that none of these operations are particularly novel) a newly specialized kind of aesthetic technology. At any rate, it will be my presupposition here that it is by way of a return to old-fashioned aesthetics—to beauty rather than to the sublime of modernism—and thence to the religion of art (following which it is only natural that the art of religion should then begin to rotate into view), that a certain aesthetic postmodernity finds itself able to produce works that give the illusion of substance (of "having-content") in its absence.

Religion is thus, to recapitulate this argument, what looks like content when you are no longer able to acknowledge the content of social life itself: in a factitious simulacrum of content very much to be distinguished from modernist abstraction. But this aesthetic function of religion today, in the postmodern, is then also to be juxtaposed with another kind of resurgence of religion in the so-called contemporary fundamentalisms (and also in certain of the neo-ethnicities, also based on religious motifs): here we have to do, not with any survivals of traditional religious custom or ritual, or with premodern folkways of this or that type—all of which have been largely swept away by the prodigious movement of modernization at one with what we call modernism and modernity as such—but rather precisely with simulacra of what, in the postmodern present, is imagined to be those older folkways, with contemporary reinventions of tradition which affirm a neo-ethnic pluralism of free choice and the free reinvention of small-group adherence (as opposed to the older constraints and indeed the doom or fate of racial or ethnic determinism in the pre-modern or early modern past).

For all these reasons, then, religion is once again very much on the agenda of any serious attempt to come to terms with the specificity of our own time; and it is in this sense that I read Derrida's insistence, at several points in the present text, on the way in which Marx's own theorization necessarily loops back into a reflection on religion as such.

This is to be sure also to be understood historically and exegetically, as the way in which any discussion of the problematic of the early Marx—or of the emergence of what might be thought of as "mature Marxism"—necessarily posits a discussion of the specific intellectual debates in which Marx's thinking was formed, and from which the Marxian problematic ("answers rather than questions") itself emerged: namely the turn of Feuerbach, the moment of Feuerbach's intellectual "revolution," in which the immense and crushing corpus of Hegel is simplified and reduced to a merely religious problematic (Marx will himself follow this line in his *Critique of Hegel's 'Philosophy of Right'*), a revolution which will then be staged in a wholly new way by positing religion as the distorted projection of human productivity and human praxis. But that debate also drew its urgency from the institutional relationship—and not only in the German principalities of the early nineteenth century and the Holy Alliance—of state religion to state power: the attack on religion in that context will thereby be a scarcely veiled mode of outright political subversion (a far more openly political intervention, for example, than in the consequences of the debate on Darwinism in the British context later on in the century): Derrida's reestablishment of a religious problematic as being henceforth inescapable in any truly renewed examination of Marx today is thus also to be thought in terms of this gap between the older (early Marxian) situation of established religion and our own world of religious "revivals" which are effectively social simulacra. This gap might be reformulated as a problem in the following sense: if a certain Hegelianism is to be grasped as the afterimage of the established religious institutions of his own time, where do we stand with respect to the *problem* of such a Hegelianism in our own time, with its very different recoding of religion?

But Derrida's methodological warning (about the fundamental role of religion in Marx's writing) also turns specifically on the twin phenomena— or perhaps one should say the dual conceptuality in Marx—of the theory of ideology and the theory of fetishism: and insofar as these are themes which emerge into full view only in the so-called mature writing of *Capital* itself, they demand a somewhat different optic from the preceding one that holds for Marx's formative years, "only the reference to the religious world allows us to explain the autonomy of the ideology [in Marx] and thereby of the efficacity of the ideological, its incorporation within apparatuses [*dispositifs*] that are not only endowed with an apparent autonomy of their own but also with a kind of 'automaticity' that is not without its similarity to the well-known 'stubbornness' of the wooden table" (*SM*, 262). In another place,

Derrida affirms "the irreducibility of the religious model in the construction of the concept of ideology" (*SM*, 236), thereby ambiguously warning us of the ambiguity of this last, which may be as tainted as a concept by outworn conceptions of the religious, by the illusions of "religion" themselves, as fully as it may constitute a drawing of the ultimate conclusions from a fundamental analysis of religions as such, which might permit us to detect religious and metaphysical remnants and survivals within the reality of contemporary secular ideology.

I myself feel that Derrida's analyses of certain foundational passages in *The German Ideology* (on Stirner's ego and its ghosts) and in *Capital* itself (the famous passage on the fetishism of commodities) point us usefully to a different way of approaching the religious phenomenon affirmed to be somehow prior here. This mode of analysis would eschew the psychological and also permit a rereading and reinterpretation of the historicist paradigm (which may be thought of as a kind of collective psychology: the stages through which groups pass, etc.). It would avoid even the traditional allegorical readings which determined the "problematic" or the shape of the debate on religion in the sixteenth and seventeenth centuries, and which was the object of the scorn of *le président de Brosses*, for example, in his 1760 book, *Du culte des dieux fétiches*, from which Marx derived his own immediate conception of fetishism. The twin faces of this traditional allegorical reading (studied magisterially in modern times by Jean Seznec)[38] lay in the assimilation of lower images to higher divinities (animals or even blocks of wood as allegorical of higher, more "monotheistic" religious belief), or on the other hand so-called *euhemeristic* solutions in which the various lower forms of the divinity prove to be in all actuality divinizations of human figures and events, of real occurrences and actors, whose historical status has been arrested and sublimated in the form of legend and then divinity.

When one examines these various forms of religion, indeed, it becomes possible to reinscribe them in a lateral way as so many forms of figuration, and indeed, of what I will call literal figuration (or figural literalization), in which an external content is then reified and rehearsed, in a second moment, as the pretext for the production of a host of new figures that take the literal surface of the older figure as their foundation and point of departure. Vico no doubt marks the eighteenth-century breakthrough towards figuration in this respect, while in the nineteenth century, and after the immense Germanic labor of Creuzer (along with Hegel's suggestive deductions), the grandest and most intelligent "summa" remains Flaubert's *The*

---

[38] *La survivance des dieux antiques*, London: Warburg Institute, 1940; in English, *The Survival of the Pagan Gods*, trans. Barbara Sessions, New York: Pantheon Books, 1953.

Temptation of Saint Anthony, a work whose various versions are virtually contemporaneous with Marx, from the elaboration of *The German Ideology* and the *Manifesto,* in the late 1840s, all the way to the elaboration of the various versions of the *Grundrisse* and *Capital* in the Second Empire (the latter appearing in 1867, while the "definitive" version of *Saint Antoine,* begun in 1848, appears in 1873). More dramatically and self-consciously than any of the Enlightenment or Romantic approaches to religious figuration, Flaubert's includes the most radical ambivalence, that is to say, a whole libidinal charge of derision and disgust along with the most appropriate fascination. Indeed, virtually our basic theme here—what is the appropriate form of "materialist philosophy" today, in postmodernity—can be found to be encapsulated in that passage from Flaubert's letters that Derrida himself chose for the pretext of one of his most interesting recent essays:

> Je ne sais pas ce que veulent dire ces deux substantifs, Matière et Esprit; on ne connait pas plus l'une que l'autre. Ce ne sont peut-être que des abstractions de notre intelligence. Bref, je trouve le Matérialisme et le Spiritualisme deux impertinences égales. (March 1968, to Caroline)[39]

De Brosses's sarcasm, for us a splendid example of eighteenth-century Enlightenment ethnocentrism, which reinscribes the gross stupidities of fetishism on the lowest rung of some supposedly evolutionary human ladder, is reproduced in a more complex and ambivalent form in Flaubert, where such forms of literality are the occasion for the dizziest loathing coupled with an irrepressible hilarity, as in the giggles of Saint Antoine, when he observes a shapeless fetish being carried along by a believer ("qu'il faut être bête de croire en cela!"). This is exactly the sensation Marx wishes to invoke by designating the "everyday commodity," the anonymous and omnipresent object world in which bourgeois daily life is pursued, as an ensemble of fetishes: at that point, then, the cultural loathing of the "advanced" or "Western" European for the most retarded of pre-modern peoples and practices, is transferred onto and surcharged on the loathing of the even more advanced socialist for that mode of production *en passe de devenir archaïque,* which is bourgeois society as such. Nor (in Flaubert fully as much as in Marx) does this jocular use of the religious analogy preclude deeper consequences, as in the hilarious yet fateful footnote in *Capital,* where the omnipresence of commodity fetishism as the backdrop of East and West alike generates the two echoing poles of a bourgeois fascination with table-turning and the occult—such as has often preceded catastrophe and obscurely foreshadowed it (for example in the penultimate chapter of *The Magic Mountain*) just as much as in the spiritualist crazes of

---

[39] Quoted in Derrida, *Psyché,* 305.

the French 1860s as they approach the multiple disasters of the 1870s—along with, among the colonized, the ferocious religious (specifically, Christian) revolt of the Taiping in China, the longest and most successful anti-Western revolution before those of the twentieth century. These two forms of religion—degraded occultism or spiritualism and subaltern fundamentalism and anti-colonial "fanaticism"—are if not dialectically then at least complementarily related as the twin excesses and volcanic exceptions of a world "normally" governed by commodity fetishism.

Flaubert can then equally serve us as the object lesson in a literal figuralism in which the gods, having assumed human form, must also by virtue of the very structure of the figure assume the latter's mortality, so that it can be posited of them that they also have it in them to die, as in the glorious scene in which the Olympians, growing old, totter feebly towards their extinction, Jupiter drops the empty cup from which rejuvenating ambrosia has utterly dried up, Atlas causes the world to fall in his weakness, etc. These internally dynamic and self-generating figures then lead us back to Hegel's discussion of religion, in which, particularly in his (to be sure, profoundly ethnocentric) readings of the swarming of Indian and Egyptian figuralities, he would seem to posit this endlessly self-referential allegorism as the result of figures unable to develop into concepts: as a kind of Lévi-Straussian *"pensée sauvage" avant la lettre* in which abstract (or Greek, post-Socratic philosophical) conceptuality is not yet possible, so that the figures must eternally revert back into themselves and use their own internal and self-designating structures as ways of desperately anticipating a meaning and a conceptuality they cannot otherwise achieve. It would also seem possible, on this occasion, to reread or reinterpret Hegelian historicism, which in the general realm of religion posits for humanity in general three stages (he will be followed in this, with modifications, by Auguste Comte), in which the obscure conceptual stirrings of religion within the figures we have illustrated is followed by the great aesthetic moment of the Greeks, and thereupon, in the famous "end of art," by philosophy itself, which breaks through the figures of both art and religion and introduces the pure Concept or *Begriff* onto the stage of history (and of modernity). What we can now suggest is that it is the attention to figuration in art which allows religious imagery to be broken open and to give rise to what it might be a little more relevant to call theory (the analogy with Paul de Man's reading of genuine texts or "Literature" as a place in which figuration becomes "aware of itself" and capable of deconstructing itself, is suggestive).

As for Derrida's dramatic rereading of the dancing-table episode (which itself stresses the overtly dramatic or "theatrical" mode of this particular presentation/representation [*Darstellung*] of value in an inert wooden thing), it seems rather to stress the ineluctability of the phantasmagoric in human and social experience, rather than the inseparable relationship of this particular phantasmagoria—the famous "fetishism of commodities"—to one particular social form or mode of production. This was in another sense always the paradox of Marx's view of capitalism itself (and thus, as will be clear in a moment, of "use value"): for precapitalist societies and modes of production are by definition never transparent, since they must assure the extraction of surplus value by extra-economic means—by family structure or the institution of slavery, by brute force or by religious and cosmological ideologies. There is thus a sense in which only capitalism pursues economics by purely economic means (money and the market), and thereby also the deduction that in a larger acceptation all of the extra-economic determinations required by other or non-capitalist modes of production may be largely termed religious (tribal animisms and fetishisms, religions of the *polis*, religions of the god-emperor, or rationalizations of various aristocracies by birth). Capitalism therefore, as in the historical narrative we have inherited from the triumphant bourgeoisie and the great bourgeois revolutions, is the first social form to have eliminated religion as such and to have entered on the purely secular vocation of human life and human society. Yet according to Marx, religion knows an immediate "return of the repressed" at the very moment of the coming into being of such a secular society, which, imagining that it has done away with the sacred, then at once unconsciously sets itself in pursuit of the "fetishism of commodities" in a kind of Deleuzian reterritorialization. The incoherence is resolved if we understand that a truly secular society is yet to come, lies in the future; and that the end of the fetishism of commodities may well be connected to some conquest of social transparencies, provided that we understand that such transparency has never yet existed anywhere: a situation in which the collective labor stored in a given commodity is always and everywhere visible to its consumers and users. This is also to resolve the problem of use value, which seems like a nostalgic survival only if we project it into what we imagine to be a simpler past, a past "before the market," in which objects are somehow used and valued for themselves: but that is to forget "real" fetishism (as opposed to the symbolic kind that attaches to modern commodities), along with the various other symbolic ways in which value was projected onto objects in the societies of the past. Use value lies thus also in the future, before us and not behind us: nor is it (and this is I think the real objection to the concept nowadays) distinct from and antagonistic to the phenomena which cluster around the function of information and communication, but must probably eventually come to include those in unimaginably complex ways.

This is in fact the other conclusion we will find Derrida drawing, at the end of this remarkable excursus in which the table dances again as it did for the first readers of Marx himself, and commodity fetishism becomes assimilated to the extraordinary agitation of poltergeists within our seemingly banal daily lives. For Derrida here wishes to assimilate the spectrality of these phenomena, which are more and other than what they seem as inert objects, to their sociality (Marx's collective production, stored labor power), and thence to their "automaticity" (what Sartre would have called the practico-inert), their power to act and cause in ways more complex and undecipherable than the individual human mind or intention. We will not be able to identify this "automaticity" plainly, however, until the final section, below.

Here we must, on the contrary, retrace our steps to the equally remarkable pages on Stirner, or rather on Marx's interminable settling of accounts with Stirner in *The German Ideology*. The polemic has known a partial rejuvenation in recent years, owing to the suggestion that Stirner (however mediocre his thinking and writing as such) stands in the place of something like a Heideggerian existentialism of that period and focuses on the "unique" specificity of being-unto-death in a Hegelian and universalizing climate: something like a Kierkegaard to whom Hegel (his place here taken by Marx) was able to find time to respond. However seriously we are to take Derrida's mild suggestions in passing as to a possible rereading of Stirner, it is clear that, as with Heidegger himself, this implies omitting the ontological pretensions and in particular the tedious social theories which are both generated in their very different ways from out of the existential datum. The Derridean qualification marks, as has been said, that reflex whereby what is interesting in Heidegger is ruthlessly separated from those "fundamental" positions (ontology, spirit, origins, the authentic, etc.) which can only be antipathetic to Derrida which he has only recently been willing to characterize as "ludicrous" (*HQ*, 86).

As for Stirner (and Marx's laborious page-by-page commentary on his book), what interests Derrida is not the historical and social speculation but rather very specifically the sections that deal with the dynamics of abstraction as such.[40] In all these passages it is a question of how abstract ideas get replaced by real bodies: we are thus at the opposite pole to the problematic of Feuerbach and his speculations as to how images of the divinity are projected out of human potentialities, or that, even more linguistic, of Marx himself on the way in which Hegel hypostasizes properties and makes adjectives over into substantives. Here it is a matter of how the abstractions of the mind as it were illicitly become incorporated in their existential bodies: in other words, how we get back, in human and individual development, from the first mesmerization of the child and the adolescent by "reified" ideas (in

---

[40] In Karl Marx and Friedrich Engels, *The German Ideology*, Moscow: Progress Publishers, 1976. See the commentary on Stirner, Part 1, "A Man's Life," 136ff; on Part 2, Chapter 2, "The Moderns," 165ff; and on Stirner's "dialectic," 289ff. Future references to this work are denoted *GI*.

whose existence belief is invested) to the possession of a concrete individual body which is mine: "in the period of spirits, thoughts outgrew me although they were the offspring of my brain ... by destroying their corporeality, I take them back into my own corporeality and *announce*: I alone am corporeal. And now I take the world as it is for me, as *my* world, as my property, I relate everything to myself" (*GI*, 137). It is a now familiar existential therapy in which reified abstractions are "reduced" to concrete existential experience; but Stirner is even more complicated, insofar as the Hegelian paradigm—how humans recognize everything in the not-I and the non-human world ultimately as being their own productivity and as "belonging" to them (so-called Absolute Spirit)—is also transferred onto an existential or individual framework: now Absolute Spirit gets an individual lived body and restores itself by reappropriating its own physical existence. Clearly, more than mere Hegelian ideologies are at work here, and much of contemporary ideology of the body and of desire might also distantly recognize itself in Stirner's ancient spotted mirror. The passage is thus also a crucial one for any intersection between "Marxism" and the various existentialisms, and it is certainly wrong (or at least not enough) to say that Marx rejects this return to the body. He could certainly not do so in the name of the abstractions Stirner himself seeks to dispel, for those are his own target (they are the phantoms or specters of the brain). Marx's dramatic insight lies in the identification of this allegedly concrete existential body (*je meiniges*) as itself being a phantom, a "body without organs," an imaginary body ("he makes his own body into a body of specters" [*GI*, 137]). The attempt to conquer and achieve concreteness via the expulsion of the specters only leads to the construction of an even mere imaginary entity, which I think of as "my self": the existential path thereby leads, not into reality, but into an even more intricate unreality. Marx does not offer a counter-therapy, but the rest of *The German Ideology* (in particular the famous opening section on Feuerbach) is there to suggest that for him individual reality is to be found and achieved there where social reality is also to be found, namely in production itself, or in other words by going around before the invasion of the cerebral and reified conceptual phantoms, and beginning again from their point of production; by circumventing them rather than traversing them into what is vainly hoped and fantasized as being a truer reality after the reign of the phantoms themselves.

Derrida's interventions then take place at two points in this polemic: the first is that of Marx's own critique of Stirner's program, which he restates as follows:

> In his abstract reconstruction of the ages of life, Stirner only offers us a "phantom shadow" that we are supposed to "confront" with his vanished body, for what he has lost in this alleged destruction of the specters is simply his own body, "life" and "effective reality." He has lost his body out of love for his body. (*SM*, 209)

At which point Derrida adds: "For this whole matter remains informed and determined by the paradoxes of narcissism and of the work of mourning." It is a whole program which we will not follow up on here but which as surely as anything else locks these discussions back into the principal concerns of Derrida's later work.

But then there is a second intervention, this one on Marx himself and on his very critique, haunted as one might well imagine by ontology as such. Marx wishes to exorcize Stirner's ghosts, the ghosts Stirner called down on himself by his own awkward and misconceived exorcisms. It is however precisely this that will be Derrida's deepest reproach to Marx, if we may put it that way: it is this that underlies the temptation to ontology elsewhere in Marx (and even more omnipresent in so-called Marx-ism), the spectral project of a Marxist "philosophy" for example, or the Marxist view of reality or of "Man" (Althusser rejected the "humanism" of the early Marx for what are surely much the same reasons). But all the ontological temptations come from this deeper source, which lies precisely in Marx's own relationship to ghosts (and thereby to the past, to history, to death, and to life in the present):

> In short, and we will incessantly return to this, Marx doesn't like ghosts any more than his adversaries do. He doesn't want to believe in them. But he thinks about nothing else. He still believes more or less in what is supposed to distinguish them from effective reality, from living effectively. He thinks he can oppose them, as death to life, as the vain appearance of the simulacrum to real presence. (*SM*, 83)

This is then Marx's fundamental mistake (if not "error"): he wants to get rid of ghosts, he thinks he can do so, and he also thinks it is desirable to do so. But a world cleansed of spectrality is precisely ontology itself; a world of pure presence, of immediate density, of things without a past: for Derrida, an impossible and noxious nostalgia, and the fundamental target of his whole life's work. But we can now go even further than this, and Derrida risks an analysis of this polemic with Stirner: "my own feeling is that Marx is afraid of himself, he obsessively pursues someone who is not far from being a perfect likeness of himself, a brother, a double, thus a diabolical image. A sort of phantom of himself. That he would like to distance from himself, to distinguish from himself: to oppose" (*SM*, 222). But this fear now needs to be reconnected with the famous opening of *The Eighteenth Brumaire*, in which the fear of bourgeois revolutionaries is evoked: their need for the ghosts of the past, for costumes and dead paradigms, to disguise this open freedom onto an uncharted future on which they are launching. It is as though Derrida, in what some call postmodernity, is in the process of diagnosing and denouncing the opposite excess: that of a present that has already triumphantly exorcized all its ghosts and believes itself to be without a past and without spectrality, late capitalism itself as ontology, the pure presence of the world market system freed from all the errors of human history and of previous social formations, including the ghost of Marx himself.

7.

Now however we must ask what spectrality holds for the future: *Hamlet* was after all not a ghost story very specifically in this, that it did not merely tell about some grisly hold of the past on the present (as in *The Turn of the Screw*), but rather showed the apparition of the past in the act of provoking future action and calling for retribution by the living. The future is also spectral in that sense: it is not at one with a present (itself "out of joint"), it has the distance from our own plenitude of the dead and of ghosts, its blurred lineaments also swim dimly into view and announce or foretell themselves: there can be *traces* of the future (to use a privileged Derridean word), and it is all of this that restores some immense temporality as tendency or Tao which has been flattened out by positivism and finally reduced to the present by the current social order.

Such traces of the future, however, need their specific entry point, which is sometimes, when it is envisaged from a human perspective, described as the prophetic, but which can also take another form which has begun to occupy a significant position in modern theory and not least in Derrida's own work, namely the messianic as such. The word recalls Walter Benjamin, whose famous passages are indeed quoted and carefully glossed by Derrida in the present text; it also suggests the cognate "messianism"— the great millenarian movements—from which Derrida is careful to distance the other verbal form.[41] Messianism, or Utopianism, or all the active forms of millenarian movements and politics, are obviously very much targets of political and hegemonic doxa today: associated with all the imaginable varieties of political movements you fear, from Hitler and Nazism to religious fundamentalism, and not at all omitting Stalin and communism in the USSR, but also, at your own discretion, Lenin, Mao Tse-tung, and, no doubt, Marx himself, whose own proper name adorns something that sometimes seems like a movement. Current liberal thought—it is of course conservative and not "liberal" in the loose American sense of the word— focuses fundamentally on such projects which it identifies as the root cause of political evil in the world: all are projects of systemic change as such,

---

[41] "*Messianique*, préférons-nous dire, plutôt que *messianisme*, afin de désigner une structure de l'expérience plutot qu 'une religion,'" *SM*, 266.

in other words of "revolution." Yet it seems important to distinguish this traditional "Marxian" concept, which we will find reappearing metamorphosed in Derrida's thought later on, as the "messianic," from other kinds of "fundamental concepts,"

> which shackle it [the spirit of Marxism] to the body of a Marxist doctrine, and of its alleged systemic metaphysical or ontological totality (and in particular to the "dialectical method" or the "materialist dialectic"), to its fundamental concepts such as work, mode of production, social class, and thereby to the whole history of its apparatuses. (*SM*, 145–146)

As materialism makes a fleeting reappearance in this passage, it is worth remarking a curious feature of the history of these various Marxisms themselves, that virtually all of them include within themselves a crucial denunciation of bad or "vulgar-materialist" Marxisms: that it has, as it were, seemed impossible for any Marxism to define itself or to assert its identity without this internal exorcism of the *frère ennemi* or ghostly double which would be the bad or vulgar Marxism, the reductive one, what "Marxism" is for everybody else, for the non-Marxists; and this from Marx himself onwards (whose "I am not a Marxist" probably no longer needs to be quoted). This surely has something to do with the contradictions within the materialist project itself, which we have already touched on, namely the paradoxes of a "materialist consciousness," which these various authentic or true Marxisms acknowledge by warning of the dangers of trying to bring that about by suppressing consciousness (or intelligence) altogether. However, the requirements of a doctrine and those of an organized party (here "institution" or "apparatus") which turn on the establishment of such a doctrine no doubt also play their role; and Derrida's "International" "without a party, without a homeland [*patrie*], without a national community … without co-citizenship, without adherence to a class" (*SM*, 142), rejoins the allergy he shares with many others today to the older political formations.

Only a few of the wiser Marxisms have reintegrated this exorcism of a vulgar Marxism into their very structure as a way of thinking and a strategy all at once: here one thinks of various notions, like that of Korsch, of the oscillation back and forth from vulgar or determinist Marxism to a voluntaristic and theoreticist kind, depending on the situation in which it is called upon to act. Brecht vulgarized this notion in an eminently usable way when he talked about that *plumpes Denken* or vulgar thought, reductive, materialist, vulgar analysis (including cynicism, debunking, and the like), which any intellectualist and hyperintellectually dialectical Marxism had to carry about within itself in order to remain authentic. The superstructure, for Brecht, needs in other words to be reanchored to the base; the thought of the superstructure needs to carry the reminder of the base around within itself. It was then a duality or double standard that Benjamin reversed and immortalized in his image of the chess player[42]: the automaton on the outside, the revolutionary party that can be seen, with a little dialectical skill, to win every historical engagement and is carried forward by the "inevitable" march of history, but whose moves are in reality made by a very different conception of history (and in the present context, of figuration), namely that represented by the dwarf of theology.

Nor was it clear either how Benjamin thought of revolution: except that as he was contemporaneous with one, in another part of space and time, namely the Soviet Union, he developed Proustian conceptions of simultaneity and coexistence to think that particular co-evality. Yet alongside that other world, there existed this one, of the Paris of the 1930s and of Hitler next door, in which revolution was very far from happening, in which indeed it was unthinkable (and his guarded reactions to the Moscow purge trials suggest that this impossibility and inconceivability of revolution later on began to extend to everything in the world). Benjamin thus offers the supreme example of the intellectual committed to revolutionary values in a world in which revolution cannot be expected to happen: it is this which makes up everything priceless in that experiment which was his life and work, and in particular gives its relevance and energy to the basic figure through which he was accustomed to think this impossibility, namely that very conception of the messianic to which Derrida appeals at the climax of his own book on Marx.

But we must be very subtle in the way in which we, particularly those of us who are not believing Jews and are very far from such kinds of beliefs, understand the coming of Messiah. Non-Jews imagine that Jews think of Messiah as a promise and a future certainty: nothing could be further from the truth. Indeed, it was Benjamin's own close friend Gershom Scholem who wrote the definitive history of this illusion in his great biography of the apostate Messiah, *Sabbatai Sevi*,[43] who marks the moment in the history of the Diaspora of a truly messianic moment that ran through the then Jewish world like wildfire. The apostasy of Sevi before the Grand Turk then profoundly marks the messianic idea, incises it with the pain of disappointment and the sharp experience of defeat. By the association of ideas at work in collective trauma a redemptive idea is soaked in the colors and dies of bitter disillusionment: it comes to mean that along with what it also continues to mean in itself. The very idea of the messianic then brings the whole feeling of dashed hopes and impossibility along with it: and it is this that it means in

---

[42] See the first thesis in "Theses on the Philosophy of History," in *Illuminations*, ed. Hannah Arendt, trans. Harry Zohn, New York: Harcourt, Brace and World, 1968.

[43] Princeton: Princeton University Press, 1973. For these and other insights I am greatly indebted to Craig Phillips.

Benjamin as well. You would not evoke the messianic in a genuinely revolutionary period, a period in which changes can be sensed at work all around you; the messianic does not mean immediate hope in that sense, perhaps not even hope against hope; it is a unique variety of the species hope that scarcely bears any of the latter's normal characteristics and that flourishes only in a time of absolute hopelessness, a period like the Second Empire, or the years between the wars, or the 1980s and 90s, when radical change seems unthinkable, its very idea dispelled by visible wealth and power, along with palpable powerlessness. It is only in those tough years that it makes sense to speak of the messianic in the Benjaminian sense.[44]

As for the content of this redemptive idea itself, another peculiar feature of it must be foregrounded, namely that it does not deploy a linear idea of the future: nothing predictable, nothing to be read in the signs of the times, in the first few swallows or shoots, the freshening of the air. "The Jews were prohibited from investigating the future ... every second of time was the strait gate through which the Messiah might enter."[45] This is the notion of the non-announced, the turning of a corner in which an altogether different present happens, which was not foreseen. It is also the sense in which, for Benjamin, the Social Democratic and then the Stalinist rhetoric of historical inevitability weigh down the historical present even more balefully: as in

---

[44]   I quote Derrida's own evocation in full: "Le messianique, y compris sous ses formes révolutionnaires (et le messianique est toujours révolutionnaire, il doit l'être), ce serait l'urgence, l'imminence, mais, paradoxe irréductible, une *attente* sans *horizon d'attente*. On peut toujours tenir la sécheresse quasiment athée de ce messianique comme la condition des religions du Livre, un désert qui ne fut même pas le leur (mais la terre est toujours prêtée, louée par Dieu, elle n'est jamais possédée par l'occupant, dit justement l'Ancien Testament dont il faudrait aussi entendre l'injonction); on peut toujours y reconnaître le sol aride sur lequel ont poussé, et passé, les figures vivantes de tous les messies, qu'ils fussent annoncés, reconnus ou toujours attendus. On peut aussi tenir cette poussée compulsive, et la furtivité de ce passage, pour les seuls événements depuis lesquels nous approchons et d'abord nommons le messianique en général, cet autre fantôme dont nous ne pouvons ni ne devons nous passer. On pourra juger étrange, étrangement familière et inhospitalière a la fois (*unheimlich, uncanny*) cette figure de l'hospitalité absolue dont on voudrait confier la promesse à une expérience aussi impossible, aussi peu assurée dans son indigence, à un quasi « messianisme » aussi inquiet, fragile et démuni, à un « messianisme » toujours présupposé, à un messianisme quasi transcendantal mais aussi obstinément intéressé par un matérialisme sans substance: un matérialisme de la *khôra* pour un « messianisme » désespérant. Mais sans ce désespoir-là, et si l'on pouvait *compter* sur ce qui vient, l'espérance ne serait que le calcul d'un programme. On aurait la prospective mais on n'attendrait plus rien ni personne" (*SM*, 267).

[45]   Walter Benjamin, "Theses on the Philosophy of History," XVIII-B, in *Illuminations*, 264.

Proust, whatever is to happen, it will assuredly not be what we think or predict. In this sense, Benjamin had a more historically vivid feeling for how revolutions actually happen, unexpected by anyone, even their organizers, a few people gathering in the streets, larger and larger crowds, suddenly the rumor spreads that the king has secretly left the city. It is this temporality which is the messianic kind, and about which the very peculiarity of the messianic idea testifies, which can thus not be "hoped" for in any familiar way; nor is "belief" in the Messiah comparable to any ordinary thinking about the future. Perry Anderson has some suggestive remarks about what constitutes the unexpectedness of revolution as such when he distinguishes between an unpredictable development in the base, in production and its accompanying economic crises, and the sudden spark generated by contact with a specific mentality in the superstructure.[46] Both of those however can exist for long periods in unrelated states: neither is fruitful of eventfulness (as Heidegger might say) in and of itself; what is unpredictable is precisely the spark that flies between these two sealed and as it were unrelated areas. This helps us "think" the messianic moment, the future event, in a somewhat more articulated way, it being understood that what the very concept of the messianic above all wishes to warn us is that the event cannot be thought in the ordinary meaning of that word; and with this we rejoin Derrida's critique of conventional philosophical thought in general as a misguided attempt to think what demands a different preparation and approach.

Yet the "messianic" must be sharply distinguished from, in Derrida's usage, the "apocalyptic", which is much more specifically the thinking of the "end" and to which the charge of critical and negative doxa that nowadays attaches to revolution and the Utopian becomes attached: but with a fundamental difference. For in Derrida, if I read him right, the apocalyptic is largely a right-wing matter, and Fukuyama becomes the textbook example in the present work and the paradigm case of an apocalyptic pronouncement on the death of the past as such, the utter disappearance of that prehistory we still call History: in other words, the definitive exorcism of specters and spectrality, the beginning of a market universe which is a perpetual present, as well as the instauration of truths.

> Whoever takes on the apocalyptic tone comes to signify to, if not tell, you something. What? The truth, of course, and to signify to you that it reveals the truth to you … Truth is itself the end, the destination, and that truth unveils itself is the advent of the end.[47]

---

[46] Perry Anderson, *Arguments within English Marxism*, London: Verso, 1980.

[47] Immanuel Kant and Jacques Derrida, *Raising the Tone of Philosophy: Late Essays by Immanuel Kant, Transformative Critique by Jacques Derrida*, ed. Peter Fenves, Baltimore: John Hopkins University Press, 1993.

This is then the sense in which we ought to be able to distinguish an apocalyptic politics from a messianic one, and which might lead us on into some new way of sorting out the Left from the Right, the new International in Marx's spirit from that in the world of business and state power. The messianic is spectral, it is the spectrality of the future, the other dimension, that answers to the haunting spectrality of the past which is historicity itself. The apocalyptic, however, announces the end of spectrality (and we remember that even in Marx it remained a temptation, and that Marx also sometimes imprudently talks about the end of history, but in the name of the beginning of a different one).

There is, however, finally another feature of the messianic that emerges in Derrida's discussion, and that unexpectedly opens this and spectrality onto another world of the real not normally deployed by these themes and images, these stolen and displaced words. This is the other face of modern or we might even say of postmodern virtuality, a daily spectrality that undermines the present and the real without any longer attracting any attention at all; it marks out the originality of our social situation, but no one has reidentified it as a very old thing in quite this dramatic way—it is the emergence, at the very end of Derrida's book, of spectrality, of the messianic, as "the differential deployment of *tekhne*, of techno-science or of tele-technology" (*SM*, 268).

The relationship between deconstruction and the machine—that is to say what cannot be thought as such or what evades humanistic categories (and one supposes in this sense that what is called functionalism escapes thinking in original but not often acknowledged ways whereas the word merely papers over a problem)—can in retrospect be seen to run through the entire corpus, most notably in that extraordinary moment in which, having demonstrated Hegel's infeodation to "vulgar" or linear conceptions of temporality, Derrida exclaims: what Hegel cannot grasp is the machine. In my view, the problem is made respectable by an appeal to Heidegger's concept of the *Gestell*, assuming anyone knows what that means: I think that the new concern with tele-technology greatly outstrips Heidegger's anti-modernist and finally very traditional distaste for science and technology ...[48]

---

[48] "Ce que Hegel, interprète relevant de toute l'histoire de la philosophie *n'a jamais pu penser*, c'est une machine qui fonctionnerait. Qui fonctionnerait sans être en cela réglée par un ordre de réappropriation. Un tel fonctionnement serait impensable en tant qu'il inscrit en lui-même un effet de pure perte. Il serait impensable comme une non-pensée qu'aune pensée ne pourrait relever en la constituant comme son propre opposé, comme *son* autre" (*MP*, 126). It might be argued that Heidegger does pose the *Gestell* as the other of thought in precisely this fashion; in any case the urgent relevance of all this to the Marx of *Capital* ought to be obvious.

As far back as *The Postcard* it had become clear to what degree Derrida's subversion of mainstream semiotics and communications theory fed into a vast "dissemination" of his own earlier concepts of writing and difference, which now emerged in the place in which a theory of communications technology would have existed were one possible.[49] But instead of becoming formalized in a new tele-technological "theory" or turn, that constellation of terms and themes is here modulated in the direction of spectrality itself:

> [Spectral differentiation, the messianic,] forces us more than ever to think the virtualization of space and time, the possibility of virtual events whose movement and speed forbid us (more than ever but also in new ways since nothing is ever completely new) to oppose their presence to their representation, or "real time" to "deferred time," effectivity to its simulacrum, the living to the non-living, in short the living to the living death of its phantoms. It forces us to think from out of this situation another space for democracy. For a democracy to come and thus for justice. We already suggested that the event around which we are here circling hesitates between the singular "who" of the phantom and the general "what" of the simulacrum. In the virtual space of all the tele-techno-sciences, in the general dis-location to which our time is condemned, along with the spaces of lovers, of families, of nations, the messianic trembles at the edge of this very event. It is that hesitation, it has no other vibration, it cannot "live" otherwise, but would no longer be messianic if it ceased to hesitate ... (*SM* 268)

So it is that Marxism and its current spectrality, which not so unexpectedly intersected the weak messianic impulses of our own period, now both emerge in some post-semiotic universe of messages and into the virtualities of the new communications technologies: original forms of hesitation, a new kind of trembling or shimmering of the present in which new ghosts now seem on the point of walking.

It will be remembered how Derrida opened up Lacan's still essentially semiotic and centered reading of Poe[50]: a letter never arrives at its destination ... a letter always arrives at its destination ... Marx's purloined letter: a program capable of keeping any number of conspiratorial futures busy ...

---

[49] But see now Richard Dienst, *Still Life in Real Time: Theory after Television*, Durham, NC: Duke University Press, 1994, for a pathbreaking study of what the fact and existence of technology do to the very possibilities of philosophizing (from Marx to Deleuze and Derrida).

[50] "Le facteur de la vérité," in *La Carte postale*, Paris: Flammarion, 1980.

Chapter 5

Deleuze and Dualism

We begin, as one so often does, without necessarily wanting to, with Hegel (heaven only knows if we will also end up in the same place). The motto will be Hegel's prescient analysis of the situation of thought in modern times, which he contrasts to the situation of nascent philosophy in ancient Greece:

> The manner of study in ancient times differed from that of the modern age in that the former was the proper and complete formation of the natural consciousness. Putting itself to the test at every point of its existence, and philosophizing about everything it came across, it made itself into a universality that was active through and through. In modern times, however, the individual finds the abstract form ready-made; the effort to grasp and appropriate it is more the direct driving forth of what is within and the truncated generation of the universal than it is the emergence of the latter from the concrete variety of existence. Hence the task nowadays consists not so much in purging the individual of an immediate, sensuous mode of apprehension, and making him into a substance that is an object of thought and that thinks, but rather in just the opposite, in freeing determinate thoughts from their fixity so as to give actuality to the universal, and impart to it spiritual life. But it is far harder to bring fixed thoughts into a fluid state than to do so with sensuous existence.[1]

So here, astonishingly, at the opening of *Phenomenology of Spirit*, we find a mature and subtle reflection on reification: reification not only in the world of everyday life, but in thinking as well, and in our intercourse with already existing concepts, with free-floating thoughts named and signed like so many books or paintings. The ancient Greeks had the task, Hegel suggests, of wresting abstract ideas ("universals") from the flux of the sensory: of transforming *pensée sauvage* into systems of abstractions, of reclaiming Reason (or the ego, Freud might say) from the morass of the immediate. This is henceforth achieved, and thinkers in the modern period are then

---

[1] G. W. F. Hegel, *Phenomenology of Spirit*, trans. A. V. Miller, Oxford: Oxford University Press, 1977, 19–20.

suffocated by the proliferation of just such abstractions, in which we swim as in an autonomous element, which suffuse our individual consciousnesses with abstract categories, concepts, and information of all kinds. What to reclaim or reconquer from this new morass, which is rather different from what confronted the Greeks in their "blooming, buzzing confusion"? And who does not see that this holds a thousand times more true for ourselves in postmodernity and late capitalism, in the society of the spectacle and the realm of the cybernetic, than in Hegel's still relatively information-poor life-world? If the Greeks transformed their sensory immediacy into universals, into what can universals themselves be transformed? Hegel's answer is generally interpreted to be reflexivity, self-consciousness, the dialectic and its distance from the concepts it wields and inhabits: that's probably not wrong, but also not very usable under present circumstances (but his own word was "actuality"). Marx had a better formula: bourgeois thought, he said (which we may also read as Greek philosophy), sought to rise from the particular to the universal; our task is now to rise—note the persistence of this verb—from the universal to the concrete.[2]

The greatness of Gilles Deleuze—or at least one of his many claims on greatness—was to have confronted omnivorously the immense field of everything that was thought and published. No one can read the two volumes of *Capitalisme et schizophrénie* (or, in a different way, those of *Cinéma*) without being stunned by the ceaseless flood of references that tirelessly nourish these texts, and which are processed into content and organized into dualisms. This is the sense in which one can speak of Deleuze as a thinker of synthesis, one who masters the immense proliferation of thoughts and concepts by way of assimilation and appropriation. (If you like dualisms, indeed, and great cosmic or metaphysical oppositions, then you can say that Derrida is his opposite in this respect, tirelessly dissolving all the reified thoughts he encounters in the tradition back into the first impossibilities and antinomies from which they sprang.) This is why it seems to me misguided to search for a system or a central idea in Deleuze: in fact, there are many of those. It seems preferable to observe the extraordinary process whereby his intelligence rewrites and transcodes its overpopulated conceptual environment, and organizes it into force fields. But that organization, often so luminously schematic, does not aim to give us the truth, but rather a series of extraordinary representations: it is a fictive mapping which utilizes as its representational language great mythic dualisms such as the Schizophrenic and the Paranoid, the Nomad and the State, space and time, molar and molecular.

---

2   Karl Marx, *Grundrisse*, in *Marx and Engels Collected Works*, Vol. 28, New York: International Publishers, 1986, 38.

I want to look further into that organizational process, but I want to come at it from a specific question. The attacks on Freud that run through *Capitalisme et schizophrénie* (particularly the first volume) have been more notorious than the defense and deployment of Marx, which is an equally persistent feature. But we know that Deleuze planned a work on Marx in his final years, and we may also suspect that Marx is a good deal more pervasive than the lengthy chapter on that part of the *Grundrisse* sometimes entitled "Precapitalist Economic Formations," which occupies so central a space in *L'Anti-Oedipe*. I think that Deleuze is alone among the great thinkers of so-called poststructuralism in having accorded Marx an absolutely fundamental role in his philosophy—in having found in the encounter with Marx the most energizing event for his later work.

Let's first examine, as it were, the sequence of events in that vast Marx chapter of *L'Anti-Oedipe*, which nonetheless and despite its energy and coherence may be taken as a set of notes on Marxism rather than some new philosophy of the latter, or some ideologically innovative reading. The chapter is itself a subdivision of a larger one, something like the philosophy of history of the Deleuze/Guattari operation, strangely entitled "Sauvages, barbares, civilisés," a classification that has more ancient roots (in Adam Ferguson, for example), but which springs in recent times (with the enthusiastic approval of Marx himself) from Lewis Henry Morgan's *Ancient Society* of 1877. I must say something more about this fascinating figure, whom Lévi-Strauss called the inventor of the kinship system and the founder of modern anthropology[3]; but I will here limit myself to the extraordinary way in which, with Morgan, all theories of the modern and of modernity meet their supplement and their hidden truth. The "modern" is of course here "civilization"; but whoever says so immediately posits an Other and a preceding stage of premodernity or precapitalism. That can simply, for most theoreticians of the modern, be the traditional and its benighted ignorance, while for others it can offer the libidinal investment of a golden age, that of the Noble Savage and the State of Nature. What is unique about Morgan is that he takes both positions simultaneously—as a supporter of the Paris Commune and an adoptive clan member of the Iroquois tribe, a lifelong admirer of the Native American mode of social organization called, from its equivalents in antiquity, the *gens*. "Barbarian" thus has no negative connotations in Morgan: it is a proud affront to the dehumanization and alienation of "civilized" industrial capitalism, a badge worn in honor and defiance. But the energy necessary to break with the modernizing social order in this way must itself be paid for; so it is that Morgan's negation of civilization generates a negation of the negation—a second, supplementary Other in the form

---

[3] For more on Morgan, see my *Archaeologies of the Future*, London: Verso, 2007, 326–327.

of the Savage—something like the remainder or waste product, the convenient result of an operation of "splitting" whereby everything unpleasantly uncivilized about the Iroquois can be separated off and attributed to "truly" primitive or tribal peoples. Morgan's libidinal horror at the "savage" can be sensed in his own expression, "the stupendous system of promiscuity," by which is meant not only unbridled sexuality before the incest taboo but also a generalized system of flux: no writing, no fixed domicile, no organized individuality, no collective memory or history, no customs to be passed down —the imagined list by which this absolute disorder can be designated is endless. Clearly, in the Deleuze/Guattari system, the valences on all this are changed: savagery becomes as close as we can get to the idyllic liberation of schizophrenia, while the already implicit hierarchies of the *gens* are, on their account of barbarism, deployed and developed into the ur-state, primal despotism, the sway of the emperor and of the signifier itself.

This grand narrative of history will then clearly reinvent the classic problem of the transition from feudalism to capitalism and will tend to emphasize the survivals of both earlier stages, and their possible recurrence, more than is the case in most Marxian accounts. The central position of power in the account of barbarism—the sacred body of the king or emperor replacing the body of the earth, the emphasis on hierarchy and the State as a historical force—will swell into the alternating terms of the great dualism of *Mille plateaux*. Contrary to first impressions, this emphasis on power (unlike what happens in Foucault) does not here assert itself as an alternative to Marxian economic analysis; rather, the latter is itself generalized throughout the Deleuze/Guattari historical narrative in such a way that the determination by the economic is argued more fully and persuasively for the primitive (or "savage") mode than in most Marxian discussions. Indeed, here, alongside the primal value given to the "code" and to inscription, which would seem to offer a still relatively structuralist interpretation of primitive society, it is the tension between filiation and alliance that perpetually reinserts the economic, in the Marxian sense, and persists all the way up to capitalism, where it becomes the internal opposition between the two uses of money itself: as capital and as purchasing power, as power of investment and as measure of exchange.

But it is to the question of the code that we need to return in order to grasp the originality of the Deleuze/Guattari account of capitalism. The latter is, indeed, seen by them as organized by an "axiomatic", which is very different from the code of the earlier moments, raising the suspicion that, as with money itself, one of the functions of the very concept of "code" in the first place is to set off this radical difference with the axiomatic, while the other function is to secure its own identity from within as a concept, described (rather than defined) as follows: "A flux is coded inasmuch as detachments of the chain and preselections of the flux operate in correspondence, embrace, and marry each other."[4] The figure is that of Louis Hjelmslev's glossematics, so highly praised here owing to the relative indifference of the content of each of its planes, along with the absolute requirement of a formal coordination between the two planes (what another system describes as the double inscription).

It would not be appropriate to mark this distinction by describing the "code" as meaningful and the "axiom" as meaningless or arbitrary, since the very concept of meaning in its traditional sense is something Deleuze aims to do away with and to replace. We might just as well say that the property of a code is to be indifferently replaceable by another code, which will look equally "meaningful" or organic; whereas with an axiom, you're stuck—you can't change it, at best you can add another one, until the axiomatic resembles those legal systems in which enormous quantities of precedents and old rulings can be found in the stacks somewhere. In mathematics, as I understand it, the axiom is the starting point, which cannot itself be grounded or justified, but rather serves as the ground or justification for all the other steps and propositions: "The choice of axioms involves a choice of basic technical terms to be left undefined, since the attempt to define all terms would lead to endless regression" (*L'AO*, 294; 247).[5] It is my understanding that modern discussions of axiomatics turn essentially on this

---

[4] Gilles Deleuze and Félix Guattari, *L'Anti-Oedipe*, Paris: Minuit, 1972, 174; my translation here. In English, *Anti-Oedipus: Capitalism and Schizophrenia*, trans. Robert Hurley, Mark Seem, and Helen Lane, Minneapolis: University of Minnesota Press, 1983, 149. Future references to this work are denoted *L'AO*; all page references will cite the French edition first, followed by the English translation.

[5] *The Harper Encyclopedia of Science*, Vol. 1, ed. James R. Newman, New York: Harper and Row, 1963, 128. And see Gilles Deleuze and Félix Guattari, *Mille plateaux*, Vol. 2, *Capitalisme et schizophrénie*, Paris: Minuit, 1980: "The axioms of capitalism are obviously not theoretical propositions or ideological formulas, but rather operatory statements which make up the semiological form of Capital, and which form constituent parts of the assemblages [*agencements*] of production, circulation, and consumption. The axioms are primary statements, which neither derive from nor depend on any other. In a way, a given flux can be the object of one or several axioms at the same time (the ensemble of such axioms constituting the conjugation of the flux); but it can also lack any axioms of its own, so that its treatment is simply the consequence of other axioms; finally, it can remain outside altogether, and evolve without limits, remaining in the state of 'free' variation [*sauvage*] in the system. There is in capitalism a constant tendency to add more axioms" (577). In English, *A Thousand Plateaus: Capitalism and Schizophrenia*, trans. Brian Massumi, Minneapolis: University of Minnesota Press, 1987, 461–462. The source for this doctrine of the axiomatic would seem to be Robert Blanché, *L'Axiomatique*, Paris: PUF, 1959. Future references to *Mille plateaux* are denoted *MiP*; all page references will cite the French edition first, followed by the English translation.

matter of presupposition and arbitrary starting points. At any rate, it is precisely as an axiomatic that Deleuze and Guattari begin their discussion of capital. Let me risk the following characterization: codes have an ephemeral self-sufficiency about them, whether they subsist in the form of decorations (bodily tattoos, for example) or in the form of custom and myth, and even though they are prone to transformation into other codes in the immense slippage of history. Axioms, on the other hand, are operational; they do not offer anything for commentary or exegesis, but rather are merely a set of rules to be put into effect. And this is the sense in which capitalism repairs itself and surmounts its contradictions by adding new axioms: you are supposed to believe in a pure market system, that is to say, a rather simple axiomatic positing undisturbed exchanges. But when there is a crisis in free trade or the gold standard, you add the more complex axioms of Keynesianism: those do not modify the axiomatic of capitalism but merely complicate the operations that make it up. There can be no return here to any simpler axiomatic or purer form of capitalism; only the addition of ever more rules and qualifications (rules against rules, for example, a dismantling of Keynesianism that has to use the latter's structures and institutions in order to enact itself). At any rate, this enigmatic but central term must, I think, be grasped in terms of what might be called a Deleuzian semiotics, and indeed, we here urgently need something like a semiotics of the axiom, provided we have already equipped ourselves with a satisfactory semiotics of the code as such. Even so, the question lingers as to the originality of the distinction: does it do much more than restate the old opposition between the mechanical and the organic, between *Gemeinschaft* and *Gesellschaft*, in new and novel terminology?

The answer given by *L'Anti-Oedipe* itself is resolutely "textual": codes are inscribed—at the outer limit inscribed on the body itself (tattoos, scars, face painting) when not on the body of the world. But the axiomatic is not a writing and leaves no traces of that kind. If you prefer the distinction to be staged the other way round, we may say "that a code is never economic and can never be" (*L'AO*, 294; 247), an observation that slowly leads us back to Marx's own account of precapitalist formations, which, although "ultimately" organized around a specific type of economic production in them —but unlike what holds for capitalism—are secured by an "extra-economic instance": "religion for the Middle Ages, politics for the ancient city-state," to which, after Morgan, the tradition has added "kinship for tribal society or primitive communism." This separation of power from production in noncapitalist societies was then theorized by the Althusserians as the distinction between the determinant—always a form of the economic—and the dominant, which in the social formations mentioned is extra-economic: only in capitalism do the two then coincide. (One of the crucial theoretical arguments about socialism today surely turns on this distinction as well, i.e., on whether socialism and other proposed alternatives to capitalism, such as Islamic fundamentalism, do not also require some "extra-economic" motivation.)

The argument about the code, then, is one of the three principal features of this subchapter. The remarkable pages on kinship, which reorganize this concept into a tension between filiation and alliance, furnish the theme of a second development, turning on the reappearance of this tension within capital itself as the two functions of money. The final discussion on the Oedipus complex happens to interest me much less, but it posits a specific and unique form of representation and the production and function of images in axiomatic society (or capitalism), of which the primal scene and the Oedipal family become the first form and the exemplar. Meanwhile, from time to time, the authors remember their initial project and ask themselves how desire can be invested in such systems; they invoke and reinterpret the "falling rate of profit"; most significantly for any political reading, they theorize the tendencies of the system: in a remarkable passage they assert that capitalism's deterritorializations are always accompanied by reterritorializations, or at least by the impulse and temptation to reterritorialize (*L'AO*, 306–307; 257).[6] Such tendencies, to reinvent the private garden or the religious enclave, to practice the sacred after hours like a hobby, or to try to libidinalize money into an exciting game—in other words, to attempt to transform bits of the axiomatic back into so many codes—is obviously at one with the way in which the various forms of precapitalism (coding and overcoding, the despotic state, the kinship system) survive in capitalism in forms that resemble their traditional counterparts, but that have in reality completely different functions. This incapacity of the axiomatic, or of capitalism, to offer intrinsic libidinal investments to its subjects—its urgent internal need to reinvent older forms of coding to supplement its impoverished structures—is surely one of the most interesting and promising lines of investigation opened up by the "Marxism" of *L'Anti-Oedipe*.

Alongside this argument, however, is the other line proposed by the overall title of the two-volume work, *Capitalisme et schizophrénie*, which affirms that, despite the homologies between the two terms of the slogan, ideal schizophrenia constitutes an alternative to capitalism and stands as its external limit. I prefer to come at this from a somewhat lower level of theorization, by way of the more empirical discussions of class. For here the assertions are more revealing: "From the point of view of the capitalist axiomatic, there is only one class with a universalist vocation, and that is the bourgeoisie" (*L'AO*, 301; 253). Deleuze and Guattari endorse the unhappy conclusion into which Sartre argued himself in the *Critique of Dialectical*

---

[6] "What [modern societies] deterritorialize on the one hand, they reterritorialize on the other."

Reason, namely, that social classes have only a serial being and that only group unities present a radically different and active principle. In that case, the proletariat cannot really have a historical vocation of radical systemic transformation, and indeed it is to the *hors-classe* (potentially the ideal schizophrenic) that a true guerrilla potential belongs (*L'AO*, 303–304; 255)

Those reflections are then continued in the chapter of *Mille plateaux* devoted to the State, "Appareil de capture" (particularly in Proposition 14), where the notion and consequences of the axiomatic are further developed and explored. The interrelationship between an increase in constant capital (machines, technology, automation, and the axiomatic itself) and the falling rate of profit is usefully appealed to here for a further elaboration of the internal contradictions of capitalism (*L'AO*, 585; 468). But the most interesting features of this chapter for us are clearly those in which Deleuze and Guattari elaborate on the notion of the *hors-classe*, and, basing themselves on contemporary Italian political thought, wish to develop the idea of a revolutionary movement completely outside the State itself. This is the point at which we get the most vivid sense of the empirical value of that Deleuzian terminology which might otherwise seem merely poetic or speculative: "decoding," "deterritorialization," the replacement of the older codes by the new capitalist axiomatic that triggers and releases "fluxions" of all kinds (translated as "flows" by Brian Massumi, but the older word is perhaps more usefully medical). These have hitherto seemed to be relatively structural; now, however, we get the real thing.

> In proportion, as ever more decoded flows enter a central axiomatic, they tend ever more to escape the periphery [i.e., the Third World] and to raise problems the axiomatic is incapable of controlling, let alone resolving (even with those special extra axioms that have been added to deal with the periphery) ... The four principal flows that torment the representatives of the world economy or of the axiomatic are the following: the flux of energy-matter [i.e., oil and other such goods], flux of population, flux of food products, flux of the urban. (*MiP*, 579; 463)

Meanwhile, the problem of the location of the working class remains central:

> As long as the working class remains defined by an acquired status, or even by a State which it has itself theoretically conquered, it still only appears as "capital," as part of capital (variable capital) and does not escape the *plane* of capital as such. That plane at best becomes bureaucratic [i.e., as in the Socialist countries]. Yet it is precisely by leaving the plane of capital, by ceaselessly exiting from it, that a mass becomes fully revolutionary and destroys the dominant equilibrium of denumerable ensembles. (*MiP*, 589; 472)[7]

---

[7] The reference is to work by Tronti and Negri.

However uncertainly poised this estimation leaves the politics of *L'Anti-Oedipe* in its Cold War situation of 1972, the analysis is prescient and prophetic in the light of the current situation, notably, the immense structural unemployment and the recent emergence of a host of social subjects who cannot be expected to take on the political role hitherto assigned to the industrial working classes, with their strategic control of the "levers" of production. When we search for the political relevance of Deleuze and Guattari's books today, it is surely in just such insights and appreciations that it must be sought. The same is true of the concomitant discussions of money and finance and banking, with the resurgence today of a novel form of "finance capital" clearly confirming the agenda of this twenty-five-year-old work: "It is the bank which governs the whole system, including the investment of desire" (*L'AO*, 272; 230).[8] These are then the two directions opened up by this prodigious analysis of the decoding and deterritorialization of the capitalist axiomatic: on the one hand, the impoverishment of subjectivity and the extinction of the older subject itself (to use a non-Deleuzian terminology); on the other, the immense power now granted to money itself and the logic of finance, as that paradoxical and contradictory form taken by the axiomatic in the everyday life and functioning of capitalism as a system.

Thus, theoretical problems arise, not so much with the descriptions of capitalism in the Deleuze/Guattari corpus as in the positing of its Other, whether the latter is to be considered the industrial working class (as is traditional) or the sub- and underclasses, the unemployed or minorities, and outside of capital and society altogether. In other words, do we face a genuine dualism in which capitalism and the State are confronted with what is absolutely not themselves, what is radically other to and outside of them? Or is this a more dialectical opposition in which the Other, the working class, is also somehow a part of, and thereby itself subordinate to, the State and to capital, a position which would seem to end up in a monism whereby there exists ultimately only the State, only capital? We will return to these issues shortly.

At this point, I want to pause to clarify my position on the exercise we have just been conducting. It is not a question, I feel, of deciding whether Deleuze (or that hybrid subject Deleuze/Guattari) is or is not a Marxist.

---

[8] This conception of the Deleuzian line of flight as the dissolution of capitalist society by way of the dispersal of its population is already envisioned on the final pages of *Capital*, Vol. 1, trans. Ben Fowkes, London: Penguin, 1976. It is also, I think, a fundamental impulse in Hardt and Negri's *Empire* and *Multitude*; and see also Paolo Virno, *A Grammar of the Multitude*, trans. Isabella Bertoletti, James Cascaito, and Andrea Casson, New York: Semiotext[e], 2004.

The various Marxisms are, no doubt, ideologies and are susceptible to analysis like other ideologies. Marxism as a body of thought, however—I hesitate to mention the word "science"—is something I prefer to call a problematic. What seems far more important to me in the present context is to determine to what degree the thought of Deleuze moves within and endorses that problematic; or, the other way round, to what degree the problematic of Deleuze includes the Marxian problematic and endorses Marxian problems and questions as urgent ones within its own field of inquiry. The current return to classical liberalism—and the return of traditional disciplines such as ethics, aesthetics, and political philosophy, which also characterizes the present intellectual climate—has tended to regress to pre-Marxian positions and problems by way of the assurance that the Marxian problematic is no longer valid for late capitalism. The crucial feature of this diagnosis lies not in the absence of the whole range of different Marxist answers and solutions to those problems, but rather in the repression of the problems themselves and the disappearance of inquiries that seek to position the logic of social life today (commodification) and the novel operation of a globalizing finance capital within the descriptions we are called upon to make of aesthetic production, the functioning of ideology, and the role of intellectuals and their conceptual innovations.

But, in my opinion, the work of Deleuze gives no aid and comfort to such regressive efforts; indeed, the whole function of this work has been not to seal off the academic disciplines from the social, the political, and the economic, but rather to open them up precisely to that larger force field. Rather than attempting to contain those realities, in other words, and to send them back to the sterilized compartments of the appropriately specialized disciplines, Deleuzian analysis displays a realm of prodigious polymorphous coding in which desire restlessly invests across the boundaries; indeed, in which the libidinal cannot be confined to the narrower realm that bourgeois thought calls subjectivity or psychology (or even psychoanalysis), but shows how the social is also a tissue of phantasms, and the narrowly libidinal itself a web of social and political representations. This breaking down of the barriers between the subjective—narrow concepts of desire and libido, even of sexuality—and the allegedly objective—the social, the political, and the economic—is one of Deleuze's most important achievements, it being understood that there are other ways of doing so. (Certain contemporary developments of Lacanian thought—I think above all of the now monumental work of Slavoj Žižek—seek to achieve this end by other means and in other forms.) As far as Deleuze and Guattari are concerned, however, let me read into the record one of the more striking moments in *L'Anti-Oedipe*, when the convulsive effort to tear down those traditional walls between the subjective and the objective can be witnessed:

How does a delirium begin? Perhaps the cinema is able to capture the movement of madness, precisely because it is not analytic and regressive, but explores a global field of coexistence. Witness a film by Nicholas Ray, supposedly representing the formation of a cortisone delirium: an overworked father, a high school teacher who works overtime for a radio-taxi service and is being treated for heart trouble. He begins to rave about the educational system *in general*, the need to restore a pure *race*, the salvation of the social and moral *order*, then he passes to *religion*, the timeliness of a return to the Bible, Abraham. But what in fact did Abraham do? Well now, he killed or wanted to kill his son, and perhaps God's only error lies in having stayed his hand. But doesn't this man, the film's protagonist, have a son of his own? Hmm … What the film shows so well, to the shame of psychiatrists, is that every delirium is first of all the investment of a field that is social, economic, political, cultural, racial and racist, pedagogical, and religious: the delirious person applies a delirium to his family and his son that overreaches them on all sides. (*L'AO*, 326; 274)

And what is dramatic and narratively foregrounded in the case of delirium is also at work in the microscopic operation of desire itself, and in general, on a daily basis. This is no longer one of those Freudo-Marxisms in which each side kept its own party structures (as in some popular-front government of the mind) and cooperated on disputed terrains, sending groups of experts to consult with each other. Rather, it underscores the will to monism in Deleuze (a matter to which I will return shortly) and the way in which that multiplicity of disciplines implied in our opening observation by Hegel is overcome by a prodigious movement of dedifferentiation: one that no doubt derives much of its force from the establishment and institutionalization of the disciplines and specializations in an earlier historical moment, but marks a new will to reestablish multiple connections among all those separated things. This is the spirit of synthesis in Deleuze I evoked above, and it therefore comes as no surprise that the other face of that monism of desire we have been considering offers precisely that multiplicity of references, that ceaseless incorporation of texts of all kinds and research from any number of fields, which must astonish any reader and which is even more dramatic in *Mille plateaux* than in *L'Anti-Oedipe*: linguistics, economics, military strategy, the building of the cathedrals, mathematics, modern art, kinship systems, technology and engineering, the history of the great classical empires, optics, evolutionary theory, revolutionary praxis, musical modes, the structure of crystals, fascism, sexuality, the modern novel—everything is grist for a mill that is no longer a simple and mechanical establishment of homologies, but rather the setting in motion and the systemic rotation of an unimaginably multidimensional reality.

All of which returns us to the central issue of philosophical representation, to which we must now, however, add a new problem: what is called the critique of ideology (or *Ideologiekritik*) in the Marxian tradition, for which a Deleuzian alternative suddenly seems to open up in *Mille plateaux*, in the form of what the authors call noology, or as they put it, "the study of the images of thought and of their historicity" (*MiP*, 466; 376). The program for noological analysis—as a mode of distinguishing and implicitly judging texts on the basis of the Deleuze/Guattari ideological dualism (Nomads versus the State)—seems to me to have more content than the more formal distinction between the "rhizomatic" and the "arborescent" (the growing out in all directions as opposed to the hierarchical) which has become so well known, but which seems to present a more abstract and more purely philosophical set of discursive features. For, as the opening chapter of *Mille plateaux*, "Rhizome" (also published separately) has something of the dogmatic force of a manifesto; the unveiling of the noological method—in the very thicket of the content of later chapters—is more concrete and argued from the opposition between "royal science" and "minor science" (on which we will touch in a moment). Whether the new coordinates do not mark a slippage of the work of Deleuze and Guattari from the economic—the modes of production that dominated *L'Anti-Oedipe*—to a conception of the political in which judgments and the taking of sides are more facile must be the open question with which we approach the new material.

At first, noology is organized around a simple checklist, and it is the characteristic originality of the authors to derive it not directly from philosophical thought but from various kinds of engineering: the building of the great cathedrals by journeymen, as opposed to the codification of building methods and engineering standards imposed later on by the State; the former is indeed characterized as an "*inexact yet rigorous*" method, one that is "inexact by essence and not by chance" (*MiP*, 454; 367). But what is thereby derived is a way of judging thought according to its conformity "with a model borrowed from the State apparatus":

> The classic image of thought, and the *striage* of mental space that it effectuates, lays a claim to universality. In effect, it operates with two "universals," the totality as the ultimate foundation of being or as an all-encompassing horizon; and the Subject as the principle which converts being into a being-for-us … [a] double point of view of Being the Subject, placed under the direction of a "universal method." (*MiP*, 464, 469; 374, 379)

I think that this kind of classification has become something of a doxa in our period, where the reaction against Marxism has produced any number of reborn anarchisms. On my view, the most welcome result of this noology is not so much its conclusion about State-oriented thought as its passionate qualification of the nomadic thinking that is its opposite—a dualism if ever there was—and that runs the risk of an association with all kinds of racisms owing to the terms in which nomadic situationality is celebrated: race, tribe, nationalism. But here the authors have a magnificent thing to say:

> The tribe-race only exists at the level of an oppressed race, and of the oppression it undergoes; there are only inferior races, minority races, there is no dominant race, a race is not defined by its purity but rather by the impurity conferred on it by a system of domination.

And so on, to the obligatory climactic quotation from the Rimbaud of *A Season in Hell* (*MiP*, 470; 479).[9] This everyone can subscribe to, it seems to me; as always the deeper truth of Deleuze and Guattari is to be found on this side of the opposition, in the remarkable intuition of the minor which emerges from their thought (and which has found something of its own codification in the now classic—the now unfortunately classic—thoughts on minor literature and inner subversive language in the Kafka book, something of a lost chapter to this one, a stray plateau to be added in here[10]).

It is thus in the analysis of nomadic texts and micrological war machines that we will expect to find the most interesting pages. (As far as the State is concerned, as the title of the corresponding chapter suggests, it is rather the operation of "capture," of appropriation and annexation, exerted by the State over its satellites, its accompanying nomad or guerrilla groups, which will make up the interest of the corresponding analyses.) It is in the magnificent set piece on blacksmiths and metallurgy that we find the demonstration of a full-blown Deleuzian ideological analysis, one based on the dualisms of Hjelmslev's linguistics and which finds its strength in the insistence by Deleuze and Guattari on exteriority. For not only is the war machine "exterior" to the State; in a sense everything theorized in *Mille plateaux* is a phenomenon of exteriority, since the language of interiority, subjectivity, identity, the warm night in which "all cows are gray," is itself one of the polemic targets of Deleuzian thinking. But exteriority, now suddenly meaning "relationship", opens a given phenomenon up to the outside. This then relates the individual phenomenon—whether it be a text of some sort, or this or that social individuality—to larger external forces.

The traditional vocabulary of ideological analysis is, to be sure, a relatively limited one, in which for any such individual phenomenon—a text, an idea, or even a social class—equivalents are sought, and a correlation is meant to be established between this or that aspect of the superstructure and conditions in the base of infrastructure. The doctrine of externality usefully

---

[9] The quotation—"Il m'est bien évident que j'ai toujours été race inférieure"—is from Arthur Rimbaud, "Mauvais sang," *Une saison en enfer*, in *Oeuvre complètes*, Paris: Pleiade, 1963, 220.

[10] Gilles Deleuze and Félix Guattari, *Kafka: Pour une littérature mineure*, Paris: Minuit, 1975.

transcodes all this and gives us a more supple, provisional way of dealing with the operation of transcoding, in which it is no longer a question of establishing some simple one-to-one correlation between two already existing entities (such as literature and society, for instance), but rather of showing how any given text knows lines of flight out beyond itself, being apparently autonomous yet in its very structure carrying a kind of referentiality, a kind of movement out of itself to something else.

Hjelmslev's linguistics is a more suitable model for this process than such widely accepted forms of semiotic or linguistic analysis as Saussure's because its two planes include four terms and are related to each other only by exteriority, by a specific or contingent intersection, rather than by some deeper, pre-established harmony. Thus the two planes of content and expression are themselves each organized into oppositions between substance and form: already the old distinction between form and content is defamiliarized and renewed by this violent reassignment of each to different zones within the linguistic phenomenon. Content now has its own logic and inner dynamic, just as expression does: there is a form and substance of content, just as there is a form and substance of expression. The coordination of the two planes yields a model in which the Deleuzian flux (the content) can now be punctually articulated in a given code (the expression), yet in such a way that these can be analyzed separately as distinct moments which find their combination historically, as an event rather than a structure. Deleuze indeed insists strongly on a significant distinction between connexion and *conjugaison* (conjunction): the latter term belongs to the side of the State, and foretells a kind of organic capture in which the autonomy of the two planes is finally lost; "connexion," however, would designate the provisionality of the meeting and the way in which each plane continues to remain exterior to the other, despite the productive interaction between them (*MiP*, 636; 510).

It is a complex model, which is best conveyed by illustration and example, particularly this striking one of metallurgy, in which for the first and only time in the work a properly Hjelmslevian table is reproduced (*MiP*, 518; 416).

For the question turns on the nature of the relationship between the general form of the nomadic war machine (which can be found in types of science and art fully as much as in Genghis Khan's social institutions) and the specific phenomenon of the blacksmith in traditional society. Oddly enough, it is the social reality of the blacksmith which is designated as the plane of content, and the war machine that of expression, perhaps because the war machine articulates the form which governs the organization of the specific social reality of metallurgic production.

Yet how can blacksmiths and metallurgy—presumably a sedentary *métier* like those of modern society and unlike the activity of, say, hunters—be characterized as nomadic? We have to look at the material relations implied in this peculiar type of matter, whose extraction, unlike that of other elements such as wood and stone, requires the linkage of fields, mountains, forest, and desert. It is this unique specificity of the raw material that both gives it a relational privilege over other natural elements and confers a social privilege on the smiths who work it. Indeed, these pages include a remarkable "praise" of metal itself as "what raises to consciousness something only hidden or buried in other raw materials and other operations" (*MiP*, 511; 410). Metal is thus seen as matter par excellence, the *machinic phylum* itself, the very source of Wilhelm Worringer's idea of a "nonorganic life" (which will also play a significant role in the first *Cinéma* book[11]). Metalworking is necessarily something more than a technique; it is a relationship to the singularities, the contingent "events" of raw material. And the blacksmith must somehow "follow" those contingencies—it is in that sense that he is more nomadic than other kinds of workers. Nomadism, in other words, is the process of following contingencies, events of matter, *haecceities* (to use the medieval expression, which Deleuze glosses at some length), across the body of the earth: the blacksmith's work is thus the specific equivalent or *analogon* of this more general process, whence his magic power and prestige in tribal societies of all kinds.

But the Hjelmslev model intervenes precisely here, in the fact that both the work of the blacksmith and the functioning of the nomadic war machine have their specific externality; that is to say, both are defined in an essential relationship to an element, a raw material, a geographical context. Thus while each is the form-term of their specific planes of content and expression, each also has a substance-term. The substance pole of the metal-lurgist lies, then, in metal itself, as the very epitome of the phylum, the flux of matter as such; the substance-term of the war machine is smooth space as such (extrapolated then into desert or ocean, and governed by a movement distinct from movement from point to point, which Deleuze characterizes as turbulence—vortices, whirlpools, eddies—a swirling which is an event and not a line drawn from place to place). These pages, rich with detail, are among the most exciting moments in *Mille plateaux* and should be analyzed at greater length; I have merely wanted to show what the operation of ideological coordination between social form and specific social institutions looks like in Deleuze, and how this particular analysis, on the side of nomadry, is a good deal more complex and interesting than the corresponding noological reading of forms associated with the State.

Now I want to move from the narrower question of the relationship to Marx to the broader question of the relationship to History, it being

---

[11] See Gilles Deleuze, *Cinéma 1: L'Image-Mouvement*, Paris: Minuit, 1983, 75–76.

understood that the test of such a relationship will come with the capacity of the Deleuzian conceptual apparatus to register (and in this case, since we are dealing with texts dating from 1972 and 1980, to *predict*) the novel structures of late capitalism—or, in other words, our own actuality. The noological inquiry, however, will pass through questions of representation not in the sense in which some very eminent contemporary studies of history have interrogated historical texts for their deeper narrative paradigms, but rather for the larger non-narrative structures that make a Deleuzian metahistory possible in the first place. You will already have suspected that chief among such non-narrative structures is that of dualism itself, or duality: it was already implicit in *L'Anti-Oedipe* in the form of the great opposition between revolution and fascism which constituted one of that book's starting points and one of its basic conceptual dilemmas. But *L'Anti-Oedipe*'s machinery complexifies this particular opposition and adds new terms at every step, denying it the status of a mythic or cosmological antithesis that the great opposition in *Mille plateaux* between the Nomads and the State seems everywhere on the point of asserting. But is the tension between the desiring-machines and the body without organs of that cosmological type? It can seem so when we retranslate it into the terms of the great opposition between the molecular and the molar. And what of the figure of the schizophrenic (in *L'Anti-Oedipe*)? As a zero degree, it does not really seem opposed to anything in that dualistic way, not even to its political opposite number, the paranoid.

Indeed, I believe that it is the unifying will of *Capitalisme et schizophrénie*, its drive towards monism, which is paradoxically the source of the later dualisms. For the principle of desire itself would be a monism: everything is libidinal investment, everything is desire; there is nothing which is not desire, nothing outside of desire. This means, of course, that fascism is a desire (something we now know well, but which was a more scandalous assertion at the time), bureaucracy is desire, the State is desire, capitalism preeminently desire, even the much maligned Oedipus complex has to correspond to a certain desire in order to take on its inveterate authority.

But how does dualism emerge from monism, when it would seem that the very vocation of monism lay in the rebuking of all those traditional dualisms and in their replacement by a single principle? It is a numerological question, finally, and Deleuzian numerology, or at least the return of the numerological throughout these pages, may afford an answer. If the mission of the One lies in subordinating illusory pairs, doubles, oppositions of all kinds, then it turns out that we are still in dualism, for the task is conceived as the working through of the opposition—the dualism—between dualism and monism. The One may overcome the Two, but it also produces it: it may then counterattack from the other end of the series and seek to undermine the Dual by the Multiple, or by Multiplicity itself—many multiplicities (one, two, three … many Vietnams) as opposed to the One of the Multiple itself.[12] Indeed, the whole dialectic becomes intensified if we go even further (as our authors do in *Mille plateaux*) and suggest that Number itself has its opposite in the Nondenumerable. This is their remarkable solution to the question of minorities within capitalism, it being understood that the solution also bears on that even more fundamental antithesis developed throughout *Mille plateaux* between major and minor (royal science versus minor science, for example) and which is, as I've said, best known programmatically from the formulation of a minor literature and a minor language in the Kafka book. Here is the fundamental statement:

> What defines a minority is thus not number, it is the relationships within number. A minority may be numerous or even infinite: just like a majority. What distinguishes the two is that the relationship within number constitutes an ensemble in the case of the majority, a completed or an infinite ensemble but one that can always be denumerated or counted; whereas a minority is defined as a non-denumerable ensemble, whatever the actual number of its elements. What characterizes the nondenumerable is neither ensemble nor elements: it is *connection* [which, as I have already said, Deleuze now wishes to distinguish sharply from conjunction], the "and" that is produced between the elements, between the ensembles, and that belongs to neither of them, which escapes them and constitutes a line of flight … The role of the minority is to bring out the power of the nondenumerable even when it consists in only one member. (*MiP*, 587, 588; 469, 470)[13]

It is an ingenious solution, which reinforces and theorizes the priority of what is outside the system (minorities, *hors-classe*) over and against what is still inside it (the working class); as such, it is perhaps more congenial to the current climate of identity politics at the same time that it clings to an older political value of subversion and contestation in order to rewrite it and give it a new theoretical justification—"the emergence of a foreign language within language itself" (*MiP*, 638; 512), as another formulation of the

---

[12] But we also need to register Deleuze's dissent from such formulas, as in *Foucault*, Paris: Minuit, 1986: "The essential feature of this notion lies in the fact that the construction of a substantive like 'multiple' ceases to be a predicate in opposition to the one, or attributable to a subject identifiable as One. Multiplicity must be utterly indifferent to the traditional problems of the many and the one … There is no one and no multiple or many … There are only the rare multiplicities, with their singular points, their empty places for whoever comes briefly to function as a subject within them … Multiplicity is neither axiomatic nor typological but topological" (23). Would it be impertinent after that to suggest that the "opposite" of this new kind of multiplicity might well turn out to be the dualism?

[13] On the English "and," see 124, n. 26.

minor puts it. But who does not see at the same time that this dialectical emergence of something other from out of the vexed system of number (one, dual, multiple, many multiplicities) also reinstates the dualism of number as such, by positing the new opposition of Number and the Nondenumerable?

I want now to make a few final remarks about *Mille plateaux* in the light of these issues, which are certainly not clarified by the extraordinarily complex and abstract, lapidary and formal conclusions to that book, where the theoretical materials (strata, assemblages, rhizomes, the body without organs, deterritorialization, the abstract machine) are laid out in such a way as to make the question of monism and dualism quite undecidable. I do want to correct the impression that the opposition between the State and the Nomads is the dominant dualism here: certainly, it is the most dramatic and the most mythic (if I can put it that way, meaning thereby also the most susceptible to narration). I also suspect that, being more accessible, these chapters are perhaps more widely read and influential than the others. But even here the issue is complicated by a terminological slippage which sometimes replaces "nomadism" with "war machine," despite the desperate and strenuously argued qualification that the aim and telos of this war machine is not at all "war" in the conventional sense.

But this may furnish the occasion for saying why the emergence of this or that dualism should be a cause for complaint or critique in the first place. Dualism is, I believe, the strong form of ideology as such, which may of course disguise its dual structure under any number of complicated substitutions. This is so, I want to assert, because it is the ultimate form of the ethical binary, which is thus always secretly at work within ideology. Thus one can say, with Nietzsche, that the opposition between Good and Evil (itself derived from that between Self and Other) is always noxious and to be eradicated at the source by way of transcendence into another mode of thinking, "beyond good and evil." This does not mean, as the fainthearted or the bourgeois liberals believe, that morals in general are to be done away with and that henceforth everything is permitted, but rather that the very idea of the Other—always transmitted through concepts of evil—is to be done away with (perhaps along with the very idea of the Self, as so many religions have taught). In passing, one can then even more strongly deplore the revival of disciplines such as ethics today, after the ebbing of that modern period in which such disciplines had proved utterly contradictory and sterile, academic in the bad sense.

What the ethical binary now means for other kinds of dualism is that it always tempts us to reinsert the good/evil axis into conceptual areas supposed to be free of it, and to call for judgment where none is appropriate. Nowhere is this more obvious than in the dualisms of Deleuze and Guattari, where the reader feels perpetually solicited to take sides with the Schizo against the Paranoid (or the body without organs) and with the Nomads against the State. But the example of the war machine may demonstrate how misguided such identification would be. The Deleuzian argument indeed turns on the reassurance that the nomadic war machine does not have war as its ultimate end or content, a proposition drawn from Paul Virilio's analysis of the contemporary "military-industrial complex," where the latter plausibly suggests the insertion of military technology—constant capital—as a new axiom, so to speak, of contemporary capitalism that now requires its incorporation as an economic function and no longer as a means of defense (*MiP*, 583–584; 467–468).[14] It is the argument with which we have grown familiar, namely, that military spending in and of itself (and not for any actual use or warlike purpose) turned out to be one of the principal post-Keynesian ways of solving the Great Depression. But on the level of judgment, or even libidinal investment, this merit of the late-capitalist war machine to solve economic crises rather than to flourish by way of new wars is probably not the same kind of endorsement as what we are asked to accord the Nomads when we decipher their hidden mission as a resistance against the State rather than as the "scourge of God" and the source of bloody raids for their own sake. To what level of icy historical contemplation the move beyond dualism, the move "beyond good and evil," raises us must be an open question; but the example shows at the very least the way in which the ethical solicitations of dualism persist, even within the most complicated continua between various phenomena.

Still, the dualism we have been looking at here—Nomads against the State—is a very late theme of this book, emerging only after some four hundred pages on other matters (less dualistic, those, and impossible to summarize, let alone to examine, here). Much of this material turns on the various forms of reterritorialization provoked by the capitalist axiomatic, and, after a long doctrinal opening about the central Hjelmslev linguistic system on which the book is based, takes the form of various accounts of the production of intensities, the capacity of the properties of phenomena to know transformation, and so forth; intensities and transformations are indeed something like that "foreign language" within our own language which mysteriously passes across the surface (like a minority, like a war machine) and then disappears again. I think that the ultimate appearance of the great, mythic State/Nomads opposition is a way of recontaining all this complex and heterogeneous material: something like a narrative and even, as I've suggested, an ideological frame that allows us to reorder it into simpler patterns. Whether that reordering is possible conceptually I am uncertain: the dense pages with which the book concludes give no particular confidence that the task could ever be carried to any satisfying conclusion.

---

[14] And on Virilio, 479, n. 64.

And this is why I think the work includes its own methodological clues, of what I hesitate to call an aesthetic nature. (But we should note that Deleuze and Guattari themselves conclude *Mille plateaux* with something like an aesthetic slow movement in the chapter on the *lisse* and the *strié*.) The clue here lies in the complex discussion of music, based on Pierre Boulez's theories, in which a dualism of slowness and speed emerges as a kind of pattern in its own right, and which can minimally authorize us to see the whole book as an immense musical score, whose alternative dualisms and monisms must also be apprehended as a pulsation of this text, and a vast interplay of modes of writing, as they recommend for reading Nietzsche, where

> the problem is not so much that of a writing of fragmentation. It is rather that of swiftnesses and decelerations: not writing slowly or swiftly, but rather such that writing itself, and everything else, should be the production of velocities and slownesses between particles. No form can resist it, no character or subject can survive in it. Zarathustra knows only fast or slow tempi, and the eternal return, the life of the eternal return is the first great concrete liberation of nonpulsed time. (*MiP*, 329; 269)

It is a rehearsal of the distinction between the two great forms of time, the Aion and the Chronos (*MiP*, 320; 262),[15] which will recur so productively in the *Cinéma* books.

It is tempting to conclude that dualism is an unstable structure, whose ultimate fulfilment must always be pragmatic rather than epistemological, performative rather than constative. The ethical binary into which it tempts and snares us then transcends itself in great prophecy, where a whole collectivity is summoned to change and to mutation (Nietzsche's transcendence of ethics was always a turning of the binary structure back against itself). Yet the oppositional structure was also detected, in structuralism and semiotics, within the most microscopic or molecular cells of meaning itself: this line of flight takes us on through the dissolution of stable substances and their reified concepts and on into process and Deleuzian flows or fluxions as such. There is, finally, the inner energy of the binary as sheer conflict: here we pause on Clausewitz, who affirmed war to be a duel, before streaming on headlong into Hegel on contradiction as the inner law of the universe and Marx on class struggle as the dynamic of History itself: strife, the Eris of the ancients, which has triumphantly absorbed its contrary into the unity of opposites.

---

[15] For an extraordinary and pathbreaking exposition of Deleuze's concepts of time and history, see Jay Lampert, *Deleuze and Guattari's Philosophy of History*, London: Continuum, 2006.

Chapter 6

History and Class Consciousness as an Unfinished Project

The actuality of Georg Lukács has in recent years always seemed to founder on two concepts: the defense of literary realism and the idea of totality. When one considers that these are virtually the two most important and central conceptual achievements of his life's work, no little discouragement tends to surround the project of "reviving" him. The story of their relationship is generally told as follows: the extreme-left "workerism" of *History and Class Consciousness* (1923) was condemned by the Comintern as idealistic (it seems clear that the attack on epistemological "reflection theory" in this book[1] was the principal motive for its scandalized reception by the party). Lukács bowed to these criticisms and, as a result of this disaster as well as of the failure of his initiative in Hungarian politics (the so-called Blum Theses, largely regarded as a forerunner of the later official strategy of the popular front), withdrew from political activity. He concentrated instead on aesthetics: the well-known essays on nineteenth-century realism and on the historical novel were the immediate results of his new orientation. Moreover, they are marked by the very reflection theory—adequation of the subject's concept to the object in the outside world—which he had denounced in *History and Class Consciousness*.[2]

---

[1] *Geschichte und Klassenbewusstsein*, Neuwied: Luchterhand, 1977, 387–393; in English, *History and Class Consciousness*, trans. Rodney Livingstone, Cambridge, MA: MIT Press, 1971, 199–204. Future references to this work are denoted *HCC*; all page references will cite the German edition first, followed by the English translation.

[2] See *Studies in European Realism*, trans. Edith Bone, New York: Grosset and Dunlap, 1964; *Writer and Critic: And Other Essays*, ed. and trans. Arthur D. Kahn, New York: Grosset and Dunlap, 1974; and *The Historical Novel*, trans. Hannah and Stanley Mitchell, Lincoln: University of Nebraska, 1983. In the 1950s Lukács reformulated many of these positions in *Realism in Our Time: Literature and the Class Struggle*, trans. John and Necke Mander, New York: Harper and Row, 1971.

There are textual problems with this now conventional narrative about Lukács. For one thing, aesthetic problems make episodic appearances throughout *History and Class Consciousness*[3] (as they could not but do, given Lukács's lifelong preoccupation with the aesthetic). More than that, one entire paragraph of the earlier book, which deals with "journalism" as the "apogee of capitalist reification" (*HCC*, 275; 100),[4] is not merely an obvious allusion to Balzac's *Illusions Perdues* but virtually a synopsis of the article he will later devote to it, one of the fundamental statements of the "realist period" and the realist aesthetic. Textual inconsistencies of this kind do not prove anything, but they alert us to the possibility of conceptualizing the relationship between the idea of "totality" in *History and Class Consciousness* and the later account of realism in some other way than as break, substitution, compensation, formation. Indeed, in my opinion,[5] what seems more plausible is rather the continuity between these two doctrines and indeed their inextricable philosophical relationship.

I. Lukács's Reception

If that remains a provocative proposition it is because what has traditionally separated the notion of totality and the concept of realism from one another is their *readership*. The political and theoretical activists who found *History and Class Consciousness* stimulating and endlessly suggestive are often the same people who find the cultural premises of the essays on realism dull and traditional. How can the prescient and systemic analysis of reification in late capitalism in the former book (along with its ringing affirmation of the epistemological priority of the working class and its unique capacity to break the process of reification and to institute radically new kinds of social relations) be reconciled (1) with the backwards-looking celebration of the tradition of the nineteenth-century *bourgeois* novel and (2) with what looks like a call for socialist society to absorb the bourgeois cultural tradition rather than to project and invent some new one? Brecht's well-known formula about the "bad new things" that we ought to prefer to the "good old things" (*das schlechte Neue* and *das gute Alte*) did as much damage to later Lukács as the Comintern did to the earlier work, and far more succinctly.

---

[3] See for example the remarks on German aesthetics (316–319; 137–139), on landscape painting (340–341; 157–158), and on classical tragedy (360–361; 175–176).

[4] Compare Lukács, "Balzac: Lost Illusions," in *Studies in European Realism*, 47–64.

[5] Expressed in *Marxism and Form*, Princeton: Princeton University Press, 1971, 162–163; and see also the invocation of *History and Class Consciousness* at the end of my essay "Third World Literature in the Era of Multinational Capitalism," in *Social Text*, Num. 15, Fall 1986, 65–88, for crosslight on the present study.

We must therefore look more closely at the doxa and the prejudices at work in Lukács's reception, for it is necessarily within that force field and against that resistance that any new conception of Lukács and his work will have to make its way. From the perspective of literary and cultural "taste," for example, Lukács's account of realism might well seem to stand as a generational statement, his "contemporary" writers (in *Soul and Forms*) having melted back into the cultural bric-a-brac of a turn-of-the-century Central Europe, while his major exhibits—Balzac, Tolstoy—have the unpleasant mustiness of the school classic. Even where the Victorian revival seems in full swing, his way with them does not look much like ours (a full-dress deconstruction of Mrs. Gaskell, for instance, producing a "text" that looks more like Philippe Sollers than like Dickens). Lukács's canon, meanwhile, carries a strong moralizing (itself Victorian) sense of duty about it. In a period that concerns itself philosophically with "pleasure" or "desire," the valorization of these long realistic novels sometimes strikes the reader as a reinforcement of all those strategic mechanisms of repression Lukács may be supposed to have made himself undergo in order to survive.[6] On the other hand, even this perception may need modification in a period—sometimes loosely called the postmodern—in which the very objects of Lukács's own principled distaste—the "great moderns"—have themselves become school classics to be repudiated by contemporary artists.

One sometimes feels that it is not Lukács's "taste" so much as his language, his conceptual and analytic machinery, which is old-fashioned. How else to understand the persistence with which his defense of realism is misread and credited to an ideal of photographic accuracy (let alone to "socialist realism" or Stalinist normativity)? In this situation one always needs to insist, not merely on Lukács's own understanding of his work on realism as a *critique* of Stalinist aesthetics, but also on the code-word function of the negative term "naturalism" as a tactical euphemism in the Moscow of the 1930s, very precisely for "socialist realism." Something may even be gained, in our own time, with its rather different intellectual and cultural priorities, by insisting on his constitutive identification of realism with narrative and storytelling. "Photographic realism," what he called naturalism, is in his aesthetic disparaged very precisely on the basis of its non- or anti-narrative structure, on the symptomatic formal influence within it of the sheerly descriptive. As for modernism—in its initial historical guise of the symbolic or the symbolistic—it is not merely the other "extreme" deplored by some *juste milieu*, but is rather grasped by Lukács as the dialectical opposite of naturalism and as its structural correlative, its

---

[6] Adorno's diagnosis, in "Erpresste Versöhnung," translated as "Reconciliation under Duress," in *Aesthetics and Politics*, London: Verso, 1977, 151–176; yet even Lukács's earlier works are imbued with a spirit of ethical puritanism.

other face. (The later views on emergent "experimental" and avant-garde literature, although more complexly argued, continue to be elaborated within this initial dialectical framework.)

What becomes clear when Lukács's positions are grasped in this interrelated and dialectical way is that their philosophical underpinnings remain those of *History and Class Consciousness* and in particular specifically presuppose the theory of reification. Lukács's conception of reification is best initially grasped as a synthesis of Marx and Weber.[7] It is a development of Marx's description, not merely of commodity fetishism and exchange but of commodity *form* itself, which is now enlarged to include Weber's account of the rationalization process; of the Taylorization not merely of the work process but also of the mind, of the scientific disciplines fully as much as of the psyche and the senses. The operative paradox of this first extraordinary *systemic* account of the logic of capitalism lies in the way in which it insists on extreme fragmentation as a social norm. It attempts to project a process which separates, compartmentalizes, specializes, and disperses: a force which at one and the same time operates uniformly over everything and makes of heterogeneity a homogeneous and standardizing power. This is the sense in which, in *History and Class Consciousness*, the prophetic invocation of some radically different class logic—the praxis as well as the new epistemological capacities of the industrial working class—stages a counterforce. This allows us to imagine a collective project not merely capable of breaking the multiple systemic webs of reification, but which *must* do so in order to realize itself. Just as the continuing preoccupation of a great range of contemporary theories with what Lukács first described as reification has scarcely been appreciated,[8] so also the fundamental message of "dereification" which *History and Class Consciousness* bears—"history is the history of the unceasing overthrow of the objective forms that shape the life of man" (*HCC*, 372; 186)—has only intermittently been audible.

But in the aesthetic works, "realism" is described as having the same function as "the consciousness of the proletariat" in *History and Class Consciousness*. It is the bearer of the force of dereification, which suggests that our stereotypical idea of Lukácsean realism as a "form" in its own right, and a constraining and antiquated one at that, may not be altogether accurate after all. The dialectic of naturalism and modernism recapitulates the fate of the object-subject relationship under intensifying Taylorization: the instrumental dismemberment and strip-mining of the object world, such that only laborious local and technical descriptions can at length be provided for

---

[7] See *The Political Unconscious*, Ithaca: Cornell University Press, 1981, 220.

[8] What Paul de Man analyzed in terms of "thematization", for example, seems to me very closely related; the topic is surely a central one for any "conversation" between Marxism and deconstruction.

it; the hierarchical specialization of the mental and psychic faculties such that only those excluded from "instrumental Reason" and marginalized are henceforth available for the now trivialized operations of culture. So far so good: Adorno and Horkheimer, it will be said, showed us as much, and in finer-grained detail, but managed to do so while in the process dispensing with Lukács's embarrassing and normative conception of realism.

This is the crucial moment in any approach to Lukács's aesthetic, for it is the moment of the fundamental misreading. It is generally assumed that the subject-object relationship is one of Lukács's basic conceptual categories: various models of a split between the subject and object in modern times seem to make up the bulk of his diagnostic of modern culture. It is then presumed that Lukács's "positive" next step will necessarily involve some restoration of the "unity" between the subject and the object, some invocation of a "reconciliation" between these fragmented and damaged zones of being. Concepts which imply such reconciliation are then quickly evaluated by conventional wisdom as nostalgic or Utopian in all the bad senses.

But this is not at all the move Lukács makes. His dialectic is a good deal more unpredictable than that and does not laboriously restore the mechanical "synthesis" (also wrongly attributed to Hegel). For what springs into being after the account of the distribution, by reification, of a whole range of structural distances between subject and object (and within them) is not their reunification. Rather, and quite unexpectedly, it is the concept of "totality," and along with it, as we will argue here, the concept of "narrative" in the aesthetic realm. The conventional expectation, in other words, of some equally conventional synthesis between subject and object is dramatically displaced. Hitherto unsuspected dimensions of the problem— "interrelationship" and "process"—are suddenly disclosed as features which transform the new solution beyond recognition.

2. Reconnecting Totality and Realism

This may also be the moment to secure some more concrete sense of the connection, in Lukács's thought, between totality and narrative, and, beyond them, between the preoccupations of *History and Class Consciousness* and those of the later works on realism. The problem of totality first enters narrative construction, as it were, vertically: it becomes visible when we begin to ask ourselves questions about the ultimate determinants of a given act or experience. The latter are generally understood as the most basic raw materials of the novel, which stages a character as an actor in a desperate struggle to achieve something (Balzac), or as the unhappy recipient of a variety of external forces and necessities (Alfred Döblin), or as the vehicle and recording apparatus for a complex new and as yet unnamed feeling about things (Virginia Woolf), or even as a perplexed self-interrogation about a lack of feeling or of desire altogether (Flaubert). What psychoanalysis has taught us (since Lukács) is the degree to which other people, and in particular family structure and history, *in reality* still actively participate in these seemingly individual passions or ambitions. What the Marxist theory of ideology has taught us is the degree to which whole collectivities, with their ideological values and mystifications, also co-participate in the way we conceive and stage such passions or ambitions. What the Marxist theory of capitalist society has taught us, in addition, is the way in which the very possibility of conceiving of a certain passionate value or of being capable of feeling a certain unique emotion is dependent on the labor of other people and on a social differentiation of production within which those particular human possibilities are available or on the other hand excluded.

But from the point of view of immediacy (in Hegel's sense) all those multiple determinants—which are in reality a very great range of *other people*, and *their* acts and passions—are absent from the scene of the novelistic act or encounter, or from the room or landscape in which a given feeling or *Stimmung* declares itself. Why we do not normally notice their absence, and the radical incompleteness of their presentation, in the everyday reading of what may still seem realistic novels to us, Lukács himself does not directly address. However, the Sartre of *What Is Literature?* (yet another now old-fashioned aesthetic text) may be appealed to for a description of the way in which social class provides a readership with boundaries of *familiarity*, with a ready tolerance for all the things and realities which do not have to be said (and which can therefore be ignored), with some properly ideological sense of when a given act or experience grasped within our own class perspective is felt to be "complete" and to "need no further explanation."

The "aspiration to totality", famously evoked by Lukács in *History and Class Consciousness* (358; 174),[9] would then in the narrative realm involve a refusal of these habitual limits and boundaries and even a defamiliarization of our habitual sense of the recognition and the understanding of human acts and passions. It projects *interrelationship* as an aesthetic by way of the tendential sense that in order to show what a given event is in reality, the novelist must somehow overcome the presentational constraints of the immediate, and *somehow* suggest the active influence and effects of that whole range of social and historical forces without which this unique event is finally inconceivable. The word "somehow" here marks the status of this expanded and "totalizing" conception of realism as an ideal, and indeed, as

---

[9] The German reads "eine Intention auf die Totalität der Gesellschaft." Husserl's technical term "intentionality" opens a description of the perceptual function of the concept which is missing from the weaker English word.

an aesthetic form or language as yet unrealized (and realizable, as well, in a great variety of unpredictable and as yet unimaginable ways).

"Somehow" is also the place in which the requirement of narrative as such will emerge. For it will not have gone unnoticed that the description of some new narrative totalization that has just been offered bears an uncanny family likeness to many of the aspirations to totality of modernism itself, and very precisely to those decried by Lukács, to those fallen into period oblivion fully as much as those whose luster has in our time redoubled, to Jules Romains and Dos Passos fully as much as to Joyce and to Robert Musil. The notion of totality may therefore mark the extreme point of Lukács's modernity, including the sense of its boundary or limit. It marks the moment beyond which his thought is unwilling to pass, returning to a conception of interrelationship which seems more traditional since it includes the requirement of transparency and the possibility of *thinking* such connections.

For the totalizing forms of the "great moderns" are imperatives to think totality—and very specifically the complexities of urban and industrial totalities—in a situation in which they have become ungraspable, and in which the sheer simultaneity of unrelated destinies in the city, the sheer contingency of random meetings and chance intersections, suggests deeper interrelationships which constitutively escape individual experience and the "point of view" of any individual actor or participant. The moderns, however, sharpen this tension by their repudiation of the older totalizing points of view, of the older omniscient novelist or even privileged witness. Even Proust's first-person narration secretly but systematically undoes its own structure.

Meanwhile, the formal presupposition of all the modernisms that totality is irreconcilable with the individual psychic subject, and even further, that any conception of totality as a form of consciousness, of total knowing or of some privileged subject position, is vitiated. (But then how can the very *concept* of totality be conceived in the first place?) The next steps are the properly poststructuralist theoretical and philosophical arguments against *all* forms of totality, above all, that of Lukács in *History and Class Consciousness*.

3. Lukács versus Modernism

Modernist totalizing works are, however, specifically excluded by Lukács as formal solutions to the modern dilemma. This is not merely because they designate themselves as necessary failures. In that, they would merely be symptomatic of the antinomies of bourgeois consciousness in general as *History and Class Consciousness* famously outlines them (in particular, the contradiction between increasing fragmentation and specialization and a "whole" becomes spurious and mystical). But to say so is also to suggest that such formal failures—which are also epistemological ones—can be *explained*, even if they cannot (in the framework of capitalist society) be *corrected*. One has the feeling, therefore, that for Lukács, these modernisms would again become (critical) realisms had they been able to stage the limits of their characters' experience—in other words, what structurally blocks *narrative* as such in the modern works—within a perspective within which such limits would become the subject and the problem of the works themselves; just as in Balzac, Hulot's sexual passions become the object of an inquiry which must finally appeal to history and the social in order for their representation to become somehow "complete."[10] What happens, however, is that in these texts narrative failure itself is reified and becomes an object of aesthetic contemplation in its own right. The result is Lukács's rhetoric of decadence, which we are free to deplore, providing we understand that it is not merely the instrument for moral and political censure, but presupposes, as a kind of shorthand, the whole systematic philosophical armature of *History and Class Consciousness* itself.

Two features of that larger analysis may be recalled on the occasion of the modernist canon. They offer descriptive possibilities which do not necessarily and automatically entail excommunication (in any case, a principled hostility occasionally notices features of an object invisible to its enthusiasts: one thinks, for example, of Yvor Winters's not unrelated diagnosis of the irrationality of the structures of modernist poetic language[11]). "Contingency" is in that sense one of the crucial features of Lukács's discussion of the limits of bourgeois thought which returns in the analysis of bourgeois or modernist narrative with genuine analytic power (we will return to other of its possibilities at the end of the present essay). Contingency is as it were the inner blind spot of bourgeois consciousness, or of the existential experience of capitalism. In the twin forms of chance and of "crisis" or "catastrophe" (*HCC*, 276–280; 101–105),[12] it marks the moment at which events that are meaningful socially or historically turn incomprehensible, absurd, or meaningless faces to individuals, who can henceforth only ratify their bewilderment with the name of "accident" or of well-nigh "natural" convulsion and upheaval. That in bourgeois science these "irrationals" or unthinkables become themselves the object of new forms of scientific inquiry and specialization—in probability theory and statistics, for example, or in crisis theory or catastrophe theory—is perhaps a rather different development from the second feature of Lukács's analysis, which designates the blind spot of the system itself, and the incapacity to grasp totality as a meaningful whole.

---

[10] See Lukács, *Writer and Critic*, 139.

[11] "The Experimental School in American Poetry," in *In Defense of Reason*, New York: Swallow Press and William Morrow, 1947, 30–74.

[12] Compare Lukács, *Studies in European Realism*, 55–58.

This is Lukács's theory of absolutes, in which the entire system is as it were reified and thematized in the form of a metaphysical or symbolic essentialism or foundationalism (to use the language of contemporary philosophy). "The absolute is nothing but the fixation of thought, it is the projection into myth of the intellectual failure to understand reality concretely as a historical process" (*HCC*, 374; 187).[13] The full weight of this diagnosis will, however, not be fully appreciable if we limit it to the obvious cases of religious or metaphysical absolutes. Lukács has indeed in mind all philosophies or systems as such: vitalism or *Lebensphilosophie*, the doctrine of "economic man" or of innate aggressivity, all secular notions of the "meaning" of either nature or human nature, even at some outer limit, existentialism itself when its anti-philosophical project imperceptibly shifts back into a philosophy in its own right (the "absurd"). Contemporary philosophy has, indeed, set itself the task of unmasking such secular absolutes, which inhabit a whole range of thoughts that no longer wear the trappings or strike the poses of the metaphysical or the religious in their older forms. Its designation of them as "essentialisms" or "foundationalisms" may, however, risk reabsolutizing them in a new way, by staging them as philosophical positions in their own right, and thereby excluding the social context from which their compensatory function as projection becomes visible.

What is, in our present context, equally significant is the operation of analogous dynamics in the aesthetic realm, and in particular the existence of formal "absolutes" in the work of art (which have nothing to do with philosophical conceptuality). Such are, for example, the various forms of symbolic totalization which confer on the (modernist) work of art its appearance as a thing complete in itself, an object which is somehow "cause of itself" and the intrinsic foundation of its own meaning, without external presuppositions or extrinsic references. Only the academic canonization of the modernist "classics" has made such issues seem less relevant than they once were, since one rarely questions the things one takes for granted about their deeper reasons for being and the justifications of their own existences. Today, however, when the modernist moment itself—in full postmodernism—seems to have receded into some radically different past, the question as to the unique and historically original natures of such works may again be expected to preoccupy us in a different way. On such questions Lukács's principled philosophical problematization of the modern confers articulation and content.

---

[13] See also 290–291, 381; 114, 194.

The War on Totality

For the moment, however, it is less with modernism as such than with the deeper inseparability between Lukács's conception of realism and his notion of totality that we are concerned, an argument that now commits us to confront a whole contemporary, poststructural, or even postmodern hostility to the very spirit of slogans like "totality" or "totalization" (Sartre's later version). Jean-François Lyotard's counterslogan, "Let us wage a war on totality,"[14] is a useful and expressive starting point for the exploration of these positions, which conflate intellectual authority (the subject that *knows* totality), social relationships (a totalizing picture of society that represses difference, or differentiation), politics (a single-party politics, as opposed to the pluralism of the so-called new social movements), ideology or philosophy (Hegelian idealization, which represses matter, the Other, or Nature), aesthetics (the old organic work of art or concrete universal, as opposed to the contemporary fragment or aleatory "work"), and ethics and psychoanalysis (the old "centered subject," the ideal of a unified personality or ego and a unified life project). In the *koiné* of contemporary theoretical debate, the name Lukács has become interchangeable with those of Hegel and Stalin as the word that illustrates the enormity of all these values by uniting them in a single program. It would be frivolous, but not wrong, to observe that the undifferentiated identification of these distinct positions with each other is itself something of a caricature of what is generally attributed to "totalizing thought" at its worst.

One argues with the specific levels or aspects of such a global position (as I will very selectively do in what follows); one does not, however, "argue" with the *Zeitgeist*, whose general thought or feeling this is. Rather, one analyzes that—which is to say, the conflation, the global identification and repudiation—*historically*, with a view towards understanding why it is that today so many intellectuals feel this way and are committed to these slogans and this language. It is a development which is clearly linked to the destiny of Marxism intellectually as well as politically in our own time. It is linked very specifically to the fate of Marxism in France, in many ways, since the war, the very heartland of so-called Western Marxism.

The "demarxification" of France, whose origins one can seek alternately in the CPF's decisions in May 1968, in the emergence of an

---

[14] Jean-François Lyotard, *The Postmodern Condition*, trans. Geoffrey Bennington and Brian Bassumi, Minneapolis: University of Minnesota Press, 1984, 82. The complexity of Lyotard's position can, however, only fully be appreciated when it is understood that "totality," in this programmatic slogan, designates both the concept and the thing itself. And see, for an illuminating review of Lyotard's work and career, Perry Anderson, *The Origins of Postmodernity*, London: Verso, 1998, 24–36.

"extraparliamentary Left" in the early 1960s, or in the launching of the Common Program in 1972, seems, as far as the intellectuals are concerned, virtually complete. It is no doubt the object of nostalgic mourning on the part of those foreigners for whom France was for centuries synonymous with the Left or political intellectuals as such. Culturally, demarxification in France has gone hand in hand with a rememoration of a now relatively more distant past, re-evoked in the style of *la mode rétro*, namely the moment of the occupation and the Holocaust, and also, curiously, of the Gulag. This makes it difficult to disentangle political positions from a whole cultural climate which may be the former's effect but could just as easily be its cause. At any rate, one's immediate first thought—that the repudiation of totality is the result of acute and more self-conscious and articulate anxieties about Stalinism—seems less plausible when some of the intervening events are recalled, such as Khrushchev, the New Left, Eurocommunism, the transformation of the Italian Communist Party, market socialism, Deng Xiaoping, Gorbachev, and even so-called Western Marxism itself. The enthusiastic republication in France today of the hoariest American Cold War literature, such as James Burnham, awakens the suspicion that at least a few of the most strident of the anti-totality positions are based on that silliest of all puns, the confusion of "totality" with "totalitarianism." I am tempted to conclude that what is here staged as a principled fear of Stalinism is probably often little more than a fear of socialism itself: something reinforced by the curiously simultaneous chronology of French demarxification and the rise, and then the electoral victory, of the new French Socialist Party itself.

Two or three more precisely theoretical points need to be made, however. For one thing, it would seem abusive, or at the least invidious, to bring the whole weight of the guilty conscience of contemporary intellectuals (at a moment when, as a species, they are in the process of disappearing) to bear on Lukács's conception of totality as though it were some Hegelian moment of Absolute Spirit which any individual intellectual were likely to invest and personally to exploit. Knowledge is power, no doubt, and "theory" is repressive and patriarchal: truths we have learned from a whole range of highly theoretical thinkers from Foucault to Luce Irigaray. But "totality" is not in that sense, for Lukács, a form of knowledge, but rather a framework in which various kinds of knowledge are positioned, pursued, and evaluated. This is clearly the implication of the phrase "aspiration to totality" which we have already quoted. Meanwhile, as we will show later on, such a concept and framework is not an individual matter but rather a collective possibility which very much presupposes a collective project.[15] Lukács's very idealization

---

[15] We owe the term "collective project" to Henri Lefebvre. On the distinction between individual and collective categories, see *HCC*, 348–349, 355–356, and 380; 165, 171, and 193.

of the role of the party in this period, which may, to be sure, be subject to other kinds of objections, is quite inconsistent with the reproach of intellectual hubris, Hegelian placelessness, or the will to power and knowledge of the clerical caste. Nor does it seem altogether proper to charge the author of the Blum Theses with a passion for Identity and the repression of social and class differences. The "workerism" of *History and Class Consciousness* means, in my opinion, something rather different, which will be discussed in its place. At best, then, one may object that Lukács lacks any place for the political sociology of intellectuals as such. To call him a mandarin is reasonable enough, provided one does not forget to add that, exceptionally among the great modern thinkers and intellectuals, he chose to live the last forty years of his life under socialism and to share the problems and dilemmas of socialist construction.

The passionate repudiation of the concept of totality is also illuminated by the proposition that it is more interesting as an anxiety to be analyzed in its own right rather than as a coherent philosophical position. The postmodern moment is also, among other things, to be understood as the moment in which late capitalism becomes conscious of itself, and thematizes itself, in terms of extreme social differentiation,[16] or in other words, of a "pluralism" which is constitutive rather than, as in an older liberalism, simply ideal. For this last, pluralism is a value, that expresses itself in terms of moral imperatives such as tolerance and democracy (in the sociological sense of the acknowledgement of multiple group interests). In late capitalism, however, it is the very complexity of social relations, the inescapable fact of the coexistence of unimaginably atomized and fragmented segments of the social, that comes to be celebrated in its own right as the very bonus of pleasure and libidinal investment of the new social order as a whole. (Consider, for example, the attraction of fantasy images of the United States, of California and Manhattan, for Europeans.)

Pluralism has therefore now become something like an existential category, a descriptive feature that characterizes our present everyday life, rather than an ethical imperative to be realized within it. What is ideological about current celebrations of pluralism is that the slogan envelops and illicitly identifies two distinct dimensions of social complexity. There is the vertical dimension of late-capitalist or corporate institutions, and then the horizontal one of increasingly multiple social groups. Celebrations of pluralism pass the first off under the guise of the second, in whose joyous and Utopian street "heterogeneity" it decks itself out. But the complexity of institutions is also a form of standardization (the very paradox of the *system* of reification as Lukács first described it in an early stage). Meanwhile, the celebration of the

---

[16] We owe the most exhaustive theorization of this process today to Niklas Luhmann.

diversity of the "new social movements" released by the 1960s obscures their increasing collectivization and institutionalization as well. The solitary Romantic rebels and nonconformists of earlier periods have all been transformed into groups and movements, each with its own specific micropolitics. The transformation marks a significant (if provisional) gain in the political power of formerly marginal or repressed individuals, who, however, thereby forfeit the power and the pathos of an older rhetoric of individual resistance and revolt.

Yet it is very precisely by way of this new institutionalization, marked, for example, by a neo-ethnic movement in culture, in which older groups now produce their "heritage" in the form of the image, that the ideologeme of "pluralism" is able to do its work. It shifts gears imperceptibly from these new group structures to the very different structures of the corporate, which can now appropriate the celebration of Difference and Heterogeneity and harness it to the celebration of consumer goods, free enterprise, and the eternal wonder and excitement of the market itself.

But why is this happening now? At the very moment in which the official dystopian imagination—in novels and films—has abandoned its older *1984*-type nightmare paradigms of the repressive Stalinist political state for new "near-future" nightmares of pollution and overpopulation, corporate control on a galactic scale, and the breakdown of civilization into a "time of troubles" of the *Road Warrior* variety, why do now old-fashioned *1984* fantasies return in the realm of political ideologies as the terror of some repression of Difference by the last remaining adherents of philosophies of totality and totalization? On the level of political strategies and tactics, "totalization" means nothing more forbidding than alliance politics and various avatars and variants of popular fronts and hegemonic blocks, including the dilemmas and the failures of those complicated and delicate enterprises. Historically, no practical Marxist politics has ever imagined that the industrial working class could ever be anything but a minority in advanced society, albeit a significant one, with equally significant "special relationships" to the nerve centers of the social order.

But at this point, the philosophical question about the "concept" of totality surely needs to dissolve into (or to "realize itself in") the analysis of the specific historical situation and conjuncture, whose contradictions do not logically imply any flaw or fatality in the concept. It was indeed the specific vice of the Stalinist form of "ideological analysis" to draw philosophical conclusions from the "symptoms" of political acts and tendencies. What is wrong here is not some category mistake, for the whole force of Marxism lies in the affirmation of ultimate connections between these areas, but rather the immediacy (in Hegel's sense), the lack of mediations in the explanatory model, that presides over such summary judgments. *History and Class Consciousness* was, of course, one of the earliest explicit proposals (in what was to become the so-called Western Marxist tradition) for a new and more complexly mediated theory of ideology.

The crucial theoretical question often raised about the politics of "totality," however, is not in my view a specifically political one, although it tends at once to awaken practical anxieties about the predominance of one faction over another in the operation of political alliances and popular fronts. This is of course the question of "priority," and in particular the priority of the industrial working class: virtually the central argument of *History and Class Consciousness* and the most notorious piece of evidence for Lukács's "workerism."

5. Lukács's Particular Epistemology

What is argued in this text is essentially an *epistemological* priority of a particular social group or class in advanced society. Whatever the group or class identified and "privileged" by such an argument, therefore, the form of the argument is itself unusual and demands attention in its own right, since in its very structure it seeks to relate a truth claim to the social structure and phenomenological experience of a specific collectivity. Epistemology thus passes over into social phenomenology in a way that cannot but be felt as scandalous, and as a kind of "category mistake," by those for whom these levels correspond to distinct academic disciplines and their strictly differentiated methodologies. Since such differentiation—epistemology, economics, sociology as three autonomous fields of study—corresponds to Lukács's previous diagnosis of the reification of bourgeois thought, his very argument here—and the polemic against such specialization, in the form of the conceptual adversary or hostile reader—is itself a kind of "unity of theory and practice" and dramatized in the text by the conceptual content of his position.

But the inverse form of formulating the issue of priority is no less misleading. It is, for example, tempting to suppose that if the matter of the practical balance of forces in alliance politics is not here immediately at stake, then the argument must somehow be a "metaphysical" one, that is, an argument about ultimate grounds or foundations, or about what the Marxist tradition notoriously calls ultimately determining instances. The shape of a metaphysical argument of this kind comes immediately into view when one replaces Lukács's designation of the working class by a classification of its abstract concept, namely, social class. At that point, one concludes that Lukács is arguing the explanatory priority of the concept of class over competing concepts or ultimately determining instances— mostly, in the contemporary situation, sorted out according to race or gender or some related social concept on the one hand, or according to language or some related "dimensional" concept on the other. The polemic, thus conceived, becomes a two-front struggle. On one hand, "Marxism" (in the person of Lukács) wages a battle against feminism and race- or ethnic-based ideologues (or even against the more general prioritization of the "new social movements" or of "marginality"). On the other hand, it responds to the philosophical threat of various language-based "structuralisms" in the largest sense (Umberto Eco's defense of the sign,[17] for example, or Habermas's communicational model). This is, however, to recast Lukács's arguments in terms of what remain so many metaphysical Absolutes, an idle form of disputation in which each side replies by reiterating its own "absolute presupposition," after the fashion of the older disputes (also still with us, however) over whether human nature is essentially good or essentially bad.

What is more significant is that this way of restaging the fundamental issue at stake in this moment of "Reification and the Consciousness of the Proletariat" omits not only what was its most original feature but also the very "move" or "step" on which the whole argument turned: namely the insistence, not on abstract concepts such as class and production, but rather on group experience. The omission characterizes Lukács's defenders fully as much as his various adversaries to the point where, today, one has the feeling that the most authentic descendency of Lukács's thinking is to be found, not among the Marxists, but within a certain feminism, where the unique conceptual move of *History and Class Consciousness* has been appropriated for a whole program, now renamed (after Lukács's own usage) standpoint theory.[18]

These pathbreaking texts now allow us to return to Lukács's argument in a new way, which opens a space of a different kind for polemics about the epistemological priority of the experience of various groups or collectivities (most immediately, in this case, the experience of women as opposed to the experience of the industrial working class). For the argument of standpoint theory now enables a principled relativism, in which the epistemological claims of the various groups can be inspected (and respected) for their "truth content" (Adorno's *Wahrheitsgehalt*) or their respective "moments of truth" (to use another convenient contemporary German expression). The presupposition is that, owing to its structural situation in the social order and to the specific forms of oppression and exploitation unique to that situation, each group lives the world in a phenomenologically specific way that allows

---

[17] As, for example, in *A Theory of Semiotics*, Bloomington: Indiana University Press, 1976.

[18] See Nancy Hartsock, *Money, Sex, and Power*, New York: Longman, 1983; Sandra Harding, *The Science Question in Feminism*, Ithaca: Cornell University Press, 1986; and Alison M. Jagger, *Feminist Politics and Human Nature*, Totowa, NJ: Rowman and Allanheld, 1983.

it to see, or, better still, that makes it unavoidable for that group to see and to know, features of the world that remain obscure, invisible, or merely occasional and secondary for other groups.

This way of describing the argument has, incidentally, the additional merit of cutting across that most notorious of all Lukács's secondary qualifications, namely the seemingly last-minute distinction between the actual experience and thinking of working-class people and their "imputed consciousness" (*zugerechnetes Bewusstsein*).[19] This distinction opens the wedge through which Lukács's various adversaries (on the extreme left as well as on the right) glimpse the wolf-in-sheep's-clothing of the Party or the Intellectual, who now conveniently gets substituted for a sociological working class that needs this entity to find out what it "really" thinks. But it should also be juxtaposed against the other crucial qualification of Lukács's (shared, one would think, by all forms of Marxism), that the "subject" in question here is not, as in the bourgeois epistemologies, an *individual* one, but is the result of "the abolition of the isolated individual" (*HCC*, 356; 171):

> The bourgeoisie always perceives the subject and object of the historical process and of social reality in a double form: in terms of his consciousness the single individual is a perceiving subject confronting the overwhelming objective necessities imposed by society of which only minute fragments can be comprehended. But in reality it is precisely the conscious activity of the individual that is to be found on the object-side of the process, while the subject (the class) cannot be awakened into consciousness and this activity must always remain beyond the consciousness of the—apparent—subject, the individual. (*HCC*, 350; 165)

The temptations of the centered subject, therefore—including the optical illusion that scientific truth could somehow be the experience and spiritual property of an individual consciousness (of Lacan's *sujet supposé savoir*, for example)—are socially generated (but "objective") mirages projected by a properly bourgeois experience of social fragmentation and monadization.

The opposite of this monadic conception of individual consciousness is not, however, some doubtful, mystical or mystified, notion of *collective* consciousness. In my view, indeed, the stirring slogan so often taken to be the climax of *History and Class Consciousness*—the proletariat as "the identical

---

19   The term is not used in the major essay on which we have drawn here, "Reification and the Consciousness of the Proletariat," but rather in the essay entitled "Class Consciousness," in *HCC*, 223–224; 51. The fateful sentence reads as follows: "Class consciousness consists in fact of the appropriate and rational reactions 'imputed' to a particular typical position in the process of production." That the word "rational" specifically mobilizes Weber's theory of rationalization may not be particularly evident in the English-language context, but obviously moves Lukács's thinking much closer to Weber's theory of "ideal types."

subject-object of history" (*HCC*, 385; 197)—is rather the local thematic climax of Lukács's intermittent engagement throughout this text with the central motifs of German idealism from Fichte to Hegel. The passing phrase marks the "solution" to those specific traditional contradictions, in their own specific language or code, which is no longer our own. It is preferable, in our own linguistic and intellectual climate, to retranslate the perspectival and subject-oriented figure of the "standpoint" into the structural notion of the positioning of a given class or class fraction in the social totality.

At that point, it becomes clear that the epistemological "priority" of "proletarian consciousness," as a class or collective phenomenon, has to do with the "conditions of possibility" of new thinking inherent in this particular class position. It is not a matter of the scientific aptitude of individual workers (although Sartre quite properly underscores the qualitative difference in thought mode of people who work with machines as opposed, for example, to peasants or shopkeepers), still less of the mystical properties of some collective proletarian "worldview." The conception of conditions of possibility then has the advantage of stressing, not the content of scientific thought, but its prerequisites, its preparatory requirements, that without which it cannot properly develop. It is a conception which includes the diagnosis of blocks and limits to knowledge (reification as what suppresses the ability to grasp totalities) as well as the enumeration of positive new features (the capacity to think in terms of process).[20]

Contemporary feminist standpoint theory was able to restore and to make again visible this fundamental line of Lukács's argument (often effaced or distorted by generations of "faithful" as well as hostile commentators), because of the central importance it gives to the problem of Western science itself and that of scientific knowledge. Lukács's work had rarely been seen in this context for two reasons: first, because of his own anti-scientific and Viconian bias, inherited by so-called Western Marxism as a whole[21]; and second, because developments in the history and philosophy of science were in the past never so propitious for the posing of such questions as they are in the effervescence of the post-Kuhnian moment of this subdiscipline, when stereotypes of Lysenko have been displaced by a new speculative willingness to grasp scientific facts and scientific knowledge as human constructs and as praxis.[22] But it is precisely only within that radically different

---

[20]   These are of course the central features of Lukács's socioeconomic description of reification in the first section of "Reification and the Consciousness of the Proletariat" and of his philosophical description in the second section.

[21]   See Perry Anderson, *Considerations on Western Marxism*, London: New Left Books, 1976, 56; on the orientation to epistemology, 52–53. Vico's *verum factum* in effect sunders history from nature as an object of possible human knowledge.

[22]   See, for example, the pathbreaking work of Bruno Latour, *Science in Action*,

framework—science as construction and invention, rather than science as discovery and as the passive contemplation of external law—that such Lukácsean issues as the class preconditions of the possible forms of scientific praxis become meaningful and even urgent.

Meanwhile, the feminist appropriation of Lukács also allows for a productive and comparative inquiry into the epistemological potentialities of the various social groups which is very different in spirit from that sterile metaphysical quarrel about ultimately determining instances to which reference has already been made. And this is also the moment in which the conception of a "moment of truth" in the various competing types of group experience becomes crucial, since it is not some abstract evaluation applied from the outside and after the fact to this new kind of epistemological and sociological description, but is rather immanent and inherent in this last. Lukács himself, for example, first characterized the phenomenological experience of the industrial working class in terms of a new capacity to see the world historically and in terms of process, which that class very specifically owed to its concrete situation as the ultimate, but very unique, commodity in the system of capitalist production. Its structural destiny, therefore, on this formulation, lay in its experience of itself as wage labor, or in other words as the commodification of labor power, a form of *negative* constraint and violence which now dialectically produces the unexpectedly *positive*, new content of its experience as "the self-consciousness of the commodity" (*HCC*, 352; 168).[23] In his 1967 preface to the book—a mature autocritique which can no longer be supposed to be motivated by any of the Galilean ambiguities of his earlier recantation—Lukács proposes a reformulation of this epistemological "exceptionality" of the industrial working class in terms of labor and praxis[24] (whether the transformation in contemporary production and machinery, the new dynamics of the cybernetic in late capitalism, modifies or enriches this descriptional option remains to be seen). Meanwhile, other forms of Marxism have thematized the uniqueness of working-class experience in further, distinct categories, such as that of a specific experience of cooperative or collective action.

If one wants to be consequent about Lukács's model, however, it seems clear that *History and Class Consciousness* must also be read, or must be rewritten, as including a description of the specific epistemological capacities of the bourgeoisie itself, the very originator of "Western science" in its

---

Cambridge, MA: Harvard University Press, 1987; and with Steve Woolgar, *Laboratory Life*, Princeton: Princeton University Press, 1986.

[23] The form of the theory (often schematically designated as the theory of "radical chains") obviously originates in Marx himself: see "Critique of Hegel's *Philosophy of Right*: Introduction," in *Early Writings*, London: Penguin, 1975, esp. 256.

[24] See, in the English-language edition of *HCC*, xvii–xviii.

current form. At that point, it will be very precisely the dynamics of reification as a social and phenomenological experience which constitute the moment of truth of the extraordinary disciplinary and specializing developments of "positivist" research. Those developments compose a long and incomparably productive period which now seems to have touched its structural limits, if the unparalleled intensity of contemporary critiques of Western "rationality," of the dynamics of the physical sciences, and of the historical and structural closure of the various disciplines, is to be believed.

Feminist standpoint theory, which has generated some of the most acute of those critiques, now stages the specific phenomenological experience of women in the patriarchal social order as a structural submission to negative constraint equally "exceptional" as, but very different from, that of the working class. That experience generates new and positive epistemological possibilities which are thematically distinct from those enumerated by the Marxist tradition. The emphases here—whose relationship varies according to the description, in this theory currently in full elaboration—include an experience of the body radically distinct from that of men, or even of male workers (even though what is presupposed is that this is an experience of the deeper truth of all bodily experience, generally masked from men's consciousness). They also include a capacity for non-reified consciousness, generally negatively characterized in the caricatured attributes of feeling or of "intuition," but which itself "leaps over" a certain historical stage of the psychic division of labor to which men have historically had to submit. Finally, feminist standpoint theory emphasizes an experience of the collective which is different from the active collective praxis of workers and already constitutively experienced as that community and cooperation which for the working-class movement still lies in the future.[25]

The black experience has its "priority" in something like a combination of both of these distinct moments of truth (that attributed to workers and that attributed to women), but a combination which is qualitatively distinct from both, including not merely an experience of reification deeper than the commodity form, but also the historic link, by way of imperialism and the plunder of what was to become the Third World, with the older stage of capitalist accumulation. These kinds of unique epistemological priorities

---

[25] See in particular Hartsock, *Money, Sex, and Power*, 231–261; Harding, *The Science Question in Feminism*, 141–162; and Jagger, *Feminist Politics and Human Nature*, 369–385. The privileged test case for the relationship between women's "standpoint" and scientific discovery has become the achievement of the molecular biologist Barbara McClintock. See Evelyn Fox Keller's biography, *A Feeling for the Organism*, San Francisco: W. H. Freeman and Co., 1983; as well as her collection *Reflections on Gender and Science*, New Haven: Yale University Press, 1984, particularly Part 3, sections 8 and 9, 150–177.

are surely presupposed in all black theory as it emerged from the 1960s and the Black Power movement, but their theoretical foundations lie in W. E. B. Du Bois's notion of "dual consciousness" on the one hand, and Frantz Fanon's rewriting of the Hegelian Master Slave struggle for recognition on the other.[26]

Meanwhile, particularly since George Steiner has so often complained of the suppression of the specifically Jewish component in the Marxian and dialectical literary tradition—if not from Marx himself, then at least from Lukács all the way to Adorno—it seems appropriate to say a word about this specific social and epistemological situation as well. We are in fact often tempted, as intellectuals, to stress the obvious formal analogies between the Talmudic tradition and its exegetical relationship to sacred texts and the intricacies of modern dialectical reading and writing. But these analogies presuppose a cultural transmission which remains obscure, and which may well be very problematic indeed in the case of assimilated urban Jews whose interest in the tradition (one thinks of Walter Benjamin) was purely intellectual and a development in later adult life. The moment of truth of the Central European Jewish situation seems to me very different from this, and cannot go unnoticed by any reader of the work of Adorno, and in particular of *Dialectic of Enlightenment*. This is not first and foremost the formal and aesthetic stress on pain and suffering, on dissonance and the negative, everywhere present in Adorno; but rather a more primary experience, namely that of collective *fear* and of vulnerability—the primal fact, for Adorno and Horkheimer, of human history itself and of that "dialectic of Enlightenment," that scientific domination of nature and the self, which constitutes the infernal machine of Western civilization. But this experience of fear, in all its radicality, which cuts across class and gender to the point of touching the bourgeois in the very isolation of his town house or sumptuous Berlin apartment, is surely the very moment of truth of ghetto life itself, as the Jews and so many other ethnic groups have had to live it: the helplessness of the village community before the perpetual and unpredictable imminence of the lynching or the pogrom, the race riot. Other groups' experience of fear is occasional, rather than constitutive: standpoint analysis specifically demands a differentiation between the various negative experiences of constraint, between the *exploitation* suffered by workers and the *oppression* suffered by women and continuing on through the distinct structural forms of exclusion and alienation characteristic of other kinds of group experience.

---

[26] W. E. B. Du Bois, *The Souls of Black Folk* (Oxford: Oxford University Press, 2007), and Frantz Fanon, *The Wretched of the Earth*, trans. by Constance Farrington (New York: Grove Press, 1963). But see, for parallel speculations, Harding, *The Science Question in Feminism*, 163–186.

What must be added at this point is that any conception of cultural tradition and transmission must begin with this shared fear of the ethnic group, which accounts for cultural cohesion and identity as a symbolic response to the more primary situation of danger and threat. Such analysis is finally not complete until the identification of the moment of truth of group experience—itself negative and positive all at once, an oppressive restriction which turns into a capacity for new kinds of experience and for seeing features and dimensions of the world and of history masked to other social actors—is prolonged by an epistemological articulation that translates such experience into new possibilities of thought and knowledge. That such new possibilities can also be thought of in aesthetic and formal ways, alongside these scientific and epistemological ones, must now be recalled and emphatically stressed, since it was in terms of this very interrelationship between the formal possibilities of "realism" and of standpoint knowledge that we argued for the deeper continuity between the Lukács of *History and Class Consciousness* and the later theoretician of the realist novel.

What emerges from the feminist project, and from the speculations it inspires, is an "unfinished project": namely the differentiation of all those situations of what I have tried neutrally to characterize as "constraint," which are often monolithically subsumed under single-shot political concepts such as "domination" or "power"; economic concepts such as "exploitation"; social concepts such as "oppression"; or philosophical concepts such as "alienation." These reified concepts and terms, taken on their own as meaningful starting points, encourage the revival of what I have characterized above as an essentially metaphysical polemic about the ultimate priority of the political, say (the defense of the primacy of "domination"), versus that of the economic (the counter-primacy of the notion of "exploitation").

What seems more productive is to dissolve this conceptuality once again back into the concrete situations from which it emerged: to make an inventory of the variable structures of "constraint" lived by the various marginal, oppressed, or dominated groups—the so-called "new social movements" fully as much as the working classes—with this difference, that each form of privation is acknowledged as producing its own specific "epistemology," its own specific view from below, and its own specific and distinctive truth claim. It is a project that will sound like "relativism" or "pluralism" only if the identity of the absent common object of such "theorization" from multiple "standpoints" is overlooked—what one therefore does not exactly have the right to call (but let it stand as contradictory shorthand) "late capitalism."

6. Lukács Now

As for the "workerism" of *History and Class Consciousness*, I have tried to suggest that it is also not an endpoint, not a "solution" or a final position on matters of group consciousness and praxis, but rather the beginning of work yet to be done, and of a task or project which is not that of ancient history, but of our own present. Towards the end of his life, in an interview conducted in the late 1960s, Lukács had this to say about the Utopian romanticism of that now bygone era:

> Today, in arousing the subjective factor, we cannot recreate and continue the 1920s, we have instead to proceed on the basis of a new beginning, with all the experience that we have from the earlier workers' movement and from Marxism. We must be clear about this, however, that the problem is to begin anew; to use an analogy, we are not now in the twenties of the twentieth century, but in a certain sense at the beginning of the nineteenth century, when the workers' movement slowly began to take shape in the wake of the French revolution. I believe that this idea is very important for theorists, for despair can very rapidly set in if the assertion of certain truths only finds a very weak resonance. Don't forget that certain things that Saint-Simon and Fourier spoke about had at the time an extraordinarily weak resonance, and it was only in the thirties and forties of the nineteenth century that a revival of the workers' movement got underway.[27]

The Communist Manifesto, in other words, let alone Lenin and the Soviet Revolution, are not behind us somewhere in time; they have yet to come into being. In some new way we are called on to achieve them through the slow and intricate resistances of historical time. Something like this is also what I would have liked to say about Lukács himself. *History and Class Consciousness* is a work whose prodigious philosophical deductions had an incomparable effect on several generations of revolutionary intellectuals. In that sense, to be sure, it is alive in the past and a perpetually fascinating object of historical meditation, among those very special dead which it is the mission of the historian, à la Michelet or Benjamin, to summon back to life. I think that it would be better, however, to consider that, like the *Manifesto*, it has yet to be written, it lies ahead of us in historical time. Our task, as political intellectuals, is to lay the groundwork for that situation in which it can again appear, with all the explosive freshness of the *Novum*, as though for the first time in which it can, once again, become both real and true.

---

[27] Hans Heinz Holz, Leo Kofler, and Wolfgang Abendroth, *Conversations with Lukács*, Cambridge, MA: MIT Press, 1975, 62.

Chapter 7

Sartre's *Critique*, Volume 1: An Introduction

There are many reasons why Sartre's *Critique* has not had the attention it deserves, and its unfinished character is the least of those (especially since, except for the plays, he never really finished anything). For one thing, it came at a moment in the early 1960s when the intellectual hegemony of existentialism—virtually universal in the immediate postwar years—was giving way to that new intellectual passion called structuralism. Claude Lévi-Strauss's rather summary attack on Sartre's "myth" of the French Revolution (and no doubt provoked by Sartre's reassimilation of nascent structuralism in the lectures in which the *Critique* was first presented) anticipated François Furet's version of the topic by twenty years without the anti-communism. (Sartre's view of "structure" as the objectification of *praxis*, its exoskeletal trace, will be revived and powerfully augmented by Pierre Bourdieu's *Esquisse d'une théorie de la pratique* of 1972, which itself in turn in many ways marked the end of the structuralist period.) But Lévi-Strauss's authority in the early 1960s was powerful enough to legitimate a wholesale reaction against, and withdrawal from, phenomenological positions in general: yet those still very much motivated the insistence of the *Critique* on the necessity for a continuity between individual and group experience.

Meanwhile, now that structuralism has followed existentialism into intellectual history, it is the notorious stylistic difficulty of the *Critique* that offers the more fundamental reason why all those who ought to be most immediately concerned by it—they include political philosophers, sociologists, militants interested in the Laclau-Mouffe dynamics of action, as well as whatever Sartreans may have survived the deluge (Bernard-Henri Lévy's enthusiastic new book suggests that there may be a whole generation of new converts waiting in the wings)—have given it a wide berth.

This very linguistic difficulty reinforces the idea that philosophers have no business reflecting on sociological issues that ought to be left to experts. The professionalization of the social sciences thus reinforces empiricist and anti-theoretical prejudices already alerted by Sartre's radical political positions and in particular his rather strident adherence to Marxism (and to the "orthodox Marxism" of the early 1960s at that!). How can he write on the French Revolution? He's no historian, he only uses secondary sources! How can he write on the history of French unions and anarcho-syndicalism? He's no labor historian! How can he write on French Malthusianism and France's peculiar economic development? He's no economic historian! And as for Chinese deforestation and the gold and silver of the Spanish New World—it's obvious that a philosopher has no expertise on any of these subjects. Perhaps, as he is a "culture worker," he might at best be granted some authority in speaking, as he does, about French "distinction" and bourgeois manners (another theme in which he is followed, far more famously, by Bourdieu later on). So the idea, from Kant to Deleuze, that the philosopher's job is to look over the shoulder of the various scientists and experts and check their thinking and their use of abstract categories—this notion of the philosopher's vocation is no longer very current among us.

Do we need, in other words, to philosophize history? In a nominalistic age, indeed, "philosophies of history" (famously rebaptized by Jean-François Lyotard as "grand narratives") are greeted with universal suspicion, even though the most tenacious of them—the story of modernization—continues to have a powerful grip on political thinking in East and West alike. Capitalism itself lives in a perpetual present; the human past seems to be a senseless accumulation of unsuccessful human efforts and intentions; yet the future of technology inspires blind and unshakeable faith. Sartre here offers to reorganize this doxa into what may at least be considered as negative meanings, in the categories of counter-finality and the practico-inert: a proposal which would, as we shall see, restore a certain philosophical meaning to historical events, at the same time as it risks projecting some new cyclical "vision of history."

As for the undoubted difficulty and occasional unreadability of this text, so thoroughly devoid of the fireworks that make up Sartre's other discursive writing, the complaint betrays something of a misapprehension as to the internal dynamics of this philosophical prose. It is meant to be a study in the status of two kinds of thinking, analytic reason and dialectical reason. But unlike so much of Sartre's philosophy, it does not have as its primary function the invention of new philosophical concepts (although new terms and concepts do emerge from it). Rather, it is an operation in matching an already existing dialectical language or code against a series of individual and collective experiences. The *Critique* is thus from this standpoint to be seen as an austere and formalistic exercise, without any instrumental coloration, like late Bach; and it invites us to judge whether the rewriting of this or that type of historical content in the terminology of, for example, the negation of the negation (or of subject and object, passive and active, multiplicity and unification, transcendent and immanent, exteriority and interiority) is successful: that is, whether the new formulations have a new and heightened kind of intelligibility in their own right. This can be an exasperating process, particularly when Sartre tries out various different versions of this matching in succession. But the reader's interest will be fully stimulated only if this unique and peculiar linguistic operation is the center of the focus. The problem can be rephrased as a testing of the validity of Engels's dialectical categories (for it is he, rather than Marx himself, who originally formulated them, in the *Anti-Dühring*) for the illumination—which is to say, the rewriting—of history, and not least of contemporary twentieth-century history (up to 1960). This means that Sartre here takes on himself a pre-existing alien language: that of Engels's three laws of the dialectic—the transformation of quantity into quality (and vice versa); the interpenetration of opposites; and the negation of the negation. He will now attempt to rewrite the problems of a philosophy of history at a level of philosophical intensity and abstraction quite different from that of the orthodox Marxist version of this philosophy to be found in Stalin's dialectical materialism—a "philosophy" still very much alive at the moment in which Sartre is writing and is attempting to work out his own practical and theoretical relationship to the existing Communist parties as well as to the other revolutionary traditions. Much is thus at stake in this seemingly formalistic exercise; I therefore recommend a preliminary approach through the form and its problems, before we hazard a judgment on the resultant content, not to speak of the success of the enterprise as a whole. Yet readers, in order to understand the work in the first place, as with most original philosophies, are here required to learn what amounts to a new language, as Sartre constructs one out of his matching and rewriting enterprise, a new artificial language he not only devised but taught himself to speak with occasionally maddening fluency. The *Critique* is thus a "language experiment," and the reader is to be reassured that with a little practice its rhythms fall into place.

This approach can be further strengthened by an awareness of the continuities between Sartre's earlier existential system (embodied in *Being and Nothingness*) and this new project which so many people have wrongly assumed to mark a break with existentialism and a philosophical as well as a political turn towards Marxism—the implication being that Sartre will now stage a wholesale replacement of his older concepts and terms. The argument for this rather different kind of matching operation, however, depends on establishing a fundamental continuity between the two moments, something Perry Anderson has succinctly evoked as a "conduit from many of the concepts of *Being and Nothingness* to those of the *Critique of Dialectical Reason*: among others, the notion of 'facticity' leading to that of 'scarcity,' 'inauthenticity' to 'seriality,' the instability of the 'for-itself-in-itself' to that of the 'fused group.'" Yet the rewriting process is far from being a static translation of the older system, in which the bleak pessimism of the existential period is replaced by the ferocious world of competition and violence in the dialectical one. I want to go further and to claim that the revisions of the *Critique* make possible a genuine philosophical solution to the dilemma that remained open in *Being and Nothingness*, namely that of "concrete relations with the other": we will return to this below.

At any rate, it seems best to skip over the methodological reflections with which the text begins (and even the questions of structure and the frustrating perspective according to which the first volume merely lays in place the philosophical instruments—seriality, group-in-fusion, etc.—which are to be concretely deployed in the second one) and to note a few basic initial presuppositions. Thus, if we are to continue the translational operation sketched out above, we will have to say that what is here called *praxis* is more or less the same as what *Being and Nothingness* called the project: The new language betokens an extension of the original concept rather than its replacement, for now what will be argued is that the freely chosen project describes not only individual action but collective acts as well; or better still, that understanding collective action is not different in nature from the understanding of the individual (existential) act. Here, in other words, we find the same fundamental existential and phenomenological bias mentioned above, but which now confronts us with the fundamental dilemma of the *Critique*, namely whether collective or historical events can be thought to have the same transparency for understanding as do individual ones. This is not at all evident, and Sartre's task is clearly a difficult one, which a mere change in terminology is unlikely to make any easier.

As if all this were not enough, the very status of Volume 1 of the *Critique* makes for some additional complications. For it is in effect a preparatory volume, and never arrives at what will presumably be the central concern of this philosophical enterprise, namely the meaning of history. What are being laid in place in this volume (the only completed one) are merely the basic sociological and even metaphysical concepts, the static instruments, required before we set "history" in motion. The division of the projected work into two general types of discourse—that of methodology and basic concepts, and the more properly philosophical argument about history's putative unity, direction, and meaning—would seem however to be a rather undialectical one: in both Hegel and Marx the *Darstellung* of the basic concepts turned into a whole dialectical exposition in its own right (in Hegel, the *Logic*, or perhaps even the *Encyclopedia* as a whole), in Marx, the first and simplest approach to capital (Volume 1), which was to have been redeveloped dialectically in the far more complex spirals of volumes 2 and 3 (along with the projected unwritten ones), which retrace the earlier simple or "basic" steps in more concrete trajectories (many capitals, capital as a whole). Nothing of the sort is here in Sartre, whose defense might take the following form: Marxism and the tradition now already exists so that it is not a question of expounding utterly new conceptualities but rather critically and dialectically reexamining those in place to restore to them a dialectical spirit which has long since evaporated in the hands of the various orthodoxies. And this is a task that probably has to proceed, à la Hobbes, in a more or less analytic fashion.

The other explanation is a reflex of Sartre's unique strengths rather than of any formal or conceptual weakness: it is simply his irrepressibly narrative spirit, which tends to convert any simple expository task into a storytelling form, something evidently related to the historical subject matter, for which "concrete" always means "event." Thus even economics—the question of inflation in imperial Spain—or sociology—the exposition of what "class interest" might mean—let alone the long illustrative sections drawn either from the French Revolution or from the Soviet Revolution down to Stalinism —all these illustrations tend to overpower the surface text and to acquire a dynamism of their own.

But this means that the reader is tempted to mistake these narrative illustrations for so many positive philosophical propositions about concrete history: something which results in the fundamental error so many readers (including myself, in an earlier effort) have made about Volume 1, namely the notion that it sets in place a cyclical view of history in which groups incessantly form and then dissolve back into seriality, leaving an essentially dictatorial structure in place behind them. We will come back to this issue.

Let me now enumerate the key moments, which is to say the key operative concepts, of Volume 1. I have already suggested that the first of these concepts, the very starting point, that of scarcity, allows Sartre to preserve the much disputed dialectical category of the negation of the negation: scarcity is seen as an initial structure of the world, or of being, which is negated and transcended by human need—the experience of lack and desire, of hunger and thirst, is then the initial way in which we organize the *en-soi* (being-in-itself) into a situation, turning a combination of chemical elements into a desert or a lush landscape. The human organism, as a meaningless fact, thereby makes itself over into a project, into a *praxis* that can henceforth have a meaning (to call it a human meaning is simply to multiply these terms unnecessarily), and thus an outcome, whether of failure or success. But to begin with scarcity is also to short-circuit and disqualify the whole false problem of human nature (something the fundamental existential tenet—existence precedes essence—sought to do on a more abstract level). Now it becomes possible to share the realist pessimism of Hobbes or Machiavelli—that beings are necessarily evil—without any metaphysical premises about nature itself. Indeed the simple fact of inhabiting a world of scarcity (a world we still inhabit even if or when our own society happens to become rich and prosperous) explains the fact of violence and aggressivity in a situational rather than a naturalistic way: "When, in the course of a migration, members of a tribal group come across a strange tribe, they suddenly discover man as an alien species, that is, as a fierce carnivorous beast who can lay ambushes and make tools" (107).[1] This is not some belated form of social Darwinism nor even a proposition out of socio-biology, it is the expression of human freedom, as well as of that of reciprocity: "In pure reciprocity, that which is Other than me is also the same. But in reciprocity as modified by scarcity, the same appears to us as anti-human in so far as this same man appears as radically Other—that is to say, as threatening us with death" (131–132). Scarcity is thus a contingent feature of our world (we can imagine science-fiction alien creatures from a world without scarcity, but then they would not be human in the ways we experience that condition). Meanwhile, generosity, cooperation, and the like are not false or fictional, but they are not features of human nature either (there is no such thing as human nature). They are, rather, other forms in which our freedom negates that initial fact of being.

Once this initial ontological (or even metaphysical) premise is given, we are in a position to name and to appreciate its transformations. Once again, these are given in the order of their emergence: that is to say, a Hegelian or evolutionary presentation is adopted which can very easily lend itself to the narrative misconceptions I have already warned about. In other words, this sequence of concepts, categories, or forms can very easily be mistaken for something like a "philosophy of history" (a misconception, to be sure, only strengthened by the decision to publish this enormous definitional section as a whole book or separate volume in its own right). Let's go even further than this, on the grounds that authors are always complicitous in the misunderstandings of their own works: this sequence then may well in reality betray something like an alternate "philosophy of history" within the larger (and never completed) text; it betrays a cyclical pattern virtual in Sartre's thinking and no doubt in contradiction with the official analysis of historical direction he meant to offer us.

At any rate, the first move in this "emergence" will follow the logical order of *Being and Nothingness*, where pure being (being-in-itself) is then initially shaped and organized by the negativity of human beings (or by being-for-itself). Here the being of scarcity is transformed into a situation of need by way of the negativity of human lack (or: inorganic being is transformed by organic being or life), and there results a first simple and fundamental form of the project, the negation of the negation: the form in other words of human action itself. In the translational scheme with which Sartreans must become familiar in order to read the *Critique*, the key term "project" is here rendered as *praxis*.

---

[1] Jean-Paul Sarte, *Critique of Dialectical Reason*, Vol. 1, trans. Alan Sheridan-Smith, London: Verso, 2004. All parenthetical citations refer to this edition.

It would be tempting indeed to pause for a lexical digression on this momentous word, recoined and placed back in philosophical circulation by Count Cieszkowski in 1838, and then almost at once appropriated by Marx in the *Theses on Feuerbach* (1845–1846), where it is defined as *sinnlich-menschliche Tätigkeit* or "sensuous human activity," that is to say a material, or materialist, action involving change. What does the new borrowing add to the plainer language of acts themselves? Well, to be sure, even the choice of the word "act" adds something to our narrative understanding of events, since it implies a unified process which leaves real traces (as opposed, in one of Sartre's favorite dualisms, to the mere gesture, on the one hand, or the immaterial thought or wish on the other—that "mere interpretation" of which Marx accused the philosophers). *Praxis* then suggests that we need to open up even the conventional conception (or better still category) of the act, to include two more dimensions: one of ontology and one of history.

Praxis thus implies and designates the deep structure of the act, as that combines being and negativity; and it also asks us to consider the humblest act in what Hegel would have called a world-historical light, or what Sartre himself terms the incarnation of the meaning of History itself: in this sense, then, the opening of a can of peas stages my whole relationship to being itself at the same time that it inflects the historical modalities of the world of capitalist industrial production (in this case, as we shall see, what Sartre calls exigency). *Praxis* does not impose those two dimensions of meaning on an act in advance, but rather opens the act up to an interrogation in terms of both or either one.

But as if that were not enough (now closing our parenthesis), the word *praxis* itself in the *Critique* is quickly doubled and outpaced by another one, a true neologism this, whose technical meaning has latterly been utterly transformed and travestied by its increasingly central role in ideological debate. This is of course the word "totalization," which Sartre coined specifically in order to differentiate himself from Lukács and the latter's keyword "totality." Unfortunately, the ideological connotation with which the Sartrean term has been more recently endowed pointedly conflates these two terms, and makes Sartre over into yet another philosopher of "totality," that is to say, not merely of universals and of Marxism, but, above all in the context of identity politics, a philosopher representative of identity itself and the hegemony of the white male Western intellectual (and no doubt characterizing the left intellectual, as opposed to the various right-wing ideologies). "Totalizing" has thus become a slogan which identifies a claim to speak from above and for all of society, as opposed to the minoritarian and differential positions of this or that Foucauldian "specific intellectual." There is thus, in the deployment of this epithet in discursive struggle, a movement out from the condemnation of the various Communist parties and their claims to truth and to hegemonic leadership towards the indictment of political intellectuals generally as those espouse this or that "total" systemic change of capitalism as a whole, as opposed to this or that specific minority-group agenda within capitalism.

Nor did Lukács himself really mean anything so offensive, even though the "standpoint of totality" will be evoked as a criterion of truth, where it means grasping the system as a whole, and characterizes a dialectic for which thinking starts not with Descartes' smallest parts or units and working upwards but with the most complex final form and working downwards. But Lukács identified this standpoint and this perspective with a class position; and he evoked the proletariat's "aspiration to totality" rather than their empirical possession of such a universal view, which the party itself was supposed to mediate, by way no doubt of all kinds of bad "totalizations."

However one evaluates Lukács's so-called standpoint theory, which has been very suggestively revived and adopted by theoreticians of gender and of race as we have seen in the preceding chapter, it has nothing whatsoever to do with Sartre's usage. Sartrean totalization was meant, indeed, to exclude any implication that multiples like the "group in fusion" have the ontological status of a totality or an organism (of a "hyperorganism," as Sartre's text will constantly warn us). For Sartre, then, a totality is precisely a static concept, a concept of being rather than of process, and one governed by analytic rather than by dialectical reason.

But these lofty philosophical issues are scarcely raised by Sartre's use of the word "totalization," which simply means *praxis* itself, organized activity with a view towards an end; and, whatever its possible extension to collective and historical movements and events, its relevance begins with the stereotypical behavior of individuals, and indeed with acts as insignificant as that opening of a can.

It is curious that Sartre should have chosen a relatively spatial word, redolent of exteriority, to characterize even the initial forms of human activity; indeed we will find it associated with unification as well, which compounds our sense of the incongruity of the choice of such terms to characterize interiority and human action. Yet they evoke the multiple and the dispersed, separation and heterogeneity, in order to dramatize what the human project most immediately confronts and what it must most immediately overcome. Indeed, I feel that the importance of the notion and the experience of multiplicity for Sartre has scarcely yet been evaluated, for it arguably governs everything from the inert things and beings of the outside world all the way to demography itself, in its twin form of philosophical otherness and of colonial subjugation.

At any rate, in this first context of the simplest acts of individuals, totalization and unification underscore what negativity, the project, human *praxis*, first does to the world of being that confronts us, which is to organize its scattered bits and pieces, its "blooming, buzzing confusion," into a unified situation: for it is only with the situation—this great leitmotif of the dynamism of Sartre's earlier work—that *praxis* can begin, as the intervention into and the transformation—Sartre says, the *dépassement*, the transcendence—of that situation it has itself initially brought into being (a dimension of the nascent act reminiscent of Heidegger's *Vorgriff*). And with this "first" human act, then, we are thrown into history itself.

For what totalization or *praxis* produces is one form or another of "worked matter," what Hegel would have called my objectification in the outside world, and as it were an inert and alienated trace of my completed act. And with this, the dialectic itself begins, and the fundamental dualism of all Sartre's philosophy rears its head, namely the radical differentiation between people and things, between my consciousness, my alienation in matter, and my alienation by other people. This, which was the tripartite organizing principle of *Being and Nothingness*, must not be confused with that dualism of subject and object, of the *pour-soi* and the *en-soi*, to which Merleau-Ponty objected, in his own effort to restore a phenomenological monism by way of the *corps propre*. (Yet Merleau-Ponty was himself guilty of this particular dualism common to all phenomenology, and the central target, not only of Heidegger's *Kehre*, but of so-called poststructuralism in general.) No, this particular dualism is scandalous precisely because it is itself the recognition of the scandal of the existence of other people, surely Sartre's central philosophical motif and the most original and durable element of his various systems. Nor is it subject to the usual critiques of dualism as such, since it is a dualism which functions as a moment in the reestablishment of monism proper. In this respect, the remarks about Marxism, which Sartre considers to be "in fact both monist and dualist," are significant:

> It is dualist because it is monist. Marx's ontological monism consisted in affirming the irreducibility of Being to thought, and, at the same time, in reintegrating thoughts with the real as a particular form of human activity … The dialectic is precisely a form of monism, in that oppositions appear to it as moments which are posited for themselves for an instant before bursting. (25, 180)

But these methodological considerations do not yet specify the concrete and fundamental dualism at work in the *Critique*, which can be understood as constituting a commentary on Marx's famous remark "Men make their own history, but not under conditions of their own choosing." On Sartre's reading, however, what will be underscored is the peculiarity of just those situations not "of their own choosing," which, however, as historical situations, were in fact the result of human action in the past, even though they may now be considered as materiality. The point here is that, although such "conditions" are material ones, they are certainly not natural, in the sense of absolute contingency unmodified by human action. (Or, to be even more precise about it, even "contingency" is the result of human reality, insofar as it has already been produced as contingency by human need and human desire.)

At any rate, Sartre will now reformulate the maxim in a new and circular way: "the crucial discovery of dialectical investigation is that man is 'mediated' by things to the same extent as things are 'mediated' by man" (79). "Matter," he observes elsewhere, is "a mediation between individuals" (113). At this point, we approach one of the great original ideas of the *Critique*, which goes well beyond the alienation theory of the early Marx. Just as theology needs to account for evil and suffering in a world otherwise attributed to God, so any conceptually satisfying "philosophy of history" needs to account for violence and failure in some meaningful way, rather than as a series of accidents that fall outside of meaning. *The Communist Manifesto* does so by underscoring the dialectical nature of capitalism, its immensely destructive power, which is at one with its immensely productive power.

Sartre's dialectic will go further than this by theorizing an anti-dialectic intertwined with the dialectic of human *praxis*, a counterfinality inextricably conjoined with the finalities of human action and production. Indeed, this new force has a bonus for us in the invention of a new concept and a new and durable philosophical term, the so-called practico-inert, as a more precise way of designating objects which are not mere things and agencies but which are not exactly people either.

But this will not be a Manichaean vision of history: that type of evil is, as we have seen, already profoundly human: it is the immeasurable brutality people visit on other people within the world of scarcity. This new kind of negative force is to be understood in a different way, and to theorize it properly would, as Sartre observes, explain how *praxis* can logically "be an experience both of necessity and of freedom" (79). Indeed, "what has never been attempted is a study of the type of passive action which materiality as such exerts on man and his History in returning a stolen *praxis* to man in the form of a counterfinality" (124). We have here to do, therefore, with a type of "unintended consequence" quite different also from the reversals of human action in history, as Marx writes their comic epic in *The Eighteenth Brumaire of Louis Bonaparte*. (Indeed this new anti-dialectic offers one more dramatization of the banality and inadequacy of current fashionable attempts to rewrite the dialectic precisely in such everyday or "common-language" terms as that precisely of an "unintended consequence.")

Counterfinality is thus a negative version of Hegel's "ruse of history" (or "ruse of reason"), which he himself derived from Adam Smith's hidden hand and Mandeville's *The Fable of the Bees*, with the qualification that what was unexpectedly positive in them becomes, characteristically enough, implacably negative in Sartre. The premise, however, remains that of the efficacy of *praxis*: what is negative in counterfinality is not the result of a matter as such, but rather of the human productivity or *praxis* invested in it, and returning in unrecognizable form upon the human beings who invested their labor in it in the first place. Sartre will also call the bearer of this new, and active, malign power "worked matter" (*matière ouvrée*), and it can be distinguished from human "totalization in course" as being very precisely an already "totalized totality." This is thus the place of the various historical forms Marx calls modes of production, and it is the concomitant of a specific form of human sociality Sartre will call the collective (among which is included the Marxian phenomenon of social class). We can better understand this important notion by observing that it can be said to have two distinct sources.

On the one hand, we may find it anticipated in the relatively phenomenological rehearsal of the oppositions between activity and passivity, and interiority and exteriority, in which (as in the other oppositions we have already enumerated) a human realm is opposed to a non-human one. For, as Sartre never ceases to remind us, in this following Heidegger as well as many of the descriptions of *Being and Nothingness*, the human agency works on exteriority by making itself exterior, and works on passivity by making itself passive. Not only is this the meaning of the tool as such, but it is also the disposition of the hand that wields the tool. But this work on the self and on my own body, which lends my body efficacy in the passive and external realm of bodies as such, also in some reciprocal yet seemingly magic fashion endows the matter on which I work with some of my human characteristics.

At which point we may take up what strikes me as Sartre's other source, namely Marx's own notion of "stored labor," and in particular the consequences of the labor process for machinery and machine-produced goods. The non-human world must for Marx be distinguished from a material one invested by labor: such material objects become "masses of crystallized labor-time," their raw material "soaked in labor." Machinery now dialectically transforms this process of investment on a higher level, adding value to its product which is distinct from but compounded with the immediate human labor also involved. This is because the machine stores up the labor which has gone into its own production and then reinvests it in its new product: "Only in large-scale industry has man succeeded in making the product of his past labour, labour which has already been objectified, perform gratuitous service on a large scale, like a force of nature."[2]

It is this peculiar temporal deferral—the possibility of storing up an initial quantity of expended labor in order to reinvest it in smaller amounts later on in a secondary product—which seems to me the most suggestive antecedent

---

[2] Karl Marx, *Capital*, Vol. 1, trans. Ben Fowkes, London: Penguin, 1976, 510.

for grasping what Sartre will now describe as a more "metaphysical" process. Nor should the fundamental opposition of multiplicity and unity be left out: for counterfinality reflects a "material unity of human actions … And passive unity, as the synthetic appearance of pure dispersal and as the exteriorization of the bond of interiority, is for *praxis* its unity as Other and in the domain of the other" (163). (This first passive activity of worked matter will find its echo in that much later objectification which is the social institution, characterized as an "active passivity.")

Two famous examples or set pieces will be called upon to illustrate the baleful effects of this "*praxis* without an author" (166): the deforestation of China and the monetary crisis which strikes the Spanish Empire at the height of its power in the New World. But it is important to remember that it is this global unity of counterfinality which also defines social class, as that shared situation which makes an agglomeration of individuals over into a class (and a collective in the larger sense): so that Sartre's excursus on class interest here (197–219) can be seen as a doctrinal obligation and a more specific contribution to Marxian class theory, and one which is in addition meant to distinguish this particular social structure from other features generally lumped together under an omnibus concept of ideology.

In Marx, the structure of labor and the structure of the commodity are two faces of the same phenomenon, two distinct languages, as it were, which characterize the same fundamental originality of capitalism like the alternating figurations of waves and of particles in quantum theory. So it is that at this point in the *Critique* that the dialectic, or anti-dialectic, of worked matter turns over into an examination of the type of social relations inseparable from it. We must here remember the paradox of the we-subject as it was described in *Being and Nothingness*: it is a form of subjectivity in which my (purely psychological) identification with other people is mediated by the "directions" on the world of things, the instructions on the box, the proper method for opening a can. But it is through such requirements (*exigences*, here translated "exigencies") that worked matter directs our activity in general. The subjectivity which accompanies this purely ideal or imaginary community with other people, other users and consumers, but other workers as well, will now be called seriality.

With this, we are at the very heart of this first, definitional volume of the *Critique* and are in a position to evaluate its central conceptual antithesis between two fundamental forms of collective existence, between the side-by-side indifference and anonymity of the "serial" agglomeration and the tightly knit interrelationship of the "group-in-fusion". This is an antithesis that is not merely a classificatory one, for as a principle of social dynamics and an empirical fact of social history, the group-in-fusion emerges from seriality as a reaction against it, its subsequent development and fate governed by the danger of its dissolution back into seriality again.

Nor is this a particularly original distinction, although Sartre's account of the internal structure of each form is remarkable and probably without precedent. Yet formally the antithesis has something of the same spirit as that traditionally attributed to the distinction between anthropology and sociology, given its now classical (modern) form by Tönnies in his famous opposition between *Gemeinschaft* and *Gesellschaft*, the former designating small clan-based or tribal, pre-modern or "traditional" societies, the latter the great urban agglomerations of modern industrial ones. In the *Critique*, however, no particular social or political form is attributed to the two terms; indeed, they are scarcely symmetrical at all in that sense, since seriality is a social condition that must extend through all kinds of societies and populations, while the group-in-fusion is hardly social form at all, but rather an emergence and an event, the formation of a guerrilla unit, the sudden crystallization of an "in-group" of any kind. (As we shall see, the formation of the group has a motivation and real historical content; but that content is quite irrelevant for the present structural description, and might range from stamp collecting to assassination conspiracies or political parties.)

The more fundamental question about the antithesis is an ethical one, for it is clear from the language of these descriptions that a judgment is implicit in them, and that the serial state, however comfortable or content its members might consider themselves to be, is one of mediocrity if not of alienation, while the group-in-fusion incarnates active human *praxis* in a uniquely heightened fashion—a kind of *praxis* all the more distinctive in that it constitutes the production, not of things, but of other people and the self, of a new kind of sociality.

Our question must then turn on the affinity between this judgment on social relations (which might in a pinch be foreshortened into a distinction between the private and the political) and the existential legacy of the concepts of authenticity and inauthenticity, which clearly spring to the tip of the tongue with any evocation of seriality and group existence. For this is an ambiguous legacy indeed, and in its first modern form, in Heidegger's work of the 1920s, it is overwhelmingly conservative in tenor: authentic is the individual's being-unto-death, and the call of a duty or mission, which if it is not overtly couched in group terms certainly evokes the soldier and the military unit. What is unmistakably authentic on the other hand is the anonymous state of what the 1920s characterized as "mass man," the faceless crowds of the big city, the "man" or "on" (German and French versions of the anybody or the impersonal "you"). Sartrean seriality is not far behind these early accounts, even though already in *Being and Nothingness* the class character of these collective actors is reversed, and it is the bourgeois we-subject which is inauthentic, while the we-object, the alienated and reified small group, is described in terms of underclass marginality and already anticipates the account of the group-in-fusion.

At a time when the very notions of authenticity and inauthenticity have come to seem suspiciously humanist and psychologizing, if not individualist, Sartre's celebration of the group may well incur the diagnosis of anarchism, or even left infantilism: the Right may well indict it for the excesses of the 1960s and their aftermath; the Left sense in it some surviving trace of left adventurism and romanticism; while Americans are likely to conjecture uncomfortable affinities with conspiratorial terrorist organizations. It would be more difficult, however, to take the other alternative offered by Sartre's antithesis and to come out with a full-throated defense and endorsement of seriality.

It is easiest to deal with the two states together, as they are in fact defined in deliberately antithetical terms. Thus in seriality, as in the now famous example of the waiting line for a city bus, "everyone is the same as the Others in so far as he is Other than himself" (260). And this otherness is as spatial as it is psychological: I am not in the center of my world, which is elsewhere, in other people (all of whom feel the same way as I do). In the group, on the contrary, each member is the center, the center is everywhere; otherness has been converted into identity. Nor, inasmuch as group formation is first and foremost an attempt to overcome the serial situation, is it surprising to find that in the group, everyone is the same as the other, and otherness has momentarily become a kind of collective identity. But it will also be clear that this second structure is necessarily far more complex than the first one, of seriality, in which people stand in a simple exteriority to one another.

Certainly seriality also knows its paradoxes: it is indeed no accident that Sartre's principal extended illustrations are those of radio broadcasts and of the free market. In fact, I believe, the notion of seriality developed here is the only philosophically satisfactory theory of public opinion, the only genuine philosophy of the media, that anyone has proposed to date: something that can be judged by its evasion of the conceptual traps of collective consciousness on the one hand, and of behaviorism or manipulation on the other. If this were all Sartre had managed to do in the *Critique*, it would already mark a considerable achievement (neglect of which may reflect the turn of current media theory towards a problematic of the image as much as anything else).

When it comes to the group-in-fusion, however, things are by no means so simple: we must reckon with what is no longer a dualism, a simple reciprocity or indifference of one person to another, but rather with a triadic form, in which (as in the group-object theory of *Being and Nothingness*) formerly serial individuals are united by the threat (or the Look) of an external third, which the emergent group must then interiorize in order to retain its coherence and its dynamic. Thus each member becomes a third to all the others, thereby grounding that omnipresent centrality of each member that was far too simply evoked in the preceding paragraphs:

> The individual, as a third party, is connected, in the unity of a single *praxis* (and therefore of a single perceptual vista) with the unity of individuals as inseparable moments of a nontotalized totalization, and with each of them as a third party, that is to say, through the mediation of the group. In terms of perception, I perceive the group as my common unity, and, simultaneously, as a mediation between me and every other third party ... the members of the group are third parties, which means that each of them totalizes the reciprocity of others. (374)

Just as this seemingly Ptolemaic system of turning thirds (*tiers*) proves to be something familiar that we know already from our daily experience, so the reader will find that, with a little practice, this rather startling prose quickly becomes readable enough.

We leave the reader to navigate it, but with an important proviso: we have here only designated the emergence of the group—famously illustrated by Sartre in the taking of the Bastille. What is not yet clear, indeed what is supremely problematic, is how it can possibly remain in being, as a group, when the threat of the external third party (the king's troops) has been withdrawn. One simple and obvious answer overshoots the mark: and that is that the group cannot remain in being; indeed it never was in being to begin with, in the ontological sense. It never had, nor can it ever acquire, any durable ontological status; it cannot therefore accede to any new form of collective being which might be expected to supercede that of the individual "being-for-itself" and thereby to cancel the famous peroration of *Being and Nothingness*. Here as there, then, "man" remains a "useless passion": yet at the same time Sartre's inveterate pessimism can here be grasped far more clearly as a critical instrument, and not merely an inheritance of the out-of-date Cartesian and phenomenological traditions of a "philosophy of the subject" centered on a purely individual consciousness. Rather, as always in Sartre, ontological failure and anxiety are energizing and the stimulus to further *praxis* and subsequent group formation:

> The group has not, and cannot have, the ontological nature which it claims in its *praxis*; conversely, each and all are produced and defined in terms of this nonexistent totality. There is a sort of internal vacuum, an unbridgeable and indeterminate distance, a sort of malaise in every community, large or small; and this uneasiness occasions a strengthening of the practices of integration, and increases with the integration of the group. (583)

It remains to indicate briefly how, in this situation and seemingly doomed to failure, the group does finally manage to become something structurally other than a mere punctual interruption of seriality.

We have already hinted at the crucial mechanism by which a few straggling "others" momentarily brought together by an external threat (from the external Other or third) solidify this momentary solidarity: it is by interiorizing the *tiers* itself (the "third party") in such a way that each member of the initial group becomes a third to all the others. Each is now both part and whole of this strange new structure, both individual member and also that now internalized exteriority which grasps all of the members ("as though from the outside") as a group. We must not say that at this stage there is no leader: on the contrary, at this stage everyone is the leader, whose task, like the tribal chieftain of Pierre Clastres's anthropology, is not to impose a line of action but merely to speak its possibility aloud, to be the mouthpiece of the situation itself before the group.

It is a Utopian state (Malraux's "lyric apocalypse") which cannot last. Everything now turns on the problem of the future, and of the future of the group: it will be clear in a moment how this problem sets vibrating the deepest existential concerns of *Being and Nothingness* at the same time that it generates its most dramatic language, its most eloquent pathos: my project is "a temporal form where I await myself in the future, where 'I make an appointment with myself on the other side of that hour, of that day, of that month.' Anguish is the fear of not finding myself at that appointment, of no longer even wishing to bring myself there." But where the group is concerned, this appointment is the pledge, and the paradigm of the French Revolution reveals that its fundamental structure is the Terror and the threat of death. The Tennis Court Oath is the moment in which this paradigm becomes fixed: the very beginning of the Revolution itself—the "revolutionary" Revolution, as opposed to the counterrevolution of the nobles against the king that preceded and triggered it. For in the Tennis Court Oath, the bourgeoisie and its hegemonic bloc, reassembled in an unused space in the palace, collectively swear, under pain of death, not to separate until the Constitution shall have been established, "sur des fondements solides" (June 20, 1789). The crucial clause, "under pain of death," is not merely Sartre's interpretation or extrapolation: it is the implied reading deduced after the fact by Robespierre's Terror, as the latter's justification. It is also the (desperate and impossible) attempt to solve the problem of future commitment already raised in *Being and Nothingness*: for this consent to my own death and execution (by all the members of the group) is not only my effort to compel the fidelity of all the others, it is also and first and foremost my attempt to protect myself against myself, to compel the fidelity of my future self to my present one (422). It is finally, also, the production of treason as such, since seriality cannot know the latter, which can only exist as the violation of this very oath of allegiance. This is the moment to remember the profound resonance of this theme of treason and the traitor throughout all of Sartre: as the "objective treason" of the intellectual never fully or ontologically committed to any cause; as the *jouissance* of treason

---

[3] Jean-Paul Sartre, *Being and Nothingness*, trans. Hazel E. Barnes, New York: Citadel Press, 1956, 36.

in the rebel (particularly in Genet), or of the *l'homme du ressentiment* (particularly in the collaborators); the great test of my authenticity as well (will I stand up under torture?), and the eternal self-doubt of the bourgeois renegade against his own class, variously elaborated in *Lucifer and the Lord* and in *Words*, if not in the interminable *Family Idiot* itself.

The pledge is now the positive side of all that, the great moment of affirmation in all of Sartre; indeed it is the very "origin of humanity" (436):

> We are the same because we emerged from the clay at the same date and through all the others; and so we are, as it were, an individual species, which has emerged at a particular moment through a sudden mutation; but our specific nature unites us in so far as it is freedom ... this fraternity is not based, as is sometimes stupidly supposed, on physical resemblance expressing some deep identity of nature. If it were, why should not a pea in a can be described as the brother of another pea in the same can? We are brothers in so far as, following the creative act of the pledge, we are our own sons, our common creation. (437)

The pledge is thus the climactic moment of constituent power: its articulation as a date and an event is what gives the French Revolution its paradigmatic quality over all those other revolutions in which it is necessarily present but only implicit as an act and as the very expression of the multitude. Its theorization places Sartre squarely in the great tradition that runs from Rousseau to Antonio Negri and passes through the Paris Commune itself.

The more sombre concluding pages of the *Critique* will then observe and bear witness to the inevitable decline from this apotheosis. They chronicle the slow ossification of the group under the pressure of some surrounding universal seriality. Indeed, they permit us to reaffirm the transformation (or sublation) of the older question of authenticity into this newer political and collective dilemma. For (as in Heidegger) authenticity is never, for Sartre, a state which one can somehow achieve and in which one can then dwell and persevere: it is a precarious space conquered from the swamp of inauthenticity itself, into which it then fatally lapses. If one can speak, indeed, of anything like a human nature, then one must say that that nature is first and foremost inauthentic, in which moments of authenticity are but fitful and evanescent episodes (it is a doctrine already anticipated in a distorted form by Christian images of sin and grace). But this raises serious questions about the implications for a philosophy of history of such a view of group authenticity.

At any rate, it would seem that Sartre foresees at least three ways in which the group can dissolve: it can of course simply disperse back into seriality, like a crowd which dissolves and goes back to its ordinary business. But this is to grasp the group-in-fusion before the defining moment of the pledge. After that, what lies in store for it is institutionalization, with its dual forms of bureaucracy and dictatorship, forms which Sartre's account—with its accounts of schism and factionality, of the passive activity of the institutional practico-inert, of hierarchy, of the externalization of authority and the emergence of the sovereign and of a henceforth serial obedience—seems to conflate and to identify together. But this is because the underlying paradigm has changed; and from now on, and throughout Volume 2 of the *Critique*, it will be the fate of the Soviet Revolution after Lenin's death which is the reference. (Thus the entire *Critique* may also be read as an elaborate historical commentary, in the spirit of Machiavelli or Gramsci, on these two supreme events which are the French and the Soviet revolutions.)

But it should not thereby be concluded that the *Critique* replicates the standard bourgeois dogma according to which revolution (here, group formation) inevitably leads to totalitarianism (or in other words, Stalinism). Nor, on the other hand, do we here discover in advance the Deleuze–Guattari vision of innumerable nomadic and guerrilla war machines forever flinging themselves against the inevitable State. In Sartre, the State itself is a reified group-in-fusion which has established itself within a milieu of seriality (perhaps on the distant analogy of those former Nomads who become the imperial ruling class). The point is, however, as has already been warned, that this first volume of the *Critique* is not intended to offer a vision of History; but only to lay in place the concepts and the categories with which such a vision might be constructed. If history is already present here, this is merely in the formal sense in which all history offers an endless spectacle of the interaction of seriality and group formation, like a great current, on which white water, ripples and swells, appear and disappear ceaselessly. Yet the river's source and its drainage, its ultimate return into the sea, are issues distinct from this steady stream into which one always steps.

Those issues, intimated at the end of this volume and then sporadically developed in what was to have been the second one, turn on the rather different matter of historical unification, and of Sartre's fundamental maxim that the many histories of the past have gradually become unified into one history. Any "philosophy of history" today must begin with this qualification that History, in that unified and universal sense, has not yet existed, but is only now coming into being. There were once many distinct and unrelated histories, many distinct modes of production, as innumerable, if not as grains of sand, then at least as the languages of the New World and of Australasia, so many separate and unrelated tribes and groups of hunters-and-gatherers, who only gradually over many millennia come to be unified, that is to say, to share the common destiny which a world capitalism gradually imposed on them. In the brief decades between Sartre's composition of the *Critique* and the visible emergence of what we now call globalization, this principle has become inescapable, and with it the very possibility of a universal history reemerges in a new way.

Chapter 8

Sartre's *Critique*, Volume 2: An Introduction

At the time (1963) many of us thought that Sartre's *Critique* was unfinished or incomplete: but of course it could at best be unfinished like Heidegger's *Sein und Zeit* (for a long time famously, "Part 1") or at worst fragmentary like Benjamin's *Arcades*. The "break" was variously accounted for: the manuscript was too long and had to be broken off somewhere; Sartre had had a mild stroke (all those uppers!); he had lost interest (having never completed anything but the plays anyway); he could not solve the problem (the "meaning of History") and had given up; he had stopped "being" a Marxist and the dialectical project thereby lost its point; or any and all of the above. Rumors about a second volume were always accompanied by the warning that it went in a very different direction, or was nothing but an assemblage of unrelated fragments (and/or both). When the remarkably edited edition of Arlette Elkaïm-Sartre's finally did appear, in 1985, it was too late. No one was even interested in Volume 1 anymore; France was submerged by a belated but strenuously dogmatic anti-Marxist fervor.

Nor did the second volume's extended and seemingly obsessive analyses of Stalinism and the history of the Soviet Revolution help matters. By the mid-eighties no one was interested in that anymore either, except to outdo each other in composing chilling pictures of Stalinist violence and adding new icons to the gallery of twentieth-century political monsters.

Meanwhile poststructuralism had long since reckoned its accounts with Sartre and his old-fashioned philosophizing. Never mind the respectful references to the *Critique* itself in Deleuze and Guattari's *Anti-Oedipus*. It was already clear to everyone that the "dialectic," whatever it is, illicitly posited in advance some subject-object dichotomy which even the deconstructionist beginner was capable of identifying as a false problem and a mistake destined for more than "erasure."

But one does not get rid of the subject-object opposition by the mere taking of thought, any more than one gets rid of what is more or less the same—the mind/body split—by affirming one's materialism or idealism, or at any rate one's monism. I hesitate to characterize these themes in some

Kantian way as eternal categories of the mind itself; still, however historical, they are certainly deeply sedimented structural features of our situation as human beings. As such the best philosophy can do, besides ignoring them, is to invent better ways of negotiating their apparent dualism, of reformulating them in terms of a kind of ambivalence, at the risk of being accused of purely verbal solutions. Sartre, with his "third way" between idealism and materialism—a philosophy of praxis—was able to articulate this ambivalence in terms of that preeminently amphibious thing, the body, both subject and object all at once, *pour-soi* and *en-soi* inextricably intermingled. The importance of this "solution" in the present context, however, is that, having been merely implicit in *L'Être et le néant*, with its voluntarism and its emphasis on freedom, it becomes the fundamental key to the *Critique* and its confrontation with history.

There is a scene in one of Sartre's novels in which one partner, giddy with some momentary euphoria, seizes the other's wrist and shakes the hand in the air as one would play with a baby. For the subject, the experience offers a peculiar phenomenological sensation, that of the hand as inert object in the world. *Being and Nothingness* had insisted over and over again that the hand as such is not an instrument or a tool, not a material implement in the service of some practical intention: it *is* that practical intention itself (to use the preferred Sartrean phrase), it embodies our practices and turns what it uses into the latter's instruments or tools. Or better still, it transforms the latter—a hammer, a tennis racket—into extensions of the body, which is to say, of my intentional action. It is not until the act is interrupted in failure— I miss the ball, or the nail—that consciousness flows back into my hand as an imperfect instrument in the world. There reigns here a latent dualism of action and the inert (which will shortly become the passive): this is no longer the dualism of the *pour-soi* and the *en-soi* (as Sartre calls the subject and the object), but it is what they have become, what they are transformed into, by the emergence of human reality as praxis and activity.

What now has to be emphasized is what makes this kind of ambivalence possible, what can account for this capability of what we call the body to pass from an active to a passive state, or better still, from what we grasp as ourselves and our action, to what we mutely contemplate as a kind of thing in the world that somehow belongs to us but which remains at a distance and is no longer altogether in our power. The lapse or failure is only one staged situation in which such ambivalence becomes phenomenologically accessible; the jiggling of the hand itself is, of course, yet another one. But the process itself—the alternation between action and inertia—must somehow be grounded in some deeper possibility within the body itself.

The characteristic Sartrean formula for this possibility is the one foreshadowed in the description of sexuality in the earlier work: "the body which desires is consciousness making itself body ... in desire I make myself flesh *in the presence of the Other in order to appropriate* the Other's flesh."[1] It is, to be sure, a rather specialized situation, which we do not often associate with work or with the world of objects. Yet already and implicitly these two situations are ontologically related: we can only confront the inertia of things, of matter, of the *en-soi*, by making ourselves inert. We make our active body a thing in order to engage the thingness of the world. The so-called body (*my* body, it is worth emphasizing) is, to be sure, not a thing for me, it is myself and action in the world. Yet we endow this bodily existence of ours with inertia in order to bring ourselves to bear on the inert; we make ourselves that *en-soi* (which we also are) in order to weigh on the *en-soi*, to intervene in it, to modify it.

> The organism ... makes itself inert and commits its subsisting functions to producing and preserving this inertia, with an actual view to transforming exteriority through exteriority. Through this negation of itself and the exterior milieu, it constitutes exteriority within itself and outside as the *means* of restoring to itself the integrity of its organic functions. The fundamental choice of this *passion*, inasmuch as it is realized through labor, is simply the *action*.[2]

It is enough: this ambivalence of what we normally and without thinking call "our bodies"—this possibility of being either *pour-soi*, intention and action in the world, or else making ourselves *en-soi* and matter, paying the price of a certain active passivity, of inertia and extension as tools in the realization of our project—this ambivalence then becomes the key to human history itself, and to the fate of human and collective action in it. The individual and collective projects which seek to intervene in the material world are then seen as endowing themselves with a kind of materiality which transfers teleology and intention, a kind of project-ness, to that world itself in such a way that it reacts back on human beings themselves, thereby producing that unique alienation we call History.

Such were the principles laid in place by the first volume of the *Critique*. One cannot characterize its distinctions as synchronic, exactly, since the structural conception of the synchronic is incompatible with Sartrean thought, every situation in the present carrying with it a sedimentation of the past and consisting as it were in layers of dead action and praxis (itself reabsorbed into the material world in much the same way as for Marx the

---

[1] *Being and Nothingness*, trans. Hazel E. Barnes, New York: Washington Square Press, 1966, 505–506; in French, *L'Être et le néant*, Paris: Gallimard, 1943, 458.

[2] Jean-Paul Sartre, *Critique of Dialectical Reason*, Vol. 2, trans. Quintin Hoare, London: Verso, 1991, 373–4; in French, *Critique de la raison dialectique*, tome 2, revised ed., Paris: Gallimard, 1985, 382. Unless otherwise noted, all page references refer to this work; page references will cite volume number, then the English edition, followed by the French edition.

machine carries within itself stored human labor). Still, the first volume ended with a promise to set all this in motion; and after that first immense "regressive" analysis of the conditions of possibility, "progressively" to reconstruct the emergence of the consequences and to observe the production of History itself.[3]

Here we inevitably confront the question of the relationship between this philosophy and Marxism itself. Sartre had already warned us in Volume 1:

> We must give notice that the investigation we are undertaking, though in itself historical, like any other undertaking, does not attempt to discover the movement of History, the evolution of labor or of the relations of production, or class conflicts. Its goal is simply to reveal and establish dialectical rationality, that is to say, the complex play of *praxis* and totalization. (Vol. 1, 39; 157)

This is not an altogether coherent or reliable statement. We may recall that in the earlier, but intimately related, *Search for a Method*, Sartre had famously declared that every age knows its own truth in the form of a dominant philosophy, of which Marxism is ours; but that currents of thought like existentialism were rather to be considered as "ideologies," whose function lay in the critique and correction of that dominant philosophy.[4]

Here, however, the clarification of the dialectic (no longer, to be sure, identified as existentialism, but retaining all kinds of intimate relations with the latter, as we shall see) is posited as an attempt to establish the truth claims of Marxism (which are, in a sense, both historical, in the sense that Marxism could only come into being in our mode of production, and transhistorical, inasmuch as the dialectic is grounded in the very nature of human action as such). Marx did not live to write his book on dialectics; and Sartre's affirmation is of a piece with any number of assertions (since Engels's invention of that rather different thing called Marxism) that the

---

[3] The "regressive-progressive method" (credited by Sartre to Henri Lefebvre) is more fully outlined in *Search for a Method*, trans. Hazel E. Barnes, New York: Vintage Books, 1968; in French, "Question de méthode," in *Critique de la raison dialectique*, tome 1, Paris: Gallimard, 1985, 19–132, and consists in reconstructing the elements of the original situation and then reimagining the historical act which, as free choice and innovation, emerges in response to it. I should add that the numerous concrete illustrations throughout the *Critique* (such as the boxing match in Volume 2) suggest the close relationship between this work of the historian and the novelistic imagination itself.

[4] See *Search for a Method*, 7–8; and "Question de méthode," 21–22. In my opinion, the idiosyncratic choice of the word "ideology" for the critical and corrective theory Sartre has in mind tends to blur those very different problems (often associated with "false consciousness") with which the word is also associated.

basic Marxist positions and principles needed to be completed by some thoroughgoing and properly philosophical justification—a conviction that has given us any number of very different Marxist "philosophies," whose characters range from positivism to Christianity, from phenomenology to pragmatism, from Lukács's reification theory to analytic philosophy.

However estimable such philosophical speculations may or may not have been—and certainly *History and Class Consciousness* and Sartre's *Critique* were fundamental contributions to the development of philosophy itself— I would prefer to grasp Marxism as something rather different from a philosophical system (incomplete or not). I believe that it shares, uniquely with psychoanalysis in our time, the character of an as yet unnamed conceptual species one can only call a unity of theory and practice, which by its very nature and structure stubbornly resists assimilation to the older philosophical "system" as such.

However this may be, it does not invalidate Sartre's inquiries into the nature of dialectical understanding and its distinction from what he calls analytic thinking (these two corresponding more or less to Hegel's distinction between *Verstand* and *Vernunft*)[5]; but the perspective does isolate rather starkly Sartre's need to ground his new "Marxist" system on what would seem a metaphysical foundation, namely the concept of scarcity, from which negation (along with the well-known negation of the negation) is said to derive. This is not the place to inquire further into this much debated and debatable "humanist" concept: except to observe that it is historicized by Science Fiction, appealed to at several key points in the present volume (319–322, 339–340; 330–333, 350–351); the point being that the primacy of scarcity only holds for this particular world of ours, others of a radically different and even Utopian type being imaginable. Such thought experiments, in my opinion, function as a way of transforming the hypothesis of scarcity into a relative proposition rather than a metaphysically absolute one (and they also include Utopian possibilities). At any rate the central humanist category of "need," exemplifying Engels's negation of the negation (Vol. 2, 277; 287) is immediately derived from the fact of scarcity—"the world is not made for man" (Vol. 2, 220; 231).

---

[5] See the discussion of "dialectical comprehension" (Vol. 2, 369–380; 378–390); and also the various discussions of science as the restricted truth of analytic reason or the thought of exteriority (Vol. 2, 417–421; 426–429. And especially Vol. 1, 57–64; 172–179). A different kind of reification emerges from the past (as what has become a kind of *en-soi* within the *pour-soi*): this is the realm of "essences" (Vol. 2, 350; 359), which thereby rejoins that whole dimension of reification which Sartre called the *psyche* in *Being and Nothingness* and which included emotions and the self, fully as much as Ideas.

As for the disclaimer in Volume 1 which we have quoted above, it is certainly not true that the *Critique* eschews all discussions of class and class struggle. On the contrary the first volume is very much concerned to distinguish the historical phenomenon of social class from those collective structures centrally identified as seriality and the group-in-fusion: it is a more historically ambiguous phenomenon, sometimes having the unity of the group, sometimes the dispersal of seriality, and sometimes the rigidity of an institution (Vol. 1, 678; 761).

Nor is it accurate to say that the *Critique* ignores class struggle: indeed the initial direction of Volume 2 takes up this theoretical challenge quite explicitly in posing the philosophical question of the unity of two distinct projects or praxes in conflict or struggle with each other. How can we affirm the dialectical unity of these two autonomous projects when there exists outside of them no third point of view, no position of the godlike observer, from which that unity might be perceived? Yet if they are not somehow unified, then History itself has no unity and is dispersed into a multiplicity of distinct human efforts whose contingent contacts and conflicts have a merely analytic meaning on the order of the intersection of random molecules.

It is a problem rehearsed and redramatized on several levels (which I will call allegorical). The first—the great phenomenological example—is that of a boxing match: as a gifted boxer in his youth, Sartre knew something about the incorrect totalizations of spectators who read a simple and essentially unified pattern of parry and riposte into such complex events. On another level altogether, it is hard not to see this whole elaborate analysis as an allegory of the Cold War itself, and a philosophical attempt to comprehend the historical unity of the struggle between the two distinct collective projects of communism and capitalism (here significantly termed directorial societies and bourgeois democracies). It is a distinction to which we will return in a moment; suffice it to add that the final level of the allegory is constituted by the existential-phenomenological requirement itself, namely to ground all these dimensions in the ultimate reality of the human body itself.

It is worth underscoring one further feature of the already quoted distinction between the *Critique*'s investigation and Marxism as such, and that is the expression "the movement of History" ("le mouvement de l'Histoire"). The *Critique*, and in particular this second volume, is in fact very much concerned with the problem of the "meaning" of history ("le sens de l'histoire"). Does this imply that Sartre distinguishes between a traditional Marxist and apparently teleological conception of the movement of History towards socialism (leaving "inevitability" out of it) and some other kind of meaning which History may or may not have? I think so: and it accounts for the conspicuous absence of any references to socialism as such in these volumes, as well as for the defense of the whole enterprise as an attempt to understand dialectical understanding as such—something which has as much to do with the question of multiplicity as with what was called the project in *Being and Nothingness*, but which is here named totalization. Sartre quite plausibly affirms that the "unity" of history is recent and itself historical: once there were many histories, innumerable ones sometimes as microscopic as the fate of individual groups of hunters-and-gatherers.[6] Today History has a meaning (and bears a capital letter) owing to the twin unifications of colonialism and imperialism. But the fundamental question remains, and it determines the whole unfolding of the arguments of the *Critique*, namely whether we can bring to this immense unification the same kind of understanding brought to bear on the acts and projects, the totalizations, of individuals. This is the sense in which History will be able to be said to have a "meaning" or not, whatever its "movement."

A final remark on the relationship between Marxism and the *Critique* imposes itself at this point. There can be no doubt that much of the *Critique* is taken up with labor and production, from the phenomenological standpoint of the workers themselves. Their opposite number, the capitalists or businessmen, are then phenomenologically grasped in terms of a structural reaction and, as it were, a defensive compensation against the existence of the workers and their various groups-in-fusion. This phenomenological bias of Sartre's, so to speak, would of course solve in advance that problem of the unity of struggle between two projects which is reformulated at the beginning of the second volume. But I believe it points to a more fundamental absence in the *Critique* itself, and that is capitalism itself: it is this glaring absence that causes readers occasionally to wonder whether this is really a Marxist work after all. Nor is it enough to observe that as the analysis of capitalism has long been achieved already (in *Capital*), Sartre did not need to cover that familiar ground again. Clearly, we need to take a closer look at the return of the phenomenological method in force here in the second volume, as well as at the status of capitalism as an anti-dialectic and the supreme form of the practico-inert in its vision of history.

Yet these terms, which it was the function of Volume 1 to define and to elaborate, remind us that the terminology of Volume 2—some of it new with respect to Volume 1 and some of it pressed into more insistent service in this shift from the synchronic to the diachronic—demands a few preliminary comments at this point. I will not return to the uninformed polemics surrounding the term "totalization," which is little more than the new dialectical word for what Sartre used to call the project, in *Being and Nothingness*, and which helps to articulate the latter (along with its correlative,

---

[6] "The signification of a history is not its *meaning* [*sens*]. An arrested history (that of Pompeii or the Incas) has no *meaning* for us. It had one for those who lived it in interiority. It may have a *signification*: if we find the ensemble of factors that arrest it" (Vol. 2, 402; 410–411).

the situation). But it is worth reminding the reader for whom this term has become a negative symptom of everything old-fashioned, bad, humanistic, or universalizing in Sartre, that it is always explicitly distinguished from any notion of an achieved totality: "totalization" is a temporal word, and can never connote completion or closure. It does, however, always designate a kind of finitude, and that is why such a reader must also be reminded that the currently modish notion of "singularity" is also very much a Sartrean term and always accompanies the identification of any totalization as such. (There was always something paradoxical, if not wrong-headed, in the denunciation of existentialism, and its philosophy of freedom and singularity, as a Hegelian universalism.)

Totalization as a concept deploys several sets of binary semes which can be folded back into each other depending on the matter or occasion. Multiplicity, for example, is a crucial feature of our encounter with the world, which inevitably calls for unification (although not for unity): readers of Sartre's novels, even more than of the philosophical works, will be aware of the role multiplicity plays in his narratives, particularly in the form of the multiplicity of people or of others in the world, as in *Le Sursis* (*The Reprieve*).[7]

But the unification (or partial unification) of such multiplicities is also related to the interiorization of what is exterior to or external in them: terms designed to replace the old unwanted subject-object dualism by process words that emphasize that ambiguous shifting back and forth between the two poles discussed above, and which then in turn produce the correlative term "exteriorization."

Yet the exterior is essentially the inert, or indeed, the old *en-soi* of *Being and Nothingness*; and the dialectic of the inert and the active is very much at the heart of things here (even though Sartre only occasionally recalls the older ontological terminology [but see vol. 2, 315ff; 320ff]) where the

---

[7] "A vast entity, a planet in a space of a hundred million dimensions; three-dimensional beings could not so much as imagine it. And yet each dimension was an autonomous consciousness. Try to look directly at that planet, it would disintegrate into tiny fragments, and nothing but consciousness would be left. A hundred million free consciousnesses, each aware of walls, the glowing stump of a cigar, familiar faces, and each constructing its destiny on its own responsibility. And yet each of those consciousnesses, by imperceptible contacts and insensible changes, realizes its existence as a cell in a gigantic and invisible coral. War: everyone is free, and yet the die is cast. It is there, it is everywhere, it is the totality of all my thoughts, of all Hitler's words, of all Gomez's acts; but no one is there to add it up. It exists solely for God. But God does not exist. And yet war exists." *The Reprieve*, trans. Eric Sutton, New York: Knopf, 1947, 326; in French, *Le Sursis*, in *Oeuvres romanesques*, Paris: Gallimard, 1981, 1,024–1,025.

characterization of the *en-soi* is however more useful in conveying the practico-inert than that of the *pour-soi* for praxis and totalization.

All of which dramatically underscores the ultimate status of the *Critique* as the philosophy of praxis par excellence: the philosophy of freedom of *Being and Nothingness* always implied a primacy of activity. Here it takes central stage, with the consequence that the opposite number of praxis, namely the anti-dialectic, the practico-inert, what corrodes human action and projects, what resists collective efforts to overcome the inertias and failures of History, must also necessarily take center stage along with it. Freedom was not accompanied by non-freedom, but rather by *mauvaise foi* (bad faith) and by facticity and contingency. Here, however, we confront a malignant force which is the very motor force of human production absorbed and turned against the latter: a force which becomes more visible in the collective, rather than the individual or existential, dimension.

So perhaps our initial query slowly shifts around into a rather different one: not how Marxist this Sartre of the *Critique* can be considered to be, but rather how existential he can be said to remain, despite the frequent insistence on singularity. At this point we also return to the question of phenomenology raised above, and we confront the omnipresence of what may be a new theme for the *Critique* but what is also an old and familiar preoccupation of *Being and Nothingness*, namely the phenomenon of incarnation.

Again, paradoxically, it was in the earlier book's pathbreaking analysis of sexuality that "incarnation" found its currency; and the sexual overtones (along with the inescapable religious ones) remain something of an annoyance for the serious understanding of the new role this word is called upon to play in the *Critique*. No less a paradox, and no doubt an equally annoying association, is its initial deployment around the person of Stalin himself. We must remind ourselves, in order to grasp this development, that no less than with a philosophical inquiry into history and historiography, Sartre was also preoccupied with the philosophical possibilities and justifications of biography as such. From the first sketchy studies of Baudelaire and Mallarmé, to the monumental book on Jean Genet, and on into the interminable and unterminated final study of Flaubert, the analysis of the determinations of an individual life remained a central question for Sartre (it will be remembered that Antoine Roquentin was himself already preoccupied with understanding the life and actions of the enigmatic M. de Rollebon).

It was therefore not only with the dynamic of the Soviet Revolution and the communist state that Sartre remained engaged here, but also with the person of Stalin himself. Why Stalin? Sartre never tired of mocking Plekhanov's airy remark that if Napoleon had not existed some other general would have done equally well in filling his place in history. Would not Trotsky have followed the same policies (maybe without killing people)? What is indeed the constitutive relationship between Stalinism and Stalin himself? Or are bourgeois pop-psychology and Sunday-supplement scandal-mongering and demonology right after all, such that everything can be explained by the fact that he was a monster? Sartre wants us to maintain the principles of what he called "existential psychoanalysis" (which differs from psychobiography in its equal emphasis on politics and the historical dialectic) in dealing with such figures; and to agree that our comprehension is not complete until we grasp the constitutive relationship between Stalin's character (itself a complex product of the historical situation) and his policies; or, to return to the language of the *Critique*, to grasp the incarnation of Stalin's totalizations in his own individual person. The concept thus designates the unavoidable mediation between the existential level and the dialectical-historical one; or, better still, it reintroduces the dialectical into the realm of the existential and of lived or phenomenological experience.[8]

This is evidently a never-ending project, an inexhaustible task (as the work on Flaubert confirms), in which the opposition between individual and collective is raised to the philosophical level of the antinomy of mind and body, or consciousness and matter—thereby becoming as unresolvable and as tantalizing and obsessive as the older ambiguity. It also reinforces a once influential criticism of Sartre from another quarter, namely the charge by Althusser of expressive causality (which the latter associated with Hegel and Hegelianism). This consisted in a residual practice of a kind of symbolic or organic thought in which every feature of a phenomenon is permeated by some central meaning, as in Spengler's concept of the spirit of the age, in which all the practices of a given period, say, the Baroque, are to be characterized as the various species of a common genus (Baroque art, Baroque statecraft, Baroque mathematics, Baroque philosophy, and so forth).[9] Here, the suspicion is awakened that Sartre's doctrine of incarnation wants to perpetuate some equally organic or symbolic view of a kind of identity between the historical process and the existential individual, from which not even the insistence on the constitutive operation of the logic of totalization on both these levels can save it. As I have hinted above, it seems to me that a rather different use of Sartre's idea may be available if we substitute the logic of

---

[8] Clearly, both *Saint Genet* and *The Family Idiot* are a great deal more dialectical than is here implied.

[9] See, for example, the remarks on Bach: "It is thus that the *meaning* of the *ancient regime* ... of the minor German courts ... of the clash between 'reason' and 'tradition,' as well as of the social hierarchy and the status of the artist, etc., is *temporally reproduced* in our ears by the playing of a Bach fugue on the harpsichord. Through this *retemporalization*—an incarnation of Bach's life itself—the conceptual ensemble we have just described is reincarnated as an ongoing process-praxis *through our time*" (Vol. 2, 296; 307).

allegory for that of the symbol; but this is not the place to develop such a suggestion further.

Still, the phenomenological problem of incarnation (and of Stalin) can at least helpfully lead us on into the other problem—that of the role of capitalism in the *Critique*—in an unexpected way. Sartre has indeed chosen to divide his topics in the second volume politically, into contrasting studies of what he calls directorial societies on the one hand (read: dictatorial or Stalinist) and bourgeois democracies on the other: about which the editor assures us repeatedly that the latter was never written. Unsurprisingly, this distinction reflects Sartre's growing loss of faith in the possibilities for the development of the Soviet Union[10]; surprisingly, however, it replicates the hoariest Cold War ideology, namely the opposition between closed and open societies (or between communist "totalitarianism" and the "free world"). We will revisit this distinction in a moment: a more serious objection to this classificatory move lies in its displacement of systemic description from the economic infrastructure to the political superstructure. The substitution of politics for economics was always a key move in the hegemonic struggle against Marxism (as in the substitution of questions of freedom for those of exploitation).

Indeed, this very substitution may explain why Sartre tired of his immense project and found it uninteresting to continue. For the notion of a directorial or dictatorial society is not only redolent of an ideology Sartre would have found it difficult to share: it also provides an attractive framework for the kind of phenomenological analysis which its opposite number—so-called bourgeois society—with its dispersal and atomization, its random currents and potentially non-unifiable and incorrigibly multiple forces, would render more arduous if not altogether impossible.[11] The very idea of incarnation itself calls for the centrality of a figure like Stalin (or the absolute monarchs of yesteryear), compared to whom the multiple office-holders of the various Western political systems offer less propitious and at best local objects of study.

But this very problem—which I would describe as a representational or even narrative one—brings us back to the absence of capitalism from Sartre's projected argument. Clearly enough, capitalism is a developed form

---

[10] Or maybe not: evoking the "science cringe" the first *Sputnik* unleashed in the US, the remarks that "one of the reasons for the American *Grande Peur* was the confused feeling in everyone of being an *object* of History, of which the Soviets were the *subject*" (Vol. 2, 319; 330n).

[11] "Marxism is strictly true if History is totalization. It is no longer true if human history is decomposed into a plurality of individual histories; or if, at any rate, within the relation of immanence which characterizes the fight the negation of each opponent by the other is on principle *detotalizing*" (Vol. 2, 16; 25).

of the practico-inert and its structures very much correspond to that seriality richly analyzed at such length in Volume 1, along with the close examinations of key related phenomena such as interest. What is missing are not the features and the pieces but rather capitalism as an actant, as a central actor on the stage of world history, as a primary agent, rather than a background system. Sartre's concept of totalization takes care adequately enough of all the players in the system, from Ken Lay to John D. Rockefeller, from the Roosevelts to Edison and Disney; but they dwindle to caricatures and bit players compared to capitalism itself as a personified system (or indeed to Stalin or Napoleon on the other, directorial side). And from that existential perspective which remained Sartre's to the very end, this satiric diminution is all to the good, and history's personification of its central forces is no doubt a mystification and a mere literary device. Yet in the ever more glaring light of Sartre's fundamental assertion—that there once were many histories and now only one—such reluctance to "name the system" is no longer helpful; and perhaps in late capitalism, in full globalization and post-modernity, we must feel the unified force of this system in a more immediate and personal way than Sartre could.

On the other hand, this recognition has what is perhaps an unexpectedly positive consequence for contemporary students of the *Critique*. For we now come to it with the conviction that Sartre's binary opposition was illegitimate and also unnecessary; and that there really is no difference between directorial societies and bourgeois democracies. Foucault played his role in the effacement of this distinction by showing how power is today everywhere at work in its microscopic developments, its capillary spread through the older social forms. The emergence of an American empire then completes the process, unveiling the prize-winning exhibit of a bourgeois democracy to be itself a state riddled with intimidation and surveillance, disinformation and conformism, corruption, unbridled exploitation and deregulated appropriative impulses, interventionist to its core and incorrigibly driven to military adventure not by its soldiers but by big business itself. This is the situation in which Volume 2's analysis of the "totalization of envelopment" (which Sartre thought characterized the Soviet Union alone) has now acquired universal value, and the *Critique* recovers its rightful place as one of the central philosophical achievements of modern times.

A final word may be in order about the title, which deliberately recalls the great Kantian precedent. Are we then to understand that Sartre's *Critique* aims, in similar fashion, to set limits to what it identifies as reason today? We have already mentioned the constitutive distinction between analytic and dialectical reason, the former being a subset of the latter projected into exteriority.[12] Comprehension as such, however—the grasping of the project or

---

[12] See note 5 above.

of totalization—is only limited by the *en-soi* itself, by contingency and the not-I, or, in Sartre's terms here, by scarcity as the fundamental fact of this particular world. Yet there are many scarcities in our world, among them the scarcity of life and the scarcity of time. This accounts for the repeated insistence, in late Sartre, that if everything is a project, if everything is totalization, then we must also acknowledge the inevitable failure of all totalizations, their finitude and their unfinished character, owing to the central fact of death. History is thus necessarily "*a history of mortal organisms*" (Vol. 2, 312; 323); death "as a contingent brutality—i.e., as a naked manifestation of facticity —is unassimilable and non-transcendable, and at the very heart of History manifests itself as a rupture of the synthetic links of interiority" (Vol. 2, 313; 323–324); and this is an altogether different kind of limit to dialectical comprehension than the anti-dialectic, which is itself generated by the human project itself.

For one thing, this accounts for the primacy of discontinuities and breaks in History: "History reveals itself to warring individuals and groups as *riddled with holes*" (Vol. 2, 313; 324). For another, it reinforces the acute consciousness modern or, perhaps even more, postmodern people have come to have of the generational break and the need to grasp the fact of generations dialectically and to include it constitutively within history (and within the collective projects themselves). Finally, this insistence on death may strengthen the reminder that to theorize the primacy of History is not necessarily the same as to celebrate it. Indeed, the *Critique*'s concluding fragment is stunning in its properly existential denunciation of History as alienation. To the question, "is History essential to man?," it answers: "No. It is the outside lived as the inside, the inside lived as an outside. It is man's own exteriority (his being-an-object for cosmic forces, for example) lived as his interiority" (Vol. 2, 450; 451).

PART IV
ENTRIES

Chapter 9

Commodification

"Commodification" designates the structural tendency in capitalism whereby matters of value are transformed into objects with a price that can potentially be sold on the market. The conceptual difficulties of grasping this process are betrayed by the very fluctuations of this word in the various national languages. In English the term is not universally recognized (and writers out of the Marxist tradition sometimes substitute the uglier "commoditization"). In French the word "commodity" is rendered by the older *marchandise*, rendering the construction of a process word (*marchandisation*) more awkward. German characteristically doubles the native word *Ware*, which presents the same problem, with the foreign loan stem, producing the term *Kommodifizierung*. And so forth.

I.

The concept of the commodity is constructed at the intersection of two phenomena, both grasped as processes or as the result of formal and structural transformations. On the one hand, the item in question must have been transformed into an object. On the other, it must be endowed with a specific value or in other words have acquired a price. Neither of these attributes is necessarily obvious: some commodities are for example not distinct physical objects in appearance, and some are seemingly natural things rather than man-made things (as Marx frequently points out to his more dogmatic followers). Nor is the exchangeability of the item, its value on the market, always clear-cut (as in the products of commercial culture).

But this means that each of these attributes must initially be examined separately. Thus, on the one hand, the analysis of commodification will lead us back to some prior discussion of the more fundamental phenomenon of objectification as such, or the organization of reality into things (or substances, as they were called in antiquity); after this initial and as it were metaphysical stage, there would then be required an analysis of reification or

Verdinglichung, the imposition of that metaphysical object form on entities which are not naturally so organized. It is then the moment of reification which enables the emergence of commodification as such; or to put it the other way around, the existence of a tendency to commodification is then what motivates reification and encourages its influence in all kinds of areas (the psychic and the cultural, for example) in which it did not previously hold sway or seem applicable. Obviously enough the most dramatic and mysterious place of reification and commodification is labor power itself, in capitalism transformed into a thing by the measurement of time, and then endowed with a price and an exchange value.

Meanwhile, the other line of analysis, that of value and price, will lead back to the market mechanisms themselves, since "exchange" implies a space in which distinct objects can be made equivalent and then mediated by way of some sort of value system. In this sense, commodification as a process will depend for its precondition on the establishment of the appropriate institutionalized market: thus the commodification of artworks depends on the system of galleries and organized markets for the sale of paintings, a system which in its turn requires the codification of values by critics and museums, a codification which the market then gradually, if indirectly and in a mediated way, brings into being.

2.

It is appropriate to trace a heightened sense of the phenomenon of thingification (*chosification* in Sartrean French) back to Schopenhauer's critique of Kant.

Schopenhauer indeed objected that Kant had omitted a fundamental category from his enumeration of a priori forms, and that was the form of the object or substance itself. However we judge the value of the observation as a philosophical critique, it stands as an attempt to defamiliarize our common-sense perception of objects in a more thoroughgoing way than any of the traditional accounts of substance, which take the form for granted. Schopenhauer is indeed here performing a thought experiment in which we are asked to go around behind our common-sense experience of the world as a collection of objects, and to confront some hypothetical reality in which the world is still that "blooming, buzzing confusion" evoked so memorably by William James. We must in other words be able to imagine the world without the object form in order to develop a more precise awareness of the role that form plays in our world.

The Marxist tradition, to be sure, offers a different kind of estrangement-effect to this same end. In Marxism what is imagined as preceding a world organized into objects is a world of human relations and human production, in which the appearance of objects is translated back into these very different realities (and in which presumably the static and immobile sense of a world of material substances is replaced by the historical mobility of innumerable processes).

The appearance of the commodity then determines and crystallizes this emergence of a world of things from a world of production and process; and it is in this context that Marx speaks of the objectification of human relations in the form of things (*Vergegenständlichung*, *Verdinglichung*). From one perspective, of course, the emergence of a notion of objectification may be located in Marx's early *Auseinandersetzung* with Hegel himself, for whom objectification and externalization was a positive and essential (if dialectical) moment of human history and progress. Indeed, in Hegel, individual and collective or historical development are posited as a ceaseless externalization of inner forms by human beings, a relentless expansion of the social and cultural object world (taken now in the widest sense, which includes figural uses). Marx's early conception of alienation springs from his differentiation of a bad and destructive form of objectification, to be found in the exploitation of the worker and his labor power, from that creative objectification which alone Hegel was able to see at work in history.

After Marx, however, and before the posthumous publication in 1929 of Marx's early writings on alienation, reification as such makes its official philosophical debut in Georg Lukács's *History and Class Consciousness*, in which the commodification of labor power—now identified in the form of a philosophical concept as reification—becomes the means to differentiate the conceptual (and cultural) worlds of the two contending social classes. The shift from a socially specific term, however, that of commodification, to the more philosophically general one of reification, meant that Lukács's pathbreaking work was crucially limited in ways which the later so-called Western Marxism then attempted to reopen.

3.

As for that indispensable feature of commodification which is the market price which alone stamps an object as a commodity, Marxism here once again confronts that central conundrum which is the distinction between value, determined by the quantity of labor time, and price, determined in addition by market forces and fluctuations. The history of the debates and polemics around this dual nature of exchange value suggests that no account of commodification can escape unscathed: the result is that contemporary discussions are divided between abstract philosophical evocations of commodification as some general cultural and economic process, and specific empirical studies of the operations of markets in various fields, specifically including their enlargement and complication in the era of globalization. The division is most glaring in the field of culture: aesthetic philosophy, as in that of T. W. Adorno, insists tirelessly on the commodification of art works as the essential or constitutive feature of the situation in which art, and in particular modern art, if not modernism as such, appears. Meanwhile an older sociology of art continues to study the economic evolution of art markets, publishing houses, distribution and statistics of reception, in ways seemingly incompatible with the larger philosophical generalizations.

The division might also be traced to a more fundamental incompatibility, which is that between the labor theory of value and the study of economic markets. The rhetoric of the latter is to be sure hegemonic in the current moment of globalization and of the pursuit by capitalism of deregulation and of so-called free-market conditions all over the world. As for the labor theory of value, it is again and again challenged by the difficulties of its application to so-called cultural values, as well as by the seeming inapplicability of its fundamental conceptions of labor time to the operations of computers and information technology. In culture, to be sure, it seems willful enough to try to apply a theory of labor time to that one line of the sonnet that "falls from the ceiling" (Valéry), even though the other thirteen lines may involve a forbidding amount of work; still, as Molière puts it, "le temps ne fait rien à l'affaire." But when it comes to the construction of the ideological concepts and categories whereby culture is itself organized into a field of commodities, some notion of collective labor (that is to say, the status of intellectuals) seems clearly relevant. The Romantic notion of "genius," for example, which Ernst Fischer saw as the supreme commodity offered on the new cultural and intellectual market of the early nineteenth century, is a collective production and construction and not an individual one. Yet other features of literary value—for example, that lack or need in the social field to which the success of a given ideological and cultural invention triumphantly replies—would seem to replicate the dynamics of supply and demand on the economic market in a merely analogical way. Yet to put it that way is to become aware of the increasing centrality of fashion and its changes and innovations in the spread of the capitalist market since the eighteenth century; and thus to reorganize the problem around the role of culture—eventually including advertising—in the dynamics of the economic market itself. Postmodern theory has indeed posited a conflation of the cultural and economic levels as one of the constitutive features of the current third stage of capitalism (the stage of globalization or of postmodernity).

Yet the whole notion of globalization today is premised on the expansive dynamic of capitalism as such, and in particular on its present-day penetration of the hitherto non-capitalist areas of the globe. This is to say that theories of globalization are all approximations of an analysis of what Marx called the world market, that is to say, the universal extension of wage labor, which breaks up the older modes of production by turning peasants into farm workers just as it reduces the proportion of agricultural production in a given traditional society from 70 or 80 percent down to 10 or 7. But to return to wage labor is very precisely to return to the matter of commodification, since in the area of production "wage labor" is defined as the commodification of labor (or vice versa), and the wage is here distinctly perceived as the price of that commodity called labor power which is bought and sold on the market. Thus what has become an even more complicated problem at the cultural or philosophical end of the spectrum here becomes an inescapably concrete reality at the infrastructural pole, where the establishment of global markets for the commodity of labor essentially determines the flight of industries from the old industrial core of First World capitalism and triggers the deepest political and social crises of the First World nation states (without necessarily endowing the new Third World labor markets with any stability either). In the *Grundrisse* Marx observes that socialism will not really be on the agenda until the world market has been established and capitalism has reached some ultimate limit to its expansion. In the universal commodification of labor power we begin to glimpse the shudder and potential convulsions of this historically new situation.

4.

As is well known, Marx's fundamental analysis of the commodity is to be found in the first chapter of *Capital*, Volume 1. It will then serve, not only as the basis for the indispensable notion of the commodification of labor power, but also of the demonstration of the structural and unavoidable embedding of exploitation and alienation within capital production as such: a central contradiction of that mode of production which cannot be eliminated by reform or by the ameliorations of social-democratic regimes.

The analysis of the commodity, that is to say of the product of exchange value, takes the form of a chiasmus across which energies are exchanged. Chiasmus has long been understood to be one of the fundamental tropes of Marx's style and imagination, as in expressions such as that of the replacement of the weapons of criticism by the criticism of weapons. Chiasmus indeed posits two terms which exchange their properties in what has to remain an unequal or uneven way which is masked by an apparent symmetry: thus, the seeming equation of value (the ten yards of linen that "equal" one coat) includes temporality yet only runs in one direction. It is not reversible, a peculiarity which announces the imminent transformation of one of the terms into a commodity which is not a commodity, or in other words, that "form of value" destined eventually to become money.

This asymmetry in the value equation is then thematized and ultimately identified in all its specificity when the commodity in question becomes labor power itself. At this point, the form of the equation has the ideological mission of suggesting that there can be a "just price" for labor and that a capitalist society can be reformed in such a way as to pay its workers equitably. But the price of that unique commodity which is labor power turned out to include surplus value along with the price of the worker's means of subsistence and can thus never really be the exact equivalent of the value of the worker's labor time.

The other outcome of this analysis of the commodity form is the religious after-effect of the mystifications implicit in the value equation. Marx derived his notion of "fetishism" from the anthropological speculations of *le président de Brosses* in the eighteenth century, and meant by the term that troubling surplus of human meaning an inanimate object is made to carry, not only in tribal versions of the sacred, but also in the capitalist commodity itself, which is famously "nothing but the definite social relation between men themselves which assumes here, for them, the fantastic form of a relation between things."[1]

Here also, then, Marx's analysis leads in two separate directions, both of which will play a part in the later fortunes of the notion of commodification: on the one hand designating the practical operations of exploitation latent in Value as such and in the money form essential to capitalism; on the other, opening a symbolic realm in which potentially religious, mystical, or idealist cultural excess can be grasped and identified, but which also projects a powerful Utopian vision in the notion of a transparent society from which the commodity form has been eliminated ("an association of free men, working with the means of production held in common, and expending their many different forms of labor-power in full self-awareness as one single social labor force").[2] Marx's deployment of the anarchist term "association" here (along with much else which is famous in Chapter 1, this passage was added to the second edition of *Capital*) goes a long way towards responding to later accusations of statism from the anarchist tradition. The notion of transparency (not Marx's word) has also been the object of deconstructionist critique on the grounds that it implies illicit and nostalgic philosophical promises of presence and immediacy.

---

[1] Karl Marx, *Capital*, Vol. 1, trans. Ben Fowkes, London: Penguin, 1976, 165.
[2] Ibid., 171.

5.

Lukács's influential conception of reification (in the 1923 *History and Class Consciousness*) seems on the face of it to be more distant from the original notion of the commodity and even from that *Verdinglichung* denounced by Marx as a mystifying substitute for human production and human relations. Yet it is important to grasp its dual use in the stunning philosophical theorization of the epistemological privilege of the proletariat in that greatest of all conceptual "reflections" of Leninism.

For Lukács, indeed, reification takes on utterly different forms and knows utterly different practical outcomes depending on whether, as an inevitable social tendency of capitalism, reification is examined as a structural limitation of bourgeois thinking or on the other hand is grasped as that feature of the life world of the proletariat which endows the latter with the structural possibility (so-called imputed consciousness) of grasping society as a whole. The reification of the proletariat—its labor power become a commodity—has as a result that workers, having become things, are utterly destitute of any other interests or libidinal investments which might generate ideologies. They are thus able to grasp the antagonistic structure of capitalism ("them" and "us") in its pure immediacy. (The theory of class suggests that the point of view from below sees the social organism as antagonism, that from above grasping it rather in analytic separation and inert juxtaposition, as strata or levels of status [Dahrendorf].) Lukács's ultimate authority for this "workerist" epistemology is Marx's early essay "Introduction to the Critique of Hegel's *Philosophy of Right*," with its theory of "radical chains" (so influentially revived in the great minority revolts of the 1960s).

Meanwhile, the effect of reification on the bourgeoisie is just the opposite of this expansive possibility of thought and lies in the constriction of the idea and the experience of society visible in the various specializations and disciplines. Reification is what prevents the bourgeoisie from grasping society as a whole or totality, and thereby from experiencing the blinding reality of class struggle: something which can also serve as a way of criticizing the ideological limits the various philosophers imposed on themselves in order to avoid thinking that reality (Lukács here rejoins an alternate conception of ideology Marx offers in *The Eighteenth Brumaire*—ideology as limit and as occultation, rather than as false consciousness).

This analysis of bourgeois thought then makes clear the operation in Lukács of a conceptual opposition between reification and totality (or rather the "aspiration to totality"). The bourgeoisie must not confront society as a totality; the reification of its thinking makes it possible to remain within the semi-autonomous limits of this or that discipline, this or that limited thematization. Reification, however, turns the proletariat as it were into a single *thing*, which can thereby be experienced as a totality. The force that was a limitation for those who merely profit from and live off social production without themselves engaging in it will be the source of truth for the exploited producers themselves. In this way Lukács rejoins the Hegel of the Master/Slave dialectic, for whom ultimately the Master is abandoned to sterile enjoyment, while the Slave's praxis is also productive of truth itself.

6.

Precisely this duality of effects characterizes the later cultural philosophy which emerges around the notion of commodification in the Frankfurt School and also in poststructuralist France in the 1950s and 1960s. Both the *Tel quel* group in France and T. W. Adorno in Frankfurt concur in their assessment of the formal role commodification plays in modernist literature.

For Adorno, the latter (which he does not explicitly identify as modernist) begins, in Baudelaire, with the commodification of works of art within the tendential commodification of the entire social field by capitalism. The (modern) work can then only resist this external commodification by commodifying itself from the inside, by making itself over into a strange kind of mirror-commodity which is also an anti-commodity. "Baudelaire was right: emphatic modern art does not flourish in Elysian fields beyond the commodity but is, rather, strengthened by way of the experience of the commodity" (298; 443).[3] "Art is modern through mimesis of the hardened and alienated … The Absolute art-work converges with the absolute commodity" (21; 39).

The *Tel quel* group draws the opposite aesthetic lesson (which might be considered a postmodernist rather than a modernist one) from the same viewpoint. Agreeing that reification is the effacement of the traces of production from the object, they argued that the only formal conclusion to draw was the recommendation of an emphasis on the work's process of production rather than on the aesthetic product in some completed art-object. The subsequent "textualization" of the work of the various members of this group (Ph. Sollers, D. Roche, etc.) constituted the attempt to put this aesthetic into practice.

Yet a third powerful statement from the period is less calculated to generate this or that future aesthetic than it is to open new directions for social

---

[3] Theodor Adorno, *Aesthetic Theory*, trans. Robert Hullot-Kentor, Minneapolis: University of Minnesota Press, 1997; in German, *Ästhetische Theorie*, Frankfurt: Suhrkamp, [1970] 1997; unless otherwise noted, all references refer to this work; page references will cite the English edition, followed by the German edition.

and cultural analysis. Guy Debord's proposition, indeed, that the image is the final form of commodity reification (*Society of the Spectacle*, 1968) throws the door open to fresh analyses of the whole new world of the simulacrum (Baudrillard) and of image or spectacle society, which characterizes the third or postmodern stage of capitalism. The impetus given here to film studies and cultural studies of all kinds is the inevitable consequence of the displacement of a language-centered modernism towards an aesthetic system in which space and the visual are dominant. Debord's proposition also suggests that a turn to image production may well include the acknowledgement of reproductive technology as a new dominant in capitalist production in general.

7.

It remains to be seen what consequences this new view of late-capitalist culture as a field of universal commodification will have for the construction of a new politics in the contemporary period. It must be said that commodification, or commodity reification, played a relatively secondary role in the Marxism of the modernist (or Leninist) period. For one thing, the countries of actually existing socialism often suffered from a lack of commodities and a deficiency in commodity production, in a situation in which the central aim lay in the industrialization of hitherto underdeveloped societies as well as in the emphasis on defense technology enforced by the Cold War.

For another, the Leninist emphasis on class struggle—save in Lukács's ingenious philosophical proposals—precluded an analysis of the social and political effects of commodification in a situation in which the stakes turned on imminent revolutionary change. It was not until the failure of world revolution in the 1920s and the complicity of the German working classes in Nazism in the 1930s that thinkers on the left began to explore possible cultural causes for these unexpected ideological developments, which were still (plausibly) accounted for by Lenin's theory of the bribery and corruption of the working classes of the West (or First World).

Finally, the emphasis on the base/superstructure distinction seemed to abandon questions of the superstructure and of culture to mere "epiphenomena" of no great or determinate significance for changes in the base.

It is not until the post–World War II period and the Cold War that so-called Western Marxists (in that distantly following the Lukács of *History and Class Consciousness*) turned to cultural analysis for explanations of the defeat of the Left.

The generation of left intellectuals coming of age in the 1920s—Sartre, the Frankfurt School—demanded a renewed Marxist attention to problems of consciousness, and to cultural phenomena which had been dismissed as merely ideological (including of course the theory of ideology itself). But the existence of the various Communist parties as the only serious and organized vehicles for political action on the Left meant that such heretical thinkers were violently attacked by the party apparatuses and themselves precluded from any active political engagement.

Today a new socioeconomic situation—that of globalization—suggests the possibility of the invention of new kinds of politics, which will grasp a globalizing capitalism and its weaknesses and contradictions in new ways which have yet to be explored. Among other things, it has become evident that commodity reification has become the central phenomenon in the enlargement and spread of capitalism around the world, taking the social form of what has come to be identified as consumerism (often identified as Americanization, after the superstate in which its purest form developed). Indeed, Adorno, always prescient of new possibilities, suggested that the practice and habit of consumption would gradually replace the necessity of ideological control and belief in these advanced societies and thus render the analysis of ideology less central for the contemporary period.

Meanwhile, it was no accident that the American New Left of the 1960s (the SDS) achieved a fundamental insight into capitalism which it was unable to follow up in any practical-political way. This was the idea that commodity consumption itself embodied a central contradiction in the system. Capitalism, as Marx and Engels already observed in *The Communist Manifesto*, produces not only new objects in wave after wave of technological innovation; it also produces new desires in a well-nigh infinite measure. The theorists of SDS then concluded that the gap between this plethora of new desires and the capacity of the system to satisfy them would prove to be the real Achilles' heel of this mode of production. Clearly, this marks a considerable break with an older Left-moralizing emphasis on the evils of commodification and a nostalgia for precapitalist and pre-commodity-producing societies. It remains to be seen which of these assessments of the dynamics of commodification will be politically more energizing for future anti-capitalist movements.

Chapter 10

Cultural Revolution

The concept of cultural revolution, although only articulated in modern times, is an essential completion of any theory of revolution or of systemic social change (and not only of Marxist theories). It has however been obscured by the fate of the Chinese "eleven years," whose official designation—the Great Proletarian Cultural Revolution—has seemed to stage it as the textbook paradigm of the process, and not some uniquely contingent historical experience.[1] Meanwhile, a linguistic variation common to several languages—should it be called "culture revolution" or "cultural revolution"?—suggests a deeper ambiguity to be addressed later on.

In fact, the expression itself was coined by Lenin in his last writings, and already theorized in *State and Revolution*.[2] The process, however, in which the formation of revolutionary subjectivity is transformed into the restructuring of collective subjectivities along the logic of a new mode of production, can already be witnessed in the French Revolution, in Robespierre's invention of the Goddess of Reason and his attempt to propagate her cult.[3] It may be assumed that all systemic revolutions have had to confront this problem, which, as in Stalin's USSR, operates on at least two levels: the production of a new culture in the narrow and specialized sense of literature, film, and the like; and the remolding of the culture of everyday life in the more general sense. Such projects then at once raise theoretical questions: the concept of culture itself and the adequacy of traditional

---

[1] Roderick MacFarquhar and Michael Schoenhals, *Mao's Last Revolution*, Cambridge, MA: Belknap Press, 2006.

[2] V. I. Lenin, "On Cooperation," in *Collected Works*, Vol. 33, Moscow: Progress Publishers, 1973; and *State and Revolution*, New York: International Publishers, 1969.

[3] Ruth Scurr, *Fatal Purity: Robespierre and the French Revolution*, New York: Macmillan, 2006; Maximilien Robespierre, *Virtue and Terror*, intro. Slavoj Žižek, ed. Jean Ducange, trans. John Howe, London: Verso, 2007; Mona Ozouf, *Festivals and the French Revolution*, trans. Alan Sheridan, Cambridge, MA: Harvard University Press, 1988.

notions of superstructures; the relationship of culture and ideology; the dialectical difference between bourgeois culture and socialist culture; and the adequacy of a Gramscian conception of hegemony as a way of addressing the shifting relationship in any such sweeping cultural change between consent and force.

But even this brief overview suggests the possibility of extending the concept of cultural revolution beyond the transition from feudalism to capitalism, or bourgeois society to socialist society: indeed, the question needs to be posed (but not necessarily answered) whether this concept might not also prove useful or suggestive in the interpretation of still earlier historical transitions between modes of production. Indeed, the transition from matriarchy to the Olympian gods has sometimes been considered as a cultural revolution specific to the transition from pastoral to agricultural society and the city-state.[4] Meanwhile, Max Weber's classic account of the transformation of peasants into wage workers, in *The Protestant Ethic and the Spirit of Capitalism*—although technically bearing on the transition from feudal to capitalist society—can serve as one kind of model of many such transitions, which have continued all over the globe well up to the present day.[5] Even Weber's analysis of religion, narrativized as an actant or agent in the change, is suggestive of a more general approach to culture as the very space or element of the transition.

The objections to an extrapolation of the original Marxian concept of cultural revolution to other historical periods and modes of production include (1) the length of such transitions, which may be assumed to last over several generations; and (2) related to that, the relatively non-intentional nature of these processes, no longer apparently linked to a collective project. On the other hand, insofar as many earlier transitions include the myth of a great law-giver, human or divine, and the granting of a constitution, they may well have more in common with modern cultural revolutions than meets the eye. Meanwhile, there is also the dialectic to be factored into such comparisons, namely the qualitative difference between them, owing to the unique dynamic of the modes of production in question. However, there have clearly been bourgeois cultural revolutions which take the form of intentional policies: as for example in Jules Ferry's program of universal lay education in the early years of the French Third Republic,[6] or in the conscription policies of many European nation-states, where the army itself is designed to be a space in which regional differences are effaced and a proper national consciousness developed.

[4]   George Thomson, *Aeschylus and Athens*, London: Lawrence & Wishart, 1946.

[5]   Max Weber, *The Protestant Ethic and the Spirit of Capitalism*, trans. Talcott Parsons, New York: Scribner's, 1958.

[6]   Eugen Weber, *Peasants into Frenchmen: The Modernization of Rural France, 1870– 1914*, Palo Alto, CA: Stanford University Press, 1976.

As for the theory of cultural revolution as training for political revolution, cultural revolution not merely as subversion of the existing order but also of preparatory construction of another one and of a new subjectivity, Gramsci is clearly the fundamental reference here (his achievement can also be augmented by Brecht's unique reflections and in a different way perhaps Peter Weiss's *Aesthetics of Resistance*).[7] The topic of cultural revolution should also include the question of the production of a viable mass culture and the failure of the socialist countries to do so (in a situation in which the dominant mass culture in the world today is produced in the heartland of capitalism, namely the United States).

A final topic suggested by the unique information technologies that organize the capitalism of the current period would then question the relevance of the notion of cultural revolution today, or at least seek to discover and project the new and original forms it would need to take in the era of globalization and postmodernity.

I. Lenin

State and Revolution (August 1917) stages the problem of cultural revolution (the term is not yet used here) in terms of the now familiar "transition" from socialism to communism: and thus, as the title of the book suggests, in terms of state power, law, and the "withering away of the state." Nonetheless, despite this thematic limitation, what emerges in Lenin's thought is the sense that bourgeois legality and bourgeois political forms ("democracy") will have to be maintained during a first period and until workers and peasants have learned what genuine social equality really is. Lenin frames this new experience in terms of "accounting and control": "the moment all members of society, or even only the overwhelming majority, have learned to administer the state themselves, have taken this business into their own hands, have set up control."[8] The prerequisites for this are clearly cultural and in particular pedagogical: "universal literacy ... then the 'training and discipline' of millions of workers by the huge, complex and socialized apparatus of the post office, the railway, the big factories, large-scale commerce, banking, etc."[9]

---

[7] Antonio Gramsci, *Prison Notebooks*, 3 vols., trans. Joseph A. Buttigieg, New York: Columbia University Press [*Quaderni del carcere*, 4 vols., Turin: Einaudi, 1977]; Bertolt Brecht, *Me-ti*, from *Grosse kommentierte Berliner und Frankfurter Ausgabe*, Vol. 18, Frankfurt: Suhrkamp, 2000; Peter Weiss, *The Aesthetics of Resistance*, Vol. 1, trans. Joachim Neugroschel, Durham, NC: Duke University Press, 2005.

[8] Lenin, *State and Revolution*, 84–85.

[9] Ibid., 87.

This is now an approach to broad cultural change and the transformation of subjectivities which will be expanded in Lenin's last published writing, "On Cooperation" [On Cooperatives] (January, 1923) in which it is asserted that the new historical epoch cannot be reached "without universal literacy, without a proper degree of efficiency, without sufficiently training the population to acquire the habit of reading books, and without the material basis for this." (This insistence on cultural revolution as education and pedagogy might also be expanded to include the issue of language revolution itself, already crucial in the various nationalisms.) It must be acknowledged that Stalin's USSR achieved these particular objectives.

"On Cooperation" now more directly addresses the problems raised by a peasantry as such (*State and Revolution* had mainly focused on workers), and it is in that context, and within the more general framework of the New Economic Policy launched in 1921, that Lenin proposes his new *mot d'ordre*: "the organization of the entire peasantry in cooperative societies presupposes such a standard of culture among the peasants ... that this cannot be achieved without a complete cultural revolution."[10] The essay concludes with a rectification of conventional theories of revolutionary dynamics: "we did not start from the end that was prescribed by theory ... in our country the political and social revolution preceded the cultural revolution, the cultural revolution that now confronts us. This cultural revolution would now be sufficient to transform our country into a completely socialist state."[11]

It is worth noting that it is essentially the formulations of *State and Revolution* which were appealed to in the Stalinist ban on Utopias, and the development of the so-called theory of nearer aims (*teoriya blizhnego pritsela*). Yet while Lenin here sternly warns against the repeated demands for a blueprint of the communist stage ("it has never entered the head of any socialist to 'promise' that the higher stage of communism will arrive"), in the final essay he calls for the universal establishment of Owen's Utopian cooperatives on the grounds that what was Utopian under capitalism is no longer to be thought of in the same way ("under our present system, cooperative enterprises differ from private capitalist enterprises").

Finally, it is worth noting the way in which the 1917 book gives us a valuable clue to Lenin's thinking about the nature of cultural revolution, for it is here that in another language he briefly but significantly characterizes the revolutionary transformation of subjectivity which cultural revolution aims to produce: "very soon the *necessity* of observing the simple, fundamental rules of human intercourse will become a *habit*." The aim is thus no longer

---

[10] V. I. Lenin, *The Lenin Anthology*, ed. Robert C. Tucker, New York: W. W. Norton, 1975, 710–713.

[11] Ibid.

to pursue class struggle (it has been successfully completed), but rather to produce new habits.

2. Earlier Forms: Cultural Revolution in the French Revolution

The interpretation of Robespierre's politics in terms of cultural revolution is based on three salient features: the appeal to "*vertu*," the significance of the popular festival, and the attempt to found a cult of the goddess Reason (and of the Supreme Being). All these policies can be traced directly back to Jean-Jacques Rousseau, whose work thereby becomes something of a theoretical handbook for the Jacobin project.[12]

The classical conception of *vertu* is derived, via Rousseau, from Plutarch, whose *Lives* can thus also be grasped as an ensemble of political lessons for this first bourgeois and neo-classical revolution. *Vertu* signifies not merely private virtue, as in honesty and incorruptibility (Robespierre's nickname), but also very much a public and civic engagement, the commitment to the collective as a dimension now subsuming mere private life. This concept thereby constitutes an initial attempt to address the perennial problem of collective mobilization during revolutionary periods: how to ensure permanent revolutionary enthusiasm, how to train people in accepting the public and the political, the properly collective, as a permanent dimension of their existential lives (and not merely an occasional experience due primarily to social disorder). It is certainly also possible to grasp *vertu* in its deterrent function as a way of securing consent to obedience and to the new law.

The revolutionary festival also bears the marks of Rousseau's influence, as the nostalgia for the popular festival plays its part in *La Nouvelle Héloïse*, the *Lettre à d'Alembert*, and even the political writings. The first great *Fête de la Fédération* (more closely associated with Lafayette than with the still unknown Robespierre) celebrated the anniversary of the fall of the Bastille, and was the euphoric expression of the first great moment of solidarity and fraternity in France (what Malraux calls the lyric illusion), preceding the dialectical and necessarily divisive dynamic of the social revolution as such (Michelet's evocation of this festival is an expression of the sublime, also theorized by Kant).[13]

Robespierre will later seek to reawaken this first spirit in his *Fête de la raison* (November 10, 1793) and above all in the *Fête de l'Être suprême* of

---

[12] Jean-Jacques Rousseau, *The Social Contract*, Cambridge: Cambridge University Press, 1997.

[13] Jules Michelet, *Histoire de la revolution francaise*; Immanuel Kant, *The Conflict of the Faculties*.

June 8, 1794 (*le 20 prairial de l'an II*). It is wrong to think of such attempts (with which Rousseau's conception of civic religion concurs) as the state imposition of eighteenth-century deism or as the perennial conviction that order and social obedience can only be secured by religious authority (although the more radical atheist revolutionaries certainly argued that Robespierre's position was an essentially reactionary or conservative one).

The religious motif also constitutes a first attempt to think through one of the central problems of a revolutionary society, namely that of the incarnate belief or fetish necessary to unite a collectivity: later on this role will mostly be taken over by the charismatic leader (although in other instances, such as the stability of the USA, it can also be occupied by an object, such as the American Constitution[14] or the nation as in later Stalinist celebrations). For analyses of the festival itself, particularly as Rousseau develops it, have shown that the popular festival is a pure form: in it participants and spectators, subjects and objects, are one and the same; it has no audience or public, no outside; and if it celebrates the community by designating itself, it has no specific content other than itself.

3. Stalin and Cultural Revolution

It seems clear than an immense revolution in culture and subjectivity necessarily took place in the industrialization and collectivization of the countryside and in the mass movement of peasants to the cities in the 1930s; the violence of the period equally clearly testifies to the partial failure of cultural revolution as a hegemonic project. It seems important for any long overdue reevaluation of the history of the USSR under Stalin to insist that the most notorious features of such a transformation—the doctrine of socialist realism, censorship, and the like—are only one dimension of that history, and also that they correspond to the emergence from illiteracy of a nascent mass public and thus constitute a first form of socialist mass culture.

There is also a sense in which the term "cultural revolution", in a far more restricted historical usage, may properly apply in a different way to the great explosion of artistic forms in the Soviet 1920s, from art and architecture and film to literature and music, whose cultural-revolutionary potential was to be theorized in various ways by Lunacharsky, Mayakovsky, and others. Liberation from the old regime fell on a soil already prepared for modernism before and during the war, but the efflorescence of modernisms of all kinds that resulted from Lenin's NEP was unique in Europe owing to the profound identification between artistic revolution and political revolution,

---

[14] Thomas Jefferson, *The Declaration of Independence*, intro. Michael Hardt, ed. Garnet Kindervater, London: Verso, 2007.

which had no equivalent in Paris or Berlin. It is this specifically modernist cultural revolution which may be said to come to an end with the first Five-Year Plan and collectivization.

4. The Great Proletarian Cultural Revolution

In China also, cultural revolution produced a specific artistic aesthetic in the reforms and projects of Jiang Qing, as well as a far more self-conscious and concerted onslaught on the whole tradition of the bourgeois and feudal pasts, particularly in the anti-Confucianism and iconoclasm of the Red Guards. If the first of these currents attempted to combine aspects of the festival with a revolutionary romanticism of positive heroes (and negative villains)—forms emerging from agitprop and continuing on in guerrilla theater today—the second current expressed a more fundamental concern with subjectivity common to all cultural revolutions (and Jiang Qing's romantic-revolutionary aesthetic was also iconoclastic in its general repudiation of bourgeois tradition and bourgeois forms).

The Great Proletarian Cultural Revolution began in late 1965 as the project of undermining the power and authority of the Chinese Communist Party as such ("bombard the headquarters!"). In this, it contained elements of an old anarchism as well as of the expectation of the "withering away of the state" and the substitution of a direct democracy inspired by the unanimity of Rousseau's General Will. It may be said that this moment of the cultural revolution came to an end with the Shanghai Commune and its repudiation by Mao Tse-tung in January 1967 (even though its radical leaders were not fully discredited until, as members of the so-called Gang of Four along with Jiang Qing, they were arrested in the months following Mao's death in 1976). The early disappearance of this experiment in socialist direct democracy (along the lines of the Utopianism of the Paris Commune,[15] as adumbrated by Marx himself as well as Lenin) may be said to have resulted in an ideological void, empty of content, which was filled by the fetish of Mao's image and person, along with his *Little Red Book*, which added a pedagogy to this "cult of the personality." But the deeper social achievements of the Chinese cultural revolution cannot be properly appreciated unless they are replaced in the generational system inherited from the feudal past: for the youth of the Red Guards, crisscrossing China en masse and often the bearers of a violent and sometimes internecine fanaticism, signified a revolutionary dissatisfaction and impatience with the authority of the elders and the hierarchical family system endorsed by Confucius. If

---

[15] Karl Marx, *The Civil War in France*, in *Marx/Engels Collected Works*, Vol. 22, New York: International Publishers, 1986.

as Gramsci suggested, subalternity is constituted, not merely by the state institutions of exploitation, but also by inner habits of obedience and sub-servience, submissiveness to traditional authority, to which we may add the psychoanalytic dimension of the Frommian "escape from freedom" and fear of autonomy, then clearly one of the functions of genuine cultural revolu-tion lies precisely in the breaking up of such habits and indeed the end of what Kant already called immaturity in the collective and political realm. However disastrous the "eleven years" have been in other respects, the destruction of such subaltern subjectivity in China is one of its enduring leg-acies. Meanwhile, the patriarchal structure of Confucian ideology itself, the family replicating the state, which itself replicates the cosmos, suggests a hitherto under-explored cultural-revolutionary potential to psychoanalysis, whether it takes the form of Wihelm Reich's Sex-pol, Fanon's "therapeutic violence," or Adorno's "authoritarian personality."[16]

5. Cuba and Cultural Revolution

The socialist movement has always included the rights of women and minorities among its aims and values, but such issues were not thematized on a mass basis, giving rise to their own autonomous emancipation move-ments, until the post–World War II era. The distinctiveness of the Cuban cultural revolution has been said to have specifically refocused these issues as part of the construction of socialism and to have pursued them actively in culture (film and literature) as well as in daily life and political directives.

Another originality of the Cuban revolution has been a conception of the end of classes based on the armed struggle of the *focos*, where intellectuals, peasants, and city workers came together on a footing of equality. It is a position which would seem closer to the privileging of veterans, as with the Yugoslavian partisans; rather than the preferences given to class affiliation (working-class families versus bourgeois families) after the revolution, as for example in higher education in China or the DDR.[17]

Finally, it is important to note that as far as culture in the more limited sense of literature and the arts is concerned, Cuba explicitly repudiated the Soviet example and declined to endorse any specific artistic mode (as was the

---

[16] Erich Fromm, *Escape from Freedom*; Immanuel Kant, "What Is Enlightenment?"; Wilhelm Reich, *Sex-pol: Essays, 1929–1934*, ed. Lee Baxandall, New York: Vintage Books, 1972; T. W. Adorno et. al., *The Authoritarian Personality*; Frantz Fanon, *The Wretched of the Earth*, trans. Constance Farrington, New York: Grove Press, 1963.

[17] Régis Debray, *Revolution in the Revolution?*, Harmondsworth, England: Penguin, 1967; and Fidel Castro, "Palabras a los intelectuales," speech, Salón de Actos de la Biblioteca Nacional, Havana, June 1961.

case with socialist realism). On the contrary, modernism, which had its own deep roots in Cuba, was welcomed fully as much as realist agitprop and the other artistic traditions of socialism. In a famous phrase, Fidel announced that within the revolution everything was permitted, a doctrine very specifically intended for artistic practice.

The significant role of Cuban nationalism in the construction of its "path to socialism" must also be noted. But this powerful sense of national identity is accompanied by a unique multiplicity of its identity contexts: a Latin American country, but also a Caribbean nation, an African country, a socialist country, and finally a culture most closely (among the other former Spanish colonies) identified with that of North America (Cuba's culture hero José Martí spent fifteen years in New York before going home to die in the wars of liberation).

6. The Yugoslav Model

In many respects the Yugoslav experience of *autogestion* and federalism was unique among the postwar socialisms, although the influence of these achievements was largely theoretical and the Yugoslav model failed to generate a parallel socialist movement elsewhere along the lines of Trotskyism or Maoism. The violent disintegration of the federal system in the 1980s—as a result of globalization and the policies of the IMF and the World Bank, as well as the disappearance of Yugoslavia's strategic position in the Cold War[18]—only serves to underscore the extraordinary success of the federal system in earlier years, particularly in the light of the collapse of Soviet federalism and the fragility of this political system elsewhere. The unique role of Marshal Tito as an emblem of this process (he was half Croatian, half Serbian) focuses the questions of the charismatic leader and the unifying fetish in a new way. Meanwhile both federalism and *autogestion* suggest that the concept of cultural revolution needs to be expanded to include what has hitherto been thought to be more purely economic, such as the forms of the labor process.

7. People's Democracies

These analyses could probably be extended to all the states of the then "actually existing socialisms" in various ways, even though for the most part little individual or comparative work has been done in this area. In Vietnam, for example, a unique anti-Confucian political pedagogy was developed in the

---

[18]   Susan L. Woodward, *Balkan Tragedy,* Washington, DC: Brookings Institute, 1995.

villages, where the Vietcong instructed the peasants, "We are not your father; you are our mother!" Peter Weiss, with his commitment to questions of revolutionary pedagogy, has made an extensive exploration of these methods.[19]

Meanwhile, a special case clearly needs to be made for so-called liberated areas, that is to say, zones within a capitalist country which are no longer under its control and which have already begun to evolve a post-revolutionary form of daily life simultaneously with a revolutionary practice of resistance.

In the German Democratic Republic, the return of the anti-fascist exiles, above all, Brecht, determined a variety of cautious experiments in literature, theater, and film, which were largely cut off by the anti-formalism decrees of the Eleventh Party Plenum in 1965. In general, what have been characterized in the West as various national versions of the "thaw," a term borrowed from the title of Ilya Ehrenburg's 1956 novel from the Khrushchev period, are better analyzed as so many emergent forms of socialist cultural revolution, rather than as nascent forms of "dissidence" (an ideological category which historically emerges only much later).

8. Cultural Revolution and the Concept of Culture

This outline of the basic issues at stake in the concept of cultural revolution has deployed the notion of culture itself in at least four ways: as the more limited and specialized sphere of the aesthetic and of artistic production as such, from literature and the visual arts to film and music; as the theory and practice of distinctive forms of socialist pedagogy, pioneered, for example, in the reeducation centers dramatized in Makarenko's *Road to Life*[20]; as the realm of daily life itself and its organization, of practices and habits, of concrete social relations; and finally as the name for what the Marxist tradition identifies as superstructures or the superstructure, as opposed to the base or the infrastructure, namely the economic (or the forces of production combined with the relations of production). It is worth briefly outlining in conclusion the problem confronted by these presuppositions.

The concept of cultural revolution evidently presupposes a well-known dualism, that of superstructure and base (or infrastructure) as the model of the distinction between culture and the economic. Western Marxism, with

---

[19] Peter Weiss, *Notes on the Cultural Life of the Democratic Republic of Vietnam*; Frances Fitzgerald, *Fire in the Lake*. See, for example, A. S. Makarenko, *The Road to Life: An Epic of Education*; and also Asja Lacis's memoir on the Soviet reeducation projects.

[20] A. S. Makarenko, *The Road to Life: An Epic of Education*; and also Asja Lâcis's memoir on the Soviet reeducation projects.

its critique of economism and its emphasis on culture as a more general political project, has widely repudiated this traditional formula (only evoked once in Marx's own works), on the grounds that it inevitably reduces culture to a reflex of the economic. More traditional Marxisms, on the other hand, have wished to retain it as an essential feature of the Marxian system, fearing that any abandonment of the doctrine of the economic as determinant in the last instance would open the system to liberal revision if not the most complete "postmodern" relativism.

When we consider the base superstructure distinction in terms of wage labor, however, it seems clear enough that money (wages) institutes a fundamental barrier between work time and "leisure." The base superstructure distinction is a theory, but also a symptom, of this social reality and can be expected to disappear only when wage labor (and perhaps labor itself) disappears as such. Such a disappearance can only be imagined thus far in Utopian (or indeed in dystopian) terms, and in the form of four possible outcomes: (1) a dystopia in which everything will have become labor; (2) a regime of automation in which no human labor is any longer necessary; (3) a society in which work has become play in the philosophical sense, or has at least been aestheticized; (4) a society in which all aspects of what was formerly called leisure have been commodified and priced.

The dualism of culture and the economic has however come to seem unproductive, particularly in the third stage of capitalism (postmodernity or late capitalism), in which these two dimensions have seemed to de-differentiate and to fold back in on each other: culture becoming a commodity and the economic becoming a process of libidinal and symbolic investment (a process not irreconcilable with Marx's analysis of the "theological niceties" of the commodity form).

For one thing, such a dualism implies an ambiguous or even un-decideable place for the political and for state power (or power *tout court*); does it imply that power itself has its infrastructure and superstructure (the monopoly of violence on the one hand, hegemony or consent on the other)? Then too, any radical distinction between the two dimensions—an insistence on the semi-autonomy of culture as such—tends not only to put culture in relationship to the economic but also to imply its radical difference from the latter and to move in the direction of some outright autonomy of the cultural. The Althusserian conception of "ideological state apparatuses" would meanwhile seem to project something like an infrastructure of the superstructures as such, an approach which might well be fruitfully generalized in both directions.

Finally, the emergence of an information society and an economy significantly reorganized in terms of computers and electronic technology would seem to require a rethinking of the traditional Marxian ideas of culture or at least an enrichment and complexification of them. The burgeoning of contemporary ideologies (or even metaphysics) of communication such as that of Habermas also demands an original Marxian response (and meanwhile reminds us that the question of ideology has scarcely been raised in this outline, despite the fact that the theory of ideology in many ways offers an alternate and competing theoretical code to that of culture as such).

Chapter 11

Persistencies of the Dialectic: Three Sites

I have the feeling that for many people the dialectic (insofar as it means anything at all) means an adjunct or supplementary kind of thinking: a method, or mode of interpretation, which is only intermittently appealed to, and somehow only occasionally added on to our normal thought processes. This means that not many people are capable of thinking dialectically all the time: and it may also mean that the dialectic is not a form of thought generated by this particular kind of society, for which positivism, empiricism, and various other anti-theoretical traditions seem more congenial and appropriate. (It is of course a dialectical thought as such to suppose that the various social formations—or more precisely, modes of production—secrete forms of thinking and abstraction that are specific to them and functional within their own particular structures: a presupposition that does something to the "truth" of those various kinds of thinking that it would be best not to call relativistic, even though this dialectical or "absolute" relativism certainly has its kinship with other progressive contemporary relativisms.)

In that case, perhaps it would be plausible to conjecture that, despite ample pioneering exploration in the works of Hegel and Marx (and intermittently of many others), the dialectic is not a thing of the past, not some chapter in the history of philosophy, but rather a speculative account of some thinking of the future which has not yet been realized: an unfinished project, as Habermas might put it; a way of grasping situations and events that does not yet exist as a collective habit because the concrete form of social life to which it corresponds has not yet come into being. Perhaps we might try to imagine a society in which the antinomies of individual versus collective being, the indivisibility of the negative and the positive, the inevitable alienation of our productive acts, and the peculiar "Heisenberg principle" presented by the ideology of our point of view, are all commonplaces, as widely understood as the old-time religions or the current Western forms of scientific common sense. It is for a society like that that the rhetoric of "transparency" has often been deployed—not because everything in it would be immediately meaningful, and no longer obscured by the structures required to legitimate capitalism (or precapitalist forms of power), as rather because of the paradoxes of the collective and the social will, which have long since been identified as such. Perhaps one should add that in a society of this kind, a henceforth dialectical society, what we call Marxism today, namely the science of capitalism, will also have disappeared in that form, giving way to the dialectical philosophy or ontology latent in it, but unable to be developed or codified in the present world: both Lukács and Gramsci have written suggestive pages on this "historicist" proposition,[1] which should probably be taken as a warning not to try to work out anything like a Marxian philosophical system or ontology in our own time.

Such a historicist view of the dialectical also demands that we account for the privileged positions of Hegel and Marx as moments in which anticipations of the dialectic were possible: both were indeed social-revolutionary periods of history, in which the window onto a radically different future was, however slightly, pushed open. Sympathy with the French Revolution allowed Hegel to form a very different concept of actuality and of history than the ones he inherited from the theology and philosophy of his own time; while for Marx, the universal commodification of labor power, or the universalization of wage labor, accompanied by the first forms of labor organization and militancy (from the 1848 revolutions all the way to the First International and the Paris Commune), enables a structural theorization of what would necessarily, until that time, have remained a visionary anticipation of a radically different society. But these "conditions of possibility" are what you work your way back to, after the fact: we cannot deduce in advance what new kinds of dialectical conceptions the current cybernetic revolution, along with the capitalist "end of history," may or may not have put us in a position to produce and to think.

I have found it useful to characterize the dialectic in three different ways, which surely do not exhaust the possibilities, but may at least clarify the discussion and also alert us to possible confusions or category mistakes, to interferences between them. The first of these directions involves reflexivity, or thinking itself: perhaps it can be described as a relatively synchronic form of the dialectic. The second raises problems of causality and historical narrative and explanation (and is thus more diachronic). Hegel and Marx are the obvious places in which these first two aspects of the dialectic are the most richly exercised, respectively.

The third feature or aspect of dialectical thinking does not seem to offer a model (as these first two might seem to do), as rather to isolate the fundamental feature of the operation itself: this is, indeed, the emphasis on

---

[1] See Georg Lukács, "What Is Orthodox Marxism?" in *History and Class Consciousness*, trans. Rodney Livingstone, Cambridge, MA: MIT Press, 1971, 1–26; and Antonio Gramsci, "The Revolution against *Das Kapital*," in *Pre-Prison Writings*, ed. R. Mellamy, trans. V. Cox, London: Cambridge University Press, 1949, 39–42.

contradiction as such, and we may honor Brecht for his insistence on this requirement, and for his lesson, in a great variety of contexts and forms, that dialectical thinking begins with the contradiction, that it means finding the inevitable contradiction at the heart of things and seeing and reconstructing them in terms of contradictions, or (if you prefer) that the various forms of non-dialectical thinking can always be identified as so many strategies for containing, repressing, or naturalizing contradictions as such. This is a less exclusive formula than the first two, and (while not exactly a method) perhaps offers the most practical hints for the application and identification of the dialectic alike.

Turning first to reflexivity—to the originality of the dialectic as a recognition of the way in which we are mired in concepts of all kinds and a strategy for lifting ourselves above that situation, not for changing the concepts exactly but for getting a little distance from them—it is certain that today self-consciousness (as this is also sometimes called) has bad press; and that if we are tired enough of philosophies of consciousness, we are even more fatigued by their logical completion in reflexivities, self-knowing and self-aware lucidities, and ironies of all kinds. The current period has been a reconquest of the superficial over the obligatory depths; while all of modern philosophy and thought (Freud included) has been in therapeutic flight before older moralizing notions of the subjective and its cultivation. Perhaps consciousness and self-consciousness have been too closely allied with various forms of repression, with various class-bound notions of the self or the ego. Those were, Adorno might have said, fruits of the entrepreneurial period of bourgeois subjectivity; now that we are in full transition from the older entrepreneurs and patriarchal robber barons to the age of transnational monopolies and the new anonymous global collectivities, the glorification of the self comes to seem an historical curiosity and an outworn, impossibly expensive luxury of the past, like a private railroad car. But perhaps the reading of Hegel in such terms was itself a projection of that bygone modernist historical period; and just as Freud has come to be rewritten without the stoicism and without the mirage of the cure (in that sense, indeed, the supreme moment of self-consciousness or reflexivity as such), so also Absolute Spirit might perhaps be readapted to the more modest and schizophrenic tastes of the present age, as sheer historical overlaying and simultaneity.

The more serious question, however, turns on the use we may or may not still have for self-knowledge: for the deeper reason why this value seems to have been first reduced in price and put on sale, and then consigned to the ashcan of history outright, is that the self has also lived its time, and that multiple selves, multiple subject-positions, no longer seem to offer anything very interesting or tangible to know. Not much knowledge there any longer, let alone much wisdom.

Let me anticipate a little here and suggest that we may be looking in the wrong place: if subject-positions are not optional changes of clothing, whose possibilities finally depend on your pocketbook, then perhaps they ought to be seen as responses to situations. That means that their multiplicity and coexistence today correspond to the way in which postmodern people live within several coexisting situations all at once: the past seems to have been simpler in this respect, pre-urban and ordered by religious repression, but then one never knows about the past and it may well be, as the Nietzscheans among us are fond of asserting, that multiple subject-positions were always with us and that the village was no less complicated than California at its most feverish. The point is, however, that in that case, what has been called self-knowledge is not really a knowledge of the self, but rather a consciousness of its situations, a way of gaining and keeping awareness of precisely that multiplicity of situations in which the self finds and invents itself. That kind of knowledge need not have any of the old subjectivist, bourgeois-introspective connotations we used to endow it with (and you could reread Hegel, for that matter, as a series or sequence of situations, rather than of essentialist forms). I do not want to dwell on any of this any longer, but would like very rapidly to associate these first remarks on the dialectic with some of Derrida's early thoughts about cancellation or "rature" in the *Grammatology*, which warned us that we could scarcely modify the concepts in our head in some Utopian fashion and leap ahead to a wholly new philosophical outlook, without utterly changing the world in the first place, and producing new situations (not his formulation) in which the new concepts might somehow find some currency or use.

But this turn in the discussion of self-consciousness now reminds us to name its other, more Marxian variant, which is to be sure the concept of ideology itself, the last and most important conceptual achievement of the Enlightenment drive to banish the idols and the superstitions. It is above all in this that deconstruction, for example, is related to Marxism, as cross cousins in some extended kinship system; and that the best way to undertake the comparison would be to begin with an analysis of deconstruction as a form of *Ideologiekritik*, as they used to call Marxism in Germany now so many years ago. Here we must return, in a new way, to imagery from the previous version, that is, to the formulation in terms of reflexivity. For the point is the same: we are submerged in our ideologies (indeed, the self itself is just such an ideology, as the dialectician Lacan has shown us) and becoming aware of our own ideologies is rigorously the same as what was then called self-consciousness. For ideology-critique begins at home, with the so-called self and its baggage and furnishings, and can only thereafter be trained with some accuracy and precision on the doings of the outside world. In this respect, Hegel once said an instructive thing about his own period: our situation as philosophers, he observed, is radically different from that of the Greeks, in that they had first of all to generate usable abstractions out of the immanence of empirical daily life; we, however—the historical situation is clearly that of the first modernity of Hegel's day—drowning in abstractions, we have to find a way of getting out of them without precisely sinking back into the sheer instinctive traditional life of the pre-philosophical.[2] That way, clearly enough, he called the dialectic; but it is further illuminated by Marx's wonderful comment, which one is tempted to take as a gloss on this one of Hegel. Bourgeois philosophy, said Marx, rises from the particular to the general; we must now rise—note the persistence of the verb—from the general to the concrete.[3] The concrete is no longer a tissue of generalities and abstractions, of universalities; but it is also no longer a mindless anti-theoretical empiricism; it is something else which we have yet to describe in any satisfactory way here, all the more so since this once so fashionable word "concrete" seems also to have run its course.

The link between Hegelian analysis and the "materialism" of *Ideologiekritik*, however, lies in the space and schematism of the philosophical "category": or in other words the mental forms that have from Aristotle to Kant been identified as intervening between us and the objects of our thought. In Aristotle and in Kant, the categories are inventoried and sorted out according to various classification schemes,[4] but they cannot be said to have been interpreted, exactly, since they do not have meanings in and of themselves but rather govern and organize meanings and to that degree stand outside of meaning as such. The originality of Hegel was to have enabled an approach to some intrinsic meaning of the categories themselves by way of a sequence of forms (through which the "concept," the use of Hegelian language, gradually and historically becomes "equal to itself"). We are today rather far from the picking and choosing implied by Croce's famous title (*What Is Living and What Is Dead in the Philosophy of Hegel*);

---

[2] G. W. F. Hegel, *Phenomenology of Spirit*, trans. A. V. Miller, Oxford: Oxford University Press, 1977:"The manner of study in ancient times differed from that of the modern age in that the former was the proper and complete formation of the natural consciousness. Putting itself to the test at every point of its existence, and philosophizing about everything it came across, it made itself into a universality that was active through and through. In modern times, however, the individual finds the abstract form ready-made; the effort to grasp and appropriate it is more the direct driving-forth of what is within and the truncated generation of the universal than it is the emergence of the latter from the concrete variety of existence" (19).

[3] *Grundrisse*, in *Marx/Engels Collected Works*, Vol. 28 New York: International Publishers, 1986, 38.

[4] Aristotle, *Metaphysics*, in *Complete Works*, Vol. 2, Princeton: Princeton University Press, 1985: "The 'what,' quality, quantity, place, time and any similar meanings which 'being' may have; and again besides all these there is that which is potentially or actually" (Book VI, chapter 2).

still, if Hegel and his works have an actuality and a practical value for us today, those cannot but lie in just this dialectic of the categories, which incites us to invent a distance from our own thoughts in which their failure and insufficiencies can be diagnosed and identified in terms of those of the mental categories we have been able to deploy. Already in Hegel, the conditions of possibility of specific mental categories (and not other, more adequate ones, for example) were the object of a properly historical diagnosis: the dialectical flaws in a given category (the way in which, for example, it might impose a false dualism upon us) are already indices of our historical situation; and with that, the way towards a certain Marxism is thrown open.

The return to Hegel today, in a variety of forms, is thereby justified: less as a scholarly and antiquarian project (although such research into the documents themselves and the history of philosophy is invaluable), than rather as a renewed effort to think through and elaborate the multiple and suggestive connections between a Hegelian analysis of categories and a Marxian analysis of ideology. I remain convinced that one of the most fruitful efforts to stage those connections lay in the ill-fated *Kapitallogik* movement, in which the categories of Hegel's logic were experimentally juxtaposed with those of Marx's analysis of capital itself.[5]

The more frequent moves in this direction, however, lay in the attempt to bypass or neutralize a kind of form-content stereotype operative in the standard comparisons of Hegel and Marx: that is, provisionally to ignore the idea (probably encouraged by the preceding remarks) that in Hegel it is a question of the form of thoughts and attitudes, whereas in Marx we have to do with their concrete or empirical class content. *Capitallogik*, indeed, may be seen as attempting to give a concrete class content to Hegel's "forms," while in other Marxian developments—most notably in Lukács's *History and Class Consciousness*—the strategy has been to reveal the categorical forms implicit in seemingly empirical class and political positions and opinions. This remains a rich area for work today, and it may also be observed to take place within our philosophical terminologies: I think, for example, of the suggestive and exciting results of the elaboration by Slavoj Žižek and his associates of the dialectics of Lacanian psychoanalysis, which are deployed very specifically in the force field opened up between Marxism and German objective idealism.

Thus, it is not so much the incompatibility of some Hegelian idealism and this or that Marxian materialism which vitiates the development of the dialectic today: on the contrary, as I hope to have suggested, such "incompatibilities" are the space in which genuine philosophical innovation can

---

[5] See Bertell Ollman, *Dialectical Investigations*, New York: Routledge, 1993, especially parts 1 and 2; Tony Smith, *The Logic of Marx's "Capital*," New York: SUNY Press, 1990.

take place. The more urgent problem today is an historical and a social one, and, if it strikes at the Hegelian dialectic by way of an omnipresent positivism and revulsion against theory itself, its consequences for the Marxian theory of ideology itself are no less momentous. For there is a question whether, today, in postmodernity and globalization, in the universal reign of the market and of a cynical reason that knows and accepts everything about itself, ideology still takes on its once classical form, and ideology-critique serves any purpose any longer. For that was once a cultural-revolutionary purpose and a collective pedagogy: not merely and not even foremost to discredit and unmask the enemies, but rather to transform the intellectual and practical habits of the collectivity itself, formed in and still poisoned by this social system. Today, and for the moment, we need more modestly to ask ourselves how ideology functions in the new moment, how the market achieves its unquestioned sway. What is paradoxical is that the crudest forms of ideology seem to have returned, and that in our public life an older vulgar Marxism would have no need of the hypersubtleties of the Frankfurt School and of negative dialectics, let alone of deconstruction, to identify and unmask the simplest and most class-conscious motives and interests at work, from Reaganism and Thatcherism down to our own politicians: to lower taxes so rich people can keep more of their money, a simple principle about which what is surprising is that so few people find it surprising anymore, and what is scandalous, in the universality of market values, is the way it goes without saying and scarcely scandalizes anyone. Why did we need in the first place to invent the elaborate Geiger-counters of ideology-critique developed on the left during the modernist period if it was all so simple all along? The implication is that the Cold War shamed the various Western bourgeoisies into complicated intellectual disguises for these motivations, which had to be deconstructed in equally complicated ways, but which no longer need the cloak of altruism or of higher philosophical justifications, now that they have no enemies any longer.

Perhaps, however, we need to entertain the idea that ideology today takes rather different forms than in the past, and in particular that our two great dominant ideologies—that of the market; that of consumption or of consumerism—are not exactly ideas in the older sense. Adorno wondered somewhere very pertinently whether today the commodity might not be its own ideology: thereby seeming independently to confirm the general conceptual movement away from an overt theory of ideology to one of practices (as in Bourdieu's work, for example). That such an "end of ideology" could never mean an end of class struggle seems obvious enough, but it would certainly entail a dilemma in the articulations of class struggle and in the opening up of new discursive spaces in which to fight it out. Perhaps this sense of the becoming immanent of ideology in late capitalism explains the renewed significance, on the left, of the theory of commodity fetishism, which was for Marx the undeveloped secret of any analysis of daily life in our social system. The renewal of a theoretical interest in religion may also have its relevance here as well (and not only in the empirical social world around us), since Marx's brief analysis is staged in religious terms. At any rate, contributions from psychoanalysis and colonial philology alike[6] have converged on this interesting matter, which also surely holds a key to practical politics in the current scheme of things.

But now it is time to move to the second way in which the dialectic has often been understood and misunderstood, and that has to do with telos, narrative, and history: with the story of change, or in other words, with the diachronic, rather than with the structures of consciousness as such. Marx has often, along with Hegel, been accused of having a "philosophy of history" (which is evidently supposed to be a bad thing; and also of being somehow religious, replicating Christian historicism unconsciously, and projecting a salvational narrative of a movement of history towards some end of time—in short, of perpetuating the noxious doctrine of a telos); and in a lesser accusation, of being not only teleological but also a proponent of historical inevitability, whatever that may mean. No reader of *The Eighteenth Brumaire of Louis Bonaparte* can believe any of these things, to which I can only reply in abbreviated form. I certainly hope that Marxism projects a salvational history; why it should be Christian I cannot particularly understand, since Christian salvation remains essentially individual, and the Day of Judgment is a figure for the end of history altogether, rather than, as in Marx's own words, the end of "prehistory." This is perhaps also the moment to deal with the much stigmatized concept of totality: it is capitalism which totalizes, which constitutes a total system, not its critics. We have to think, however, in terms of a totalizing transformation of the social system precisely because this system is itself a total one (something Foucault teaches even better than Marx, by the way, and which is also implicit in Derrida's ideas of the closure of conceptuality in the *Grammatology*). Salvational is then that kind of transformation: that it is inevitable we are, chastened by the lessons of the last few years, no longer supposed to say. But here too it was never socialism that was inevitable, but the implosion of the contradictions of capitalism. Marx allows as much when he pointedly observes that some world-historical conflicts end "not with the reconstruction of society as a whole, but rather with the mutual ruin of contending classes."[7] Indeed,

---

[6] Slavoj Žižek, *The Sublime Object of Ideology*, London: Verso, 1989; William Pietz, "The Problem of the Fetish," in *Res*, Num. 9, Spring 1985.

[7] Karl Marx and Friedrich Engels, *The Communist Manifesto*, in *Marx/Engels Collected Works*, Vol. 6, Moscow: Progress Publishers, 1976, 484.

the two things are not "on all fours" as the philosophers like to say: capitalism is a system and a machine with irresolvable internal contradictions; socialism is a human and a collective act, a collective project. The fate of the former does not depend on us; that of the latter is at one with our collective praxis.

But these perspectives—sometimes supposed to be "grand narratives"—are not really narratives at all; they are axiology and Utopian vision. They enable the construction of this or that historical narrative, but are not themselves narrative as such. If we look for a moment at those texts in which we can speak of some genuinely dialectical narrative—I mentioned *The Eighteenth Brumaire* a moment ago—what we observe is indeed the very opposite of this allegedly pious rehearsal for longed-for truths, of history written as wish-fulfillment and as the simple-minded interaction of a few abstractions. Rather *The Eighteenth Brumaire* makes us witness to a narrative which is at every point a perpetual and dazzling, sometimes bewildering, cancellation of previously dominant narrative paradigms. Here the dialectic is a constant reversal of older stereotypes of causality, of historical or narrative efficacy and efficiency: it constantly underscores the absolutely unforeseeable consequence, the bitterly ironic reversal, the inversion of human (individual) intention, and the progress inherent in the worst rather than the best, in failure rather than victory. History puts its worst foot forward, as Henri Lefebvre liked to say, and not its best, as bourgeois or Whig, progress-oriented historiographies claim and try to demonstrate by their own narratives. To be sure, the great forefather of this historiographic practice was again Hegel (he had his own precursors in Adam Smith and Mandeville), and in particular his notion of the "ruse of reason" or the "ruse of history," the way in which a collective history uses the passions and intentions of individuals, and even of individual nations, behind their backs in order to produce some utterly unexpected result. But in that programmatic form, the dialectic is still too simple and itself becomes predictable: the dialectic of history in Marx wishes to escape just that predictability. But here we now draw closer to an understanding of the dialectic as a set of operations, in situation, rather than as some static "view" or even "philosophy"—in this case of history itself. Among our inner ideologies, in other words, are notions of what an event is, how things happen, what effective causes are, how change can best be influenced: the dialectic wishes ceaselessly to interrogate and undermine those narrative and historical ideologies, by allowing us to see and grasp historical change in a new and more complex way. But this is the difference with postmodern historiography in general: the dialectical one still does wish to give a provisional picture of historical change, a provisional narrative, with provisional interpretation of the events, and therefore still implies that those events are not altogether meaningless, and that historical narration is not an altogether ideological process.

Now at a certain point along the way, it seems to me that such dialectical narratives froze over and became codified; so that new narrative procedures had to be invented to undermine them in their turn. The two I would above all wish to single out for twentieth-century historiography are Freud's *Nachträglichkeit*, his so-called retroactive effect, whereby the arrival of puberty, for example, triggers events that have in some sense already happened at the age of three, but in another sense have not yet happened at all; and alongside that, Derrida's notion of supplementarity, in which, following Jakobson's notion of the synchronic, a new moment in the system comes complete with its own brand-new past and (as in Husserl) reorders our perception around itself as a center (whose permanence is then projected back endlessly into time). I believe that both these historiographic forms have occasionally been understood as critiques of the dialectic, and I understand why; but I hope it will also be clear why I now perversely consider both as contributions to a dialectical rewriting of history rather than some newfangled post-dialectical inventions.

It all depends, you will say, on how we define the dialectic in the first place. No doubt; and the first Derrida we know, the Derrida of the recently published master's thesis of 1953, the dialectical (rather than anti-dialectical) Derrida, grasped dialectics as essentially a matter of mediation. The dialectic is what lets us think the unity of opposites, and (in that particular case, which was the critique of Husserl's philosophy) the identity of activity and passivity, of constituting and constituted, even of subject and object, and so forth. What of that particular version of the dialectic? This is the point at which we must touch on the third of our topics, namely contradiction; and in which we must bring in other, less philosophical names, and in particular that of Brecht, supposed to be the student, in dialectics, of Karl Korsch.

I will omit that obligatory digression, however, and simply repeat Brecht's stress that what defines the dialectic above all is the observation—everywhere and always—of contradictions as such. Wherever you find them, you can be said to be thinking dialectically; whenever you fail to see them, you can be sure that you have stopped doing so.

My reason for drawing Brecht into the discussion in so seemingly arbitrary a fashion (besides implicitly shedding a little crosslight on his adversary, Lukács) is to restore some of the forgotten prehistory of contemporary anti-dialectical positions, which we mostly lump under the designation "poststructuralist." I have come to believe, indeed, that much in the arsenal of attacks on the dialectic actually derives from the dialectical tradition itself, and specifically from Brecht, whose plays exploded like a thunderbolt in summer 1954, in a Parisian intellectual atmosphere dominated absolutely by so-called existential Marxism.

The body of critical writing that most vigilantly and intelligently transmitted the Brechtian ethos to France and to the French intellectual and political climate of those years, which is to say to the nascent French sixties and nascent poststructuralism, is the work of Roland Barthes, whose *Mythologies* constitutes a splendid series of Brechtian estrangement-effects, including a theory of estrangement rewritten for French usages. I am, however, more interested in Barthes' attacks on identity, which seem to me faithfully yet creatively and imaginatively to transmit the Brechtian positions on this particular theme. In particular, what seems to be Barthes' semiological undoing of the individual "subject"[8]—its fragmentation into multiple semes, its x-raying into overlapping actants, the death of the author-subject as well, and finally the dissolution of the writing subject into the un-self-sufficient moments of textual production—this actually can be seen to derive from Brecht's dramaturgy; not only the reconstruction of the individual subject in *Mann ist Mann*, or the positive and negative personae of *The Good Person* (but of many other plays as well), but above all, the sense that subjectivity itself is in reality *gestus*, that we do wrong to try to empathize with this or that inner feeling of the character, and indeed that in any given gesture a multiplicity of motivations overlap. Barthes' further dismantling of the event, in his so-called proairetic code, is very reminiscent of the Brechtian staging of the *gestus*, and the insistence on showing the audience that any number of other versions of these gestures and reactions might have been possible in other frames and other situations. The practice of multiple subject-positions, therefore, is already present in Brecht (despite his lack of interest in what is still simply Freudian psychoanalysis); and the persistent undermining of the whole range of forms taken by an illusory identity is his most inveterate critical posture.

In Barthes as well (who however benefited from a double lesson on the subject, having also learned it from his other master, Sartre), we find the fundamental Brechtian insistence on the primacy of the situation, whether this has to do with political choices, subject-positions, or literary theories and forms. This insistence on the situation as such is what makes it so difficult to codify this dialectic, about which it becomes evident that its terms and emphases must vary according to the demands of circumstance and of strategy. Brecht is not the only modern thinker to have insisted on the relationship between strategy and thought, between strategy and dialectics: but his lesson has been enormously influential.[9]

Where, finally, do we find contradiction in all this? In the structure of the situation itself, first of all; but also in the relationship of the gesture or *gestus* to the situation it tries to change; and finally within the *gestus* and the subject-position itself, where the sheer multiplicity of elements itself constitutes a contradiction. The misunderstanding would lie in imagining

---

[8] Roland Barthes, *S/Z*, Paris: Seuil, 1970.

[9] For a fuller discussion, see Fredric Jameson, *Brecht and Method*, London: Verso, 1998.

that Brecht desired this multiplicity and these contradictions to be done away with; that with him, as in those caricatures of the Hegel alongside whom he now lies buried, some "synthesis" must necessarily follow on the proverbial thesis and antithesis; or else, at the outside limit, we will find ourselves forced to evoke a "dialectic without a synthesis," as though that were not simply the nature of the dialectic *tout court*. Where, however, this distinction has been drawn in a programmatic way, and a perpetual movement back and forth between opposites or within a dualism contrasted with some alleged dialectical "totalization" in which the opposites and the contradictions are supposed to be laid to rest, then I think one can contrast the notion of the contradiction and that of the antinomy, which is the form taken by contradictors in so much anti-dialectical poststructuralist thought, and on which I have commented elsewhere.[10]

I want to add, returning to the beginning of this discussion, that I think notions of the mediation as a solution or bridge between contradictories are also something of a misunderstanding, and attribute to the dialectic philosophical and ontological ambitions it must not have: this notion of the mediation is redolent of the old Hegelian and dialectical-materialist notion of a dialectics of nature, for example; while the Brechtian position I have tried to outline here would I believe be more inclined to identify mediation and contradiction as such: where you can perceive a contradiction, there you already intuit the union of opposites, or the identity of identity and non-identity. Mediation is thus not some strange and fluid event in the world: it characterizes the way our spectatorship and our praxis alike construct portions of the world with a view towards changing them.

---

[10] Fredric Jameson, *The Seeds of Time*, New York: Columbia University Press, 1994.

Chapter 12

Lenin as Political Thinker

On the night of June 25, 1935, Trotsky had a dream:

> Last night, or rather early this morning, I dreamed I had a conversation with
> Lenin. Judging by the surroundings, it was on a ship, on the third class deck.
> Lenin was lying in a bunk; I was either standing or sitting near him, I am not sure
> which. He was questioning me anxiously about my illness. "You seem to have
> accumulated nervous fatigue, you must rest …" I answered that I had always
> recovered from fatigue quickly, thanks to my native *Schwungkraft*, but that this
> time the trouble seemed to lie in some deeper processes … "Then you should
> *seriously* (he emphasized the word) consult the doctors (several names) …" I
> answered that I already had many consultations and began to tell him about my
> trip to Berlin; but looking at Lenin I recalled that he was dead. I immediately tried
> to drive away this thought, so as to finish the conversation. When I had finished
> telling him about my therapeutic trip to Berlin in 1926, I wanted to add, "This
> was after your death"; but I checked myself and said, "After you fell ill …"[1]

This "singularly moving dream," as he puts it, is analyzed by Lacan in his
sixth seminar (on "desire and its interpretation") in the lecture of January 7,
1959. Readers of Lacan will recognize its affinity with themes with which
Lacan was particularly fascinated, most notably Freud's own dream about
his father ("he was dead, but he didn't know it"). The situation in question
accumulates a number of Lacanian motifs: the big Other, barred, castrated,
dead; God as dead (without knowing it); the unconscious as the place of this
non-knowledge of death, very much like that noumenon which for Kant is
the subject and which we can never know. I will rapidly summarize his
observations: Lenin's non-knowledge in the dream is the projection of
Trotsky's own non-knowledge, not only of his own death (he is beginning
to feel the weight of illness and age, the diminution of his extraordinary
energies), but also of the very meaning of his dream. He has also projected
onto Lenin the fact and experience of pain itself, the pain of Lenin's last

---

[1] Leon Trotsky, *Trotsky's Diary in Exile, 1935*, trans. Elena Zarudnaia, Cambridge,
MA: Harvard University Press, 1976, 145–146.

illness, the "suffering of existence" (as Lacan calls it elsewhere), which emerges when desire ceases to conceal it. In the dream Lenin, the dead father, is also the shield against this existential dread, a perilous footbridge over the abyss, as Lacan puts it: "the substitution of the father for the absolute Master, death."

Lenin does not know he is dead: this will be our text and our mystery. He doesn't know that the immense social experiment he single-handedly brought into being (and which we call Soviet communism) has come to an end. He remains full of energy, although dead, and the vituperation expended on him by the living—that he was the originator of the Stalinist terror, that he was an aggressive personality full of hatred, an authoritarian in love with power and totalitarianism, even (worst of all!) the rediscoverer of the market in his NEP—none of those insults manage to confer a death, or even a second death, upon him. How is it, how can it be, that he still thinks he is alive? And what is our own position here—which would be that of Trotsky in the dream, no doubt—what is our own non-knowledge, what is the death from which Lenin shields us? Or, to put all this in a different terminology (that of Jean-François Lyotard), if we know what "the desire called Marx" is all about, can we then go on to grapple with "the desire called Lenin"?

The premise is that Lenin still means something; but that something, I want to argue, is not precisely socialism or communism. Lenin's relationship to that is on the order of absolute belief: and since it never gets questioned, we will also find no new thinking about it in his work: Marx is a big Other, the big Other.

Then what about something which everyone agrees to have been his most original thought: what about the party and the party structure, is this still what Lenin means to us? To be sure, except for the fact that no one nowadays wishes to raise the question or to mention the unmentionable term "party." The word seems to carry with it layers of material and associations from which the current mentality recoils with acute displeasure: first, the authoritarianism and sectarianism of Lenin's first party form; then the murderous violence of the Stalin era (trained as much, to be sure, on the original Bolshevik party members as on the latter's opposition); the corruption, finally, of Brezhnev's party, held out to us as a horrible object lesson in what happens when some party or "new class" becomes comfortably encrusted in its power and privileges. These offer so many reasons for repressing the problematics of the party altogether; or at least, for turning away from that in the quite reasonable conviction that new times and a new historical situation demand new thoughts about political organization and action, to be sure: but my impression is that most often the appeal to historical change is little more than an excuse for avoiding these problems altogether; in a period whose political atmosphere is largely anarchistic (in the technical sense of the term), it is unpleasant to think about organization, let alone institutions. This is indeed at least one of the reasons for the success of the market idea: it promises social order without institutions, claiming not to be one itself. Then, in another way, what I am calling Lenin's sectarianism perhaps sends its own image back in a wholly unwanted and undesirable way (its own bad smell, as Sartre puts it) to a left which (at least in the United States) is utterly given over to the logic of sectarianism and fission/proliferation.

I will say more about the party later on. But perhaps at this point I can raise some conceptual problems which offer a different and a defamiliarizing approach to the matter. Let me put it this way: is the problem of the party a philosophical problem? Is the party itself a philosophical concept which can be thought or even posed within the framework of traditional philosophy? This is not a question that can be answered in the traditional terms of some Leninist "philosophy," which has generally, and even in Althusser, involved the problem of materialism. I'm not very interested in that metaphysical question; nor will I take up the newer assertion of Lenin's Hegelianism (about which more later on). Meanwhile Badiou's stimulating book, which sees the party as a combination of an expressive and an instrumental function,[2] certainly succeeds in philosophizing the party, as the "organization of politics, the organization of the future anterior"[3]; but it does not raise my question, which I prefer to leave in the form and status of an unasked question, namely, what kind of philosophical concept does the problem or the idea of the party constitute, if any?

Yet, it will be observed, there is such a thing as political philosophy, a recognized branch of traditional philosophy as such, which includes Hobbes, Locke, and Rousseau, and accommodates certain modern thinkers, Carl Schmitt in one way, Rawls perhaps in another. Presumably, in a problematic which raises the question of the state and civil society, of freedom and rights, even of political representation as such, there might be found some neglected corner in which Lenin's reflections on the party could be offered storage space. Still, with the signal exception of Schmitt, this collection of philosophers does not seem unduly preoccupied with the philosophical status of political philosophy as such, and rarely seeks to found or to ground it. Questions about representation and constitutions meanwhile quickly slide down into some empirical realm in which they rejoin the Leninist party as some purely instrumental and historical set of recipes. Or to put it the other way round, can one not raise the same question about those issues and equally pose the question of the status of constitutions and parliaments, for example, as properly philosophical concepts? Even in Hegel, so intensely

---

[2] Alain Badiou, *Peut-on Penser la Politique?*, Paris: Sevil, 1985, 107–108.

[3] Ibid., 109.

preoccupied by the interrelationship of his various subsystems, we do find little more than a grounding of political and state forms in something like a deduction from human nature, or, in other words, in an ontology quite different from the dialectical one of the *Logic*. These questions no doubt convey some of my own doubts and suspicions about political philosophy in general; and I'll come back to those later on as well.

Finally, there is a more naïve and impressionistic way of talking about all this, which does, I think, have its value and remain suggestive. This is the feeling we all have, and which we sometimes express like this, in the form of a kind of amazement and admiration, namely, that Lenin is always thinking politically. There is not a word that Lenin writes, not a speech that he gives, not an essay or a report that he drafts, which is not political in this sense—even more, which is not driven by the same kind of political impulse. This can of course strike others as obsessive and repulsive, inhuman: an anxiety before politics which mobilizes the nobler word "reductive" for such single-minded and unblinking attention. But is this reduction of everything to politics, to thinking politically, reductive? What is reduced, what is left out or repressed? Is it not extraordinary to witness what happens when all of reality is grasped through the Absolute of this focus or optic, or to contemplate this unique concentration of human energy? Better still, proceeding by the negative, can such absolute reduction be considered a desire? And if so, a desire for what, a desire called what? Or is this truly the instrumental in its most nightmarish ultimate form, the transformation of everything into a means, the translation of everyone into agency or counter-agency (Schmitt's friend or foe)? What possible end could justify this omnipotence of political thinking, or, as I prefer, of thinking politically? So I slowly make my way back to my initial question: is thinking politically incompatible with philosophical thought? What could justify its centrality and its new status, which might be comparable to the role of the cogito in other philosophical systems? Does thinking politically offer a resource of certainty and a test for doubt around which some utterly new philosophical system or stance might be organized? It will at any rate have become clear that whatever thinking politically is, it has little enough to do with traditional conceptions of politics or political theory, little enough also with that untranslatable distinction that has had its fortune in France in the last years, namely the distinction between *le politique* and *la politique*. May we then venture to say that in that sense Lenin has nothing to do with politics, if it means any of those traditional or contemporary things?

But now we need to confront another alternative, a traditionally influential one, even if it has suffered the same opprobrium in recent years as the problem of the party. This alternative to the political is the economic, by which I must first and foremost mean the economic in the Marxian sense, Marxist economics: a field and a category which immediately raises philosophical questions in its own right, and most notably the question as to whether Marxist economics is an economics at all in the traditional sense. Surely the critique of political economy leads out of political economy altogether, a departure which has at least the merit of barring those tempting paths that lead down into the flatlands of bourgeois economics and positivism. If so many people are trying to feel their way back to political economy today, it is in order to locate that other path that can lead out of it in the other direction of Marxism, which is henceforth how I will more simply identify Marxist economics as such in everything that is distinctive about it.

Marxism in this sense—neither an economic ontology nor either a purely negative critique or deconstruction—is presided over by two generalities, two universal and abstract names, whose philosophical status we also need to worry about: capitalism and socialism. Capitalism as a machine whose dynamism and perpetual expansion result from the irresolvable contradictions it carries within it and which define its essence; socialism as that sketch or possibility of collective or cooperative production some of whose traits can already be glimpsed within our own (capitalist) system. Are either of these "systems" philosophical concepts? Certainly philosophers have over and over again attempted to translate them into more respectable—if paradoxical—philosophical concepts, such as the one and the many; translations which, however stimulating, always seem to lead us back into the most sterile ideological judgments and classifications, not least because, like any binary pair, the one and the many keep changing places. For Marxists, it is capitalism which is the one (whether in the form of the state or the system), while for the others it is socialism which is the bad totalitarian one, and the market which is somehow a more democratic space of pluralism and difference. The problem is that neither "concept," if that is what they both are, is empirical; both designate the empty yet indispensable place of the universal. As a thinker Lenin begins to approach all this through his late Hegelian moment and his return to the *Greater Logic*, as Kevin Anderson and others have so luminously demonstrated. But at that point we are far enough from economics in the Marxian sense (even though we are fairly close to Marx's *Capital*, in the dialectical one).

Is Lenin an economic thinker? Certainly, there are wonderful Utopian passages in *State and Revolution*; everyone agrees that *The Development of Capitalism in Russia* is a pioneering classic of socioeconomic analysis; and *Imperialism* certainly underscores one of the fundamental contradictions of capitalism, if only one. Nor is it to be doubted that the external situation of the revolution in wartime Russia and then even more during the Civil War is such that meditations on socialism as such could never have been at the very forefront of Lenin's agenda.

But I would also like to point to a deeper structural issue. It has always been my feeling that the peculiarity of Marxism as a thought system (or better still, like psychoanalysis, as a unique "unity of theory and practice") —but also its originality—lies in the way in which in it two complete Spinozan modes overlay each other and coexist, the one that of capitalist economies, the other that of social class and class struggle. These are in one sense the same; and yet different vocabularies govern each in such a way that they are not interrelated within some metalanguage, but constantly demand translation—I would even want to say, transcoding—from the one language into the other. If this is so, then Lenin's dominant code is clearly that of class and class struggle, and only much more rarely that of economics.

But I also want to insist on the priority, within Marxism, of economics as some ultimately determining instance. I know that this is not a fashionable position (even though, in the era of the worldwide sway of the market, it may come once again to have its attractiveness). It should be clear, by the way, that when I use the words "economics" and "economic", it has nothing to do with that purely trade-union consciousness and politics Lenin designated by the term "economism" long ago and in another situation (even though the phenomenon called economism is certainly still very much with us). To be sure, the term economics is no more satisfactory to characterize Marxism than "sexuality" is to characterize Freudian psychoanalysis: the latter is not an erotics, not a form of sexual therapy, and when psychoanalysis is described in terms of some sexual ultimately determining instance, this is a very generalizing and impressionistic characterization indeed. Still, whenever Freud sensed a movement of his disciples towards a formulation calculated to dilute the sheer empirical scandal of the sexual and generalize libido out into the more non-specific and metaphysical areas of power or spirituality or the existential—such are for example the well-known moments of Adler, Jung, and Rank—he draws back theoretically with some sharp and one may even say instinctual sense of the focus and boundaries of his object as originally constituted: and these are indeed the most admirable and heroic moments in Freud, the one in which he most stubbornly keeps faith with his own discoveries and insights. Thus one cannot say positively that sexuality is the center of Freudianism, but one can say that any retreat from the fact of sexuality opens up a kind of revisionism which Freud himself was always quick and alert to criticize and to denounce.[4]

Something like this is what I would have wanted to argue for the centrality of economics in Marxism: this is clearly not an economics in any traditional sense, yet all the attempts to substitute another thematics for the economic, or even to propose additional and parallel thematics—such as those of power, or the political in any of its traditional senses—undo everything that made up the originality and also the force of Marxism as such.

---

[4] Does this mean that Freud's late concept of the death instinct is something like Freud's NEP?

The substitution of the political for the economic was of course the standard move of all the bourgeois attacks on Marxism—to shift the debate from capitalism to freedom, from economic exploitation to political representation. But since the various left movements of the 1960s, since Foucault on the one hand, and the innumerable revivals of anarchism on the other, Marxists have been relatively unvigilant—whether for tactical reasons or out of theoretical naïveté—about such crucial substitutions and surrenders. Then too—beginning, I believe, with Poulantzas, and in the light of all the well-publicized abuses in the Soviet Union—the conviction became increasingly widespread that the crucial weakness of Marxism was that it structurally lacked a dimension of political (and juridical) theory; that it needed to be augmented with some new doctrines of socialist politics and socialist legality. I think this was a great mistake, and that the very force and originality of Marxism was always that it did not have a political dimension of this kind, and that it was a completely different thought system (or unity of theory and practice) altogether. The rhetoric of power, then, in whatever form, is to be considered a fundamental form of revisionism. I should add that the unpopular opinion I am expressing may be more seasonable today than it might have been in previous (Cold War or Third World-liberational) decades. For now it is clear that everything is economic again, and this even in the most vulgar-Marxist senses. In globalization, in its external dynamics as well as its internal or national effects, it should be clearer once again to what degree even things that looked like purely political or power issues have become transparent enough to glimpse the economic interests at work behind them.

But now we have a problem; for I have asserted that Marxism is based on the structural priority of economics over politics, at the same time that I have conceded that Lenin is to be considered a fundamentally political thinker rather than a theoretician of economics, let alone of socialism. Does this mean that Lenin is not a representative Marxist thinker? Or perhaps it explains why a hyphenated "Leninism" needed to be added to "Marxism" in order properly to identify the new doctrine and to suggest that Lenin in fact had something unique and different, supplementary, to add to Marx?

The solution to the paradox lies, I think, in the introduction of a third term, one in which it would be tempting to say that these two alternatives, the political and the economic, somehow come together and become indistinguishable. And I think that that is so, but this in the temporal sense, in that of Badiou's Event, rather than in any structural fashion. This term, which is the very center of Lenin's thinking and action, is as you will perhaps already have guessed the term "revolution". This is also not a popular concept nowadays, and is even more of an embarrassment than any of the other traditional slogans I have mentioned. That revolution can be a truly philosophical concept far more readily than notions like the party and capitalism I think could be demonstrated throughout the philosophical tradition; even though we may wish to wait further for some fully developed philosophy of revolution for our own time.

If I dared to sketch in my own requirements for such a philosophy to come, I would insist on two distinct dimensions which are somehow united and identified, however fleetingly, in the moment of revolution. One is that of the Event, about which one must say that it achieves some absolute polarization (Schmitt's definition of "politics" is thus in reality merely a distorted apprehension of revolution as such). And this polarization constitutes the one moment in which the dichotomous definition of "class" is concretely realized.

Revolution is also that unique phenomenon in which the collective dimension of human life comes to the surface as a central structure, the moment in which a collective ontology can at least be seized, otherwise than in some adjunct to individual existence or in those euphoric moments of the manifestation or the strike which are in fact so many allegories of the collective, just as the party and the assembly are its allegories. (I will return to this crucial notion of the allegorical in a moment.)

But all these features still tend to summon up archaic images, which foreground violence, about which it is crucial to say and repeat that in the revolutionary situation, violence first comes from the right, from reaction, and that left violence is a reaction against this reaction. Still, the great peasant revolts (which Guha has taught us are very far from being spontaneous), the French Revolution, the desperate revolt of the Luddites (which Kirkpatrick Sale has in so timely a fashion restored to the properly revolutionary tradition), Lenin's putsch in October, finally, and the triumphant flood tides of the Chinese and Cuban revolutions—none of these images of the punctual seizure of power seem very appropriate or reassuring when we come to the postmodern age, the age of globalization.

This is why, at this point, we must insist that revolution has another face or dimension, equally essential, which is that of process itself (as opposed to Event). Revolution is then, seen from that angle, the whole lengthy, complex, contradictory process of systemic transformation: a process menaced at every turn by forgetfulness, exhaustion, the retreat into individual ontology, the desperate invention of "moral incentives," and above all the urgency of collective pedagogy, of the point-by-point cartographic charting of the ways in which so many individual events and crises are themselves components of an immense historical dialectic, invisible and absent as an empirical perception at every one of those points, but whose overall movement alone gives them their meaning. It is precisely this unity of the absent and the present, of the universal and the particular, unity indeed of the global and the local so often insisted on today—it is this dialectical unity which I call allegorical, and which demands at every step a collective awareness of the way in which revolution is being played out symbolically and actually in each of its existential episodes.

Now perhaps it will be clearer why the true meaning of Lenin is neither political nor economic, but rather both fused together in that Event-as-process and process-as-Event we call revolution. The true meaning of Lenin is the perpetual injunction to keep the revolution alive: to keep it alive as a possibility even before it has happened, to keep it alive as process at all those moments when it is threatened by defeat, or worse yet, by routinization, compromise, or forgetfulness. He didn't know he was dead: this is also the meaning of the idea of Lenin for us, it is the keeping alive of the idea of revolution as such, in a time when this word and idea has become a virtually biblical stumbling block or scandal.

Those who have wished to do away with it have found it necessary to perform a very enlightening preliminary operation: they have had first to undermine and discredit the notion of totality, or, as it is more often called today, the notion of system as such. For if there is nothing like a system, in which everything is interrelated, then it is clear that it is both unnecessary and improper to evoke systemic change. But here contemporary politics, and in particular the fortunes of social democracy, have the decisive lessons for us. I speak as one who is very far from endorsing Lenin's sectarianism as a practical political strategy, his intransigent refusal of the compromisers and the social democrats (in our modern sense). Today, speaking at least from the perspective of the United States, but also, I venture to say, from that of the Europe of the European Union countries, the most urgent task seems to me the defense of the Welfare State and of those regulations and entitlements which have been characterized as barriers to a completely free market and its prosperities. The Welfare State is of course the great postwar achievement of social democracy, even though in continental Europe it knows longer and older traditions. But it seems to me important to defend it, or better still to give social democracy and the so-called Third Way a chance to defend it, not because such a defense has any prospects of succeeding, but rather very precisely because from the Marxian perspective, it is bound to fail. We must support social democracy because its inevitable failure constitutes the basic lesson, the fundamental pedagogy, of a genuine Left. And I hasten to add here that social democracy has already failed, all over the world: something one witnesses most dramatically and paradoxically in the Eastern countries about which it is generally only said that in them communism failed. But their rich and privileged historical experience is much more complex and instructive than that: for if one can say of them that they experienced the failure of Stalinist communism, one must also add that they then experienced the failure of orthodox capitalist free-market neo-liberalism, and that they are now in the process of experiencing the failure of social democracy itself. The lesson is this, and it is a lesson about system: one cannot change anything without changing everything. Such is the lesson of system, and at the same time, if you have followed my argument, the lesson of revolution. As for the lesson about strategy, the lesson of *What Is to be Done?*, I hope I've suggested an important differentiation between strategy and tactics in these remarks: one need not, in other words, slavishly imitate Lenin's divisive, aggressive, sectarian recommendations for tactics, to grasp the ongoing value of a strategy which consists in tirelessly underscoring the difference between systemic and piecemeal goals, the age-old differentiation (and how far back in history does it go after all?) between revolution and reform.

He didn't know he was dead. I want to conclude these remarks with a different kind of problem: one absolutely related to Lenin's revolutionary meaning, as you will agree, but whose relationship to that meaning remains a puzzle and a problem. The problem is philosophical, I continue to think, but how it is philosophical is part of the problem itself. Maybe I can quickly encapsulate it with the word "charisma" (itself a part, the tip end so to speak, of the fuzzy ideological notion of totalitarianism, which means repression on the one hand, and dependence on the Leader on the other). Every revolutionary experience or experiment we know about has also been named for a Leader, and has equally often been bound up with the personal fate of that Leader, however biologically. We must feel something scandalous about this: it is for one thing allegorically improper for a collective movement to be represented by a single named human individual. There is something anthropomorphic about this phenomenon, in the bad sense in which over so many decades of modern or contemporary thought we have been taught an alert suspicion, not only about individualism and the mirage of the centered subject, but about anthropomorphism in general and the humanisms it inevitably brings with it. Why should a political movement, which has its own autonomous systemic program, be dependent on the fate and the name of a single individual, to the point of being threatened with dissolution when that individual disappears? The most recent explanation, that of these generations we have suddenly discovered miraculously at work in history, is not a particularly satisfying one (and indeed requires some historical explanation—as a theory and an historical experience—in its own right).

The individual seems to signify unity, ran the explanation from Hobbes to Hegel; and there certainly would seem to be much empirical truth to the function of such an individual in holding an immense collective together, and in damming up that tide of sectarianism, fission, and secession that menaces revolutionary movements like a flaw in human nature. Charisma is, however, an utterly useless pseudo-concept or pseudo-psychological figment: it simply names the problem to be solved and the phenomenon to be explained. Lenin was in any case, we are told, far from being a charismatic speaker like many, but not all, of the other favorite great dictators. There is a weight of legend that gets elaborated later on, but what is its function?

There is the matter of legitimization and violence or terror, but what is legitimization in the first place?

Is all this to be explained psychoanalytically, whether in terms of the father or the big Other? If so, what follows does not bode well for any revolutionary or collective movement. One thinks, in passing, of Lacan's four discourses, and in particular of the Master, of transference, and of the discourse of the University, which is characterized (the Master observed) by the need to connect everything up to proper names (this is Hegelian, this is Lacanian, this is Spinozan, Deleuzian, Leninist, Gramscian, Maoist, or whatever). "Transference" does seem to be a better word for the problem than simple "charisma" on the other hand, political philosophy, even the models of a representational politics, has not even begun to address its complexities. I do think, however, in passing, of Elizabeth Roudinesco's remark, in her history of the politics of the Lacanian movement itself, that the latter's political structure offered the unique spectacle of an absolute monarchy combined with an equally absolute anarchist democracy at the base. It is an interesting model, whose results, however, seem to have been as catastrophic as the sequels to most of the revolutionary movements one can think of.

I myself imagined a different one, which is so grotesque as to merit mentioning it in passing. Tito was still alive then, and it occurred to me that there was a place, in revolutionary theory, for something like a concept of socialist monarchy. The latter would begin as an absolute one, and would then, in the course of things, be phased down into something exceedingly limited like a constitutional monarchy in which the named and charismatic Leader has reduced himself to a mere figurehead. However desirable, that does not seem to have happened very often either, if at all. And so I much appreciate Slavoj Žižek's return to the allegedly conservative Hegel, in which the place of the monarch, indispensable and yet external to the system, is a merely formal point without content: this would be something like paying its tribute to anthropomorphism while placing it as it were under erasure. Is this the way to deal with Lenin, dead without knowing it?

Shall I end with a question, or with a proposition? If the former, it's done; if the latter, one would only want to observe that if one wants to imitate Lenin, one must do something different. Imperialism represented Lenin's attempt to theorize the partial emergence of a world market; with globalization, the latter has come into view far more completely or at least tendentially completely, and, as with the dialectic of quality and quantity, has modified the situation Lenin described beyond all recognition. The dialectic of globalization, the seeming impossibility of delinking—this is the "determinate contradiction" to which our political thought remains shackled.

Chapter 13

Rousseau and Contradiction

The philosopher of the general will is not likely to be the favorite political thinker of an age of microgroups and new social movements, which, along with so many other political philosophizers nourished by the classics, he would have considered to be so many "factions." So within the history of the twentieth century he is most likely to have been characterized as totalitarian. But there are other Rousseaus, and indeed other Jean-Jacques: Sparta may have been totalitarian (in some rather different and unique way), but the simple and hardy pastoral villages of which Rousseau also dreamed are perhaps rather to be described as regressive; and as for the famous "state of nature" (so often wildly misconstrued), it is better to follow Claude Lévi-Strauss in considering it a contribution—the first and the most glorious!—to the scarcely even nascent discipline of anthropology.[1]

Meanwhile, Rousseau's self-portrait was so decisive in fixing an image of his subjectivity for all time—and like any image, it is only that, a construction—that we may well have some difficulty in taking seriously the thinking of an autodidact, a dreamer, a masturbator, a paranoid, and a pretentious imitator of antiquity. I want to argue that we can learn much that is useful about thinking and reasoning politically from Rousseau, without in any way having to endorse his ideas or opinions. Indeed, I see that as the purpose of any reconsideration of political philosophy: namely, to identify the form of genuine political thinking, whatever its content, in such a way that we can rigorously separate the political text from expressions of mere opinion or ideology. This is, to be sure, not a very satisfying approach for those—and I admire them—who feel that our duty and our vocation as intellectuals lies in the identification and denunciation of right-wing and even liberal positions. My own skepticism and pessimism are, however, so all-encompassing as to make me feel that such an approach has little chance of teaching us anything new or surprising.

---

[1] Claude Lévi-Strauss, *Tristes tropiques*, Paris: Plon, 1955, 421.

So I will not unmask or denounce Rousseau today, although it is worth pointing out how uneasy his critics have always been, how ambiguous their judgments, how unsettled a place he continues to occupy in literary or philosophical history. He has been as embarrassing for the Marxists—was he not some kind of predecessor?—as for the fascists or the liberals: only Jacobin republicans have given him pride of place in their national pantheon. So perhaps the paranoid Jean-Jacques was right after all, and his greatest achievement was to have been loathed and attacked by all sides.

After that, it always comes as a shock to remember those slashing formulas by which Rousseau stunned the age and planted a dagger in its heart: "Man is born free, and everywhere he is in chains."[2] "The first man who, having enclosed a piece of ground, to whom it occurred to say *this is mine*, and found people sufficiently simple to believe him, was the true founder of civil society."[3] These astonishing sentences, which only Rousseau could have written, on the mode of declamation, are, it should be noted, temporal in their ambition: they aim to isolate, identify, and make dramatically visible not so much a fundamental Event as a fundamental change. That change can also be said to be the beginning of history, or, what is for Rousseau the same thing, the beginning of civilization: the beginning of something which, for him, and for Lévi-Strauss following him, had accidental causes and need never have happened in the first place. And indeed, we know today that it did take a very long time to happen: perhaps hundreds of thousands of years, compared to which our own history and civilization is a mere flash in the pan. Is a society without the state also a society without politics? In that case, it is the beginning of the political which is also at stake here; and I will not review the literature which, from the 1960s on, from Pierre Clastres to Michael Mann, has sought to solve the riddle and answer the question of the mechanisms whereby human beings were able to avoid state power for so long. In a way, Rousseau is less interested in solving the problem than in posing and articulating it: but we'll come to that distinction in a moment. And perhaps I should also add an historical observation—that the classical tradition, from Plato to More, from Locke to Fourier, always firmly identified the coming into being of so-called civilization with the coming into being of private property; but in the contemporary period, and not least in the modern Marxist tradition, civilization has been associated with power,

---

[2] Jean-Jacques Rousseau, *Du contrat social* (the so-called *Social Contract*), in *Oeuvres complètes*, Vol. 3, Paris: Gallimard, 1964, 351. All translations from this work are mine. Future references to *Oeuvres complètes*, Vol. 3, are denoted *OC*.

[3] Jean-Jacques Rousseau, *Sur l'origine de l'inégalité* (the so-called *Second Discourse*), in *OC*, 164; in English, *Second Discourse*, in *The Discourses and Other Political Writings*, ed. and trans. Victor Gourevitch, New York: Cambridge University Press, 1997, 161. Future references to the English edition are denoted *DOP*.

and with state power at that, rather than with property and private owner-ship. It is, on my view, a momentous distinction, and ought to have its relevance in the definition for us today of the political.

I don't want to lose sight of Rousseau, however, and particularly of his texts, of his sentences, which must somehow for us today be inseparable from his thinking, and offer a more reliable object of study than those philo-sophical positions and ideas in which only idealists still believe. I would therefore want to say that the analysis of Rousseau's political thinking must somehow be inseparable from the analysis of his style: except for the palpa-ble fact that with Rousseau we have to deal, not with style—that modern, personal, idiosyncratic appropriation and production of language—but rather with rhetoric, and with the clumsy and grandiloquent imitation of ancient rhetoric at that. Who does not hear the oratorical accents of Rousseau's declamations, of his great rhetorical periods and perorations, of the grandiloquent egotism with which the speaker announces his intent to take a stand on all the great problems of the age? This eloquence is not personal; indeed, the only personal feature of this language is the awkward-ness and self-consciousness of the classical imitation, while Rousseau's "ideas"—virtue, freedom, Sparta, self-sufficiency, physical hardiness, etc.—are the baggage the classical or rhetorical sentence carries within itself. Another generation or two, and all this will be swept away by Romanticism.

But now I need to say what is truly original, historically original, with Rousseau; and I suppose that in the history of ideas it bears the name of Enlightenment or Reason or one of those periodizing labels that have little enough to do with texts and a lot more with ideology and opinion in their most general sense, or with those peculiar fictive entities called values. Thus "Enlightenment" has something negative to do with religion and supersti-tion; "Reason" is another word for "secularization"; and so forth. What I have in mind is not Reason, however, but reasoning; and when we look at it more closely, we may find ourselves drawing closer to Rousseau's own opinion: namely, that he has little enough in common with the other *philosophes*.

Let's look at a specific passage: that climactic moment in the *Second Discourse* when he introduces the concept of perfectibility. It is an odd word for Rousseau to use; or rather it functions as something like camouflage, or a ruse, for his intellectual public, who all presumably have a firm belief in human progress. But it is not the ideas—we already know, from the position of the *Second Discourse* itself, that Rousseau is far from believing in perfect-ibility in any conventional sense—that we need to analyze; it is rather his reasoning's shape and the sequence of ideas into which it is inserted that offer a more significant clue to everything unique and peculiar about Rousseau.

In a first mention, indeed, Rousseau endorses the commonplace view that it is perfectibility that distinguishes human beings from animals. At that point, we are astonished by a perverse and characteristic association of ideas, for in the next sentence Rousseau asks: "Why is man alone liable to become imbecile?" (*DOP*, 141; *OC*, 142). He neither lists the positive achievements that would normally document the claim of perfectibility nor narrates the stages whereby "man" rises from an animal condition to an ever more perfected state. It is true that he will tell that story later on, but for a rather different, we may even say Lévi-Straussian, purpose; namely, to show that history and what we call civilization need never have taken place; that what we call perfectibility is the result of a series of accidents, that

> perfectibility, the social virtues, and the other faculties which natural man had received in potentiality could never develop by themselves, that in order to do so, they needed the fortuitous concatenation of several foreign causes which might never have arisen and without which he would eternally have remained in his primitive condition. (*DOP*, 159; *OC*, 162)

But I read this somewhat differently than Lévi-Strauss does (although the latter remains the appropriate reference) and will come back to this difference shortly.

For the moment, and returning to the initial passage already quoted, in which Rousseau associates man's perfectibility with his devolution into old age and senility, I want to observe that in his reflection on the matter, Rousseau characteristically isolates the form rather than the content of the idea of perfectibility. He sets aside the positive valence of the latter, retaining only the formal identity of perfectibility with change or history. And this is all the more astonishing inasmuch as the ethical judgment, the eudaimonic framework in which notions of attraction and repulsion, pleasure and pain, good and bad, come into play—this framework will be the indispensable framework of the *Second Discourse* as a whole, which reaches the well-known conclusion that civilization and civil society are harmful states which generate class inequalities. What then is this faculty of judgment suspended in the passage that immediately concerns us, to the point where not even the paradoxical effect of illustrating perfectibility with senility is allowed to distract us? The fact is that Rousseau is not interested in what will later on (in Part 2) be his fundamental conclusion; he is not here interested in judgment or content; rather, he is intent on observing the abstract form of historical change itself. And it is at this point that I would wish to specify Lévi-Strauss's interpretation more sharply, yet very much in his spirit. For it seems to me that here Rousseau anticipates that great discovery which remains associated with Lévi-Strauss's name and work, namely, the distinction between the synchronic and the diachronic. The diachronic—change and history—is neither meaningful nor thinkable: it is the result of a series of accidents. Only the synchronic—here the famous state of nature—is thinkable and meaningful; only the synchronic has genuine content, while the diachronic is an abstract sequence of events whose content or meaning is variable and lacks necessity. Clearly enough, this is the point at which it would be appropriate to raise the issue of narrative as such—the issue of causalities, of telling the story of this sequence of meaningless events, or indeed (in Lévi-Strauss's system) of transforming such a sequence into a narrative myth, in which meaning is generated by borrowing terms and oppositions from the synchronic as such.

But that is not my topic here, for I have only wanted to use this first brief passage in order to demonstrate the way in which Rousseau is prepared to follow his own thinking into the unthinkable. Let me now offer a much larger and more dramatic illustration of this process, in which confidence in reasoning leads the thinker on fearlessly into a cul-de-sac. It is the famous digression on the origin of language (not to be confused with Rousseau's later and equally unsuccessful attempt to confront this problem, in a fragment henceforth rendered famous by Jacques Derrida's commentary in the *Grammatology*, but which exceeds the discussion in the *Second Discourse* by raising the additional issues of writing, climate, music, and the like).

What the proportionally considerable digression in the *Second Discourse* offers is the astonishing spectacle of a reasoning so self-punishing in the demands it makes on itself that it renders the problem insoluble and in effect incapacitates itself: "Let me be allowed briefly to consider the perplexities regarding the origin of Languages" (*DOP*, 145; *OC*, 146). The digression is an enlargement of the discussion of the emergence of thinking and abstract ideas among those "natural beings" who only know needs and passions and do not as yet think any more than they speak. I summarize the various obstacles which Rousseau places in the way of thinking the emergence of language: (1) why language should have been necessary in the first place; (2) how abstract meanings could ever have been communicated; (3) how the cry as such could have been domesticated and articulated in such a way as to serve the needs of everyday life; (4) how propositions and sentences could have emerged from that first form of language which was the individual word; (5) how general terms could have emerged from names of individual things; (6) a more concentrated summary of all of the above, involving the distinction between the intellect and the imagination (this moment will also be the point of departure for Lévi-Strauss's theory of *pensée sauvage*):

> Hence one has to state propositions, hence one has to speak in order to have general ideas: for as soon as the imagination stops, the mind can proceed only by means of discourse. If, then, the first Inventors could give names only to the ideas they already had, it follows that the first substantives could never have been anything but proper names. (*DOP*, 148; *OC*, 150)

At this point Rousseau breaks it off:

> By means which I cannot conceive ... I pause after these first steps ... as for myself, frightened by the increasing difficulties, and convinced of the almost demonstrated impossibility that Languages could have arisen and been established by purely humans means, I leave to anyone who wishes to undertake it the discussion of this difficult problem.

And finally: "quoiqu'il en soit de ces origines"—"whatever may be the case regarding these origins ..."

Rousseau has talked himself out of his own illustration; by the peculiar power of the reasoning proper to him, and which is at present our object of study, he has so effectively multiplied the problems involved in thinking the origin of languages that he has proved to his own satisfaction that they could not have come into being in the first place! It is no doubt a comic spectacle, akin to being too smart for your own good. But there is something salutary in the shock as well, and something temporally perverse and retroactive, with a kind of family likeness to Freud's *Nachträglichkeit*. The point is that the event to be modeled has already happened; we are in the process of foretelling the past, predicting what already exists behind us, as it were framing a guilty man. And the shock lies in the fact that the most airtight reasoning proves that it can never have happened in the first place. Thus, in the gap between our reasoning and the facts, a mystery suddenly emerges fully blown, which is the mystery of time and of historicity, the mystery of the Event itself, as a scandal and a stumbling block. The apparent discovery that we cannot think the diachronic does not abolish history, nor, as Lévi-Strauss believed, does it discredit historical thought: on the contrary, it establishes history for the first time in all its arresting freshness and unpredictability. The flight of the owl returns upon the world of daylight to confer a grisly clarity upon it, in which every leaf stands out without a shadow.

This is then an altogether remarkable outcome, which surely does not demonstrate the weakness of Rousseau's capacity for thought and his philosophical abilities so much as it exhibits their very power and his frightening resolve to follow his own reasoning wherever it leads him—a peculiar enough character trait to find in so inveterate a daydreamer and fantasist.

I see several ways of interpreting this peculiarity. One will predictably be the reading of Lévi-Strauss, on which we have already touched several times, and which again rehearses the opposition between the synchronic and the diachronic. But in the present context this opposition takes on unusual content. First of all, we confront the obvious fact that no one ever has accounted for the origins of language: this has to do at least in part with the absence of anthropological data (but it should be noted that Rousseau himself takes into account just such scientific lacunae: "Comparative Anatomy has as yet made too little progress," etc. [*DOP*, 134; *OC*, 134]); and the linguistic paradox is given yet another twist by virtue of this very absence, which results from the necessary non-existence of writing in such an early period. But Lévi-Strauss's position is not merely an agonistic one: he affirms that language could never have come into being piecemeal, gradually, bit by bit (beginning with the cry and the gesture, and slowly passing into articulated sounds and so forth). Rather, as a synchronic system, language had to appear all at once, complete and fully developed—a requirement that may well make the origins of language even more unthinkable than they were in Rousseau.

But we may also come at this from the vantage point of another reader of Rousseau, this time a follower from his own century, for whom the reading of Jean-Jacques was fully as decisive: Immanuel Kant. For was not at least one of Kant's great discoveries the conclusion that the human mind is constitutionally limited in what it can think and in its proper objects? And is this not one of the most dramatic lessons of Rousseau's procedures here—that when making the most rigorous demands on itself, the mind sometimes comes up short against the unthinkable? The conclusion Kant draws from this lesson, indeed, is the impossibility of thinking about origins (the first paralogism in the *Critique of Pure Reason*, or in other words "the antinomy of pure reason": "the world has a beginning in time," "the world has no beginning," etc.).[4] But as with language in Rousseau, this is not exactly a false problem: for clearly enough, like language, the world did have a beginning inasmuch as it exists. What is at stake is not that evident fact, but our capacity to think it in any adequate way.

Yet somehow both these readings (and Rousseau himself) tend to affirm the impossibility, if not of history, then at least of historical thinking. And this is very clearly the consequence Lévi-Strauss draws in his famous polemic with Sartre.[5] I want to suggest a somewhat different conclusion, which will affirm Rousseau's relationship to the then emergent dialectic and to dialectical thinking as such: for it seems to me that what his thinking arrives at, as its momentary terminus, is neither impossibility nor diachronic incoherence, nor is it the antinomy as such, but rather contradiction, the very motor power of the dialectic itself.

But let's now, in conclusion, try to see this at work in an eminently political text, namely the *Social Contract*. Here it is not so much a question of the origin of that bad thing civilization or civil society and its history, as of that second-best thing which is the social contract in its most vigorous and uncorrupted form, as it succeeds the so-called state of nature. The idea of

---

[4] Immanuel Kant, *Critique of Pure Reason*, eds. and trans. Paul Guyer and Allen W. Wood, New York: Cambridge University Press, 1997, 470–471.

[5] Claude Lévi-Strauss, *La Pensée sauvage*, Paris: Plon, 1962, 336.

the contract—that is to say, Rousseau's motivation in retheorizing it, since it is itself a very ancient idea—Rousseau's interest in the idea of the contract must be explored in several directions. One—and it is the great originality of this unique text—lies in the production of a new mental category: that of a relationship between the individual and the collective which is neither that of simple homology—the collectivity is simply the individual writ larger, it is a collective subject of some kind—nor that of an aggregate of individuals, a single individual multiplied in such a way that notions of majority, plurality, minority, and so on are ontologically relevant. Indeed, Rousseau wishes to establish something like a radical ontological difference between the individual and the collective whole, without the existence of any mediating groups or instances. Does he succeed in achieving this new category of thought, which would be, if it existed, distinct in form from oppositions like universal and particular or general and individual? The answer has never been clear or definitive, and the negative judgment, that the exclusion of factionalism and intermediate groups is simply totalitarian—an accusation powerfully reinforced by the Jacobin practice of Rousseau's idea—is as plausible as it is contradicted by the text.

For one of the other purposes of the *Social Contract* is to exclude the idea that a people can contract into slavery or voluntarily accept tyranny: the inalienability of freedom then gives content to and poses limits on the consequences of the contract as such, and inscribes the right to rebel in human nature.

But what interests us here, in the present context, is rather the slippage of the idea of the contract. It was designed to identify the deep structure of that social contract which replaced the state of nature—in such a way that disparities between the original contact and an increasingly corrupt modern society are underscored. Here, as always, there is a confusion and an interference between the political and the economic: is the degradation of modern society the result of private property, as the *Second Discourse* affirms ("whoever first said this is *mine*"), or is it, as the language of the *Social Contract* seems to imply, a matter of freedom and its loss? This second possibility would seem to be more a cultural or superstructural consequence, a waning of the consciousness of some original freedom, rather than, as with private property, the institution of new kinds of infrastructural constraints. Two rather different "revolutionary" solutions would then be implied by the alternatives; but I want to focus on the fact that either seems to imply a solution, that is to say, that the idea of an original contract seems fatally to suggest the possibility of returning to it and of somehow rectifying the present fallen state of society.

In fact, in another part of his mind, Rousseau would seem to be convinced that a revival of the contract is possible only under very specific conditions which in modern times only rarely obtain. *The Project for a*

Constitution for Corsica, the *Considerations on the Government of Poland*, and Part 3 of the *Social Contract* underscore the unique historical opportunities of these two areas still relatively uncorrupted by "modern society," whose inhabitants still retain something of the vigor and independence of the simpler mountain tribes of ancient Switzerland, say. Indeed, the weaknesses of Corsica and Poland in the modern world are precisely their social strengths when it comes to a return to the virtues and strengths of an older Spartan state (to be sure, they are quite different weaknesses: in Corsica underdevelopment, in Poland feudal decentralization and Russian oppression). As for the so-called advanced nations of Western Europe, however, they are incorrigible, and no return to societal health or to the original contract is to be fantasized for them. We can already guess, from this pessimism, the presence of that mental operation we have already underscored: an attempt to fantasize, which is at every step interrupted and blocked by a kind of reality principle of the imagination itself, which combines its demands with an insistence on the difficulties of constructing the fantasy in the first place, and finally multiplies them to the point at which it talks itself out of the very possibility of conceiving an optimistic projection altogether.

We do not, however, have to deduce the operation of this characteristic process in Rousseau: we can observe it again in detail at one specific point, namely, that moment in the *Social Contract* when Rousseau describes the inauguration of the contract itself and the agency whereby it is first brought into being. I have already observed that Rousseau's formulations waver between base and superstructure, so to speak: between institutions and cultural habits, between the laws of the city and the practices and daily life of its inhabitants. At his weakest, he makes this hesitation, this alternation, visible as an inconsistency; at his strongest, he insists on the political necessity of uniting the two in a kind of cultural revolution. Meanwhile, and very much in the spirit of the Althusserian reading of the *Manifesto* as a form,[6] he will not be content until he drives his imagination on to the very point of origin itself and confronts the necessity of grasping the agency responsible for the foundation of the new system. This agency is still an individual one, like Machiavelli's prince; and it lies in the past, as an historical act of foundation which is certainly exemplary and perhaps inimitable.

Everyone who has absorbed the atmosphere of neoclassical eighteenth-century political culture and has confronted the inescapable reference to Sparta in it will scarcely be surprised by the looming presence, in this discourse, of Lycurgus, the mythic founder. Plutarch's *Lives* then take their place alongside Plato's *Republic* as one of the fundamental Utopian texts, something like the life of Utopus himself, whose inauguration of the perfect

---

[6] Louis Althusser, "Machiavel et nous," in *Écrits philosophiques et politiques*, Vol. 2, Paris: Stock/IMEC, 1995.

commonwealth is, in More, shrouded in mystery, not least because, like Lycurgus himself, he then seems to have programmed himself out of the system, if not out of history and legend.[7] Meanwhile, Heidegger assures us that the founding of a state is, along with the work of art, the philosophical concept, and the ominously named "essential sacrifice," one of the fundamental places of truth and of the disclosure of being.[8]

Rousseau observes all this with characteristic and we may even say remorseless lucidity. But given his method, as we have just outlined it, he arrives at a somewhat different perspective on the conclusion. We may translate this method into contemporary terms as follows: Rousseau's reasoning is the reconstruction of history in thought. It is neither an historiographic narrative nor an historical representation exactly: something we can verify by comparing that first part of the *Discourse on Inequality*, of which we have already spoken, with the second, in which he attempts to recuperate his losses and paper over the extraordinary train of reasoning of the first with a far more conventional historical story of the stages of the emergence of civil society and class injustice. Rather, it seems to me more appropriate to compare Rousseau's procedure—the reconstruction of historical development by way of presuppositions and preconditions—with what Althusser called the concrete-in-thought, a nonrepresentational mode which often has surprises in store for us.

Let's follow the process in the case of Rousseau's "reconstruction" of Plutarch's Lycurgus. We are warned of the looming thunderclouds of paradox and antinomy by the opening sentence, which posits the need, in the founder, of "une intelligence supérieure, qui vit toutes les passions des hommes et qui n'en éprouvât aucune" (*OC*, 381).[9] Rousseau is very clear that the transformation of human nature itself, as he says, means the end of the individual and the creation, in his place, of the group itself. Meanwhile, this rare and unusual process requires a very distinctive kind of agency: the lawgiver cannot impose his new constitution either by force or by rank or position. A strict differentiation must be established between conventional rules and their offices and this one: "Si celui qui commande aux hommes ne doit pas commander aux lois, celui qui commande aux lois ne doit pas non plus commander aux hommes" (*OC*, 382).[10] (It would have been worth

---

[7] Plutarch, "Lycurgus," in *The Lives of the Noble Grecians and Romans*, trans. John Dryden and Rev. Arthur Hugh Clough, New York: Random House, 1932, 49–74.

[8] Martin Heidegger, "The Origin of the Work of Art," in *Philosophies of Art and Beauty*, eds. A. Hofstadter and R. Kuhns, New York: Random House, 1964, 685.

[9] "A superior intelligence, capable of contemplating all human passions without feeling any of them."

[10] "If he who has authority over men should have no authority over the law, he who has authority over the law should not have authority over men."

pausing here to note the emergence in Rousseau of that trope of the dialectical chiasmus which is omnipresent in Marx and which is indeed the sign and symptom of a whole new mode of thinking.)

At any rate, it is clear that the lawgiver, the founder of the state, cannot himself be an individual exactly: it is the inverse and the logical concomitant of the social contract: the people as a whole must function as something more and other than a collection of individuals, while the individual who sets the contract in place must stand outside that collection, and in no way constitute a part of the whole of which he is the godlike cause. Thus, just as the collectivity of the social contract requires a new conceptual category, different in kind from either that of the individual or that of the multiple, so also the founder must be conceptualized in a new way: "Ainsi [concludes Rousseau] l'on trouve à la fois dans l'ouvrage de la législation deux choses qui semblent incompatibles: une entreprise au dessus de la force humaine, et pour l'éxécuter, une autorité qui n'est rien" (*OC*, 383).[11] Were we to continue our juxtaposition of Rousseau with the thinking of modern structuralism, we would be inclined to feel that Rousseau has here discovered the essentials of what Lévi-Strauss calls a myth, namely, a figure which unites incompatible semes or signifying traits. I would thus conclude that Rousseau has (as with the invention of language) proved that Sparta never was founded (and, indeed, could never have existed in the first place). But now I want to draw a further conclusion from this conclusion: that what Rousseau has discovered here (if he has not indeed invented it) is what will shortly, in the emergent dialectical tradition, be called a contradiction. Indeed, the greatness of Rousseau lies precisely in this, to drive his thought on until it reaches that ultimate limit which is the contradiction, what is incompatible and ultimately unthinkable. That this has something to do with his fantasy-production and his inclination towards daydreaming I have already hinted; and perhaps I can theorize that connection by evoking the reality-principle within fantasy itself, and the rigorousness with which a certain daydreaming makes demands on itself and attempts to secure the conditions of possibility of its own fantasies. At any rate it is that peculiar rigor which we find here and which impels Rousseau towards the implacable undoing of his own fantasies in contradiction as such.

Meanwhile, this is no ordinary contradiction, insofar as it has as its object history and temporality: here, indeed, is the revolutionary vicious circle which the mystery of the founder and the contradictory myth of Lycurgus contains within itself:

---

[11] "We thus find two seemingly incompatible things in the work of legislation: an enterprise beyond all human powers, and, for its execution, an authority which is nothing."

Pour qu'un peuple naissant pût goûter les saines maximes de la politique et suivre les regles fondamentales de la raison d'Etat, il faudrait que l'effet put devenir la cause, que l'esprit social qui doit être l'ouvrage de l'institution présidât à l'institution même, et que les hommes fussent avant les loix ce qu'ils doivent devenir par elles.[12]

It is an astonishing conclusion, in no way vitiated by the feeble Enlightenment appeal to persuasion and reason by which Rousseau attempts to cut his Gordian knot and solve his irresolvable problems.

So Rousseau was not only the impossible founder of structuralism; he was the equally impossible founder of the dialectic itself. He was not only the discoverer of the tension between synchrony and diachrony; he also stumbled upon that necessity of the dialectic which is rooted in the historicity of language itself. (I have often, to this effect, quoted the extraordinary footnote in *Émile* on the relationship between words and modes of production.[13]) But it would be enough to return to the *Second Discourse* to observe the same dialectical lucidity at work in his frequent identifications of anachronism in the language of his philosophical opponents. What can the word "misery" mean, when applied to the state of nature? he responds to Hobbes (*DOP*, 150; *OC*, 152); "explain to me what the word *oppression* means" in such a state, he adds (*DOP*, 158; *OC*, 161); and finally, how could the words "power" and "reputation" have any significance for those people you

---

[12] "In order for an emergent people to enjoy the healthy maxims of politics and to follow the fundamental rules of the state's reason [the untranslatable *raison d'État*], it would be necessary for the effect to become the cause, and for the social spirit which was to have resulted from this institutionalization to have presided over the founding of the institution itself, in other words, for men to have been before law what they were to become by virtue of its existence" (*OC*, 383).

[13] Jean-Jacques Rousseau, *Émile*, in *Oeuvres complètes*, Vol. 4, Paris: Gallimard, 1969, 345 note: "J'ai fait cent fois réflexion en écrivant qu'il est impossible dans un long ouvrage de donner toujours les mêmes sens aux mêmes mots. Il n'y a point de langue assez riche pour fournir autant de termes, de tours et de phrases, que nos idées peuvent avoir de modifications. La méthode de définir tous les termes et de substituer sans cesse la définition à la place du défini est belle mais impraticable, car comment éviter le cercle? Les définitions pourroient être bonnes si l'on n'employoit pas des mots pour les faire. Malgré cela, je suis persuadé qu'on peut être clair, même dans la pauvreté de notre langue; non pas en donnant toujours les mêmes acceptions aux mêmes mots, mais en faisant en sorte, autant de fois qu'on emploie chaque mot, que l'acceptions qu'on lui donne soit suffisamment déterminée par les idées qui s'y rapportent, et que chaque période où ce mot se trouve lui serve, pour ainsi dire, de définition. Tantôt je dis que les enfans sont incapables de raisonnement, et tantôt je les fais raisonner avec assez de finesse; je ne crois pas en cela me contredire dans mes idées, mais je ne puis disconvenir que je ne me contredise souvent dans mes expressions."

call "savages" (*DOP*, 187; *OC*, 193)? This is the other face of the opposition between the synchronic and the diachronic; it reflects the secret historicity of this apparently historical and antihistorical opposition—the history revealed by the inapplicability of the elements of our own synchronicity, our own historical system, to a radically different one.

So it is that Rousseau discovers revolution as the unthinkable gap between two systems, the untheorizable break between two distinct synchronicities: perhaps it would be enough to evoke a contemporary rediscovery of that mystery, such as Antonio Negri's notion of constituent power,[14] to glimpse again the positive energies that begin to emanate from this seemingly negative and self-defeating act of thought. I believe that political thinking is to be surprised here, as it were in its moment of emergence, and by that very method of the implacable reduction to conditions of possibility which was Rousseau's own historical invention.

---

[14] Antonio Negri, *Insurgencies*, Minneapolis: University of Minnesota Press, 1999.

Chapter 14

Ideological Analysis: A Handbook[1]

> … *le geste essentiel de l'analyse ideologique semble consister*
> *à "condamner" un texte …*
>
> G. Genette

The theory of ideology is Marxism's better mousetrap. How many ambitious ideologues have left their textual bones behind in the fruitless attempt to discover, not merely a better one, but the thing itself! So it is that one reads with a sinking heart and the proverbial mixed feelings the fateful opening words: What is ideology? Ideology is—. Yet to take one's distances prudently and to restrict oneself to a neutral account of the various positions that have been proposed on this topic is to indulge the "history of ideas" in its most relativistic and vacuous, antiquarian form.

A certain tactical modification might, however, be available in the intent to measure the analytic or diagnostic value of the various competing conceptions of ideology, rather than to fight ontologically about the substantive itself: it is a move analogous to contemporary discussions of that other hotly debated concept social class, where the defense of an operation called class *analysis* seems at least initially sufficient to short-circuit endless debates about what "a" class might be, if indeed such a thing existed it the first place.

Still, it seems obvious that one cannot do ideological analysis very effectively without using the word (although, paradoxically, I will argue below that some forms of contemporary and not so contemporary thinking in fact do just that), and so a few preliminary terminological remarks are in order. I suspect that people are in general more disposed to an occasional use of the adjective "ideological" than the noun from which it comes: judiciously, strategically placed, this qualifier still has a shock value which is less a matter of invective than of an *estrangement* which is also a *positioning*. And this seems to me one of the fundamental functions of the terminology and

---

[1] This text was first composed as a "course" for Australia's Open University Deakin University in Geelong, in 1981, and published in pamphlet form. The prospect of a later publication prompted the addition, in 1990, of sections viii to xii, in order to "bring it up to date." Yet in 2008 a much more comprehensive reevaluation seemed necessary, which is found in the afterword.

conceptuality of ideology even today: none of the competing terms ("world-view," for instance) is able in the same way to preserve the elements and the structure of a given object (a "philosophy," for example) while radically shifting the discursive framework in which it is seen—bracketing it as it were, so as to make its constitutive features of belief, socially symbolic praxis and group mediation, visible to the naked eye.

If the substantive "ideology" is less frequent in contemporary academic discourse, this is not merely due to the intellectual threat theories of ideology in general pose for a largely liberal conception of ideas as such, but above all because the term is also a declaration of adherence to a particular interpretive community, in this case to Marxism as a problematic and a praxis. I observe this fact of life, not to warn outsiders away but rather to emphasize a situation in which all distinctive or marked theoretical terminology today functions in much the same way, although the group dynamics of other such interpretive communities may be at first glance less obvious or visible.

It is the very centrality of the problem of ideology to Marxism which, far from rendering it too specialized, constitutes its signal conceptual strength and advantage. The centrality I have in mind here is not necessarily that of a key concept (like the labor theory of value, for instance), but that of a unique type of interpretive operation—the strongest form, perhaps, of what the dialectical tradition calls a mediation. Ideological analysis does not commit one in advance to any of the specific "theories" of ideology that will be outlined in the following pages (indeed, one of the purposes of this survey or overview is to disengage us from the temptation of deciding which of these competing and often incompatible theories is the true or correct one); what it does do is to condemn one to a renewed confrontation with the problematic from which such theories arise—a problematic which it is difficult enough to formulate (since all the specific formulations of these issues are themselves then by definition "solutions" to them and theories of ideology in their own right), but which has sometimes been described in terms of the relationship of a particular system of ideas (or a linguistic or textual articulation of such a system) and that something else or other which is its outside or ground: a relationship generally characterized in terms of a representation of some reality or as the expression of a group praxis or ethos. The more local problems of "context" and of "intention" as they have been developed (or stigmatized) in the area of intellectual and cultural history are thus, for example, at one and the same time features implicit in any work of ideological analysis, and also competing or alternative ways of formulating the problematic as such. What is argued here, however, is that the problematic of ideology—or better still, the framework of ideological analysis as a method and an operation—offers a more complicated, but also a more interesting and more adequate, perspective in which to confront matters which, under the nomenclature of "context" and "intention," may be considered false problems.

The notion of ideological analysis therefore allows us to subsume and to sublate a whole range of traditional problems not solvable in their own terms: this is to say that it allows us to rewrite such problems more strongly; indeed, one of the incidental features that this review of theories of ideology can be assumed to involve is a displacement of stereotypical narratives of the history of contemporary theory, and the rewriting, and estrangement, of that narrative around the question of ideology (to which now a certain number of classic or contemporary "theories" of various kinds—Freud and Nietzsche, Derrida and Foucault—are rewritten as so many contributions and proposals; as subsets or variants, in other words, of the theory of ideology itself). This is an alternate historical paradigm which may at least be expected to produce new evaluations and distinct positionings than those currently accepted.

The most consequent objections to the terminology and the conceptuality of ideology will, however, be those which challenge the claims of dialectical language as such. The very notion of a "problematic," which is somehow distinct from the whole range of terms and concepts derived from it—some of them radically antithetical to each other, as for example in the incompatibility of notions of ideology as false consciousness or error and those notions for which ideology is either a necessary feature of social thinking or an indispensable dimension of all group praxis—will no doubt pose problems for the analytic mind. They are problems one must respect, on account of the rigorous standards they enforce on thinking and writing alike. On my view, however, the ambiguity and the semantic slippages in a term like "ideology" are as productive as they are intolerable; the dialectical use of such a term specifies it in a local textual situation, but mobilizes the presence of competing meanings, not in order the more effectively to exclude them, but rather as a means of problematizing the issues themselves and making their complexity less avoidable.

i.

Although in its modern usage it is an essentially Marxian concept, the theory of ideology inscribes itself in the whole series of specifically nineteenth-century contributions to the study of the complexities of consciousness and culture, and may initially be understood as one moment in what Freud will later call the Copernican revolution in thought.

By this expression, Freud meant to designate the waning of the eighteenth-century confidence in reason, and the increasing sense throughout this period that consciousness is not really the master in its own house; that deeper forces of various kinds are at work beneath and behind the immediate appearance of conscious experience and thinking. In other words, it came to be believed that, as with the solar system, reality does not revolve around human reason and consciousness, but the latter obey the force of gravity of other laws, hidden from us, which the analyst must uncover, decode, detect, reveal.

Other significant moments in this discovery, or Copernican revolution, include the following:

1. Hegel's notion of the "ruse of reason," or the "ruse of history," namely, that history uses individuals and their private ambitions for ends that may have little enough to do with their own conscious intentions (thus, for example, we can say that Hitler's conscious anti-communism *objectively* ended up enlarging the Soviet bloc and spreading socialism throughout the world).
2. Darwin's theory of evolution, which not only shattered some traditional religious illusions, but also reinserted human history into natural history.
3. Nietzsche's "genealogy of morals," which demonstrated the operation, within ostensibly charitable or philanthropic or altruistic actions, of the dynamics of the struggle for power between the weak and the strong ("will to power"), and the presence, within such "positive" impulses, of the negative force of *ressentiment*.
4. Freud's own theory, finally, which constructed perhaps the most powerful and influential model of this "decentering" of consciousness and launched the fortunes of the concept of an *unconscious*. (Modern or twentieth-century thought will then add to this list the discovery of language, and of our programming by essentially linguistic systems: expressed most notably in the structuralism of Claude Lévi-Strauss.)

Marx's theory of ideology occupies a unique position in this series: formulated in essentially nineteenth-century or pre-Freudian terms (that is, lacking a theory of the unconscious proper), it has proved capable in the twentieth century of developing rich new variants that take into account later discoveries. We will therefore want to examine both classical forms of Marxian ideology theory and some of its modern versions (which are often termed neo-Marxist).

There is another significant reason, however, why Marxism requires a theory of ideology in order to complete itself. In common with all other theories that attempt to build a model of the world that is different from the experience of common sense, from what Hegel calls the "immediacy" of daily life and of sense perception, Marxism must answer an initial question: if the world is as Marxism describes it, how is it that human beings have had to live through so much history in order to arrive at this "discovery"? More than that, if this particular "truth" about the world has finally been revealed to us in modern times, how is it that so many people continue to refuse it and insist on seeing the world in quite different terms? And why is it that this description of the world by way of the dialectic is so elaborate and convoluted a process?

Like Freudianism, like existentialism, Marxism must therefore posit a *resistance* to its often unpleasant and painful teachings and must account for that resistance, *within* the terms of its own system, in an account of its own difficulties of reception and of its apparent disparity with daily life and common-sense experience: this account will essentially be the Marxist theory of ideology.

As for the historical part of the problem—why humanity had to wait for Marx in order to obtain his essential discovery, the labor theory of value —Marxism also includes an account of this paradox, and this is what characterizes Marxism as an historicism, that is, a philosophy for which human thought and science are seen as conditioned and limited by the historical moment and by social developments. Marx's historicism asserts that the dynamics of value could not become visible to analysts, or accessible to scientific thought, until a social formation—capitalism—emerged, in which for the first time human labor is universally transformed into a "commodity" or in other words, "commodified." Thus, although Aristotle had some intuitions about the nature of work and value, his insights were structurally limited by the social organization of Greek society, in which slavery and slave labor played a predominant part[2]: and slave labor is distinct from the free modern proletariat in that slaves do not sell their labor power and are not paid wages. Nor is the labor of the serfs of feudalism commodified labor in this sense either. Thus, the discoveries of Marxism could only emerge in a mode of production which, for the first time in human history, universally transforms the labor of producers—the new factory workers, but also the peasantry in a capitalist system of agriculture—into wage labor, or commodified labor—labor power which can be bought and sold like commodities.

It is indeed very precisely this historicist approach to science and scientific discovery which explains the significance within Marxism of a theory of "modes of production," or in other words of a typology of various structurally distinct kinds of human societies. In the classical Marxian view,[3] there have been essentially five distinct modes of production or types of human society in history (primitive communism or tribal society; the "ancient mode" or in other words the slave-holding system of the Greek *polis* or city-

---

[2] Karl Marx, *Capital*, Vol. 1, trans. Ben Fowkes, London: Penguin, 1976, 151–152; and see G. E. M. de Ste. Croix, *The Class Struggle in the Ancient Greek World*, Ithaca: Cornell University Press, 1981.

[3] See for example "Forms Which Precede Capitalist Production," in Karl Marx, *Grundrisse*, London: Penguin, 1973, 471–514.

state; the "Asiatic mode," or the great systems of the so-called oriental despotisms as in ancient India, China, and the Middle East; feudalism; and capitalism) with one more—communism or socialism—yet to come in the future. What is "dialectical" about this view of the series of modes of production (not necessarily a linear or evolutionary theory) is the qualification that each of these modes of production has its own unique and distinct laws and, in particular, that the emergence of capitalism determines a complete dialectical transformation of all earlier ways of life.

The remarks on Aristotle, meanwhile, suggest a theory of the breakdown of the classical world: limited by slavery, the ancient city-state (in which commerce and certain commodity forms are already very much present) is unable to develop into genuine capitalism on account of the availability of slaves. This in turn suggests a further reflection on the specificity and originality of capitalism: it is dialectically distinct from all preceding societies in its prodigious and well-nigh infinite possibilities of expansion. Hence its superiority to the older social forms, which it ruthlessly breaks down and assimilates into itself—a process known as imperialism, and one that is still under way (witness the so-called modernization of Third World countries and societies, into which industry, the market, the money system, the commodification of labor, continue to penetrate).

Finally, the example of Aristotle may serve as a first lesson in a specific form of Marxian ideological analysis. Aristotle's incapacity to grasp the hidden truth of labor and value exemplifies only one feature of the dynamics of ideology and will illustrate only one of the ways in which Marx conceived the possibilities of error and the structural difficulties of and resistances to "truth." This particular model of a Marxist theory of ideology suggests that history and social development impose objective structural limits on the capacity of even the finest minds to penetrate reality and that people cannot think beyond the level to which their social life and organization have developed. Later, as in *The Eighteenth Brumaire* (1852), this theory will be applied to social classes, which are similarly limited by their positioning within a social totality and which cannot think beyond those limits.[4]

It should be noted carefully that this particular model of ideological limitation does not necessarily involve "false consciousness" or error: Aristotle was neither deluded nor under the spell of religious or metaphysical illusion. What he could see he saw clearly, but the total social process necessarily escaped his view, owing to the objective limits of his social formation. Marx will later apply the same kind of ideological critique to the economic thinkers (or "political economists") of the periods immediately preceding his own, most notably Adam Smith and above all David Ricardo: here too an

---

[4] Karl Marx, *The Eighteenth Brumaire of Louis Bonaparte*, New York: International Publishers, 1994, 50–51.

insufficient development of capitalism as a system, as well as the "blinkers" of a particular class formation, prevent these thinkers from developing their key insights into labor, money, and commodities, into that fully scientific system *Capital* purports to unfold. Still later, the most important Marxist philosopher of the twentieth century, Georg Lukács, will in his seminal book *History and Class Consciousness* (1923) apply this model of the structural limits on thinking to a magisterial analysis of classical German philosophy and its "ideological" limits, particularly in Kant, Schiller, and Hegel. This is the chapter (on "Reification and the Consciousness of the Proletariat") in which Lukács's controversial theory of "totality" (widely under attack today both by Marxists of the so-called Frankfurt School and by those following Louis Althusser) is most amply developed and laid out.

Returning to the function of the concept of ideology within Marxism— an account of the inevitable *resistance* to the doctrine—it is obviously in the reality of social class (structuring of capitalism around the class antagonism and opposition between producers and owners, proletarians and capitalists) that such resistance will always ultimately be located and explained. But ideology can take many different forms (some of them not evidently or immediately of a class character): this means that Marxism can imply a whole range of models of ideology and a whole range of distinct methods of ideology, and a whole range of distinct methods of ideological analysis. Below, we will try to sort out and typologize a few of the most important. But first a few preliminary remarks still need to be made.

First of all, Marxism attempts to distinguish itself from purely philosophical systems (and also from untheoretical or ideological political movements of various kinds) by positing itself as a "unity of theory and practice." This means that the attempt to deflate and dispel ideology can be waged on two distinct levels, that of theory and that of praxis. In other words, we can attempt to grasp and "demystify" the operations of ideology in an analytic or theoretical way, by looking at various ideological texts or historical forms of ideology in order to understand their dynamics and their functions. But we can also seek to dispel ideology by way of praxis, by action and by the attempt to change the objective situations and circumstances that have brought those ideologies into being and made them necessary in the first place. After all, we are all ourselves caught in ideology, and ideological critique must therefore also take the form of self-analysis and self-consciousness, of self-critique. *Ideology is in one sense the form taken by alienation in the realm of consciousness or thought: it is alienated thought.* But a concept of alienation necessarily implies some (perhaps unformulated) notion of a non-alienated state (otherwise we would never be aware of our alienation in the first place). So too a theory of ideology necessarily implies some account of its opposite (truth, science, class consciousness, or whatever, varying according to the model of ideology used). But the great discovery of the

"Theses on Feuerbach" (written at the same time as *The German Ideology*) was precisely that discovering the truth and elaborating it is inseparable from action, from changing ourselves and the society from which our illusions sprang. The most famous of these theses, the eleventh, stated: "The philosophers have only interpreted the world, in various ways; the point is to change it." Thus ideological critique, for Marxism, must always involve this or that effort at liberation, not merely from ideology but also from alienation itself. The classical Marxist view of such liberation sees it in terms of collective and political action: but clearly some of the counter-cultural movements of our own time have also had a revolutionary and liberatory potential: alongside these two strategies for liberation must also be mentioned feminism, one of the most important movements of the present day.

Next a word on the dialectic itself may be in order. Briefly, the dialectic may be said to be thinking that is both situational (situation-specific) and reflexive (or conscious of its own thought processes). That is, it follows from what we have said above about history and about ideology, that (1) no transhistorical or absolute thinking or understanding is possible, so that thought must somehow attempt to approximate its own concrete historical situation, and (2) that as we are ourselves always involved in ideology, our thinking must include the attempt to reckon ourselves as observers into the process.

But also implied here is the idea that the very nature and strategies of the dialectic will change according to its historical situation and according to the objects or ideologies it seeks to understand or to combat. The young Marx, owing to the social circumstances of his own time (a still feudal Germany which had neither made its revolution against the *ancien régime* nor essentially known a theoretical, scientific, and secularizing revolution in thought of the type of the eighteenth-century French *philosophes*), was still essentially engaged in combating ideologies of a religious or metaphysical type. Later, however, as his targets shifted to the ideologies of a commercial, secularized, and fully capitalist England, the dominant emphasis on religion gave way to something else, which can be called bourgeois ideology, marked above all by the ahistorical categories of nature (including human nature), and a static or analytic (non-dialectical, and later positivist) thinking particularly in the emergent field of political economy; here, then, the thrust of ideological critique must change, and denounce the repression of history from such ideological forms. Thus, if the Marx of the critique of religion strategically affirms Marxism as materialism (that is, as opposed to the idealisms of religion and metaphysics), the later strategies of Marxian ideological critique tend to stress history and process as such. That the two strategies are interrelated is of course underscored by the definition of Marxism as historical materialism. Still, such shifts in emphasis, explained by the changing historical situations in which Marxism has struggled and worked, may account for the inconsistency between the three models of ideology that we now briefly describe.

ii.

The classical formulation of ideology as "false consciousness" is often taken to be the fundamental version of the Marxian theory of ideology; in what follows, we will see that, influential as it is, it represents only one of several alternative models for Marxism.

We have already suggested a break between the eighteenth-century belief in reason and those later nineteenth-century forms of mistrust of reason that include the theory of ideology. "Breaks" are ways of structuring an historical narrative and should be regarded as fictions or constructs rather than facts. This proposition (it involves the whole problem of what is called periodization) can now be demonstrated, since we will now rather be concerned to stress the *continuity* between the present theory and the polemic thrust of the Enlightenment *philosophes*. From this point of view, then, the Marxian theory of false consciousness will be studied as a still relatively eighteenth-century theory.

The project of the philosophers was the secularization of reason and the disengagement of scientific and political inquiry and speculation from the shackles and taboos of the older religious orthodoxy. In a sense, therefore, for them, religion was an ideology, to which they opposed reason and science. (Indeed, later we will be able to refine this proposition and to suggest that in certain precapitalist societies, such as the feudalism of the *ancien régime*, religion is very precisely the form taken by ideology, that is, the value system and hegemonic cultural institutions that ensure social control and the social reproduction of the system from one generation to another.)

The *philosophes* defined their target—religion—as "error" and "superstition," that is very much in the same way that our present Marxian model of ideology will use terms like "idealism" and "metaphysics." This is still then very much an epistemological model of ideology, still stressing the individual knower, knowledge, or error as such, and the primacy of individual reason after it has been purified of its habits of error. There are two essential limits on this view of ideology. First, it is still confined to what the Althusserians will later call the viewpoint of the individual subject. Second, from a political standpoint, this view leads to the notion (still current among some centrists today) that political change and progress are a matter of rational persuasion, for example, that the electorate, if properly educated and informed, will automatically make the right choices. Here too the confidence in the essential rationality of human beings overlooks those deeper unconscious or nonrational forces that move collectivities and that have become only too evident in the nineteenth and twentieth centuries (fascism and Nazism are surely something a little more complicated than mere false consciousness, or even mere irrationality). Note that, at this period, it was the enemies of the *philosophes*, the defenders of a conservative and organic view of society and history—above all, Edmund Burke, in his *Reflections on the Revolution in France*—who undertook the critique of Enlightenment rationalism and stressed some of those other nonrational forces, most notably tradition and organic social cohesion.

There is a sense in which these objections to Enlightenment rationality still hold for this first Marxist model of ideology: the doctrine of false consciousness implies the possibility of reason, which in the Marxian traditions takes the form of science. The theme of the opposition of ideology to science is one of the great (and controversial) leitmotifs of the whole Marxist tradition. Meanwhile, as has been suggested in the first section, this view is still very much in polemic opposition to the hold of religious and hierarchical dogmas in pre-1848 Germany; so it is no accident that its formulations, which take as their targets idealism and metaphysics, generate a slogan, "materialism," that itself emerges from the most radical eighteenth-century thinkers.

This said, we also note another tendency in the eighteenth-century Enlightenment, which, alongside the opposition reason/error, is keenly aware of the institutional infrastructure of power in the *ancien régime*. When the *philosophes* denounced superstition and dogma, they at the same time denounced the Church, which they saw clearly as one of the institutional pillars and mainstays (the Althusserians will later call this kind of institution an ideological state apparatus) of the whole hierarchical quasi-caste system of the *ancien régime*. Hence Voltaire's revolutionary cry, "Écrasez l'infâme!" or, in other words, "Destroy the Church, root and branch!" The eighteenth-century formulations of this relationship between a superstitious and false system of ideas (religion) and an institution (the Second Estate, or Church hierarchy) often have an old-fashioned ring to us today. Think only of Voltaire's rewriting of the Oedipus story, in which the seer Tiresias becomes the representative of a repressive Church hierarchy, and the tragedy of Oedipus becomes the crushing of reason by superstition. Still, this problem —the relationship between ideology as individual consciousness or as a thought system and the function of ideology in the external social institutions—will be a crucial one for all later theories of ideology, which can be sorted out according to the ways they seek to link these two distinct dimensions. Indeed, our next model will show how the Marxian theory of social class permits a decisive reformulation of this whole eighteenth-century "problematic."

iii.

The eighteenth-century *philosophes* were indeed representatives of the Third Estate (even when technically aristocrats, some of them by birth) and thus ideologues of an essentially bourgeois revolution and of the conquest of power by a secular and commercial bourgeoisie. For Marxism, this determines some of their limits, which become visible when one acquires something the bourgeoisie was unwilling or unable to recognize, namely, a conception of social class and of the class dynamics of social change. Briefly, the Marxian doctrine of class struggle implies that classes do not exist in isolation (either ideologically or culturally) but essentially define themselves against each other. The Marxian theory of economics and politics implies that at least under capitalism, there are basically only *two* fundamental classes: the owners and masters of the production process, on the one hand; its producers or proletarians, on the other. All the other "classes"— the peasantry, the petty bourgeoisie, and the remnants of a vanquished aristocracy—are ancillary classes—former castes—that are capable of taking *effective* political action only when they attach themselves within an "historical bloc" (Gramsci) to the decisive struggles of these two classes.

What is the role of ideology in this perpetual struggle between the two major classes (the bourgeoisie seeking to extract even more surplus value and to extend the working day, the proletariat seeking covertly or overtly to shorten it and to resist such extensions by slowdowns, sabotage and strikes, and other forms of union or organizational action)? From this vantage point, we can see that the first essentially epistemological model of ideology does not help us much, for it is not a question of the truth or error of a thought system that is now decisive, but rather that of its function and use and effectiveness in class struggle. The task of a ruling-class ideology is now seen as that of "legitimation" and "hegemony" (contemporary terms drawn from Habermas and Gramsci respectively). In other words, no ruling class can ever permanently secure its rule by brute force, although that may well be necessary in moments of social crisis and upheaval. Rather, it must depend on some form of consent, or at least passive acceptance, and the function of a great ruling-class ideology will thus essentially be to convince people that social life should remain as it presently is, that change is futile, that social relations have always been this way, and so on. Meanwhile, of course, the function of an oppositional ideology—for example, Marxism itself, now seen as the *ideology* of the proletariat, rather than as the science of society—will be to challenge, undermine, sap, and discredit this hegemonic ideology and to develop its own counterideology as part of a more general struggle for political power.

In this second model, then, philosophical systems, values, and cultural products are grasped in terms of their social functionality; and the kind of ideological analysis developed here, one of the most original contributions of Marxism, lies in its ambition to *demystify* what look like mere thoughts, positions, ethical or metaphysical options, and opinions by revealing their role as instruments and weapons of legitimation in an ongoing class struggle. Such analysis is often said to be reductive, and of course it is; it means brutally to reduce what had the appearance of pure thought to its more unlovely practical function in the social world. This is a Copernican revolution quite as extensive as Freud's own (and, of course, the Freudian demystification of conscious experience and values is fully as reductive as this one, but in terms of the ruses of the unconscious and desire rather than the objective class interest of this or that collective group, which the individual may never consciously be aware of).

An "illustration" of these propositions may now be offered which continues to have thematic significance in the more modern thinkers to be dealt with later: this is the idea of nature. One can, of course, grasp the idea of nature as a pure thought, which can be analyzed in epistemological terms for its coherence, its truth or falsity, its adequacy to reality and to science, and so on. The traditional history of ideas displays the variants of this pure thought in terms of purely philosophical developments, in which successive formulations of the concept are compared and their evolution explained.

For Marxism, however, the concept of nature is precisely an ideology in the sense of our second model; indeed, it is one of the most significant ideologies in the arsenal of the bourgeois revolution proper. The concept of nature is immensely useful because it includes within itself "human nature" as well, so that it can generate both a view of the *ancien régime* and a theory of human nature that implies a whole conception of social life and its organization.

The denunciation of the essentially class and bourgeois ideology of nature is thus a significant leitmotif in Marxism, and returns in modern times in thinkers such as Brecht, Roland Barthes (who denounces the illusions of what he calls naturality) and Louis Althusser (whose notion of humanism is essentially in all its forms that of a vision of "human nature" as a static, eternal, unchanging essence—an ideology or "essentialism" of human nature also powerfully denounced by Sartrean existentialism). Does this mean that the Marxist analysis of this ideology is wholly negative and destructive? That would perhaps be true if we were still working with our first model, that of false consciousness, which would imply that the bourgeois concept of nature is nothing but error and superstition, idealism and metaphysics.

On the contrary, the evaluative judgments of this second model are no longer exactly those of truth and error, but something different, something often formulated in terms of an opposition also traditional in Marxist terminology: progressive and reactionary. From this standpoint, we can see that this particular system of bourgeois ideology (like many of the social and economic achievements of the bourgeoisie generally) is quite literally ambiguous, having both positive and negative, both progressive and reactionary, functions. It is therefore not to be denounced in some unequivocal way, but to be analyzed precisely in terms of those ambiguous and situational functions.

Thus, in its struggle against the caste society of the aristocracy and the *ancien régime*, the bourgeois conception of nature is positive and progressive: the hierarchy of the *ancien régime* depended on the legitimizing notion (and ideology) that the various social groups (middle-class merchants, peasants, great aristocrats) are somehow different and distinct in their very natures, in their blood (this is not yet modern racism, but has certain affinities). Thus, each "estate" has its own form of justice and legality, which is appropriate to its own particular "nature." In this context, it is clear that to assert a universal human nature, a genuine equality between all human beings, is to perform a subversive and profoundly revolutionary act and to generate an ideology for which people will be willing to fight passionately and, if necessary, to die.

But when the bourgeoisie comes to social and political power, the ideology of nature begins to change its function. Now it has a new social antagonist, no longer the aristocracy, which must be dislodged from its position of power, but rather the laboring classes, which must be kept in their place and prevented from realizing a revolution of their own that would seize power in turn from the bourgeoisie. Now the idea of nature and of an equal human nature comes to mean something rather different, namely, the equivalence of human beings in the market system, their equivalence as exchange value and commodified labor power, their "freedom" to sell their labor on the market.[5]

The notion of equivalence thus functioned to discredit, in advance and by anticipation, the Marxian idea of social classes as well as the practical experience of class realities by individuals: in the market system, we are ostensibly faced, not with the dialectical relations of social classes, but rather with the "atomized" competition of a host of equivalent individuals or monads. Belief in nature and human nature will therefore now serve the legitimizing function of forestalling collective or class consciousness.

Meanwhile, the static and eternal aspects of the concept of human nature now also function to "repress" the idea of history. If human nature is always and everywhere the same, it would be chimerical and Utopian to imagine it radically transformed, and with it the social relations of the present system. Marx himself denounces this static view of human nature when he

---

[5] See C. B. Macpherson, *The Political Theory of Possessive Individualism*, Oxford: Clarendon Press, 1962.

speaks of the bourgeois political economists who believe that the market, exchange, and the commodity form are part of human nature, are unchanging elements of all imaginable social arrangements: they thus, as he says, strategically project the *Homo economicus* of capitalism back onto all other social formations and modes of production, both in the past and in the future.

This same view is brought out even more sharply in the cultural context today by Barthes, who draws importantly on Brecht's conception of the estrangement effect: the point of the latter, and for Brecht the task of a political culture, was essentially to estrange and distance people's experience of daily life, which they have been trained (precisely by the bourgeois ideology of nature) to think of as natural and eternal. The estrangement effect is a way of drawing back from "immediate" experiences, from the illusions of daily life in the market system, and seeing them as something peculiar, quite unnatural, odd and inhuman—in other words, as Brecht put it, a way of revealing that what has been thought to be natural (human emotions, such as competitiveness and aggressiveness, fully as much as human institutions) is in reality something quite different, namely, *historical*. In that case, if our social system is not eternal and natural but the result of historical development, if people once lived differently, then they can do so again, and to say that a thing is historical is also to suggest that it can be changed by human action. The Brechtian assault on the concept of nature is thus a revolutionary act.

Barthes, in his *Mythologies*, now trains the Brechtian estrangement effect on contemporary society, and, in particular, on the media and advertising, whose effort he shows to be that of convincing us that pursuing particular commodities of consumer society (smoking a particular brand of cigarette, purchasing a particular car, using credit cards, accumulating masses of false needs and disposable objects) is deeply natural rather than artificial and historical, springing from an eternal desire to consume that is rooted in "human nature."

With analyses like these, however, we seem to be moving beyond the limits of our second model. Is the telling of the "naturality" of, say, smoking (images of beautiful people inhaling tobacco in a pastoral setting) still a class ideology, a conceptual system, in the sense of our second model? Perhaps not; perhaps we now need to make room for yet another model, in which the lived experience of daily life—irrespective of people's official opinions and intellectual values—has something ideological about it in its own right. This will then serve as the transition to a different model of ideology, reification.

iv.

This third model is implicit in the Marxist classics but has been more abundantly developed in modern times; we will here restrict ourselves to its initial forms, reserving later developments for a fourth model, which may in some ways be seen as a dialectical permutation of this one. The term "reification" is associated with the work of the philosopher Georg Lukács, in his book *History and Class Consciousness*, which attempts to work out something like the philosophical presuppositions of Marxism in a way not attempted by its founders. It will be remembered that the latter sometimes spoke of Marxism as transcending or, alternatively, as *realizing* philosophy—in either case rendering traditional philosophical speculation idealistic and unnecessary. Meanwhile, *Capital*, even in its present four-volume form, was only the reduction of a far vaster project of Marx's, which purportedly would have developed a theory of the state, ideology, and culture and thus eventually have projected Marxism as a "philosophical" system in its own right. Engels later gave his version of this system in the *Anti-Dühring*, which was to be the foundation of Soviet Marxism, with its distinction between historical materialism (essentially a method, which we have been outlining here) and dialectical materialism (a whole worldview and metaphysic), which sees the dialectic itself as the "eternal" law of nature.

Lukács's great book, however, proposes a wholly different reestablishment of Marx's "lost" philosophical system in which reification is called on to play a key role. The concept of reification—the transformation of human relations into things or relationships between things, Carlyle's "cash nexus," the transformation of the social world into exchange value and commodities—is, of course, present in *Capital*, with its notions of *Verdinglichung* and the fetishism of commodities. Lukács gives this view a decisive permutation by associating it with the ideas of his own intellectual master, Max Weber, on rationalization, in which the emergence of the modern world is seen essentially as a process whereby traditional activities (particularly in precapitalist societies) are reorganized in terms of efficiency, measurability, and means-ends rationality. Clearly, something will happen to the worker or artisan in this process—hitherto a skilled craftsman, an artist who has a mastery over his material and products: the rationalization of production will little by little tend to turn him into one more instrument within it. The process of rationalization is perhaps most strikingly exemplified in modern factory management, and, in particular, in what is called Taylorization, after its inventor Frederick Winslow Taylor, whose researches dictated widespread industrial reform and transformation of the labor process. "Taylorization" means the thoroughgoing fragmentation and atomization of productive activity, the breaking of each operation down into its smallest quantifiable segments, and the setting of workers to supervise each of those tiny segments in such a way that, unlike the older artisan, the individual worker can no longer have any sense of the meaning of the process as a whole or of his position within it. Clearly, Henry Ford's invention of the assembly line is little more than a genial extrapolation of Taylor's method.[6]

Lukács and Weber were then able to describe some consequences of this process as a more general social one, and, more important, to take account of its effects on human subjectivity and human experience. Weber's notion of rationalization can, for example, be extended to the quantification of space that began with the Galilean and Cartesian worldviews, in which the older sacred and discontinuous space of precapitalist societies (with, for example, their sacred forbidden cities at the center of the cardinal points of space) is broken up and homogenized in order to produce the gray equivalence of Cartesian extension, everywhere exactly alike. It can also be extended to time, and, in particular, to the introduction of quantifiable, measurable clock time.[7] The point would be to see these and analogous rationalizing processes, not as scientific discoveries about the measurability of, for example, forces of the scientific worldview, but rather as a total social "great transformation" in which all the qualitative and multifold dimensions of the precapitalist world are systematically reorganized by the new capitalist rationality on all levels, from those of sense perception to those of science and thought. (Marx's distinction between concrete labor and labor power clearly fits in here as a distinction between older qualitative craft activities and the new measurable and commodified empty time of labor power which the worker must sell every day in advance.)

Most relevant in the present context, however, is the effect of this total process on the mind, the psyche, human experience, and the very nature and organization of subjectivity (and thus of its products in culture and thought and the like). The innovation of Lukács was to have extrapolated Weber's description of social processes and tendencies (in the external object) to the subject itself. He here links up with an older tradition of German idealism, still apparent in the early Marx, but most fully expressed in Schiller. This is the application of Adam Smith's notion of the division of labor to the human mind itself, the view that in modern times the very psyche itself is subject increasingly to a kind of division of labor in its own right. So, for instance, under Weberian rationalization, those parts of the mind that perform calculating, mathematical, and measuring functions will undergo specialization and find themselves separated out from other less socially useful mental functions such as qualitative perceptions, fantasy, and so on.

---

[6] See Harry Braverman's classic discussion in *Labor and Monopoly Capital*, New York: Monthly Review Press, 1975.

[7] See E. P. Thompson's article on the role of the chronometer in early labor struggles, "Time, Work-Discipline, and Industrial Capitalism," *Past and Present*, Num. 38 (1967).

The latter will become marginalized and people who feel more at home with them—bohemians, artists, and so on—will themselves, in a business society, become marginals. As in early Marx, Schiller's diagnosis of the fragmentation of the modern psyche proposes a powerful counterimage of psychic reunification, of a psyche in which all these now disparate and specialized functions will be somehow reintegrated (an ideal that for Marx requires collective rather than individual transformation).[8]

This concept of reification may now be linked to another diagnosis of the modern world, already present in Hegel's conception of "civil society," in the early Marx's analysis of the state and bureaucracy, and later in Habermas's notion of the public sphere. This is the notion that in modern society, virtually for the first time in human history, the public has been radically sundered from the private, such that we live in two distinct worlds, the world of work, from nine to five, and our more "genuine" experience of the private life that we take up when we leave the workplace and the public realm.

In the present context, this can be seen as yet a further instance of rationalization and reification; and one of the ideals of a Marxian politics will then be to restore a social order in which the opposition of private and public, of the individual and the collective, of work and "leisure"—in short, the world of alienation—no longer obtains.

Like Weber, Lukács described his insight essentially in epistemological terms, in terms of science and knowledge and the deformation of these by reification. The immense suggestiveness and influence of his book spring, however, from the possible extension of the "division of labor" to the realm of the senses. The evolution of painting and that of music suggest that in modern times each of these senses has become "semi-autonomous," a whole world of activity in its own right. The body is itself fragmented, and Marshall McLuhan's insight into the opposition of an oral culture to a print culture based on the eye can also be read as a contribution to an extended version of Lukács's theory.

The originality of this third model of ideology lies in the way in which it locates the ideological, not in opinions or errors, worldviews or conceptual systems, but in the very process by which daily life is systematically reorganized on all its levels (the body and the senses, the mind, time, space, work process, and leisure) by that total quasi-programming process that is rationalization, commodification, instrumentalization, and the like. Unlike our two first models, this is somehow a process without a subject. No one plans

---

[8] We might now, however, in the light of postmodern "distraction," prefer to see Marx's "humanist" ideal less in terms of a unified subject than in those of Fourier's butterfly consciousness, the swift readaptation of the individual to a bewildering variety of projects and desires (what Marx also calls "new needs").

it that way, not even the "ruling class"; it is part of the ruling class, it is part of the very dynamics of capital, so that one might say, metaphorically, that the subject of this process is not an individual or a group but rather capital itself.

In retrospect it becomes clear that the first model had as its "subject" the individual mind, the second model rather something like a "collective consciousness of the subject." Yet in the first two models, something like resistance to ideology was still possible, and both projected counterimages of science or class praxis. In this new model, of a total system, you may believe it is harder to imagine forms of resistance, except as Lukács does—as a total systematic change, the abolition of capital and all its processes, and the coming into being of a new and radically different social system. Or the resistance to rationalization-cum-reification may be conceived, as it was by Schiller first and Marcuse much later, as the spirit of play, the resistance of the aesthetic itself (marginalized in the business world) as a space in which what is crippling about reification is refused. Or perhaps life under reification might be imagined as a series of small-scale microscopic guerrilla actions and symbolic protests on the order of the work stoppage. At any rate, the "pessimistic" dimension of this new theory of ideology as objective process (Weber's idea of the "iron cage" that was settling down irrevocably over human life) should not be minimized.

V.

The sequel to this story is generally told as follows: the "method" of *History and Class Consciousness*, which comes as an awakening shock for a younger generation of Central European thinkers, is prolonged in the work of the so-called Frankfurt School (Horkheimer, Adorno, Marcuse, more distantly Benjamin), where it acquires extraordinary philosophical and cultural subtlety and is in the process purged of its vulgar-Marxist (read: Stalinist) elements. But to read the Frankfurt School against the problematic of ideological analysis greatly complicates this scheme and renders it rather trivial as well.

The "instrument" borrowed from Lukács can be identified, if at all, as a reduced conception of reification, namely that of commodification, whose more limited range excludes the organization of production and centers the analytic process on consumption proper. The Frankfurt School took a decisive step in this respect in their reevaluation of the classical tripartite Kantian distinction between knowledge, practice, and aesthetics: the distinction had remained significant for Lukács, who continued to see the aesthetic realm as a privileged one, in which alone, in this society, some "reconciliation" of subject and object was possible; Lukács, however, transformed the aesthetic into a figure for the possibility of a non-alienated society generally (before proposing a more limited conception of novelistic realism as a critical norm in which such "reconciliation" can be observed in the realm of art). This figural power of the aesthetic again disappears from the work of the classical Frankfurt School (except for Marcuse), along with any sense of the historic possibility of systemic social alternatives. What the focus of the Frankfurt School on processes of commodification revealed, however, was that the aesthetic as such—the Utopian space of classical German philosophy—now lay open to the full force of commodity logic and was itself in the process of commodification. The pathos of this discovery—which corresponds to a somewhat later sense that the unconscious itself, under the reign of the commodity, was slowly being colonized by reification—obviously depends on the preservation, as an ideal value, of what is thereby lost: namely the aesthetic in its most authentic form, which hindsight allows us to identify as the aesthetic of high modernism. But that remains only as a punctual and fragile, vulnerable experience, subject to historical mortality (the extraordinary achievement of Adorno's *Aesthetic Theory* lies precisely in this tension between the authentic experience of modernism and the acknowledgement of its historicity); just as the implacable commitment to the denunciation of commodification in thought is reduced to the sheer point without dimension of the "negative dialectic." It is also clear, however, that the passionate commitment of the Frankfurt School to the identification of such often microscopic yet omnipresent processes of commodity reification could know an urgency and an immediate relevance in the United States (where Adorno's intuitions were confirmed and elaborated) that more conceptual forms of ideological analysis might not seem to have. This displacement of the object of analysis from ideational structures to forms and practices is significant, and will later be prolonged and developed in original ways.

As for ideology in the older sense, the strategic euphemism for its analysis adopted by the Frankfurt School—"critical theory"—unlike Gramsci's terminological displacement ("hegemony"), significantly conflates its practice with Marxism as a whole, something which is probably not irrelevant to the group's later depoliticization. Paradoxically, however, in no other body of work (save perhaps certain pages of Sartre) is the analysis of ideology as sheer false consciousness so triumphantly vindicated as in Adorno's devastating and exemplary polemic analyses (in *Prisms* and in later debates)—destructive criticism which, attentive to the social and class functions of its objects, nonetheless in its range and penetration goes a great deal beyond the perfunctory identification of this or that class affiliation which passes for a garden-variety ideological critique.

One may here occasionally have the feeling (which I have allowed myself to express about some of Kenneth Burke's work elsewhere) that the conception of ideology which guides such analyses is a somewhat old-fashioned 1930s one—certainly the Freudian elements pressed into service here strike one today as rather antiquated. If the essential vocation of the intellectual is critique and the permanent hyperconscious negation of everything that is, then that role has never been so energetically and vibrantly fulfilled; if on the other hand the left intellectual is called upon to play a supporting function in other social movements, then the free-floating autonomy of the negative and the critical may come to seem somewhat more problematic (and to involve a veritable ideology of intellectuals and their practice as such), and this is how the Frankfurt School has come to be regarded in recent years.

Yet the prolongations of that work are multiple and may be identified in a variety of ways (which do not all involve direct influence). The stress on the commodification of culture, for example, which finds its slogan in the identification of the nascent media structures as the Culture Industry,[9] points ahead to what we will call institutional analysis. The essential problem with such analysis—the difficulty of passing from a study of commodified forms to the infrastructural dynamics of this or that industry or technology—is however not solved; meanwhile it is also in this specific area that the limits of a conception of Ideology as false consciousness take their toll. For the tendency to dismiss all of manipulated mass culture as false consciousness then leaves unused and deprives of their very reason for being the very rich instruments of formal analysis also developed by Adorno, which in his work only come to find their fullest application in the decipherment and deconcealment of the formal contradictions at work in the monuments of high culture.

Still, it has not seemed self-evident to those who came after the Frankfurt School that its conception of some deep Utopian force and instinct—the longing for gratification and fulfillment, the Utopias of childhood and memory, the *promesse du bonheur* inherent in the aesthetic as such, what will later on be evoked in a distantly related sense as Desire—need be limited to the works of high culture and have no relevance at all to the "degraded" products of media entertainment.

Meanwhile the very rhetoric of repression and desire, of the instinctual scars left on works of art by social and historical contradictions (a rhetoric which originates more in the Freud of *Civilization and Its Discontents* than in Marx), was itself subjected to a certain critique by that member of the Frankfurt School most alert to the historical modifications and developments of late capitalism: Herbert Marcuse indeed raises the crucial issue of the historical destiny of repressed impulses and their force in a whole new world in which, by way of what he called repressive desublimation, the old force of taboo and repression no longer seems necessary. Marcuse also, in

---

[9] In Max Horkheimer and T. W. Adorno, *Dialectic of Enlightenment*, trans. E. Jephcott, Palo Alto, CA: Stanford University Press, 2002.

One-Dimensional Man, offers the bleakest historical picture of a social situation in which the vocation of the negative, of critical distance, along with the very sense of history itself, is sapped by the all-pervasive cultural logic of what we have come to call postmodernity.

This term (which implies an historical perspective on the modernism to which the group's members were committed which could not have been that of the Frankfurt School itself) suggests a final way of rewriting the group's heritage, and in particular of reinvigorating the group's great central theme of commodification. It is given in an extraordinary insight of Guy Debord, in his *Society of the Spectacle*: that the final form of commodity fetishism is the *image*. This mediation now releases the possibility of a kind of ideological analysis which passes beyond the contradicted structure of an individual text to the more general cultural processes of late capitalism in general: a whole system of image-production and of simulacra which has itself an ideological function, over and above its immediate local messages, and can be related both to issues of everyday life and to those of cultural imperialism.

In retrospect, it is clear that one of Sartre's great lifelong preoccupations was also the image, as a process of derealization closely linked to the aesthetics of the historical bourgeoisie itself and its religion of art and social uses of culture; but where Sartre stressed the impulse of *ressentiment* at work in image culture, Debord and his group, the *situationnistes*, opened this working notion up to the very problem of space itself as an ideological field, something to which we will return below.

All these developments, however—the critique of false consciousness as well as the conception of commodification as the production of an image culture—are pre-structuralist, in the sense in which their theoretical projections do not seem to require any particular stress on unique properties of language and the symbolic as such, or on a linguistic dynamic which might intervene between the subject and the object and problematize that traditional form of dialectical analysis. Still, all these post-Lukácsean developments do in one way or another register the social and historical modifications of capitalism from which structuralism itself as an intellectual movement (or an intellectual revolution) springs: most notably the prodigious expansion of the media and the transformation or destruction of traditional forms of culture. It may therefore be presumed that they will continue to be relevant for us beyond the structuralist "break"; or, if you prefer, that such a break—however historically and experientially evident to those who lived through it—must be grasped in terms of a systemic modification in social life in general, of which the newer theories of language are themselves only among the most dramatic intellectual features.

Still, it seems fair to say that if "Western Marxism," as it emerges after Lukács, is characterized by a renewed emphasis on consciousness and culture which always includes an awareness, in whatever form, of Freud and psychoanalysis, contemporary theories of ideology now all necessarily include the problematic of language itself (including newer "linguistic Freudianisms"), no matter how they formulate this new third term which does not in its autonomy seem to be a mediation in any easy traditional sense. If indeed, one cares to rewrite this version of the history of Marxian theories of ideology in terms of the realism/modernism/postmodernism paradigm, then it would not seem altogether incorrect to stage it as a shift of emphases from the social and class function of culture, through an autonomization of the problems of culture and the unconscious, to some heightened but more fragmentary sense of the autonomy of language and symbolic systems as such (with a "return of the repressed" of some equally new and problematic sense of the autonomy of what may be called part-institutions or the institutional in general).

vi.

The most influential and dramatic rethinking of the traditional Marxist conception of ideology, the most ingenious and suggestive new model of ideological processes, is clearly that proposed by Louis Althusser in "Ideology and Ideological State Apparatuses."[10] Published relatively late in the development of postwar Marxism, it marks something of a break (or "displacement") in Althusser's own work, which had previously turned on the issue of the discontinuities in social structure (as a "complex overdetermined structural totality") and had sought to unite a general but now much more distant conception of its "determination in the last instance" (in Althusser, a determination by the structure as a totality rather than by the economic level itself alone) with a new and productive emphasis on the "relative autonomy" of the various levels of social life.

The essay on ideological state apparatuses does not imply any repudiation of those theses, but strikes out in a completely new direction, which brings together and seeks to codify a number of newer trends in the area of ideological analysis: so that its interest as such lies as much in the way it will allow us to articulate those in their variety, as in its influence (which was at one time great but relatively specialized and limited). Like much of Althusser's work, however, the essay is programmatic and speculative: it is not a full-dress philosophical position, but rather an agenda, still incompletely fulfilled.[11] Indeed, the collapse of the Althusserian movement by the mid-1970s, (and the suffocation of the few conceptual advances in the new theory of ideology under

---

[10] See Louis Althusser, "Ideology and Ideological State Apparatuses," in *Lenin and Philosophy*, trans. Ben Brewster, New York: Monthly Review Press, 1971.

[11] The complete version of the original seminar has now, however, been published, as *De la reproduction*, Paris: Presses Universitaires de France, 1995.

a weight of now conventional Althusserian polemic jargon, have obscured what is still stimulating, suggestive, and even urgent about this unfinished theoretical business, which will also have the merit of revealing deeper problems involved in any Marxist theory of ideology than did the classical texts discussed earlier.

In this respect, it is significant that Althusser's essay falls into two separate parts, each of which has been influential in a different way with different groups of theorists. The main body of the essay explores the thematics announced in the title, and seeks to ground ideology materialistically, in the concrete social institutions which produce it, and which are to be seen as distinct from the official institutions of the state and of state power. (The point of the title's slogan, therefore, is to differentiate "*ideological* state apparatuses" from "state apparatuses" in the conventional sense: the army, the police, the juridical apparatus, and so forth.) The ISAs (as they have come to be known) are rather pedagogical and formative machineries (the Church, the school system, the family being explicitly mentioned), whose relationship to the state is conceived of more functionally than formally (in France, for example, the school system is immediately dependent on the centralized state; but the decentralization—and in some cases the private character—of the educational system in the United States would no less be characterized in terms of the concept of the ISA, owing to its function to reproduce the system of which the state is itself a part).

This emphasis on institutions—that is, on the institutional preconditions of ideology—is a new and original contribution of the theoretical work of the 1960s and 1970s to the theory of ideology, which must be sharply differentiated from the older, more global and unmediated affirmations of the organic links of ideology to classes or the state. Except in Althusser's own exercise in grand theory in the essay aforementioned, work in this area has been more empirical and sociological, beginning with the historical realities of the specific institutions in question, as in Pierre Bourdieu's influential and paradigmatic studies of the educational system, the museum, and photography, which indeed largely preceded Althusser's essay and probably inspired it. In some obvious senses, these kinds of investigations may be said to reflect precisely that "semi-autonomy" of social levels addressed by Althusser's earlier work, or if you prefer, may be seen to spring from the multiple concrete realities and structural complexities which that earlier work itself registered as a new theoretical problem.

The language of mediation was of course always available to deal with this kind of problem, in which it is, for example, a question of showing how dialectical links are made between a given class ideology in general and a specific expression or "utterance" (the school system as mediation; but also daily life as mediation, everyday speech as mediation, the media as mediation, individual psychobiography as mediation). The doctrine of "mediation," in other words, seemed to solve this conceptual dilemma a little too rapidly, preventing the mediatory institution from emerging in all its historical specificity and density; such older dialectical language also seemed to abridge the moment of existential scandal that gives the newer institutional research its materialistic edge—the scandal of the "extrinsic," the shock of the determination of the "spiritual" by institutional realities of another order, which have their own laws and dynamics and their own inertia, as well as their specific forms of struggle and contested terrain. This is why it seems possible to explain the emergence of this new institutional perspective, not merely in terms of the autonomous development of theory itself (in the social sciences as well as the linguistic ones), where it comes as something of an unexpected reversal, but also as the moment in which a discipline touches its constitutive limits and boundaries; not only as a consequence of the ongoing differentiation of social reality in the increasingly prosperous postwar period, but also in the French context of a Left which on the one hand confronts the new institutional inertia of a modernizing Gaullist society after 1958, and on the other begins, particularly from its newly emergent extra-parliamentary wing, to interrogate the institutional persistence of a more traditional French Communist Party as well.

This is to say that the institutional theory of ideology will have specific political consequences in its various specialized sectors. In literature and the arts, for example, and not only in France, the younger generation will feel that it is more urgent to unmask and to challenge Literature itself as an institution, rather than to interpret and "demystify" this or that specific literary text; more significant to focus militantly on the nature of the museum and of the system of the art galleries and their relationship to ideological production on the one hand (the journals, the forms of art criticism and commentary) and to business, finance, and the state on the other (as, for the United States, in the matter of tax laws and investment possibilities)—rather than to pursue an art history or an art criticism of an older interpretive type.

Such a shift in emphasis only *seems* to clarify and simplify the possibilities of political action, and the history of the 1960s has been read (by its right-wing interpreters) as little more than a series of vandalizing attacks on a whole range of just such ISAs, from the university itself on down. In hindsight, the very operative distinction of institutional analysis—that between the state as such and local or non-state ISAs—ought to have foreclosed an essentially anarchist identification between the "withering away of the state" and the rather different aim of abolishing social institutions altogether. If it is a matter, not of destroying a normative social system altogether, but rather of transforming it into a system of a radically different type (socialism), then the unremitting and negative critique of individual institutions or ISAs needs to be accompanied by reflection on their possibilities for structural transformation as well as on the nature of the new kinds of collective institutions into which they are to be transformed (a reflection which in the Marxist tradition is for better or for worse associated with the problem of "cultural revolution").[12]

What should be understood is that the new requirements and imperatives of institutional analysis do not simplify the task of ideological analysis but make it more complicated in all kinds of new ways. The newer explorations of ideology which we will examine below (and which are by no means all associated with Marxism) reflect that more general contemporary sense of the need to incorporate infrastructural realities in the study of texts which is overtly articulated in the conception of ISAs and in what we have been calling the "institutional" tendency of ideological analysis today. But the concept of ISAs can also be used to test these other approaches and to measure the adequacy of their account of institutional production. However, as has already been observed, the very conception of ISAs and the practice of "institutional analysis" as such still very much confront us with theoretical unfinished business: very little in Althusser's own theory or in the concrete studies of this or that cultural institution helps bridge the conceptual gap between discussions of social institutions (such as the school and the museum) and readings of specific texts, a gap which remains the fundamental dilemma (if not aporia) of all contemporary ideological analysis.

This is a dilemma which has always been registered in one form or another (without resolving it) by the most lucid theorists of ideology: by Terry Eagleton, for example, in his pertinent distinction (in *Criticism and Ideology*) between the "general ideology" of an author and his or her more specifically "aesthetic ideology."[13] What is meant here clearly is the difference between a discussion of the "values" of a given writer in social or class terms (Balzac's monarchism, for example) and the more implicit formal commitments and practices of the writer in question to "ideologies" of representation; organic form, "realistic" writing, and the like: it being understood, in our present context; that these last ultimately lead us into the specific questions of institutional analysis proper, namely, the relationship of writing practices to the institution of Literature (and its appropriate ISAs). But Eagleton's fateful distinction (which is also one between an "old" Marxist criticism and a "new" Marxist criticism—between Plekhanov, say, and the *Screen* collective) absolutizes the gap we have designated and makes it difficult to see how one could ever work one's way back from questions of *écriture* to questions of "petty bourgeois ideology."

Althusser himself handles the problem in a somewhat different way, as a distinction between a "general theory of ideology"—a theory of ideology "in general" (the conception of the ISAs)—and specific accounts of individual

---

[12] See Chapter 10, above.

[13] Terry Eagleton, *Criticism and Ideology*, London: Verso, 2006.

ideologies, which must remain concrete and historical and bound to this or that situation of class struggle. This is also, in effect, to absolutize the dilemma and to perpetuate it in the form of that tension which has so often been remarked in Marxism in general between sociology and history, between an abstract model-building account of a synchronic structure (or even a process) and a situational or narrative account of unique historical events: the tension between *Capital* and *The Eighteenth Brumaire*, if you like; or between Althusser himself and E. P. Thompson.

It is by no means out of any wish to trivialize this crucial issue that I now propose a parallel with a more traditional philosophical dilemma: for this is, after all, the Marxian version of the old mind/body problem (or rather, the mind/body problem can be seen as the anticipation, in bourgeois philosophy, of what will, with Marxism, become the more collectively framed and focused problem of base and superstructure). This is to say, not that the terms of the problem are the same—since the transformation of an individual body into a collective phenomenon marks a genuine dialectical leap—but rather, more ominously, that all the false solutions seem to resemble each other structurally: the road to the El Dorado of the pineal gland as the ultimate locus of the cog between matter and spirit knows fateful parallels in the adventures of the wandering "break" or "bar" between infrastructure and superstructure in Marxian theory, at the same time that it suggests a useful thematic interrogation for a whole range of such theories, namely, how the issue of this key "mediation" is staged, handled, or eluded.

vii.

The Althusserian school has some interesting answers to these questions, but they are, paradoxically, not spelled out in Althusser's own programmatic essay, which abruptly, after its sketch of a theory of ideological state apparatuses, shifts to the ideological superstructure, and to a no less remarkable and original new theory of the subject of ideology. The terms of his formulation—"ideology is a 'representation' of the Imaginary relationship of individuals to their Real conditions of existence"—are Lacanian in origin and in use, but their specific combination here generates a rush of new speculations and, as a kind of theoretical definition, seems to offer a conceptual instrument rather different from anything to be found in Lacan's own work, which is destined for the formation of analysts in training.

Indeed, of the three Lacanian "orders" (the Imaginary, the Symbolic, the Real) two make an official appearance in Althusser's formulation. The Real—as absent cause, as "that which resists symbolization absolutely," as the source of anxiety but also the locus in which we can alone come to provisional terms with our "desire"—is here the social totality itself, something no individual can ever grasp or "represent," and which is as it were invisible at the same time that it is omnipresent and inescapable. Here the objections based on misconceptions of Lukács's notion of social totality are decisively excluded in advance: there is no menace of a centering of power and knowledge around "totality," since this word designates what no human individual can grasp, let alone possess, yet whose existence is affirmed (and experienced existentially).

Meanwhile, the loss of that epistemological possibility by individuated subjects motivates a rather different and politically significant revision of the traditional Marxist concept of ideology by Althusser, namely the logical conclusion that there can never be an end of ideology, that all social formations (including socialism and whatever Utopian arrangements can be imagined after it) must necessarily include what I have called a "mapping" mechanism, a way in which distinct individual subjects represent their relationships to reality and to the social totality to themselves. Were we to undertake a thought experiment in which a species were fully embodied in a single individual—as for example in the sentient ocean of Stanislaw Lem's *Solaris*—then it might be possible to deduce a situation in which science and ideology somehow coincide (that imaginary entity is of course the God of the Western tradition); but even here it is difficult to see how the form of "consciousness" to be attributed to such a being could altogether do without some equivalent of that "self-consciousness" whereby we attempt to "see" the self and grasp its relations to its objects (that mapping function, again, which Althusser calls ideology).

The terminology of the "self" however immediately resituates us in the realm of what Lacan calls the Imaginary, namely some dual relationship to self and to other (normally rehearsed in terms of his well-known thesis on the "mirror stage"). The image, and representation in general therefore, participate in the multiple illusions of this inescapable house of mirrors which is the Imaginary (yet which also consists essentially in a shadow realm, that haunts the real, but can never be confronted directly in its own right: the existential lining of our experience, as it were, never fully coinciding with that experience itself). The explicit articulation, however, of the links between "representation," the Imaginary, and ideology is the decisive move in the new formulation, since it grounds the whole poststructuralist thematics of "representation" (generally understood in a binary system, in which representation and mimesis are "bourgeois" and ideological, while the generally modernist breaking through of such surface orders is taken to be subversive, revolutionary, or the index of some deeper and more authentic "desire"). It is clear from the way Althusser restages this theme that "representation" can never be achieved nor be dispensed with: it is a process both permanent and impossible which is something a little more than a mere "aesthetic ideology" (although any number of "ideologies of representation" certainly exist, and they would include among their number that very poststructuralist repudiation of "representation" which has just been referred to). Meanwhile, the constitutive relationship established between ideology and representation now tends to move ideological analysis out of the history of ideas and opinions, where it has so often been reduced to a rather trivial activity of labeling and identification, and into the new field of narrative analysis.

Yet as we observed in passing, the third of Lacan's "orders"—the Symbolic —is at least thematically or lexically absent from the Althusserian "definition" of ideology: an absence which must make itself felt conceptually when we remember that the "consciousness" of self, the image of the self, its "representation" (even in its relations to reality), cannot, on the Lacanian account, be even adequately or practically completed by the logic of the Imaginary all by itself. The Imaginary is no doubt the very space of "images" of the self (and everything which is illusory about them, everything which encourages a belief in the consistency of that "psychic object"); it is also, however, when uncorrected by the logic of the other orders, the space for an endless and interminable propagation of selves and mirror images and doubles within which no relatively stable functioning of the psyche (and ideology) is any longer conceivable.

What intervenes in this process to endow it with structure is very precisely the Symbolic Order, that is, the relationship to an absolute Other (capital A in the French notation), a very different relationship from the multiple alter egos of the mirror stage and one which includes the relationship to the adults or parents (and their language) and to language itself, as that which is addressed to the Other, or better still, which responds to what is felt to be the Other's wish, address, desire, or expectation of us.

The indispensability of this new psychic syntax accounts for the apparent shift in Althusser's account from the formulation as it has already been discussed to an even more famous discussion of "interpellation," that is, the designation by some absent but absolute Other of my potential subject-position (and the form taken in Lacanian theory by the Hegelian concept of "recognition" in the Master/Slave dialectic, and by the Sartrean Look). It is because the Other lays down the terms of the subject-positions available to me (and there is a certain multiplicity available to me within these limits; I can be the opposite—the structural inversion—of what is expected, for example, a naughty child rather than a well-behaved one, a rebel or criminal rather than a good citizen) that I can finally achieve the functional aim of "ideology," namely the "representation of *my* Imaginary relationship" to the Real: the self can in other words only constitutively play its part in this representational process when it has been able to assume a subject-position, something dependent on the Other.

At this point, therefore, a whole rich new area of research opens up which has at the present been most energetically explored in film criticism: what kind of subject-position does a given disposition of the camera and its images offer me? Am I invited to assume a Look which is gendered in a particular way and which preselects "me" in terms of race or class? The Sartrean version of this analysis—in *What Is Literature?*—was predicated on a reading situation in which a given text selected or excluded certain kinds of readers, and in which the excluded ones, then, simply let the book fall in bewilderment, boredom or incomprehension. In film, however, once we are in the movie theater, the operations on us of the various subject-positions seem more intense, although one would not wish to think this in a mechanical way, in terms of some absolutely passive receptivity (we can become uncomfortable, indignant, and occasionally even leave the theater)—film theory therefore has had to confront more theoretically an issue which can more easily be evaded in the study of reading. There is, however, a risk of impoverishment in an emphasis on subject-positions and interpellation which obscures the other dimension of the Althusserian conception of ideology, namely the representation of the way in which such subjects—albeit in an Imaginary mode—conceive of their relations to their Real (that is, collective) conditions of existence.

Finally, the Althusserian discussion includes a suggestive account of the way subject-positions are formed and reinforced: such programming—in the very spirit of the definition—is better conceived of as active rather than passive, as something the subject does to himself or herself, on the occasion of outside constraints and limits. It is in other words necessary at this point to break through the ideological double bind of freedom and manipulation and to find formulas and terms which escape the force field of that particular ideological resonance:

> Where only a single subject … is concerned, the existence of the ideas of his belief is material in that his ideas are material actions inserted into material practices governed by material rituals which are themselves defined by the material ideological apparatus from which derive the ideas of that subject.[14]

Actions, practices, rituals, ISAs: such is the mediation which now leads back from the formation of ideological subjects to the "materialism" of the earlier section of Althusser's essay. In particular (as we shall become aware in the following pages) the conception of "practice" and "practices" has known a remarkable theoretical success, as a putative replacement for seemingly old-fashioned or reductive conceptions of ideology and a concept which offers a two-fold advantage: (1) a way into the whole concrete world of daily life, with its routines and its apparently non-philosophical concerns (think of the early films of Godard, for example!); and (2) a way of concretizing and

---

[14] Althusser, "Ideology and Ideological State Apparatuses," 169.

materializing things like opinion, "values," and *Weltanschaungen* (to which ideology had too often been traditionally reduced). The richest theorization of this conception of practice remains Pierre Bourdieu's *Outline of a Theory of Practice* (1972/1977). The disadvantage of the terminology of practice and practices is however at one with these strengths, for a discussion couched exclusively in these terms can easily elide the conceptual and social dimensions of ideology altogether, and offer a nominalistic account of various proto-narrative experiences and incidents which cuts us off once again from the historical function of ideology in class struggle.

It is worth noting that Michel Foucault's account of what used to be called repression in the sexual area, and his interesting isolation of the new institution of "confession" are closely related to the Althusserian model, as it were seen from its other angle: in confession, we talk ourselves into a given subject-position; our own "practice" of self-examination, introspection, and verbal avowal is thus very precisely an exemplification of the Althusserian analysis of ideology. Meanwhile, religious accounts of "kerygma," as in Paul Ricoeur—the message from the Other or the Subject—are also consistent with this analysis, and it is significant that Althusser's one concrete illustration of the matter is the religious one (since his is a theory of ideology "in general," it will apparently not make much difference, according to him, what historical illustration he chooses).

The historical character of the illustration, however, awakens a troubling suspicion as to the ahistorical or "eternal" validity of the new Althusserian model. Is a situation of religious interpellation, in which an absolute Other still exists, really consistent with contemporary life? That we possess ISAs which are the equivalent of the Church in the older social formation—indeed that we witness a proliferation of new and secular ISAs—is indisputable: yet the Symbolic pole of the absolute Other was also indispensable to the account, and, save in the exceptional situation of fascism and the "charismatic" leader, does not seem to suggest any easy analogies in late capitalism (itself, in the multinational era, radically decentralized).

Meanwhile, other tenacious questions begin to return at the term of the Althusserian account, for its persuasive dramatization of ideology in terms of the individual subject now seems to have made the conceptual return to historical and social phenomena, and in particular to the great social and class ideologies of a collective nature, very problematic indeed. We are perhaps now, in other words, in a much better position to grasp the way in which my personal ideology situates and maps me in the world (and even, at the limit, in late-capitalist "conditions of existence"): but what can that personal ideology, that Imaginary representation, have to do with matters of "petty bourgeois ideology," the Whig theory of history, the liberalism of the American middle classes in the New Deal era, the free-market convictions of the present day, and other such "ideologies," which may now seem old-fashioned constructs, but which it was the specific merit of the Marxist analysis of history to place insistently on the agenda of historiography and social analysis?

These objections seem to me very well founded if one restricts oneself to the essay of Althusser himself which we have been reconsidering here; when one looks at the much less familiar work of some of his disciples, unexpected and provocative new answers to some of these questions emerge, answers which are not necessarily definitive but which open up as yet unexplored fields of investigation and speculation. After a brief detour through certain other related yet competing models of what must still be called ideological analysis, we will conclude with a brief summary of these new findings (which are often designated by the term "discourse analysis").

viii.

The advantages of some reformulation of ideology in terms of practice or practices seemed, as we have seen above, to be two-fold: first, for whatever reasons (which surely include the transformation and complexification of modern societies), practices are a more concrete object of study than ideological opinions or "values." With the onset of consumer society, indeed, it becomes an open question whether the practices of consumption are not more effective ideological mechanisms to ensure social reproduction than some more traditional form of the "internalization" of values or beliefs. Meanwhile, from the point of view of the intellectual, the study of practices, the elaboration of some new "hermeneutic" of practices (how gestures and concrete behavior can somehow bear ideological and even "conceptual" content within themselves), is an attractive task, which at the outer limit promises some reunification of conceptual and narrative analysis (contemporary semiotics is the ideal model for such a reunification, even though semiotics itself came rather late to such issues).

Second, the very conception of practice implies activity on the part of ideological subjects and thereby seems to offer an escape from the implications of passivity and of manipulation which the older models of ideology (including the conception of an image-society) seemed to entail. We have seen indeed how in Althusser's formulation of "interpellation," practices are specifically appealed to as the mode in which individual subjects train themselves and make themselves "ideological." Clearly, any conception of ideology must necessarily retain some sense of ultimate externality and of the kind of imposed false consciousness suggested by conceptions of manipulation: the various theories of practice do not pose the active behavior of their subjects in terms of any absolute freedom of choice either, but they tend to inscribe such externality structurally, as a limit on the form and content of practices available to the individual subject (where the freedom to revolt then often takes the form of mere structural inversion within the system, as opposed to a different kind of internal resistance which consists in modifying the system itself and its range of practices). For this reason, the conception of practices requires some accompanying paradigm of the field in which practices are ordered and determined; and it seems clear that the most influential way in which such a field has been theorized is the historically new conception of "daily life," "everyday life," or the quotidian.

The notion that daily life could be an object of study in its own right is a relatively recent one. Traditional anthropology studies, to be sure, customs and taboos, spatial organization, and ritual time of primitive societies, but the idea is that these are fairly rigidly organized, and that tradition in such societies imposes a set of firm patterns that can be isolated by the anthropologist. Daily life in the modern world, on the contrary, is apparently characterized by a weakening of tradition in this sense. For the late Middle Ages, this sapping of binding routine was felt as a kind of freedom—the so-called freedom of the city. One may compare this positive evaluation of the absence of law to Durkheim's concept of *anomie*—lawlessness—which literally means the same thing but designates the pathology of the individual in the great agglomeration, and indeed, as a concept, emerged from Durkheim's study of suicide.

The reference to the city, however, suggests that the first form in which thinkers began to approximate a conception of daily life was in the preoccupation with the city as such. Indeed, the great novelists and poets—most notably Baudelaire and Flaubert, but also Dickens, and later Zola and Dreiser—may be said to have launched the study of daily life in the modern city, which then culminated in the theoretical work of people like Georg Simmel (and later Walter Benjamin, writing about Baudelaire).

The next step in the development of a theory of daily life may be said to have emerged with so-called phenomenology. Building on the work of Husserl, for whom the meaning of experience was in some sense immanent, so that a "phenomenological" description of a particular reality can be expected to yield its meaning without external or causal explanation, Alfred Schutz proposed the elaboration of a phenomenological sociology, which would describe the institutions of society, not as external things, but rather as processes in construction. No one has ever seen a social institution—such as a law or a kind of power or authority—so it is already a "reification" when social scientists give us a picture of these as things. Clearly a very different account emerges when we try to describe the process in which we feel and submit to authority (with its undoubted external signals and signs, which are however not yet the phenomenon itself). But, of course, when one says "process," one at once introduces time into the picture, and greatly complicates the task of description. The most accessible account of this kind of sociology is given in Berger and Luckmann, *The Social Construction of*

Reality, whose very title usefully conveys the spirit of this approach—and adds the new feature of "construction" as a way of doing justice to the temporal character of our experience of social life.

A somewhat eccentric American offshoot of this tradition is to be found in so-called ethnomethodology (Harold Garfinkel, Irving Goffman), which attempts to study social processes by way of the verbal accounts the participants themselves give of them, and whose work tends to center on those privileged situations in which social custom breaks down: moments of embarrassment, hesitation, reaction to marginal phenomena (one of Goffman's major books is called *Stigma*), in which the very uncertainty about the social order can be allowed to make the latter more visible than it is under normal circumstances. This school has often been described as literary, and it is certain that their accounts—still immanent and phenomenological—are closer to the work of the great novelists than to, say, statistical studies of the conventional sociology of institutions.

The stress of ethnomethodology on "accounts" reintroduces the problem of language in the "social construction of reality" and makes a bridge to the contemporary semiotics of daily life. Now social processes are seen as a set of signs, and the experience of those processes and "institutions" as a kind of reading. Thus Michel de Certeau has analyzed the different kinds of walks one can take in different parts of the city or in different cities as so many quasi-verbal tropes (metaphor, metonym, synecdoche, and so on).

The central Marxist figure in the analysis of daily life is, however, Henri Lefebvre, whose pioneering studies in this area date back to the immediate postwar years (1947) and seem to have emerged independently of the phenomenological tradition. Lefebvre's intellectual trajectory is an exemplary one, which led him first to a new analysis of the city (whose historical transformation from a locus of nascent capitalism to a subordinate feature in a capitalist world system are analyzed in terms of the transition from the use value of space and buildings to their exchange value). The city is a site of revolt and festival (Lefebvre's enormous and varied work includes historical studies of the Paris Commune and of May '68), but also of the production of instrumental ideologies—so-called theories of urbanization (of which Lefebvre has been an outspoken critic and analyst). It is also the place of a very special kind of aesthetic and ideological practice, namely architecture—a realm in which the problems of contemporary cultural production are perhaps more acute and contradictory than any other. Lefebvre worked closely with practicing "avant-garde" architects over a long period, and has had thereby a more immediate practical influence on cultural production than any other contemporary philosopher or theorist: always maintaining a Utopian demand for the transformation of the city (and of society itself) which has left its mark on architectural, urban, and Utopian theories as well as on the practices of building, and also on certain practical political forms of rhetoric (in particular the French Socialist Party's program for the transformation of daily life in the early 1980s).

These multiple philosophical themes (as well as a range of other interests which cannot be examined here) ultimately reconverge in Lefebvre's magnum opus, which proposes nothing less than a whole new philosophy of *space* itself. *The Production of Space* (1976) in effect elaborates a new and historical category of space and its production as the central mediation in what we have been calling ideological analysis. For Lefebvre, the category of space projects a three-fold dialectic governing practices (the practices of daily life), scientific representations, and aesthetic and cultural production:

> [1] Spatial praxis, which includes production and reproduction ... [2] representations of space; linked to production relations ... and to forms of knowledge ... [3] spaces of representation ... offering complex ... symbolisms, linked to the clandestine and underground dimension of social life; but also to art, which might eventually be redefined; not as the code of space proper, but rather as the code of spaces of representation.[15]

Lefebvre's pioneering work on spatial analysis offers what would seem to be the most stimulating designation of a whole new unexplored form of ideological analysis, whose categories cut across some of the earlier false problems raised by other theories of ideology (such as the alternatives of activity and passivity mentioned above). It is significant that the major theoretical work on the analysis of "practices" as such—Pierre Bourdieu's *Outline of a Theory of Practice*—also turns on the mediations of space in the production and reproduction of ideologies (his concrete illustrations are spatial analyses of the Kabyle village and the Kabyle house as machines for inscribing ideology on individual and collective subjects). Bourdieu's influential and innovative work—centrally positioned, not in philosophy or the humanities, but in sociology itself, the very heartland of the social sciences —has made fundamental and authoritative contributions to both the theory and the practice of interpretation, and ranges from the spatial study of precapitalist or traditional cultures (as in those just mentioned) to institutional studies of contemporary or capitalist ISAs, such as the school system— studies which as we have seen parallel Althusser's program discussed above, as well as some of the discursive investigations to which we will come shortly. Yet this fundamental distinction in the objects of study (precapitalist, capitalist) seems to involve a dialectical shift in methods of analysis which will remain an unresolved problem in the work to which we now turn, and which can be generally designated as the study of "symbolic" practices.

---

[15] Henri Lefebvre, *La production de l'espace*, Paris: Anthropos, 1974, 42–43.

ix.

The term can scarcely be said to name a method or even a unified school or movement, yet it certainly names one of the dominant tendencies of much of the work in the humanities and social sciences today, which share a "family likeness" by way of their attention to the political and ideological meaning of concrete practices which range from the rituals of traditional societies to the more secular routines and behavioral patterns of everyday life in late capitalism. The theoretical reference points of such analyses span the newer anthropology of Clifford Geertz and Victor Turner, the historio-graphic investigations of "mentalities" developed by the Annales School (which often return to the area of traditional superstructures, as in Keith Thomas's related *Religion and the Decline of Magic*, as well as to newer family history), and finally various essentially historiographic works by Michel Foucault, which cover fields like medicine, insanity, prisons, education, and sexuality, but which have also seemed to promise some new more properly theoretical orientation, particularly in their development of themes of power. The life-work of the Soviet critic Mikhail Bakhtin, on carnival (but also on the dialogical and the polyphonic), has only more recently and belatedly joined this constellation of references, models, and authorities. The writings of the late Michel de Certeau, which are beginning to exercise an influence in the United States on what is sometimes called the new historicism, seem to offer something of a paradigm for some future "method" of symbolic analysis, by their extraordinary variety of objects of study, which include witchcraft, mystical discourse, early travel narratives, psychoanalysis, contemporary daily and urban life, and historiography.

The appeal of what we will call, for convenience's sake, symbolic analysis (meaning by that the study of "symbolic practices," rather than any refer-ence to the Lacanian conception of the Symbolic Order) can perhaps be accounted for in a two-fold way. This tendency for one thing seems to open up an enormous new area for interpretive activity, at the same time that it seems to offer a satisfying codification of a new and complex interpretive method. Older literary works on myth or ritual still seemed to be relatively specialized and "interdisciplinary" experiments (in their "application" of anthropological materials and methods to this or that literary text); the new approach, however, comes at a moment when such disciplinary categories are in the process of collapsing and new fields (social history as anthropol-ogy, for instance) as well as new and creative possibilities of transcoding are in full emergence. The fundamental contribution to ideological analysis of this newer tendency can be described as the dissolution of one such bound-ary, namely that which distinguished between outright political phenomena (and officially political texts) and other forms of social life and practice, con-sidered to be somehow non-political. For the analysis of symbolic practices, as the term also suggests, everything is henceforth at least *symbolically* political; all forms of social practice and cultural production can therefore be considered ideological in some larger sense yet to be defined. We have yet to show how this deeper proto-political or even "ideological" significance of the various "symbolic" texts is theoretically secured; but even at the outset it is worth observing an unfortunate paradox, namely that at the same moment in which symbolic analysis affirms the deeper politicality of other, non-political forms of practice or of text, it tends in the very heat of this interpretive discovery to assign to overtly political practices and texts a lower level of interest. One is reminded of the one theoretical precursor Freud was able to uncover in his review of earlier approaches to the interpretation of dreams: an obscure tribal society which had in fact come to the working conclusion that all dreams had an essentially sexual meaning and content— except for overtly sexual dreams, which meant something else! There is certainly a tendency or a temptation of this kind at work in symbolic analysis as well, for which everything is politically symbolic, except for the officially political: and that this is itself politically symbolic becomes clear in the concrete interpretations, which valorize the symbolic practice of resistance (in daily life, for example) over the more conventional forms of outright political resistance and protest.

All of which brings us to the second great attraction of symbolic analysis, namely that what gives it its interpretive content is also potentially the source of a whole ideological stance (it can descriptively be identified as anarchism) which has known a remarkable rebirth since the 1960s and has competed very successfully with Marxism in recent years for the allegiance of radical intellectuals. For the essential theme or interpretive code in which symbolic analysis does its work and in terms of which it rewrites its objects or texts is that of power (or domination)—something middle-class intellectuals always tend to feel more immediately and existentially than the traditionally drier realities of economics or of modes of production (which include domination and power relations, but only as projections of a somewhat different category, exploitation). Here the theoretical implications of Michel Foucault's work have been if anything more influential than his historiography, since a whole complex of contemporary concerns with "power" in general and specific forms of domination in particular seemed at a certain point to crystallize around this "signature" in an ideologically explosive way.

For Marxism, the overemphasis on power and domination can be read as a symptom of a strategic displacement of the social and historical "problematic" from the economic to the political level, from the determination "in the last instance" of the economic to a new kind of determination in the last instance of the political which, in virtual Cold War terms, shifts the focus of discussion from capitalism to bureaucracy, and from the factory and the commodity form to the grid of power relationships in everyday life and the various forms of "repression." Max Weber's sociology is an early form of this essentially anti-Marxist displacement strategy, and Foucault's theories (which ran through a number of variable positions on Marxism itself) seem to serve much the same function today.

Rhetorical emphases on power and liberation obviously need to be distinguished from more consistent ideological and philosophical positions on this subject. A specifically Marxian examination of the state and of the space of political power has emerged in recent years from the Althusserian insistence on the "semi-autonomy" of the various social levels, including the political one; the work of Nicos Poulantzas can be evoked in passing, which includes a trenchant critique of Foucault, as well as an emphasis on the spatial nature of his analyses of power which suggests some interesting links to the proposal for a properly spatial "ideological analyses" which has been mentioned earlier.

X.

Meanwhile, it is also clear that the Marxist tradition encompasses reflections on a number of elements and features central to the symbolic analysis of power and domination, which cast a somewhat different light on those themes.

The most influential of such currents has its source in Hegel's chapter on the master and the slave in the *Phenomenology*. Marxism also draws on this chapter, stressing the way in which the salvation of the slave is achieved through production and labor on matter (while the master vegetates away in luxury and a non-productive culture and existence). But if one leaves this feature of Hegel's rather mythic fable, what emerges is something quite different, namely, the *agon* or antagonistic confrontation between the two persons of master and slave, who struggle for recognition and dominance over each other.

Sartrean existentialism reworked this figure in a powerful model, in which it is the Look which mediates between two individuals or two groups struggling for primacy. In Frantz Fanon's works, written at the height of the Algerian revolution (*Black Skin, White Masks*; *The Wretched of the Earth*), this model was generalized out into one of the most influential ideologies of political struggle in the Third World and in minority struggles generally. For Fanon, revolution is essentially a process whereby the colonized must learn through praxis to shed their imposed sense of inferiority and marginality, their sense of belonging to inferior races and of passive obedience to the colonial master and his hegemonic values. This therapeutic and liberatory act is achieved by violence, in which the slave rises up and by terror forces the master to recognize his humanity in turn. This model remains in one way or another that of ethnic politics, and of some forms of feminism and other marginal or minority strategies.

It was then generalized by Michel Foucault into a whole theory of structural exclusion: in his book on madness, for example, Foucault shows how the very concept of madness is historically generated by the emergence of the concept of reason, which needs an excluded or marginalized term in order to affirm its own centrality (these concepts of the center and the eccentric or marginal also form the political content of much of Jacques Derrida's work). It is clear, however, that the politics of decentering, of contesting the center, of violently achieving recognition, are quite different in character from the traditional Marxist aim of destroying the commodity form and transforming social life by the invention of new social forms.

Foucault in some of his later works has abandoned this conflictual model, most notably in his book on prisons (*Discipline and Punish*), which although clearly about exclusion (the emergence of the prison is like the emergence of the asylum as a repressive institution), now focuses on a gradual penetration of life and society in general by a gridwork of control (Sartre's Look here becomes surveillance and measurement of a quasi-impersonal kind). As with our earlier theories of reification, the repressing subject (whether master, colonist, or ruling class) has virtually disappeared and we have instead the model of a quasi-objective process which seems virtually irrevocable. This process of control extends to the experience of the body itself, hence Foucault's description of his current work as "the political technology of the body." It is clear that to describe this particular "great transformation" in terms of domination rather than of commodification is significantly to transform the thrust of the account. (Note that in the Frankfurt School also, with the influence of Nietzsche, there had already been a certain stress on domination—science and Enlightenment as the domination of nature, leading to Auschwitz.)

Elsewhere, however, Foucault stresses the linguistic character of exclusion, suggesting that its fundamental form is the appropriation of other people's speech. Either they are repressed from speaking, or we speak for them, as we do for those marginals called children, insane people, sick people, inferior races, and so forth. This conception of the repressive character of language and speaking itself anticipates issues of linguistic alienation which will be raised in a different way in our final section.

xi.

We must finally note a rather different tendency in the general turn towards the analysis of practices (and daily life) from that of symbolic analysis. This is a reflection on the opposition between public and private life, or the public and the private spheres (Jürgen Habermas's terms), which seems to entertain much closer affinities with the dialectical tradition (and in particular with conceptions of "civil society" developed by Hegel and the young Marx). In fact, however, Hannah Arendt's central development of these themes makes its descendency from the Aristotelian tradition explicit: her ingenious theory, that the eclipse of the public in contemporary life is to be accounted for by an unparalleled expansion of the private and of privatization, can thus be seen to be dependent on the historically exceptional structure of the ancient *polis*, in which a unique kind of public sphere and public space was secured by demographic circumstances and by the exclusion of women and slaves.

Nonetheless a different kind of "ideological analysis," in the most expanded sense, has been generated by this conceptual opposition, most notably in Habermas's *The Structural Transformation of the Public Sphere* (along with the attempts of Negt and Kluge to theorize a properly proletarian public sphere) and in Richard Sennett's *The Fall of Public Man*. The concrete readings and analyses made possible by such a hermeneutic (particularly in Sennett's book) suggest that the thematics of the public and the private offer much more revealing interpretive codes in the study of contemporary society than do the thematics of symbolic analysis (based, as we have seen, on forms of power and domination).

The problem with this particular interpretive code is not merely its irreducibly dualistic—and therefore ideological—nature; it is more concretely that this dualism, and the very split between public and private itself, is an ideological projection of capitalism, and would therefore as such seem peculiarly unsuited as a conceptual instrument with which to study this last. When one considers the public and the private in our society, indeed, questions begin to arise about two crucial areas: work or factory space (which is certainly not part of private life, although it is also private in the juridical sense) and "daily life," which used to be public in the traditional street and the spaces of the traditional city, but which no longer seems to be public any longer in that sense, although it is certainly not private either. Such considerations suggest that the public/private opposition is exceedingly valuable in raising the problems and issues of such contemporary historical developments, on condition that it can be dialectically deconstructed and abandoned after it has done so; and they also suggest that the category with which we began—the category of "daily life"—remains a more effective framework in which to interpret them.

xii.

Paradoxically, although the newer forms of ideological analysis spring from what we have called the break, which consisted in the discovery of the centrality of the Symbolic and of representation and language itself, very few of them have been ambitious enough to project a theory of the "pineal gland" itself, that is, to work out a mediation such that the essentially linguistic transformational mechanism which can be said to relate institutional phenomena to representational or ideological ones is identified as such. The very rich and interesting developments in contemporary semiotics generally seem to presuppose a conception of language as the "ultimately determining instance," a solution which effectively blots out the problem by removing its institutional or infrastructural pole. Otherwise, the primacy of the linguistic model has been effectuated by importing it into the other sciences while abandoning the study of its primary object—speech and text—in the process: here too the theoretical dilemma does not arise, since the invocation of language has become largely structural and metaphorical or analogical (so that language ceases to perform any mediatory function). Another way of putting this is that neither semiotics nor structural anthropology is interested in the problem of ideology as such—the problem of mediation par excellence—which they decree resolved in advance.

Homologies also seem an unsatisfactory way of conceptualizing these issues. Ferruccio Rossi-Landi's very rich and interesting work on the analogies and influences between the commodity form and the forms of language, between the emergence of Value and the abstractions of speech, is ultimately theoretically unsatisfying owing to its unproblematic affirmation of the identity between social and linguistic forms (something which can probably also be said of Pierre Bourdieu's striking hypotheses about "cultural capital"). Meanwhile, studies of contemporary linguistic alienation, such as Herbert Marcuse's description of the bureaucratization and impoverishment of everyday language in *One-Dimensional Man*, which has a clear theoretical relationship to theories of commodification and of the image outlined in an earlier section, fail nonetheless to isolate that rather different mediatory problem which obtains between discursive practices and "psychological" reification. Habermas's own conceptions of ideal or Utopian communication and its alienation by way of deformations of the public sphere generate weak visions of social democracy without offering any instruments for concrete textual analysis.

As we have seen above, Althusser's programmatic essay on ideology had the merit of dramatizing the problem and the dilemma of this ultimate form of mediation by its problematic and peremptory separation of the "two halves that don't add up," namely the theory of institutions and the theory of subject-positions. What must now be shown in conclusion is that some of his followers have in fact been able to propose ingenious and at least provisionally satisfying ways of functionally reuniting these two dimensions by way of the relationship between sentence structure or "levels" of linguistic competency and that obviously key ISA which is the school system.

The crucial contribution to this theory is the achievement of Renée Balibar, whose important 1974 book *Les français fictifs* (by which she means "fictive languages," "fictive forms of the French language") goes well beyond the usual affirmation of the ideological influence of the school system and traces this influence concretely into the very forms of the sentence itself. Such a solution ingeniously strikes at the problem of "general ideology" and "aesthetic ideology" in an unexpected place: the class character of discourse is here located not in its content but rather structurally, in the relational position of one kind of discourse to other possible forms of discourse, which include "literariness," as we will see in a moment, so that her position returns to the institutional challenge to such social institutions as Literature but in a new way, and from within the text.

The crucial mechanism in this process is the "tracking system," the function of the school in general, with its various levels of scholarship, to reprocess its subjects along various class tracks such that they emerge into the appropriate class positions. This is an institutional process that has been exhaustively studied by Bourdieu, and which is also invoked by Althusser himself (but in the institutional section of his essay):

> [The School] takes children from every class at infant-school age, and then for years, the years in which the child is most "vulnerable," squeezed between the family State Apparatus and the educational State Apparatus, it drums into them, whether it uses new or old methods, a certain amount of "know-how" wrapped in the ruling ideology (French, arithmetic, natural history, the sciences, literature) or simply the ruling ideology in its pure state (ethics, civic instruction, philosophy). Somewhere around the age of sixteen, a huge mass of children are ejected "into production": these are the workers or small peasants. Another portion of scholastically adapted youth carries on: and, for better or worse, it goes somewhat further, until it falls by the wayside and fills the post of small and middle technicians, white-collar workers, small and middle executives, petty bourgeois of all kinds. A last portion reaches the summit, either to fall into intellectual semi-employment, or to provide, as well as the "intellectuals of the collective laborer," the agents of exploitation (capitalists, managers), the agents of repression (soldiers, policemen, politicians, administrators, etc.) and the professional ideologists (priests of all sorts, most of whom are convinced "laymen"). Each mass ejected en route is practically provided with the ideology which suits the role it has to fulfill in class society ...[16]

What Balibar will now show is the way in which each of these three tracks acquires the capacity for the production of a certain kind of (increasing complex) language: the first-level students learn to produce simple declarative sentences, and their linguistic productivity remains at this level their

---

[16] Althusser, "Ideology and Ideological State Apparatuses," 155.

whole life long, in such a way that the simple sentence is class-marked, is the sign of a certain class affiliation. The middle-level students then acquire grammar: that is, they learn to complicate the basic simple sentence with incidental clauses and a variety of other syntactic devices and relationships. Only the upper level of the student population, now greatly diminished in numbers, reaches "rhetoric" or the embellishment of the lower forms of sentence structure by the tropes, including irony. Indeed, irony is the very dialectical mechanism par excellence by which upper class students sublate what they must preserve, namely the class-marked structure of the simple sentence and the Latinate or grammatic "periodic" sentence: the tropes allow a "critical distance" from these sentence forms even as they are being used, and Balibar suggests that the "critical" or "negative," ironic consciousness of (even radical) intellectuals is to be traced back to this institutional basis, in the three dimensions of the sentence itself as they correspond to the fundamental class-tracking systems of the schools.

These are by no means the only "structures" inscribed by institutions on syntax, language, and the texts themselves: elsewhere in her book, Balibar notes the presence of interference effects between the two basic models of the writing lesson in French elementary schools: the *rédaction* (a practice of narrative) and the *dissertation* (a practice of what we call the essay form). These planes of discourse, whose intersection marks the composition of Camus' *Stranger* in symptomatic ways on her reading, also lend an institutional infrastructure to Michel Pêcheux's analysis of scientific discourse in *Language, Semantics and Ideology* (*Les Vérités de La Palice*), a complex syntactic "deconstruction" of Frege's problematic of sense and reference which marks an important additional contribution to the new type of syntactic-institutional ideological analysis we are presenting here.

It is evident that any approach of this kind, situation-specific to the point of linking linguistic structures to historical and social institutions, will not be immediately transferable to other languages and other systems of schooling. Still, this work which is concretely linked to the historical specificity of French education, bears some distant family likeness to a few developments in the area of the English language. Basil Bernstein's correlation between "restricted" and "general" practices of discourse and class situation and formation comes at these issues from yet another direction; while Labov's work on American Black English (in spite of his polemic with Bernstein) is obviously also very relevant indeed.

Two final points need to be stressed about the type of discourse analysis opened up by Balibar. The first is that in such analysis, the concrete mediation between subject-positions and institutional structures has finally been theorized: but the mediatory hypothesis only works on condition that these subject-positions are grasped in differential relationship to each other, as part of a total system of possible class positions. This is to say that if we restrict our discussion, as Althusser himself seems to do, to the "individual" interpellation which generates the subject-position of an "individual," the class content of such subject-formation will not emerge, since it can only become visible as such when we grasp the positioning of that particular subject against radically different interpellations. Within the individual "consciousness" this differential relationship must remain external; it is not experienced from within, but interpretively added on by some apparently omniscient commentator. In reality, however, the relationship of the various positions within a single social totality is given by the differential unity of the institution of the school itself.

Finally, the concrete nature of these readings must be underscored, which do not content themselves with vague generalities about oppression, class, exclusion, and the like, but do the work and make the articulated links between base and superstructure. Balibar's reading of the opening sentence of Flaubert's *Un coeur simple* (in which all three types of syntactic competence—simple declaration, Latinate case-relations, tropes—are present and superimposed) is a model of a literary analysis which has left the double bind of the intrinsic and the extrinsic behind it, and which has new things to tell us about the emergence of the effect of "literariness" from the dialectic of class as it informs language production.

Ideological Analysis: An Afterword

All these forms of ideological analysis—modern as well as traditional—were predicated on the presupposition that a space existed outside the system, no matter how cramped, illegal, or movable. This space—the Archimedean point of ideology—could ordinarily be formulated in intellectual terms, as a place or point from which something else could be thought, from which negativity could be projected, like a Scud missile from over the border: yet it was always dependent on a social launch pad of some sort—whether the existence of a radically different national space abroad (the USSR, Cuba, certain Third World countries) or the existence of classes, underclasses, concrete groups, and collectivities here which were not completely incorporated into the system.

What seems to characterize capitalism's third stage—globalized, postmodern, post-Fordist, or however one wishes to identify what began to be more visible since Reagan and Thatcher—is then indeed the definitive incorporation of all these remainders, all these spaces outside the system; or if you prefer, it is the final penetration of the logic of the system into all these excluded or neglected, "undeveloped" vacant lots in which a logic of difference flourished, if that is the word for such a precarious form of existence. The filling up of all these uncolonized holes and gaps was then completed by the consignment of everything leftover into the great geographical black holes of global capitalism—places of famine, of massacre, of concentration camps.

It is then scarcely surprising that since the last, mostly retrospective review of the theories of ideology very little in the way of theoretical innovation could be detected in this area, where only tired conceptions of subversion, contestation, and deconstruction continued to be rehearsed. After the Cold War, the ideology of Western capitalist, in either its "liberal" (social-democratic) or conservative (free-market) forms, no longer needed the intellectual disguises forced upon it by its communist competition. But it was precisely those disguises that ideological analysis had the task of dismantling or unmasking. In the new climate, it was no longer obscene to endorse the profit motive, but rather somewhat philanthropic (defending, after all, that very tide that raised all boats together). Now all the complex and subtle forms of evasive and ideological philosophy shriveled back down to the original simplicity of the right to make money; while the new climate of cynical reason rendered the exposés and discoveries of ideological analysis unscandalous and even uninteresting: everyone knew it already, the system was non-functional, people were corrupt and untrustworthy, Utopianism of whatever sort was both impractical and old-fashioned, and ultimately a more reliable path towards disillusionment and the shame of surrender and conversion to the system than any silent acquiescence in advance.

To what degree do the youth revolts (anti-globalization) and the various international forms of resistance to the United States change this bleak picture or constitute signs of the emergence of new anti-systemic movements? Both possible trajectories face the same dilemma in practice that ideological analysis faces in theory: namely that of delinking, of the possibility of separating or seceding from the system at a time when all the former spaces outside the system have been extinguished.

The dialectical way with a dilemma of this kind is to turn the problem into a solution in its own right. In this case, the mutation required of ideological analysis will turn on the issue of replication. We are no longer in the position of evaluating whether a given thought system or aesthetic form is progressive or reactionary, to use an older language: this is to say that opinion as such is no longer, in the realm of cynical reason, of much importance, having been relegated to the sphere of the individual subject and of individual temperament. (In any case, in the era of globalization, the reactionary response—US protectionism—might well turn out to be more progressive than the progressive one—free trade!) This devaluation of sheer opinion (but its philosophical pedigree extends at least as far back as Plato's denunciation of doxa) was already at work in the dissolution of classical ideological analysis, and detectable in the various attempts to substitute something like the concept of practice for that of old-fashioned ideology: not what I say but what I do.

It is, however, as we have already seen, not so easy to achieve satisfying ideological analyses of practices and of daily life, although the notion of an "ideology of daily life" might be usefully defamiliarizing, as in Adorno's remark somewhere that today the commodity might well turn out to be its own ideology. Still, that leads us back to practices and reinforces my point, namely that it is increasingly difficult to retain the concept and the term "ideology" when analyzing such concrete processes (as so many theorists have brilliantly done in the last few years). But the burden of the preceding essay has consisted in the argument that something fundamental—something practical and political, as well as something theoretical, something, indeed, of Marxism itself—is lost when the word "ideology" disappears.

This is the point at which the very notion of a system comes to the rescue: or perhaps I should say, *the* system, for in the long run there is only one, a totality that includes everything. Ideological analysis today consists in revealing the traces of that system in a given text (which can range from political programs and their vocabularies to literary texts, from personal addictions to the experience of space, from affect to science), that is to say, in demonstrating the patterns and the functions or operations of the system as it is replicated in all the multitudinous subsystems that make up postmodern life today everywhere. I can only lend a little density to this proposition by referring to earlier stages in my own work: *The Political Unconscious*, for example, posited three levels of interpretation—that of daily events or the news, that of group dynamics or class struggle, and that of the economic or in other words the patterning system of late capitalism. In *Postmodernism, or, the Cultural Logic of Late Capitalism*, I then observed a displacement in cultural analysis, from language to the visual or spatial, and from literature to mass culture: which I interpreted, not only as the reason for the emergence of cultural studies, but above all as the necessity for a different kind of focus, no longer on the text as an object, but on the object as a process. That process was precisely the patterning system identified in *The Political Unconscious*, which I here want to specify in terms of replication.

Is this then to say that we find ourselves back in the logic of modernism to the degree that, while everything replicates the system, it is the minute change or variation in that system that makes it count as subversion or reappropriation, as critique or Brechtian *Umfunktionierung*? (Adorno's notion of radical art as a homeopathic strategy is more subtle, but perhaps still to be ranged under these older categories of art as negation.)

My own inclination would be if not to replace, then at least to enlarge, those often still interesting analyses of an older and more familiar kind, with an analysis grounded in the dialectical union of opposites, and positing an ambivalence of replication and Utopia. Marx taught us that if anything like socialism was possible, it would have to be found developing within capitalism itself: he thought that the emergence of collective labor (so-called cooperation) within industry, as well as the gradual emergence of monopoly (which he called concentration and centralization) as such, were the two faces of an emergent socialism.

But in Marx's original demonstration the forms he singled out were dialectical, and could be indifferently inflected in both negative and positive directions. "Cooperation"—that is to say, collective labor—could provide an organization of labor power that intensified exploitation along with production, just as readily as it offered a form of collective human energies (an "association of free men"). Nor can there be any mistake about the ambiguities fostered by such a dialectical union of opposites: as witnessed in the enthusiasm of Lenin and Gramsci for Taylorism and Fordism, as well as the later excesses of Stakhanovism. Yet the form—Utopian or exploitative—is the same, and the lever of difference—the decision-making process, management versus councils or *autogestion*—is the place of an unresolved contradiction in both (inasmuch as the capitalist tension between owners and managers offers a mirror image of the socialist hesitation between Stalinism and self-management). Indeed, each of these forms emerges from history, including within itself a contradiction not even defined let alone resolved or resolvable, which is the very mark of its historicity, of its status as an earlier stage in a development which will replace it with something else, with something contradictory at a higher level and a greater complexity. As for the ideological replication of this form—what leaves its imprint on the organization of the various superstructures, whether theoretical, political, or artistic—we might suggest that it can be observed in the structure of the nineteenth-century novel, with its immense increase in personnel and their reorganization around protagonists and levels of secondary or minor characters, organized into a kind of proletarian, anonymous background.[17]

When we move from Marx's vantage point in the nineteenth century to that of twentieth-century monopoly, it becomes clear that it is a corporate system that takes the place of the older or earlier one, and whose form is reflected everywhere from fascism to the New Deal, from Soviet communism to Bellamy's *Looking Backward*, and all the other state-centered Utopias which marked the limits of the political-economic imagination of this period. I would also want to argue that not only the most obvious ideological superstructures, such as the juridical and the philosophical ones, are shaped and limited by this now corporate form, but even scientific

---

[17] See Alex Woloch's extraordinary *The One vs. the Many*, Princeton: Princeton University Press, 2003, 25, in which the minor characters of the nineteenth-century novel are divided into workers and eccentrics.

experiment and theorization itself, which cannot think, except in rare anticipatory moments, beyond the social limits of the period (in keeping with
Marx's notion of ideological limits—"in their minds they do not get beyond
the limits which the latter [the social class represented by the politicians in
question] do not get beyond in life"[18]).

This is why I have argued that the most fruitful way of approaching a
Utopian text or project lies not in judging its positive elements, its overt representations, but rather in seeking to grasp what it cannot (yet) think, what
lies in it beyond the very limits of its own social system and of the empirical
being it seeks to transcend.

In our own situation, for example, it is evident that Utopias of decentralization are everywhere in current political fantasy, from the regional projects
of the older centralized nation-states to the organization of business firms
themselves. The anarchist resistance to centrality and state power is fully as
reflective of this new value as the conspiracies of the various central governments to "give power back to the states," that is to say to relieve their
financial obligations by transferring fiscal responsibilities back to cities and
localities. The naïve left enthusiasm about the "Japanese way" in factory
organization has its obvious kinship with the theoretical excitement of the
ideologists of so-called post-Fordism or flexible capitalism: and it is in this
sense that a whole range of liberal, philanthropic, or Utopian values and
projects in fact simply replicate the system of late-capitalist economic production, in a regime of electronic globalization. It finds its concrete
exemplification, however, not so much in official political representation
and legal business as in the real (or nineteenth-century "realist") production
and distribution systems of the so-called Neapolitan Camorra, as Roberto
Saviano has made it visible for us:

> To satisfy this new desire, dealing had to become flexible and free of criminal
> rigidities. The supply and sale of drugs had to be liberalized. The Di Lauro clan
> was the first to make the leap in Naples. Italian criminal cartels traditionally prefer
> to sell large lots. But Di Lauro decided to sell medium lots to promote small drug-
> dealing businesses that would attract new clients. Autonomous businesses, free
> to do what they want with the goods, set their own prices, advertise how and
> where they choose. Anyone can access the market, for any amount, without
> needing to go through clan mediators. Cosa Nostra and 'Ndrangheta have exten-
> sive drug businesses, but you have to know the chain of command, and to deal
> through them you have to be introduced by clan members or affiliates. They insist
> on knowing where you'll be peddling, what the distribution will be. But not the
> Secondigliano System. Here the rule is laissez-faire, laissez-passer. Total and abso-
> lute liberalism. Let the market regulate itself. And so in no time Secondigliano
> attracted everyone eager to set up a small drug business among friends, anyone

---

[18] Marx, *The Eighteenth Brumaire of Louis Bonaparte*, 50–51.

wanting to buy at 15 and sell at 100 to pay for a vacation, a master's degree, or a mortgage. The total liberalization of the market caused prices to drop ...

This is the logic that shapes the economic imperative. It's not the Camorristi who pursue deals, but deals that pursue the Camorristi. The logic of criminal business, of the bosses, coincides with the most aggressive neoliberalism. The rules, dictated or imposed, are those of business, profit, and victory over all the competition. Anything else is worthless. Anything else doesn't exist. You pay with prison or your skin for the power to decide people's lives or deaths, promote a product, monopolize a slice of the economy, and invest in cutting-edge markets. To have power for ten years, a year, an hour—it doesn't matter for how long. What counts is to live, to truly command ...

This is the new rhythm of criminal entrepreneurs, the new thrust of the economy: to dominate it at any cost. Power before all else. Economic victory is more precious than life itself. Than anyone's life, including your own ...

What clients anywhere in the world are really interested in is quality and design. And the clans provide just that—brand as well as quality—so there really is no difference. The Secondigliano clans have acquired entire retail chains, thus spreading their commercial network across the globe and dominating the international clothing market. They also provide distribution to outlet stores ...

The clans affiliated with the Secondigliano Alliance—the Licciardi, Contini, Mallardo, Lo Russo, Bocchetti, Stabile, Prestieri and Bosti families, as well as the more autonomous Sarno and Di Lauro families—make up the Directory, whose territory includes Secondigliano, Scampia, Piscinola, Chiaiano, Miano, San Pietro a Patierno, as well as Giugliano and Ponticelli. As the Directory's federal structure offered greater autonomy to the clans, the more organic structure of the Alliance ultimately crumbled. The Directory's production board included businessmen from Casoria, Arzano, and Melito, who ran companies such as Valent, Vip Moda, Vocos, and Vitec, makers of imitation Valentino, Ferré, Versace, and Armani sold all over the world ...

Investigations conducted by the Naples anti-Mafia prosecutor reveal that the Camorra's flexible, federalist structure has completely transformed the fabric of the families: instead of diplomatic alliances and stable pacts, clans now operate more like business committees. The Camorra's flexibility reflects its need to move capital, set up and liquidate companies, circulate money, and invest quickly in real estate without geographic restrictions or heavy dependence on political mediation. The clans no longer need to organize in large bodies. (But, of course, "neoliberalism" is just one ideological representation among others.)[19]

Postmodernity, then, as an historical stage of capitalism which includes everything from the labor on the ground to the form of the thoughts and fantasies in people's heads, constitutes a dominant ideological patterning

---

[19] Roberto Saviano, *Gomorrah*, trans. Virginia Jewiss, New York: Farrar, Straus and Giroux, 2007, 66–67, 113–114, 39, 40, 45.

system which forms a structural limit to all our superstructural as well as infrastructural realities. Even the representation of this immense totality— a globalization characterized on the one side by advanced information technologies and on the other by a population explosion in which all the repressed subjects on the globe are finding their voices and emerging as subjects in their own right—is necessarily always thematized or biased by an ideological standpoint: a Real which can never find its "objective" scientific knowledge but which must always be triangulated by the attempts of those who seek to represent it to include their own absolute epistemological and historical and class limits within their impossible representation.

It is then the conception of replication as an ideological phenomenon which can alone furnish an Ariadne's thread in the process of hypothesizing the noumenon behind these phenomena: the replication of the system of late capitalism even within the thoughts and projects that seek to challenge, let alone to overthrow, it can alone today furnish the clue to current ideology and offer some chance at the intermittent approximation of the Real.

PART V

POLITICS

Chapter 15

Actually Existing Marxism

The end of the Soviet State has been the occasion for celebrations of the "death of Marxism" in quarters not particularly scrupulous about distinguishing Marxism itself as a mode of thought and analysis, socialism as a political and societal aim and vision, and communism as an historical movement. The event has clearly enough left its mark on all three of these dimensions, and it can also be agreed that the disappearance of the state power associated with a given idea is likely enough to have an adverse effect on its intellectual prestige. Thus, we are told that enrollment in French courses dropped sharply when General de Gaulle resigned from his presidency in 1970; but it would presumably take a more intricate argument to link this decline in intellectual fashion with any more objective deterioration in the "validity" of French itself.

In any case, the Left in the West, and Marxism in particular, was in trouble long before the wall came down or the CPUSSR was dissolved, owing to three distinct types of critique: first, a distancing from the political traditions of Marxism-Leninism at least as old as the secession of Maoism in the late 1950s; then, a philosophical "post-Marxism" dating from the late 1960s, in which an emergent new feminism joins forces with a variety of poststructuralisms in the stigmatization of such classical Marxian themes as totality and totalization, telos, the referent, production, and so forth; finally, an intellectual Right, slowly emerging in the course of the 1980s, which seizes on the dissolution of Eastern European communism to affirm the bankruptcy of socialism as such and the definitive primacy of the market.

What is more paradoxical is the way in which a remarkable form of mourning—what, alongside that well-known affect called wishful thinking, I am tempted to characterize as "wishful regret"—seized on even the least likely suspects, and stole over those currently attempting to squeeze dry the lemon of their hostility to a phantasmatic communism fully as much as over those who always claimed the Soviet Union had nothing whatsoever to do with what they fantasized as genuine socialism in the first place. It was as though, despite assurances to the contrary, in their heart of hearts they still believed that the Soviet Union was capable of evolving into genuine social-ism (in hindsight, the last moment for which this seems plausible was the aborted Khrushchev experiment). It is a different kind of wishful regret from the one that saw in the existence and the structure of the Communist parties themselves (particularly in the West) a flawed political instrument without which we would, however, be poorer (and at best merely in a posi-tion to evolve more rapidly into the classic two-party system of the Western liberal states).

Nor are the various national situations often given much attention in this context. The end of socialism (for we have now slipped insensibly into that version of received opinion) always seems to exclude China: perhaps the fact that it still has the highest economic growth rate in the world has led west-erners to imagine (incorrectly) that it is already capitalist. The informed will reserve an expression of real pathos for the disappearance of East Germany, which seemed for the briefest of moments to offer a chance at a radically different kind of social experiment. As for Cuba, one can only feel rage at the prospect of the systematic undermining and destruction of one of the great successful and creative revolutionary projects; but then, it is not over yet, and if Cuba offers the lesson, on the one hand, of the intensified dilemmas of "socialism in one country" within the new global system, if not, indeed, the impossibility of autonomy for any national or regional area (socialist or not), it also raises the question of social democracy, or of a mixed economy, in a backhanded way by forcing us to wonder what you are supposed to call something that is supposed to have ceased being socialist, without for all that having developed into anything structurally classifiable as capitalist (the political dimension, and the qualification of parliamentary democracy, are complete red herrings here). But the new market doxa now shuts off the substantive task of theorizing the possibility of a "mixed economy," since the latter is now most often seen negatively as the tenacious survival of older forms of governmental involvement, rather than as a specific and positive form of economic organization in its own right. But this effectively excludes the possibility of social democracy itself as an original solution, and as any-thing more than an impartial administrator of capital in the interests of all of its fractions (Aronowitz). In any case in recent years no social-democratic government has come to power anywhere that did not capitulate to the neo-conservative dogmas of fiscal responsibility and budget austerity.

Nonetheless, whatever identifies itself as a purer or more authentic Left than the Socialist parties should also find time to mourn the end of social democracy as well. Social democracy has an historic function, and its victories should be welcomed for more fundamental reasons than the achievements of some Scandinavian countries, along with the relief most people feel when after long conservative administration its party finally comes to power (although that is itself no small thing). The social-democratic program has a pedagogical value which emerges from its very failures when these are able to be perceived as structurally necessary and inevitable within the system: it thus shows what the system is incapable of achieving and confirms the principle of totality to be outlined below. That politically educative value is, to be sure, considerably diminished when social democracy capitulates of its own free will; something that should, rather, provide the demonstration that even minimal demands for economic justice cannot be achieved within the market framework by committed and "liberal," let alone "socialist," people and movements.

What is certain is that the collapse of the Eastern European party states (while confirming Wallerstein's prescient assessment of them as anti-systemic, rather than as constituting the nucleus of some new world system in their own right) has been everywhere accompanied by what Christopher Hill calls "the experience of defeat." This mood is worth generalizing well out beyond the despair that people have felt before at other moments of some palpable and absolute "end of history"; and it is also to be distinguished from the astonishing spectacle of the opportunism of so many left intellectuals, for whom the matter seems to have boiled down to the question of whether socialism works or not, like a car, so that your main concern is what to replace it with if it does not work (ecology? religion? old-style scholarly research?). Anyone who thought the dialectic was a lesson in historical patience, as well as those few remaining Utopian idealists who may still harbor the conviction that what is unrealized is better than what is real or even than what is possible, will have been too astonished to be depressed by the rush of Marxist intellectuals for the door; and no doubt surprised at themselves as well for having assumed that left intellectuals were leftists first and foremost rather than intellectuals.

But Marxism has always been distinguished from other forms of radicalism and populism by the absence of anti-intellectualism; so it is necessary to specify that the situation of the intellectual is always difficult and problematic in the absence of mass movements (something American leftists have had to confront far more often than their counterparts elsewhere); and that this kind of left opportunism is better explained by the more pervasive atmosphere of immediate returns generated by present-day society. The demands thereby encouraged are difficult to square with one of the fundamental peculiarities of human history, namely that human time, individual time, is out of sync with socioeconomic time, and in particular with the rhythms or cycles—the so-called Kondratiev waves—of the capitalist mode of production itself, with its brief windows of opportunity that open onto collective praxis, and its incomprehensible inhuman periods of fatality and insurmountable misery. One does not have to believe in the mechanical alternations of progressive and reactionary periods (although the market cycles do justify such alterations to a certain degree) to understand that, as organisms of a certain life span, we are poorly placed as biological individuals to witness the more fundamental dynamics of history, glimpsing only this or that incomplete moment, which we hasten to translate into the all-too-human terms of success or failure. But neither stoic wisdom nor the reminder of a longer-term view are really satisfactory responses to this peculiar existential and epistemological dilemma, comparable to the science-fictional one of beings inhabiting a cosmos they do not have organs to perceive or identify. Perhaps only the acknowledgment of this radical incommensurability between human existence and the dynamics of collective history and production is capable of generating some new ethic, whereby we deduce the absent totality that makes a mockery of us, without relinquishing the fragile value of our own personal experience; capable, as well, of generating new kinds of political attitudes; new kinds of political perception, as well as of political patience; and new methods for decoding the age as well, and reading the imperceptible tremors within it of an inconceivable future.

Meanwhile, it was not merely Wallerstein who was right about the failure of the Bolshevik and the Stalinist experiments to develop into the enclave from which a whole new global system would develop; it was a certain Marx as well (the Marx of the *Grundrisse*, perhaps, more than of the more triumphalist passages of *Capital*), who tirelessly insisted on the significance of the world market as the ultimate horizon of capitalism, and thereby on the principle, not merely that socialist revolution would be a matter of high productivity and of the most advanced development rather than of rudimentary modernization, but also that it would have to be worldwide. The end of national autonomy, in the world system of late capitalism, seems far more radically to exclude episodic social experiments than did the modern period (where they survived, after all, for a considerable number of years). To be sure, conceptions of national autonomy and autarchy are very unpopular today indeed, and are energetically discredited by the media, who tend to associate them with the late Kim Il-sung and his doctrine of *juche*. This is perhaps reassuring for countries like India and Brazil, intent on abandoning their national autonomy; but we must not give up the attempt to imagine what the consequences of trying to secede from the world market could be and what kind of politics would be necessary to do so. For there is also the question of what secures such an implacable integration of the new world market, and this is a question whose answer, above and beyond the development of a dependence on imports and the destruction of local production, must surely today be largely cultural, as we shall see later on. This longing to be integrated into the world market is clearly enough perpetuated by world information circuits and exported entertainment (mainly from Hollywood and American television), which not only reinforce just such international consumerist styles but even more importantly block the formation of autonomous and alternative cultures based on different values or principles (or else, as in the case of the socialist countries, undermine whatever possibilities for the emergence of such an autonomous culture might have hitherto existed).

This clearly enough makes culture (and commodity-reification theory) into a far more central political issue than it ever was in previous moments of capitalism; at the same time, while suggesting a relative redistribution of the significance of ideology under other more influential cultural practices, it confirms Stuart Hall's idea of "discursive struggle" as the primary mode in which ideologies are legitimated and delegitimated today. The saturation with a culture of consumerism was accompanied by the systematic delegitimation of slogans and concepts ranging from nationalization and welfare all the way to economic rights and socialism itself, once thought to be not merely possible but also desirable, yet today universally held to be chimerical by an omnipresent cynical reason. Whether cause or effect, this delegitimation of the very language and conceptuality of socialism (and its replacement by a nauseatingly complacent market rhetoric) has clearly played a fundamental role in the current "end of history."

But the experience of defeat, which includes all these things but transcends them all, has even more to do with the well-nigh universal feeling of powerlessness that has dawned on an immense range of social strata around the globe since the end of the 1960s, a deeper conviction as to the fundamental impossibility of any form of real systemic change in our societies. This is often expressed as a perplexity in the identification of agencies of change of whatever type; and it takes the form of a sense of the massive, permanent, and non- or post-human immutability of our immeasurably complex institutions (despite their own ceaseless metamorphoses), which are most often imagined in high- or late-technological terms. The result is an instinctive belief in the futility of all forms of action or praxis, and a millennial discouragement which can account for the passionate adherence to a variety of other substitutes and alternative solutions: most notably to religious fundamentalism and nationalism, but also to the whole range of passionate involvements in local initiatives and actions (and single-issue politics), as well as the consent to the inevitable implied by the hysterical euphoria in visions of some delirious pluralism of late capitalism with its alleged authorization of social difference and "multiculturalism." What seems important to stress here is the gap between technology and economics (just as we will observe Marxism elsewhere to insist on the distance between the political and the economic or the social). Technology is indeed something like the cultural logo or preferred code of the third stage of capitalism: it is late capitalism's own preferred mode of self-representation, the way it would like us to think about itself. And this mode of presentation secures the mirage of autonomization and the feeling of powerlessness already described; in much the same way in which old-fashioned mechanics no longer have anything to say about automobile motors organized around computer programs. It is, however, crucial to distinguish between this technological appearance, which is of course equally a cultural phenomenon, and the socioeconomic structure of late capitalism that still corresponds to Marx's analyses.

In saying so, however, I anticipate the substance of the present essay, which will recapitulate the relevance of Marxism for our current situation, and will thereby need to deal with the following topics. (1) What is Marxism then, exactly, if the media and the various right-wing blowhards have it all wrong? (2) What is socialism in that case, and what might it be (or be thought of being) in the future? And, above all, (3) what can the relationship of both be to that supremely stigmatized traditional concept called revolution? (4) What then was communism, and what happened to it? (5) And lastly, and as a logical conclusion to all of the above, what is late capitalism, and what does Marxism imply for any of the new politics that can be expected to accompany it? What new theoretical tasks does late capitalism set for the new or third-stage Marxism that has begun to emerge along with it?

I.

What is Marxism? Or if you prefer, what is Marxism not? It is not, in particular, a nineteenth-century philosophy, as some people (from Foucault to Kolakowski) have suggested, although it certainly emerged from nineteenth-century philosophy (but you could just as easily argue that the dialectic is itself an unfinished project, which anticipates modes of thought and reality that have not yet come into existence even today).

In part, this answer can be justified by the assertion that Marxism is not in that sense a philosophy at all; it designates itself, with characteristic cumbersomeness, as a "unity of theory and practice" (and if you knew what that was, it would be clear that it shares this peculiar structure with Freudianism). But it may be clearest to say that it can best be thought of as a "problematic": that is to say, it can be identified, not by specific positions (whether of a political, economic, or philosophical type), but rather by the allegiance to a specific complex of problems, whose formulations are always in movement and in historic rearrangement and restructuration, along with their object of study (capitalism itself). One can therefore just as easily say that what is productive in the Marxian problematic is its capacity to generate new problems (as we will observe it to do in the most recent encounter with late capitalism); nor can the various dogmatisms historically associated with it be traced to any particular fatal flaw in that problem-field, although it is clear that Marxists have not been any freer of the effects of intellectual reification than anyone else, and have, for example, consistently thought that base-and-superstructure was a solution and a concept, rather than a problem and a dilemma, just as they have persistently assumed that something called materialism was a philosophical or ontological position, rather than the general sign for an operation which we might term "de-idealization," an operation both interminable in Freud's classic sense and also unrealizable on any permanent basis and for any durable length of time (inasmuch as it is idealism which is the most comfortable assumption for everyday human thought).

The initial problematic of Marxism developed around the specificities—the structural and historical peculiarities—of the production of value in industrial capitalism: it took as its central conceptual space the phenomenon of surplus value, which offered the signal advantage of being able to be multiply transcoded: that is to say, the problem of surplus value could be translated into a number of seemingly distinct problems and areas which corresponded to specialized languages and disciplines, many of which did not yet exist at the time in their current academic form. Surplus value could be approached, for example, through the phenomenon of commodity production, leading on into the social psychology of commodities and consumerism (or what Marx called commodity fetishism). It could also be tracked out into the area of money theory (banks, inflation, speculation, the stock market, not to speak of what Simmel calls the philosophy of money). It transforms itself, in the most astonishing of mythological mutations, into the living and breathing presence of the social classes themselves. It leads a second or shadow life under legal forms and juridical categories (and in particular in the various historical, traditional, and modern forms of property relationships). Its very existence calls forth the central dilemmas of modern historiography (as the narrative of its own emergence and its various destinies).

Surplus value has most often been thought of—a thought which we might therefore have some interest in resisting or postponing—as a matter of economics, which has, for Marxism, most often taken the form of an investigation of crisis and of the falling rate of profit, and of the implications and consequences of the fundamental mechanism of capital accumulation (the economics of possible or feasible socialisms also belongs here). Last but not least, the concept would seem to authorize—but also to require—any number of theories of ideology and of culture, and to take as its ultimate horizon the world market (as the outer limit of its structural tendency to accumulate), including the dynamics of imperialism and its later equivalents (neo-colonialism, hyper-imperialism, the world system). The transmutation of the notion of surplus value into these very different disciplinary languages or fields of specialization constitutes the problematic of Marxism as an articulated conceptual space (which one could map), and can also account for the variability of any number of specifically Marxist ideologies and political programs or strategies.

The crises in the Marxian paradigm, then, have always come punctually at those moments in which its fundamental object of study—capitalism as a system—has seemed to change its spots, or to undergo unforeseen and unpredictable mutations. Since the old articulation of the problematic no longer corresponds to this new configuration of realities, the temptation is strong to conclude that the paradigm itself—after the Kuhnian fashion of the sciences—has been overtaken and outmoded (with the implication that a new one needs to be devised, if it is not already taking shape).

This is what happened in 1898, when Eduard Bernstein's *The Presuppositions of Socialism and the Tasks of Social Democracy* proposed radically to "revise" Marxism in the light of its alleged failure to do justice to the complexity of the modern social classes as well as to the adaptability of contemporary capitalism. Bernstein advised the abandonment of the Hegel-derived dialectic along with the notion of revolution itself, and the consequent reorganization of Second International politics around mass democracy and the electoral process. It is very precisely these features of the first post-Marxism that reappeared in the 1970s of our own era, when more sophisticated versions of that diagnosis and its prescription alike begin to reappear in ever greater numbers (no single pronouncement marks this cyclical reappearance of post-Marxism as dramatically as Bernstein's, but Hindess and Hirst's 1977 book on *Capital* may be taken as a first swallow, while Laclau and Mouffe's *Hegemony and Socialist Strategy* of 1985 shows the migration in full course across the sky).

The emphases of these various post-Marxisms (whether they still attempt to cling to the named tradition or rather call for its outright liquidation) vary according to the way they stage the fate of the object it was the vocation of Marxism to analyze in the first place, namely capitalism itself. They may for example argue that classical capitalism no longer exists, and has given way to this or that "post-capitalism" (Daniel Bell's idea of a "post-industrial society" is one of the most influential versions of this strategy), in which the features enumerated by Marx—but most particularly the dynamic of antagonistic social classes and the primacy of the economic (or of the "base" or "infrastructure")—no longer exist (Bell's post-capitalism is essentially organized by scientific knowledge and run by scientific "philosopher-kings"). Or one can try to defend the idea that something like capitalism still exists, but has become more benign and has for whatever reason (reliance on more widespread commodity consumption, mass literacy, an enlightened awareness of its own interest) become more responsive to the popular will and to collective needs; so that it is no longer necessary to posit radical systemic changes, let alone revolution. This is, or so one supposes, the position of the various surviving social-democratic movements.

Finally, it can be maintained that capitalism does indeed still exist, but that its capacity for producing wealth and for ameliorating the lot of its subjects has been significantly underestimated (particularly by the Marxists); indeed, that capitalism is today the only viable road to modernization and universal improvement, if not affluence. This is of course the rhetoric of the market people, and it seems to have won out over the other two arguments in recent years (although they are all affiliated and far from being mutually exclusive).

Far more plausible is the counterposition to this one, propounded most dramatically by Robert Kurz in books like *The Collapse of Modernization* (Frankfurt, 1992), namely that it is precisely the capacity for producing new surplus value—in other words, the capacity for modernization in the classic sense of industrialization and investment—that has disappeared in late capitalism. Capitalism may thus well have triumphed, but its outcome is increasingly marked by dizzying paper-money speculation on the one hand, and new forms of "immiseration" on the other, in structural unemployment and in the consignment of vast tracts of the Third World to permanent unproductivity. If this is so, the situation would presumably also call for some kind of post-Marxism, but of an utterly different kind from that deduced by the more optimistic view of capitalism outlined above.

Before analyzing the historical significance of the various post-Marxisms, however, it will be appropriate to respond to the views of capitalism on which they are based, which all presume some mutation in the basic structure described by Marx himself. Bell's idea that the dependence of modern business on science and technology has displaced the older capitalist dynamic of profit and competition is surely the easiest to dispose of, in the light of any number of contemporary debates or scandals that turn on the commercial exploitation of scientific products—patents from the rainforest, for example, or the various AIDS drugs—and in the light of the ever more desperate search of the theoretical scientists for relatively "disinterested" research funding.

Inversely, it can easily be shown that no business in the world today (of whatever nature or complexity) is at liberty to suspend the profit motive even locally: in fact, we can witness its global generalization in the reorganization of areas hitherto relatively exempt from the more intense pressures to postmodernize—areas that range from old-fashioned book publishing to village agriculture, where the old ways are ruthlessly extirpated, and high-powered monopolies reorganize everything on a purely formal basis (in other words, in terms of profit or investment return) with no regard to the content of the activity. It is a process (Marx calls it subsumption) that takes place within the relatively more underdeveloped enclaves in the advanced countries (often cultural or agricultural) as well as accompanying the penetration of capital into hitherto uncommodified zones in the rest of the world.

So it is a mistake to suppose that the historically original dynamics of capitalism have undergone a mutation or an evolutionary restructuration; and the ongoing drive to maximize profit—or in other words to accumulate capital as such (not a personal motivation, in other words, but rather a structural feature of the system, its necessity to expand)—can be seen to be accompanied by other equally familiar features from mankind's recent past: the vicissitudes of the business cycle, the fluctuations of the labor market, including massive unemployment and capital flight, and the destructiveness of the ever increasing tempo of industrial and technological change, albeit on a global scale that makes such persistent features seem unprecedented.

About democracy, and in addition to the inveterate failures and capitulations of social democracy that have already been mentioned, it is enough to observe the ever more systematic servility of all governments today in the face of business orthodoxies (balancing the budget, for example, or IMF policies generally), to come rapidly to the conclusion that the system brooks no collective demands that are likely to interfere with its operations (this is not to suggest that it can ever operate very smoothly). Less than ever, now that the Soviet Union has disappeared, are episodic attempts tolerated which show the intent to chart an autonomous national course or to shift the priorities of government economic policy in any dramatic way that might injure business interests: the Allende coup is the paradigmatic response to these ever more enfeebled velleities of populism or national autonomy.

As for the market, its rhetoric is of course an ideology, which mobilizes belief with a view towards action and political results. It seems just as plausible to believe in the apocalyptic scenario whereby the market will dramatically fail to improve the lives of two-thirds of those living on the globe; but as a matter of fact this scenario is also furnished (for the price of one!) by the market people themselves, who sometimes like to outline those parts of the world (Africa, the poorer countries of Eastern Europe) that will never successfully feel the beneficent modernizing effect of the appropriate market conditions. What they omit is the role of the new world system itself in this desperate pauperization of whole populations on a global scale.

I take it therefore as axiomatic that capitalism has not fundamentally changed today, any more than it can be thought to have done in Bernstein's period. But it should be equally clear that the resonance of Bernstein's revisionism, as well as the persuasiveness of a whole range of contemporary post-Marxisms, is no mere epiphenomenon either, but a cultural and ideological reality which itself demands historical explanation: indeed, insofar as all such positions centrally imply a breakdown in the very explanatory powers of an older Marxism in the face of the new developments, it would be best if the explanation were itself a Marxian one, and thereby a vindication in this respect as well.

We have mentioned in passing one of the fundamental features of Marx's analysis of capitalism, namely that capital must ceaselessly expand, it can never call it a day and sit back to rest on its achievements: the accumulation of capital must be enlarged, the rate of productivity constantly increased, with all the well-known results of perpetual transformation, wholesale trashing and fresh construction, and the like ("all that's solid …"). Furthermore, capitalism is also supposed to be contradictory and constantly to paint itself over and over again into corners in which it confronts the law of the falling rate of profit in the form of diminishing returns, stagnation, unproductive flurries of speculation, and so forth. Because these effects largely derive from overproduction and from the saturation of available markets, Ernest Mandel has (in *Late Capitalism*) suggested not only that capital tends to extricate itself by technological innovation that reopens those markets for products of wholly new kinds, but also that the system as a whole has had thus to rejuvenate itself at several crisis points in its three-hundred-year-old career. Meanwhile, positing a somewhat longer time period, Giovanni Arrighi (in *The Long Twentieth Century*) has detected the presence of a phase of speculation and finance capital very similar to what we today observe in the First World, at the close of each of the ever-expanding cycles of the world system (Spanish-Genoese, Dutch, English, and now American). For Mandel, it is the introduction of radically new kinds of technology that rescues capitalism from its cyclical crisis, but which also, along with a shift in its center of gravity, determines a convulsive enlargement of the system as a whole and the extension of its logic and its hegemony dramatically over ever vaster areas of the globe.

It does not seem to be an accident that these momentous systemic transmutations should correspond faithfully to the emergence of the moments of a post-Marxism which have already been mentioned. Bernstein's was the age of imperialism (Lenin's monopoly stage), in which along with the new technologies of electricity and the combustion engine, and the new modes of organization of the trust and the cartel, the market system was itself projected out beyond the "advanced" nation-states in a relatively systemic carving up of the globe into European and North American colonies and spheres of influence. The extraordinary mutations in the realm of culture and consciousness, familiar to students in various disciplines of the human sciences—the emergence of modernism in all the arts, preceded by the twin harbingers of naturalism and symbolism, the discovery of psychoanalysis, echoed by a variety of unfamiliar new forms of thought in the sciences, vitalism and machinism in philosophy, the apotheosis of the classical city, alarming new types of mass politics—all of these late nineteenth-century innovations, whose ultimate links with the infrastructural modifications we have mentioned can be demonstrated, now seemed to propose and to demand modifications in an essentially nineteenth-century Marxism itself (that of the Second International).

The moment of the first post-Marxism is thus that of the Modern, or modernism, in general (if we follow the scheme according to which a first, national-capitalist period, from the French Revolution on, is termed a moment of realism, or secularization; while the latest moment of capitalism, the restructuration of capitalism in the nuclear and the cybernetic age, is now generally referred to as postmodern). Bernstein's revisionism can today be seen as a response to changes in content associated with this momentous transition between the first (post-feudal or national) and the second (modern or imperialist) stages of capitalism: even though only the effects of the new imperialist system (set into place around 1885) are registered in Bernstein's analysis of the increasing prosperity of the working class, the appearance of innumerable class fractions unlikely to identify directly with it, and the shift in stress to political aims (an enlargement of democracy) rather than socioeconomic ones. (Indeed, imperialism will only enter the debate in the Second International a few years later, around the time of the First World War, with Kautsky's notion of "ultra-imperialism"—the union of all the imperialist rivals against their "Others"—which today seems extraordinarily prophetic of our own situation.)

The first post-Marxism, in other words, drew plausible conclusions about the inadequacy of the traditional Marxian problematic on the basis of internal social conditions, without attention to the enlargement of the international, or global, frame, itself instrumental in modifying those conditions in the first place. (Lenin's notion of the corruption and complicity of the First World proletariat by an internal prosperity owed to imperialism itself is a rather crude corrective to this narrow focus.)

But the precedent of Bernstein's revisionism allows us new insights into our own contemporary post-Marxisms, which begin to emerge, in analogous fashion, at the very moment in which one stage of capitalism (now the imperialist stage itself) begins to give way to another one, involving new technologies and also an immensely expanded world scale. Indeed, the beginning of the nuclear age and of cybernetics and information technology on every level of social life, from the quotidian to the organization of industry and warfare as such, coincides with the end of the older colonial system and with a worldwide decolonization that has taken the form of a system of immense transnational corporations mostly affiliated with the three centers of the new world system (the US, Japan, and Western Europe). Expansion in this third or postmodern age of capitalism has thus not taken the form of geographical exploration and territorial claims but rather the more intensive colonization of the older areas of capitalism and the postmodernization of the newer ones, the saturation with commodities and the remarkable post-geographical and post-spatial informational simultaneity that weaves a web far finer and more minute and all-pervasive than anything imaginable in the older semaphore routes of cable and newspaper and even those of airplane and radio.

From this perspective it can be argued that just as Bernstein's revisionism was a symptom and a consequence of social changes that resulted from the organization of classical imperialism—or in other words, a reflex of modernity and modernization as such—so also contemporary post-Marxisms have found their justification in extraordinary modifications of social reality under late capitalism: from the "democratization" resulting from the emergence of all kinds of "new social movements" and subject-positions into an immensely expanded media space (if not exactly "public sphere" in the classical sense) to a worldwide restructuration of industrial production that has paralyzed national labor movements and problematized the very concept of the local itself (living your whole life in one place, with one job or career, in a relatively stable institutional and urban setting). It is changes on this level that have led the post-Marxisms variously to insist on the irrelevance of a stable idea of social class, on the unworkability of the older party politics and the delusions of the classical concept of revolution as the "seizure of power," on the outmodedness of concepts of production as well in the era of mass consumption and the theoretical disintegration of labor theories of value in the face of information bits. I leave out of the picture here the more abstruse philosophical polemics, around the now allegedly discredited and "Hegelian" notion of contradiction, in a world of sheer surface differences; on the stigmatization of the idea of a telos as just another bourgeois conception of progress (both concepts unseasonable at the end of history and in a world in which deep temporality and all kinds of ideas of the future as such have seemed extinct); polemics against notions of ideology and false consciousness as well (but also, more tactfully, against the Freudian unconscious itself) in a stream of Deleuzian flux inhabited by all kinds of decentered subjects.

It is clear that each of these critical themes has something significant to tell us about changes in social life today, if it is examined as a conceptual symptom rather than as a feature of some new postmodern doxa. But it should also be clear that, like Bernstein's critical vision, a fresh contemporary focus has been bought at the price of the totality or of the global frame itself, whose shifts constitute the invisible but operative coordinates in which local empirical phenomena can alone be evaluated. For it is only within the structure of the third phase, the new world system, of capitalism itself that the emergence of the new internal-existential or empirical-social phenomena can be understood: and this is clearer today, in a greatly enlarged world system, than it was in Bernstein's time, when "imperialism" could still be grasped externally and extrinsically, as something outside domestic national experience. Today, it is clearer than ever before that late capitalism defines itself at one and the same time in its global dynamics as well as in its internal effects: indeed the former now seem to impose a return on the latter, as when we speak of the way in which an "internal Third World" and a process of internal colonization have seemed to eat away at the First World itself. Here the view of Marx the theoretician of the world market (particularly in the *Grundrisse*) not only supersedes current post-Marxisms, but can be seen as essential to the analysis of the earlier stages of capitalism as well.

But it is a dialectical view of the continuities of capitalism that is proposed here, in place of an overestimation of the latter's breaks and discontinuities: for it is the continuity in the deeper structure that imposes the experiential differences generated as that structure convulsively enlarges with each new phase.

2.

About socialism ("the death of"), as distinguished from Soviet communism as an historical development, a word needs to be said in honor of its necessity as a political, social, and imaginative ideal (which would have to be reinvented should it ever suffer extinction); as a future program which is also a Utopian vision and the space of a radical and systemic alternative to the present social system. The incidentals generally thought to be "socialist" in the generic sense seem to come and go in predictable rhythms: so that it is only apparently a paradox that at the very moment in which the "Soviet model" has seemed utterly discredited, the American public seemed on the point of seriously reconsidering the possibility of a somewhat more socialized medicine for the first time in sixty years. As for "nationalization," itself long since a casualty of "discursive struggle" and a slogan even the most orthodox socialists have been reluctant to brandish in public, its reappearance in all kinds of unexpected situations and contexts cannot be precluded (although it seems possible that it will be right-wing or business governments that find strategic nationalizations useful for cutting their own costs). In any event, the denunciation of government intervention by market rhetoricians is rendered ludicrous by the omnipresent prestige of the Japanese model, in which government intervention is so prominent as to suggest that the system as a whole might well be characterized as state-managed capitalism. Meanwhile, after the Reagan/Thatcher period, in which private business celebrated orgies of a type not witnessed since the Gilded Age of the previous century, the trend seems to be flowing back towards a reinterrogation of the minimal social responsibilities that must be assumed by the state in any advanced industrial society; here the continental and in particular the

German tradition of a welfare state dating back to Bismarck has been obscured by Cold War polemics but now seems in the process of becoming visible again against the rhetoric of privatization sponsored by Anglo-American capital.

At the same time, and despite the experimental ideas of the Clinton administration about private investment in ecological industries and technology, it would seem ever clearer that ecological reform can only be achieved by the state itself, and that the market is structurally inadequate to the immense changes required not merely by control and limitation of existing industrial technologies but also by the revolution in daily life and consumption habits such limitations would require for their motivation and enforcement. Ecology has at times been seen to be in tension with socialism as a political objective, particularly where the latter has brandished a rhetoric of modernization and a "Promethean" attitude towards the conquest of nature (which has often wrongly been attributed to Marx himself). Nonetheless, any number of disappointed socialists seem to have transferred their political practice to the ecological sphere, so that for a time the Green movements seemed to have replaced the various left political movements as the principal vehicles for opposition in advanced countries. At any rate, what needs to be affirmed here is the dependence of ecological political aims on the existence of socialist governments: it is a logical argument, and has nothing to do with the abuse of nature and the ecology by communist governments in the East who were ruthless and desperate in their pursuit of rapid modernization. Rather, it can be determined a priori that the ecological modifications are so expensive, require such massive technology, and also such thoroughgoing enforcement and policing, that they could only be achieved by a strong and determined government (and probably a worldwide government at that).

Meanwhile, it should also be understood that the project of an ironically named "transition to capitalism" in the East is at one with Western "deregulation" and, very specifically hostile to all forms of welfare security, dictates the systematic dismantling of all the tattered safety nets still in existence. But this is what has not been generally visible to the citizens of the socialist countries: discounting as propaganda the few truths their governments actually did tell them about the West, they clearly believed that we retained the equivalent of their own safety net, their medical and social services and public-education system, while somehow having managed, magically, to add on top of all that the goods, gadgets, drugstores, supermarkets, and video outlets that they now coveted: it seems not to have been clear to them that the conditions for having the latter—the goods—was the systematic renunciation of the former—namely, the social services. This fundamental misunderstanding, which lends the Eastern European stampede towards the market its tragicomic resonance, also omitted any sense of the difference between the simple availability of commodities and the frenzies of consumerism itself, something like a collective addiction with enormous cultural, social, and individual consequences which can only be compared, as a behavioral mechanism, to the related addictions of drugs, sex, and violence (that in fact tend to accompany it). Nothing human can be alien to any of us, of course; and perhaps it was as historically important as it was necessary for human society to have gone through the experience of consumerism as a way of life, if only in order more consciously later on to choose something radically different in its place.

It should be clear that the features enumerated above—nationalizations, government interventions of various kinds—scarcely suffice to define the socialist project as such: but at a time when even the welfare state is under attack by the new world-market rhetoric, and when people are encouraged to loathe big government and to fantasize about private solutions to social problems, socialists should join with liberals (in the American, centrist sense of the word) to defend big government and to stage their discursive struggle against such attacks. The Welfare State was an achievement; its internal contradictions are those of capitalism itself and not a failure of social and collective concern; at any rate, where it is in the process of being dismantled, it will be important for the Left to seize and articulate the dissatisfactions of ordinary people with the loss of those achievements and that safety net, and not play into the hands of the market rhetoricians. "Big government" should be a positive slogan; "bureaucracy" itself needs to be rescued from its stereotypes, and reinvoked in the terms of the service and class commitment it has had at certain heroic moments of bourgeois society (while reminding people that the largest bureaucracies are in any case those of the big corporations). Finally, it is crucial to undercut the use of private or personal analogies—one's own monthly income and budget, "spending beyond your means," etc.—for the understanding of national debts and budgets. The problem of paying interest on an enormous national debt is a problem of the world monetary system as a whole, and should be thought of in those terms and analyzed as such.

But those are only the necessary reactive strategies for current discursive struggle and for reestablishing a climate in which a properly socialist vision can be projected: for one thing many of these seemingly left-wing or social-democratic proposals—that of a guaranteed minimum annual wage, for example—can perfectly well suit the purposes of a Bonapartist or even a fascist Right. All the more reason, then, to stress the other absence in a merely reactive strategy, namely the failure to name the alternative, to name the solution, fully as much as to "name the system." Not only is it the systematicity of socialist solutions, the interrelationship of all of the measures proposed within a larger project, that marks the difference between revolution and piecemeal reform; it is also the characterization of such measures as socialist which necessarily draws the line between a genuinely left movement and a left-center, or welfare reformist-politics.

In a basic book on the American Left (*Ambiguous Legacy*), James Weinstein indeed demonstrates that as radically different from one another, as virtually unrelated to each other, as were its three high points in modern times—the Socialist Party of Eugene Debs before the First World War, the American Communist Party in the 1930s, the New Left in the 1960s—they all shared a common failing, namely, the conviction that you could not use the word "socialist" to the American people, and that social aims, even those which attracted widespread support among the voters, ought always to be disguised as essentially liberal or reformist measures in order not to alienate the American masses. This means that even if achieved, and enshrined in collective popularity, such individual aims are always open to confiscation by centrist movements; and indeed, as in a famous Jules Feiffer cartoon, the main function of the American Left generally is to have invented new ideas to replenish the imagination and the political arsenal of an eclectic moderate movement (most often, the Democratic Party itself), whose bankruptcy follows swiftly on the disappearance of its secret source of inspiration. But social-democratic or welfare measures cannot contribute politically to the development of socialism unless they are labeled as such: socialism is a total project, whose various components must be registered allegorically, as so many emanations and figures for its central spirit, at the same time that they are justified in their own right, in terms of their own local appropriateness. The collective project always operates on the two levels of the microcosm and the macrocosm, the individual or empirical issue in all its burning urgency, and the bigger national or international picture, the micropolitical here being placed in perspective by the overall totalizing umbrella party or alliance strategy.

Yet the line between the critical or reactive and the positive or Utopian, the construction-oriented, runs through both micro- and macropolitical levels: discursive struggle, the discrediting of the hegemonic market model, runs out into the sands unless it is accompanied by a prophetic vision of the future, of the radical social alternative, whose problems today are obviously compounded by the discrediting of older "modern" or "modernist" images of socialism or communism (as well as the contemporary emergence, in the gaps left by the latter, of a range of micropolitical and anarchist substitutes).

Socialism has surely always meant cradle-to-grave protection for human beings: the ultimate safety net, which provides the beginnings of an existential freedom for everyone by providing a secure human time over and above practical or material necessity: the beginnings of a true individuality, by making it possible for people to live without the crippling anxieties of self-preservation ("ohne Angst leben," as Adorno, who most abundantly has developed this theme philosophically, characterized music), along with the less widely identified but equally paralyzing anxieties of our powerless yet well-nigh visceral concern for others (the majority of people spoiling their lives, as Oscar Wilde put it in *The Soul of Man under Socialism*, "by an unhealthy and exaggerated altruism," indeed, being "forced so to spoil them"). This is the sense, indeed, in which socialism means guaranteed material life: the right to free education and free health care and retirement support, the right to community and association, let alone grassroots democracy in the most thoroughgoing sense (that of Marx in his lectures on the Paris Commune); the right to work as well—no small thing from the social and political perspective of the present day, in which massive and permanent structural unemployment can be foreseen as a requirement of late-capitalist automation; and finally the right to culture and to a "leisure" uncolonized by the formal stereotypicalities and standardizations of current commercial "mass culture."

This vision in its turn is ideologically rent and deformed by the seemingly incompatible poles of an existential or individual focus on the one hand (the private alienations of late capitalism, the scars left on individual subjectivity) and a communitarianism on the other, whose essential collective focus is currently in the process of being confiscated by liberal and even right-wing ideologues. Lafargue's scandalous "right to laziness," on the one hand; the Utopias of small agricultural or even Native American tribal communities on the other: such are only some of the thematic terms in which the possibility of imagining socialism is conflicted on the Left itself.

Here, clearly enough, the anxiety about Utopia takes the form of an apprehension of repression: that socialism will involve renunciation, that the abstinence from commodities is only a figure for a more generalized puritanism and a systemic willed frustration of desire (about which even Marx showed us that capitalism was the latter's stimulant and an immense machine for producing new and unforeseeable desires of all kinds). This is then also the point at which Marcuse's meditation becomes indispensable, posing for the first time since Plato the question of true and false desires, true and false happiness and gratification: it is significant, then, that the repudiation of Marcuse at once takes a political and an anti-intellectual form (who is the philosopher-king appointed to adjudicate between the true and the false in these matters, etc.?). The paradoxes of the synchronic indeed allow us to grasp, but only from the outside, how difficult it may be to relinquish the compensatory desires and intoxications we have developed in order to make the present livable. The dilemma is not to be solved by debates on human nature, surely, but in terms of a collective decision and a collective will to live in a different way: the freedom necessarily implied by such a collective choice can then respect itself only by acknowledging individual freedoms to opt out or to secede, temperamentally to refuse the pieties of the majority. Meanwhile, it is Marxism's weakness as well as its strength always to find its insistence on the economic (in the broadest and loosest sense) countered by essentially political considerations and worries: indeed, I tend to think that the strength of current free-market rhetoric depends on the use of the image of the market as a symbolic political fantasy rather than a specifically economic program.

This particular fear of socialism—the libidinal one, the anxiety about repression—then logically develops into a more openly political concern with power as such. Bakunin was not the first to associate socialism with political tyranny and dictatorship (the reproach had already been developed by the Utopian socialists), nor was Wittfogel the last, although his book *Oriental Despotism*, which juxtaposed Stalin with the god-emperors of the earliest hydraulic civilizations, made a lasting mark on right-wing propaganda. It is probably not enough to observe that government and the state—in whatever political form—always by definition hold the monopoly of force. Yet the reproach does not seem particularly consistent with the equally current right-wing notion that real democracy is ungovernable and that the demands awakened by socialism are likely to bring the social machine to a standstill. To that inconsistency may be added another, historical one: namely the virtually unanimous consensus of this doctrine—that socialism means the absolute state—as a result of the collapse of that state structure and that particular political order in the first place.

Most often, however, particularly in the conditions of a market climate and of the momentary hegemony of market rhetoric, the envisioning of socialism and of Utopia must make its way through the ideological conflict between a command society on the one hand and a largely individualistic or atomized, decentered, "invisible hand" society on the other. Even Robert Heilbroner, in his pre-1989 book *Marxism: For and Against*, speaks up for the vitality of this alternative vision in terms of the collective choice and prioritizing of a relatively fundamentalist way of life which, like current stereotypes of so-called Islamic fundamentalism, attempts to secede from the world market by way of a kind of ethical puritanism and a libidinal renunciation. It is a vision that places a welcome premium on the possibilities of collective choice no less than on the price to be paid for the achievement of a different kind of social life; at the same time, however, it feeds into deep unconscious fears and anxieties about Utopia itself, and confirms one's sense that any projection of socialist visions today must come to terms with the fear of Utopia fully as much as with the diagnosis of the pathologies of late capitalism.

As for the stigmatization of planning as the image of a "command society" libidinally invested with images of Stalinism along with deeper stereotypes of "oriental despotism" that extend back into ancient history (the statist adversaries of the ancient Hebrews and Greeks alike), a beginning might be made with those contemporary endorsements of socialism that attempt to formulate the great collective project in individualistic terms, as a vast social experiment calculated to elicit the development of individual energies and the excitement of a truly modern individualism—as a liberation of individuals by the collective and an exercise in new political possibilities, rather than some ominous social regression to the pre-individualistic and the repressively archaic: here, for example, the great pre-Stalinist Soviet "cultural revolution" might be appealed to as a powerful ideological counterforce.

But Heilbroner's defense remains useful to the degree to which it stresses the nature of "Utopia" as an alternative social system, rather than the end of all social systems; and underscores the structural necessity for any social system or mode of production to include mechanisms which as it were immunize the existing system of relationships against destructive or radically transformative novelties (thus, for example, a certain—coincidentally anti-Marxist—anthropology took it on itself to demonstrate the ways in which small tribal societies structurally prevent and exclude the accumulation of wealth and the coming into being of power as such and eventually of what will become the state).

In particular, the systemic incompatibility between the market and socialism is here presupposed, and was surely confirmed by the destructiveness of the market in Eastern Europe, not merely in the disintegration of social relationships after the collapse of the communist state, but also in the superstructural corruption by commodity fantasies and Western mass culture that preceded that collapse and prepared it. Polyani's strictures on the catastrophic effects of the market can thus today be enlarged to include the devastation of consumerism and of the social and cultural habits of commodification, all of which no doubt presupposes the necessity for any socialist system to generate a culture which somehow neutralizes those influences, but which does so in a vital and positive way, as a collective choice rather than a regime of censorship and secession. At the same time it should be stressed that the violence and physical repression to be observed in the history of the no longer actually existing socialisms (and in particular the communist states as such) were always the response to genuine threats from the outside, to right-wing hostility and violence, and to internal and external kinds of subversion (of which the US blockade of Cuba still offers a vivid illustration).

Philosophically, the point to be made against the Right is that the "freedom of choice" of consumer goods (in any case greatly exaggerated by the celebrants of a "flexible" and "post-Fordist" dispensation) is scarcely the same thing as the freedom of human beings to control their own destinies and to play an active part in shaping their collective life, that is to say, to wrest their collective future away from the blind necessities of history and its determinisms: surrender to the famous "market mechanisms" of the invisible hand is in this sense the abdication of the challenges of human freedom, rather than some admirable exercise of human powers (the whole issue then becoming trivialized by the realization that such an ideal and idealized free market has never existed anywhere in history and is not likely to do so).

All of which takes a somewhat different turn when it is rephrased in the theological or metaphysical terms of a Niebuhr-like original sin, or a *hybris* of the kind Edmund Burke attributed to the Jacobin project: here human nature is itself indicted, along with the perniciousness of the Utopian as such. It is a language which seems to have caught on in the former East, where post-socialist intellectuals have imputed the destructiveness of everything political from Bolshevism to Stalin himself to the evils of a Utopian will to transform society; unfortunately, the decision to stop willing such transformations merely amounts to passing the decision-making power on to someone else (nowadays generally a foreigner). As for the conviction about the sinfulness of human nature, and although it might well seem to be a demonstrable empirical fact that human animals are naturally vicious and violent and that nothing good can come of them, it also might be well to remind ourselves that that is an ideology too (and a peculiarly moralizing and religious one at that). The fact that cooperation and the achievement of a collective ethos are at best fragile achievements, at once subject to the lures of private consumption and greed and the destabilizations of cynical *Realpolitik*, cannot strip them of the honor of having occasionally existed.

Meanwhile, the belated wisdom of a François Furet–like disillusionment expresses itself in the law-and-order ethos of what I am tempted to call neo-Confucianism: the "respect" for even the most unprepossessing authority and the preference for the most disreputable state violence over the most humanly comprehensible forms of chaos and revolt.

Not only does violence always begin on the Right, triggering the infinite chain reaction of counter-violence that makes up so much of recent history; it is important to take into account at least the possibility that the destructive passions of the great right-wing movements, from fascism to nationalism and, beyond it, to ethnic and fundamentalist fanaticisms, are essentially substitutes—not primary desires in themselves—that spring from rage and bitter disappointment at the failures of Utopian aspirations, and from the consequent, and deeply held, conviction that a more genuinely cooperative social order is fundamentally impossible. As substitutes, in other words, they reflect the situation in which, for whatever reason, revolution itself seems to have failed; and this is the moment to turn to that related, but distinct, topic.

3.

For the critique of the very concept of revolution is virtually the centerpiece of most recent post-Marxisms (as it already was in Bernstein), and this for theoretical as well as for political reasons. I will assume, perhaps unjustly, that political reasons most often motivate the philosophical debates around this question—those that swirl around the concepts of totality and telos, around notions of the centered and decentered subject, around history and narrative, skepticism and relativism or political "belief" and commitment, around the Nietzschean perpetual present and the possibility of thinking radical alternatives (it being understood that the more visceral and ideological motivations of such philosophical choices do not exclude the necessity of arguing them on a purely philosophical basis as well). I believe that the concept of revolution has two somewhat different implications, both of which are worth preserving, particularly under current circumstances. The first implication has to do with the nature of social change itself, which I will argue to be necessarily systemic; the other implication has to do with the way in which collective decision-making is to be conceived.

But this kind of discussion cannot begin to make headway until we disentangle from the conceptual questions the encumberment of representation and image with which they are so often invested. This involves not merely the unwanted "persistence of vision" of stereotypical older pictures of revolutions that took place in the earliest stages of modernization, let alone in the transition out of feudalism itself: which is not to say that the histories of such revolutions, from the great French Revolution itself to its English predecessor (or even from the Hussites or the peasant wars, let alone from the Spartacus uprising) all the way to the Chinese and the Cuban revolutions, are without important historical and dialectical lessons, besides offering stirring narratives still more interesting than most countries' history books, let alone their novels. Nor is it only a matter of the obvious, namely that radical social transformation in conditions of more complete modernization (not to speak of postmodernization) will necessarily raise very different problems and generate very different kinds of collective activity. Rather, we need to do without these images because of the ways they constrict the political imagination, and encourage the illicit reasoning that consists in discrediting the concept of revolution on the grounds that, for example, the postmodern city, or rather the communicational sprawl of the post-city, renders the agency of street mobs inoperable for strategic political and revolutionary intervention. In fact, however, it is the image of the mob itself which is ideological, extending back at least as far as the great revolutionary "days" of the French Revolution, and rehearsed like a nightmare in virtually all the great bourgeois novelists of the subsequent century, from Manzoni to Zola, from Dickens to Dreiser, where the reader can sometimes feel that anxieties about property and about the well-nigh physical violations of intimacy are being exploited and abused for essentially political purposes, in order to show what monstrous things happen when social control is relaxed or weakened. But if this is the case, then it seems particularly important that any serious reflection about the concept of revolution rid itself of such pernicious ideological imagery.

In fact, here too we observe what was already noticed above, namely the persistence of political anxieties—better still, the persistence of the motif of power—in such arguments. Even when not stigmatized as such (for instance, in the more philosophical analyses, such as those, most subtly of all, developed by Laclau and Mouffe, and following them, by most so-called post-Marxists), what is always at the bottom of the quarrel about the term is the conception of revolution as violent, as a matter of armed struggle, forceful overthrow, the clash of weapons wielded by people willing to shed blood. This conception explains in turn the appeal of what may be called demotic Trotskyism, that is, the insistence on adding the requirement of "armed struggle" to whatever socialist proviso is at issue: something that would seem both to substitute effect for cause and unnecessarily to raise the ante on salvation. Rather, this proposition needs to be argued the other way around: namely that the other side will resort to force when the system is threatened in genuinely basic or fundamental ways, so that the possibility of violence becomes something like the test of the authenticity of a given "revolutionary" movement seen retroactively, by Hegel's owl of Minerva or Benjamin's angel of History (they are in fact the same being under different disguises). This involves something like the paradoxes of predestination and election in theology: to choose violence is the outward sign and it always comes afterwards, it cannot be reckoned on in advance, as when social democracy cautiously plots a course calculated to offend no one. But if the course arrives at a genuine systemic change, then resistance necessarily occurs, virtually by definition, but not because the planners wanted it that way. So a peculiar politico-economic Heisenberg principle is at work here (as in Weinstein's critique of left-wing American strategies, touched on above): we seem incapable of grasping diachronic change except through our synchronic and systemic lenses; history has always happened already; class realities, only detectable in hindsight, cannot be second-guessed.

The attempt to think revolution (or to "refute" it) thus necessarily involves two kinds of issues: that of system and that of class (Marx himself having been the theoretician who combined them).

The argument about system, namely, that everything in society is ultimately connected to everything else, and that in the long run it is impossible to achieve the most minimal reforms without first changing everything—this argument has most often philosophically been conducted around the much-stigmatized notion of totality. Those long-dead philosophical intellectuals for whom the concepts of system and totality were conquests and fundamental weapons against the trivialities of empiricism and positivism and the degradation of the rational into commercial and pragmatic reifications would have been astonished by the latter-day transmogrification of these same quite unphilosophical empirical and anti-systemic positivist attitudes and opinions into heroic forms of resistance to metaphysics and Utopian tyranny; in short, to the State itself. "Waging war on totality" seems somewhat misplaced when it is a question of intellectual systems (such as Marxism) for which the very representation of the social totality is itself fundamentally problematic: the imperative to totalize and to achieve a representation of totality by way of the very dilemma of representation itself—this process seems less plausibly characterized as totalitarian than the specific party structure and mass politics such critics also have in mind.

At any rate, it may be enough in the present context to insist on the derivation of the concept of a totality or a system from practical, social, and political experiences that are not so often discussed in this connection. For the notion of a social system is above all suggested by the incompatibility between various kinds of social motives or values, and in particular between a logic of profit and a will to cooperation. The one, indeed, tends to drive the other out; something that makes even the most carefully controlled "mixed economy" a problematic matter. This can also be said the other way around, by stressing the immense moral and collective fervor that has to be mobilized in order to achieve, not merely fundamental social change, but the social construction of new collective forms of production. Such moral and political passion—singularly difficult to sustain under any circumstances, and corresponding to what we have called the ideal of socialism, as opposed to its immediate, local tasks—is itself profoundly incompatible with the profit motive and the other values associated with it. These basic incompatibilities are what first and foremost suggest that a system, a totality, or a mode of production is a relatively unified and homogeneous things that cannot long coexist with systems or modes of a different kind. The concept of revolution is then given with this particular reading of history; entailed by the very concept of system itself, it designates the process, untheorizable in advance, whereby one system (or "mode of production") finally replaces another one.

But it is perhaps the very structure of this concept which interferes with its representation, and continues to generate those outmoded images of the revolutionary "seizure of power" we have already complained of, while instituting a new binary opposition or aporia in its turn, namely the antithesis of the democratic and the electoral path to power (it should be added that today, no one seems to believe in the latter any more than they do the former). But we have other and different examples of what a revolution might look like that transcends this kind of opposition: Allende's Chile comes to mind, and it is time to rescue this historical experiment from the pathos of defeat and the instinctive libidinal anxieties about repression. It is also the moment to take the point of the post-Marxists about the falseness of the conception of the "instant" or "moment" ("revolutionary" or otherwise), but to complain about their omission of "process" in favor of some Nietzschean infinite stream of heterogeneous time. Left electoral victories are neither hollow social-democratic exercises nor occasions in which power passes hands definitively: rather, they are signals for the gradual unfolding of democratic demands, that is to say, increasingly radical claims on a sympathetic government which must now, in obedience to that development, be radicalized in its turn, unless it sells out to the appeal for order. The revolutionary process in this sense is a new legal dispensation in which repressed popular groups slowly emerge from the silence of their subalternity and dare to speak out—an act which can range, as in Allende's revolutionary Chile, from the proposal of new kinds of laws to the seizure of farm lands; democracy necessarily means that kind of speaking out, which can also be identified as the truest form of the production of new needs (as opposed to consumerism). It is then clearly an immensely disorderly process which threatens to overwhelm control in all directions and generates the kinds of political fears we have already commented on (and of which the fate of Allende's regime is a grisly illustration). But it is a process thoroughly consistent with democracy as such (as opposed to republican institutions), in terms of which all the great revolutions can be rewritten.

As questionable as such notions of systematicity may be on the Left today, it is worth observing that they have long since become acquired wisdom on the Right, with its eye on the so-called transition to capitalism. For the market propagandists have themselves insisted over and over again on the incompatibility of the market system as such with either residual or emergent features of other, different socioeconomic systems. It is not necessary to refer to the agonies of "deregulation" in the former socialist countries: one has merely to remember the unremitting pressure the United States has brought—on Canada, to do away with socialized medicine; on Japan and France, to do away with farm supports; on Europe in general, to do away with the "unfair competition" of government welfare structures; and on virtually everyone to do away with the protection of national forms of cultural production—in order to get a vivid picture of the way in which a "purer" market system must necessarily seek to eliminate everything that is other than itself in order to continue to function. Surely such demands, which have in actual practice been pursued by US foreign policy everywhere since the end of World War II, before reaching their paroxysm in the Reagan and NAFTA/GATT years, persuasively infer the very same essentially systemic conception of a society or a mode of production that is normally associated with the ideologically rather different ones of revolution and of totalization.

Perhaps this merely suggests the Utopian nature of standard market rhetoric as well: which is no doubt the case if it simply means that the market, as evoked in current conservative and media usage, never existed and never will. On the other hand, the consequences of the systematic are real enough; and I think of that story Joel Chandler Harris tells about a sufferer who met the most amazing difficulties in getting his raging tooth extracted. The barber tried, the blacksmith tried: finally an enterprising dentist of a new type, with all kinds of new equipment, managed to get purchase on the offending molar—which, however, attached to the jawbone, and then to the backbone, rib cage, pelvis, and tibia, finally proved to be hooked onto the big toe; so that by the time they got the tooth out, the whole skeleton came with it and the patient had to be sent home in a pillowcase. Some fore-knowledge of the social anatomy might well help us avoid this unhappy fate (which might well serve as the allegory of Reaganite deregulation).

The other implication of the concept of revolution can be glossed more rapidly, for it simply takes the revolutionary process as a whole as the con-densed figure for the recovery, by the social collective, of the very possibility of praxis, of collective decision-making, self-formation, and the choosing of a relationship to nature. Revolution in this sense is the moment in which the collective takes back into its own hands a popular sovereignty (which it may in fact never have enjoyed or exercised in historical reality), in which people recover a capacity to change their own destiny and thereby to win some measure of control over their collective history. But to put it this way is at once to understand why the concept of revolution has fallen on hard times today, for—as has already been observed—there have been few moments of modern social history in which people in general have felt more powerless: few moments in which the complexity of the social order can have seemed so forbidding and so inaccessible, and in which existent society, at the same time that it is seized in ever swifter change, has seemed endowed with such massive permanence.

Indeed, it has been argued that it is precisely this quantum leap in systematicity in the postmodern, or in late capitalism—an intensification marked somehow as scientific and technological, and imputed to cybernetic processes—that has rendered the scale of human agency, whether individual or collective, derisory: it seems more prudent, however, to retain the feature of scale and to bracket the issue of technology itself. For it is also plausible that such confusion and the feelings of helplessness it inspires (along with the consequent of the paralysis of action, the apathy of those concerned, the cynicism of leaders and followers alike) are themselves a function of the con-vulsive expansion of the system, which now confronts us with new measures and quantities to which no one has yet adjusted, and with new geographical processes (and temporal ones too, insofar as time today is spatial and some new informational simultaneity has to be reckoned back into our categories of the degree and the interval) for which we have not yet grown organs.

One of the most striking results of the new scale onto which the system has been projected is the inadequacy of previous categories of agency, and in particular the perception that the notion of social classes is outmoded, or indeed that class in the older (Marxian) sense has ceased to be relevant, if it has not disappeared altogether. This perception thus already conflates the distinct levels of theory and empirical sociology, and requires a more complicated answer, in which the empirical is easier to dispose of (although not for all that particularly gratifying). Globalization, which has spelled the crisis in national production, and thereby in the institutions of a shrinking national workforce, can be expected to bring into being international forms of production with the corresponding class relations, yet on a scale so far unimaginable to us, whose forms cannot be deduced in advance, and whose political possibilities cannot yet be predicted, let alone computed. It is necessary to insist both on the inevitability of this new process of global class formation and also on the representational dilemmas with which it presently confronts us: not only is the geological tempo of such class formation imperceptible to organisms condemned to human time (as has been said, we exist simultaneously in both these incommensurable temporal dimensions, which do not often communicate with one another); but the schematisms whereby we might begin to map this inaccessible reality (comparable to the problems raised by the passage from a limited or perceptual segment of heavenly space to cosmologies so immense as to escape our mental categories) have also not yet been determined.

Indeed, newer categories of representation (or renewed and transformed categories of representation that have fallen into disrepute)—in particular everything clustering around the problem of allegory and implying multidimensional forms of unconscious signification—may serve to document this claim and to testify to the pressure now being exerted on what were formerly common-sense figures for the larger realities. However, at a moment in which international business is in the process of reorganizing itself and developing new relationships across the former national boundaries, and while the technologies of contact, exchange, and network-creation have begun to impose their own inevitability, with all kinds of unexpected consequences, it would be surprising indeed if wage workers from different national zones of the world economy were unable to develop new and original ways of reasserting their own interests. Yet to invoke the future in this way (although in this instance it offers no grounds for facile optimism) is also unreasonable, in a situation in which postmodernity also means an imprisonment in the system of a present of time from which the narrative categories of change seem excluded. Meanwhile, the deterioration of the national factory work-force has given way to the emergence of masses of unemployed people, who have now come to seem more plausible agents of political action (or "subjects of history"), and whose new dynamics are registered in the emergence of the radical new categories of marginality and subalternity. Yet all the inherited wisdom about political organization was acquired on the basis of wage work and the spatial advantages it presents, which are not available in the situation of the unemployed (save in such special cases as involve squatters and *bidonvilles* or tent cities).

The question of class is so often taken to be the central practical objection made to Marxism today that it is worth adding a few more remarks. They would have to begin with the reminder that the alleged incompatibility between a class politics and the priorities of the "new social movements" reflects a very American perspective indeed, insofar as race (and today gender) have always seemed to loom larger than class in the US experience, where sectarianism and the tendential and inevitable fragmentation of larger political movements have each been as American an impulse as religious fundamentalism and anti-intellectualism, if not violence and apple pie. It should also be added that few Marxists in recent times have ever believed that industrial factory workers could come to constitute a numerical majority of the population of advanced and differentiated modern societies: this is why left politics in the twentieth century has consistently taken the form of an alliance politics (no matter how heavy-handed such programs have been, or how fraudulent the regimes that claimed to embody such alliances were in practice). Gramsci's remains the most usable form of such theorization today; which does not exclude a certain general propensity within Marxisms of the modern period towards a workerism whose unspoken presupposition (spelled out by Sartre and Brecht, for example) lies in the feeling that people who work with machines have a different kind of intelligence of the world and a different relationship to action and to praxis than other classes.

But all this still amounts to treating "class" as the badge of one group of individuals, who line up to be counted across the room from those other groups of individuals wearing badges that read "race" or "gender" (or perhaps "friends of the earth"). What needs to be argued is the difference in conceptual status between the idea of social class and that of race or gender: and this means something more than the evident fact—often triumphantly produced in evidence against it—that the category of class is a universalizing one and a form of abstraction capable of transcending individuality and particularity in a more successful and also more productive way (insofar as the upshot of that transcendence is envisioned to be the abolition of the category itself). In this sense, class is often supposed to be an "ontological" category like "matter" or "materialism," which implies and perpetuates the error of substance and substantiality (of truth, presence, etc.). In fact, the "truth" of the concept of class (to speak like the Hegelians) lies rather in the operations to which it gives rise: class analysis, like materialist demystification, remains valid and indispensable even in the absence of the possibility of a coherent "philosophy" or ontology of class itself.

It would however be equally important to show how what is sometimes over simply called class consciousness is as internally conflicted as categories like race and gender: class consciousness turns first and foremost around subalternity, that is around the experience of inferiority. This means that the "lower classes" carry about within their heads unconscious convictions as to the superiority of hegemonic or ruling-class expressions and values, which they equally transgress and repudiate in ritualistic (and socially and politically ineffective) ways. Few countries are as saturated with undisguised class content as the United States, owing to the absence here of any intermediary or residual aristocratic level (whose dynamics can thus, as in Europe, overlay the modern class oppositions and to a certain degree disguise and displace or even defuse those): all points in which the classes come into public contact in the US, as in sports, for example, are the space of open and violent class antagonisms, and these equally saturate the other relations of gender, race, and ethnicity, whose content is symbolically invested in class dynamics and which express themselves as through a class apparatus when they are not themselves the vehicles for the expression of class dynamics as such. Yet it is very precisely just such internalized binary oppositions (for class relations are binary and tend to reorganize the other collective symbolic relationships such as race and ethnicity into binary forms as well) which ought to render such phenomena privileged spaces for detecting multiple identities and internal differences and differentiations. It should also be noted that everything that can be said in this respect about subalternity holds for hegemonic or ruling-class consciousness itself, which bears within itself the fears and anxieties raised by the internalized presence of the under-classes and symbolically acts out what might be called an "incorporation" of those dangers and class hostilities (not to speak of class guilt) which are built into the very structure of ruling class consciousness as a defensive response to them.

Finally, it should be stressed that class investments operate according to a formal, rather than a content-oriented, dynamic: it is according to a binary system that phenomena become assimilated to the fundamental play of class antagonisms. Thus, to take a now classic example, the electoral struggle between Kennedy and Nixon in the early 1960s was strongly coded according to class: yet paradoxically it was Kennedy, the liberal figure, whom the American masses consciously or unconsciously perceived as upper class, owing to his wealth and his Harvard education, while Nixon, who clearly suffered the inferiorities and "stigmas" of a petty bourgeois class background, became at once translated into a representative of the lower classes. Yet other oppositions, drawn from all the ranges of social experience, become recoded in much the same way: thus, in the modern period, the opposition between mass culture and high art acquires a very obvious class symbolism in the United States, despite the oppositional and anti-bourgeois stance of "high art" in Europe; while with the arrival of theory and nascent postmodernity, it is theory which comes to be coded as foreign and thereby upper class, while "true" creative literature—including both "creative writing" and commercial television culture—is rewritten as a populist ethos.

Class is thus both an ongoing social reality and an active component of the social imaginary, where, with post–Cold War globalization, it can currently be seen to inform our various (mostly unconscious or implicit) maps of the world system. As a dichotomous phenomenon (there are only two fundamental classes in every mode of production), it is able to absorb and refract gender connotations and oppositions (along with racial ones); at the same time it is itself concealed and complexified by the survival of older residual class images and attitudes, aristocratic or (more rarely) peasant components intervening to distort and enrich the picture, so that Europe and Japan can be coded as aristocratic in the face of a plebeian US, while the Third World is joined by Eastern Europe as a generally subaltern area (in which the distinction between working class and peasant is blurred by notions like "underdeveloped," which do not articulate the surplus value transferred from Third to First Worlds over the course of history). As soon as the focus changes from a world system to a regional one—Europe or the Middle East, for example—suddenly the class map is rearticulated in new ways, just as it would be even further if the frame were that of a single nation-state with its internal class oppositions. The point to be made is not, however, that all such class mappings are arbitrary and somehow subjective; but that they are inevitable allegorical grids through which we necessarily read the world, and also that they are structural systems in which all the elements or essential components determine each other and must be read off and defined against each other. This was of course most notably the case with the original dichotomous opposition itself, whose historical emergence in capitalism has been shown to involve a constant process whereby a working class becomes aware of itself in the face of business repression, while the ruling class is also forced into an ever greater self-definition and organization by the demands and the threats of a labor movement. This means in effect that each of the opposing classes necessarily carries the other around in its head and is internally torn and conflicted by a foreign body it cannot exorcise.

But if we can accustom ourselves to thinking of class as a category (rather than as an empirical property, like a birth certificate or property statement), then perhaps it will prove more natural to think of class as always being contingent and embodied, as always necessarily having to realize and specify itself by way of the categories of gender and race. It is this increasing sense of the need to grasp such categories as a triangulation that accounts for the recent fortunes of such terms and concepts as "articulation," concepts which do not supply instant recipes for alliance building, but at least impose a requirement to make a complete circuit on the occasion of any local analysis, and to make sure that none of these categories is omitted, of which it can safely be said that when you forget any one of them, it does not fail to remember you. But in the United States it is the category of class that is the most likely to be neglected: so that it has celebrated its own kind of "return of the repressed" in the ways in which the various new social movements have all in their different fashions run into trouble on the invisible and subterranean realities of class conflict. Perhaps it is appropriate to conclude this section by observing that class is also that analytic category which makes it most difficult to avoid grasping the social as a systemic entity which can only be changed in a radical and systemic way.

4.

As for communism, what needs to be affirmed is that the recent developments (which spelled the demise of so many of the regimes that bore that name) are due, not to its failure, but to its success, at least as far as modernization is concerned. Left-wing economists are by no means the only ones who have sung the praises of Marxism-Leninism (about which it will have become clear that I here distinguish it sharply from Marxism as such) as a vehicle for modernization: one can even find editors of *The Economist* who have saluted the one-party state as a useful path towards the rapid industrialization of underdeveloped societies (particularly in Africa). This makes it all the more amusing to hear the day's more reactionary revisionist historians regret the heights of productivity that Russia would more peacefully have been able to reach had the liberals remained in power; let alone to watch them point to the prosperity of Taiwan today as proof of the superiority of Chiang Kai-shek's economics over that of his mainland rivals. The fact is that Stalin modernized the Soviet Union, at a tremendous cost, transforming a peasant society into an industrial state with a literate population and a remarkable scientific superstructure. Stalinism was thus a success and fulfilled its historic mission, socially as well as economically, and it is idle to speculate whether this could have happened in some more normal, peaceful, evolutionary way. For the crucial distinction remains, namely that Soviet communism was a modernization strategy which (unlike Japanese state capitalism, for example) used a variety of socialist methods and institutions. Its use of those institutions, its deployment of socialist rhetoric and values, indeed its very origins in a very different and surely proto-socialist revolution, had the result of developing some aspects of a socialist life world as a byproduct and also of representing the embodiment of socialist hopes and values to the outside world for an extended period. But one wishes today, particularly where modernism is complete or where it is no longer on the agenda, to insist on the radical differences between socialism, which Marx and Engels expected to develop, at the end of capitalism, out of a regime of high industrial productivity, and the heroic and grisly, thrilling and horrifying saga of the forced modernization of that particular Third World country.

At any rate, it is rather the collapse of this system that now needs to be addressed: to be explained precisely in terms of its success (rather than in terms of hidden flaws and weaknesses) and in a way that documents the continuing explanatory powers of Marxian theory in a situation which has often been taken to discredit it. Once again, it will be the prodigious expansion of the capitalist system, the "scaling" upwards of its global reach into a new and more intensive kind of international relationality, that provides the most satisfying account of the Soviet Union. It is an account that does not exactly function in terms of the competition between the two "systems," although it must certainly draw attention to the enthusiasm with which the Soviet leaders of the "period of stagnation" sought to attach themselves ever more closely to the emergent new world system, in part in order to borrow heavily and to consume ever more of the West's attractive (and essentially high-tech and communicational or informational) products.

Meanwhile, I believe that competition in defense spending, and the tactic whereby the Reagan administration led the Soviet Union on into ever greater military outlays beyond its own means—to which the Soviet collapse is most often attributed—is also to be understood in this fashion as yet another form of typically Western-style consumption, encouraging the emergence of the Soviet state from the shelter of its own system in a misguided (although perfectly comprehensible) attempt at the emulation of products for which it had no economic or systemic need (unlike the Americans, whose postwar prosperity has largely depended on just such state-military spending). Of course, counterrevolutionary strategy has often involved just such long-term systemic threats which transform democratic revolutions into states of siege, including ever larger surveillance and police activity and the classic development of the Terror, as can be observed at least as far back as the French Revolution. But the unique timing of this particular effort, at the watershed between modern and postmodern production, determined a kind of cooptation, a transfer of values and habits of consumption, unusually destructive to such revolutionary institutions as still subsisted. This also suggests a significant cultural dimension of the process, to which we will return later on.

But systemic interrelationship is a two-way street, and many are the cybernetic images of what you lay yourself open to when you link up to an external network. I myself prefer figures of high pressure: by way of the Debt and developing commercial coexistence, the Soviet Union, hitherto isolated in its own specific pressure area as under some ideological and socioeconomic geodesic dome, now began imprudently to open the airlocks without its space suit on, and to allow itself and its institutions to be subjected to the infinitely more intense pressures characteristic of the world outside. The result can be imagined as comparable to what the sheer blast pressures did to the flimsy structures in the immediate vicinity of the first atomic bomb; or to the grotesque and deforming effects of the enormous weight of water pressure at the bottom of the sea on unprotected organisms evolved for the upper air. These figures are to be understood, less in sheer physical ways as characterizing the punctual impact of late capitalism on this or that individual form, than rather as systemic vulnerability: the exposure to a wholly different dynamic and as it were a different set of physical and natural laws altogether.

Three examples of just such systemic incompatibilities can be found in the phenomenon of the national debt, and in the dominant imperatives of efficiency and productivity. The Debt, to be sure, comes in two forms, one of which, seen from the outside, can be witnessed in the catastrophe of the Third World countries; the other, more internal, seems to turn rather on the national budget. The politics of the latter is of course complicated by an Imaginary that solicits the assimilation of governmental priorities to people's individual handling of their own private incomes—a highly psychoanalytic matter whose analogies do not particularly make for rational thinking about the national debt itself, about which Heilbroner has tried to explain that it would be a disaster to "pay it off" and that it is misguided and bad politics to think of the matter in these terms. What seems to be at stake in these arcane discussions is essentially the credit of a given nation-state, that is to say, the way in which other nations assess its economic viabilities. That is obviously a very important consideration when it comes to borrowing on the outside, or securing foreign capital investment; but older values of autarchy (and not only Stalinist versions of those) put a premium on avoiding that kind of financial dependence in the first place. It has been said repeatedly that national autonomy of this kind is no longer possible; it is certainly obvious that it is not possible to retain autonomy if you are eager, on the other side, to be a part of the transnational system as it functions today; and Cuba and North Korea are supposed to demonstrate the unviability of trying to go it alone. If, on the other hand, you imagined that autonomy, or in other words resistance to various binding norms of late-capitalist economic practice, might under certain circumstances be a matter of national pride, then a convenient rhetoric lies to hand in which nationalism is itself denounced as a barbarous collective fantasy and the source of unmitigated violence (at this point, somehow the phenomena of the national and the ethnic suddenly find themselves inextricably identified and conflated). At any rate the loss of national autonomy, whether deliberate or not, has the immediate effect of subjecting the nation-state to external financial regulation, at the same time that the Debt does not vanish along with the communist regimes that first began to accumulate it.

"Efficiency" is yet another of those international norms that may not have been particularly relevant for countries operating on other principles; the reproach of inefficiency—archaic factories, ancient cumbersome technology, wasteful production methods—is of course a favorite one with which to beat the (now expired) Soviet donkey, and it has the advantage of implying a much simpler historical lesson than the one elaborated here, namely that the Soviets "lost" because their production was shoddy and unable to stand comparison with our own (and, as a bonus in the form of a secondary ideological conclusion, because socialism is itself fundamentally inefficient). But we have just shown that such comparisons or competitions were far from being relevant as such and in themselves, becoming operative only at the moment in which the Soviets decided to join the world market. (As suggested above, warfare, whether it be Hitler's against Stalin, or the Americans in the Cold War, imposes its own kind of forced competition; the race in defense spending can thus be seen as a way of forcing the Russians to join the world system.)

But initially efficiency is not an absolute but a priority which may well sometimes take second place to other, no less rational considerations. Indeed, Sweezy and Magdoff showed years ago, about both the Chinese and Cuban revolutions, that in the construction of socialism, industrial production could also be thought of as a form of collective pedagogy: not merely the reeducation in practice of peasants, whose mentalities are to be modified by the enlarged literacy of the machine itself, but also the political education of factory workers in forms of self-government and *autogestion*. One can imagine that for a social revolution in course (and which had overcome more urgent problems of sheer hunger and misery) those might sometimes be values that override a conception of efficiency whose essential function is the promotion of comparisons between the levels of various kinds of national and international production, and whose relevance is thus ultimately found in the matter of productivity itself.

But productivity, as Marx taught long ago in *Capital*, is itself no timeless absolute against which the individual labor process can be mysteriously evaluated once and for all: it is produced, and indeed produced by the unified market itself, which then allows a standard of comparison to come into play between the various firms, ultimately driving out those that are unable to keep pace with the newer methods. It is in this sense that a shoe factory operating in a perfectly satisfactory way in some isolated village and province whose needs it is there to meet, is suddenly transfixed as a virtually unworkable anachronism when, absorbed by a more unified system, it has to meet the standards of the metropolis. This is the sense in which, on a comparative scale, higher productivity means not only newer machinery, but newer technology, that can compete with the standards set elsewhere: the point is, however, precisely that productivity is a comparative concept and not an absolute one, and that it only makes sense across space, in which different forms of productivity come into contact in the market and can thereby be compared. In such contacts between isolated factories or between whole regions, the boundary of the context is everything, and its opening up can prove disastrous to the more modest but often no less successful operations on the wrong side of the divide.

But all this is precisely what happened to the Soviet Union and its client states when they formed the project of plunging into the capitalist world market and of hitching their star to the newly emergent world system of late capitalism as that has itself taken form in the last twenty years.

We may also want to take into consideration the possibility that this period of stagnation, in which economic corruption and the moral deterioration of the leadership went hand in hand with the loss of political will or ambition, with cynicism and with a generalized feeling of powerlessness, was in fact not restricted to the Soviet Union of the Brezhnev era, but had its equivalents worldwide. What, for example, Hisham Sharabi describes (in his book of the same name) as "neo-patriarchy" in the Arab world seems strictly comparable, as do of course the more fashionable and Western excesses of the Reagan and Thatcher regimes. It would be wrong to think of this universal stagnation (accompanied by stupefying quantities of loose and unproductive riches) as a cyclical matter by virtue of which the political 1960s were succeeded by a new period of unbridled speculation, itself presumably to be replaced by this or that return of government responsibility and state intervention.

Stagnation, at any rate, seems to have coincided with the emergence of the Debt—possibly as its very reason for being—as First World banks began to lend their uninvestable surpluses with abandon to the Second and Third Worlds in the early 1970s; and also with the invention of the word and of the strategy "deregulation" around 1976. But the more fundamental historical question about such a periodization turns on the issue of modernization itself, and what its status might be under what has now widely come to be known as postmodernity.

In the grim and implacably argued work referred to above, Robert Kurz has recently suggested that we link modernization and the modern (or "modernity") together far more inextricably than we have had the habit of doing, and that we draw thereby the ultimate conclusion that it is modernization itself—read: industrialization, the construction of new plants, the setting in place of new productivities—that is over and done with; and that whatever else postmodernity may be, it no longer involves modernization or production in any meaningful sense.

Kurz's book asks us to imagine the extraordinary mobility of what have become unparalleled amounts of capital sloshing around the globe, like water in a basin, at speeds that approach instantaneity as their outer limit. Its touchdown points are governed, however, by the prevailing rates of return, themselves geared and attuned to high-tech industry or postindustrial postmodernity: the most basic laws of capital—indeed its very definition—excluding investments in those older, purely modern forms of productivity that we associate with the old-fashioned industrial age itself. Not only are their rates of profit far lower than what obtains in high-tech, but the velocities of the new international transfers make it much easier for mobile capital to escape these sluggish backwaters of the older factories and to teleport onwards to fancier arrangements. But it was precisely those older forms of modern productivity that underdeveloped countries (and even those now unwillingly underdeveloped parts of the developed or advanced countries) needed in order to "develop" and to "modernize," to endow themselves with a varied infrastructure that might afford a certain industrial autonomy. International capital will no longer tarry for them, or for any modernization in this classical sense. The conjuncture is thus supremely unfavorable, not to say contradictory: for the great majority of Third and former Second World nations, the clock still calls for modernization in an ever more peremptory and urgent fashion; while for capital, moving rapidly from one low-wage situation to the next, only cybernetic technology and postmodern investment opportunities are ultimately attractive. Yet in the new international system, few countries can seal themselves off in order to modernize on their own time and at their leisure: most have already bought into an international circuit of debt and consumption from which they can no longer extricate themselves. Nor is the new cybernetic technology of any immediate use to such developing countries, for social as well as economic reasons: it creates no new jobs or social wealth; it does not even minimally provide import substitutions, let alone a basic national source of ordinary necessities. As Kurz puts it, "remorselessly the law of profitability must sooner or later reassert itself—a law which specifies that only production has market value that corresponds to the international level of productivity today."[1]

This is then the more fundamental meaning of the end of the modern as such: the discovery that modernization is no longer possible for anyone. It is the only possible meaning that postmodernity can have, which is merely trivialized if it is understood to designate nothing more than changes in fashion and in dominant ideas and values. But it was this arid wind of postmodernity that caught the Soviets unaware when they timidly ventured out of "socialism in one country."

Such stories can always be told another way: indeed, it is becoming imperative always to do so, since only a variety of possible narratives can begin to model the "absent cause" that underlies them all and that can never

---

[1] Robert Kurz, *Der Kollaps der Modernisierung*, Leipzig: Reclam, 1994, 196.

be expressed as such. (Nietzschean relativism and fictionality is thus most productively used as a mode of triangulation or of the deployment of parallaxes, rather than as some idle flight from "linear history" or "old-fashioned" notions of causality that are themselves in reality mere narrative forms.)

So an alternative narrative may be sketched in here which underscores the essentially cultural failures of communism: for its propensities to consume, its fascination with Western products of all kinds, but above all with the specific products of the postmodern age (information technology in the most general sense)—these fatal weaknesses, that impelled communism towards the great market of the Western world system, are fundamentally signs of cultural weakness, symptoms of the failure of any specifically socialist collective culture to emerge; or at least to consolidate a mode of daily living and a practice of subjectivity that could both keep pace with Western fashions in these matters and constitute a viable (and systemic) alternative. The prestige of Islam today indeed stems in no small measure from its unique claim to offer such an alternative to Western "culture." But the argument is, to be sure, circular, since this use of culture is so broad as to envelop the hitherto "merely" economic within itself: not only is "entertainment" a basic US industry, but shopping and consumption are fundamental American cultural activities (along with religion). So this chicken is in reality its own egg: and it does not matter much whether the Eastern European "cultural fever" caused them to take the plunge into the Western market or merely served as the symptom that they were in the process of doing so.

Are we then, finally, to consider the disappearance of the Soviet Union a good thing? There are radicals who believe, plausibly enough, that the disappearance of communism will make left politics in the US more viable, if only by cleansing it of the taint of the foreign and the imported, as well as of "tyranny." Such movements for national liberation as still exist in the outside world, meanwhile, must bitterly regret the evaporation of that material aid and support with which (to give them their due) the Soviets were often so generous.

As far as the rest of the world is concerned, not to speak of our own self-knowledge and moral welfare, it does not seem particularly desirable for Yankee hypocrisy and self-righteousness triumphantly to remain alone in the field. We have never had much understanding of genuine cultural difference, particularly as we do not perceive our kind of capitalism and our kind of electoral system to be cultural (rather than simply the most obvious aim and end of all history). Once upon a time, and for whatever reasons of their own, the sheer existence of the Soviets constituted something of a brake on these tendencies, and often allowed this or that collectivity to assert its national identity and independence and to proceed to the rudimentary social revolution still desperately necessary in every country of the globe today. The Iraq War is there to show how we behave when such restraints no longer obtain: nor do Europe or Japan seem likely to be able to assume this role of moral counterweight, since there is a very real question as to whether they still constitute autonomous cultures in their own right or whether Americanization has not eaten away at the very substance of what once seemed primary traditions, albeit in more subtle and imperceptible ways than its dissolution of putatively socialist traditions in the European East.

5.

This now leads us into our final topic (which we have, of course, in reality been discussing all along), namely the nature of late capitalism or the world system today and the place of Marxism within it. It is a question that probably needs to be enlarged by another, more preliminary one—namely, which Marxism?—since few intellectual movements have known quite so many internal schisms. That between a theoretical or highly intellectualized Marxism and a practical or even vulgar, demotic Marxism, for example, is not exactly the same as the opposition between so-called Western Marxism and the much-stigmatized Soviet kind, nor even between Hegel and Marx, or historical materialism and dialectical materialism—but there is certainly some affinity between all these unholy dualisms, whose adherents can often be observed in passionate conflict. Every hyperintellectual or philosophical Marxism ought to carry a vulgar one inside it, Brecht once said: while the very founder of that same Marxism-Leninism that is for most people the purest form of the vulgar doctrine par excellence was once heard to exclaim, "All Marxists should, *ex officio*, constitute a '*société des amis matérialistes de la dialectique hegelienne*'!"

This polarity no doubt betrays the irresolvable slippage, in Marxism as elsewhere, between subject and object, between the irreconcilable starting points of consciousness and of the world. Vulgar Marxism has clearly fared the less well of the two: since its "grand narrative" of the modes of production, and of the transition to socialism, falls under the two-fold verdict leveled, first on narratives as such, and then on socialism in particular. This is not only to point to the void in political praxis left by the crisis of the Communist parties and the abdication of the Socialist ones; but also to designate the very empty place of any vision of History which might inform local and national praxis at the same time that it offers a motivation for theory and analysis in the first place. Into that void, of course, the various Manichaeanisms and their apocalypses have flowed; nor is it improbable that out of their raw materials, some new vision of history may gradually be refashioned: to say that it will necessarily be Marxian in the most general sense is merely to recognize the fact that of all the current competing ideologies only Marxism stubbornly retains its constitutive relationship with History as such, that is to say, with a redemptive vision of the future—without which it must necessarily falter as a political project, but also as a field of scientific research.

The more philosophical or, if you take the worst-case scenario, more academic Marxism has never been more flourishing, as witness the extraordinary richness of contemporary Marxian economics and historiography: somewhat paralyzed, it is true, by their current reluctance to end their narratives on a triumphalist note, with singing futures. If the first, practical Marxism, of labor unions and political parties, was a Marxism of the base, one is tempted to identify this one with the superstructure, provided it is understood, first, that the very opposition stems from "vulgar" or demotic Marxism rather than from its more sophisticated counterpart, and second, that at the heart of all such current theoretical economic and historiographic analyses of capitalism that have just been referred to there dwells a sometimes unspoken premise that the very relationship of superstructure and base has itself been profoundly and structurally modified in late capitalism. This proposes a more paradoxical interrelationship of base and superstructure than had been conceptualized earlier, and thereby produces a demand for more complex theoretical solutions and models; indeed, it implies a whole new theoretical agenda for Marxism about which only a few basic points can be made here. For one thing, these developments—the structural modifications of late capitalism—explain something of a shift in "theoretical Marxism" from philosophy to culture. The philosophical themes that predominated in so-called Western Marxism remain significant ones; above all, the theorization of totality, always correctly perceived by post- and anti-Marxists to be an indispensable feature of the Marxist project—practical as well as theoretical—insofar as it must necessarily grasp capitalism as a system and must thereby insist on the systemic interrelationships of contemporary reality. Of the competing worldviews, presumably only ecology demands totalizing thought in the same way; and we have tried to suggest above that its agenda—as immediate and urgent as it is—necessarily presupposes the socialist one.

But even the vulgar repudiation of totalization in social and cultural terms—it means "totalitarianism," or the primacy of the intellectual over the people, or a single political party in which all differences are suppressed, or male universalism over the various localisms, or class politics over gender and race, etc.—betrays a weakening of conceptual thought and its supersession by various kinds of knee-jerk doxa that are essentially cultural in origin. Meanwhile some of the other great polemic spaces of the preceding period—structural causality, ideology, the waning of the negative, the relationship to psychoanalysis, and the like—can today better be appreciated as essentially cultural problems. Marxism traditionally made a place for these issues, but it can in hindsight be seen to be a relatively restricted and specialized place, which can perhaps best be initially identified as so-called reification theory, or the analysis of commodification and commodity fetishism. What needs to be suggested in conclusion, therefore, is that this hitherto minor preoccupation will in the immediate future, in the force field of late capitalism, become the primary focus of theoretical Marxism as such.

It is perhaps worthwhile to consider the relationship of commodity theory to practical politics, and in particular the advantages of the Marxian analysis of late capitalism over its liberal and conservative rivals. For the critique of commodification is surely the central issue in any examination of what is original about late capitalism and also in any analysis of the political and social issues that seem most hotly debated in it. What then becomes clear is that most political critiques of consumption in late capitalism—which pass insensibly over into a critique of American society as a whole—tend fatally to mobilize an ethical or a moralizing rhetoric and make judgments which are inseparable from such stances. But surely it is a rhetoric which is singularly ill suited to the kind of society this has become, a society in which religion has been trivialized into an ethnic badge or a hobby of small subgroups, while moralism is at best a harmless generational tic and at worst a matter of *ressentiment* and historical bitterness; as for great prophecy, were such a thing still conceivable, it could only take the form, today, of crank oratory or mental aberration. (Indeed, the return of ethics as a philosophical subdiscipline and its subsequent colonization of political philosophy is one of the most regressive features and symptoms of the ideological climate of postmodernity.)

It seems appropriate, therefore, to exclude moralizing positions on consumption from the outset, for practical-political as well as philosophical reasons. Such ethical mobilizations as have been successful in the US in recent years have taken xenophobic or racist forms and have been accompanied by other reflexes that only too obviously betray the deeper fears and anxieties of the white majority. Only in historically oppositional subgroups, such as the black community, has righteous moral indignation transmitted the great political message of a call for universal justice (for values can only be grounded in the "social equivalent" of lived collectivities). What remains of those ethico-political "grand narratives" on the secular or liberal Left is as shrunken as the "political correctness" as which the majority caricatures it. But religion itself today is effective only when (following its etymology) it can express and coordinate a group experience that under present circumstances necessarily risks becoming parochial and exclusionary or sectarian, rather than universal.

There is a second version of the moralizing or religious critique of consumer society whose replication of the latter's philosophical flaws and political weaknesses may well be less evident: this is what may be called variously the psychological or the culturalist critique. In this form a steady stream of books and articles on "American life" issue forth which, energetically essentializing their subject matter, are intellectually incapable of grappling with consumerism as a socioeconomic process or of evaluating it as an ideological practice. Durkheim's principle still articulates the fundamental philosophical objection to such thinking, namely that whenever we confront a psychological explanation for a social fact, we may be sure that it is wrong. It is axiomatic that social facts are of a different order of reality from than the individual data of psychological or existential experience (and we have already observed Marxism to multiply such differentiations on a far greater scale, in its systematic distinction of the economic from the political, and of both from the social and the psychic, all of which are governed by their own semi-autonomous laws and evolve at distinct rates on very different planes from each other). At any rate, to deploy the categories of individual and existential experience for the understanding of social phenomena—whether such categories are put to moralizing or psychologizing uses—is to make a fundamental "category mistake" whereby the collective is anthropomorphized and the social allegorized in individual terms.

To characterize the Marxian account of consumerism and commodity fetishism in contrast to this anthropomorphic one as a "structural" explanation may not do justice to the implications of dialectical explanations as such, but it at least serves to emphasize the way in which consumption is here grasped as an objective and impersonal process, one structurally indispensable to capitalism itself, and which cannot simply be diminished, let alone omitted, on whatever moral or cosmetic grounds. Such an account would in effect reunite the French and German traditions, and incorporate the work of the Frankfurt School on reification and commodity fetishism into a post-Althusserian perspective which no longer seeks to bracket such seemingly existential and experiential materials, which are however objects just as real, just as objective and historical, as the various disciplinary and institutional levels to which Althusser tended to oppose them.

The advantage today in beginning with the functional role commodity fetishism plays in late capitalism as a system lies not only in the way in which it allows us to distinguish this description of postmodernity from the other, mainly culturalist and moralizing, versions; but also in the historic originality it attributes to this kind of society as such. There is certainly an ethical dimension to this analysis, but it takes the complex and dialectical form of the evocation of capitalism in general in the *Manifesto*, where the latter's simultaneously destructive and progressive features are celebrated, and its simultaneous capacity for liberation as well as for wholesale violence is underscored. Only a dialectical view can do justice to this fundamental ambiguity or ambivalence, which is far from being mere indeterminacy, and which can be seen to recapitulate itself in the positions on postmodernism and postmodernity today, where it seems simplistic either to welcome the new social pluralism of the postmodern or to regret its apolitical one-dimensionality in any univocal way. Thus, the fundamental ambivalence of capital has clearly not been modified by its transformation into this third or postmodern stage; and it has seemed to me that only the Marxian dialectic remained capable of thinking the system adequately, without ideological oversimplifications.

The challenge remains to avoid that ethical binary, which is the root form of all ideology: to find a position which neither recapitulates the puritanisms and moralizing denunciations of certain older Marxisms and radicalisms (and not only of them) nor surrenders to the mindless euphorias of a market rhetoric reinforced by high-technological enthusiasms; in short, to try to think a beyond of late capitalism which does not imply a regression to earlier, simpler stages of social development but which posits a future already latent in this present, as Marx did for the capitalism of his day.

Globalization and information technology are indeed the principal novelties of the new "postmodern" stage of capitalism and it is these developments to which Marxism will wish to attach its intellectual and political commitments. It is only from the perspective of the world system as such that reification theory, with its essentially cultural perspective, can be grasped as being at one with the crisis theory of the economists, and the new and permanent structural unemployment understood as an integral part of the totality in which financial speculation and the mass-cultural postmodernities are also inseparable constituents. It is only from such a perspective that new forms of international political praxis can be developed, which promise to grapple with the loss of national autonomy implicit in the new world system and to find ways of drawing strength from the enfeeblement of the national labor movements as well as the rapidity of capital transfers. Nor should the transnational organization of radical intellectuals be omitted here, for its possibilities illustrate the ways in which the new communications systems can be used positively by the Left, fully as much as by the business power structure.

All of which suggests that the age demands a politics of ambivalence or ambiguity (assuming the word "dialectical" is still unfashionable); the emphasis on a great collective project whose focus must be on structural impossibilities, the commitment to a globalization for which the loss of autarchy is a catastrophe, the necessity of a cultural focus to be primarily economic and of economic research to grasp the essentially cultural nature of late capitalism, the mass democratization of the world market by world information technology on the very eve of mass starvation and the permanent downsizing of industrial production as such—these are only some of the paradoxical contradictions and contradictory paradoxes which a "late" or postmodern Marxism must confront and embrace as its destiny.

This will be surprising only for those who thought Marxism was "dead," or imagined it somehow merely to "survive" in vestigial form, as though bereft of the context and the ecosystem in which it once flourished, however minimally. But it seems paradoxical to celebrate the death of Marxism in the same breath with which you greet the ultimate triumph of capitalism. For Marxism is the very science of capitalism; its epistemological vocation lies in its unmatched capacity to describe capitalism's historical originality; its fundamental structural contradictions endow it with its political and its prophetic vocation, which can scarcely be distinguished from the analytic ones. This is why, whatever its other vicissitudes, a postmodern capitalism necessarily calls a postmodern Marxism into existence over against itself.[2]

---

[2] I have summarized the positions of this essay in the form of "Five Theses on Actually Existing Marxism," which are to be found in *Monthly Review*, Vol. 47, Num. 11, 1996, 1–10.

Chapter 16

Utopia as Replication

We ordinarily think of Utopia as a place, or if you like a non-place that looks like a place. How can a place be a method? Such is the conundrum with which I wanted to confront you, and maybe it has an easy answer. If we think of historically new forms of space—historically new forms of the city, for example—they might well offer new models for urbanists and in that sense constitute a kind of method. The first freeways in Los Angeles, for example, project a new system of elevated express highways superimposed on an older system of surface streets: that new structural difference might be thought to be a philosophical concept in its own right, a new one, in terms of which you might want to rethink this or that older urban center, or better still, this or that as yet undeveloped sunbelt agglomeration. For a time then, the Los Angeles concept is modern; whether it is Utopian is another matter altogether, although Los Angeles has also been a Utopia for many different kinds of people over the years. Here is Brecht on Hollywood:

> The village of Hollywood was planned according to the
>   notion
> People in these parts have of heaven. In these parts
> They have come to the conclusion that God
> Requiring a heaven and a hell, didn't need to
> Plan two establishments but
> Just the one: heaven. It
> Serves the unprosperous, unsuccessful
> As hell.[1]

A true dialectic; a true unity of opposites! Will it be possible to untangle the negative from the positive in this particular Utopia, which has perhaps also, like all the other Utopias, never existed in the first place? Something

---

[1] Bertolt Brecht, *Poems 1913–1956*, eds. John Willett and Ralph Manheim, London: Eyre Methuen, 1976, 380.

like this will be our problem here; but we need to work through some further preliminaries before we get that far.

I.

For the hypothetical example of a new kind of city that sets an example for the building or reorganization of other new kinds of cities to come is based on a conviction we may no longer be able to rely on, namely, the belief that progress is possible and that cities, for example, can be improved. What is Utopian is then identified with this now traditional and much-criticized bourgeois idea of progress, and thus implicitly with teleology as such, with the grand narrative and the master plan, with the idea of a better future, a future not only dependent on our own will to bring it into being but also somehow inscribed in the very nature of things, waiting to be set free, lying in the deeper possibilities and potentialities of being, from which at length and with luck it may emerge. But does anyone believe in progress any longer? Even keeping to the realm of the spatial we have taken as an example, are the architects and urbanists still passionately at work on Utopian cities? The Utopian city was surely a staple of modernism: one thinks of everybody from Le Corbusier to Constant, from Rockefeller Center to the great Nazi or Soviet projects.[2] At a lower level, one thinks of urban renewal and of Robert Moses.[3] But modernism is over, and it is my impression that the postmodern city, west or east, north or south, does not encourage thoughts of progress or even improvement, let alone Utopian visions of the older kind; and this for the very good reason that the postmodern city seems to be in permanent crisis, and to be thought of, if at all, as a catastrophe rather than an opportunity. As far as space is concerned, the rich are withdrawing ever more urgently into their gated communities and their fortified enclosures; the middle classes are tirelessly engaged in covering the last vestiges of nature with acres of identical development homes; while the poor, pouring in from the former countryside, swell the makeshift outskirts with a population explosion so irrepressible that in a few years none of the ten largest cities on the globe will include the familiar First World metropolises any longer. Some of the great dystopias of the past—I think of John Brunner's novels from the early 1970s[4]—centered on what was then the alleged nightmare of

---

[2] See, for the canonical account, Sigfried Giedion, *Space, Time and Architecture: The Growth of a New Tradition*, Cambridge, MA: Harvard University Press, 1967.

[3] Robert Caro's biography of Moses, *The Power Broker*, New York: Knopf, 1974, is an indispensable resource.

[4] *Stand on Zanzibar* (1968), *The Jagged Orbit* (1969), *The Sheep Look Up* (1972), *The Shockwave Rider* (1975).

overpopulation; but that was a modernist nightmare, and what we confront today is perhaps not a dystopia either, but rather a certainty lived in a rather different way and with a properly postmodern ambivalence; which at any rate distinctly forecloses the possibility of progress or of solutions.

Indeed, it suffices to think of the four fundamental threats to the survival of the human race today—ecological catastrophe, worldwide poverty and famine, structural unemployment on a global scale, and the seemingly uncontrollable traffic in armaments of all kinds, including smart bombs and unmanned drones (in armaments, along with pharmaceuticals, good and bad, progress does apparently still exist!)—it suffices to think of these four trends alone (leaving pandemics, police states, race wars, and drugs out of the picture) for us to realize that in each of these areas no serious counter-force exists anywhere in the world, and certainly not in the United States, which is itself the cause of most of them.

Under these circumstances, the last gasp of a properly Utopian vision, the last attempt at a Utopian forecast of the future transfigured, was a rather perverse one, I mean so-called free-market fundamentalism as it seized the moment of globalization to predict the rising of all boats and the wonder-working, miraculous powers of worldwide unregulated global markets. But this was a Utopia which, drawing on the unconscious operations of Adam Smith's invisible hand, and in sharp contrast to the hyperconsciousness of the Utopian "intentional community," gambled everything on the uninten-tionality of its universal panacea, for which any number of populations around the globe proved unwilling to wait. Nor did this waning Utopian effort recover much strength by shifting to a different code, from economics to politics, and rebaptizing the freedom of the market as the freedom of democracy. To that degree, as a political slogan, the banner of Utopia has been passed to the critics and the enemies of free-market globalization and has become the unifying rallying cry or "empty signifier"[5] of all those varied new political forces which are trying to imagine how another world might be possible.

Yet an empty signifier seems far enough away from the Utopian visions with which we are familiar from More and Plato on down, and this is proba-bly the right moment to say a word about the long book on Utopias I have just published and of which this essay is something of a reconsideration, if not a supplement. What has tended to perplex readers of this book, *Archaeologies of the Future*,[6] if not to annoy them, is not only the repeated insistence on the form rather than the content of Utopias, something that would on the face of it scarcely be unusual in literary criticism, no matter

---

[5] See Ernesto Laclau and Chantal Mouffe, *Hegemony and Socialist Strategy: Towards a Radical Democratic Politics*, London: Verso, 1985.
[6] London: Verso, 2005.

how deplorable, but also another thesis more likely to catch the unwary reader up short, namely the repeated insistence that what is important in a Utopia is not what can be positively imagined and proposed, but rather what is not imaginable and not conceivable. Utopia, I argue, is not a representation but an operation calculated to disclose the limits of our own imagination of the future, the lines beyond which we do not seem able to go in imagining changes in our own society and world (except in the direction of dystopia and catastrophe). Is this then a failure of imagination, or is it rather simply a fundamental skepticism about the possibilities of change as such, no matter how attractive our visions of what it would be desirable to change into? Do we not here touch on what has come to be called cynical reason, rather than the impoverishment of our own sense of the future, or the waning of the Utopian impulse itself? Cynical reason, as the concept has evolved far beyond what Peter Sloterdijk named so many years ago,[7] can be characterized as something like the inversion of political apathy. It knows everything about our own society, everything that is wrong with late capitalism, all the structural toxicities of the system, and yet it declines indignation, in a kind of impotent lucidity which may not even be bad faith. It cannot be shocked or scandalized, as the privileged were able to be at earlier moments of the market system; nor is the deconcealment of this system, its analysis and functional demonstration in the light of day, any longer effective in compelling critical reactions or motivations. We may say all this in terms of ideology as well: if that word has fallen on hard times, it is perhaps because in a sense there is no longer any false consciousness, no longer any need to disguise the workings of the system and its various programs in terms of idealistic or altruistic rationalizations; so that the unmasking of those rationalizations, the primordial gesture of debunking and of exposure, no longer seems necessary.

The waning of Utopias is thus a conjuncture between all these developments: a weakening of historicity or of the sense of the future; a conviction that no fundamental change is any longer possible, however desirable; and cynical reason as such. To which we might add that it is the sheer power of excess money accumulated since the last great world war, which keeps the system in place everywhere, reinforcing its institutions and its armed forces. Or maybe we should also adduce yet a different kind of factor, one of psychological conditioning—namely that omnipresent consumerism which, having become an end in itself, is transforming the daily life of the advanced countries in such a way as to suggest that the Utopianism of multiple desires and consumption is here already and needs no further supplement.

---

[7] Peter Sloterdijk, *Critique of Cynical Reason*, Minneapolis: University of Minnesota Press, 1987.

So much for the limits on our capacity to imagine Utopia as such, and for what it tells us about a present in which we cannot any longer envision that future. But it would clearly be wrong to say that the representational Utopia has everywhere today disappeared; and another significant critique of my book suggested that I failed to do my duty as a Utopian insomuch as I omitted any mention of these surviving Utopian visions, which mostly center on the anti- or post-communist conviction that small is beautiful, or even that growth is undesirable, that the self-organization of communities is the fundamental condition of Utopian life, and that even with large-scale industry the first priority is self-management and cooperation: in other words, that what is essential in Utopianism is not the ingenious economic scheme (such as the abolition of money, for example) so much as it is collectivity as such, the primacy of the social bond over the individualistic and the competitive impulses.

The great Utopias of the 1960s (and 1970s) tended to stage such visions in terms of race and gender: thus we have the unforgettable image of male breast-feeding in Marge Piercy's *Woman on the Edge of Time* (1976), and the ideal (in Le Guin as well) of the villages of the First Americans. Later on, at a different historical moment, in France, at the moment of the socialist electoral victory of 1981, we have Jacques Attali's image of free collective tool shops, where anyone in the neighborhood can find the materials to repair, to rebuild, to transform space; along with the periodic festivals that, as in Rousseau, reaffirm the collective project itself.[8] In our own time, meanwhile, with the resurgence of anarchism, a variety of vivid representations of workers' self-management restore the sense of class to these concerns, as in Naomi Klein's admirable film *The Take,* about the seizure of a factory in Argentina by workers who have been abandoned by their bankrupt owner. Such intermittent visions of the structural transformation of the shop floor itself have energized and revitalized political action from Marx's lectures on the Commune all the way to the program of Yugoslavian *autogestion* and to *soixante-huitard* films like *Coup pour coup* (Marin Karmitz, 1972); and they clearly persisted in America yesterday and do so today.

It is not appropriate to raise practical political objections to these enclave Utopias, always threatened by the hegemony of private business and monopoly all around them, and at the mercy of distribution as well, not to speak of the dominant legal system. I would rather speak of the genre of the revolutionary idyll: and indeed, in his *Some Versions of Pastoral* (1960), William Empson went a long way towards assimilating socialist realism in general to such a form, which, with its shepherds and shepherdesses and its rural peacefulness and fulfillment, seems to have died out everywhere in the literature of the bourgeois age as such. William Morris famously subtitled his great

---

[8] Jacques Attali, *Les trois mondes: pour une théorie de l'après-crise*, Paris: Fayard, 1983.

Utopia "an epoch of rest": and this is indeed what, on an aesthetic level, the idyll or the pastoral promises as a genre: relief from the frenzied anxieties of the actual social world, a glimpse into a place of stillness and of transfigured human nature, of the transformations of the social relations we know today into what Brecht memorably called "friendliness." To that degree, what I've been calling representational Utopias today do seem to take the form of the idyll or the pastoral; and assuredly we do need to recover the significance of these ancient genres and their value and usefulness in an age in which the very psyche and the unconscious have been so thoroughly colonized by addictive frenzy and commotion, compulsiveness and frustration.

So I do see a place for the representational Utopia, and even a political function for it: as I tried to argue in *Archaeologies,* these seemingly peaceful images are also, in and of themselves, violent ruptures with what is, breaks that destabilize our stereotypes of a future that is the same as our own present, interventions that interrupt the reproduction of the system in habit and in ideological consent and institute that fissure, however minimal and initially little more than a hairline fracture, through which another picture of the future and another system of temporality altogether might emerge.

Yet today I also want to project a different way of invoking that future and to propose a different function for the Utopian; and in a sense it is premised on the distinction I proposed at the very beginning of my book between the Utopian program and the Utopian impulse, between Utopian planners and Utopian interpreters, so to speak, or if you like, between More and Fourier or Ernst Bloch. The Utopian program, which aims at the realization of a Utopia, can be as modest or as ambitious as one wants: it can range from a whole social revolution, on the national or even the world scale, all the way down to the designing of the uniquely Utopian space of a single building or garden: what all have in common, however, besides the Utopian transformation of reality itself, is that closure or enclave structure which all Utopias must seemingly confront one way or another. These Utopian spaces are thus on whatever scale totalities; they are symbolic of a world transformed; as such they must posit limits, boundaries between the Utopian and the non-Utopian; and it is of course with such limits and with such enclave structure that any serious critique of Utopia will begin.

The interpretation of the Utopian impulse, however, necessarily deals with fragments: it is not symbolic but allegorical: it does not correspond to a plan or to Utopian praxis, it expresses Utopian desire and invests it in a variety of unexpected and disguised, concealed, distorted ways. The Utopian impulse therefore calls for a hermeneutic: for the detective work of a decipherment and a reading of Utopian clues and traces in the landscape of the real; a theorization and interpretation of unconscious Utopian investments in realities large or small, which may in themselves be far from Utopian in their actuality. The premise here is then that the most noxious phenomena can serve as the repository and hiding place for all kinds of unsuspected wish-fulfillments and Utopian gratifications; indeed, I have often used the example of the humble aspirin as the unwitting bearer of the most extravagant longings for immortality and for the transfiguration of the body.

2.

This kind of Utopian analysis, however, may seem to foreground the subject and subjectivity and to risk transforming the Utopian impulse itself into inconsequential projections which carry no historical weight and imply no practical consequences for the social world as such. This objection seems to me to be overstated to the degree to which human desire is itself constitutive of the collective project and of the historical construction of social formations, within the limits imposed by objective conditions of possibility. Still, it may be best to lay in place a view of those objective conditions before continuing; and to outline a model of the objective possibilities of Utopian social transformation against which the interpretations in terms of some putative Utopian impulse might be measured.

Indeed we might well want to argue that the Marxian view of historical change combines both these forms of Utopian thinking: for it can be seen as a practical project as well as a space of the investment of unconscious forces. The old tension in Marxism between voluntarism and fatalism finds its origins here, in this twin or superimposed Utopian perspective. A Marxist politics is a Utopian project or program for transforming the world, and replacing a capitalist mode of production with a radically different one. But it is also a conception of historical dynamics in which it is posited that the whole new world is also objectively in emergence all around us, without our necessarily at once perceiving it; so that alongside our conscious praxis and our strategies for producing change, we may also take a more receptive and interpretive stance in which, with the proper instruments and registering apparatus, we may detect the allegorical stirrings of a different state of things, the imperceptible and even immemorial ripenings of the seeds of time, the subliminal and subcutaneous eruptions of whole new forms of life and social relations.

At first this second model of temporality is expressed by Marx through the most banal of essential mysteries, which no longer carries much figural power for us. "No social order ever disappears," he tells us in 1859, "before all the productive forces for which there is room in it have been developed"—so far, so good—and it is an observation which was not sufficiently meditated upon in the eighties and nineties of the last century. And then he goes on: "and new, higher relations of production never appear before the material conditions of their existence have matured in the womb of the old society."⁹ Yet this is so far nothing but a metaphor; and childbirth does not necessarily seem to be the best figure for dynamics of the Utopian impulse as Bloch described it, or for the allegories of Utopian investment and the Utopian libido, the hidden traces and signs of Utopianism that lie in wait in the world about us, like Rimbaud's flowers that begin to observe us as we pass by.

Meanwhile, we need to add that both Marx and Lenin wrote specifically Utopian works, both of them based on the Paris Commune. Marx's lectures on the commune ("The Civil War in France") are indeed something like a blueprint for a Utopian democracy beyond the structures of bourgeois parliamentarianism. Lenin's *State and Revolution* then expands on this model of direct democracy, famously breaking off in August 1917 with the apologetic remark that it is more entertaining to make a revolution than to write about one. Both of these texts, however, deal with political rather than economic Utopias, and it is clearly the latter that poses the greatest conceptual difficulties for us today.

To be sure, the anarchist strain in Marx is not to be underestimated. When, early in *Capital,* he asks us "to imagine, for a change, an association [*Verein*] of free men, working with the means of production held in common, and expending their many different forms of labor-power in full self-awareness as one single social labor force,"¹⁰ it is still not clear whether this is not merely some expanded collective "Robinsonade" or Robinson Crusoe fantasy, nor indeed whether we are not still at the stage of petty commodity production, as in yeoman farming or the Germanic mode of production.

The decisive statement will come later on, and will, as Marx himself puts it, "flirt with the Hegelian dialectic":

> The capitalist mode of appropriation, which springs from the capitalist mode of production, produces capitalist private property. This is the first negation of individual private property, as founded on the labour of its proprietor [a reference to the yeoman system I just mentioned]. But capitalist production begets, with the inexorability of a natural process, its own negation. This is the negation of the negation. It does not reestablish private property, but it does indeed establish individual property on the basis of the achievements of the capitalist era: namely cooperation and the possession in common of the land and the means of production produced by labour itself. (*Cap*, 929)

---

⁹ Karl Marx, Preface, *A Contribution to the Critique of Political Economy,* in *Basic Writings on Politics and Philosophy,* ed. Lewis S. Feuer, New York: Doubleday, 1959, 44.

¹⁰ Karl Marx, *Capital,* Vol. 1, trans. Ben Fowkes, London: Penguin, 1976, 171. Future references to this work are denoted *Cap.*

Note that childbirth still persists somewhere in these figures, which mean to describe "the centralization of the means of production and the socialization of labor"—in other words, what the Frankfurt School significantly called *Vergesellschaftung* ("societalization") in a variety of contexts (and what Italian thinkers today, following the Marx of the *Grundrisse,* call General Intellect[11]). Still, not only does the metaphor of pregnancy not go away, the child is actually born in this paragraph! The centralization and socialization just mentioned are now a few lines later in a famous peroration declared "incompatible with their capitalist integument" (in other terms, the new infrastructure becoming incompatible with the older superstructures): "This integument is burst asunder. The knell of capitalist private property sounds. The expropriators are expropriated." This is very much a figural climax, or the realization of several different kinds of figures all at once (although not the ones we will shortly be concerned with). What is at stake in the account generally is, of course, the growth of monopoly; and it will actually be a monopoly which I perversely wish to identify as a Utopian phenomenon. But before I do so, it seems to me appropriate to quote a little more of Marx's description of the approach of what Lenin will then theorize as capitalism's second (or "highest") stage, as it seems to me extraordinarily contemporary and powerfully relevant for our own third stage of capitalism, what we generally call globalization:

> This expropriation is accomplished through the action of the immanent laws of capitalist production itself, through the centralization of capitals. One capitalist always strikes down many others. Hand in hand with this centralization, or this expropriation of many capitalists by a few, other developments take place on an ever-increasing scale, such as the growth of the cooperative form of the labour process, the conscious technical application of science, the planned exploitation of the soil, the transformation of the means of labour into forms in which they can only be used in common, the economizing of all means of production by their use as the means of production of combined, socialized labour, the entanglement of all peoples in the net of the world market, and, with this, the growth of the international character of the capitalist regime. Along with the constant decrease in the number of capitalist magnates, who usurp and monopolize all the advantages of this process of transformation, the mass of misery, oppression, slavery, degradation and exploitation grows. (*Cap,* 929)

It is then appropriate to prolong this standard Marxian picture of the transition from capitalism to socialism with Lenin's analyses, which omit the

---

[11] Karl Marx, *Grundrisse,* trans. Martin Nicolaus, London: Penguin, 1973, 706; and see also Paolo Virno, "The Ambivalence of Disenchantment," in Paolo Virno and Michael Hardt, eds., *Radical Thought in Italy: A Potential Politics,* Minneapolis: University of Minnesota Press, 1996, 20–24.

image of childbirth but insist even more vehemently on the ways in which the future society is "maturing within" the present one—in the form, not only of the socialization of labor (combination, unionization, etc.) but above all monopoly. Indeed, we are here at a certain watershed in radical or socialist thinking: where a progressive bourgeoisie seeks to deal with monopoly by breaking up the great corporations into smaller ones again, in order to permit the return of a healthier competition; and where anarchism denounces concentration as a figure for the state itself, which is to be destroyed at all costs and wherever its power appears—for Lenin the "withering away of the state" consists very specifically in the seizure of the monopolies and in their management by the producers themselves, which at one stroke does away not only with the managerial class but also with the political state and bureaucracy that runs its affairs. Take, for example, the following passage on finance capital (something already quoted in Chapter 1, above, and still very relevant to us today):

> Capitalism has created an accounting *apparatus* in the shape of the banks, syndicates, postal service, consumers' societies, and office employees unions. *Without big banks socialism would be impossible* ... The big banks are the "state apparatus" which we *need* to bring about socialism, and which we *take ready-made* from capitalism; our task here is merely to *lop off* what *capitalistically mutilates* this excellent apparatus, to make it *even bigger*, even more democratic, even more comprehensive. Quantity will be transformed into quality ... We can "lay hold of" and "set in motion" this "state apparatus" (which is not fully a state apparatus under capitalism, but which will be so with us, under socialism) at one stroke, by a single decree.[12]

Now I have quoted these very representative passages at some length because their very defense of size and monopoly is shocking today, both on the right and on the left, for admirers of free markets as well as for those who believe that "small is beautiful" and that self-organization is the key to economic democracy. I often share these sympathies, and do not particularly mean to take a position here; but I would observe that in both cases—regulation and the breaking up of monopolies in the name of business competition on the one hand, and the return to smaller communities and collectivities on the other—we have to do with historical regression and the attempt to return to a past that no longer exists. But it is apparently difficult for us to think of an impending future of size, quantity, overpopulation, and the like, except in dystopian terms. Indeed, the difficulties in thinking quantity positively must be added to our list of obstacles facing Utopian thought in our own time.

---

[12] V. I. Lenin, quoted in Neil Harding, *Leninism*, Durham, NC: Duke University Press, 1996, 145–146.

3.

This is the point at which I wish to propose a model for Utopian analysis that might be taken as a kind of synthesis of these two subjective and objective approaches. I want to develop two examples of this kind of interpretation, which will be what I want to identify, not as the Utopian method as such, but at least as one possible method among others: and these examples will draw on history and theory respectively. My theoretical example will be drawn from the now burgeoning field of manifestos for a politics of the "multitude"; my historical example will however propose a new institutional candidate for the function of Utopian allegory, and that is the phenomenon called Wal-Mart. I trust that this proposal will be even more scandalous than Lenin's celebration of monopoly, all the more so since information research tells us that an enormous percentage of Wal-Mart shoppers are themselves sharply critical and even negative about this corporation (and that the critics also shop there.)[13] The negative criticisms I think everyone knows: a new Wal-Mart drives local businesses under and reduces available jobs; Wal-Mart's own jobs scarcely pay a living wage, offer no benefits or health insurance; the company is anti-union (except in China); it hires illegal immigrants and increasingly emphasizes part-time work; it drives American business abroad and also itself promotes sweatshops and child labor outside the country; it is ruthless in its practices (mostly secret), exercises a reign of terror over its own suppliers, destroys whole ecologies abroad and whole communities here in the US; it locks its own employees in at night, etc., etc. The picture is unappetizing, and the prospects for the future—Wal-Mart is already the largest company, not only in the US but in the world!—are positively frightening and even, particularly if you have a bent for conspiracy theory, dystopian in the extreme. Here, rather than in the trusts and monopolies of Theodore Roosevelt's time, is the true embodiment of the Marxist-Leninist prophecy of concentration and the monopoly tendency of late capitalism; yet as its commentators observe, the emergence of this entity—like a new virus, or a new species—was not only unexpected but also theoretically unparalleled and resistant to current categories of economic, political, and social thinking:

> Wal-Mart is something utterly new ... carefully disguised as something ordinary, familiar, even prosaic ... Yes, Wal-Mart plays by the rules, but perhaps the most important part of the Wal-Mart effect is that the rules are antiquated ... At the moment, we are incapable as a society of understanding Wal-Mart because we haven't equipped ourselves to manage it. (*WME*, 221–222)

---

[13] Charles Fishman, *The Wal-Mart Effect*, New York: Penguin, 2006, 220. Future references to this work are denoted *WME*.

What we must add to this, however, is the reminder that there is a type of thinking which can deal with this strange new phenomenon lucidly, at the same time that it explains why traditional thought is unable to do so: and that is the thinking called the dialectic. Consider the following analysis:

> That kind of dominance at both ends of the spectrum—dominance across a huge range of merchandise and dominance of geographical consumer markets—means that market capitalism is being strangled with the kind of slow inexorability of a boa constrictor. (*WME*, 234)

And if this sounds like mere journalistic rhetoric, we have the observation of a nameless CEO who flatly affirms of Wal-Mart—"they have killed free-market capitalism in America" (*WME*, 233). But what is this peculiar contradiction but the contemporary version of what Marx called the nega-tion of the negation? Wal-Mart is then not an aberration or an exception, but rather the purest expression of that dynamic of capitalism which devours itself, which abolishes the market by means of the market itself.

This dialectical character of the new reality Wal-Mart represents is also very much the source of the ambivalence universally felt about this business operation, whose capacity to reduce inflation and to hold down or even lower prices and to make life affordable for the poorest Americans is also the very source of their poverty and the prime mover in the dissolution of American industrial productivity and the irrevocable destruction of the American small town. But this is the historically unique and dialectical dynamic of capitalism itself as a system, as Marx and Engels describe it in the *Manifesto* in pages which some have taken as a delirious celebration of the powers of the new mode of production and others as the ultimate moral judgment on it. But the dialectic is not moral in that sense: and what Marx and Engels identify is the simultaneity of "more and more colossal produc-tive forces than all preceding generations together" along with the most destructive negativity ever unleashed ("all that is solid melts into air"). The dialectic is an injunction to think the negative and the positive together at one and the same time, in the unity of a single thought, there where moraliz-ing wants to have the luxury of condemning this evil without particularly imagining anything else in its place.

So it is that Wal-Mart is celebrated as the ultimate in democracy as well as in efficiency: streamlined organization that ruthlessly strips away all unnec-essary frills and waste and that disciplines its bureaucracy into a class as admirable as the Prussian state or the great movement of *instituteurs* in the late nineteenth-century French lay education, or even the dreams of a streamlined Soviet system. New desires are encouraged and satisfied as richly as the theoreticians of the 1960s (and also Marx himself) predicted, and the problems of distribution are triumphantly addressed in all kinds of new technological innovations.

I enumerate a few of the latter: on the one (informational) hand, there is the evolution of the UPC or the so-called bar code, one of what Hosoya and Schaeffer call bit structures, and which in general they define as "a new infrastructure in the city, providing unprecedented synchronization and organization in seeming formlessness. Bit structures reorganize the pattern of the city and allow its destabilization."[14] The bar code, meanwhile "reverses the balance of power between retailer and distributor or manufacturer," via the introduction, in the early 1970s, of "a whole new generation of electronic cash registers," which were now able to process the mass of information registered on the bar code from inventory to customer preferences: technological innovation pioneered, according to the oldest logic of capitalism, "as a remedy to a time of stagnation that forced competing manufacturers to cooperate."[15] The Utopian features of the bar code project it as something like the equivalent, in the world of commodities, of the Internet among human subjects; and the reversal of dominance from production to distribution somewhat parallels the emergence of the ideologies of democracy in the social realm.

Yet on the side of the material object, there is another relevant development, as fundamental as this one but quite different from it, and that is the invention and emergence of containerization as a revolution in transport, whose multiple effects we cannot explore further here.[16] This spatial innovation would be something like the response to demography and overpopulation in the social realm, and also leads us on into a dialectic of quantity and quality. Indeed, both these ends of the so-called supply chain demand philosophical conceptualization and stand as the mediation between production and distribution and the virtual abolition of an opposition between distribution and consumption.

Meanwhile the anarchy of capitalism and the market has been overcome and the necessities of life have been provided for an increasingly desperate and impoverished public, exploited by its government and its big businesses over whom it is scarcely able to exercise any political control any longer. Anyone who does not appreciate this historic originality of Wal-Mart and

---

[14] Chuihua Judy Chung, Jeffrey Inaba, Rem Koolhaas, and Sze Tsung Leong, eds., *The Harvard Design School Guide to Shopping*, Köln: Taschen, 2001, 157. This book is Volume 2 of Koolhaas's monumental *Project on the City*. And see also on technological innovations "The Physical Internet," *The Economist*, 17 June 2006; and Thomas Friedman, *The World Is Flat: A Brief History of the Twenty-first Century*, New York: Farrar, Straus and Giroux, 2005, especially 128–141.

[15] Chung, et al., *The Harvard Design School Guide to Shopping*, 158.

[16] But see Marc Levinson, *The Box*, Princeton: Princeton University Press, 2006.

its strengths and accomplishments is really not up to the discussion; mean-while—and I say this for the Left as well—there is an aesthetic appreciation to be demanded for this achievement, an appreciation of the type Brecht reserved for one of his favorite books, Gustavus Myers's *History of the Great American Fortunes,* or which we might today be willing to grant the manipu-lations and strategies of those arch-criminals the Russian oligarchs. But such admiration and positive judgment must be accompanied by the absolute condemnation that completes the dialectical ambivalence we bring to this historical phenomenon. Nor is Wal-Mart itself wholly oblivious to its own ambivalence: after avoiding journalists altogether for fear of letting slip damaging facts, its publicity people now come to expect mixed feelings in which the harshest criticism will inevitably be accompanied by celebratory concessions (*WME*, 145–146).

I am tempted to add something about the ambivalence of the dialectic itself, particularly with respect to technological innovation. It is enough to recall the admiration of Lenin and Gramsci for Taylorism and Fordism to be perplexed at this weakness of revolutionaries for what is most exploitative and dehumanizing in the working life of capitalism: but this is precisely what is meant by the Utopian here, namely that what is currently negative can also be imagined as positive in that immense changing of the valences which is the Utopian future. And this is the way I want us to consider Wal-Mart, however briefly: namely, as a thought experiment—not, after Lenin's crude but practical fashion, as an institution faced with which (after the revolution) we can "lop off what capitalistically mutilates this excellent apparatus," but rather as what Raymond Williams called the emergent, as opposed to the residual—the shape of a Utopian future looming through the mist, which we must seize as an opportunity to exercise the Utopian imagination more fully, rather than an occasion for moralizing judgments or regressive nostalgia.

I now need briefly to address two further but extremely pertinent objec-tions to this paradoxical affirmation, before moving on to a Utopian exercise of a rather different kind. First, it will be said that Wal-Mart may be a model of distribution but it can scarcely be said to be a model of production in the strict sense, however much we might talk of the production of distribution, etc. This cuts to the very heart of our socioeconomic contradictions: one face of which is structural unemployment, the other the definitive outstrip-ping (dated in the US from 2003) of "productive" employment by retail employment. (Computerization and information would also have to be included in these new contradictory structures, and I think it is evident that Wal-Mart's special kind of success is dependent on computers and would have been impossible before them.) I want to look at this from the perspec-tive of the dictatorship this retail company exercises over its productive suppliers (or "partners," as Wal-Mart likes to call them); it is a devastating power, in which the giant firm is able to force its suppliers into outsourcing, into a reduction in quality of materials and product, or even to drive them out of business altogether. It is worth noting that this power could be exercised in exactly the opposite way: "using its enormous purchasing power," Fishman suggests, "not just to raise the standard of living for its customers, but also for its suppliers"(*WME*, 181). (The example is the proposal that Wal-Mart impose ecological standards on the Chilean salmon fisheries it has itself virtually created; one might imagine a similar positive dictatorship over working conditions and labor relations.) It is a Utopian suggestion, to the degree to which the valences of this power—from retail monopoly to the various producers—could be reversed without structural change.

But I also want to suggest that—as at the end of Eisenstein's *Old and New* (a.k.a. *The General Line*; 1929), where the aviator and the peasant swap roles, the worker becoming an agriculturist and vice versa—it seems possible that the new system offers a chance to suppress this opposition altogether—this binary tension between production and distribution, which we do not seem to be able to think our way out of—and to imagine a wholly new set of categories: not to abandon production and the categories of class in favor of consumption or information, but rather to lift it into a new and more complex concept, about which we can no longer speculate here.

The other objection has to do with the profit motive itself: after all, the very driving force of Wal-Mart is that it is a capitalist industry, and the failures of socialism all seemed to lie in the slackness encouraged by the command economy, in which corruption, favoritism, nepotism, or sheer research ignorance led to the scandals in which, famously, the basements of the GUM were filled with illimitable quantities of identical lampshades that no one wanted to buy. All socialism seemed to be able to offer as a counterforce to the profit motive were the famous "moral incentives" Che invoked in Cuba, which require repeated mobilizations and exhausting campaigns, in order to reinvigorate failing supplies of socialist enthusiasm.

What has to be observed here is that Wal-Mart is also driven by moral incentives: the secret of its success is not profit but pricing, the shaving off of the final pennies, so fatal to any number of its suppliers. "Sam valued every penny," observes one of the founder's colleagues (*WME*, 30), and it is a fateful sentence: for this imperative—"Always Low Prices"—is in fact driven by the most fundamental motive of all, the one Max Weber described as the "Protestant ethic," a return to that thrift and obsessive frugality which characterized the first great moment of the system and which is recaptured (with or without its religious component) in the hagiography of Sam Walton and the heroic saga of his company. Perhaps, then, even the explanatory appeal to the profit motive is essentialist and part of an ideology of human nature itself projected from out of the necessities of the initial construction of capitalism. It should be added that Marxism is not psychologically reductive in an essentialist way, and asserts, not determinism by greed or acquisitiveness, but rather the determination by the system or mode of production, each of which produces and constructs its own historical version of what it would like to call human nature.

4.

Now I need to describe with more precision the theory and practice of this new type of Utopia my account of Wal-Mart seems to presuppose. Indeed, the discussion will assert that theoretical approaches to it are sometimes to be found in positions explicitly characterized as "anti-Utopian." This is the case with our next example, which will turn on the now well-known concept of the multitude, as developed (borrowing a term of Spinoza) by Michael Hardt and Antonio Negri in their books *Empire* and *Multitude.* It is worth noting that their own specific denunciations of Utopianism, while consistent with a good deal of poststructuralist doctrine, have the immediate political and historical reference of Stalinism and of the historic Communist parties coming out of the Leninist tradition (despite the latter's own internal critique of Utopianism from Lenin on). Here Utopia is identified with slogans of historical inevitability and of "tomorrows that sing," the sacrifice of present generations for some future Utopian state, and particularly with the party structure.

As for the concept of multitude itself, it seems to me, however flawed, to constitute an attempt to provide a new and more serviceable substitute for older theorizations of collectivity and collective agents, such as those of "the people" (in populism) and of social class (in workerisms that excluded gender and race, and even sometimes the peasantry, from their narrow political definitions). Every new approach to collectivity is on my view worth welcoming in an atomized and individualistic society (but I will come back to individualism in a moment). The older collective concepts were also clearly flawed in their own very different ways; at the same time that they expressed the social reality of the emergence of new forms of collective agents or subjects. But I will not here enter the debate on multitude, since I am rather trying to identify a methodological innovation. In order to do so, however, I will not draw on the massive and complex books of Hardt and Negri, but rather on a briefer intervention in this discussion, a luminous exposition of some of the consequences of this new theoretical position (which is by now a new tradition) by one of the most remarkable philosophical minds of the era, the Italian philosopher Paolo Virno, still too little known over here.

His book *A Grammar of the Multitude* may be read as a series of notes on the changes the concept of multitude should be expected to bring to the phenomenology of everyday life in postmodernity (not his word) and indeed to our attitudes towards and evaluations of those changes. I will not touch on all his themes and intentions here, but essentially on the book's revision of certain standard Heideggerian positions which are still very much with us today, in liberal as well as in conservative culture, and indeed in Western bourgeois daily life in general.

You will recall that Heidegger called for a purgation of the decadent habits of bourgeois comfort by way of anxiety and the fear of death; and that he saw modern life as dominated by inauthenticity and urban collectivity. You may also remember the four forms of degradation into which *Dasein's* daily life is alienated in the daily life of modernity, namely, "das Gerede, die Neugier, die Zweideutigkeit, das Verfallen,"[17] or, as the translations of *Sein und Zeit* have it, "idle talk, curiosity, ambiguity, and falling" (or "falling prey"). It is essentially these categories, and the very concept of inauthenticity, that Virno has it in mind to revise (leaving Nazism and the later theories of technology out of it, as we will also do).

What is important to grasp, however, is that these diagnoses of "modernity" are not specific to Heidegger; they are part and parcel of a whole conservative and anti-modernist ideology embraced by non-leftist intellectuals across the board in the 1920s, from T. S. Eliot to José Ortega y Gassett, by traditionalists from China to America. This ideology expresses a horror of the new industrial city with its new working and white-collar classes, its mass culture and its public sphere, its standardization and its parliamentary systems; and it often implies a nostalgia for the older agriculturalist ways of life, as in the American "Fugitives," in the idealization of English yeoman farmers, or in the Heideggerian *Feldweg*. It is unnecessary to add that this ideology is informed by an abiding fear of socialism or communism, and that the corporatisms that dominate the political life of the 1930s, from Roosevelt's New Deal to Stalin's Five-Year Plans, from Nazism and Italian fascism to Fabian social democracy, are from this perspective to be seen as so many compromises with such traditionalism as it resists the so-called modernities of the age of so-called mass man.

Those compromises have, to be sure, now for the most part entered history (leaving contemporary social democracy in some disarray, it may be added, in a situation in which free-market fundamentalism is so far really the only serviceable new practical-political ideology); but I want to argue that the general social attitudes of the older conservative ideology I have just outlined (and of which Heidegger is only the most extraordinary philosophical theorist) are still largely with us and still intellectually and ideologically operative.

---

[17] Martin Heidegger, *Sein und Zeit,* paragraphs 35–38.

I will do so by returning to the issue of representational Utopias I raised earlier. Indeed, the standard way of dealing with the social anxieties that inform the old anti-modernist ideology has been to accept it while assuring us that in whatever future "more perfect society" all of the negative features it enumerates will have been corrected. Thus, in these pastorals, there will be no social insecurity to generate anxiety (and even death will be postponed), idle gossip will presumably be replaced by a purified language and by genuine human relationships, morbid curiosity by a certain healthy distance from others as well as an enlightened awareness of our position in the social totality, "ambiguity" (by which Heidegger means the lies and propaganda of mass culture and the public sphere) will be cured by our more authentic relationships to the project and to work and action in general, and *Verfallenheit* (our loss of self in the public dimension of the *man*, or the inauthenticity of "mass man") will be replaced by some more genuine individualism and a more authentic isolation of the self in its own existential concerns and commitments. Now these are all no doubt excellent and desirable developments; but it is not hard to see that they are also essentially reactive: that is to say, they constitute so many obedient replacements of the reigning negative terms by their positive opposites. But this very reactivity of the Heideggerian response tends to confirm the priority of the negative diagnosis in the first place.

It may also be confirmed by current dystopian visions in which the multidimensional fear of all those unknown others who constitute "society" beyond my immediate circle of acquaintances is once again, under postmodern or globalized conditions, concentrated into the fear of multiplicity and overpopulation. Clearly an ancient tradition of satire from the Hebrew prophets onward rehearsed this horror of the collective other in the form of the denunciation of a sinful or fallen society; just as philosophical speculations such as Descartes' assimilation of the other to the automaton expressed the scandal in a different way from its theological version (the stream of soulless employees going to work across London Bridge in *The Waste Land*) or from journalistic "culture critiques" of alienation. The science fiction of the 1960s, particularly with John Brunner's classic tetralogy, gave non-ideological expression to various figures of social crisis, dissolution, or degradation; while the image of soulless clones or brainwashed zombies expressed some more overt denunciation of the unreformable stupidity of the modern democratic masses. Yet even in these expressions of crisis, the symptoms (pollution, atomic war, urban crime, the "degradation" of mass culture, standardization, impoverishment, unemployment, predominance of the service sector, etc., etc.) remained differentiated and gave rise each to a different kind of monitory representation. It is only in postmodernity and globalization, with the world population explosion, the desertion of the countryside and the growth of the mega-city, global warming and ecological catastrophe, the proliferation of urban guerrilla warfare, the financial collapse of the welfare state, the universal emergence of small-group politics of all kinds, that these phenomena have seemed to fold back into each other around the primary cause (if that is the right category to use) of the scandal of multiplicity and of what is generally referred to as overpopulation, or in other words, the definitive appearance of the Other in multiple forms and as sheer quantity or number. Predictably, the representational response to this crystallization has taken the twin positive and negative forms of a vision of "sprawl," as a seemingly dystopian urbanization of enormous sectors of the older global landscape, and of a retreat into precisely those pastoral visions of smaller collectivities evoked above. Few have been those who, like Rem Koolhaas, with his embrace of a "culture of congestion"[18] and his projection of new and positive spaces within which overpopulation can joyously flourish, have seized on a strategy of changing the valences and of converting the gloomy indices of the pessimistic diagnosis into vital promises of some newly emergent historical reality to be welcomed rather than lamented.

It is indeed just such a strategy that I will want to find at work in *A Grammar of the Multitude,* whose themes may now be briefly (and incompletely) passed in review. For the insecurities of both fear and anxiety (sharply differentiated in Heidegger), Virno substitutes a wholesale attack on bourgeois security as such, to which we will return, only observing that security is also a spatial concept (related to Heideggerian "dwelling") and posits some initial physical separation from my neighbor which is also ideologically interrelated with concepts of property (in that sense, only the rich are truly secure, in their gated communities and their carefully policed and patrolled estates, whose function lies in occulting and repressing the existential fact of collectivity itself). The operator of the transvaluation recommended here, from anxiety to affirmation, is the Kantian notion of the sublime, which incorporates fear within its very *jouissance*; yet the practical consequences of such a transformation will also transform the pathos of Heideggerian homelessness into the animation of Deleuzian nomadism, as we shall see.

Nomadism, however, would also seem to characterize contemporary labor, in a situation in which, the economists solemnly warn us, no one should any longer expect to hold down a single lifelong job (they do not generally add the increasingly obvious supplement, namely that many should not expect to hold down any job at all). Virno's discussion of contemporary labor, which undertakes to challenge and to dismantle the traditional Aristotelian distinction (revived by Hannah Arendt) between labor, politics, and philosophy, would also seem to aim at a Utopian

---

[18] Rem Koolhaas, *Delirious New York*, New York: Oxford University Press, 1978, 7; and see also, on city size, his *S, M, L, XL*, New York: Monacelli Press, 1995, 961–971.

restructuration of the whole notion of alienation, as it has been degraded from Marx's early analysis of industrial labor into some all-purpose cultural characterization. The Hegelian notion of externalization, of which Marx's concept was both a critique and a restructuration, itself constituted a kind of Utopian celebration of handicraft activity and production, no longer relevant in the industrial era.[19] Virno now proposes a notion of production as virtuosity, a concept which redeems the old 1960s ideal of an aesthetization of life, as well as resituating in a more positive way the even more contemporary denunciations of contemporary society in terms of the spectacle (Debord) and the simulacrum (Baudrillard).

We must first note the specificities of labor today, as Virno outlines them, drawing the ultimate conclusion from the movement of all modern philosophy from categories of substance to categories of process. Modern (or perhaps I should say postmodern) work is a matter of process, an activity for which the end has become secondary and the production of an object a mere pretext, the process having become an end in itself. This is comparable to virtuosity in the aesthetic realm, and indeed we here meet an unexpected avatar of the old left dream of an aesthetic disalienation of the world, from Schiller to Marcuse and the sixties. Yet this one will have none of the saving graces of the older aestheticism, it will be a culture of minding the machines, a post-work culture, an activity of language-sharing and linguistic co-operation. This move then also entails the resituating of labor—hitherto ambiguously differentiated from both private and public spheres (it is not private life, but its framework is still owned by the capitalist and not open to the public)—within some new space from which the opposition between private and public has disappeared, without the reduction of one to the other.

This last is now a "publicness without a public sphere,"[20] a transformation which in its turn entails a series of other Utopian consequences. For one thing, so-called mass culture is itself transformed, becoming "an industry of the means of production" (*GM*, 61). Its clichés and commonplaces are now an enactment of collective sharing and participation, and come to have the redemptive innocence of childhood repetition: indeed, at this point, Virno sketches out what might be a theory of the cultural equivalent of that theory of General Intellect, which, drawing on Marx's *Grundrisse*, has been so crucial in the way in which Italian philosophy today has sought to disclose

---

[19] Hegel's discussion of "die Sache selbst" ("the matter at hand") is to be found in *Phenomenology of Spirit,* trans. A. V. Miller, Oxford: Oxford University Press, 1977, 237–252.

[20] Paolo Virno, *A Grammar of the Multitude*, trans. Isabella Bertoletti, James Cascaito, and Andrea Casson, New York: Semiotext[e], 2004, 40. Future references to this work are denoted *GM*.

the profound socialization and collectivization of late-capitalist social life and work. In this context, then, where science and language have soaked into the everyday and permeated all the pores of our daily life, making everyone an intellectual (as Gramsci famously put it), a henceforth globalized mass culture and omnipresent communication themselves have a very different significance. The multitude has its own new kind of linguistic and cultural literacy, everywhere on the globe: there are no prehistoric peoples, no premodern survivals: tribals listen to their portables and nomads watch their DVDs; in mountain villages without electricity as well as in the most dismal refugee camps the dispossessed follow world current events and listen to the vacuous speeches of our president. Yet in that dedifferentiation of culture and politics which characterizes postmodernity, it must also be understood that such "publicness without a public sphere" also grounds and prepares what Virno calls "the feasibility of a non-representational democracy" (*GM*, 79).

It is evident that within this extraordinary reversal of the traditional judgments on mass society and its "degradations," Heidegger's existential inauthenticities will also be transformed. To the existential philosopher's enumeration (idle talk or gossip, curiosity, ambiguity, and *Verfallenheit*) Virno adds two more—opportunism and cynicism—which have perhaps attracted more explicit and fulsome condemnation in recent times. Perhaps it is increasingly obvious that gossip, as in Proust, is preeminently the mark of a human age and of the preponderance of the human other over the former relations between man and nature. But curiosity—particularly in the classic form of voyeuristic envy analyzed so long ago by St. Augustine— is also to be accorded its Utopian transfiguration. Benjamin's paradoxical defense of "distraction" may now be reread as the designation of a new type of perception within a world of habit and numb routine:

> The media trains the senses to consider the known as if it were unknown, to distinguish "an enormous and sudden margin of freedom" even in the most trite and repetitive aspects of daily life. At the same time, however, the media trains the senses also for the opposite task: to consider the unknown as if it were known, to become familiar with the unexpected and the surprising, to become accustomed to the lack of established habits. (*GM*, 93)

As for opportunism, very much in the spirit of Hegel's defense of utilitarianism, it marks the indispensable emergence of the tactical and strategic *coup d'oeil*, the capacity to size up and evaluate the situation itself, the makings of a new and intensified sense of orientation in this new world of the Utopian masses: "opportunism gains in value as an indispensable resource whenever the concrete labor process is permeated by a diffuse 'communicative action' and thus no longer identifies itself solely with mute 'instrumental action' "

(*GM*, 86). As for cynicism itself, today at the very center of liberal political reflection, it clearly also develops a new and original stance with respect to the knowledge of the way in which our system functions, renouncing "any claim to a standard of judgment which shares the nature of a moral evaluation" (*GM*, 88) and thereby, according to Virno, repudiating the very principle of equivalence on which moral judgments themselves are founded. Cynicism thereby abandons the universalism of equivalence (read: exchange value) for that new kind of multiplicity that traditionalists call relativism, but which is a new effect of the multitude rather than some inherited philosophical position. With these few remarks, Virno opens up the whole urgent problem of cynical reason today for some original retheorization.

If "ambiguity" designates Heidegger's anxiety about the degradation of language in the modern world of mass culture and universal literacy, *Verfallenheit* characterizes the more general way in which, according to him, the inauthentic *Dasein* is abandoned to the collective order and "falls prey" to the "world" of others, in which it forgets itself and loses its individuality—that is to say, for Heidegger, its existential solitude and that isolation in which it can alone know its freedom, its "being-unto-death." This loss of self in the crowd, the submersion of individuality in the multitude, has been the central indictment proposed by counterrevolutionary ideology since its invention, knowing its high points in the grisliest mob scenes of the French Revolution (and in their analysis by Le Bon and Freud as the overcoming of the rational ego by collective irrationality), as well as in deplorable outrages to private property in practically any large-scale revolt you can instance.

And this is also the way our bourgeois tradition has from time relatively immemorial observed the crowd or the mob—that is to say, from a safe distance, and deploring the excesses and the way in which its subjects run to and fro aimlessly, shouting and gesticulating, released from the constraints of law and decency, and as it were under the spell of a kind of shamanistic possession. What Virno has to tell us about this is extremely timely: these inherited pictures and prejudices, he argues, suggest that our traditional view of what we like to call modernity (First World bourgeois capitalism) presupposes our emergence as individuals from some inchoate pre-individualistic mass, and our fear of being resubmerged back into a post-individualistic "multitude" in which we will again lose everything we have painfully achieved as individual subjects. The multitude is on the contrary the very condition for individuation, it is alone in the multitude and the collective that we arrive at our true singularity as individuals. We must abandon the habit of thinking of a host of things—language, culture, literacy, the State, the nation—as goals to be achieved in some arduous yet beneficent process of modernization. On the contrary, they are long since all achieved, everyone is modern, modernization has been over for some time. "Unity," Virno tells us, "is no longer something (the State, the sovereign), towards which things converge, as in the case of the people; rather it is taken for granted, as a background or a necessary precondition. The many must be thought of as the individualization of the universal, of the generic, of the shared experience" (*GM*, 25).

The premise of unity articulated here is, to be sure, based on that understanding of General Intellect alluded to above: the recognition of an immense expansion of the cultural sphere in late capitalism or postmodernity, the generalization of knowledge (very much including science) in that end of nature and the natural, that tendential humanization of the world implicit in Marx's "universalization of wage labor" and the approach of a genuine world market. It also casts a different light on the politics of difference, which has a meaning after the totalizations of capitalism that it could not possibly have had in early capitalist (or precapitalist) thought and experience. Even the unification of groups in some great collective project must necessarily work differently after the consolidation of a system of nation-states than it did when the very construction of the nation, incomplete, was a heroic and a progressive process.

So much, then, for some of the constitutive features of this new world of the multitude, which we are to train ourselves to welcome as the first fresh stirrings of the very storm of Utopia itself. The last-mentioned aspect of the multitude's curiosity, however—"the lack of established habits"—will bring us back to the second theme I wanted to explore in Virno's book, and that is found in the very opening remarks about security and shelter. For established habits are also a security and a shelter, and perhaps the most fundamental feature of the new situation from which that new thing, the multitude, emerges, can be addressed in that way, as some new and utter absence of security and shelter, as some new homelessness no longer to be reminded with nostalgia or bourgeois comfort, with Heideggerian "dwelling" or the protection of the State—a new and permanent crisis situation in which we are all refugees whether we know it or not. What we are calling the multitude is then the population of those refugee camps as they supplant the promise of suburbs and the mobility of freeways which have become permanent traffic jams.

Virno associates two kinds of actions with this new multitude, Utopian or not. The first is civil disobedience, the refusal of the State, to which can already be opposed the self-organization of the camps and *bidonvilles* themselves, which have fallen below the State's radar. The second is his version of Deleuzian nomadism, namely emigration, as the latter hovers above modern Italian history (in Gianni Amelio's great film *Lamerica* [1994], for example) but also reappears in the very last chapter of *Capital*, where the European laborers are seen to desert the old country for the American East Coast, only in a few years to "desert the factory, moving West, towards free lands. Wage labor is seen as a transitory phase, rather than as a life sentence"

(*GM*, 45). The camps, the frontier: such is the deeper unseen reality of the world of the multitude which Virno asks us to embrace in Nietzschean fashion, not as some forever recurring of the present, but as the Eternal Return of the future and of Utopian possibilities to be celebrated as though we had chosen them in the first place.

5.

Now I need to clarify the Utopian "method" presupposed here and to give a theoretical account of the rather peculiar and even perverse readings I have offered of my two illustrations. Just as I hasten to assure the reader that I do not mean to celebrate Wal-Mart, let alone to forecast the emergence of anything good and progressive from this astonishing new post-monopoly institution, so also my discussion of Paolo Virno was not to be taken as an endorsement of some putative new politics of multitude nor even as a practical-political discussion—something he is perfectly capable of conducting in his own voice and indeed which the final chapter of his *Grammar* (on which I have not touched) begins to lay out. Or to put it in a different and more accurate way: it does not matter what I think personally about the future of the Wal-Mart-type business operation or about the "politics of multitude"; I have been using both topics and both occasions to illustrate a method, about which it is now important to say that it is meant to be distinct from any of those outlined at the beginning of this chapter.

The hermeneutic I have wanted to demonstrate is therefore not predictive, nor is it symptomological: it is not meant to read the outlines of the future within the present, nor is it meant to identify the operations of collective wish-fulfillment within the rather unpleasant phenomena (monopoly, overpopulation) which are its objects of examination. The latter approach —generally identified with Ernst Bloch's work—would have to take the opinions and ideologies, the ways of life and situations, of actually existing social groups far more seriously and empirically into consideration than this exercise has done. The former line of inquiry, that of practical politics and programs, and identified here with Marx and with Lenin, would have to assess the concrete world situation in its economic and political objectivity, as well as in the balance of ideological forces, from a strategic perspective rather than from isolated data.

I consider the Utopian "method" outlined here as neither hermeneutic nor political program, but rather something like the structural inversion of what Foucault, following Nietzsche, called the genealogy. He meant by that to distinguish his own (or perhaps even some more generalized post-structural or postmodern) "method" in sharp contrast from both empirical history and the evolutionary narratives reconstructed by idealist historians.

The genealogy was in effect to be understood as neither chronological nor narrative but rather a logical operation (taking "logic" in a Hegelian sense without being Hegelian about it). Genealogy in other words was meant to lay in place the various logical preconditions for the appearance of a given phenomenon, without in any way implying that they constituted the latter's causes, let alone the latter's antecedents or early stages. To be sure, inasmuch as those genealogical preconditions almost always took the form of earlier historical events, misunderstanding—and the assimilation of the new construction to the older historical approaches (chronology, causality, narrative, idealist continuity)—was always inevitable, and could not be warded off by Raymond Roussel's immortal anecdote of the tourist who claimed to have discovered, under glass in a provincial museum, "the skull of Voltaire as a child."

There is so far no term as useful for the construction of the future as "genealogy" is for such a construction of the past; it is certainly not to be called "futurology," while "utopology" will never mean much, I fear. The operation itself, however, consists in a prodigious effort to change the valences on phenomena which so far exist only in our own present; and experimentally to declare positive things which are clearly negative in our own world, to affirm that dystopia is in reality Utopia if examined more closely, to isolate specific features in our empirical present so as to read them as components of a different system. This is in fact what we have seen Virno doing when he borrows an enumeration of what in Heidegger are clearly enough meant to be negative and highly critical features of modern society or modern actuality, staging each of these alleged symptoms of degradation as an occasion for celebration and as a promise of what he does not—but what we may—call an alternate Utopian future.

This kind of prospective hermeneutic is a political act only in one specific sense: as a contribution to the reawakening of the imagination of possible and alternate futures, a reawakening of that historicity which our system—offering itself as the very end of history—necessarily represses and paralyzes. This is the sense in which utopology revives long-dormant parts of the mind, organs of political and historical and social imagination which have virtually atrophied for lack of use, muscles of praxis we have long since ceased exercising, revolutionary gestures we have lost the habit of performing, even subliminally. Such a revival of futurity and of the positing of alternate futures is not itself a political program nor even a political practice: but it is hard to see how any durable or effective political action could come into being without it.

Chapter 17

Globalization as a Philosophical Issue

I.

Four positions on our topic seem logically available. The first affirms the opinion that there is no such thing as globalization (there are still the nation-states and the national situations, nothing is new under the sun). The second also affirms that globalization is nothing new, there has always been globalization; and it suffices to leaf through a book like Eric Wolf's *Europe and the People without History*[1] to see that as far back as the Neolithic, trade routes have been global in their scope, with Polynesian artifacts deposited in Africa, and Asian potsherds as far afield as the New World.

Then I suppose one should add two more: one which affirms the relationship between globalization and that world market which is the ultimate horizon of capitalism: only to add that the current world networks are only different in degree and not in kind; while a fourth affirmation (which I have found more interesting than the other three) posits some new or third, multinational stage of capitalism, of which globalization is an intrinsic feature and which we now largely tend, whether we like it or not, to associate with that thing called postmodernity.

Meanwhile, above and beyond all this, there are the judgments: one can deplore globalization or celebrate it, just as one welcomes the new freedoms of the postmodern era and the postmodern outlook, and in particular the new technological revolutions, or on the other hand elegiacally laments the passing of the splendors of the modern: the glories and possibilities of modernism in the arts, the disappearance of History as the fundamental element in which human beings exist, and, not least, the end of an essentially modernist field of political struggle in which the great ideologies still had the force and the authority of the great religions in earlier times. But I do think we have an interest in at least provisionally separating this now

---

[1] Eric Wolf, *Europe and the People without History,* Berkeley: University of California Press, 1982.

familiar postmodern debate from the matter of globalization, all the while understanding only too well that the two issues are deeply intertwined and that positions on the postmodern are bound to make their way back in eventually.

Let's start from the principle that we already somehow know what globalization is, and try rather to focus on the concept of globalization, on its ideological structure, if you like (it being understood in advance that this word "ideology" is unpejorative, and that a concept can be ideological and also correct or true all at once). I believe that globalization is a communicational concept, which alternately masks and transmits cultural or economic meanings. We have a sense that there are both denser and more extensive communicational networks all over the world today, networks that are on the one hand the result of remarkable innovations in communicational technologies of all kinds, and on the other have as their foundation the tendentially greater degree of modernization in all the countries of the world, or at least in their big cities, which includes the implantation of such technologies.

But the communicational focus of the concept of globalization is essentially incomplete: I defy anyone to try to think it in exclusively media or communicational terms; and we can find a point of contrast and distinction in the images of the media in the earlier twentieth century, that is to say in the modernist period. There did then seem to be a certain semi-autonomy about the development of the media: radio did seem to penetrate for the first time into remote areas (both at home and abroad); the progress of film around the world was both a swift and a startling one, which seemed to bring some new kind of mass consciousness with it; journalism and reporting, meanwhile, were somehow at their outer reaches heroic acts, which shed new light and brought back new information. No one can feel that the cybernetic revolution is like that, if only because it builds on those first, already established, networks. The communicational development today is no longer one of "enlightenment" in all its connotations, but rather of new technologies.

This is why, along with the communicational concept of globalization, one always finds other dimensions smuggled in. Thus, if the newer phenomenon essentially distinguishes itself from the older modern one by technology rather than by information (even though this term is then itself reappropriated and ideologically developed today on a grand scale), what happens is that the technology and what the computer people call information begin to slip insensibly in the direction of advertisements and publicity, of postmodern marketing, and finally of the export of television programs, rather than the return of startling reports from remote places. But this is to say that the surface concept, the communicational one, has suddenly acquired a whole cultural dimension: the communicational signifier has been endowed with a more properly cultural signified or signification. Now the positing of an enlargement of communicational nets has secretly been transformed into some kind of message about a new world culture.

But the slippage can also take another direction: the economic. Thus, in our attempt to think this new, still purely communicational, concept, we begin to fill the empty signifier in with visions of financial transfers and investments all over the world, and the new networks begin to swell with the commerce of some new and allegedly more flexible capitalism (I have to confess that I have always found this a ludicrous expression). We begin remembering that the newly flexible production was made possible by computerization precisely (a loop back to the technological again), and we also remember that computers and their programs and the like are themselves among the most hotly exchanged forms of goods among the nations today. In this variant, then, the ostensibly communicational concept has secretly been transformed into a vision of the world market and its new-found interdependence, a global division of labor on an extraordinary scale, new electronic trade routes tirelessly plied by commerce and finance alike.

Now I think we are better equipped to understand the flows of debate and ideology around this slippery concept, whose twin and not altogether commensurable faces now seem to produce two distinct types of position, which are however themselves reversible. Thus, if you insist on the cultural contents of this new communicational form, I think you will slowly emerge into a postmodern celebration of difference and differentiation: suddenly all the cultures around the world are placed in tolerant contact with each other in a kind of immense cultural pluralism which it would be very difficult not to welcome. Beyond that, beyond the dawning celebration of cultural difference, and often very closely linked to it, is a celebration of the emergence of a whole immense range of groups, races, genders, ethnicities, into the speech of the public sphere; a falling away of those structures that condemned whole segments of the population to silence and to subalternity; a worldwide growth of popular democratization—why not?—which seems to have some relationship to the evolution of the media, but which is immediately expressed by a new richness and variety of cultures in the new world space.

If, on the other hand, your thoughts turn economic, and the concept of globalization becomes colored by those codes and meanings, I think you will find the concept darkening and growing more opaque. Now what comes to the fore is increasing identity (rather than difference): the rapid assimilation of hitherto autonomous national markets and productive zones into a single sphere, the disappearance of national subsistence (in food for example), the forced integration of countries all over the globe into precisely that new global division of labor I mentioned before. Here what begins to infuse our thinking of globalization is a picture of standardization on an unparalleled new scale; of forced integration as well, into a world system from which "delinking" (to use Samir Amin's term) is henceforth impossible and even unthinking and inconceivable. This is obviously a far more baleful prospect than the preceding joyous vision of heterogeneity and difference; but I'm not sure that these visions are logically incompatible, indeed they seem somehow to be dialectically related, at least on the mode of the unresolvable antinomy.

But now, having achieved these first twin positions, having in some first moment rotated the concept in such a way that it takes on these distinct kinds of content, its surface now glittering in light, and then obscured again by darkness and gloom—now it is important to add that the transfers can begin. Now, after having secured first initial structural possibilities, you can project their axes upon each other. Now, in a second moment, the baleful vision of Identity can be transferred onto the cultural realm: and what will be affirmed, in some gloomy Frankfurt School fashion, is the worldwide Americanization or standardization of culture, the destruction of local differences, the massification of all the peoples on the planet.

But you are equally free to do the inverse, and to transfer the joyous and celebratory Difference and multiple heterogeneities of the first, cultural dimension, onto the economic sphere: where as you may well imagine the rhetoricians of the market pop up and feverishly reassure us as to the richness and excitement of the new free market all over the world, and the increase in sheer productivity which open markets will lead to, the transcendental satisfaction that human beings have finally begun to grasp exchange, the market, and capitalism as their most fundamental human possibilities and the surest sources of freedom.

Such are the multiple structural possibilities and combinations made available by this most ambiguous ideological concept and its alternating contents, through which we may now provisionally explore a few paths.

2.

One obvious one is the sense in which globalization means the export and import of culture. This is, no doubt, a matter of business; yet it also presumably foretells the contact and interpenetration of national cultures at an intensity scarcely conceivable in older, slower epochs.

It is enough to think of all the people around the world who watch exported North American television programs to realize that this cultural intervention is deeper than anything known in earlier forms of colonization or imperialism, or simple tourism. A great Indian filmmaker once described the ways in which the gestures and the gait of his teenage son were modified by watching American television: one supposes that his ideas and values were also modified: does this mean that the rest of the world is becoming Americanized? And if so, what do we think about that; or perhaps one should ask, what does the rest of the world think about that, and what might Americans think about it?

For I must now add here a basic point about cultural pluralism and diversity, even about linguistic pluralism and diversity. We have to understand, in this country, something that is difficult for us to realize, namely that the US is not just one country, or one culture, among others; any more than English is just one language among others. There is a fundamental dissymmetry in the relationship between the United States and every other country in the world, not only Third World countries, but even Japan and those of Western Europe, as I will try to suggest in a moment.

This means that there is a kind of blindness at the center, which reflection on globalization may help us partly correct. American blindness can be registered, for example, in our tendency to confuse the universal and the cultural, as well as to assume that in any given geopolitical conflict all elements and values are somehow equal and equivalent, in other words are not affected by the disproportions of power. I happen to think this poses interesting and relatively new philosophical problems, but I want to illustrate the consequences in more concrete terms.

Take for example the question of languages in the new world system: are they all equal, and can every language group freely produce its own culture according to its own needs? The speakers of the smaller languages have always protested against that view; and their anxieties can only be heightened by the emergence of a kind of global or jet-set transnational culture in which a few international hits (literary or cultural) are canonized by the media and given a heightened circulation inconceivable for the local products they tend in any case to squeeze out. Meanwhile, it is important for us here to realize that for most people in the world English itself is not exactly a culture language: it is the lingua franca of money and power, which you have to learn and use for practical but scarcely for aesthetic purposes. But the very connotation of power then tends in the eyes of foreign speakers to reduce the value of all forms of English-language high culture.

By the same token, American mass culture, associated as it is with money and commodities, enjoys a prestige which is perilous for most forms of domestic cultural production, that either find themselves wiped out—as with local film and television production—or co-opted and transformed beyond recognition, as with local music. We do not here sufficiently notice —because we do not have to notice—the significance, in the GATT and NAFTA negotiations and agreements, of the cultural clauses, and of the struggle between immense US cultural interests, which want to open up foreign borders to American film, television, music, and the like, and foreign nation-states which still place a premium on the preservation and development of their national languages and cultures and attempt to limit the damages—both material and social—caused by the leveling power of American mass culture. Material on account of the enormous financial interests involved; but social because of the very change in values likely to be wrought by what used to be called—when it was a far more limited phenomenon—Americanization.

3.

All of which suggests that we need to open a long parenthesis on the significance of the GATT and NAFTA agreements, which constitute stages in a long American attempt to undermine a politics of cultural subsidies and quotas in other parts of the world but primarily in Western Europe.

French resistance to this American pressure has mostly been presented over here as a cultural eccentricity, like frogs' legs. I want to argue, however, that it sets a fundamental agenda for all culture workers in the next decade and may be an adequate focus for reorganizing the equally old-fashioned or eccentric notion of cultural imperialism and indeed of imperialism generally, today, in the new late-capitalist world system.

The becoming cultural of the economic, and the becoming economic of the cultural, has often been identified as one of the features that characterizes what is now widely known as postmodernity. In any case it has fundamental consequences for the status of mass culture as such. The GATT talks are there to remind us that American film and television fall under base and superstructure alike as it were; they are economics fully as much as they are culture, and are indeed, along with agribusiness and weapons, the principal economic export of the United States—an enormous source of sheer profit and income. This is why American insistence on opening the quota barriers on film in foreign countries should not be seen as a North American cultural eccentricity either, such as violence or apple pie, but rather a hardheaded business necessity—a formal economic necessity irrespective of the frivolous cultural content.

Our GATT cultural policy must thus also be seen as a drive for economic expansion—the logic of capital generally being an irresistible drive for expansion, or positing a requirement for enlarged accumulation that cannot be slowed or arrested, suspended or reformed, without mortal damage to the system itself. It is in particular important, ironically, to distance the rhetoric of freedom—not merely free trade, but free speech, the free passage of ideas and intellectual "properties"—which accompanies this policy. The material side of ideas or cultural items always lay in the institutions of reproduction and transmission: those are today, however, everywhere visible as enormous corporations based on a monopoly of the relevant information technology:

so the freedom of those corporations (and their dominant nation-state) is scarcely the same thing as our individual freedom as citizens. Meanwhile the accompanying politics of copyright, patent, and intellectual property indissociable from the same international politics reminds us sharply that the sought-after freedom of ideas is important because the ideas are private property and designed to be sold in great and profitable quantities. I won't discuss this important feature of the latter any more (which has its ecological equivalent in the attempt to patent chemicals derived from Third World rain forests and the like), but will return to the free market later on.

The other side of this particular freedom I do want to comment on, however, is that it is literally a zero-sum game in which my freedom results in the destruction of other people's national culture industries. Those of you who think the politics of socialism is dead—those of you now inveterately prejudiced against the intervention of the state, and fantasizing about the possibilities of non-governmental organizations—might do well to reflect on the necessity of government subsidies in the creation of any independent or national film industry: West Germany's *Länder* have long been a model for the subsidizing of avant-gardes, France has had intricate and valuable provisions for supporting younger filmmakers out of commercial film profits, England's current new wave, around Channel Four and the BFI, would not exist without the government and its older BBC and socialist traditions, Canada finally (along with Québec) offers a range of precedents for a really productive and stimulating role of the state in culture and even cultural politics. The point is that the GATT talks were designed, at least in the eyes of the American state lobbyists, to dismantle all these local and national subsidies as forms of unfair international competition; these subsidies were direct and explicit targets of the currently suspended free-trade-in-entertainment drive; and I hope it is also obvious that success in this area would at once mean the tendential extinction of new national cultural and artistic production elsewhere, just as the free movement of American movies in the world spells the death knell of national cinemas elsewhere, perhaps of all other national cinemas as distinct species. To talk about this in terms of a telos or an intention may seem conspiratorial, but surely the two sides go together—your own securing of advantage and the destruction of your enemy's: in this particular instance the new freer market emphatically does not result in an increase in your competitor's business as well. Already, as long ago as the Marshall Plan, American aid to the postwar Western European countries was accompanied by foresightful provisions about the quantities of American film to be lawfully admitted to the European markets; in several instances, the English, the German, and the Italian most notably, this flooding of the theaters by American films effectively killed off the respective national industries, which had to specialize or go Third World to survive at all. It is no accident that the French industry alone retained its national character, and that it should therefore be in France that the greatest consciousness of these dangers is to be found.

This destruction of a national film production—and along with it, potentially, that of national or local culture as a whole—is now what can be witnessed everywhere in the Third and Second Worlds. It should be understood that the triumph of Hollywood film (from which I won't here separate out television, which is today just as important or even more so) is not merely an economic triumph, it is a formal and also a political one. It was a significant theoretical event, I think, when in their 1985 book, *Classical Hollywood Cinema,* Bordwell, Staiger, and Thompson pronounce the death of the various 1960s and 1970s filmic experiments all over the world and the universal hegemony of the classical Hollywood form.[2] This is of course in another sense a relatively final death of the modern, insofar as independent filmmakers all over the world could be seen to be guided by a certain modernism; but it is also the death of the political, and an allegory of the end of the possibility of imagining radically different social alternatives to this one we now live under. For political film in the 1960s and 1970s still affirmed that possibility (as did modernism in general in a more complex way), by affirming that the discovery or invention of a radically new form was at one with the discovery or invention of radically new social relations and ways of living in the world. It is those possibilities—filmic, formal, political, and social—which have disappeared as some more definitive hegemony of the United States has seemed to emerge.

Now it will be said that there is a good reason for all this, namely that people like Hollywood films and that they can probably also be expected eventually to like the American way of life, insofar as it can be extended to them. Why do Hungarian or Russian audiences flock to Hollywood films rather than what remains of their own once prestigious national film production? Why is it to be feared that with privatization the hitherto sealed and protected film culture of India will begin to melt away like snow, despite the extraordinary size and popularity of traditional Hindi comedy? The rapidity of the editing of American films and the sensuous attractions of its essential violence can be appealed to as explanations; but in that form such explanations still sound rather moralizing. It is easy to become addicted to Hollywood films and television, indeed I imagine most of us are; but it would be preferable to look at it the other way around and measure the degree to which each national culture and daily life is a seamless web of habits and habitual practices, which form a totality or a system. It is very easy to break up such traditional cultural systems, which extend to the way people live their bodies and use language, as well as the way they treat each

---

[2]   David Bordwell, Janet Staiger, and Kristin Thompson, *Classical Hollywood Cinema,* New York: Columbia University Press, 1985, 381–385.

other and nature. Once destroyed, those fabrics can never be re-created. Some of the Third World are still in a situation in which that fabric is preserved. The violence of American cultural imperialism and the penetration of Hollywood film and television lies in its destruction of those traditions, which are very far from being precapitalist or quasi-religious traditions but are rather recent and successful accommodations of the old institutions to modern technology.

The point is therefore that, alongside the free market as an ideology, the consumption of Hollywood film form is the apprenticeship to a specific culture, to an everyday life as a cultural practice: the practice of which commodified narratives are the aesthetic expression, so that the populations in question learn both at the same time. Hollywood is not merely a name for a business that makes money but also for a fundamental late-capitalist cultural revolution, in which old ways of life are broken up and new ones set in place. "But if these other countries want that ..." it will still be asked. The implication is that it is in human nature; and further, that all history has been moving towards American culture as its apotheosis. But it is rather a matter of whether we want that ourselves; because if we can imagine nothing else then obviously we have nothing to warn other cultures about either.

4.

We must thus now return to the American standpoint, and to stress the point of fundamental dissymmetry between the US and other cultures. There can, in other words, never be parity in these areas: in the new global culture there are no take-off stages; other languages will never come to equal English in its global function, even if they were systematically tried out; just as other local entertainment industries are most unlikely to supplant Hollywood in any global or universally successful form, particularly owing to the way in which the American system itself undertakes to incorporate exotic elements from abroad—samurai culture here, South African music there, John Woo films here, Thai food there, and so forth.

This is indeed the sense in which the new explosion of world culture has seemed to so many to be an occasion for celebration; nor is it desirable to choose between the two very different views of the matter, but rather to intensify their incompatibility and opposition such that we can live this particular contradiction as our own historic form of Hegel's "Unhappy Consciousness." On the one hand, there is the view according to which globalization essentially means unification and standardization. By the intermediaries of the great mostly American-based transnational or multinational corporations, a standard form of American material life, along with

North American values and cultural forms, is being systematically transmitted to other cultures. Nor is this simply a matter of machinery and buildings, which increasingly make all the places of the world look alike. It is not only a matter of values either—although Americans always find it shocking when foreigners suggest that human rights, feminist values, and even parliamentary democracy are not necessarily to be seen as universals, but rather merely local American cultural characteristics that have been exported as practices valid for all peoples in the world.

That kind of shock is good for us, I want to say; but I have not yet mentioned the supreme form in which American economic interest and American cultural influence coincide to produce the export of a way of life itself. People often evoke "corrosive individualism" and also consumerist "materialism" as ways of accounting for the destructiveness of the new globalization process. But I think these moralizing concepts are inadequate to the task, and do not sufficiently identify the destructive forces which are North American in origin and result from the unchallenged primacy of the United States today and thus the "American way of life" and American mass-media culture. This is *consumerism* as such, the very lynchpin of our economic system, and also the mode of daily life in which all our mass culture and entertainment industries train us ceaselessly day after day, in an image and media barrage quite unparalleled in history. Since the discrediting of socialism by the collapse of Russian communism, only religious fundamentalism has seemed to offer an alternative way of life—let us not, heaven help us, call it a lifestyle—to American consumerism. But is it certain that all of human history has been, as Fukuyama and others believe, a tortuous progression towards the American consumer as a climax? And is it meanwhile so sure that the benefits of the market can be extended so far as to make this new way of life available for everyone on the globe? If not, we will have destroyed their cultures without offering any alternatives: but it has also been argued that all the other recrudescences of what people think of as local and nationalist violence are themselves reactions and defense mechanisms in the face of heightened globalization. Here is for example Giovanni Arrighi:

> Entire communities, countries, even continents, as in the case of sub-Saharan Africa, have been declared "redundant," superfluous to the changing economy of capitalist accumulation on a world scale. Combined with the collapse of the world power and the territorial empire of the USSR, the unplugging of these "redundant" communities and locales from the world supply system has triggered innumerable, mostly violent feuds over "who is more superfluous than whom," or, more simply, over the appropriation of resources that were made absolutely scarce by the unplugging. Generally speaking, these feuds have been diagnosed and treated not as expressions of the self-protection of society against the disruption of

established ways of life under the impact of intensifying world market competition—which for the most part is what they are. Rather, they have been diagnosed and treated as the expression of atavistic hatreds or of power struggles among local bullies, both of which have played at best only a secondary role.[3]

Whatever the validity of Arrighi's diagnosis here, he at least gives us a strong lesson in thinking about current events in terms of the current situation of globalization, rather than in culturalist terms (which generally end up being racist ones).

It is hard to give voice now to more positive views after such catastrophic visions without trivializing the other side of the coin, the celebration of globalization and postmodernity. But this is also a very persuasive view which I think many of us, particularly in the United States, tend to share unconsciously and practically to the degree to which we are ourselves the recipients of the new world culture, in a position to benefit from globalization in the activation of a host of new intellectual networks and the exchanges and discussions across a variety of national situations which have themselves become standardized by globalization to the degree to which we can now speak to each other. My sense is that the old and fundamental opposition, in the colonized world, between Westernizers and traditionalists, has almost completely disappeared in this new postmodern moment of capitalism. That opposition was so to speak a modernist one, and it no longer holds for the very simple reason that tradition in that form has everywhere been wiped out. Neo-Confucianism or Islamic and Hindu fundamentalism themselves are new, are postmodern inventions, not survivals of ancient ways of life. In that sense also the opposition between the metropolis and the provinces has also disappeared, both nationally and on a global scale; and this not necessarily for a very good reason either, since it is essentially standardization that effaces the difference between the center and the margins. And while it may be an exaggeration to claim that we are all "marginals" now, all "decentered," in the current good senses of those words, certainly many new freedoms have been won in the process whereby globalization has meant a decentering and a proliferation of differences. You see how this view grasps the arrival of globalization in exactly the opposite way from the pessimistic one, for which it meant unification and standardization: yet these are indeed the two antithetical features of that elephant we are here blindly attempting to characterize.

In the realm of culture, no one has given a more powerful expression to the celebratory picture of globalization than the Mexican theorist Nestor Garcia-Canclini, in his conception of culture as hybridization[4]: on this view,

---

[3] Giovanni Arrighi, *The Long Twentieth Century: Money, Power and the Origins of Our Times*, London: Verso, 1994, 330–331.

[4] Nestor Garcia-Canclini, *Culturas Hibridas*, Mexico City: Grijalbo, 1989.

then, the eclectic contacts and borrowings enabled by globalization are positive and healthy, they positively encourage the proliferation of new cultures (and indeed, I think it is implied by this view that in any case culture always functioned this way, by impure and disorderly combinations, and not by situations of isolation and regulated tradition). Garcia-Canclini's work thus gives ammunition to the most vital Utopian visions of our own time, of an immense global urban intercultural festival without a center or even a dominant cultural mode any longer. I myself think this view needs a little economic specificity, and is rather inconsistent with the quality and impoverishment of what has to be called corporate culture on a global scale.

But its clash with the previous pessimistic view of the globalization process is the shock from which I hope the sparks will fly, and in any case this is surely one of the most important debates of the current period.

(The other very important and surely related opposition is that which obtains between the older values of autonomy and self-sufficiency—both in culture and economics—and current visions of systemic interdependence in which we are all points in a net or global web. There too powerful cases can be made on both sides, and perhaps they will be here, but I mention this particular debate only in passing and in order to read it onto some enlarged agenda.)

But now I need to move back to the trilateral possibility, and say why, if Garcia-Canclini proves to be wrong about the continuing cultural vitality and production of the so-called Third World, we might not continue to expect a counterbalance to Americanization in the two other great world centers of Europe and Japan.

In the present context I would rather present that as a problem than a mere opinion, namely whether, in our time, the relationship between culture and economics has not fundamentally altered. At any rate, it does seem to me that fresh cultural production and innovation—and this means in the area of mass-consumed culture—are the crucial indexes of the centrality of a given area and not its wealth or productive power. This is why it was extraordinarily significant when the ultimate Japanese moves to incorporate the US entertainment industry—Sony's acquisition of Columbia Pictures and Matshushita's buyout of MCA—both failed: it meant that despite immense wealth and technological and industrial production, even despite ownership itself and private property, the Japanese were unable to master the essentially cultural productivity required to secure the globalization process for any given competitor. Whoever evokes the production of culture at the same time means the production of everyday life: and without that your economic system can scarcely continue to expand and implant itself.

As for Europe—more wealthy and culturally elegant than ever, a glittering museum to a remarkable past, most immediately the past of modernism itself—I also want to suggest that its failure to generate its own forms of mass-cultural production is an ominous sign. Is it possible that the death of modernism also meant a certain end for a certain type of hegemonic European art and culture? I happen to find the effort, stimulated by the EEC, to conjure up new European cultural synthesis, with Milan Kundera substituting for T. S. Eliot, an equally ominous, if more pathetic, symptom. The emergence of a host of local popular cultures all over Europe is a welcome bonus of postmodernity, as it is everywhere in the world, but by definition renounces the old European hegemonic project.

By the same token, the former socialist countries have largely seemed unable to generate an original culture and a distinctive way of life capable of standing as an alternative, while, as I have already suggested, in the Third World the older traditionalisms are equally enfeebled and mummified, and only a religious fundamentalism seems to have the strength and the will to resist Americanization. But here the operative word is surely "seems"; for we have yet to see whether these experiments offer positive social alternatives, or merely reactive and repressive violence.

5.

The celebration of market "freedom" has so often seemed to place these ominous developments in a wholly new and positive light, that it seems worthwhile, in conclusion, to interrogate this concept in its turn; and to determine the interference of philosophical categories activated by the identification of globalization with the market as such. These inner conceptual contradictions can at first be registered as so many conflations of otherwise distinct and differentiated "levels" of social life.

Thus, in a splendid work to which I have often referred,[5] A. O. Hirschman documents the ways in which the earliest Renaissance pamphlets and treatises about the benefits of commerce and of what was shortly to develop into capitalism itself celebrated "la douceur du commerce"—the beneficent influence of trade on savage or violent, barbaric mentalities, the bringing in of cosmopolitan interests and perspectives, the gradual implantation of the civil among rude peoples (not least those of feudal Europe itself, I may add). Here already we have a conflation of two levels: that of exchange is conflated with that of human relations and everyday life (as we would now say today), and an identity between them affirmed. Meanwhile in our own time the ineffable Hayek has proposed a similar identification, but on a grander political scale: the identity between free enterprise and political democracy. Lack of the latter is supposed to impede development of the former; and

---

[5] Albert O. Hirschman, *The Passions and the Interests*, Princeton: Princeton University Press, 1977.

therefore it must follow that development of the latter—democracy—is dependent on development of the free market itself. It is a syllogism enthusiastically developed by the Friedmanites and neo-conservatives, and most recently brandished by all those carpet-bagging free-world economists who raced to the benighted countries of the former East after 1989 to offer advice on how to build this particular better mousetrap.[6] But even within this system of ideological identifications there is a more basic ambiguity, and it concerns the market itself: the use of Marx's own categories suggests that this very "idea" or ideologeme involves the illicit conflation of two distinct categories, that of distribution and that of production (there may also be a slippage into consumption itself at various points in the rhetorical operation).

For capitalist production is what is generally being defended here, but in the name and under the guise of distribution—the extraordinary and heterogeneous varieties of market exchange—of which we know that precisely one of the fundamental crisis points in capitalism always comes when those things do not function in sync: overproduction, piling up of goods in warehouses, that nobody can buy, and so on and so forth. Meanwhile the libidinization of the market—if I may put it that way—the reason so many people now feel that this boring and archaic thing is sexy—results from the sweetening of this pill by all kinds of images of consumption as such: the commodity as it were becoming its own ideology, and in what Leslie Sklair calls the new transnational "culture-ideology of consumption" changing traditional psychic habits and practices and sweeping all before it into something allegedly resembling the American Way of Life.

Supposing, however, that what are here identified as so many levels of the same thing were in reality in contradiction with each other: for example, supposing that consumerism were inconsistent with democracy, that the habits and addictions of postmodern consumption block or repress possibilities of political and collective action as such? We may remember, for example, that historically the invention of mass culture as a component of Fordism was the very source of the famous American exceptionalism: that is to say, that what permitted a federalism, a melting pot, a management of class struggle, in the United States, as against most other countries in the world, was very precisely our unique system of mass culture and consumption as that displaced energies in new consensus-governed directions. It becomes ironic, then, when mass culture is offered as a space of democratization, let alone of resistance, as many participants in the globalization debate have tended to do.

---

[6] But see Maurice Meisner's *The Deng Xiaoping Era*, New York: Hill and Wang, 1996, for powerful evidence about the possibilities for capitalist development offered by "non-democratic" systems.

But some of these confusions can be clarified by the situations them-selves; others by the disentanglement of levels I have been proposing here. Let's look more closely at the celebration of the liberating effects of commer-cial mass culture, particularly as that has been expressed with special emphasis in the Latin American areas, by scholars and theorists like George Yúdice, and particularly in the area of popular music (and in Brazil, of television).[7] In literature, language protects the great modern literary pro-ductions—the Latin American Boom, for example—which in many ways reverse the direction and conquer North American and European markets. In music, the point is made, not only that local music wins out over imported or North American kinds, but also and even more importantly, that the transnationals actually invest in these, in the local music and record-ing industries (and also, in Brazil, in the local television networks). Here then mass culture would seem to offer a mode of resistance to a general absorption of local and national production into the orbit of transnational business, or at least, in the latter-mentioned case, a way of co-opting and deflecting that to your own local and national advantage. On the other hand, even this particular national success story does not constitute the rule rather than the exception, given the way in which television in some other (not merely Third World) countries is almost wholly colonized by imported North American shows. It is no doubt proper to distinguish between eco-nomic and cultural dependence as a rule of thumb: what I want to point out is that even such a banal distinction reintroduces the philosophical dilem-mas, and in particular the problems of category and level I have wanted to stress here. What is indeed the justification for distinguishing these two levels of the economic and the cultural when in the United States today, as we have already seen, the cultural—the entertainment business—is along with food one of our most important economic exports, and one the Ameri-can government is prepared to go to great lengths to defend, as witness the struggles within the GATT and NAFTA negotiations?

From a different theoretical point of view, meanwhile, the theory of postmodernity affirms a gradual dedifferentiation of these levels, the eco-nomic itself gradually becoming cultural, all the while the cultural gradually becomes economic. Image society and advertising can no doubt document the gradual transformation of commodities into libidinal images of them-selves, that is to say, into well-nigh cultural products; while the dissolution of high culture and the simultaneous intensification of investment in mass-cultural commodities may be enough to suggest that, whatever was the case at earlier stages and moments of capitalism (where the aesthetic was very precisely a sanctuary and a refuge from business and the state), today there

---

[7] George Yúdice, "Civil Society, Consumption, and Governmentality in an Age of Global Restructuring," in *Social Text*, Num. 45, Winter 1995, 1–25.

are no enclaves—aesthetic or other—left in which the commodity form does not reign supreme.

The proposition, therefore, that the cultural realm can in certain circumstances (Brazilian television) enter into conflict with the economic realm (dependence), while neither illogical nor unthinkable, needs further elaboration, one feature of which would no doubt lie in Brazil's unique status as an immense market of virtually continental dimensions, an explanation I prefer to the more traditional ideas of cultural difference, national and linguistic tradition, and the like, which themselves need to be translated back into materialist terms.

Yúdice's proposition, however, remains to be examined: that under certain circumstances culture—but now let's restrict it to popular music in order to simplify matters—can serve as a proving ground for democracy by offering new conceptions and exercises of something like citizenship; in other words, that there are practices of consumer choice and personal autonomy that train the otherwise subaltern individual in a new kind of freedom that can be seen (as Schiller did long ago[8]) as a preparation for political freedom. This is clearly to posit a "fusion" of the levels of culture and politics with a vengeance, and our restriction to music (not just contemplative bourgeois listening, but dance and musical practice in general) makes the proposition far more plausible than it sounds when a John Fiske, for example, rehearses it for commercial television.[9] Nor should we forget that the great and (alas) abortive Utopian blueprints for the changes French socialism never made when it came to power were patterned specifically and explicitly on the model of music by their principal theoretician, Jacques Attali, himself a musician and an economist (who frequently stressed the kinship between these two "levels").[10] But it is perhaps Stuart Hall who has most persuasively spoken out for a new conception of culture, particularly in his recent "new times" (I hesitate to call it postmodern) period or turn; leaving aside the question of Hall's Marxism or socialism today, Hall's account of the way in which the new musical culture of postmodernity functions to overcome the subalternities of the various minority groups in Britain is a powerful one, and goes a long way towards restoring political potentialities to art in a different sense than we have been accustomed to thinking about them.[11] This cultural multiplicity is however no doubt aimed at two forms of unity or oneness: the oneness of the racist state and

---

[8] Friedrich Schiller, *On the Aesthetic Education of Man,* trans. Elizabeth Mary Wilkinson and Leonard Ashley Willoughby, Oxford: Clarendon Press, 1967.

[9] John Fiske, *Television Culture,* London: Methuen, 1987.

[10] Jacques Attali, *Les Trois Mondes,* Paris: Seuil, 1983.

[11] Stuart Hall and Martin Jacques, *New Times: The Changing Face of Politics in the 1990s,* New York: Verso, 1991.

the unity of the white (Protestant) citizens represented by that state. (We're talking now about the antagonistic structure of imaginary relations, and not about the empirical social realities of this or that locality in Britain.)

It is a model which can now clarify the widespread theoretical and political emphasis on culture and the market in Latin America as well. For it is often stressed (by no one so forcefully as by Garcia-Canclini himself) that everywhere in Latin America culture and its support are identified with the state, in Mexico with the post-revolutionary state. Power in these countries is itself identified with the state, rather than, as in so-called First World countries, with capitalism itself. Thus, an emphasis on commerce and trade in a situation of state power amounts very precisely to a privileging of the moment of multiplicity as a place of freedom and resistance: the market in the sense of exchange and commerce thus functions in Latin America very much as do the so-called NGOs (non-governmental organizations) in Asia and Africa, as what also escapes the unenlightened domination of the state itself. But in the Anglo-American First World, I am tempted to say, the state can still be a positive space: its powers are what must be protected against the right-wing attempts to dissolve it back into private businesses and operations of all kinds. The state is the place of welfare and social legislation, the source of the safety net of a whole range of crucial legislative powers (over employment, health, education, and the like), which must not be surrendered to the fragmenting and disintegrating effects of American business.

Yet there is a way in which these two radically different situations can be compared: in the one, Latin America, multiplicity is celebrated against an oppressive unity; in the other, North America, a positive unity is defended against an oppressive multiplicity. But these simply change the valences on the terms, the mode of evaluation remains the same. Such changes and similarities are, I believe, to be grasped as structural peculiarities, not yet of globalization as such, but rather of the older international system: in other words, a level of abstraction and interrelationship in which what holds at a national level is reversed at a distance. If that sounds exceedingly obscure, let me cite the most dramatic example of it I have found, from C. L. R. James's great history of the Haitian Revolution, which he significantly entitled *The Black Jacobins*.[12] The title is itself the paradox I have in mind: because what transpires in James's narrative is that so-called subjects of history play very different roles across the international network. We have been taught, indeed, that the most radical force in the French Revolution was the *sans-culottes*: not yet a proletariat exactly, a mixture of petty bourgeoisie, apprentices, students, lumpens, and the like. These constituted the army of the Jacobin movement and of Robespierre. What James shows us is that in

---

[12] C. L. R. James, *The Black Jacobins*, New York: Vintage Books, 1963.

Haiti the *sans-culottes* (along with their revolutionary culture exported from France) become the forces of reaction, the principal forces who oppose the revolutionary movement and the enemies of Toussaint L'Ouverture. It is too easy to evoke simple racism in this situation: I propose that it rather be read as a dialectical reversal which is itself determined by the coming into being of relationships which are no longer internal national ones (I hesitate to use a word like "transnational," which for all its literal applicability has much more recent connotations; just as I hesitate to pronounce the word "imperialism," which is also anachronistic; nor can slavery be thought of in simple colonial terms either). And I think the dialectical shift from positive to negative in this matter of unity and multiplicity, in the differences between the North American and the Latin American situations, is also to be theorized in something of the same way.

But now I want to develop this dialectic a little more broadly. We have in this particular instance observed the endowment of the abstract opposition of Identity and Difference with a specific content of unity versus multiplicity. Yet it is also possible to transcode all this into the terms of the current postmodern debates: in the Latin American case, I believe that the positive force of culture is not meant to designate mass or popular culture exclusively, but rather includes high culture and very specifically the national literature and language: samba, let's say, is opposed to Guimarães Rosa, but identified with his literary achievement and enveloped within the more general pride of an autonomous national culture as such. Yet one can also identify national situations—and I use this clumsy circumlocution deliberately, to forestall the usual endless debates about whether there still are such things as "nations" and what their relationship to that other mysterious thing called nationalism might be—in which the defense of national autonomy takes the form of what may seem a more traditional modernism: the defense of the powers of art and high culture, the deeper kinship between such artistic modernism and the political power of the collectivity itself, now however conceived as a unified political power or collective project rather than a dispersal into democratic multiplicities and identity positions.

India is a very vast and multiple place indeed, and one finds both modernisms and postmodernisms in full development there. But I have been thinking in particular of a specific vision which unites the social-democratic project of the older Congress Party and Nehru's fellow-traveling non-alignment with a whole aesthetic and artistic politics which is quite different from the cultural-studies politics (if I may put it that way) which we have touched on in the Latin American situation. But is this just the older modernism belated and warmed over? Does it really amount to a defense of Identity over against Difference, and in that sense does it reinforce the attacks on modernism current everywhere, which always seem to have the effect of discarding a modernist politics along with a modernist art, and thereby leaving us politically aimless, as so many people complain today?

It is not out of any wish to mediate, to resolve all these differences and turn theoretical debates and battles into harmony—but rather because I want to stage the powers and benefits of the dialectic itself—that I would propose the following hypothesis: that these differences do not have to do with Difference so much as with where it is located or positioned. Who could be against Difference on the social or even the political level? Indeed, behind many of these essays stands the validation of a new democratic politics (in the First as well as in the Third Worlds) stimulated by the vitality of markets as such, peasant and otherwise: it is a more exotic sociological variant of that age-old defense of commerce and capitalism in terms of exchange and political freedom which has already been mentioned. Yet everything depends on the level at which a malign and standardizing or despotic identity is discerned. If this is to be found in the existence of the State itself, as a national entity, then to be sure, a more micropolitical form of difference, in markets and culture, will be affirmed over against it as a force for the resistance to uniformity and power: here, then, the levels of the cultural and the social are summoned to stand in radical conflict with the level of the political. And at certain key moments in arguments of this kind, something like an affirmation of federalism is invoked, as a future ideal, notwithstanding recent historical developments, about which one might also affirm that they document the failure and death, not of communism, but rather very precisely of federalism as such (the USSR, Yugoslavia, even Canada).

However, when one positions the threats of Identity at a higher level globally, then everything changes: at this upper range, it is not national state power which is the enemy of difference, but rather the transnational system itself, Americanization and the standardized products of a henceforth uniform and standardized ideology and practice of consumption. At this point nation-states and their national cultures are suddenly called upon to play the positive role hitherto assigned—against them—to regions and local practices in the preceding paradigm. And as opposed to the multiplicity of local and regional markets, minority arts and languages, whose vitality can certainly be acknowledged all over the world (uneasily coexisting with the vision of doom of their universal extinction), it is striking to witness the resurgence—in an atmosphere in which the nation-state as such, let alone "nationalism," is a much-maligned entity and value—of defenses of national culture on the part of those who affirm the powers of resistance of a national literature and a national art. Such defenders identify the levels of art and politics by linking the vitality of a national and a modernist culture (here perhaps one could indeed oppose to Gramsci's "national-popular" strategy a genuine "national-modernist" one, despite the fact that Gramsci himself was probably also a modernist in such matters) to the possibility of a great collective or national political project such as was envisioned on the left and on the right during the modernist period.

This position presupposes that it is only by way of such a possibility that the encroachments of the world market, of transnational capitalism along with the great capital-lending power centers of the so-called First World, can be opposed. That in the process it must also oppose the dispersals of a postmodern mass culture then places it in contradiction with those for whom only the activation of a truly grassroots culture of multiplicities and differences can oppose, first the national state itself, and then presumably what lies beyond it in the outside world (even though paradoxically it is often elements of that outside and transnational mass culture which are appropriated for such resistances: Hollywood films being sometimes the source of resistance to hegemony as well as the form such hegemony ultimately takes).

Now I have little enough time to summarize what may seem to have been a never-ending series of paradoxes: such an impression would already mark a useful beginning, insofar as it awakens the suspicion that our problems lie as much in our categories of thought as in the sheer facts of the matter themselves. And that would be, I think, the meaning and function of a return to Hegel today, as over against Althusser. The latter is surely right about his materialist dialectic, his semi-autonomous levels, his structural casualty, and his overdetermination: if you look for those things in Hegel you find what everybody knew all along, namely that he was simply an idealist. But the right way of using Hegel is not that way; it lies rather in precisely those things he was capable of exploring because he was an idealist, namely the categories themselves, the modes and forms of thought in which we inescapably have to think things through, but which have a logic of their own to which we ourselves fall victim if we are unaware of their existence and their informing influence on us. Thus in the most famous chapter of the *Greater Logic,* Hegel tells us how to handle such potentially troublesome categories as those of Identity and Difference.[13] You begin with Identity, he says, only to find that it is always defined in terms of its Difference from something else; you turn to Difference and find out that any thoughts about that involve thoughts about the "identity" of this particular category. As you begin to watch Identity turn into Difference and Difference back into Identity, then you grasp both as an inseparable Opposition, you learn that they must always be thought together. But after learning that, you find out that they are not in opposition; you find rather, that in some other sense, they are

---

[13] G. W. F. Hegel, "The Essentialities or Determinations of Reflection," in *Science of Logic*, trans. A. V. Miller, London: George Allen and Unwin, 1969, Book 2, Section 1, Chapter 2.

one and the same as each other. At that point you have approached the Identity of identity and non-identity, and in the most momentous single reversal in Hegel's entire system suddenly Opposition stands unveiled as Contradiction.

This is always the point we want to reach in the dialectic: we want to uncover phenomena and find the ultimate contradictions behind them. And this was Brecht's notion of dialectic, to hold fast to the contradictions in all things, which make them change and evolve in time. But in Hegel, Contradiction then passes over into its Ground, into what I would call the situation itself; the serial view or the map of the totality in which things happen and History takes place. I like to think that it is something like this movement of the categories—producing each other, and evolving into ever new viewpoints—that Lenin saw and learned in Hegel, in his reading of him during the first weeks and months of World War I.[14] But I would also like to think that these are lessons we can still put to use today, not least in our attempts to grasp the still ill-defined and ever emerging effects of that phenomenon we have begun to call globalization.

---

[14] Kevin Anderson, *Lenin, Hegel and Western Marxism*, Urbana: University of Illinois Press, 1995.

Chapter 18

Globalization as Political Strategy

Attempts to define globalization often seem little better than so many ideological appropriations—discussions not of the process itself, but of its effects, good or bad: judgments, in other words, totalizing in nature; while functional descriptions tend to isolate particular elements without relating them to each other.[1] It may be more productive, then, to combine all the descriptions and to take an inventory of their ambiguities—something that means talking as much about fantasies and anxieties as about the thing itself. In what follows we will explore these five distinct levels of globalization, with a view to demonstrating their ultimate cohesion and to articulating a politics of resistance: the technological, the political, the cultural, the economic, the social, very much in that order.

I.

One can talk about globalization, for instance, in purely technological terms: the new communications technology and the information revolution —innovations which, of course, do not simply remain at the level of communication in the narrow sense, but also have their impact on industrial production and organization, and on the marketing of goods. Most commentators seem to feel that this dimension of globalization, at least, is irreversible: a Luddite politics does not seem to be an option here. But the theme reminds us of an urgent consideration in any discussion of globalization: is it really inevitable? Can its processes be stopped, diverted, or reversed? Might regions, even whole continents, exclude the forces of globalization, secede, or "delink" from it?[2] Our answers to these questions will have an important bearing on our strategic conclusions.

---

[1] See, for a sampling of views, Fredric Jameson and Masao Miyoshi, eds., *The Cultures of Globalization*, Durham, NC: Duke University Press, 1998.

[2] The allusion is to Samir Amin's useful term *la déconnexion*, see *Delinking: Towards a Polycentric World*, London: Zed, 1985.

2.

In discussions of globalization at the political level, one question has predominated: that of the nation-state. Is it over and done with, or does it still have a vital role to play? If reports of its demise are naïve, what then to make of globalization itself? Should it, perhaps, be understood as merely one pressure among many on national governments—and so on? But lurking behind these debates, I believe, is a deeper fear, a more fundamental narrative thought or fantasy. For when we talk about the spreading power and influence of globalization, aren't we really referring to the spreading economic and military might of the US? And in speaking of the weakening of the nation-state, are we not actually describing the subordination of the other nation-states to American power, either through consent and collaboration, or by the use of brute force and economic threat? Looming behind the anxieties expressed here is a new version of what used to be called imperialism, which we can now trace through a whole dynasty of forms. An earlier version was that of the pre–First World War colonialist order, practiced by a number of European countries, the US, and Japan; this was replaced after the Second World War and the subsequent wave of decolonization by a Cold War form, less obvious but no less insidious in its use of economic pressure and blackmail ("advisers"; covert putsches such as those in Guatemala and Iran), now led predominantly by the US but still involving a few Western European powers.

Now perhaps we have a third stage, in which the United States pursues what Samuel Huntington has defined as a three-pronged strategy: nuclear weapons for the US alone; human rights and American-style electoral democracy; and (less obviously) limits to immigration and the free flow of labor.[3] One might add a fourth crucial policy here: the propagation of the free market across the globe. This latest form of imperialism will involve only the US (and such utterly subordinated satellites as the UK), who will adopt the role of the world's policemen, and enforce their rule through selected interventions (mostly bombings, from a great height) in various alleged danger zones.

What kind of national autonomy do the other nations lose under this new world order? Is this really the same kind of domination as colonization, or forcible enlistment in the Cold War? There are some powerful answers to this question, which mostly seem to fall under our next two headings, the cultural and the economic. Yet the most frequent themes of collective dignity and self-respect lead in fact less often to social than to political considerations. So it is that, after the nation-state and imperialism, we arrive at a third ticklish subject—nationalism.

---

[3] Samuel Huntington, *The Clash of Civilizations and the Remaking of World Order*, New York: Touchstone, 1998.

But is not nationalism rather a cultural question? Imperialism has certainly been discussed in such terms. And nationalism, as a whole internal political program, usually appeals not to financial self-interest, or the lust for power, or even scientific pride—although these may be side-benefits—but rather to something which is not technological, nor really political or economic; and which we therefore, for want of a better word, tend to call cultural. So is it always nationalist to resist US globalization? The US thinks it is, and wants you to agree; and, moreover, to consider US interests as being universal ones. Or is this simply a struggle between various nationalisms, with US global interests merely representing the American kind? We'll come back to this in more detail later on.

3.

The standardization of world culture, with local popular or traditional forms driven out or dumbed down to make way for American television, American music, food, clothes, and films, has been seen by many as the very heart of globalization. And this fear that US models are replacing everything else now spills over from the sphere of culture into our two remaining categories: for this process is clearly, at one level, the result of economic domination—of local cultural industries closed down by American rivals. At a deeper level, the anxiety becomes a social one, of which the cultural is merely a symptom: the fear, in other words, that specifically ethno-national ways of life will themselves be destroyed.

But before moving on to these economic and social considerations we should look a little more closely at some responses to those cultural fears. Often, these downplay the power of cultural imperialism—in that sense, playing the game of US interests—by reassuring us that the global success of American mass culture is not as bad as all that. Against it, they would assert, for example, an Indian (or a Hindu?) identity, which will stubbornly resist the power of an Anglo-Saxon imported culture, whose effects remain merely superficial. There may even be an intrinsic European culture, which can never really be Americanized; and so forth. What is never clear is whether this as it were "natural" defense against cultural imperialism requires overt acts of resistance, a cultural-political program.

Is it the case that in casting doubt upon the defensive strength of these various, non-American cultures, one is offending or insulting them? That one is implying that Indian culture, for instance, is too feeble to resist the forces of the West? Would it not then be more appropriate to downplay the power of imperialism on the grounds that to overemphasize it is to demean those whom it menaces? This particular reflex of political correctness raises an interesting representational issue, about which the following remark may briefly be made.

All cultural politics necessarily confronts this rhetorical alternation between an overweening pride in and affirmation of the cultural group's strength, and a strategic demeaning of it: and this for political reasons. For such a politics can foreground the heroic, and embody forth stirring images of the heroism of the subaltern—strong women, black heroes, Fanonian resistance of the colonized—in order to encourage the public in question; or it can insist on that group's miseries, the oppression of women, or of black people, or the colonized. These portrayals of suffering may be necessary—to arouse indignation, to make the situation of the oppressed more widely known, even to convert sections of the ruling class to their cause. But the risk is that the more you insist on this misery and powerlessness, the more its subjects come to seem like weak and passive victims, easily dominated, in what can then be taken as offensive images that can even be said to disempower those they concern. Both these strategies of representation are necessary in political art, and they are not reconcilable. Perhaps they correspond to different historical moments in the struggle, and evolving local opportunities and representational needs. But it is impossible to resolve this particular antinomy of political correctness unless one thinks about them in that political and strategic way.

4.

I have argued that these cultural issues tend to spill over into economic and social ones. Let's look first at the economic dimension of globalization, which, in fact, constantly seems to be dissolving into all the rest: controlling the new technologies, reinforcing geopolitical interests, and, with postmodernity, finally collapsing the cultural into the economic—and the economic into the cultural. Commodity production is now a cultural phenomenon, in which you buy the product fully as much for its image as for its immediate use. An entire industry has come into being to design commodities' images and to strategize their sale: advertising has become a fundamental mediation between culture and economics, and it is surely to be numbered among the myriad forms of aesthetic production (however much its existence may problematize our idea of this). Erotization is a significant part of the process: the advertising strategists are true Freudo-Marxists who understand the necessity of libidinal investment to enhance their wares. Seriality also plays a role: other people's images of the car or the lawnmower will inform my own decision to get one (allowing us to glimpse the cultural and the economic folding back into the social itself). Economics has in this sense become a cultural matter; and perhaps we may speculate that in the great financial markets, too, a cultural image accompanies the firm whose stocks we dump or buy. Guy Debord long ago described ours as a society of images, consumed aesthetically. He thereby designated this seam that separates culture from economics and, at the same time, connects the two. We talk a good deal—loosely—about the commodification of politics, or ideas, or even emotions and private life; what we must now add is that that commodification today is also an aestheticization—that the commodity, too, is now "aesthetically" consumed.

Such is the movement from economics to culture; but there is also a no less significant movement from culture to economics. This is the entertainment business itself, one of the greatest and most profitable exports of the United States (along with weapons and food). We have already looked at the problems of opposing cultural imperialism solely in terms of local tastes and identities—of the "natural" resistance of an Indian or an Arab public, for example, to certain kinds of Hollywood fare. In fact, it is all too easy to acquaint a non-American public with a taste for Hollywood styles of violence and bodily immediacy, its prestige only enhanced by some image of US modernity and even postmodernity.[4] Is this, then, an argument for the universality of the West—or, at least, of the United States—and its "civilization"? It is a position which is surely widely, if unconsciously, held, and deserves to be confronted seriously and philosophically, even if it seems preposterous.

The United States has made a massive effort since the end of the Second World War to secure the dominance of its films in foreign markets—an achievement generally pushed home politically, by writing clauses into various treaties and aid packages. In most of the European countries—France stands out in its resistance to this particular form of American cultural imperialism—the national film industries were forced onto the defensive after the war by such binding agreements. This systematic US attempt to batter down "cultural-protectionist" policies is only part of a more general and increasingly global corporate strategy, now enshrined in the WTO and its efforts—such as the abortive MAI project—to supercede local laws with international statutes that favor American corporations, whether in intellectual-property copyrights, patents (of, for example, rainforest materials or local inventions), or the deliberate undermining of national self-sufficiency in food.

Here, culture has become decidedly economic, and this particular economics clearly sets a political agenda, dictating policy. Struggles for raw materials and other resources—oil and diamonds, say—are, of course, still waged in the world: dare one call these "modernist" forms of imperialism, along with the even older, more purely political, diplomatic or military

---

[4] I have made an approach to such an analysis in *The Cultural Turn*, London: Verso, 1999; and see also Chapter 8 of *Postmodernism, or, the Cultural Logic of Late Capitalism*, London: Verso, 1991.

efforts to substitute friendly (that is, subservient) governments for resistant ones. But it would seem that today the more distinctively postmodern form of imperialism—even of cultural imperialism—is the one I have been describing, working through the projects of NAFTA, GATT, MAI, and the WTO; not least because these forms offer a textbook example (from a new textbook!) of that dedifferentiation, that confluence between the various and distinct levels of the economic, the cultural, and the political that characterizes postmodernity and lends a fundamental structure to globalization.

There are several other aspects of globalization's economic dimension which we should briefly review. Transnational corporations—simply "multinationals" in the 1970s—were the first sign and symptom of the new capitalist development, raising political fears about the possibility of a new kind of dual power, of the preponderance of these supranational giants over national governments. The paranoid side of such fears and fantasies may be allayed by the complicity of the states themselves with these business operations, given the revolving door between the two sectors—especially in terms of US government personnel. (Ironically, free-market rhetoricians have always denounced the Japanese model of government intervention in national industry.) The more worrying feature of the new global corporate structures is their capacity to devastate national labor markets by transferring their operations to cheaper locations overseas. There has as yet been no comparable globalization of the labor movement to respond to this; the movement of *Gastarbeiter* representing a social and cultural mobility, perhaps, but not yet a political one.

The huge expansion of finance-capital markets has been a spectacular feature of the new economic landscape—once again, its very possibility linked to the simultaneities opened up by the new technologies. Here we no longer have to do with movements of labor or industrial capacity but rather with that of capital itself. The destructive speculation on foreign currencies seen over recent years signals a graver development, namely the absolute dependence of nation-states outside the First World core on foreign capital, in the form of loans, support, and investments. (Even First World countries are vulnerable: witness the pounding received by France for its more leftist policies during the initial years of Mitterrand's regime.) And whereas the processes that have eroded many countries' self-sufficiency in agriculture, leading to import-dependence on US foodstuffs, might, conceivably, be described as a new worldwide division of labor, constituting, as in Adam Smith, an enhancement of productivity, the same cannot be said of dependence on the new global finance markets. The spate of financial crises over the last five years, and the public statements by political leaders such as Prime Minister Mahathir of Malaysia, and economic figures such as George Soros, have given stark visibility to this destructive side of the new world economic order, in which instant transfers of capital can threaten to impoverish whole regions, draining overnight the accumulated value of years of national labor.

The United States has resisted the strategy of introducing controls on the international transfers of capital—one method by which some of this financial and speculative damage might presumably be contained; and it has, of course, played a leading role within the IMF itself, long perceived to be the driving force of neo-liberal attempts to impose free-market conditions on other countries by threatening to withdraw investment funds. In recent years, however, it has no longer been so clear that the interests of the financial markets and those of the United States are absolutely identical: the anxiety exists that these new global financial markets may yet—like the sentient machinery of recent science fiction—mutate into autonomous mechanisms which produce disasters no one wants, and spin beyond the control of even the most powerful government.

Irreversibility has been a feature of the story all along. First mooted at the technological level (no return to the simpler life, or to pre-micro-chip production), we also encountered it, in terms of imperialist domination, in the political sphere—although here the vicissitudes of world history should suggest that no empire lasts forever. At the cultural level, globalization threatens the final extinction of local cultures, resuscitatable only in Disney-fied form, through the construction of artificial simulacra and the mere images of fantasized traditions and beliefs. But in the financial realm, the aura of doom that seems to hang over globalization's putative irreversibility confronts us with our own inability to imagine any alternative, or to conceive how "delinking" from the world economy could possibly be a feasible political and economic project in the first place—and this despite the fact that quite seriously "delinked" forms of national existence flourished only a few decades ago, most notably in the form of the Socialist bloc.[5]

5.

One further dimension of economic globalization, that of the so-called culture of consumption—developed initially in the US and other First World countries but now systematically purveyed all round the world—brings us, finally, to the social sphere. This term has been used by the Scottish sociologist Leslie Sklair to describe a specific mode of life, generated by late-capitalist commodity production, that threatens to consume alternative forms of everyday behavior in other cultures—and which may, in turn,

---

[5] I have taken the unpopular position that the "collapse" of the Soviet Union was due, not to the failure of socialism, but to the abandonment of delinking by the Socialist bloc. See Chapter 15 above. This intuition is authoritatively confirmed by Eric Hobsbawm, *The Age of Extremes*, London: Vintage, 1994.

be targeted for specific kinds of resistance.[6] It seems to me more useful, however, to examine this phenomenon not in cultural terms as such but rather at the point at which the economic passes over into the social, since, as part of daily life, the "culture of consumption" is in fact a part and parcel of the social fabric and can scarcely be separated from it.

But perhaps the question is not so much whether the "culture of consumption" is *part* of the social as whether it signals the end of all that we have hitherto understood the social to be. Here the argument connects to older denunciations of individualism and the atomization of society, corroding traditional social groups. *Gesellschaft* versus *Gemeinschaft*: impersonal modern society undermining older families and clans, villages, "organic" forms. The argument, then, might be that consumption itself individualizes and atomizes, that its logic tears through what is so often metaphorized as the fabric of daily life. (And indeed daily life, the everyday or the quotidian, does not begin to be theoretically and philosophically, sociologically, conceptualized until the very moment when it begins to be destroyed in this fashion.) The critique of commodity consumption here parallels the traditional critique of money itself—where gold is identified as the supremely corrosive element, gnawing at social bonds.

6.

In his book on globalization, *False Dawn*, John Gray traces the effects of this process from Russia to Southeast Asia, Japan to Europe, China to the US.[7] Gray follows Karl Polanyi (*The Great Transformation*) in his estimation of the devastating consequences of any free-market system, when fully implemented. He improves on his guide in identifying the essential contradiction of free-market thinking: namely, that the creation of any genuinely government-free market involves enormous government intervention and, de facto, an increase in centralized government power. The free market does not grow naturally; it must be brought about by decisive legislative and other interventionist means. This was the case for Polanyi's period, the early nineteenth century; and, with particular reference to the Thatcherite experiment in Britain, Gray shows it to be very precisely the case for our own.

---

[6] See Leslie Sklair, *Sociology of the Global System*, Baltimore: Johns Hopkins University Press, 1991.

[7] John Gray, *False Dawn*, New York: New Press, 1998. It should be noted that his official target is not globalization as such, which he regards as technological and inevitable, but rather what he calls the "Utopia of the global free market." Gray is an admittedly anti-Enlightenment thinker for whom all Utopias (communist as well as neo-liberal) are evil and destructive; what some "good" globalization would look like, however, he does not say.

He adds another ironic dialectical twist: the socially destructive force of Thatcher's free-market experiment not only produced a backlash among those whom it impoverished; it also succeeded in atomizing the "popular front" of Conservative groups who had supported her program and been her electoral base. Gray draws two conclusions from this reversal: the first is that true cultural conservatism (to wit, his own) is incompatible with the interventionism of free-market policies; the second, that democracy is itself incompatible with this last, since the great majority of people must necessarily resist its impoverishing and destructive consequences—always provided that they can recognize them, and have the electoral means to do so.

An excellent antidote, then, to much of the celebratory rhetoric about globalization and the free market in the US. It is precisely this rhetoric—in other words, neo-liberal theory—that is Gray's fundamental ideological target in this book, for he considers it to be a genuine agent, an active shaping influence, of disastrous changes around the world today. But this keen sense of the power of ideology is best seen, I think, not as some idealist affirmation of the primacy of ideas, but rather as a lesson in the dynamics of discursive struggle (or, in another jargon, of the materialism of the signifier).[8]

We should stress here that the neo-liberal ideology which Gray sees as powering free-market globalization is a specifically American phenomenon. (Thatcher may have put it into practice but, as we have seen, she destroyed herself and, perhaps, British free-market neo-liberalism in the process.) Gray's point is that the US doctrine—reinforced by American "universalism," under the rubric of "Western civilization"—is not shared anywhere else in the world. At a time when the reproach of "Eurocentrism" is still popular, he reminds us that the traditions of continental Europe have not always been hospitable to such absolute free-market values but have rather tended towards what he calls the social market—in other words, the welfare state and social democracy. Neither are the cultures of Japan and China, Southeast Asia and Russia, innately hospitable to the neo-liberal agenda, although it may succeed in ravaging them as well.

At this point, Gray falls back on two standard and in my opinion highly questionable social-science axioms: that of cultural tradition, and that—not mentioned yet—of modernity itself. And here a parenthetical excursus on another influential work on the global situation today may be useful. In *The Clash of Civilizations*, Samuel Huntington, too, emerges—if perhaps for all the wrong reasons—as a fervent opponent of US claims to universalism and, in particular, of America's current policy (or habit?) of police-style military interventions across the globe. In part, this is because he is a new kind of

---

[8] See, on this and the general lessons of the Thatcherite strategy, Stuart Hall, *The Hard Road to Renewal: Thatcherism and the Crisis of the Left*, London: Verso, 1988.

isolationist; in part, it is because he believes that what we may think of as universal Western values, applicable everywhere—electoral democracy, the rule of law, human rights—are not in fact rooted in some eternal human nature, but are, rather, culturally specific, the expression of one particular constellation of values—American ones—among many others.

Huntington's rather Toynbee-like vision posits eight currently existing world cultures: the West's, of course; the culture of Russian Orthodox Christianity; those of Islam, of Hinduism, of Japan—limited to those islands, but very distinctive—and of the Chinese or Confucian tradition; finally, with some conceptual embarrassment, throwing in a putative African culture, together with some characteristic synthesis or other that we may expect to see emerging as a Latin American one. Huntington's method here is reminiscent of the earliest days of anthropological theory: social phenomena—structures, behavior, and the like—are characterized as "cultural traditions," which are in turn "explained" by their origin in a specific religion —this latter, as prime mover, needing no further historical or sociological explanation. One might think that the conceptual embarrassment posed by secular societies would give Huntington pause. Not at all: for something called values apparently survives the secularization process, and explains why Russians are still different from Chinese, and both of these from present-day North Americans or Europeans. (The latter are lumped together here under "Western civilization," whose "values," of course, are called Christian—in the sense of some putative Western Christianity, sharply distinguished from Orthodox Christianity, but also potentially distinguishable from the residual Mediterranean Catholicism expected to materialize in Huntington's "Latin American" brand.)

Huntington does remark in passing that Max Weber's thesis of the Protestant work ethic would seem to identify capitalism with a specific religious-cultural tradition; apart from this, however, the word "capitalism" scarcely appears. Indeed, one of the most astonishing features of this apparently antagonistic world survey of the globalization process is the utter absence of any serious economics. This is truly political science of the most arid and specialized type, all diplomatic and military clashes, without a hint of the unique dynamics of the economic that makes for the originality of historiography since Marx. In Gray's work, after all, the insistence on a variety of cultural traditions was noteworthy for the delineation of the various kinds of capitalism they could produce or accommodate; here the plurality of cultures simply stands for the decentralized, diplomatic and military jungle with which "Western" or "Christian" culture will have to deal. Yet ultimately, any discussion of globalization surely has to come to terms, one way or another, with the reality of capitalism itself.

Closing our parenthesis on Huntington and his religious wars, let us return to Gray, who also talks about cultures and cultural traditions, but here rather in terms of their capacities to furnish forth different forms of modernity. "The growth of the world economy," writes Gray,

> does not inaugurate a universal civilization, as both Smith and Marx thought it must. Instead it allows the growth of indigenous kinds of capitalism, diverging from the ideal free market and from each other. It creates regimes that achieve modernity by renewing their own cultural traditions, not by imitating western countries. There are many modernities, and as many ways of failing to be modern.

Significantly, all these so-called modernities—the kinship capitalism that Gray traces within the Chinese Diaspora, the samurai capitalism in Japan, chaebol in Korea, the "social market" in Europe, and even Russia's current Mafia-style anarcho-capitalism—presuppose specific, and pre-existing, forms of social organization, based on the order of the family—whether as clan, extended network, or in the more conventional sense. In this respect, Gray's account of the resistance to the global free market is finally not cultural, despite his repeated use of the word, but ultimately social in nature: the various "cultures" are crucially characterized as able to draw upon distinct kinds of social resources—collectives, communities, familial relationships—over and against what the free market brings.

In Gray, the grimmest dystopia lies in the United States itself: drastic social polarization and immiseration, the destruction of the middle classes, large-scale structural unemployment without any welfare safety net, one of the highest incarceration rates in the world, devastated cities, disintegrating families—such are the prospects of any society lured towards an absolute free market. Unlike Huntington, Gray is not obliged to look for some distinct cultural tradition under which to classify American social realities: they spring rather from the atomization and destruction of the social, leaving United States a terrible object lesson for the rest of the world.

"There are many modernities": Gray, as we have seen, celebrates "regimes that achieve modernity by renewing their own cultural traditions." How is one to understand this word, "modernity," exactly? And what accounts for its prodigious fortunes today, in the midst, after all, of what many call postmodernity, and after the end of the Cold War, and the discrediting of both Western and communist versions of "modernization"—that is to say, of the local development and export of heavy industry?

There has certainly been a recrudescence of the vocabulary of modernity —or, perhaps better, of modernization—all over the world. Does it mean modern technology? In that case, nearly every country in the world has surely long since been modernized, and has cars, telephones, airplanes, factories, even computers and local stock markets. Does being insufficiently modern—here generally implying backwards, rather than properly premodern —simply mean not having enough of these? Or failing to run them efficiently? Or does being modern mean having a constitution and laws, or living the way people in Hollywood movies do?

Without stopping too long here, I would hazard the notion that "modernity" is something of a suspect word in this context, being used precisely to cover up the absence of any great collective social hope, or telos, after the discrediting of socialism. For capitalism itself has no social goals. To brandish the word "modernity" in place of "capitalism" allows politicians, governments, and political scientists to pretend that it does, and so to paper over that terrifying absence. It betokens a fundamental limitation in Gray's thought that he is forced to use the word at so many strategic moments.

Gray's own program for the future emphatically disdains any return to the collective projects of old: globalization in the current sense is irreversible, he repeats over and over again. Communism was evil (just like its mirror image, the Utopia of the free market). Social democracy is pronounced unviable today: the social-democratic regime "presupposed a closed economy … Many of [its] core policies cannot be sustained in open economies" where "they will be rendered unworkable by the freedom of capital to migrate." Instead, countries will have to try to alleviate the rigors of the free market by fidelity to their own "cultural traditions": and global schemes of regulation must somehow be devised. The whole approach is very much dependent on discursive struggle—that is to say, on breaking the hegemonic power of neo-liberal ideology. Gray has remarkable things to say about the sway of false consciousness in the US, which apparently only a great economic crisis can shatter (he is convinced that one will come). Markets cannot be self-regulating, whether global or not; yet "without a fundamental shift in the policies of the United States all proposals for reform of global markets will be stillborn." It is a bleak yet realistic picture.

As for the causes: Gray attributes both the preconditions of the global free market and its irreversibility not to ideology, as such, but to technology; and with this, we arrive back at our starting point. In his view, "The decisive advantage that a multinational company achieves over its rivals comes finally from its capacity to generate new technologies and to deploy them effectively and profitably." Meanwhile, "the root cause of falling wages and rising unemployment is the worldwide spread of new technology." Technology determines social and economic policy—"New technologies make full employment politics of the traditional sort unworkable." And finally: "A truly global economy is being created by the worldwide spread of new technologies, not by the spread of free markets"; "the main motor of this process [of globalization] is the rapid diffusion of new, distance-abolishing information technologies." Gray's technological determinism, palliated by his hopes for multiple "cultural traditions" and politicized by his opposition to American neo-liberalism, finally turns out to offer a theory fully as ambiguous as that of so many other globalization theorists, doling out hope and anxiety in equal measure, while adopting a "realist" stance.

7.

Now I want to see whether the system of analysis we have just worked out—disentangling the distinct levels of the technological, the political, the cultural, the economic, and the social (very much in that order); and revealing in the process the interconnections between them—may not also be helpful in determining the shape of a politics capable of offering some resistance to globalization, as we have articulated it. For it may be that to approach political strategies in this same way might tell us which aspects of globalization they isolate and target, and which they neglect.

The technological level could evoke, as we have seen, a Luddite politics—the breaking of the new machines, the attempt to arrest, perhaps even reverse, the onset of a new technological age. Luddism has been notoriously caricatured historically, and was by no means as thoughtless and "spontaneous" a program as it has been made out to be.[9] The real merit of evoking such a strategy, however, is the skepticism it causes—awakening all our deepest-held convictions about technological irreversibility or, to put it another way, projecting for us the purely systemic logic of its proliferation, perpetually escaping from national controls (as witness the failure of the many government attempts to protect and hoard technological innovation). The ecological critique might also find its place here (although it has been suggested that the will to control industrial abuse might offer a stimulus to technological innovation); as might various proposals such as the Tobin plan to control capital flight and investment across national borders.

But it seems clear that it is our deep-seated belief (true or false) that technological innovation can only be irreversible that is itself the greatest barrier to any politics of technological control. This might stand, then, as a kind of allegory for "delinking" on a political level: for to try to envisage a community without computers—or cars, or planes—is to try to imagine the viability of a secession from the global.[10]

Here we are already slipping over into the political, with this conception of seceding from a pre-existing global system. This is the point at which a nationalist politics might rear its head.[11] I take Partha Chatterjee's argument

---

[9] See Kirkpatrick Sale, *Rebels against the Future*, Reading, MA: Addison-Wesley, 1995.

[10] It is no accident that when one tries to imagine delinking in this way it is always the technology of the media that is at stake, reinforcing the very old view that the word "media" designates not only communication but transportation as well.

[11] The words "nationalism" and "nationalist" have always been ambiguous, misleading, perhaps even dangerous. The positive or "good" nationalism I have in mind involves

on the subject to be established and persuasive—or, in other words, to demand refutation, if an unmodified nationalist politics is to be endorsed.[12] Chatterjee shows that the nationalist project is inseparable from a politics of modernization, and inherently involves all the programmatic incoherencies of the latter. A nationalist impulse, he argues, must always be part of a larger politics that transcends nationalism; otherwise the achievement of its formal goal, national independence, leaves it without content. (Which is not necessarily to say that any larger politics can do *without* some nationalist impulse.[13]) It does indeed seem clear that the very goal of national liberation has demonstrated its own failure in its realization: any number of countries have become independent of their former colonial masters, only to fall at once into the force field of capitalist globalization, subject to the dominion of the money markets and overseas investment. Two countries that might currently seem to be outside that orbit, Yugoslavia and Iraq, do not inspire much confidence in the viability of some purely nationalist path: each in its very different way seeming to confirm Chatterjee's diagnosis. If Milošević's resistance is in any way linked to the defense of socialism, we have not been able to hear about it; while Saddam's last-minute evocation of Islam can scarcely have been convincing to anyone.

It becomes crucially necessary here to distinguish between nationalism as such and that anti-US imperialism—Gaullism, perhaps[14]—which must today be a part of any self-respecting nationalism, if it is not to degenerate into this or that "ethnic conflict." The latter are border wars; resistance to US imperialism alone constitutes opposition to the system, or to globalization itself. However, the areas best equipped in socioeconomic terms to sustain that kind of global resistance—Japan, the European Union—are themselves deeply implicated in the US project of the global free market and

---

what Henri Lefebvre liked to call "the great collective project," and takes the form of the attempt to construct a nation. Nationalisms that have come to power have therefore mainly been the "bad" ones. Perhaps Samir Amin's distinction between the state and the nation, between the seizure of state power and the construction of the nation, is the relevant one here (Amin, *Delinking: Towards a Polycentric World*, 10). State power is thus the "bad" aim of "national bourgeois hegemony," while the construction of the nation must finally mobilize the people in just such a "great collective project." Meanwhile, I believe it is misleading to confound nationalism with phenomena like communalism, which strikes me rather as a kind of (for example) Hindu identity politics, albeit on a vast and, indeed, "national" scale.

[12] Partha Chatterjee, *Nationalist Thought and the Colonial World*, London: Oxford University Press, 1986.

[13] Cuba and China might be the richest counter-examples of the way in which a concrete nationalism could be completed by a socialist project.

[14] This is not exactly his take on it, but see anyway Régis Debray's wonderfully provocative and sympathetic *A Demain de Gaulle*, Paris: Gallimard, 1990.

have the usual "mixed feelings," defending their interests largely through disputes over tariffs, protection, patents, and other kinds of trade issues.

Finally, one has to add that the nation-state today remains the only concrete terrain and framework for political struggle. The recent anti–World Bank and anti-WTO demonstrations do seem to mark a promising new departure for a politics of resistance to globalization within the US. Yet it is hard to see how such struggles in other countries can be developed in any other fashion than the "nationalist"—that is to say, Gaullist—spirit I have evoked above: for example, in fighting for labor-protection laws against the global free-market push; in the resistance of national cultural "protectionist" policies, or the defense of patent law, against an American "universalism" that would sweep away local culture and pharmaceutical industries, along with whatever welfare safety net and socialized medical systems might still be in place. Here, the defense of the national suddenly becomes the defense of the welfare state itself.

Meanwhile, this important terrain of struggle faces a clever political countermove, as the US co-opts the language of national self-protection, using it to mean the defense of American laws on child labor and the environment against "international" interference. This turns a national resistance to neo-liberalism into a defense of America's "human rights" universalism, and thus empties this particular struggle of its anti-imperialist content. In another twist, these struggles for sovereignty can be conflated with Iraqi-style resistance—i.e., interpreted as the struggle for the right to produce atomic weapons (which another strand of US "universalism" now restricts to the "great powers"). In all these situations, we see the discursive struggle between the claims of the particular and those of the universal—confirming Chatterjee's identification of the fundamental contradiction of the nationalist position: the attempt to universalize a particularity. It should be understood that this critique does not entail an endorsement of universalism, for in the latter we have seen the United States in fact defending its own specific national interest. The opposition between universal and particular is rather embedded as a contradiction within the existing historical situation of nation-states inside a global system. And this is, perhaps, the deeper, philosophical reason why the struggle against globalization, though it may partially be fought on national terrain, cannot be successfully prosecuted to a conclusion in completely national or nationalist terms—even though nationalist passion, in my Gaullist sense, may be an indispensable driving force.

What, then, of political resistance at the cultural level, which includes in one way or another a defense of "our way of life"? This can be a powerful negative program: it ensures the articulation and foregrounding of all the visible and invisible forms of cultural imperialism; it allows an enemy to be identified, destructive forces to be seen. In the displacement of national literature by international or American bestsellers, in the collapse of a national film industry under the weight of Hollywood, of national television flooded by US imports, in the closing down of local cafés and restaurants as the fast-food giants move in, the deeper and more intangible effects of globalization on daily life can first and most dramatically be seen.

But the problem is that the thus threatened "daily life" itself is far more difficult to represent: so that while its disaggregation can be made visible and tangible, the positive substance of what is being defended tends to reduce itself to anthropological tics and oddities, many of which can be reduced to this or that religious tradition (and it is the very notion of "tradition" that I wish to call into question here). This returns us to something like a Huntingtonian world politics; with the proviso that the only "religion" or "religious tradition" which does seem to show the energy of a resistance to globalization and Westernization ("Westoxification," the Iranians call it) is—predictably enough—Islam. After the disappearance of the international Communist movement it would seem that, on the world stage, only certain currents within Islam—generally characterized as "fundamentalist"—really position themselves in programmatic opposition to Western culture, or certainly to Western "cultural imperialism."

It is equally obvious, however, that these forces can no longer constitute, as Islam may have done in its earliest days, a genuinely universalistic opposition; a weakness that becomes even clearer if we pass from the domain of culture to that of economics itself. If it is, in reality, capitalism that is the motor force behind the destructive forms of globalization, then it must be in their capacity to neutralize or transform this particular mode of exploitation that one can best test these various forms of resistance to the West. The critique of usury will clearly not be of much help unless it is extrapolated, in Ali Shariati's fashion, into a thoroughgoing repudiation of finance capitalism as such; while the traditional Islamic denunciations of the exploitation of local mineral wealth and of local labor by multinational corporations still position us within the limits of an older, anti-imperialist nationalism, ill equipped to match the tremendous invasive force of the new, globalized capital, transformed beyond all recognition from what it was forty years ago.

The concrete power of any religious form of political resistance derives, however, not from its belief system as such, but from its grounding in an actually existing community. This is why, finally, any purely economic proposals for resistance must be accompanied by a shift of attention (which preserves within it all the preceding levels) from the economic to the social. Pre-existing forms of social cohesion, though not enough in themselves, are necessarily the indispensable precondition for any effective and long-lasting political struggle, for any great collective endeavor.[15] At the same time these

---

[15] Eric Wolf's classic *Peasant Wars of the Twentieth Century*, London: Faber and Faber, 1971, is still instructive in this regard.

forms of cohesion are themselves the content of the struggle, the stakes in any political movement, the program as it were of their own project. But it is not necessary to think of this program—the preservation of the collective over and against the atomized and individualistic—as a backwards-looking or (literally) conservative type.[16] Such collective cohesion can itself be forged in struggle, as in Iran and Cuba (although, perhaps, generational developments there may now threaten it).

"Combination", the old word for labor organization, offers an excellent symbolic designation for what is at issue on this ultimate, social level; and the history of the labor movement everywhere gives innumerable examples of the forging of new forms of solidarity in active political work. Nor are such collectivities always at the mercy of new technologies: on the contrary, the electronic exchange of information seems to have been central wherever new forms of political resistance to globalization (the demonstrations against the WTO, for example) have begun to appear. For the moment, we can use the word "Utopian" to designate whatever programs and representations express, in however distorted or unconscious a fashion, the demands of a collective life to come, and identify social collectivity as the crucial center of any truly progressive and innovative political response to globalization.

---

[16] Anyone who evokes the ultimate value of the community or the collectivity from a left perspective must face three problems: (1) how to distinguish this position radically from communitarianism; (2) how to differentiate the collective project from fascism or Nazism; (3) how to relate the social and the economic level—that is, how to use the Marxist analysis of capitalism to demonstrate the unviability of social solutions within that system. As for collective identities, in a historical moment in which individual personal identity has been unmasked as a decentered locus of multiple subject-positions, surely it is not too much to ask that something analogous be conceptualized on the collective level.

PART VI

THE VALENCES OF HISTORY

Chapter 19

The Valences of History

Part I. Making Time Appear

L'Histoire, c'est le Temps.
—Michelet

I. Temporality and Figuration

"In a certain sense, it is always too late to talk about time."[1] This startling comment by Derrida comes in the middle of a polemic against the existential category of authenticity, which had seemed to offer new kinds of ethical and hermeneutic solutions since the 1920s, and whose dismissal was a crucial move in post-Sartrean philosophy in France (and also a cornerstone of the Frankfurt School's critique of Heidegger in West Germany). In fact, in both strands of existentialism, the ethical gives way fairly rapidly to the political: in Sartre, authenticity is a weapon against the complacencies of the bourgeoisie and its collaboration, first with the German occupation, and then with the American Cold War. In Heidegger, meanwhile, the evocation of the so-called being-unto-death, awakening the older resonances of solitude and anguish, nonetheless issued into a military ethic and the decisionist "sacrifice" of the soldier. Both of these seemingly ethical positions thus eventuated in a political space which demanded a defense in its own right, a defense which Sartre went on to try to provide.

But it was perhaps the secondary after-effect on hermeneutics which became the most significant target for poststructuralism: the distinction between the surface and its deeper meaning, which had always been at work in phenomenology but to which the existential thematics of authenticity and inauthenticity gave a different kind of life and dramatic urgency.

---

[1] Jacques Derrida, "Ousia et Grammé," in *Marges de la philosophie*, Paris: Minuit, 1972, 47; in English, "*Ousia* and *Grammé*: Note on a Note from *Being and Time*," in *Margins of Philosophy*, trans. Alan Bass, Chicago: University of Chicago Press, 1982, 42.

It will not be necessary here to follow any of these polemics through: that would require a larger historical account of the displacement of existential systems everywhere in the course of the immediate postwar period. What I want to take more immediately from this general movement is its specification in the narrower context of an argument about theories of temporality. For it is this which is at stake in the essay in which Derrida makes the remark quoted above; and intellectual accountability would seem to require some initial reconstruction of that argument, not least because it involves some of the major players in what follows.

The starting point for Derrida is (as usual) a fragment: in this case a footnote, in which Heidegger distinguishes his own theory of temporality from Aristotle's (along with Hegel's, a complication that will be omitted here).[2] Aristotle's constitutes, he tells us, the "vulgares Zeitverständnis," which we may translate as the "common" or "everyday" understanding of time, it being understood that this characterization also marks it as the inauthentic understanding of time—Aristotle's has already been valorized as a peerless phenomenologist of the everyday (and the *Rhetoric* celebrated as "the first systematic hermeneutics of the everydayness of collective being [*Miteinandersein*]"[3]); but from the standpoint of *Sein und Zeit* this specification also consigns Aristotelian phenomenology to the domain of inauthenticity. Indeed, all the authorities are more or less in agreement that the Aristotelian compendium of remarks about time (*Physics*, 4.10–4.14[4]) includes just about every aspect of temporality, every theme connected to the subject of time, which will be dealt with in all subsequent philosophical discussions. Whatever its coherence, therefore—and Heidegger makes a powerful case for the inner cohesion of what can often seem to be a random inventory in Aristotle of all the things people say about time—Aristotle's account of time and temporality is thus the necessary starting point for any theory that wishes to transcend it.

Aristotle begins with the ontological problem of time, the paradox, in other words, of something which both is and is not, a now that is coupled with a past and future which are not, but whose not-beings are quite different respectively: the "was" or "has happened" being distinct from the not-yet (and often considered to be more substantial in its no-longer-being than the fragile anticipatory not-yet-being of the future). These ontological paradoxes or antinomies probably demand a whole new conception of Being as such, which, to be sure, Heidegger is prepared to offer us (not without a

---

[2] Martin Heidegger, *Sein und Zeit*, Tübingen: Niemeyer, 1957, 432–433.

[3] Ibid., 138.

[4] Unless otherwise noted, all references to *Physics* and *Poetics* will cite the numerals of the 1831 Greek text furnished by Jonathan Barnes's edition of the *Complete Works of Aristotle*, Princeton: Princeton University Press, 1984.

good deal of support from the Augustinian tradition, as Ricoeur will point out and as we shall see later on).

For the moment, however, the ontological dilemma does not interest us nearly as much as the problem of what Aristotle calls the "nature" of time. But is this a matter of essence or of definition? That is, is it a problem of content or structure, of grasping what time really is, its component parts, its raw material, its organization—as one might ask the question, what is matter? Or is this a linguistic problem, not merely to find the words for time but also to bind them together in some unified formulation? We do not here, to be sure, face any narrow conception of definition (things cannot be defined, Nietzsche famously said), but rather a process where we first list all the different kinds of things that can be said about time, in order at length to try to link those aspects and themes together in some kind of conceptual unification which can be modeled in a single sentence. And here it is: "time is the number of motion in respect of 'before' and 'after' " (*Physics*, 219b1), to which he will shortly add, "and continuous, since it is an attribute of what is continuous" (*Physics*, 220a23).

We may now ask what kind of a sentence this is: it is not insignificant that it sends us back, over and over again, and via any number of translations in the various modern languages, to the Greek original. "In respect of," "with respect to": what can that possibly mean close up and magnified by the philosophical glass of rigor and clarity, of subdivision into its smallest component parts, as Descartes might put it? Well, the Greek is simply *kata*: *kata to proteron kai usteron*. Liddell and Scott have a number of listings of the functions and uses of this preposition, but are charier about English equivalents. The ones that probably fit our situation are "according to" or "answering to"; and "in relation to" or "concerning."

Does it make any sense to ask what the correct rendering or translation of this word is? Or even, in the absence of an exact equivalent, to ask what the original Greek meaning is or was? These frustrating questions lead us into a very peculiar topic, namely the philosophical meaning or function of the preposition as such. The consequence of a focus like this is, of course, to underscore the deceptive simplicity of nouns, which philosophically stand for substances; and of verbs, which philosophically name processes: and to bring out sharply the way in which we tend to assimilate thinking and conceptualization to those two categories and to ignore the other linguistic components of the sentence (which also include adverbs and, in Greek, the untranslatable particles).

These are what are called the syncategorematic parts of speech and they throw a very different kind of light, not only on the sentence itself, but on the thinking it is supposed, somehow, to express.

Something of all these reemerged dramatically in the modernist descent into language; and perhaps the example of Mallarmé makes the point more vividly than these older philosophical texts and their translations. For we may assert that one of the fundamental words in Mallarmé—those obsessive verbal centers which function as a mysterious center of gravity of style and a glowing resonance beyond all meaning—is neither a favorite noun or adjective nor a recurrent verb, but rather very precisely a preposition: it turns out that in fact the word *selon* is the exact equivalent of the Greek *kata* which has suddenly appeared in our path.

> Mais proche la croisée au nord vacante, un or
> Agonise selon peut-être le décor
> Des licornes ruant du feu contre une nixe ...[5]

Selon and its equivalents thus suddenly transform a homogenous surface and a continuity of signifiers into a mere collage, in which these syncategorematics have as their function the humble and thankless task of mere juxtaposition, of linking one idea, one image, one set of nouns, with another: of mere contact between segments, materials, images, concepts, which they claim to meaningfully combine or mediate, but of which they merely signal an operation of spatial contact without thought.

"According to the before and after" thereby simply asks us to think the beforeness and afterness together with the other parts of the sentence: to add this part to those other parts (movement and number). Aristotle's sentence is an imperative to think an impossible thought, and not at all the expression of the thought itself.

If so, what is then time after all (*Was aber war die Zeit?* as Hans Castorp puts it in his native *style indirect libre*)? Is it simply this collage of features, or is it finally as unthinkable as Augustine would have it ("but when you ask me, I cannot say"[6])?

This hesitation, linguistic and conceptual all at once, and also mystical and existential, requires us to reformulate the problem in a different way, which short-circuits philosophical conceptuality or purely verbal and linguistic analysis: and this will be articulated in terms of what I prefer to call

---

[5]   Yet near the empty northern windowframe
      A gold is dying, against the background (perhaps [*sic!*])
      Of unicorns kicking sparks against a nymph ...

This is the famous *ptyx* sonnet, whose camera scans an empty room (that of the absent Master) until it picks up the glint registered in these lines, whose sparks (as the field of vision passes through the window itself) slowly in the poem's finale become the stars of the Big Dipper.

[6] Augustine, *Confessions*, trans. R. S. Pine-Coffin, London: Penguin, 1961, Book 11, par. 14.

figuration. The concept of the trope, indeed, implies a linguistic determinism still too redolent of the structuralist period; while "representation" opens a philosophical field and a problematic which far exceed that area of language "according to which" and "in relationship to which" I want to continue to raise the question of thinking and expression or formulation. Indeed, I see figuration and formulation as related categories, both of which imply an operation, impossible or not, rather than some mere turning on or off of a function, some mere designation of a property or possibility. To pose the problem in terms of figuration is to ask questions distinct from the traditional philosophical ones about truth (or even, from Kant on, about the possibilities and limits of understanding); as well as from literary questions about style or metaphor.

At any rate, it is in terms of figuration that I continue this brief review of Aristotle's treatise on time, which may be summarized by separating the three elements conjoined in the alleged "definition" we have quoted above: they are movement, number, and before-and-after. Several problems are raised in advance by this starting point; and first of all its omissions. What about change as such, surely a fundamental part of any discussion of time? Oddly, Aristotle inflects both time and change in the direction of deterioration or passing away: "we regard time in itself as destroying rather than producing" (*Physics*, 221b3), a standpoint which would seem to neglect growth, *physis*, emergence. But we have to understand that, for the Greeks, change and movement are inextricably intertwined: even decay is by them figured as a kind of movement, and to that degree no doubt we can assume that change is a subset of the topic of motion as such.

And then we must ask about the analysis of the "now," surely the most unique embodiment of that thing we call time: "the immense privilege of the present," as Hegel called it. The question of the now is, of course, everywhere in Aristotle's discussion: yet to include it in the definition or formulation of the nature of time would involve a vicious circle, since, unlike the other three topics, it can scarcely exist outside of the temporal, it is an inextricable part of the latter, and thus cannot be extracted as a separate feature with which to characterize it.

Then too, as later discussions will show us, to insist on the question of the now will inevitably lead us in a subjective or even a phenomenological direction: how to talk about the now without evoking consciousness, and without attempting to delve into the differences between this now and older or anticipated times, which by virtue of memory or anticipation remain strictly attached to individual (private or subjective) experience. Consciousness, indeed, appears only once in Aristotle's discussion, taking the rather Cartesian form of a thought experiment: "even if it were dark and we were conscious of no bodily sensations, but something were 'going on' in our minds, we should, from that experience, recognize the passage of time" (*Physics*, 219a7).

The more stubbornly we insist on the subjective experience of time, all the more dangerously do we enlarge the gap between existential time and the time of the world (it is, needless to say, to the latter that Aristotle's guiding theme of movement will lead, which ultimately touches on the wheeling of the stars in the heavens, and beyond that to that "perfect" figure of movement which is the circle). On the other hand, it must be added that it is on this gap which later discussions of temporality focus (and not least in the texts of Ricoeur on historical time to which we will come shortly). Leaving aside historical differences between Greek and modern subjectivities (if this is really something it is possible to posit and to analyze), Aristotle's remark makes it clear that he considers objective time to be prior, in the sense in which we will be able to talk about subjective time only after we have formulated the nature of objective time, but not the other way round: he is corroborated to the degree to which later, existential analyses of human or subjective time, very much including phenomenological ones, all seem to end up in desperate aporias that replay the subject-object opposition endlessly without reaching conclusion.

It is worth adding that contemporary, or better still poststructural, philosophy "solves" the matter by leaving the individual subject (or the cogito) out and reverting to a kind of Pre-Socratic vision of universal being, whether this be the Heideggerian ontology after the *Kehre* or Deleuzian flows and psychoanalytic structures for which the "self" is an effect of the unconscious. But these omissions and shortcuts do not solve the problem either, and we will in a moment find Ricoeur postulating a still classical alternative to Aristotle's objective time in Augustine's *Confessions*.

Returning to the preliminary problems mentioned above (change, the now), we may add a query about the topics themselves, and in particular the category of beforeness-and-afterness, which would indeed seem richly to merit Derrida's strictures in advance: for is it not already profoundly temporal, does it not already presuppose the very experience of time that it was supposed in some sense to specify if not to define?

Still, it is first only fair to register Heidegger's objections (in advance) to such a critical reading. The phenomenological translation he gives of the "according to," or *kata*, makes this appropriation of the Aristotelian text for phenomenological purposes dramatically visible, for he translates *kata* as "in the horizon of."[7] With this phenomenological keyword everything changes: rather than a series of features on a single plane, our three topics are now suddenly aligned in depth, and the before-and-after becomes the horizon within which the "number of movement" is grasped as time. It is a genial

---

[7] Martin Heidegger, *Die Grundprobleme der Phänomenologie*, Gesamtausgabe Band 24, Frankfurt: Klostermann, 1975, 347; in English, *The Basic Problems of Phenomenology*, trans. Albert Hofstadter, Bloomington: Indiana University Press, 1982, 245.

interpretation; but must be grasped in that spirit as an interpretation: an appropriation of the Aristotelian text for the later philosophical project, to which, with this slight "modification," it assuredly lends itself to telling effect.

For the new reading now introduces ontological priority among these elements, a priority it might be better to describe as phenomenological rather than logical: moving from surface phenomena, grasped in everyday terms, to deeper underlying experiences of being. But it is precisely this priority— the ontological underlying the ontic, Being underlying the multiplicity of beings or existents, and finally the authentic underlying the inauthentic— that is the object of Derrida's critique, which rejoins contemporary nominalism insofar as the new priority scheme is meant to replace the old unsatisfactory one of universals which ground particulars. This is why, to the translational modification noted above, we must also add the problem of *akolouthein*, which Heidegger reads as "following," not in the physical sense of any material or spatial before-and-after, but rather precisely in terms of just such phenomenological priority: Aristotle "does not reduce time to space nor does he define it merely with the aid of space, as though some spatial determination entered into the definition of time. He only wants to show that and how time is connected to motion."[8] In that case, the spatial misreading of Aristotle (as in Bergson) becomes the same as inauthentic temporal experience, as the common or vulgar everyday experience of time. But Derrida's question was whether any other kind existed.

The problem is inseparable from the question of the now just raised: for it is in connection with the idea of a series of "nows" one after the other that the before and the after arise in the first place. Even when the essential and structural ambiguity of the now is addressed—it is point and line alternately, a "divider" and a "unifier" (*Physics*, 22a19), a center and a mere boundary, two functions which can never be simultaneous or combined—this fundamental temporal component is always, by Aristotle, imagined as something additive: even though it may be supposed to stand for a pure present, even an eternal present, the now is also something which piles up in past time and which succeeds itself indefinitely in the future. To simplify this whole discussion rather brutally, we will observe that, for the later commentators who are critical of Aristotle (and despite Heidegger), this conception of the now is seen as being fundamentally a spatial one. Thus, even the category of beforeness-and-afterness is deeply spatial in character and conveys the sense of a series of points on a line and their relationship to each other: "before" and "after" do not convey any authentically temporal experience, but rather a degraded and reified spatial picture of that genuinely temporal experience (and here clearly Bergson again becomes the fundamental reference).

---

8   Ibid., 344–345; in English, 243–244.

But, with this discussion we have already returned to our three dimensions of the Aristotelian formulation: "time is the number of motion in respect of 'before' and 'after'," a pseudo-sentence we have treated as a collage between three distinct figures: that of number, that of movement, and that of space as such. It is not necessary to descend into the metaphysical mysteries of these three zones of being: what I have in mind is the simpler operation of determining where each of them stands with respect to that equally primordial mystery which is that of time or temporality as such and of determining their relationship to each other. In fact, it turns out that any single one of the three topics will lead us back to the structural principle to be disclosed here at work. The theme of movement, for example, will show not only that movement in and of itself is not identical with time, but also that it cannot be omitted from any discussion of time. "Time is neither movement nor independent of movement" (*Physics*, 219a1); or in a more articulated translation: "Time is neither identical with movement nor capable of being separated from it." Time "pertains" or "belongs" to movement and the same is true of number and before-and-after: a seemingly frustrating (and untranslatable) conclusion, until we reformulate the problem in figural rather than conceptual terms.

For from the standpoint of figuration, these conclusions and the ruminations which have led to them amount to so many attempts to make time appear: for the Greeks, clearly, and however else time appears, it is in movement that its presence becomes unavoidable. Yet movement is very far from being "the same" as time: it is merely that other thing which must be there in order for time—itself invisible, unfigurable, inexpressible—to emerge in such a way that we can feel its absent presence somehow behind movement; or better still, to stick to the language of the text, alongside it, accompanying it, in connection with it. The crucial word here, preposition or particle, is *hama*: and much of Derrida's discussion will turn on the way in which Aristotle with this word *hama* ("en même temps") presupposes the very temporality he is concerned to analyze in the first place (whence Derrida's dry comment with which we began).

But this is perhaps a logical problem rather than a figural one; and I would say the same for Ricoeur's equally startling but far more wide-ranging pronouncement, that there can be no pure phenomenology of time,[9] a

---

9   Paul Ricoeur, *Temps et récit*, Vol. 1, Paris: Seuil, 1983, 21, 125; vols. 2 and 3 were published by Seuil (Paris) in 1984 and 1985, respectively. The three volumes appeared in English as *Time and Narrative*, trans. Kathleen Blamey and David Pellaver, Chicago: University of Chicago Press, 1984, 1985, and 1988, and the above quotations are found on pages 6 and 83 of the first volume. Future reference to this work are denoted *TR*; all references will cite the French editions first, followed by the English translation. I should add that Ricoeur's later work *La Mémoire, l'histoire,*

statement which, coming from the most eminent contemporary phenomen-ologist and authority on Husserl, really amounts to a death sentence on philosophy itself. It cannot, the statement assures us, deal with time in its own terms; it must resort to extra-philosophical references in order to do justice to time; philosophy (here identified with phenomenology as such) can never be an autonomous discipline: whence Ricoeur's recourse to litera-ture in the volumes we are about to examine here, or to the figure of metaphor more generally, which for him always transcends itself and its own verbal or linguistic limits. But was this not the very foundation of phenom-enology as such in the first place? For the doctrine of intentionality,[10] on which the edifice was grounded in Husserl, posits the emptiness of con-sciousness, its constant referral out beyond itself: an initial consternation of the emptiness of philosophy, its insufficiency, its self-canceling movement, at the very moment in which it gave phenomenology what seemed to be a starting point for its own construction as a philosophy in the first place.

At any rate, with figuration we reach one pause or *Umschlag* in the discus-sion, one which bears to speak crudely on its methodological perspective. This will be a perspective in which not the content of theories of time will be interrogated but rather their form; or to be more specific, not the concept of time or temporality but its figuration and the way in which it makes the latter appear (even though, qua time, it will have been there all along without our being able to intuit it as an object). But now we need to specify the problem even further, for our interest here is not necessarily the gap between subjective or existential time and the objective time of the world (and the planets) which has dominated the discussion from Aristotle on down, and which will certainly recur again here. It is the addition of a third

---

l'oubli, Paris: Seuil, 2000, has not been taken into account in what follows above. The phenomenon of memory—almost completely absent for *Time and Narrative* (as from my discussion of it)—returned to claim Ricoeur's attention in an ambitious sequel, *Memory, History, Forgetting* (2004), almost as long as the first three-volume study and recapitulating much of the same ground (including the moralizing turn at the end, which here becomes a meditation on forgiveness). That such a topic could be so completely "forgotten" the first time round (save for its relevance to Augustine's theory of temporality) makes me think that there is a way in which time and memory constitute alternate codes or conceptual languages for the same reality. There is also a more political dimension to the foregrounding of memory, insofar as it grounds the construction of recent history and in particular determines the erection of monu-ments (Pierre Nora's influential and symptomatic *Les Lieux de memoire* dates from 1984, the period of Ricoeur's first "trilogy"). At this point, then, history takes second place to group politics if not individual subjectivity.

[10] See Jean-Paul Sartre's exciting presentation, "Une idée fondamentale de Husserl," in *Situations I*, Paris: Gallimard, 1947.

kind of time, neither existential nor objective, which is historical time as such.

Even if the subject-object problem is solved, the subject will always have been conceived as an individual subject (nor can we think the collective in terms of a subject as such). But history is not geological time either (as Fernand Braudel finds when his *longue durée* of the Mediterranean, which looks at first like objective time, turns out to inflect this last towards the geopolitical—see below). The *longue durée* in other words can only register geological time to the degree to which it is transformed by human projects, human settlement, and the like, into a proto-historical collective human time—the purely material history of the universe thus escaping us again. So, above and beyond the problem of making individual time appear, we will now wish to give ourselves the task of making historical time appear (it being an open question whether the time of the world—objective time, Aristotle's time of the stars—can ever appear in either fashion).[11]

2. Ricoeur's Project

As much as to Derrida's little article on Heidegger, however, the following discussion owes its impulsion to the far more ambitious work of Paul Ricoeur on *Time and Narrative*, which, very specifically touching on the distinction between existential and historical time that interests us here, adds a third topic to the mix, as his title suggests; or at least offers a new turn of the screw to the emphasis on figuration I have just proposed by identifying it in advance, and specifying it as some properly narrative figuration. I am at least postmodern enough to be willing to defend the proposition that everything is narrative (something which requires a defense against traditional positions based on truth, but also against the objections of comrades like Slavoj Žižek who feel that the relativity of narrative versions also menaces that unique conception of historical truth embodied in Marxism). From this perspective, we may observe that Ricoeur retreats at the very moment in which his own argument might be more usefully prolonged; and assimilates narrative figuration to metaphor, whose ontological analysis in *La métaphore vive* (*The Rule of Metaphor*) is the most durable part of his own work and his most original contribution to contemporary philosophy. My criticism of Ricoeur's three-volume work on narrative will thus be an affirmation of its strengths, and will bear mainly on its limits, which are to be identified in his humanism, a term I use in its strong Althusserian sense. His is in fact a stunning example of the dialectic—a strength which is also a weakness (or vice versa), inasmuch as it is Ricoeur's essentially humanist

---

[11] These two sections of the essay can be read independently of each other.

perspective and emphasis which enable a whole series of pertinent critical readings of and engagements with other philosophical texts—most notably those of Heidegger—on which we need to draw here and for which we must be productively grateful.

Ricoeur is clearly a traditional philosopher, with a vested interest in the discipline as such: I enumerate several signs of this affiliation: the appeal to ethics, the systematic refusal of all positions that might be classed under the heading of poststructuralism, the silence under which all the Marxian discussions of these same issues are passed, and finally the confidence in the philosophical tradition itself (fundamental solutions borrowed from Plato and Aristotle), as though that tradition were not itself something historically constructed. Closely related to these philosophical features are surely his religious orientation (our debt to the dead, a skeptical but still sympathetic hearing for the concept of eternity) and his general humanism (the unification of mankind). Another sign is his sympathy with an older tradition of literary criticism, from Northrop Frye to Käte Hamburger, of which he provides something like a monumental summary at the very moment (the 1980s) when it has definitively expired; and also his sympathy, both critical and religious, with Frank Kermode, from whom he derives theoretical substance (*The Sense of an Ending* as trace or foreshadowing of apocalypse, personal death, and the Last Judgment all rolled into one).

First, however, it will be worthwhile to set in place a few further remarks about Ricoeur, whom the Left has frequently mistreated, particularly during the structuralist and poststructuralist period; and to say why he is so precious a resource, although far from being an ally. The very horror of what he significantly calls "schism," a word which combines the religious category of universal brotherhood with his own personal experience of the 1960s, conveys something of the generosity of his philosophical relationship to his targets here (mostly literary semiotics), which does not exclude the most unrelenting critical dissection and analysis (but which coolly omits the polemics). Indeed, it is from such principled ideological hostility (I think of both Yvor Winters and Lukács on modernism, for example) that we are often best and most productively served. Ricoeur's example richly demonstrates the superiority of his own attitude to the younger generation's refusal of tradition and even a dialogue (for it is this, I think, that "schism" means, and not mere disagreement over principles): but we must also set in place the most powerful and appropriate reply, Lyotard's *Le différend*, which asserts, over against Habermas's humanist value of universal communication, the existence of irresolvable differences, of radical quarrels between codes that can never be adjudicated within a single framework, since they are themselves the frameworks in question. (But perhaps this particular quarrel may also be allowed, as an aporia, to resolve itself by becoming more complicated and intense.)

I specify all this, not as a criticism exactly (for I greatly admire Ricoeur, but also Kermode and Frye as well), but in order to demonstrate the stakes, and how difficult it may be to persuade post-traditional generations that this kind of inquiry has any interest for them. The discussion will therefore often involve a translation of the traditional problematic into the (now) more familiar jargon of so-called poststructuralism as well as the introduction of postmodern themes that might have modified these positions or at least allowed them to be more fully explored.

But it should be added that Ricoeur is one of the great readers, as one speaks in literary study of a critic of uncommon subtlety and verbal perception who also knows how to articulate the tempo and the connotations of a style; except that here we have to do with philosophical texts, whose inner mechanisms are rarely undone with this patience and pertinence. Such readings, in which critique has the neutral matter-of-factness of observation and demonstration, might well merit the name of deconstruction, if that term were used in the sense of approbation: even what is conservative in them is an instrument of exploration and discovery, as in Ricoeur's famous characterization of structuralism as a "Kantianism without a transcendental subject." Indeed, *Time and Narrative* rejects most of what passes for poststructural achievement today, yet in so generous and courteous a spirit the accusation is slow in disclosing this tendency, given away only at length by the disappointingly humanist familiarity of what is proposed in its stead.

But in order to avoid the reproach of humanism seeming mere empty invective and the slinging of epithets, we have to look more closely at the project of Ricoeur's *Time and Narrative*, which not merely involves the opposition between objective time and existential temporality, but also asserts the priority of the latter by way of a substitution, for Aristotle's account of time, of the Augustinian one, which develops on into Heidegger and *Sein und Zeit*.

What is bold in the ambition of the work itself is not only the vindication of narrative as a primary instance of the human mind, but also the equally daring conception of temporality itself as a construction, and a construction achieved by narrative itself. The apologia for the narrative function is then as stunning as what Ricoeur was able to do for metaphor in *La métaphore vive*, in which the starting point is similarly enlarged to include ontology and even thought itself. Here the philosophical enlargement of the initial problem is confronted with an even more indigestible object to be assimilated, namely history as such. The exemplary nature of this gesture, however, is not weakened by its ultimate afterthoughts: can one really speak of Time as one? Can one possibly think (or name) History as one? Are there not ultimate things which lie beyond the boundaries of narrative (whereby he thinks of death, whose centrality in Heideggerian thought he had so courageously repudiated in the earlier sections of the work)? These ultimate doubts about the viability of the enterprise that has been undertaken, and at this point completed, are less damaging for it than the failure to show how it can address the problems of our postmodern actuality—something I want to try to sketch out here—and the consequent lapse back into conventional notions of literature (he unnecessarily worries about the abandonment of "plot" by the avant-gardes of the 1960s and 1970s) and of history (he recommends we abandon "Utopian," that is to say systemic and revolutionary, political schemes; and, obviously enough, that we attempt to avoid "schism," thereby reaffirming canon and tradition alike).

In thus building on what I have to modify in order to develop it further, I follow his own critical method in this work, which is the emphasis on the aporia as such. As we shall see, in Ricoeur's hands the aporia is neither to be resolved, nor to be exhibited (as in Derrida's essay) as the sign of the futility of the philosophical project in the first place: it is to be made productive by expansion, by generating further, more complex and interesting aporias out of itself. But it is very precisely a mark of the limits I have alluded to that Ricoeur is unwilling to identify this method as the very essence of the dialectic as such, and equally unwilling to pronounce the telltale word "contradiction" in relation to his conceptual paradoxes. And indeed it is disappointing to find so few references to the Marxist tradition at the moment of that very discussion of historiography and historical narrative at which they might have suggested the prolongation I want to sketch out here, rather with the pious and universalizing ethical chapters with which his great project so lamely concludes. In what follows, I will restore such references and try to give a new direction to what might have been an exploration of collective time and historical narrative.

Instead of that, we find in *Time and Narrative* an exhaustive treatment of the literary and narrative theory of the period, in a series of chapters which may serve as a kind of monument to that rich moment in purely literary theory which, as I have noted, came to an end more or less at the very moment in which Ricoeur was summarizing it: Frye's *Anatomy* is central here (along with key texts of Kermode, whose secondary function is to place death on the agenda in a different way than Heidegger); there are discussions of point of view and voice, and in short a whole grammar of the novel whose source is Henry James's prefaces and in which modernism nervously scrutinized the heritage of the great realist novels from which it had uneasily emerged. It would be of historical interest to determine why this whole problematic of the novel's structure and form disappears at the very moment that the postmodern emerges.

Ricoeur's interest in the novel is, however, not innocent: although the new discussion is very relevant for the extension of Aristotle's dramatic theory to that far more extensive and complex system of mimesis that comes into the world with the historically new form of the novel as such.

Meanwhile, his theory of the "triple mimesis" (to be discussed below) finds a good deal more raw material in the novel than in the tragedies to which Aristotle rather sparsely refers, particularly in the area of the mimesis of subjectivity.

Ricoeur's polemic target here is, to be sure, complicated by the presence on his agenda of not one, but two key texts of Aristotle, namely the *Poetics* and the *Physics*, which are evaluated positively and negatively respectively: the first staging an essentially anthropomorphic account of human time in terms of narrative, while the second offering, as we have already seen, a philosophical description of temporality which omits the distinctiveness of the human or existential dimension. The crucial attack on narrative semiotics which lies at the heart of this essentially traditionalist project of Ricoeur is aimed explicitly at what he considers to be semiotics' willful and perverse substitution of abstract categories for anthropomorphic ones.

As for Aristotle's *Physics*, however (which Ricoeur will take up much later than we have in this inquiry), the old reproach of the reification of time—all these "nows" added up to make up linear time—is from the very outset contrasted with Augustine's conception of time as an expansion and contraction of consciousness: the three-fold "now of the past, now of the present, now of the future"[12] already foreshadowing Heidegger's three temporal ek-stases. We must leave aside the obvious retort that Augustine does not resolve the aporia of objective versus subjective time either: for the moment it is enough to identify humanism with this ideological commitment to the latter over the former.

But this is certainly not enough to convince anyone of the relevance of such arguments for a postmodern age. My previous observation, about the way in which philosophers today, very much including the Heidegger of the *Kehre*, bypass the whole question of consciousness and of the existential, merely presumes resolved in advance the painful aporia Ricoeur tried twenty years ago to reopen, like a wound which has not yet properly healed.

It is in his discussion of narrative semiotics that we may find our answer and a certain relevance for postmodern times. (The analogous historical references, to older discussions about historiography, which deal with the opposition of historical laws and causality to the role of narrative in history, have not worn well; Hayden White is only incidentally touched on, although Ricoeur borrows White's key term "emplotment" for his own purposes; and only Braudel emerges as a figure of permanent interest.) The literary theory of the period, however, is, as I have said, massively summarized, and contrasted with the "theoretical" analysis which follows it, namely, Greimas'

---

[12] Augustine, *Confessions*, Book 11, par. 20.

attempt to reduce the various surface components of storytelling—those very everyday or common-sense categories of Mimesis I or the phenomenology of everyday life—to the structural interaction of more abstract (and epistemological) semes. As we shall see below, this is indeed to attempt to dechronologize with a vengeance and to substitute objective processes for largely subjective or experiential perceptions: a human act, for example, being dissolved into a play of oppositions between *pouvoir* and *vouloir*, a human character being reduced to a combination of two kinds of actants, a readerly effect being prismatically dissociated into the interaction of a given semiotic opposition. This evidently substitutes typology for chronology, logical permutations for narrative ones.

Yet one need not endorse the scientific pretensions of the various semiotic systems to appreciate the heuristic value of such research, which not only enables the differentiation of various levels in a given plot and makes visible the heterogeneity of a given act of emplotment; but also permits a more microscopic scrutiny of the intellectual or semic content of works normally dismissed as pure entertainment or at best mythic representation. But the latter direction promises to make contributions to the study of ideology and of unconscious investments, an area with which Ricoeur's philosophy of consciousness or the subject is unconcerned, unless it be to deny the very existence of such impersonal forces; while the former tendency swims strongly against the valorization of unity and unification which presides over Ricoeur's analyses here (even though it is not inseparable from them: to posit the very act of unification, for example, can underscore the multiplicities and heterogeneities thus unified fully as much as it can serve as an ideological fetish of Identity).

The polemic against Greimas will then be waged in terms of the necessarily anthropomorphic content of the latter's categories and semes. Just as it is always too late to talk about time, inasmuch as the terms in which one sets out to talk about it are themselves profoundly temporal in advance, so also our human standpoint necessarily determines an essentially anthropomorphic projection within all the abstractions of action and value from which we scientifically attempt to cleanse it: our objectivities remain subjective, and Greimas has thus, for Ricoeur, succeeded only in formulating his own mimesis of the representations of human action in a pseudo-scientific jargon, when they are more adequately analyzed in the more openly anthropomorphic studies of the novel in the Jamesian tradition, as these have been enumerated above. It is, to be sure, a powerful objection; but does not really address the usefulness of Greimassian or other narrative semiotics for the literary and cultural analyst (in whose disciplinary projects Ricoeur shows little interest). At this point, then, we might observe that the critique of semiotics tends to turn anti-theoretical, implicitly to deplore theoretical jargon and the new kinds of "inhuman" abstractions theory has brought to bear on the cultural world, and to express nostalgia for an older tradition of *belles lettres* and its cultivated or high literary discourse.

This is a blind spot which will have consequences when Ricoeur comes to his own literary examples, about which he has many useful insights, as we shall see, but which he signally fails to identify as essentially modernist works which do not necessarily exemplify the range of possibilities which his own method might otherwise be capable of opening up. In any case, the humanist argument is tailor-made for all the contemporary anti-intellectual attacks on interpretation as such (as elitist, manipulative, totalizing, etc.), in the name of that nostalgia for the older defenses of literature in terms of the enlargement of our possibilities and the eternal themes of death and finitude and the concern with the Other, with which in fact his great project concludes.

3. Aristotle vs. Semiotics

Still, what is original in Ricoeur's approach to narrative is the presupposition, not merely that Aristotle's was the first narratology, but even more fundamentally, that the descriptions worked out for ancient tragedy are valid for all narrative as such, and not merely for the tragic genre or mode. None of the discussions of modern tragedy—is it still possible? What forms could it take? How would we have to adapt the older categories for modernity?—have ever gone so far as to extend Aristotle's fundamental categories to all narrative, although the slippery notion of catharsis (not convincingly elucidated by Ricoeur here either) is more often appealed to as a shorthand for this or that effect or type of reception.

It is a delicate argument to sustain: to the degree to which Aristotle's account does justice to Greek tragic drama in some well-nigh definitive way, to that degree will it presumably be inapplicable to other forms and genres. Conversely, to the degree to which it can be abstracted from that context in order to furnish a more universal pattern for all narrative change, to that very degree its status as the formulation of tragedy's *differentiae specificae* will be subject to doubt and to skepticism. Meanwhile, few other specific genres have proved capable of inspiring more general accounts of narrative as such: the signal exception here is of course Propp's *Morphology of the Folktale* (the Bible and supreme reference of all modern narratology). Henry James's prefaces do not particularly dwell on the content of action, but on the vehicles of its observation and presentation (point of view, voice, etc.). Northrop Frye's summa is meanwhile essentially a generalization of Aristotle, on the basis of the latter's remarks about the status of the protagonists (better than we are, the same, or worse/lower): this standpoint tends to focus our attention on what the reader's attitude towards the narrated characters does to the mode in which a given action is received.

But the strength of Aristotle was to have insisted on the primacy of the action over the characters: if anything turns out to be usefully generalizable about his analysis, it will certainly have to do with the way in which this position allows us to distance ourselves from that more modern tendency towards subjectification and psychology which we associate with the novel as a form. (Even Lukács's *The Theory of the Novel* is organized around the four fundamental *Weltanschauungen* of the protagonists of his four basic novel-types.) But this is a warning that may already alert us to possible mis-steps in Ricoeur's approach, whose whole project takes sides with the human and its existential subjectivity as over against the objectivity of facts, acts, events as such.

Still, returning to Propp, it is paradoxical that so rudimentary a form as the folktale or fairy tale could yield a universal pattern (Frye's genius was to have extrapolated a set of tale-types or narrative variants and alternatives from his starting point in class and status, without for all that privileging a single form and the specific action associated with it as the deeper ontological structure of all narrative). In my opinion,[13] the serviceability of Propp's paradigm lies in the fundamental option it offers between the functions of "villain" and "lack" as alternate formulations of the obstacle the protagonist-hero must confront and overcome. Thus, plot is conceived as a quest for whatever object of desire, which is interrupted and complicated by one or the other of these two obstacles: which are however assuredly not on the same categorical level at all. The villain is clearly an anthropomorphic actant who is driven by whatever motive you want to endow him with (absolute evil, lust for power, envy, his own projects, etc.); while lack is a state which can be called on to characterize desire as such (but virtually everything else resulting from the essential finitude of human life in time). To be sure, the villain can also be driven by lack: but then we have something of a reversal of the plot, like a second-degree rewriting that comments on the original (Iago's life story, for example, seen through his own eyes). It will indeed be of some interest to compare categories like this—Propp's master-plot or archetype—with Aristotle's.

But first we must note Ricoeur's objection: it is profound, and goes a long way towards giving concrete content to his humanism as well as revealing the deeper motivation behind the philosophical problem as a whole. For here, and in the following sections which analyze the work of Claude Bremond (the logic of actions) and A. J. Greimas (the semiotics of narrative) respectively, the reproach singles out not so much the substitution of abstractions for anthropomorphic representations as it does the essential operation of dechronologizing the narrative as such. Here the primacy of

---

[13] See *The Prison-House of Language*, Princeton: Princeton University Press, 1972, 64–69.

time affirmed by Ricoeur's project returns with a vengeance: and it is abundantly clear that the substitution of the categories of Greimas's semiotic square removes narrative action from its place in temporal storytelling and transforms it into a set of spatial relationships about which it becomes difficult to tell what direction they move in and what the order of their succession could possibly be. The same result obtains when a specific act or event is abstracted into a set of semes (*vouloir, pouvoir, savoir*, for instance), whose logical combination and interrelationship is then substituted for the sheer passage in time of the event or act as such. Here Ricoeur's humanism moves palpably in the direction of Heidegger's analysis of *Dasein* as time itself. If temporality is the essence of human life, of human projects and their stories, of human desires and the acts we perform to satisfy them, then clearly to omit time from the process is to overleap their most fundamental truth, as well as their very lived quality.

To this criticism will later on be added another, which has to do with the reception of narrative: the attribution to *Dasein* of what Ricoeur calls "narrative intelligence," the capacity to "follow" a story, the definition of narrative itself in terms of "followability."[14] Greimas no doubt posits a kind of narrative unconscious (which, like the original unconscious, is presumably outside time); but the followability of his narrative objects is only addressed insofar as they flex or inflect epistemological categories, such as causality. But, as Ricoeur is quite right to point out, the operations by which these deeper semic or categorial oppositions are "manifested," that is to say, are translated into the surface appearances of characters and everyday recognizable actions—anthropomorphic representations, whose semic content at some deeper level of abstraction is here affirmed—such semiotic operations remain quite mysterious (even though endowed by Greimas with a formidable complexity and a bristling nomenclature).

I believe we must distinguish between two directions in such analysis: in my own appropriation of Greimas, for example, I have found it illuminating to work back from the "surface" narrative representation, the story embodied in the text, to just such underlying semic systems. But the other direction, a "verification" of this procedure which would demonstrate the generation of the text from out of just such underlying semic systems, seems to me an impossible and perhaps even undesirable project. The first operation is what we call interpretation: contrary to populist bias, it does not assert the superiority of the interpreter or "intellectual" over the apparently more plebeian readership (but then, in that sense, we are all plebeians when we read). It simply offers interpretive hypotheses which the reader or re-reader is free to explore or to abandon (as sterile, as far-fetched, or as mistaken). What the reader is not free to abandon is the interpretive process

---

[14] The term is W. B. Gallie's. See *TR*, Vol. 1, 104; 66.

itself, which always involves the substitution of a different kind of text for the original one: Ricoeur's humanist interpretation—that, for example, the modern novel enlarges human potentialities by awakening the reader's mind to a fuller experience and exercise of temporal possibilities than before—is just another such substitution of interpretive generalities for the concrete narrative text. My objection to it is not made on the basis of the operation of substitution, however, but on the basis of the second or interpretive code itself, which is not very interesting.

But the other or second direction of analysis—that of demonstrating the production of the final text from out of its micro-semic elements or its geno-code—seems to me a poor imitation of what is fantasized as being true scientific method: it also clearly amounts to an attempt to reintroduce diachrony into a synchronic analysis and to return to a kind of historical or evolutionary narrative. The recovery, therefore, of a black box in which the various Greimassian levels are mysteriously transformed into recognizable human storytelling is quite unnecessary, whether we have to do with Greimas' own justification for his research or Ricoeur's objections to its results.

What is perhaps more significant is the seeming discordance here between the spatial and the temporal, for in the long run it is to all such spatializations of the temporal that Ricoeur has objected in his various critiques of structuralism; and the very pertinent reproach of dechronologization needs to be completed by a discussion of the spatial into which Ricoeur never enters, presuming in advance that the "achronic" as he calls this aspect of contemporary theory is simply to be evaluated as a distortion and repression or occultation of the temporal (that is to say, of the human and of concrete human experience, as well as of phenomenology). Two responses need to be laid in place here.

The first is that contemporary theory has certainly taken a spatial turn, and not only in the ideological battles waged over the Saussurian distinction between synchrony and diachrony. Graphs are everywhere in contemporary theory, from Lévi-Strauss's various models all the way to Lacanian mathemes and their representations, Foucault's more outrageous maps in *Les mots et les choses*, and even Deleuze's notion of diagrammicity. I think it is appropriate to approach these first and foremost as pedagogical operations, in which it is felt that complex systems can be better grasped as a web of visible relationships, along with their gaps and empty slots (which thinking is called on to fill in and complete), and whose temporality consists in the demonstration or *Darstellung* itself, as the pointer moves from one element to the next and back. Greimas' semiotic squares are certainly to be counted in that scrapbook of theoretical graphs, and they are pedagogically effective and useful.

Clearly they do presuppose a conception of system and ultimately some notion of the increasing synchrony—and also synchronicity!—of contemporary life: a presupposition wrapped up in the very notion of postmodernity itself, which Ricoeur could not have addressed in the 1970s and 1980s when he composed his book. This has indeed so often been characterized as the supersession of time by space that it is worth specifying a little more closely what is at stake here. In its crudest form as a slogan, the predominance of the spatial designates little more than the abandonment by contemporary writers of that great theme of deep time and memory, as it was pursued and elaborated by modernism (and very specifically in the novels we will see Ricoeur choosing to analyze). To be sure, memory returns today in trauma theory, but the very notion of postmodernity incites us to find new ways of describing this new theoretical symptom which are not mere returns of eternal human preoccupations, nor even regurgitations of an older modernist thematics (it would be enough to adduce the obsession with false memories[15] to suggest the quite different shape of the new concept).

But what is most crucial here is to cleanse the notion of the synchronic from those traces of achronicity with which Ricoeur has taxed it (it is his own authorities, such as Augustine and some of the novelists, who are more obsessed with "eternity" than are the structuralists[16]). If for "synchrony" we substitute "synchronicity" for a moment, we will find ourselves confronting an idea which is anything but atemporal: indeed it posits a rich experience of temporality as an historical emergence, but it is an experience of temporality quite different from any of the traditional ones: and it is always worth noting that despite his brilliant appropriation of Heidegger's complex temporal analyses, Ricoeur is apparently unwilling to entertain any possibility that human time has in late capitalism undergone a kind of structural mutation. But this is precisely what postmodern synchronicity implies, namely that the multiplication of relationships in the present (sometimes ideologically identified as information) has been accompanied by an inevitable shift of attention from antecedent causal lines in the past to newer notions of system which have all kinds of momentous consequences for theory and philosophy as well as for human practice. Indeed, Braudel himself very specifically singles out just such a new synchronicity as the "cause" of contemporary transformations in the discipline of history-writing[17] (or perhaps, since the word "cause" has fallen victim to this shift, we would do better to claim this development as one optional symptom in which the shift can be detected). But this simply means a new kind of time and not any literal "end of

---

[15] See on false memory, Ian Hacking, *Rewriting the Soul*, Princeton: Princeton University Press, 1995.

[16] See Ricoeur's somewhat bemused discussion of "eternity" in *TR*, Vol. 1, 41–53; 22–30. And see also *TR*, Vol. 2, 163–164, 193, 214; 109–110, 130, 144.

[17] Fernand Braudel, in *Écrits sur l'histoire*, Paris: Flammarion, 1969.

temporality" (a phrase I once used to dramatize just such "momentous consequences" for contemporary thinking).[18] The attention-deficit disorders of contemporary postmodern life no doubt bring on new problems with which an older slower world did not have to deal: but they also confront us with remarkable new possibilities, with new kinds of texts and new kinds of philosophical problems (not least in the area of time and temporality) which offer exciting prospects and permit us to avoid repeating and rehashing all the old solutions under the aegis of the canon, perennial philosophy, the tradition, or whatever other ideological label may be affixed to the "eternal human" of the various regressive essentialisms.

4. The Phenomenology of Narrative

Ricoeur is on a more productive track when he associates his (to my mind misguided) critique of semiotics with a richly merited attack on the older discussions of historical laws and the nomothetical possibilities of historiography. Those have certainly disappeared, but are not to be replaced with any return to traditional narrative history or historiographic storytelling. The very innovations of the Annales School (about which he has mixed feelings) are there to prove it, but also to suggest that we need to move on further in our approach to historical narrative: and here also to prolong Ricoeur's questions and investigations in new ways.

Historiography, he tells us, seems to offer a less complex variety of temporal structures than do literary or, better still, fictional, texts. This is an impression to which we can assent, even though a little thought suffices to make it an astonishing pronouncement: how could the variety of existential temporalities, indeed, ever hope to compete with the extraordinary multiplicity of all the temporalities included in the experience of human history? It is enough to make us suspect that historiography has not been up to the task; but also to wonder, very much in Ricoeur's spirit, whether narrative itself could ever be, and what its possibilities and limits then really are.

It is an interrogation he himself begins by an encyclopedic examination of a certain kind of literary criticism, one which, as I have already suggested, is no longer actual, no longer prevalent or influential, but of which, having done his homework with admirable thoroughness, Ricoeur presents us with a kind of summa.[19] As I have noted these references range from Kermode

---

[18] See the essay titled "The End of Temporality" in *The Ideologies of Theory*, London: Verso, 2008, pp. 636–658.

[19] Or perhaps it might be better to observe that by the time he came to write *Time and Narrative* all the major or foundational contributions to narratology had already been made. At any rate, literary analysis has rarely been the beneficiary of so rigorous and

(the possibility of narrative or generic mutations), through Benveniste, Käte Hamburger, and Weinrich (on tense systems), all the way to Günther Müller and Genette (on *énoncé* and enunciation), and ending with voice and point of view (in Dorrit Cohn, Stanzel, Uspensky, and Bakhtin). How to summarize so magisterial a summary?

We can only do so by holding to Ricoeur's own red thread which is the possibility of the narrative representation of time. Indeed, in this chapter (which follows the one on narrative semiotics), we confront for the first time a shift in attitude of which Ricoeur is himself perhaps not altogether aware, but which is of great importance for my argument. It involves his appreciation of the separation in the linguistic critics between tense systems and lived experience.

The consequence of this separation would seem to offer a replay of the objections to Greimas: the "grammarians" have tried to substitute an abstract nomenclature of tense systems for the lived experience of human temporality. But this opposition does not quite play itself out in the same way. For a debate is now glimpsed in which two antithetical possibilities solicit a new and third solution (inasmuch as Greimas' squares do not exist in the real world, but language and its tenses do). On the one hand, we have the psychological school, which claims that tenses merely express more fundamental human experiences of temporality; on the other, the structuralists who claim that language and its forms produce that effect or epiphenomenon of lived temporal experience in the first place. Nor is Ricoeur's phenomenological third way—namely that reading the deployment of linguistic tenses itself expands and modifies our experience—very satisfactory either (and it may be added that if structuralism, semiotics, and theory are extinct, surely the proliferating theories of reading that followed them have long since been awarded their multiple obituaries as well). But we do not need any substantive resolution or synthesis here: it is enough to express some astonishment that at this point Ricoeur is unwilling to take the side of phenomenological experience over against the linguistic system as such. And this is quite enough to suggest a very different outcome, namely that it is the intersection—if not even the incommensurability—of these two

---

lucid a purely philosophical attention (not always to its advantage). The aestheticians never had much that was useful for the literary critics, and only with phenomenology did the two disciplines begin productively to approach one another (with Roman Ingarden, for example); yet even Sartre's literary criticism remains distant enough from the phenomenological practice of *L'Imaginaire*. My impression is that the interest of the philosophers has always tended to focus on the question of fictionality (or Husserl's "neutralization," Sartre's "derealization"), a problem no doubt more unavoidable in dealing with the nature of time (fictive or otherwise) than with that of plot or language.

dimensions of temporality (the verbal one and the experiential one) which is the crucial fact here and which suggests a new methodological key.

The key is indeed one we have already had in our possession without knowing it, from our examination of philosophical theories of time: as the latter are figurations, we found that each one of them taken by itself will generate a representational illusions, the mirage of a substantive "definition" of time which any serious philosophical investigation will quickly dispel (time is not movement, it is not number, it is not space, etc.). The intersection of all three, however, allows us to triangulate the "reality" of time and temporality beyond any specific finite representation or figuration. Or perhaps it would be more accurate to say that figuration is itself this intersection between several incommensurable representations.

At any rate, we here for the first time glimpse a figural possibility capable of being transferred to narrative as such: what gives us an insight into the temporalities of (fictional) narrative is not the virtue of one of these accounts over the other, it is their very multiplicity as such, their intersection. (And perhaps it is necessary to reassure those for whom the notion of experiential or phenomenological time is not a text at all, but something ineffable and irreducible, something concrete but unrepresentable—very much like time itself as a concept: in fact, the phenomenological position is grounded in the body, and the so-called experiential temporality is the time of the body as such—yet another text, as the structuralists would reassure us.)

So now, with this relational thread, we may safely wind our way through the labyrinths of the various literary and linguistic theories of time that follow. The once inescapable opposition between *énoncé* and *énonciation*, for example, between the utterance and whatever goes on inside it temporally, and the time of enouncing or speaking it, of putting it into language— an opposition which had the effect of turning every literary text into autoreferentiality and an inescapable reference back to its own production process (an effect then baptized "reflexivity")—this opposition can now be seen to draw its power from precisely the intersection of the two temporalities of the content of the sentence and the act of speaking it in the first place (thus returning to Arthur Danto's maxim—"To have a narrative sentence, there must be two events mentioned, one that is referred to and one that provides the description in terms of which the first is considered"[20]— provided this maxim is now grasped formally in the sense of the present discussion). Time does not appear unless both these dimensions are held together in the "configuration" (why not use Ricoeur's excellent term?) of a single (literary) act. And with this, we can now proceed on into the concluding paradoxes of narrative voice and point of view, which may or may not always be with us, but which reach their classic foregrounding in that

---

[20] See the discussion in Ricoeur, *TR*, Vol. 1, 203–211; 143–149.

game with time associated with the first eighteenth-century English realists (*Tristram Shandy:* "I am this month one whole year older than I was this time twelve-month; and having got, as you perceive, almost into the middle of my fourth volume—and no farther than to my first day's life," etc. [Book 4, Chapter 8]). These sentences produce time for the first time, or, if you prefer, they make visible and available something operative but unspoken and unseen from the outset, namely the emergence of the great personification of Time from its multiple intersections. Time can only appear at the intersection of various times. Indeed, is not the paradox of the point and the line already just such an experience, in which under our very eyes the now suddenly wavers in a *Gestalt* alternation—at first being a period in its own right, the center of something, and then turning into a divider, a break between two periods? Are we the marker of the break, or do we only exist strongly in and of ourselves, as Schelling says, by the act of repudiating the past?

More important however (Ricoeur's lesson, following as we shall see from an insight of Heidegger's) is the multiplicity of the intersections. But, if this is so, then the pursuit of a single essence of time, or Time rising like an allegorical personification out of this multiplicity of times, is not only a will-o'-the-wisp and a mirage, it is the source of the contested notion of authenticity. The moderns no doubt pursued this mirage—*was aber war die Zeit?*—with a stubborn persistence that led them to their various absolutes above and beyond the multiple temporalities we have in mind here. We can however just as easily evoke the complacency of the postmoderns, wallowing in their various time-intersections without any concern for any ontological universal of Time that might possibly arise from them. This is, once again, the truth of the principle that difference relates, and it may now be expected to take us on, from literature, into the appearance of historical Time in its appropriate moment. But now we need to go all the way back to the beginning, to Ricoeur's own starting point.

5. Augustine vs. Aristotle

Indeed, the opening juxtaposition between the Hebraic and the Greek tradition, between Augustine and Aristotle, may remind us in passing of the starting point of Auerbach's *Mimesis*. Here also it is a question of the juxtaposition of two types of temporality, or rather, in this case, of two theories of time: the one—that of Aristotle—is the time of the before-and-after, of the chronology we observe in the heavens and in the natural or objectal world: the other—that of Augustine, Husserl, and Heidegger—is the world of the past and the future, held powerfully together by the expansive power of the now, as it extends its protensions and retensions, as it convulsively and dynamically projects its temporal ek-stases and lives outside of itself in memory and anticipation and even in the passionate *intentionalities* (in the phenomenological sense) of the presence to the world itself. The Husserlian and Heideggerian overtones of the account are deliberate: for the latter powerfully develop the three-fold insight of Augustine while slowly reversing an Augustinian bias towards the past into a projective and Heideggerian celebration of the future and of *Dasein*'s propulsion towards it.

For Augustine's distention and intention—like the systole and diastole of breathing itself—powerfully foreshadows Husserl's great breakthrough in the theorization of human time as a protension and retension of consciousness.[21] From this it is but a short leap to the Heideggerian notion that *Dasein* is its own temporality, which, a finitude projected forwards towards death, grasps the world as time by way of its own being.[22] We are our own pasts as well as our own futures: such is the solution to the Augustinian dilemma: "I am divided by time gone by and time to come, and its course is a mystery to me."[23] Yet it is a mystery Augustine himself had gone a long way towards solving:

> It is not strictly correct to say that there are three times, past, present and future. It might be correct to say that there are three times, a present of past things, a present of present things, and a present of future things.[24]

Here already, save for the powerful unifying activity of Husserl's temporality and Heidegger's three temporal ek-stases, we approach the phenomenological view of time which will inform that human (or humanist) tradition Ricoeur seeks here to oppose to the Aristotelian conception of an objective time of the universe. Yet we need to add a fourth Augustinian temporal dimension into this manifold, and that is the Augustinian doctrine of eternity, or a simultaneity of times in God: it is a form of temporality about which Ricoeur maintains a wise agnosticism, but which reappears in his analysis of the three great modern novels of temporality which, along with Fernand Braudel's historiography, will serve as his fundamental exhibits. This time of eternity may well strike us as a kind of religious substitute for the objective time of the universe, equally out beyond the bounds of existential experience: but it is also somehow a version which—like Hegel's attempt to transform system or substance, Spinoza's universe of being, into subject—gropes for a more human or subjective representation of this dimension, and

---

[21] See Edmund Husserl, *The Phenomenology of Internal Time-Consciousness*, trans. James Churchill, Bloomington: Indiana University Press, 1964.

[22] Heidegger, *Sein und Zeit*, par. 45.

[23] Augustine, *Confessions*, Book 11, par. 29.

[24] Ibid., Book 11, par. 20.

seeks to draw world time back inside human time, if only as the latter's cancellation. Heidegger's great revolution is then to have reversed Augustine's emphasis on the past and on memory by stressing that dimension of the future which orients and defines us by way of the project. The reservation any Sartrean will have about this energizing temporal reorientation—and which Ricoeur clearly shares, but with some mixed feelings—is the Heideggerian emphasis on the future as death and the being-unto-death, which not only carries military (if not even fascist) overtones with it,[25] but also discredits the great collective projects that bear on the future as well. But let us turn to the central issue it is Ricoeur's merit to have raised, namely the usefulness of this Heideggerian-Augustinian temporal analysis for the writing and reading of historiography as such.

I will first want to enter what is for me an important footnote here, about the representation of temporality. I have already noted one of Ricoeur's philosophically most audacious statements—the affirmation that "there can be no pure phenomenology of time." This means in fact that there can be no purely philosophical definition of time; we now need to rephrase this in terms of a more familiar contemporary and post-contemporary theme, namely that of representation. Aristotle says that time is not movement, but somehow always appears alongside movement; what can this mean except that time, in itself unrepresentable, can only be represented through the representation of something else—the movement of wind in the trees for example? If so, then we can at once understand Ricoeur's appeal to the literary or the non-philosophical text, which betrays a figuration of time unavailable to abstract thought or, as he puts it, to "pure phenomenology." Indeed, this is the immense advantage of Ricoeur's inclusion of his narrative examples—*Mrs. Dalloway*, *The Magic Mountain*, Proust—whose lesson adds something new to the doctrine of figuration I have just outlined. What these examples show is that it is only in the intersection of multiple kinds of temporality that Time itself—if one can speak of such a thing—can be made to appear. It is an idea one would like eventually to juxtapose with Deleuze's notion, alongside an action cinema or movement-image, of a time-image, a cinema of time; yet another path we must here leave unexplored. Nor have we yet said what these multiple temporalities are that intersect in such texts—and not only in the literary ones, as the supreme example of Fernand Braudel's three durations will bring out.

---

[25] However, I will try to show elsewhere that Heidegger's is preeminently a philosophy of revolution. His Nazism, however—one party official referred to it derisively as "Professor Heidegger's private National Socialism"—is an idealist program for a revolution which omits economics. See for the essentials of the matter Charles Bambach, *Heidegger's Roots: Nietzsche, National Socialism, and the Greeks*, Ithaca: Cornell University Press, 2003.

In reality, however, the deeper philosophical debate turns, not on the compatibility of Aristotelian narrative with Augustinian temporality, but rather with the incompatibility between the latter and Aristotelian time. Here indeed we find counterposed two kinds of temporal theories, the objective one to be found in Aristotle's classical synthesis, the subjective or existential one which first emerges in language and in history in the eleventh book of Augustine's *Confessions*. It has already been shown that Aristotle's time is the time of chronology, the time of the before-and-after, the time of the world measured by the cosmos, the revolving constellations of the heavens, the decay and rebirth of nature, the movement of objects. Augustine's existential alternative meanwhile anticipates that of *Dasein*, the world of the past and the future, held dynamically together by the expansive power of the now and of human consciousness, as it extends what Husserl will call its protensions and retensions, and convulsively projects what Heidegger and Sartre will call its temporal ek-stases so as to live outside itself in memory and anticipation and even in the passionate intentions (in Husserl's phenomenological sense) of its presence to the world itself.

Ricoeur's essential humanism is thus already present in this starting point, whose more hidden drama lies not in the juxtaposition of Augustine and Aristotle's *Poetics*, but that between Augustine's theory of time (the three-fold "now of the past, now of the present, now of the future") and Aristotle's *Physics*, in which the objective or common-sense notion of time as mere sequence is definitively laid out for the philosophical tradition. The opposition is thus, in fact, another version of our old friend the split between the subject and the object: Augustine's time is the time of the now, of human or existential experience; Aristotle's is the time of the sequence of events, of chronology, of the merely objective before-and-after but also the time of the stars, of the cosmos. All of Ricoeur's attacks on semiotics and other newfangled philosophical, structural, and theoretical approaches come down to this, that they try to objectify human time; that they remove human consciousness, the person or the subject, from events which not only depend on human choice, but also must be grasped by a human understanding of what a story is—by what he calls narrative intelligence, or phenomenological followability. But it is not so much this humanist position, and this suspicion of the scientificity or pseudo-objectivity of semiotics, that I want to question now; it is the rigorous limitation to individual human consciousness and the individual subject, and the refusal to theorize any agency on the level of the collective.

We must therefore follow this new thread back through our discussion of time as such: Aristotle opposed the subjective time of human beings to the objective time of the universe, the great wheel of the stars, the perfect circular movement, whose very existence tends to reduce individual temporal experience to mere projection. Augustine then inaugurates the modern tradition of the analysis of temporality by deepening this very existential temporality, and assimilating transcendental objectivity to the synchronicity and eternity of God. We thus confront four terms, four candidates for any complete theory of temporality: the time of the world, the eternity of God, the temporality of the individual, which as we have already seen, was refracted in Heidegger into the vulgar time sense (that precisely of Aristotle himself), and some more authentic temporality, which in the closing pages of *Sein und Zeit* seemed to touch on history. Our question will now bear on this last one, and will seek to ascertain whether, alongside objective and existential temporalities, there may not exist some third one which is neither of these and which may be characterized as the very time of history itself.

6. Ricoeur's Three Mimeses

But that moment has not yet come; and we now need to return to Aristotle's *Poetics*, of which Ricoeur gives us an extraordinary reading, at the very least in order to separate the familiar parts of Aristotle's treatise—as for example the dictum that plot is the imitation of an action rather than the portrait of a character—from Ricoeur's appropriations. Is he the only (or the first) commentator to have insisted that mimesis is an operation or a process, rather than a static representation? Probably not: but the reminder is a timely one in a situation in which discussions of representation inevitably slip towards the visual, and in which realism always seems to end up being a picture of things people look at and compare with the reality of its original, rather than something the writer does to the world, an intervention, a selection, and a shaping performed on it. Indeed, Ricoeur's otherwise cumbersome system of the three mimeses does have at least a positive consequence, namely that it becomes difficult not to think of each of the three as a process rather than a set of reflections (in whatever mirror).

I summarize these three mimeses in order to convey the architecture of Ricoeur's inquiry, before returning to the second, literary or properly Aristotelian one, which alone interests us here—namely the fashioning of the plot as such and the various components and modes of the work, whether theatrical or narrated.

Ricoeur's first mimesis, however, which precedes that one, lies deep in phenomenology itself, and governs the emergence of the raw materials, the building blocks, of the literary mimesis, from the pre-linguistic magma of wordless experience, from that "blooming, buzzing confusion" of our first perceptions and desires. But it is not a genetic or historical link which is designated here: rather simply the grounding of words and concepts in experience itself—something language is capable of, in its semi-autonomization, of making us forget (so that, for example, we can live at the level of words, at the level of ideas, without making the phenomenological link back to their original referents[26]). Thus gestures come before us as already meaningful, but they had to be carved out of some earlier experience of people and their bodies in situation; the notion of a given act (along with its name), the very name for a hitherto wordless affect, the ranging of other people into characterological typologies, the sense of a causality linking one event to another in a meaningful way—all this has to have emerged preformed and in distinct units in order for the composition of the Aristotelian mimesis (Ricoeur's Mimesis II) to proceed. Curiously, this lower-level experience and raw material is also the reservoir of semiotic elements as well, and another site in which the dispute opposing pre-verbal experience and semic systems might be expected to be invoked. It is, of course, also very much the place of culture and its specific formations, for it is here a question of cultural raw materials far more than mere individual quirks and private meanings. Mimesis I, then, may be said to mark one of the moments in which the self-transcendence of phenomenology, its founding principle of "intentionality," namely that every act of consciousness is consciousness *of* something and designates an outside of itself, finds affirmation and confirmation.

Mimesis III, the activation of the work by reading and reception, is, we need hardly add, the other such space, and indeed grounds Ricoeur's argument for reference in the literary work. It is an argument he needs to make in order to answer the obvious question about the distinction between fact and fiction in this attempt to assimilate both fiction and historiography in their different ways to narrative as such. It is then the reader who will perform the essential work of reference here in Mimesis III; and as has been observed above, what results (drawing on the Gadamer and Konstanz School reception theory) is a rather vacuous humanist evocation of the transformation of the reader ("making a new kind of reader appear" [*TR*, Vol. 3, 238; 164]), and the way in which Mimesis III (the "reconfiguration" of the text) "places its readers in the position of finding a solution for which they themselves must find the appropriate questions, those that constitute the aesthetic and the moral problem posed by a work" (*TR*, Vol. 3, 254; 173); in which it "sets the reader free for new evaluations of reality that will take shape in rereading" (*TR*, Vol. 3, 259; 176). The latter phrase identifies catharsis as its theoretical cause; and reminds us of that enigmatic concept in

---

[26] This possibility, indeed, grounds what may be called Husserl's own theory of alienation or reification, in *The Crisis of the European Sciences and Transcendental Phenomenology*, Evanston, Northwestern, 1970. The translation of a fragmentary note for this work, "The Origins of Geometry," constituted Derrida's first publication (in 1974) and served as the starting point for his critique of the notion of authenticity.

the original text of Aristotle which justifies the appeal to aesthetics of reception and reading in the first place.

But it cannot be said that Ricoeur's reading of catharsis is very satisfying, although it is no less plausible than anyone else's:

> It results from the fact that the pitiable and fearful incidents are ... themselves brought to representation. And this poetic representation of these emotions results in turn from the composition itself ... I myself have elsewhere suggested treating catharsis as the integrating part of the metaphorical process that conjoins cognition, imagination, and feeling. (*TR*, Vol. 1, 831, 50)

This develops a useful philosophical bridge to Ricoeur's magisterial theory of metaphor (to which he will later more explicitly attempt to link the reference theory of the narrative books in general); but it is also open to an interpretation which achieves the opposite of what he seems to be claiming here. For it may be argued that even if catharsis lies in the transformation of real suffering into its representation, it may also be described as a passage into the imaginary, a distancing of the real, a diminution of emotion owing to the way in which the original reference has precisely turned into art and image and has lost its grounding: far from provoking the right kind of horror and indignation, the artistic rendering of a murder may well make it pleasurable and transform it into an image of fascination.

We do not need to pursue this discussion of the aesthetic any further here (it will return in our discussion of history, below), but merely to separate these postulates of Mimeses I and III which organize the trilogy from the Aristotelian theory of narrative to which we now return, retaining only the proviso that this mimesis (like the other two) is grasped as an operation, a putting together of elements, an "emplotment" (Hayden White), or, as Ricoeur puts it, a configuration, and indeed the operation of configuring, rather than a mere reified object.

The conception of mimesis as a configuration is indeed the central contribution of Ricoeur to a new interpretation of Aristotelian mimesis (in his terms, Mimesis II). We may summarize the three fundamental aspects of that interpretation in advance. They are: (1) the presumption that the three basic plot lines identified by Aristotle—peripeteia, or reversal; anagnorisis, or recognition; and pathos, or suffering[27]—are the central features of narration as such (and indeed we will later on follow his lead in extending these plot-forms to history and even to the dialectic); (2) the eudaimonic dimension of Aristotle's theory—a passage from good fortune to bad, from happiness to unhappiness—marks the necessary insertion of the subject into the narrative process (and will clearly become crucially problematic for the

---

[27] Aristotle, *Poetics*, 1452b10. And see also Ricoeur, *TR*, Vol. 1, 72; 43.

examination of history and historiography); (3) the notion of closure and significance ("an action of a certain importance and magnitude"), which will evidently return us to the question of unity, whether under the form of the unity of the manifold or the multiple (of sheer difference), or of the process of unification as such.

For first it is with the overall process of mimesis that we have to do, and indeed what Ricoeur, borrowing from White, terms emplotment. For him it is a mental operation which is to be identified as a "judgment" in Kant's sense: "The configurating act presiding over emplotment is a judicative act, involving a 'grasping together'" (*TR*, Vol. 2, 92; 61): an identification he glosses by stressing the originality of this narrative judgment as over against Kant's original

> distinction between a determining judgment and a reflective one. A determining judgment is wholly caught up in the objectivity it produces. A reflective judgment turns back upon the operations through which it constructs aesthetic and organic forms on the basis of the causal chain of events in the world. In this sense, narrative forms constitute a third class of reflective judgment that is a judgment capable of taking as its object the very sort of teleological operations by which aesthetic and organic entities take shape. (*TR*, Vol. 2, 92; 174, n. 1).

The separation of narrative judgments from aesthetic ones here is particularly noteworthy, and obviously designed to make a place for historical narrative alongside fictional kinds. Meanwhile, the classification as a judgment then implicitly reintroduces the very specification of the latter in Kant as an appearance of necessity (the second of the approaches to catharsis discussed above). Emplotment will thus impose a feeling of necessity on the events, characters, and elements thereby configured together: and it is the arousing of this sense of necessity which brings the action to its close, that is, whose closure unifies the multiplicity of the elements that make up the narrative.

It is clear, then, that multiplicity here is to be understood as dissonance, antagonism, clash, and struggle: and also as the unexpected or the unforeseen, something Aristotle himself paradoxically factors into the process when—building on his own famous dictum that history only narrates what did happen, while "poetry" narrates what might happen, what is probable or necessary—he then turns around to observe, following Agathon, that "it is quite likely that many things should happen contrary to likelihood."[28] So even the unlikely and the improbable can with a successful emplotment be rendered necessary. It is that sense of necessity—it had to be that way or, in Pound's words, "it all coheres!": a feeling akin to relief but on some other

---

[28] Ibid., 1456a24.

tragic level—which constitutes the more plausible reading of catharsis offered by Ricoeur: "it is these discordant incidents the plot tends to make necessary and probable. And in so doing, it purifies them, or, better, purges them" (*TR*, Vol. 1; 74, 44).

This insistence on the negative materials of the plot, on antagonism and contradiction, on suffering, on dissonance and incompatibility, will now find definitive expression in Ricoeur's account of plot as "discordant concordance," provided this last is grasped as a temporal process, and one which can also be understood as an act in its own right or in other words an emplotment, which "grasps together" the discordant in such a way as to confer on the latter unity and necessity. In this form it will surely not seem terribly perverse to characterize the historian's work in much the same way as the emplotment of a narrative such that all kinds of seemingly random or unrelated events fall into place in the web of necessity: nor does the specification that emplotment is an act as well as a process need to imply some external shaping force over history, but rather only the discovery of an underlying causal logic or objective unity that it is the art of the historian and his essentially narrative intelligence to make visible. We leave aside for the moment the philosophical question it was the merit of Ricoeur to have linked to this one, namely whether such emplotment can also make Time visible (or, in this second case, History).

As for the three shapes of this completed action—peripeteia, anagnorisis, and pathos—we will come back to them in a different way in the second part of this essay. Suffice it to say for the moment that each seems to govern a rather different abstraction of the concrete or the empirical. The last of the three is the most startling, and is not normally included in traditional accounts of Aristotle's concept of plot. The spectacle of suffering as such would seem indeed to have more to do with Artaud's famous "theater of cruelty" than with Sophocles (despite the palpable fact that there is plenty of raw suffering in Sophocles, as in the *Ajax*): Euripides' *Medea* might be a more apt illustration, with its exhibition of the slaughtered children. Are we then to grasp Aristotelian pathos as a heightening of the visual or of spectacle —the Laokoon—over the other elements of plot? Yet, in the *Poetics*, visual spectacle has already been assigned, as *opsis*, a relatively secondary role in the construction. It seems preferable here to invoke a kind of heightening and intensification of the action as such, a *Steigerung*, in which human endurance is pushed to its very limits (but which need not be limited to the personal experience of a single character). It will perhaps already have become clear to the reader that I mean to inflect this notion in a Heideggerian direction, as an aesthetic form of the *phainesthai* of his phenomenology, the appearance as appearing and as event, the moment in which as he describes it Being itself somehow appears through and beyond individual beings and the present is expanded to include past and future all at once. The solemnity with which

Heidegger means to mark this idea and to distinguish it from the trivial-izations of words like "vision" is appropriate here as well, even though the event of appearance can never be guaranteed (not even by invocations of death, which is so to speak the standard Heideggerian method for lifting such instants into a quasi-religious mode). We do not need to retain such reverential sobriety, indeed sometimes it defeats its own purpose (we may recall Derrida's irreverent snicker[29]); all we need to retain is the transforma-tion of the moment in which pathos comes together in its concordance of dissonance, indeed in its dissonant concordance, into an event—the changing of its valence from static well-nigh or quasi-visual spectacle into something that both happens and is grasped as the source or well of all happening: or, if you prefer, the coming into view of the sublime.

Yet the event of the pathos, which can also be conceived as a prodigious yet ephemeral unification, also wears a different set of valences, for it can take the form of a vision of the world as nightmare, or alternately—since we mean here, with Ricoeur, to disengage the concept of plot as such from the merely tragic—as the transport of a kind of superhuman joy or world trans-figuration. Either of these states is "suffered" in the sense in which the spectators are the recipients, as are in the last analysis the characters them-selves. We may well for example here adduce states of euphoria, the redemptive, or the salvational, fully as much as the blackest depression: enthusiasm or the manic-depressive seems indeed the fundamental para-digm for the affective as it realizes itself in pathos and externalizes itself in that ultimate immobilized spectacle which is in some way the very moment of closure and the sign that emplotment has been triumphantly achieved.[30]

The other two plot-shapes seem equally necessary to successful emplotment, but in quite different ways. Peripeteia can be semically reduced to change as such, the fundamental temporal structure of the mimetic process. Yet this reduction of Aristotle's idea raises two different kinds of questions, one of content and the other of form. The question about content involves the very nature of the New, of what emerges when something changes. In the structuralist period, with its emphasis on the synchronic, the emergence of the New was always a kind of mystery, as though the essential data, the givens and the counters, were present in advance, making it difficult enough to see how anything fresh and different, anything hitherto nonexistent in the world, could possibly have emerged from their mere shuffling and reor-ganization. One was always tempted to follow Rousseau's example, and to argue the problem so rigorously that the only possible result would be the

---

[29] Jacques Derrida, *Heidegger et la question*, Paris: Galilée, 1987, 86.

[30] For a more extensive discussion of these propositions, including Kant's appeal to enthu-siasm, see Section 14 of Part II of this Chapter. Indeed, the subsequent remarks on peripeteia and anagnorisis are similarly preparations for sections 12 and 13 respectively.

conclusion that change itself could not possibly exist in the first place. If the starting point is an equation, indeed, how can any trading of places result in the unexpected appearance of a new term? And yet change, and the New, exist. Peripeteia can perhaps then simply stand as the name for this mystery, or for its perpetual reenactment on the scene of representation as such.

But does all change amount to a peripeteia or reversal? For example, Aristotle's own conception of time (in the *Physics*) as a slow decay from which nothing positive emerges, but many things disappear, would require some structural adjustment to fit the plot scheme of the *Poetics*. Yet perhaps it is precisely the operation of just that structural adjustment which is at stake in emplotment.

All of which leads insensibly to the question of form, that is to say, the nature of the abstraction in which this idea consists. How is it reconcilable, for instance, with Propp's fundamental paradigm of the quest (let alone with lack and the villain)? Lack, perhaps; a reversal from deficiency to plentitude. As for the villain, presumably this could simply amount to a passage from resistance, opposition, antagonism, to concord or harmony; if not from evil to good. But Propp's categories remain far more stubbornly empirical, far closer to the narrative surface; they are still anthropomorphic in character and never attain the degree of abstraction that governs the Aristotelian concept.

With the idea of change itself, of course, we approach a further type of semic abstraction which is that of reversal; the latter endows the former with a specific shape, namely that of the movement back and forth between two poles. Change thus finds a specific shape or form imposed on itself; or better still its elements are reorganized into a recognizable and nameable event. Thus, peripeteia would seem to involve a reorganization of the world (or at least of this particular narrative world) into oppositions (and Propp's plot-types are merely specific instances of possible oppositions). Here, then, paradoxically, the Aristotelian analysis can be at least prolonged to the borders of Greimassian semiotics, if only in the fundamental role of opposition in the process of emplotment.

Anagnorisis is an even tougher nut to crack and goes in a very different direction, for recognition can have empirical content and more immediately assume an anthropomorphic appearance. In the narrowest acceptation, for example, we find it to be a staple of melodrama—the long-lost parents united with the long-lost children—effects now mostly relegated to comedy, but also capable of shattering effects in whatever survives of the tragic ("Electre, je suis Oreste"[31]). Yet this folding of the plot-shape back into family dramas of all kinds is not some mere accident: indeed, in his monumental commentary on the *Poetics*, Gerald F. Else identifies in this

---

[31] Jean-Paul Sartre, *Les Mouches*, in *Théâtre complet*, Paris: Gallimard, 2005, 36.

particular event a mark and survival of the older clan system from which the classical Athenian *polis* emerged.[32] Peering back into that more archaic darkness, we can discern the presence of the vendetta[33] and whole societies organized around the often antagonistic and always suspicious relations of the great family systems to one another (antagonisms descending even into the household itself, since the husband and wife can often be of different lineage systems, cementing an alliance, always heavy with possible treachery and discord). In anagnorisis, then, a primal form emerges which is the discovery that the antagonist in fact belongs to me, to my family and clan; that seeming enemies are in fact blood relations, a discovery that transforms the whole structure of power oppositions. It is a momentous discovery which can be enriched with ethnic dimensions, as well as racial and even gender ones: anagnorisis is thus in this sense as much the identification or production of a community or collectivity, as it is the simple revelation of a name or of a family relationship. And obviously enough this discovery can work both ways, and can just as easily eventuate in the discovery that a longtime friend is in reality a blood enemy as it can in the narcissistic bonding of a community. It is as divisive as it is associative, and can thus be said to embody Eros or Thanatos alike.

Yet this enlargement of the concept leaves us with a lingering and far from insignificant question, namely that of the destiny of this plot (into which Propp's helpers and adjuvants can also be unceremoniously lumped) in a social world in which clans and extended families are less and less the building blocks of society let alone the agents of change and history. The nostalgia for the Mafia and its "families" is in this situation to be read as a compensatory formation rather than a sign and symptom of contemporary social trends.

What survives alongside this kind of group nostalgia or cultural envy is a different legacy of the archaic which is the very demand for recognition itself ("respect," "honor"): Hegel still sensed this at the dawn of the bourgeois era when he wrote out several versions of the dialectic of the Master and the Slave,[34] as the fundamental struggle that eventuates in the demand for the

---

[32] Gerald F. Else, *Aristotle's Poetics: The Argument*, Cambridge, MA: Harvard University Press, 1967, 349–350.

[33] René Girard's discussion of the vendetta in *La Violence et le sacré*, Paris: Grasset, 1972, remains one of the most compelling meditations on the blood feud as a central phenomenon in human history.

[34] The two earliest versions of the Master/Slave dialectic both seem to have been elaborated in the Jena lectures (the so-called *Realphilosophie*) of 1802–1804 and 1805–1806. They are translated respectively as *System of Ethical Life*, eds. H. S. Harris and T. M. Knox, Albany: State University of New York Press, 1979, 238–40; and *Hegel and the Human Spirit*, ed. L. Rauch, Detroit, MI: Wayne State University Press, 1983, 191–193.

recognition of "my" freedom. It is a demand which in a world of proliferating and indistinct identities involves a good deal more than the mere naming of a person; it includes the acknowledgement of the clan itself, something Hegel's language knows even if he does not. Anagnorisis thus designates an event—one around which is also a punctual contact or encounter, struggle or confrontation, from which hierarchy and a whole map of higher and lower social groups necessarily emerge: it is preeminently the place of the other, just as peripeteia is the place of time, and pathos the fate of the body. We will be returning to these forms of plot and emplotment in connection with historiography in the second part of this chapter.

7. Eudaimonics

Now we need to move on to the next important consideration about the *Poetics* and Ricoeur's appropriation of it, namely that which seeks to grasp the role of the eudaimonic in narrative, and the significance of the passage from happiness to unhappiness (not excluding the reverse, which was probably the organizational thread of Aristotle's lost chapters on comedy). At first glance the matter scarcely seems to pose a problem. To be sure, we here endow peripeteia with a specific content, and the reversal is now grasped in terms of a reversal in our luck or good fortune, as we like to put it. As far as figuration is concerned, we are apparently here preeminently in the domain of the anthropomorphic: what is more human indeed than happiness or misery, itself a kind of abstraction from that specific content which would make us happy in the first place? And what is more universally human than these states to which others, the reception, audience and public, might be expected to respond in the greatest immediacy? The facial and physical signs of distress provoke a kind of sympathetic mimesis; happiness is a radiance that transfigures everyone who is touched by it. If not quintessentially human, then perhaps the eudaimonic has something to do with biological life itself, whose fragility or plenitude expands and contracts across the species, and finally gets its ultimate identification in the vigor of the organism itself, in health or the debilitations of fever or infirmity. *Schadenfreude* is already the confirmation of this immediacy, and of the envy it arouses in individuals and in groups—as full a participation in its rhythms as their celebration in sympathy and fellow feeling.

More than this, the very category of pathos itself would seem to demand the ritual of some unabashed and boastful, full-frontal exhibition of this great good fortune, or else its mourning in the form of cries and shrieks, the pantomime of expressive suffering and the unanswered calls of the tortured and the dying. At this point, pity and fear become mere adjuncts to what looks like a ritual confirmation of the centrality of happiness and its fragility in human life—"Let no man call himself happy ..."—which may or may not tell us something about this classical form, and even about the vulnerability of human time, but which seems to have moved us very far away from the questions of narrative with which we began and about which it would seem difficult to affirm similar functions universally.

But it is also necessary to grasp the social content of what may at first appear a merely individual and corporeal spectacle. Aristotle's is a class-based conception of happiness whose supreme realization has as its paradigm a healthy and well-born male endowed with a substantial fortune and an extended family along with a circle of friends: this evocation (in the *Nicomachean Ethics*[35]) is clearly the ideal of the patriarch; and the leisure which he is serenely to devote to spiritual and intellectual pursuits has as its precondition this classical vision of good fortune, about whose fragility tragic drama undertakes to warn us. Athenian drama thus proposes and presupposes a general social consensus around this class value, of which the spectacle is itself the "recognition" in the larger sense proposed above.

We thus come back to the semic and ideological overtones of words and phrases like "good luck" and "fortune" in connection with Aristotelian *eudaimonia*; and we can all the more gratefully appreciate Northrop Frye's extrapolation of Aristotle's remarks about the status of protagonists—better than ourselves, equal to us, worse or lower than ourselves—whose class content is now inescapable. Most of us sitting in the bleachers will not be on the level of the great clans whose triumphs and baleful destinies are acted out on the tragic stage; nor will we identify with those lower beings, ugly, deformed, lower class or even newly manumitted, vessels of envy and *ressentiment*, impotent rage and revolt, along with all the other vices, who are the butts and principal exhibits of comedy either. Nietzsche's suggestion, that our first archaic conceptions of good and evil derive from just such class-based systems (linked back into the self and narcissism by way of the great clans and their blood recognition), would seem to find no little confirmation here and is helpful in shifting the analysis of narrative from seemingly psychological questions both of well-being and of sympathy with others to the more formal problem of whether narrative is not always organized in this way around some primal egotism (in Freud's terms: good for me, bad for me[36]) from which more superficial ethical effects derive (provided we grasp that egotism in the larger social sense of the group or clan, as I have suggested above).

---

[35] And see also Aristotle, *Rhetoric*, in *Complete Works of Aristotle*, ed. Jonathan Barnes, Vol. 2, 1360b18–30, 2163.

[36] Sigmund Freud, "Creative Writers and Daydreaming," in *The Standard Edition of the Complete Psychological Works of Sigmund Freud*, Vol. 9, London: Hogarth Press, 1959, 150.

The question of the eudaimonic thus finds itself heightened into the more collective allegory of the fate or destiny of group or nation, and thereby comes to touch the relationship of such questions to historiography as such, where the older national histories (so significant, indeed, in the very formation of the nation-states) have been thought to have been rendered obsolete by information, reflexivity, objectivity, and all those other and newer virtues in terms of which contemporary historians celebrate their emplotments. Perhaps, on the contrary, it is because the nation-state is no longer felt to be an object worthy of some properly collective cathexis that we find an attempt to read contemporary historiography in Aristotle's eudaimonic terms to be naïve and utterly misplaced. In commercial society like this one, however, we may lower the bar a little and recode happiness or downfall in terms of success or failure, categories which may well find a more significant exercise in modern narratives, historical or not, than do their older Aristotelian forms. Is not, for instance, the fascination with Hitler's downfall and the last days in the bunker a spectacle of pathos worthy of the more barbaric Greek theaters of cruelty? And is not the reading of bestsellers and the true-life story of the great entrepreneurs, let alone celebrities, the rehearsal and delectation of success in all its forms? Indeed, the moment of exclusion of such success stories from high literature —it happens with naturalism, and of their migration into the bestseller—is a historically significant one for the history of narrative itself (and for its split into high and low culture). But the very significance of such categories— human, all-too-human—would seem to reinforce Ricoeur's more humanist point about the way in which "time becomes human to the extent that it is articulated through a narrative mode" (*TR*, Vol. 1, 85; 52)—it being under- stood that narrative is human very precisely because of the way in which its viewpoints are organized around what we have been calling the eudaimonic and its successes and failures (which are bound up with action).

8. Closure of the Act

Now I must come to the third of Ricoeur's observations about Aristotle, the one that has to do with closure and with the magnitude of the action ("a minutely small creature would not be beautiful," he says [*Poetics*, 1450b39]; but he lived before the microscope and color photography). In fact, however, everything here has to do with the relationship to the time of reception. Indeed, Aristotle seems to fold two separate things back on each other: the "importance" or "significance" of the action, and the time required to inspect it: the minutely small creature "would take almost no time to see"; an action too long and complicated would not be "easily held in the memory." From this standpoint, then, *Ulysses* or Blake's grain of sand would scarcely be unimportant or insignificant; but we must also clearly grasp the latter characterizations in the social terms laid out above. What happens to the margins of daily life is not likely to be extended in time and thus worthy of public attention, unless the crimes in question or even the small miseries of the everyday are allegorical of larger matters.

But it is the importance of closure that will be most relevant here, at a moment when literary history has disposed of a number of the traditional problems related to it: we no longer feel the requirement of the famous "unities" (of time, space, and action) to be an indispensable part of the etiquette of our aesthetics, and to be resisted or dispensed with only by the most daring. Indeed, to return today to those particular closures is often itself a bravura act and an exhibition of extraordinary constructive skill. Meanwhile, incomplete things—the Chekhov short story, the fragment, the plotless novel—having been promoted to genres in their own right, are now no longer to be considered as open, but present a new kind of closure, as are most of the forms theorized by Eco in *The Open Work*. This is why Ricoeur's speculations about the end of narrative are not particularly relevant: his fears of schism, the irresolvable debates and antagonisms of the 1960s, as those prolonged themselves in aesthetics like those of *Tel quel* whose "texts" no longer seemed to be classifiable as narratives any longer—these fears have been dissipated by the very fate of the works themselves, which, insofar as they prove successful and durable, invent a new kind of generic closure for themselves, or else sink into unreadability and oblivion.

What is more significant for us here is the very principle of closure which presides over this reinterpretation of narrative and which has already been characterized in terms, not so much of unity, as of unification. But the very idea of unity or unification today functions ideologically, as a signal of identity and of the reduction of the multiple to the same, whether by inclination or violence. "Closed form" has become as stigmatized an expression as "linear time" or "linear history;" and it would be interesting to follow the details of these genealogies of an essentially postmodern lexicology. Our present context, however, reveals this discipline-to-come to be both political and aesthetic all at once: closed societies are condemned, but also closure in works of art. The grounds of such condemnations are at first liberal ones, but with the replacement of the "openness" of "democracy" by the valorization of the multiple and of difference, the other term swings into radicalism and anarchism, and clearly sets off resonances of 1960s textual experiments of all kinds, experiments which (for Ricoeur) clearly awaken the dangers of schism and irresolvable antagonism: a political position in which, as has been noted, Habermas's certainty of the possibility of universal communication runs head-on into Lyotard's *différend*, with its insistence on antagonisms which are irresolvable, and codes which cannot be translated into each other, cases which cannot be adjudicated.

To attempt to mediate these antagonistic positions would inevitably place one on Habermas's side virtually by definition and in advance (since it is the very idea of mediation that is under fire here). I prefer to insist on what I will call a postmodern principle of collage, in which it is the sheer fact of juxtaposition, rather than that of synthesis or harmonization, which is the operator of a new kind of unity or closure. There does not need to result, from this juxtaposition, any explicit meaning; what counts is the fact that the two irreconcilable items are held together for a moment within the bounds of a single act of consciousness, like the snapping of a photograph at random. Consciousness here stands for the registering of the materials of the photograph and not for thinking or interpretation, neither of which is here directly addressed. This is no doubt still to maintain some kind of aesthetic frame, but one which has as its sole function to mark the limits of attention, or even the spaces of what cannot be thought. For the modernists this was still the operation of contingency or the aleatory, and in that form it was still a thought, it still signified. Now our postmodern juxtaposition simply registers the operation "Difference relates"; and if this is at all susceptible to philosophical analysis, I would like to think of it in terms of Ricoeur's aporias, which can never be solved but only enlarged, complexified, and raised to a higher level.

So it is here, and our new aesthetic or perceptual aporias can only be intensified and not celebrated as some new formal principle. If so, however, then the notion of the discordant concordance can be adapted to precisely this kind of postmodern sensibility; and the act of unification can be preserved across the divide, while endowing it with a rather different aesthetic spirit. What is however abandoned of the 1960s here is rather the Utopian notion that the boundaries of the aesthetic will be shattered, the latter spreading out to colonize the world itself: the world, in the aesthetics of the Happenings or of Marcuse, would then be transformed into art: just as for Morris and Ruskin, longer ago, work itself would have become aesthetic labor, the individual work itself as an object disappearing in the process.

There can be no doubt that this prophecy has since been realized, but in a rather different sense than the spirit in which it was launched, that of the consumer rather than the producer. For it is the society of the spectacle, advertising, commodification, and the image, which have spread out and aestheticized the world: thereby also producing a new situation and a new set of problems for whatever still wishes to call itself art. The latter must now appeal to a certain violence in reestablishing what must remain merely provisional or ephemeral frames: the mode of perception must also be historically altered, borrowing from that type of attention Benjamin discovered in our consumption of architectural space and which he called distraction,[37]

---

[37] Walter Benjamin, "The Work of Art in the Age of Mechanical Reproduction," in

in order perhaps to fashion a new kind of attention which we may call directed distraction, and which is closest in spirit to Freud's association of ideas—a most rigorous process indeed, in which the old self and the older habits of consciousness are to be held in check and systematically excluded.

At any rate, if such an art is conceivable, then it will not need to refute Ricoeur's account of closure as a traditional aesthetic ideology, but simply readapt it to contemporary works and conditions which he could not have taken into account and for which he cannot be suspected of having any sympathy. As in the older modern music, dissonance has itself become the newer consonance; concordance is there merely to help us feel the intolerable force of all the discord pressing against it, while the memory of identity itself generates difference, and the differences of difference, in a new and vivid way. In historiography, such differences are the emergence of the demographic other, the surging of countless millions of new subjects to be somehow taken into account within the framework of what was once simply a story of kings and queens, prime ministers, legendary rebels, and nation-states, not to speak of superior races. We will now need to see under what conditions emplotment can still function in historiographic postmodernity, and whether new kinds of time are here to be registered, whether narrative has the capacity to move the cumbersome machinery of collective entities around in any persuasive or satisfying new way.

9. Modernism and the Categories of Time

However, before we address the question of collective entities (and their consequences for the subsumption of historiography under the more general rubric of narrative), we need to see what lessons Ricoeur's reading of literary narrative has for us, particularly as it bears on the problem of making time appear. We have already observed in advance that Ricoeur's three examples —*Mrs. Dalloway*, *The Magic Mountain*, and Proust—are all staples of the modernist canon; and one does not deal with this question of periodization and form adequately by simply noting (as he does) Mendilow's distinction between "tales of time" and "tales about time" (*TR*, Vol. 2, 150–151; 100–101). The postmodern turn in the direction of space has made the complicity between modernism and the theme of temporality far more vivid, while at the same time sharply problematizing the distinction between the undoubtedly temporal structure of the so-called great realist novels and those of the modern period. If the question of the persistence of narrative in general across fundamental mutations in narrative structure is a crucial

---

Illuminations, ed. Hannah Arendt, trans. Harry Zohn, New York: Harcourt, Brace and World, 1968, 239.

preliminary issue in Ricoeur's project, then it demands at least as much attention as the shift from Aristotle's Greek tragedies to those of modern times (and in particular to the structures of the novel, which everyone recognizes to be a peculiar and historically unique form).

Meanwhile, another important literary question has here also been elided, namely that of the historical novel as such. Indeed, all three of the modernist texts dealt with here can also be considered historical novels (albeit of very different types, which differ among themselves fully as much as they do from the "traditional" historical novel, such as Tolstoy's *War and Peace*). Thus, *Mrs. Dalloway* offers a view of London in the immediate post–World War I years which is already obsolete when the novel appears in 1925; *The Magic Mountain* (1924) clearly evokes a pre-war reality which has been swept away by that conflict (whose peacetime sequel the novel leaves open); finally, Raoul Ruiz's great film demonstrates the degree to which *Le temps retrouvé* is already a historical novel in its own right (Paris during the war), a generic development foreshadowed by *Jean Santeuil*'s representation of the Dreyfus case (and the Zola trial). That these works all tell us something about the ways in which Time can be made to appear in the novel is unquestionable: but the blurring of generic distinctions prevents us from asking the two questions I have implied above, namely, (1) whether modernism has developed its own distinctive ways of making Time appear (which may also no longer be ours today); and (2) whether these novels, by virtue of their historical material, do not make historical time appear in rather different ways than do the standard realistic novels about peacetime (from *La Cousine Bette* to *Our Mutual Friend*; from *Madame Bovary* to *Middlemarch*).

For it is in any case a distinction between everyday existential time and the time of History which is operative here. Indeed, Ricoeur invents several useful categories to mark the intervention of the latter into the former, categories themselves inspired by Heidegger. But the latter's versions are not themselves to be found in *Sein und Zeit*, a work hastily written for purposes of tenure (his return to Freiburg) and, particularly in the concluding sections, exceedingly sketchy on the possibility of a level of historical time distinct from either the inauthentic time of the everyday or the authentic time of individual or existential *Dasein*. Indeed, the variety of temporal levels there projected by Heidegger—I count at least five: *Sorge* (the time of the individual *Dasein*), the time of work or the project (*Zuhandenheit*), the inauthentic time of the masses (the *man*), the authentic time of the individual being-unto-death, and finally the (presumably still authentic) collective time of the generation and its "mission"—suggests some fundamental objections to Heidegger's first system (which he can himself be thought to have anticipated and corrected in the *Kehre* or the turn to a philosophy of Being). Still, the seminar he gave in the year following the publication of *Sein und Zeit* (published towards the end of his life under the title *Grundprobleme der Phänomenologie*) adds some useful categories to the undeveloped hints of that volume. In particular, the four categories of what he there calls "ausgesprochene Zeit" (or "expressed time," time humanly projected and constructed in language) are suggestive: they are *Bedeutsamkeit, Datierbarkeit, Gespanntheit*, and *Öffentlichkeit*, or, in the English translations: significance, datability, spannedness, and publicness.[38]

"Significance" has to do with the time I need to complete my projects, that is to say (in philosophically incorrect language) that it implies a passage from my subjective desires and values to the reckoning of the time objectively necessary to implement or realize them: "significance," in other words, designates not just "meaning" in some vague sense, but the negotiations with the world which are necessarily for *Dasein* in its very life in time.

"Datability" then situates *Dasein* in the web of other lives, simultaneous, long gone, or yet to come, in which individual time finds itself implicated in what we sometimes call history, namely the immense flows and multiplicities of other people and their temporalities.

The awkwardly translated "spannedness" recapitulates that ek-static structure of time which constitutes Heidegger's development of Augustine and Husserl: namely the "stretching" of temporality's protensions and retensions —the possibility of my "now" to expand and to include past and future (or on the other hand to shrink to some immediate corporeal attention to the sensations of the here-and-now). The term thus now begins to designate historicity itself, as the possibility of including past and future in my time-sense, or on the other hand losing any sense of history, finding myself reduced to the body and the present. At this point, then, the very possibility of making historical Time appear is grounded in the ek-static nature of *Dasein*'s temporality as such, the strange way in which I am "ahead of myself"[39] and also drag my past along behind me like a ball and chain (to use Sartre's expression).

"Publicness," finally, is the way in which the "now" passes into language, or is already somehow pre-linguistic in the fact of its being able to be expressed in speech; or, better yet, its impossibility of existing except as that which can be spoken or expressed. Ricoeur will then later give a structuralist twist to this complicity between the present and the language by translating it into the terms of enunciation: the present is and can only be (he claims) the time of enunciation, *le temps de l'énonciation* (*TR*, Vol. 3, 159; 108–109): and this constitutes a peculiar refinement on the older notions of temporal experience which not only leads on into the various structuralist and

---

[38] Heidegger, *Die Grundprobleme der Phänomenologie*, 369; *The Basic Problems of Phenomenology*, 261.

[39] Ibid., 375; 265.

poststructuralist ontologies of textuality but also, in Ricoeur's hands, gives rise to a new complicity between the act of enunciating and the *énoncé*—the content of the utterance, or in other words the possibilities of narration as such.

But it should be noted that all these categories of Heidegger presuppose mediation—a kind of translation from the time of *Dasein* to the time of history: a translation which is itself no doubt a *Steigerung*, a lifting up and an intensification, and very possibly also an occasion for the parting of the ways between authenticity and inauthenticity. But, in any case, such categories also suggest a kind of continuity within experience, a natural movement from individual to collective time, a way in which the temporality of *Dasein* is already historical and collective in advance, and simply requires the articulation and specification of categories already present in the existential.

Ricoeur's alternative categories, however, which he describes as "connectors between lived time and universal time" (*TR*, Vol. 3, 153; 104), could seem to imply more of a disjunction between the two levels than do Heidegger's. Here we find, if not the brutal intervention of History into individual time as the novels will document it, then at the very least an insertion of those categories into an everyday life which can remain innocent of them. "Reflexive instruments" he calls them, and they constitute a third temporal option, which,

> arising from our rumination on the aporias of the phenomenology of time, consists in reflecting upon the place of historical time between phenomenological time [individual, or existential, lived time] and the time phenomenology does not succeed in constituting, which we call the time of the world, objective time, or ordinary time [a time which Heidegger ignores, without for all that imprisoning himself in Augustine's purely subjective temporality —*FJ*]. (*TR*, Vol. 3, 153; 104)

These three mediatory "instruments" (a term well chosen to distinguish them from "categories" as such) are the calendar; the succession of generations; and the archives or traces. But the deployment of these instruments would seem to presuppose or to depend on a particular kind of space, the possibility of a public space as opposed to a private one, a space in which the intersection of historical and existential temporalities can happen as an event.

It should be clear that this event is not the same as the Event of history itself: here perhaps we might have begun our differentiation of these modernist historical novels from the traditional ones celebrated by Lukács, which do indeed attempt to take on the great historical convulsions head-on and to represent them directly: as in the burning of Moscow, or even Fabrice's failure to recognize the Battle of Waterloo as a named event. But in

Mrs. Dalloway, the event is not World War I as such, it is the moment in which that level of history becomes visible in the everyday of the immediate postwar period, in which it suddenly and brutally, in the space of the Joycean single day, intersects the peacetime world of the household and of the reception Mrs. Dalloway has planned for that very evening. And the mark of this intersection is that it also awakens a series of other temporalities which are not on the same level or in the same rhythm or duration as the agonizing four years of wartime: thus Septimus no doubt remembers the war and the trenches, which haunt and torment him in Woolf's version of what the period baptized shell shock; but Mrs. Dalloway herself remembers her childhood and youth, reawakened by the return of Peter from his imperial service in British India, which he himself also remembers in a personal way, even though it inscribes its own larger public temporality on this novel, which thereby becomes as anti-imperialist as it is anti-war and pacifist.

We do not need to assert any kind of causality in order to affirm the intimate relations between the eruption of these temporalities and the public ones inscribed first in the tolling of Big Ben (the national time) and in the passage of the prime minister's limousine (the time of the state). To these we may add the time of the male power structure as it is incarnated in the authority of the society doctor, whose decision to isolate Septimus is responsible for the latter's suicide; and also the way in which the great temporal coexistence of the reception is honeycombed with the time of gossip and rumor, brushed by occasional vague perspectives of the future of the family and of children; all these temporalities then presided over by what seem to be moments of timelessness. What is to be noted here is less the unification of these disparate temporalities than rather their surcharge and overlap, and the multiple intersections with which they endow the immense power center of empire (whose essential blindness is quite different from the lucid experience of dependence and subalternity recorded in the colonized space of a Dublin under military occupation in *Ulysses*, which otherwise furnishes the formal model for Woolf's "experiment").

The spatial precondition of *The Magic Mountain* is in many ways the opposite of this one, for it presupposes an absolute and well-nigh hermeneutic separation from those "flatlands" in which History will shortly begin to take place. Here the temporal heterogeneities we have begun to observe in *Mrs. Dalloway* are registered in a very different formal manner, namely in the carefully segmented and uneven temporal durations in which the novel consists, and which deploy chapter lengths and narrative divisions to express the tensions between hours, days, weeks, and years, a unique enclave of multiple temporalities from which the ordinary (common or "vulgar") time of the flatlands is explicitly excluded, even though it includes both the existential and the historical, both the everyday of peacetime and the wartime of history yet to come.[40] It is as though the instrument of temporal registration which is Mann's novel demanded a radical secession from ordinary time in order the better to make it appear as an object in its own right. Ricoeur's analysis, however, makes the revealing point that this is achieved by a peculiar alternation in the very process of reading and interpreting the novel, which refuses to be reduced to any one interpretive option. Thus, we may certainly take it as a philosophical exploration of time itself; yet that reading periodically finds itself interrupted by the barometer of the temporalities of sickness and the body in fever; but also, at other moments, by ruminations on the fate of Europe as its elites stumble and blunder passionately into war. Each of these alternating temporal options constructs a different "aspect" of Time (to use Husserl's technical term), a variety reinforced by those moments of timelessness also isolated by Ricoeur (which in my opinion serve a very different and more narrative function than the positing of God's eternal timelessness in Augustine).

Yet it is difficult to argue away the moments of timelessness in Proust as well, those famous moments of bliss and blinding recollection of a present from the past outside the dreary everyday of jealousy or the frustration of a vacuous high society and its rituals, along with the gnawing personal defeats as Marcel's literary ambitions sink fatally into neurasthenia. But Ricoeur's reading of these "eternities" is deployed, not to develop some new or old theory of Proustian temporality (as in Poulet, for example). Rather, the old interpretation of Proust in terms of involuntary memory and ultimate revelation is played off against the newer Deleuzian reading of *À la recherche* in terms of signs and their decipherment: and it is this conflict between two incommensurable readings which not only constitutes Ricoeur's "interpretation," but also moves us on towards an understanding of the way Time in Proust is made to appear by means of the very heterogeneity of these interpretations and the temporalities they superimpose on each other.

For the traditional interpretation in terms of quest and revelation in effect erases the entire novel that has preceded the ending: the account of a false time in which the relationship of artistic production to individual experience was not understood or, better still, was repressed. The story of that repression then suddenly becomes of little interest in the light of the "adoration perpétuelle," the characters themselves being revealed as a mere teratology of deformed and pitiful, pathological specimens.

But, on the Deleuzian reading, the work breaks down into a series of "spots of time" or hermeneutic occasions and perceptions. All are equal in value to each other, there can be no particular hierarchy in the deeply satisfying labor by which each one is expressed and translated, transfigured in

---

[40] For a different interpretation of the segmentations of *The Magic Mountain*, see Fredric Jameson, *The Modernist Papers*, London: Verso, 2007, Chapter 3.

language itself, such that it only then—in this second time of writing—happens "for the first time." It is only in appearance that these minute phenomenologies lead up to any ultimate reflexivity or self-consciousness about the process, which had to have been understood before Proust began writing in the first place.

Temps de l'énoncé, temps de l'énonciation: as in the standard eighteenth-century references Ricoeur first used in his discussion of this distinction (Fielding, Sterne, the letter novel as such), what is at stake here is really less a conflict of interpretations than an interference between two kinds of temporality (or, if you prefer, two kinds of reading time). Proust's voluminous pages contain many more kinds, however, as the great movements of expansion and contraction—the eternal luncheons, lasting hundreds of pages; the leaps from period to period—testify. What we have not yet sorted out is the way in which existential and historical times intersect in such works; and in particular how a multiplicity of existential times, an opening up of the representational fan to register and include a variety of personal temporalities, might be expected to pick up the vibrations of the more properly historical ones; or whether some external force—events, social structure, the awakening of the collective—is required for historical time to become manifest.

We thus return to Ricoeur's three temporal mediations—the calendar, the generations, the trace—for an x-ray or CAT scan of the temporalities at work in these novels. The calendar marks the spot, no doubt, of the measurability of time: of that Bergsonian spatiality and visibility which he opposed to some deeper, more natural or organic flow, in a vitalist dualism no longer philosophically very stimulating after Heidegger, or even after Deleuze's own revival of Bergsonianism, and an interpretive code no longer generally acceptable for Proust either. Yet calendar time—both public and galactic all at once—does suggest that it may have been premature for Ricoeur to exclude objective time from his field. Ricoeur has in effect painted himself into a corner by insisting on the replacement of precisely that Aristotelian time of the rotation of the stars by some lived phenomenological or Augustinian temporality: this replacement then necessarily draws the objective time of the universe back into our own subjectivities where it necessarily takes on the form of a projection or a fantasy (or even a myth, a dimension Ricoeur acknowledges at the same time that he repudiates it: pre-historical or archaic time, perhaps, the pre-modern, the superstitious?). But as Ricoeur's trilogy is also haunted by death (in discussions that run from Kermode to Heidegger, and on into ethics), it might be worthwhile asking ourselves whether there are not intersections of objective and existential time to be determined which are objective events that are at the same time unassimilable or incomprehensible. At that point, not only does death itself come as a marker of that incompatible external time of the world, but also a range of just such interventions shows up on the narrative apparatus of the novel.

The ground bass of sickness and the feverish body in Thomas Mann, for example, would certainly seem to mark the outer limit of what subjectivity can interiorize: pathos is here reserved for the sickness and death of the others, like that of cousin Joachim; but Hans's own fevers happen to him from the outside (and are certainly very different in character from his historical death in the trenches of World War I, if indeed he does die during that conflict). Sickness as a corporeal experience is not particularly vivid in Proust, who paradoxically knew a good deal more about it personally: but aging certainly is, as in the *bal de têtes* of the final volume (we will come back to it under the rubric of the generations, a category which seeks precisely to recuperate this purely material and biological fact for historical experience). What is even more relevant, as a marker of the geological time of organic life on earth, is the omnipresence of the zoological in Proust, which not only betrays the operation of kinship in the clan—no doubt a more historical and social category—but rejoins the fact of aging as an inevitable emergence of hereditary structure from out of the individuality of the young and active. Thus the beak-like features of the Guermantes, as they reemerge in the older Saint-Loup before his death on the front, draw biological fatality up into the text and into the experience of time in the present: an even deeper layer of reality than the family likenesses that mark this caste of people more decisively than their mental and verbal tics. The metaphorics of animality here is indeed very different from that of Proust's great mentor Balzac, for whom the animal kingdom of human society is a place of vices and virtues, of ferocities and vulnerabilities, rather than a realm of collective species evolving out of the mists of a time in which the history of France itself is but a passing episode (Braudel's *longue durée*).

This objective time of the organic (as it replaces that galactic time whose markers, the stars, we so rarely live with in the age of electric lights) is however itself scarcely compatible with Ricoeur's calendar, no matter what kind of numbers the biologists try to use to convey it. The human calendar is not a space of sheer number or numerical succession either. We may recall here (to anticipate a more extensive discussion later on) one of Lévi-Strauss's cheaper debating points against Sartre's historicism[41]: calendar time here is a grid consisting of parallel lines of dots, which serves Lévi-Strauss as a demonstration of the way in which what Sartre calls History is a jumbled superimposition of very different models of time: the centuries, the years, the revolutionary days—all of which have their distinct tempos which are not susceptible to any grand synthesis or unified theory of history. From our own standpoint here, however, this very heterogeneity confirms the

---

[41] Claude Lévi-Strauss, *La Pensée sauvage*, Paris: Plon, 1962, Chapter 9.

intuition to be developed, namely, that it is out of this jumbled superimposition of different kinds of temporal models that History does in fact emerge.

Ricoeur's more decisive insight about the calendar, however, has to do with the operative presence in it of what he calls the axial event, a mythic or absent starting point which provides the occasion for a Year One, whether that be the hegira, the death of the last emperor, the birth of Christ, the conjunction of the stars, or whatever is taken as the zero degree at which the clock can begin ticking and calendar time again begin its long countdown. Even chronological time as such, the much-maligned "linear" time of the chronicles or of the reified "nows" lined up in a row that extends to infinity without becoming any less spatial, is not what it seems, and conceals within itself that indispensable reference to a transcendent moment, which is neither a beginning (in the narrative sense), nor out of time altogether (like the various eternities of Ricoeur's philosophical and literary references), but rather endowed with the primordiality of the Event and ideologically charged to express the inception of something new in the world, something the humble calendar faithfully promises to record and keep track of.

So, in all three of our modernist novels, World War I stands as the axial event, even where, owing to the convolutions of these forms, it occurs in the present tense (in Proust) or even in the future (as in Mann). But it is as if this brutal temporal break multiplied smaller and more ghostly versions of itself along the continuum: so the various personal or childhood pasts in Woolf take on a portentous if faint sense of possibilities missed, while in Mann minor events in the past suddenly reemerge like premonitions, in a secular replay of those biblical typologies in which events in the Old Testament announce and allegorically foretell the New. It is in Proust, however, that paradoxically the axial event never fully happens: to be sure, a Proustian experience is by definition an incomplete event, something like Ernst Bloch's emptiness of the present. Then too the war itself is not yet over by the time the novel ends: instead, it functions as a transformation of Paris and some final degradation of everyday life and its original cast of characters. Yet the war replicates in its reshuffling of the guest lists that earlier event which now does prove to be axial: the Dreyfus case itself, which the young novelist first proposed to seize *sur le vif* in *Jean Santeuil*, but which instructively eluded any direct full-face representation.

Indeed, it is as if the axial event—which was the indispensable precondition for the existence of an historical continuum, but which in reality served to disrupt synchronic time and reveal the latter as a heterogeneous pattern of surcharged layers—is mostly visible by its absence, and evoked most intensely there where it is strongly argued against. So it is that among the historians, Fernand Braudel's tripartite narrative structure in the Mediterranean book has as its secret mission to undermine the historical significance of the Battle of Lepanto and indeed to demystify the legend of this event as the great turning point in the struggle between Spain and the Ottoman Empire, very much in keeping with the very program and mission of the Annales School, which as we shall see was intent on sapping the very category of the Event as such and of the narrative history which issues from it.

Meanwhile, the strong political form of this onslaught on the very category of the Event as such (only foreshadowed by Lévi-Strauss's polemic with Sartre, to which I return) finds its embodiment in François Furet's anticommunist attack on the centrality of the French Revolution in French political consciousness, and his attempt to erase it from the slate of the present (without for all that substituting an equivalent). For the French Revolution was an axial event if there ever was one (the analogous efforts of English historians to dismiss the significance of their own revolution pale in contrast). In any case, Ricoeur's theorization has the merit of insisting on the reality of the axial event, despite the fact that it is in another sense absent and even nonexistent or mythic: as a principle of structuration, in other words, it can never be considered a mere subjective projection or collective fantasy, although it is itself the very center of ideology as such.

The second of Ricoeur's categories—that of the generations—was apparently first foregrounded and theorized by Wilhelm Dilthey, in a famous essay footnoted by Heidegger in *Sein und Zeit*.[42] The latter publication— hastily redacted—disposes of the category with a brief but ominous mention of the "mission" of this his own generation. We now know, however, that his teaching, both before and after Hitler's accession to power, was only too explicit about the nature of that mission and the duty of his students to fulfill it.[43]

The concept of the generation, however, is perhaps grasped as a category rather than as an idea with specific content: it has less to do with premonitions of mortality and the supersession of the superannuated by the young and vigorous (Frye's very definition of comedy as such) than with an opening onto the existence of other people and of the collective. Less than the occasion for intergenerational hostility or envy (what Ricoeur seems to mean when he so frequently deplores "schism"), it is rather to be seen as the coexistence and solidarity, for good or ill, of "my" contemporaries; and in this sense we must suggest that not every "generation" feels itself to be a true generation, and that there are moments of dispersal, seriality, mere temporal vegetation, in which people do not particularly feel themselves united in this unique and active contemporaneity. Indeed, it is to be doubted whether a generation can be defined passively, by what it suffers from without: thus it seems less plausible that the victims of the Holocaust are to be considered to

---

[42] Heidegger, *Sein und Zeit*, 385.

[43] See above, note 25.

have been a generation, than rather several waves of contemporaries who followed them: the founders of Israel, and after them, the still later contemporaries of various nations who revive the memories of the Holocaust and redefine themselves as Jews.

The experience of generationality is, however, a specific collective experience of the present: it marks the enlargement of my existential present into a collective and historical one, one somehow associated, if not by specific collective acts, then at least, as Heidegger rightly suggests, by that intimation of praxis which is the "mission." Avant-gardes are so to speak the voluntaristic affirmation of the generation by sheer willpower, the allegories of a generational mission that may never come into being (or, perhaps one should even say, that can never come into being).

At the same time, it is perhaps not so paradoxical that generationality also involves a struggle against the present, insofar as the present is not yet that space of collective presence which the future must be summoned up to be.

> On traverse un tunnel—l'époque—celui, long le dernier, rampant sous la cité avant la gare toute-puissante du virginal palais central, qui couronne ... Mal informé celui qui se crierait son propre contemporain, désertant, usurpant, avec impudence égale, quand du passé cessa et que tarde un futur ou que les deux se remmêlent perplexement en vue de masquer l'écart.[44]

Mallarmé's search for the present, in an essay which opposes and combines political action and writing, is reproduced by the generation, which like Heideggerian temporality itself is always ahead of itself or lagging behind, but without benefit of any temporal plentitude in the now as such.

This is perhaps the moment to evoke a curious discussion of that "neutralization of the present" in narrative which Ricoeur rightly associates with Proust. The occasion is Harald Weinrich's reduction of the past tenses to mere signals of narration:

> Does not the signal marking the entry into fiction make an oblique reference to the past through the process of neutralization, of suspension? Husserl discusses at great length this filiation by neutralization. Following him, Eugen Fink defines *Bild* in terms of the neutralization of mere "presentification" (*Vergegenwärtigen*). By this neutralization of the "realist" intention of memory, all absence becomes by analogy a *quasi-past*. Every narrative—even of the future—speaks of the irreal *as if* it were past. How could we explain that narrative tenses are also those of memory, if there were not between narration and memory some metaphorical relation produced by neutralization? (*TR*, Vol. 2, 110–111; 74)

---

[44] Stéphane Mallarmé, "L'action restreinte," in *Oeuvres complètes*, Paris: Gallimard, 1945, 371–372.

If so, generationality itself becomes a kind of narrative we seek to impose on a recalcitrant present, mastering it in view of a triumphant story of the future. Contemporaneity is perhaps what is achieved last, while the early presence of the others not only gives rise to the mirage (and the reality) of the big Other, it also generates my own individual subjectivity. This shadowy presence of all the others behind individual figures is what equips narrative with its allegorical possibilities, of which the sense of the type, if not the stereotype, is only one modulation. As the conjuncture of the generations varies with the historical situations themselves, the only narrative generalization that can be ventured is the hypothesis that they will become more visible in moments of intense conflict, in a kind of rivalry of temporalities whose struggle for power consists in the claim of each on the present of time. The difficulty in representing such generational intersection is then to be identified in the reification of the other, his immobilization in a single moment of age, his assimilation to that mask of permanence which Proust's *bal de têtes* seeks to dissolve back into the multiple selves stationed along the unimaginable and unrepresentable time line. But this is a struggle against "the immense privilege of the present" (Hegel) which obliterates its multiple pasts and incorrigibly sustains forgetfulness. Historiography also represses the generational fact, which however sinks to a kind of metaphysical presupposition or steady unheard accompaniment, rather than disappearing altogether. In Marx generational time is replaced by labor time as well as by the circulation time of capital, which can be said to be capitalism's objective or cosmological temporality, despite the fact that revolutions are made by young people and by women. In revolutions, indeed, the temporality of the generations is concentrated in a single instant—"time's livid final flame!"—which is no doubt another way of obliterating it.

Yet if the present is the time of enunciation, the present of the generation is also the time of collective enunciation of the attempt to say "we" (after the awakening of the "us"). In this sense, generationality also marks the attempt to insert the subject into the collective, by seeking to enlarge the former to the dimensions of the latter: here Ricoeur's invocation of reading is an appropriate figure, inasmuch as it now grasps the temporalities of the novel as what have to be somehow reactivated by those of the reader. Ricoeur's Mimesis III thus becomes a process of contact and mutual restructuration between two complex temporal systems (which I have elsewhere characterized as a four-term rather than two-term intersection, where the reader and the writer in effect serve as the mediation between a contact between two historical situations and moments[45]).

History is, of course, most clearly the place in which we are called upon, not merely to confront a certain present of the past, but also to summon up

---

[45] See my "Marxism and Historicism," in *Ideologies of Theory*, London: Verso, 2008.

the past of that present and the future it momentarily included in the form of anxiety and anticipation, of fear and desire. The "horizon of expectations" of Gadamer can mean little unless it includes the way in which that present of a given past must be imagined as bearing its own unique burden of past and its own uniquely feverish hopes and projects within itself. The modern novel involved the reconquest of these multiple temporalities and the effort to invent a narrative language which could suggest that existential present of its characters as their experience "outside itself" in all three temporal ek-stases. Modern literary historiography then seeks to step outside that invention and to include the unique temporalities of the authorial situation itself within an increasingly complicated act of reading, in which the literary work itself—the twenties of Woolf, Mann, and Proust—has itself become somehow generational. Yet it is an act easily enough disguised as an aesthetic operation in some pure or eternal present.

Ricoeur's final site of temporal intersection—the trace—makes such occultations of the past impossible, owing to its peculiar ontology, in which being and not-being coexist in a fashion unconceptualizable by philosophy (this is an aporia if there ever was one). For the trace exists simultaneously in the present and in the past: it is too easy to evoke this double life in terms of the sign (whose mysteries no doubt derive from it), unless you are (wrongly) willing to grant the sign a full being as an object in the present. One is tempted to say, as Ricoeur does for time itself, that there can be no pure phenomenology of the trace but that it has at least this in common with the sign; that it must be read, deciphered, tracked like a clue, interpreted like a missing narrative; it demands a reconstruction in which it would itself qua trace disappear utterly. These are, as it were, the black holes that honeycomb the present without being visible: and if fictional narrative can make them appear by means of this or that narrative of detection (or of so-called involuntary memory), most historiography—save for the history of history—seems to have passed through them to the other side before its stories begin to be told: the notes have been taken, the registers examined, the archives closed.

These were then the mediatory categories whereby existential time can be grasped as historical: mediatory codes, perhaps, in which the temporality of *Dasein* can be written or rewritten in terms of this or that version of history—the generation, the nation, the collectivity, or however we wish to formulate this elusive dimension ideologically.

But this very way of putting it suggests its own questions, namely whether that existential temporality is historical through and through, and simply demands translation into historical terms; or whether the possibility of a mediation with history is itself discontinuous and only breaks into private life at fitful or intermittent moments (which can themselves be euphoric or nightmarish); or, finally, whether the temporality of history is not situated on another dimension altogether—the collective—which therefore demands a privileged situation in which to reveal itself.

With this third possibility we seemed to have moved from some quotidian hermeneutic towards the more transcendental model of the Heideggerian *Kehre*, in which, from time to time, the empirical experience of existents—*Seiendes*, the ontic variety of what exists within the world—is suddenly enveloped and eclipsed by the fleeting glimpse of Being itself—*das Sein*—whose fundamental property (if one can use such language) is to wax and wane, to withdraw in the very moment of its self-disclosure and unfolding, to be accessible only in the form of a felt absence.

But if this is the form of Ricoeur's interrogation, then it slowly becomes clear that two questions have here been superimposed: that of the appearance of Time and that of the appearance of History. Meanwhile, both questions have been ambiguated by a second or dialectical axis, a new dimension of ambivalence, in which a passive receptivity of the experience of Being or totality has the possibility of giving way to its active provocation, whether on the part of the philosopher or the artist, not to speak of the political leader. In a fallen world, in which the experience of the grace of this opening is contingent and seemingly arbitrary, a new question arises, namely whether it can be made to appear, and whether the preconditions of the calling up of such a dimension can be actively implemented (even if they are theoretically known).

But this question cannot be addressed until the answer to the first one is clarified. It would certainly seem that Ricoeur's humanist and anthropomorphic framework limits him to the study of individual time itself. His interrogation centers on the problem of whether we can make Time itself appear, and how. It does not, despite his historiographic materials, appear to posit some properly historical time, or in other words history itself, about which one might ask the analogous but quite distinct question, how we might make History appear as such. Indeed, the historiographic materials would seem rather to be pressed into service to illuminate the literary ones, whose machinery of temporal intersections and the superposition of the various temporal dimensions are given priority in this search for Time.

But is there such a thing as Time itself? Are there not many varieties of temporality, whose attempted unification in a single concept is the source of innumerable false problems, ultimately accounting for the failure of philosophy to overcome its endless aporias? The answer to this lies in the structure of the question, which is organized around a personification: that supreme actor, Time, *le Temps*, who makes his appearance in Proust's last pages. But such a figure is always, according to Ricoeur, a sign of emplotment, and therefore demands an answer commensurate with the three mimeses, with the translation of reality into narrative, rather than on the barren cosmological level of world time, the time of the stars and the universe, from which it can receive no response. Thus, in an echo of Sartre's response to the question about the unification of history—or of the emergence of the personification called History, if you like—we must answer, not that time is one, but that it becomes one: it wins its absolute status as a personification by being unified; and being unified, Ricoeur might have added, by narrative mimesis itself. The unification of time is thus the correlative of the closure of the work: it is what makes of multiple discords a single discordant concordance. But this formula, as we have seen, is misleading to the degree to which it still suggests an older, modernist if not even traditional, conception of what concordance and unification might be in the first place.

What we actually observe in the novels, however, is the multiplication of the temporalities they collect and include, a multiplicity which goes well beyond the dualism of subjective and objective time, of my individual experience of time passing and the objective placement of the moment in the universe of stars and galaxies. Nor is it productive, at this stage, to reduce to this simple opposition the range of temporal levels we confront in narrative, which include that of daily life and that of collective history, that of short-term memory and that of the long term (what Husserl distinguished as retention and recollection), that of other people and that of the nation, or the dead, or the human race, that of the project and that of a fixation on the past—Heidegger's authentic and inauthentic time, Thomas Mann's moments of eternity, postmodernity's acceleration, so rapid it seems to have been suspended in a kind of freeze-frame, as opposed to the slowness of peasant life, trudging the spring furrows in van Gogh's or Heidegger's wooden shoes. These multiple temporalities are not primarily distinguished by their content, but rather constitute so many different and distinct forms of time, which can only be superimposed or surcharged on each other, but not fused together in one overarching form or even two opposing ones. Each of these temporalities presents a distinct philosophical problem in its relations with the others: the literary text, however, seems to jumble them pell-mell together in an immense omnibus of time frames whose random and multiple intersections are regulated only by the emplotment, and accessible only to narrative interpretation and not philosophical systematization —to narrative intelligence rather than abstract reason. The interruption of some inner personal time of daydreaming and free association by the metallic vibrations of Big Ben would not seem to solve any of our aporias but rather produce them in the first place.

But this is for Ricoeur—or so it seems to me—very precisely the privilege of literature over philosophy, about which we recall that "there can be no pure phenomenology of time." Indeed, the superiority of literature over philosophy—if one can put it in such trivializing language—lies in the fact that the latter generally takes its function as the solution of aporias and the overcoming of contradictions, whereas the mission of the former consists in producing them in the first place.

This is the point at which we may return to the question of Aristotle's catharsis in a new way: it becomes the name of what results from the transmutation of real phenomena—good or bad fortune, real suffering—into their aesthetic representations. But it is important to distinguish here between some banal account of mere aesthetic effects and that process of aestheticization, that transformation of reality into aesthetic representation, which is an act and an operation—indeed, a form of production. The first alternative simply registers the existence of a strange kind of object among other objects, which turns out to have unique effects which other existents lack. The latter, however, is something we do to reality, and its resultant transformation is no less real than the objects on which it is performed. This operation can now be better specified by abandoning the term "aesthetic"— already suspiciously redolent of art appreciation and luxury or leisure activity —and returning to our starting point in narrative itself: for emplotment gives a far more vigorous and productive sense of this operation, whereby at one and the same time something happens to its initial quotient of misery. Catharsis, as Ricoeur reads it, is the name for that transformation of affect, most often traditionally grasped in terms of discharge or purgation or at best purification: dismissive formulations which give us to understand that we have merely distanced ourselves from what was strongly and disturbingly felt, and have now managed to get rid of the oppressive feelings somehow. "Emplotment" has by now, however, absorbed cognitive connotations from its association with historiography; and the gamble is that it can now be grasped as an activity of construction and the production of a new reality: an enterprise with at least as much dignity and practical value as, say, the Freudian talking cure.

That value will be enhanced if we now return to the philosophical side of the matter, and reexamine the impact of catharsis—grasped in this new way —on the conceptual stalemates of the aporetic. Indeed, Ricoeur's patient and extensive demonstrations suggest, not only that Time can never be represented (a conclusion already reached by Kant), but also that the gap between cosmological and existential or phenomenological time can never be closed by philosophical conceptualization, but remains, at whatever level of complexity, an aporia resistant to mere thinking. The narrative view then presupposes a skepticism about solutions, which nonetheless places a premium on the rigorous demonstration of their impossibility. This is the sense in which we may speak of the production of such aporias: a formula suggested by Althusser's language, in another context—that of ideology in literature—in which he says:

THE VALENCES OF HISTORY: PART I

Ce que l'art nous donne à *voir*, nous donne donc dans la forme du *"voir,"* du *"percevoir,"* et du *"sentir"* (qui n'est pas la forme du *"connaître"*), c'est *l'ideologie* dont il naît, dans laquelle il baigne, dont il se détache en tant qu'art, et à laquelle il fait *allusion*.[46]

This view endows art with a cognitive and constructional function consistent with its own specific mode of existence (and not imported from philosophy); and it suggests a useful way of grasping the nature of the operation of emplotment, now understood as the production of aporias, their demonstration before us (as one might demonstrate a new machine and put it through its paces), and thereby the modified status of their being (which the enigmatic word "catharsis" also seeks to convey). In other language, art's function is to produce contradictions, and to make them visible. The formulation of Lévi-Strauss, that of imaginary solutions to real contradictions—or closer to home, "real toads in imaginary gardens" (Marianne Moore)—is satisfactory to the degree to which we grasp such "solutions" as ways in which the contradiction in question is deployed and offered for examination in all its discord or dissonance (for it is important, in the light of our discussion of postmodern differentiation, to forestall the harmonizing overtones of words like "resolution").

The literary inventory of these aporias then comes as a better alternative to the repeated demonstration of the impotence of philosophy than any retrenchment in skepticism and nihilism. The repeated failure to make Time appear in some pure state, to think it head-on as an unmediated phenomenon (most recently again in Husserl[47]) thereby gives way to a collection of all the symptoms of time, the traces it leaves of its invisible omnipresence. But those traces—and this is the second conclusion we may now draw from Ricoeur's great project—can be identified and registered only at the intersections of several distinct temporalities. Even within the most subjective reduction of temporal experience, the thing itself only becomes visible at moments of temporal coexistence, of simultaneity, of the contemporaneity without coalescence of several distinct subjectivities at once.[48]

---

[46] Louis Althusser, "Lettre sur la connaissance de l'art," in *Écrits philosophiques et politiques*, tome 2, Paris: Stock/IMEC, 1995, 561.

[47] See Derrida's demonstration of the irrepressible recurrent contradictions in Husserl's quest: *Le problème de la genèse dans la philosophie de Husserl*, Paris: PUF, 1990.

[48] Without returning to the inevitable reference to Einstein, we find a luminous reflection on the growing simultaneity of the social in Benedict Anderson, *Imagined Communities*, London, Verso: 1991, 24–25: "Our own conception of simultaneity has been a long time in the making, and its emergence is certainly connected, in ways that have yet to be well studied, with the development of the secular sciences. But it is a conception of such fundamental importance that, without taking it fully into account, we will find it difficult to probe the obscure genesis of nationalism. What

But it is precisely this capacity of the literary text to make Time itself appear, even fitfully, that also constitutes the superiority of the postmodern aesthetic over its modernist predecessor in this respect. For while the latter pursued that mirage of unification which it still shared with philosophy, the former chose to embrace dispersal and multiplicity; and the slogan "Difference relates," which I have evoked above, turns out to be the best working program for this deployment of temporal levels we have found to be required for any mediated approach to time, in the absence of the thing itself. The works in question not only distend (in Augustine's language) and stretch (in Heidegger's): they strain painfully to touch the scattered dimensions in which time manifests itself, like so many walls the body's extended arms manage to brush with outstretched fingers; and this corporeal metaphor may stand in for that ultimate human agency Ricoeur identifies as Mimesis III, or in other words reading. Reading is then the momentary and ephemeral act of unification in which we hold multiple dimensions of time together for a glimpse that cannot prolong itself into the philosophical concept.

10. The Time of the Historians

It is therefore now appropriate to turn to the historiographic exhibits themselves, and in particular to compare the formal processes at work in the "novels of time" with what transpires in more properly historical texts, and in particular in Fernand Braudel's great book, *The Mediterranean and the Mediterranean World in the Age of Philip II*. This monumental work deploys that temporal structure Braudel was famously to theorize as the three *durées*—the three temporalities of, first, the *longue durée* of geological time, then the middle time of the waxing and waning of institutions, and finally the short *durée* of historical events (a tripartite scheme I myself adapted in *The Political Unconscious*, it should be noted in passing).

Here too, of course, we may object that Braudel's historiography also might be characterized as modernist in the way in which the Annales

---

has come to take the place of the mediaeval conception of simultaneity-along-time is, to borrow again from Benjamin, an idea of 'homogeneous, empty time,' in which simultaneity is, as it were, transverse, cross-time, marked not by prefiguring and fulfillment, but by temporal coincidence, and measured by clock and calendar.

"Why this transformation should be so important for the birth of the imagined community of the nation can best be seen if we consider the basic structure of two forms of imagining which first flowered in Europe in the eighteenth century: the novel and the newspaper. For these forms provided the technical means for 're-presenting' the *kind* of imagined community that is the nation."

historians waged their fundamental campaign against that central category of all narrative, the event, and thus may in some sense be thought to take an anti-narrative position on history writing, wishing to abandon the emphasis of traditional history on the great political events and turning points and on the great historical actors and figures.

The Annales School, however, and in particular this its most exemplary representative, famously retained history's emphasis on change and can be seen rather as enlarging the latter's framework by its inclusion of the *durées* or time frames, and thereby transcending the single anthropomorphic level of individuals and their acts (the old domain of the nineteenth-century narrative history, with its great historical figures and its dramatic events). Now, alongside this level, or perhaps one should say beneath it, there appears the much longer temporal movement of institutions as such, cultural, political, religious, and economic, and even below that, the famous *longue durée* of space itself and geology: in Braudel's great work, this is the very ecology of the Mediterranean from its earliest geological appearance between the two great landmasses of Alpine Europe and Africa, a stage on which emerge the properly Mediterranean institutions and cultures at their own speed and with their own (internally differentiated) temporalities, and upon the foreground of which the recognizably human figures of history strut and gesticulate, claiming no less permanence for their own minuscule agitations (Braudel has confessed that he was very reluctant to write this third panel of his story, inasmuch as it unavoidably turns on that great individual narrative and historical event which is the Battle of Lepanto.)

The question therefore first lies in the applicability of the traditional, properly narrative categories to the first two *durées*, which nonetheless surely have "events" and even characters appropriate to their respective rhythms of change. As a result of his repudiation of narrative semiotics along with Marxist historiography, Ricoeur is content to deal with Braudel's three *durées* in terms of what look like the second-best categories of quasi-event, quasi-character, and quasi-plot, even where the technical apparatus of semiotic terminology such as that of the actant (or narrative agent) would have, one would think, generated all kinds of newer and more interesting problems.

The Mediterranean and the Mediterranean World in the Age of Philippe II is in fact organized in three parts which correspond very precisely to the three durations in question: the first, a three-hundred-page disquisition on its geography—the littorals, the Turkish and Spanish limits, but above all the various smaller seas into which the sea itself is divided, and across which maritime routes pass which are as fixed as roads on land, and as subject to military and maritime contestation. The second section of the two-thousand-page work is devoted to what may be called a middle duration of institutions, cultures, and economic rhythms; while the final one, the one Braudel was so reluctant to add, includes the short duration of "narrative history"—conquests and dynasties, events and protagonists. This section ends with the death of Philip II: an event which is somehow emblematic of the relative marginalization of the great inner sea itself, ceasing to be the battleground between the two last great world empires (in Wallerstein's sense) as Spain turns towards the Americas and the route to the East is now relocated externally, around Africa, at the same time that at Lepanto the Ottomans are turned back from European waters.

The positing of the three levels of temporality of the *durées* is thus only the framework for the detection of other kinds of time—the time of the peasant's seasons on the land, for example, or of the merchant's coastwise journey from port to port; the time of the great political decisions, or of the slow trickle-down of new ideological pronouncements; the time of the circulation of Spanish gold, and of the introduction of oil painting from Flanders into Italy; the time of torture or the time of conquest ... All of these temporalities are not only skillfully positioned in their punctual interactions with each other; the grasping of them in provisional montage is designed to be unavoidable.

Clearly it is the first or longest *durée* which constitutes the most fundamental challenge for Ricoeur's humanism and over which he scores an important victory we need to take into account. This new kind of historiographic unconscious is geography itself and perhaps even geology—the oldest realm in which deep history was discovered in the nineteenth century and from which the very word "diachrony" is derived (in Lyell). The geological ages themselves, indeed, offer a serious problem for anyone who, like Ricoeur, seeks to read history in terms of Aristotelian plot.

Let us therefore follow some of the geographical trails through Part 1 in order to see how Braudel integrates it into what is after all a history and not a geographical treatise. The trails must be ruthlessly simplified to a mere thread, given the variety of directions, and also the extraordinarily rich underbrush and vegetation of facts, customs, places, civilizations through which they lead. We must very briefly talk about mountains, which emerge in geological deep time with the convulsive appearance of the mountain ranges of various ages that ring the inland sea: also a narrative, it should be remarked, but one without people (at least for a page or so). Note that the mountains, as a fundamental boundary which closes off the Mediterranean from virtually all sides, also define the narrative of the latter's history to come: it is the first closure to define the object of study, and to unify it as a single object and a single history.

It is also a different kind of outside limit: "can we define the mountains as the poorest regions of the Mediterranean, its proletarian reserves?"[49]

---

[49] Fernand Braudel, *La méditerranée et le monde méditerranéen à l'époque de Philippe II*, Paris: Armand Colin, 1990, 27; in English, *The Mediterranean and the Mediterranean*

Generally, Braudel agrees: but he begins with a counterstatement: "the mountains are a refuge from soldiers and pirates, as all the documents bear witness, as far back as the Bible. Sometimes the refuge becomes permanent" (*MM*, 27; 31). Yet these permanent settlements are also a culture in their own right:

> One thing at least is certain. Whether settled in tiny hamlets or in large villages, the mountain population is generally insignificant in comparison with the vast spaces surrounding it, where travel is difficult; life there is rather like life in the early settlements in the New World, which were also islands set in the middle of wide open spaces, for the most part uncultivable or hostile, and thereby deprived of the contacts and exchanges necessary to civilization. The mountains are forced to be self-sufficient for the essentials of life, to produce everything as best they can, to cultivate vines, wheat, and olives even if the soil and the climate are unsuitable. In the mountains, society, civilization, and economy all bear the mark of backwardness and poverty. (*MM*, 29; 32–33)

The very figures of this passage ("islands set in the middle of wide open spaces") inconspicuously assert the priority of the sea as the fundamental reference or trope in a description which develops the pre-conceptual category of the enclave. Meanwhile, the very negation here underscores the construction of this world in terms of travel and trajectory, of transport by water, at the same time that the isolation of the mountain enclaves seems to determine, not merely a different historiographic approach from other areas, but even an exclusion from historiography altogether.

> The mountains are as a rule a world apart from civilizations, which are an urban and lowland achievement. Their history is to have none, to remain always on the fringe of the great waves of civilization, even the longest and most persistent, which may spread over great distances on the horizontal plane but are powerless to move vertically when faced with the obstacle of a few hundred metres. (*MM*, 30; 34)

This is also, obviously enough, the source of the freedom always associated with the mountains, whether we are thinking of refugees or brigands, or of the oppressions of conquest and colonization or sheer power or hegemonic influence. Now insofar as difference is also a relationship, we may also note that here we find inscribed as its verso the more propitious ecology of the non-mountainous areas with which they are already being implicitly compared: the plateaus, hills, and foothills of the next section, and finally the plains themselves.

World in the Age of Philip II, trans. Siân Reynolds, New York: Harper and Row, 1972, 30. Future references to this work are denoted *MM*; all references will cite the French edition first, followed by the English translation.

It should be noted that Braudel takes pains to show us that none of these distinct ecologies is really a final stopping point, none is truly complete and self-sufficient in itself: the plateaus are places of transport and the carrying trade, epitomized by "these unending processions of beasts of burden, mules and donkeys invisible under their loads ... that enabled Castile to maintain the links between the peripheral regions of the peninsula which surround it and in places separate it from the sea" (*MM*, 49; 54–55). The plateau is thus, to anticipate, a surrogate for the sea itself.

The hillsides, in contrast, are at first glance the true paradisal space: the traveler "arriving in spring ... is greeted by a green landscape already bright with flowers, and cultivated fields where white villas stand among vines, ash, and olive trees ..." (*MM*, 50; 56). Yet the "fragile economy of terraced crops on the hillside is infinitely complex and variable with the passage of time ... These crops were forced to compete with each other according to market prices ... and with the produce of neighbouring regions ..." (*MM*, 53; 59). Finally this is a very narrow and frequently interrupted band of fertility around the Mediterranean itself, in that comparable to the oasis, yet another kind of enclave, and the hills are open to invaders and marauders from below and above alike.

As for the plains, nothing in these early pages is quite so striking as Braudel's sharp rebuke to the stereotypes: far from being rich and fertile, they are at first places of swamp and malaria, and only at the price of heavy labor over many generations and intelligent investment by towns, land-lords, or princes, do they take on their modern appearance. Meanwhile, as areas that developed relatively late, they are also the place of monocultures and big estates, and of the worst kind of landowners—namely those whose operations lead to serfdom or slavery.

It is in the light of the strengths and weaknesses of these other fundamental regions that we now return to the mountains: first in the mobile form of transhumance and nomadism, and then in that of the general spilling down of population out of the mountains. Overpopulation? Well, at least "in relation to their resources" (*MM*, 37; 41). The description of place is now set in motion by the movement of its inhabitants: from the mountains, first raids into the prosperous valleys; then peddlers and merchants of all kinds; workers in the docks; beggars; and finally, sailors. Thus the deeper sense of the initial characterization of the mountains as the Mediterranean's "prole-tarian reserves" is filled out and given content. This immigration from the mountains will be a resource in manpower: and will later on come to be identified as the ultimate stock of personnel for that fundamental vocation of the inland sea to bear the multitudes of vessels that will make up its fortune and its unique identity.

Thus the historian gradually turns his static landscapes into populations and their histories. Ricoeur captures this subtle transformation brilliantly when evoking the historian's problem of passing from Part 1 of his work to Part 2: "geohistory," he tells us, "is rapidly transformed into geopolitics" (*TR*, 291; 209); and to be sure this reconfirms his own humanist agenda, which consists, by way of Aristotle's anthropomorphic conception of plot, in turning all narrative back into its underlying human forms. We will see later, however, that even on Ricoeur's analysis, let alone Braudel's own working method, it is crucial that the transformation not be complete; that the mountains, nature, the non-human, not be completely dissolved back into human praxis; that there remain a somehow slight yet fundamental gap between Part 1 and Part 2.

For the moment, however, let us note two further points about the gradual emergence of people from these places, and the population of the various ecosystems by distinct forms and types of human individuals. For one thing, the very theme of population itself—which has here led to the consideration of an overpopulation which then supplies the needs of the expanding coastal regions with their industry and commerce for more and more manpower—this theme also heralds the future doom of the Mediterranean as a whole, as a semi-autonomous region, as "an actor on the stage of world history" (as Ricoeur will put it later on). For one of the basic forms of the dialectic is, as we shall see, the way that success brings failure, winner loses, and good fortune brings all kinds of new problems which in the end may well prove fatal. So here it is finally the problem of population which limits the development of the Mediterranean itself, as a narrow littoral around a landlocked body of water: at the height of its prosperity there are no longer enough sailors, there are no longer enough workers to build the ships, even encouraging immigration from the most far-flung regions of its influence and attraction is not enough, and this fundamental limit will sound the knell of the region and the conclusion of the book itself, the closure of the historical period it claims for its narrative.

But what is almost more important for us at this point is the role of travel, transport, immigration itself: for it is this which becomes the narrative at this stage; or to put it another way round, travel is the narrative specific to geography and to a spatial level, it is the form storytelling takes on this level and with the elements available to it. Even more significant than that, however, is the further narrative resource hidden away within this seeming abstraction under which movements, invasions, population transfers, exiles, caravans, and journeys of all kinds are ranged. For they are not merely a variety of forms of movement and displacement: they are linking operations, in which that more fundamental cast of characters (at this stage, the geographical regions, and the enclaves corresponding to them) is set in motion in the form of a structure *combinatoire* or permutation scheme. Here, indeed, we are at the very heart of Braudel's "method" (at least in this specific work with its unique constraints): it does not consist in inventing general types under which to range the dizzying variety of his raw materials. That would be relatively simple and Weberian: to isolate all the gardening hillsides as an ideal type of which we then deploy the variety; or the various mountain villages; or the kinds of plains and their characteristic crops. No, the generalizing mechanism here is directed to the types of relationship between these regions: transhumance versus nomadism, for example, and indeed within that, the two types of transhumance.

Now it is time to come to the crux of the matter, which is, indeed, relationship; or better still interrelationship as such. There are good and bad forms of this, as I have already begun to hint. Mingling present and past or, better still, blasting open a continuum between today's globalization and Braudel's late sixteenth-century Mediterranean, we may say that it was indeed something like globalization that happened to the inland sea, to the Mediterranean world of Philip II and the sultan: the opening of the Spanish Empire onto the Americas, the turn of the Ottomans towards Persia and then, after Lepanto and Transylvania, the stabilization of a kind of iron curtain in Europe—all these signs accompany the decline of the Mediterranean as a stage of world history. But is this not very precisely the effect of globalization as such, to shift stages at will? To flee areas in which wages are high for others in which cheap labor can still be found? To abandon otherwise prosperous spaces, allowing their currency to stagnate, and to create wholly new centers of production and commerce, indeed to lend the old world "center" a new and more alarming, if more philosophical, meaning? At any rate, it is in this way that the Mediterranean of the Renaissance is decentered by a prodigious expansion of global space and relegated to the sidelines of history, Spain and Turkey, but also Italy and North Africa, becoming the "sick men" not only of Europe but of this formerly world-historical geographical zone as a whole.

These glacial and inhuman masses, then, the great mountain ranges that hold the Mediterranean and its littorals within their borders, are in reality swarming with micro-narratives: even the next entities up on the scale of being, the plants and then the animals, are what attract, nourish, and are sometimes even the result of human activity, whether settlements, invasions, depopulation, transhumance, or nomadism. On the level of relationships, the mountains at once begin to betray their links with piedmont, plain, port, and the sea itself: with exploitation, invasion, emigration, transportation. But on the diachronic level each geographical feature becomes the occasion for a micro-narrative of settlement, of humanization, in short of praxis.

And it is here that we encounter Ricoeur's magnificent and pertinent formula: "geohistory is rapidly transformed into geopolitics" (*TR*, 291; 209). In other words, the fundamental narrative of Part 1 is in effect a metanarrative: it is the story of the transformation of temporality 1, geographical being, into temporality 2, the middle-range duration of human settlement of the region, with all the economics, technology, culture, religion, and warfare that such a transformation brings with it. A spiral is thus launched, in which Part 2 follows the trajectory of Part 1 at what it might be abusive to call a higher, but certainly a more human, level, and at a faster, and yet still transgenerationally slow-moving, temporality. At this point in their gradual identification with each other, levels 1 and 2 gradually become indistinguishable, leaving us with what looks very much like the old Marxian duality of base and superstructure, except that here the base includes culture, while the superstructure of temporality 3 becomes that froth of events Marxist historiography sometimes imprudently dismissed as "epiphenomenal," as reductive and abstract.

In this spiral let us examine a few encyclopedia sentences about the very formation of the Mediterranean itself, identified as

> the main existing fragment of the Tethys Sea, which before the Alpine-mountain-building period girdled the eastern hemisphere. The structure and present form of the basin and its bordering mountain system have been determined by the convergence and recession of the relatively stable continental blocks of Eurasia and Africa … The corresponding troughs of the fold system and the later foundering of areas encircled by the fold system and the later foundering of areas encircled by the folds created the major basins within the sea …[50]

It is probably unnecessary to add that this account is also a narrative, with agents and events. Still, a fundamental ambiguity remains: is this *longue durée* a form of time, or is it not rather a non-time, in which nothing happens and nothing changes? From the standpoint of human history, in other words, long duration, geography, let alone geology, is what does not change; whereas Braudel's vocabulary and formulation lead us to believe that it is still a kind of change and a kind of history, only a much slower one, a temporality so deep the human senses and even human storytelling, historical memory, the records and the archives, cannot register it.

Yet we have seen that it is a kind of story the geologists can tell; and that therefore the ambiguity is a structural one—from the point of view of human characters, the physical framework does not change and represents a kind of being-in-itself; but seen from its own perspective (if that is the right way to put it), it has its own temporality and its own narrative possibilities, just as the solar system does, or the galaxies. How does one put these two antithetical perspectives together? Well, in another masterpiece of contemporary historiography, Robert Caro's *The Power Broker* (which is disguised as a biography of Robert Moses), we can see precisely how. When the protagonist takes on his first great imperial task, the reconstruction of Long

---

[50] *Encyclopedia Britannica*, 1961, Vol. 15, 209.

Island and the building of the great parkways and beaches, Caro stops abruptly, and gives us a hundred-page geographical description of this physical formation, from its origins.

But in either case, it is clear that a gap between these levels is required and necessary: the shock comes in the montage, in the juxtaposition of these two radically different kinds of realities and temporalities, which are the evolution of the landscape on the one hand, and the fate of human projects, all intertwined with money and power, on the other. They must be separated in order to be related; they must be related by virtue of their very separation. It is a law which somehow combines Hegel and Luhmann: difference relates, radical difference is itself a form of identity. Or, as Ricoeur puts it in his version of the Aristotelian plot: it is a concordance made of discord, a discordance so deeply probed as to reveal itself as a consonance beyond dissonance. This is the form taken in historiography of the requirement of totality, whose attributes for Aristotle are sufficient magnitude, closure, and necessity (among other attributes such as happiness or unhappiness, to which we will return shortly).

Still, in this formulation, we have only succeeded in naming the phenomenon (in Braudel), we have not yet shown how it functions. What we can observe is that his Part 1 also includes narrative sentences, and is indeed made up of them; but they are not the kind of narrative sentences the encyclopedia offered about geological formulations. But to grasp the function of these narrative sentences, we need to note (as Ricoeur does) a fundamental ambiguity about this first or geological level. To be sure, the official time-span of the book is limited to 1550–1600; but that is scarcely adequate to figure a truly *longue durée* in and of itself, as there can have been very little geographical shift in the Mediterranean in that fifty-year period or any fifty-year period for that matter (although it could still include geographical events—that is to say, catastrophes—like that of 179 AD). Still what counts is the gap between the two, and that remains in Braudel:

> It thus becomes impossible to make these two series coincide, the series of economic conjunctures and that of political events in the broad sense, the series of events that contemporaries chose to consider most significant, especially in a century in which, despite everything, politics led the way. (*TR*, Vol. 1, 297; 213)

On Ricoeur's analysis, this gap will be negotiated (if not actually filled in or eliminated) by two complementary readings, from beginning to end, and from end back to beginning. Each of these readings disengages a different plot: on the first, it is the fate of the Mediterranean itself which organizes the plot, and the latter can be described as follows: "The decline of the Mediterranean as a collective hero on the stage of world history ... the end of the conflict between the two political leviathans [Spain and the Ottoman

Empire] and the shift of history toward the Atlantic and Northern Europe" (*TR*, vol. 1, 300; 215). In this case the plot is not complete in 1600 but rather several decades later.

On the other reading or rereading, it is precisely the death of Philip II in 1598 which comes as the completion of Part 3 and thus also completes the transformation of this whole immense spiral into something closer to narrative history and the old-fashioned narrative history of events and world-historical figures. This is how human beings will periodize the matter and transform these multitudinous realities into a narrative they can remember, a narrative on the scale of their own temporal existences.

Yet it is important that this second narrative remain a kind of failure and thereby retain its metanarrative signal, which is to convey the Annales position on the insufficiency of narrative history, events, anthropomorphic characters, and the like. The individual history of Philip II must therefore at one and the same time designate closure (for the narrative as a whole, on its three levels, that is to say for the book itself) and also designate its own insufficiency as a merely individual event. How can it fulfill these two contradictory functions at one and the same time?

> What frames the plot of the Mediterranean? We may say without hesitation: the decline of the Mediterranean as a collective hero on the stage of world history. The end of the plot, in this regard, is not the death of Philip II. It is the end of the conflict between the two political leviathans and the shift of history toward the Atlantic and Northern Europe. (*TR*, Vol. 1, 300; 215)

In Ricoeur's splendid reading, however, these two deaths, that of the Spanish ruler and that of the Mediterranean itself as a central terrain of History, do not make up a simple parallelism or homology, they are not coterminous. If it is true that plot is always to some extent a synthesis of the heterogeneous, the virtual plot of Braudel's book teaches us to unite structures, cycles, and events by joining together heterogeneous temporalities and contradictory chronicles. This virtual structure permits us nevertheless to judge between opposite ways of reading *The Mediterranean*.

> The first subordinates the history of events to the history of the long time-span and the long time-span to geographical time—the main emphasis is then placed on the Mediterranean. But then geographical time is in danger of losing its historical character. For the second reading, history remains historical insofar as the first level itself is qualified as historical with respect to the second level, and, in turn, the second level derives its historical quality from its capacity to support the third level. The emphasis is then placed on Philip II. (*TR*, Vol. 1, 302; 216)

The disparity between the two readings of course expresses the deeper aporia of the objective and the subjective, of Aristotelian cosmological time as opposed to Augustinian existential or phenomenological temporality. The crucial feature structurally is, however, the requirement of a gap between the three levels, of an incommensurability between them that must be acknowledged and held open in order to reveal the aporia but also to be able to express time itself through that very aporia. The alternate readings are, however, clearly not even-handedly assessed in Ricoeur: the only real event is the existential one, which takes the point of view of Philip II in his study and ends with his death. The other reading, the "pseudo-narrative" of the Mediterranean rivalry between the empires, is for Ricoeur a kind of semiotic construct, by way of which the historians imitate the followability of an existential narrative, the rhythms of an individual human drama. All the more ironic is this in the light of the Annales School's hostility to mere narratives of events as such, those of the great historical figures and the great battles, the great turning points: it is as though in their attempt to abandon such narratives and to replace them with the "deeper" levels of mentality, institution, and geography they found such apparently non-narrative discourses slowly turning back into narratives, albeit ones in which "real" or anthropomorphic events and characters are replaced by what Ricoeur will call pseudo-events and pseudo-actors.

Ricoeur's agenda thus turns out to stand in opposition to this official program of the Annales movement: and if his philosophical critique of their position is argued less aggressively than his attack on semiotics, this probably has something to do with Braudel's surrender to narrative realism or representationality, and his concession of a return to events and more traditional narrative of the period in his concluding section of *The Mediterranean*. Meanwhile, Braudel's theoretical code—the three *durées*—encourages a return to the traditional philosophical dilemmas of the conceptualization of temporality (in which Ricoeur is preeminently at home, as we have seen), without posing the conceptual and terminological alternative of a full-blown theoretic and anti-humanist semiotics whose very existence would imply a radical break with the philosophical tradition, and very specifically with phenomenology and existentialism.

Yet, from another perspective, this very polemic is not only ideologically useful; it also advances Ricoeur's inquiry in an unexpected way, by positing the possibility of an alternate dimension of temporality and an alternate reading and methodological code even if that possibility is argued to be erroneous. For Ricoeur's own procedure inclines him to move from antinomy to antinomy on an ever widening scale, never solving any of them, never "producing" a new and more satisfactory conceptual solution, but rather using each dilemma to produce a new and richer antinomy. He therefore needs just such radical conceptual alternatives, just such unacceptable but theoretical and philosophical antagonists, in order to keep his own inquiry going: so that his ideological preference for what we have called a humanism of anthropomorphic representation—if finally affirmed and settled on definitively, as it is in the last volume—impedes everything that is productive in his own argument: and it is in this sense that both the semiotic dimension and the anti-narrative program of the Annales are essential to that argument (and indeed to his own "narrative").

This means that Ricoeur's approach to Time—and our own parallel approach, superimposed on his but vaster in scope, to History—to require the existence of gaps, of incommensurabilities between the dimensions, of irreconcilable readings, of aporias that cannot be solved, and of multiple dimensions of Time and of History whose intersection and discordance alone allow the thing itself to appear.

It is in this spirit that we must reinterpret the alternative readings Ricoeur proposes of Braudel's vast text: the story of individual and collective projects, struggles and outcomes, which concludes with the death of Philip II in 1598, or that of the dissolution of the Mediterranean as the very center of History, which takes place over the course of the next century. And it is in much the same way that we must assess the multiple temporalities of the modern novels Ricoeur had paradigmatically disengaged, each of which projected a thematic center of the work it affirmed as the correct reading in preference to any of the others.

But in practice it is not the multiplicity of options which is crucial for the temporality—indeed the historicity—of the fictional or historiographic text: it is their intersection which allows time or history to appear. The gaps between these readings are necessary, their incommensurability and the antinomies they generate do not pose a problem but rather constitute in some sense the solution.

In other words, at this point we need something like a theory of "intersection" itself as a structural phenomenon (which may well have its correlation and its equivalent in extra-textual "reality"). We may agree that for such texts a first and temporal experience is required, and that the various temporalities determine a reading imperative we may compare to the obligatory *raverse* or crossing through of all of them, as the narrative constructs multiple paths and varied trajectories, the working through, in time, of the various dimensions of time it projects. Yet the appearance of Time or History as such depends not on the multiplicity and variety of these trajectories, but rather on their interference with each other, with their intersection now understood as dissonance and as incommensurability rather than as a conjuncture which augments them all, in the fashion of a synthesis, by the central space of some harmonious meeting and combination.

We must therefore retain this violence and negativity in any concept of intersection, in order for this dissonant conjunction to count as an Event, and in particular as that Event which is the ephemeral rising up and coming to appearance of Time and History as such. Nor is this a purely textual or

philosophical matter: for it is the same discordant conjuncture that constitutes the emergence of time and of history in the real world, the world of
real time and of real history. The moment of intersection, indeed, is also
that in which Time suddenly appears to individuals as an existential or
phenomenological experience (or, if you prefer, as the radical interference
with such private experience, as what breaks into it from the outside and
renders it vulnerable and the plaything of unimaginable forces outside
itself).

> When the house of the great collapses
> The lowly are also many of them crushed.
> Those who do not share the fortunes of the mighty
> Often share their misfortune. The lurching wagon
> Drags the sweating oxen with it
> Into the abyss.[51]

And such a moment, on a vaster scale, is constituted by the intersections of
multiple forces and dimensions which make History itself rise up before us,
moments of sudden possibility or of unexpected freedom, moments of revolution, moments also of defeat and of the bleakest hopelessness. These
moments are not any more subjective than the existential ones: as we shall
see, they are enabled, in a Heideggerian opening of Being whose valences
can be negative as well as positive, by a conjuncture in the forces of the world
itself; and this is why it is appropriate at this point to recall the Althusserian
notions of overdetermination and structural causality, which in my opinion
attempt to theorize a comparable reality and which will play a significant
role in the second part of this chapter ("Making History Appear").

If I have been reluctant to invoke these concepts until now, it is not only
because Ricoeur systematically passes over all such possible engagements
with Marxian theories of time and history in silence,[52] but also and far more

---

[51]   Wenn das Haus eines Grossen zusammenbricht
        Werden viele Kleine erschlagen.
        Die das Glück der Mächtigen nicht teilten
        Teilen oft ihr Unglück. Der stürzende Wagen
        Reisst die schwitzenden Zugtiere
        Mit in den Abgrund.

Der Kaukasische Kreidekreis, in Bertolt Brecht, *Werke*, Vol. 8, Berlin: Aufbau, 1992, 107.

[52]   Perhaps we should also add a word about Ricoeur's relationship to the dialectic: inter-
        preting it as narrowly as the Deleuze of *Difference and Repetition*, he assumes its
        conception of opposition as negativity to have already been refuted by the Kant of the
        "Attempt to Introduce the Concept of Negative Magnitudes into Philosophy"
        (1763), in which Kant asserts that there are no negations in nature.

pertinently in order to be able to demonstrate their insufficiencies in the light of everything we have examined here. Althusser's ambivalence about the dialectic is well known, although he is willing to use this word (sparingly) about the dialectic of structural causality. But his anti-Hegelianism is not particularly at issue for us here.

What is far more important is the absence of negativity in the Althusserian concepts themselves. To be sure, their negative and critical value can be restored philologically, when we replace them in their original polemic situations and read them in function of the conceptual targets they were devised to undermine and to replace. Overdetermination is in that sense a welcome effort to retheorize what in the stereotypes of vulgar or orthodox Marxism is grasped as a kind of monocausal determinism, and in particular a determinism by the economic. Structural causality, meanwhile, is an enlargement of this program to ward off the dangers of an idealist alternative to Marxist historiography (so-called expressive causality), from which the economic is silently omitted and which sees the historical conjunction in terms of a quasi-Spenglerian unity of style and of spirit.

Yet in our present context, the new versions—overdetermination, structural causality—which were certainly very welcome and beneficial in their own time and situation, seem now to suggest a kind of pluralism and relativism more appropriate for liberal and bourgeois views of history than for any Marxism. Overdetermination now seems to imply that a singular event, in all its uniqueness, has many causes whose conjuncture is aleatory (and which could conceivably omit the economic); while structural causality formulates the differential relationship of the various levels with one another in terms of a specific distance which is itself an effect of "structure." Even if the latter is understood as a moment of the mode of production itself, then, the concept remains a positive (or even positivist, or affirmative) one, from which negativity has been removed, or in which it is at least imperceptible. And this is to say that the central mechanism of the dialectic—contradiction itself—is still somehow here lacking or is at least hardly underscored and foregrounded by the concept itself.

It is this negativity which the notion of intersection is meant to restore, and in the light of which Ricoeur's antinomies can be grasped in their dialectical form as contradictions. And it is in the light of this theoretical correction that we may now finally part company with Ricoeur in order to confront the more basic issue his work raises for us, namely the compatibility of his Aristotelian narrative scheme with the dialectic itself, and in particular with its Marxian form. At this point, in other words, we may now consider that the investigation of Time and the manner in which it can be made to appear is concluded; and turn our attention to the possibility of the appearing or apparition (*phainesthai*) of History itself.

The Valences of History

Part II. Making History Appear

1. Taking Sides

For now it becomes essential to disentangle these problematics, and to assume, unlike Ricoeur (insofar as he thematizes the matter), that the appearance of Time will not always be accompanied by that of History, even though the latter may well require the incorporation of the former. This does not mean that we must reject Ricoeur's juxtaposition of the novel and historiography at this late stage, but only that we need to reverse his priorities, and to argue that what the novels have in common with Braudel is not so much the latter's narrativity as the former's historicity. It is not so much because Braudel's work lends itself preeminently to the perspective of the Aristotelian narrative poetic that Ricoeur's subsumption of both fiction and history under the rubric of narrative is persuasive; but rather because the novels he chooses are themselves constructed in order to register the deeper processes of history itself. They may well be novels "of time," but they are also novels "of history" as such.

That said, we must now set in place one of the great unanswered questions or problems raised by this comparison of the novel and the history, which has to do with the insertion of the subject into narrative, so to speak, or better still, the matter of side-taking in narrative and in history itself. The anthropomorphic texts of fiction or tragedy present no particular problems in this respect (although even there the issue can get very complicated). But who takes sides with pseudo-characters in the outcome of the great collective pseudo-events of History? This was, to be sure, Lévi-Strauss's influential attack on historical thinking as such,[53] which we can summarize by observing, with him, that before modernity, before the French Revolution, the question of taking sides in history becomes confused indeed: who should we

---

[53] See above, note 41.

cheer for in that muddled event which was the Fronde, let alone in the inter-minable internecine wars of the tribes of pre-Columbian Brazil? But if we cannot take sides in this earlier human history, how to reactivate Aristotle's category of the eudaimonic for history, and to assess the various passages from happiness to unhappiness which, the very motor of tragedy itself, become exceedingly problematic when we shift to matters of historical judgment?

Yet what survives of the *Poetics* is mainly devoted to tragedy—but might as well be exemplified in phallic comedy (the triumph of the younger generation over the old), in the bestseller (with its degraded fantasies of success and good fortune), or finally in what I have elsewhere termed providential narrative.[54] But that description must still be thought in conjunction with the requirements of closure and of significance ("worth serious attention"), this last being largely defined in terms of class as what distinguishes the nobler actors of tragedy from those beneath us (combining Aristotle with Frye's inventive redefinition)—the first alone having a fortune and a high station to lose. Happiness is thus here conjoined with the good fortune of class status, while "closure" designates the tragic fall itself, from the first insignificant signs of reversal to the moment in which it has clearly become definitive and irreversible. Death is only the crudest external marker for this irreversibility, just as war and battle are in collective narratives.

The latter, however, pose the problem of their constituent actors, the subjects of the completed action to be narrated, what Ricoeur calls quasi-characters—a description that excludes the most interesting theoretical questions and problems in advance. If the history has already been written, it can be interrogated by semiotic means, and the actants around which its narrative is structured can be identified and disengaged: thus, a technique such as perspective might well function as an actant in a history of painting, while a phenomenon like Foucauldian "discipline" might be the hero of a quasi-*Bildungsroman*, with ancestors and a moment of maturity on the world stage. The discussion of Braudel above, however, reminds us that such narrative structures can be ambiguous, and present the possibility of several different readings, that is to say several different narratives with distinct protagonists and a varying emphasis from one destiny (that of the Mediterranean) to another (Philip II and his individual project and fate). We can even read such narratives against the grain (as we shall see in a moment), detecting the tragic narrative of the vanquished at work beneath the official success story of the victors. Yet, in all these cases, it would seem that we need to bring a certain sympathy to the fundamental subject of the historical narrative (it is this which survives of the older Aristotelian pity and

---

[54] See my "The Experiments of Time," in Franco Moretti, ed., *The Novel*, Vol. 2, Princeton: Princeton University Press, 2006.

fear): we have to embrace the political or historical stakes, if only in the most disinterested way, in order to bring our apprehensions and our expectations to bear on the matter of its success or failure, its happy or unhappy outcome. And this is perhaps another reason why Aristotle insists on the primacy of the action rather than of the character: we can more easily appreciate the project and observe its successful completion or its unexpected undoing with interest and attention, than sympathize on command with a winning protagonist whom everything might on the contrary bring us to despise or to detest.

What can be the justification for this anthropomorphic survival of side-taking and partisanship in what ought to be objective historiographic undertakings? Are we to think of the requirement of sympathy in psychological terms? In that case it is likely to be an infantile drive which is sublimated into those ethical philosophies denounced by Nietzsche; Freud himself observes, of what he calls the egocentric fantasy,

> that the other characters are sharply divided into good and bad, in defiance of the variety of human characters that are to be observed in real life. The "good" ones are the helpers, while the "bad" ones are the enemies and rivals, of the ego which has become the hero of the story.[55]

In either case, it would seem that the goal of enlightenment is precisely to extirpate such traces of a childish egocentrism and to reach a stage of objectivity and stoicism in which there are no more villains or heroes and our attention to the unfolding narrative is the neutral one of assessing its dynamic and evaluating its outcome.

This is indeed precisely Lévi-Strauss's objection to History as such, not merely that it implies a conflation of all kinds of heterogeneous time frames, from days to epochs, from years to reigns, all subsumed under the calendar (about which we have already seen that it is precisely this heterogeneity that enables History to stand as a unification of multiplicities); but above all the necessary partisanship presupposed by an axial event—in his critique of Sartre it is the French Revolution itself—which governs our historical sympathies and divides the historical cast of characters up into heroes and villains. But what do we do, asks Lévi-Strauss, about events which have taken place before the radical simplification operated by the inaugural date as such?[56] It is the problem of the "noble pagans" for the Church Fathers, or

---

[55] Freud, "Creative Writers and Day-Dreaming," in *The Standard Edition*, 150.

[56] Yet *The Conflict of the Faculties*, trans. Mary J. Gregor, Lincoln: University of Nebraska Press, 1992, 153, Kant asserts that certain events "find in the hearts of all spectators … a wishful participation that borders closely on enthusiasm." This conception of history, which is related to his notion of the universal claim of aesthetic judgment, will be discussed in some detail below in Section 4.

of the writers before 1848 and the *Manifesto* for Lukács: a problem now pressed home by the complicated enigma of the Fronde (1642)[57] in which we find, confronting each other in fundamental antagonism, the great nobles, the court, the people of Paris, the regent, her son the boy king Louis XIV, Mazarin, le cardinal de Retz, and so forth. Where is the momentum of history in this confused uprising and with whom are we to take sides, in a situation in which the so-called people of Paris are to be understood as notables, lawyers, shopkeepers, and their apprentices, and very far indeed from anything resembling a proletariat or downtrodden and oppressed masses? Lévi-Strauss does not mention the even more immediate reference for an anthropologist, namely the immemorial wars between various tribal peoples in Brazil, where it would be a poor thought indeed to determine the more prosperous or powerful and then to take sides with their victims. The identification with the victim is indeed very much a contemporary tendency among twenty-first-century citizens trained in genocide and expert in ethnic oppression: but it remains an ideological or merely ethical choice, and to that degree demonstrates the inseparability of historical narrative and the structural presupposition of an ideological point of view, to which even omniscient or objective narrators remain secretly in thrall.

"All history is the history of class struggle," said Marx and Engels in a decisive pronouncement, which turns out to have been a rather curious generalization. For in the most technical sense, classes only emerge as such in modern capitalism, where they take the dichotomous form of workers and owners. The idea of the class fraction (the petty bourgeoisie, for example) is a function of the social relationship to these two fundamental classes and has

---

[57] "At first sight, there seems no doubt on one side the privileged, on the other the humble and exploited; how could we hesitate? We are Frondeurs. However, the people of Paris were being manoeuvred by noble houses, whose sole aim was to arrange their own affairs with the existing powers, and by one half of the royal family which wanted to oust the other. And now we are already only half Frondeurs. As for the Court, which took refuge at Saint-Germain, it appears at first to have been a faction of good for nothings vegetating on their privileges and growing fat on exactions and usury at the expense of the collectivity. But no, it had a function all the same since it retained military power; it conducted the struggle against foreigners, the Spaniards, whom the Frondeurs invited without hesitation to invade the country and impose their wills on this same Court which was defending the fatherland. The scales, however, tilt the other way again: the Frondeurs and Spaniards together formed the party of peace. The Prince de Condé and the Court only sought warlike adventures. We are pacifists and once again become Frondeurs. But nevertheless did not the military exploits of Mazarin and the Court extend France to its present frontiers, thus founding the state and the nation? Without them we should not be what we are today. So here we are on the other side again." Claude Lévi-Strauss, *The Savage Mind*, trans. John and Doreen Weightman, Chicago: University of Chicago Press, 1966, 255.

been mainly appealed to in ideological analysis. As for the peasants and the landlords, who certainly survived well into the first century of capitalism, before being converted into farm-workers and capitalists in their own right, they are better characterized as feudal castes which function in a somewhat different way, just as the category of slaves cannot be assimilated to that category of wage workers who alone constitute the industrial proletariat. And as far back as tribal society and hunters-and-gatherers, who is willing to defend the idea that in the domination of the village elders over the young and over women we still have to do with class struggle?

We can, of course, see why Marx and Engels wanted to put it this way: they wanted to foreground the relationship of exploitation to the production process. The "nightmare of history" (Joyce) is no doubt a dizzying accumulation of violence and cruelty, but to think of it exclusively in this way is to encourage an ethical pathos which can be made productive only if we displace the object of this vision of history from human nature to social structure; meanwhile the concept of class includes the injustices of power without essentializing the lust for power either. The famous slogan thus directs our attention to the systems of exploitation in the human past, and at the same time aims to demystify the ethical and humanist prejudices which ignore those systems and tend to conceal them by fragmenting them into merely individual and empirical wrongs.

But our present context also offers another reason for this rhetorical exaggeration on Marx and Engels's part: it is to narrativize the interminable balance sheets of human history and to stage it very precisely in such a way as to encourage that taking of sides which Lévi-Strauss deplored. But we need to be careful here to respect the complications not always apparent in the narratological position. It is indeed not a question of setting up a "point of view" from which these various pre-histories are observed and evaluated: that is to say that even the much-criticized notion of some "subject of history" is not really implicit here, let alone Lukács's notion of "partisanship" (*Parteilichkeit*) (Sartre's notion of *engagement* or commitment may be a little closer). But all these concepts, beginning with that of narrative point of view, reflect what are essentially modern or post-Cartesian categories of the individual subject. In the history of narrative as such, we may assert, following Benveniste,[58] that it is the third person which comes first and which precedes first-person narrative: the later return to the third person in *style indirect libre* then enriches the former with all the subjective acquisitions of the I-narrative.

Aristotelian poetics is indeed far from specifying a point of view, partly owing to its theorization in terms of the collective reception of drama, and partly because of its links with what Ricoeur calls archaic and mythic

[58] Émile Benveniste, *Problèmes de linguistique générale*, Paris: Gallimard, 1966, and see also Harald Weinrich, *Tempus*, Stuttgart: Kohlhammer, 1964.

thought, in which forces hold sway rather than human individuals, the vision of the gods effectuating only a partial and limited anthropomorphism. This is the moment to return to the affective qualification—happiness or unhappiness—with which Aristotle was careful to invest his account of the complete action. These eudaimonic characterizations do not necessarily, for pre-individualistic reception, imply the presence of modern individual subjects, either as observers or as protagonists: happiness and misery are here free-floating states of the world, which at the outer limit might be personified as Good and Bad Luck, the later *Fortuna* or the even later Chance. Even the Heideggerian notion of *Stimmung* is probably too subjective to render this state of the world, now ominously darkened, now struck by sunburst: Taoist notions of world harmony and world imbalance are more satisfactory.

It is surely something like the range of these pre- or post-individualistic concepts which is more appropriate for the contemplation of the multiple pasts of human history, which no witness and no Absolute Spirit could encompass: Spinozan substance rather than Hegelian subject—such as been the post-contemporary bias of a generally philosophical consensus for the decentered, which must necessarily make a place for the apprehension of stretches of genuine misery and moments of liveliness and invention in the long countdown towards Utopia or extinction.

Yet we have not exhausted the implications of the narrativization of history which Marxism proposes (and which again vanishes in some free-market end of history in which there survive only the most rudimentary Manichaean stories of goodness—ourselves—and evil—the Other). For now what the Marxist dialectic enjoins, as a historically new and original thought mode, is the conflation of Good Luck and Bad Luck, and the grasping of the historical situation as happiness and unhappiness all at once. The *Manifesto* proposes to see capitalism as the most productive moment of history and the most destructive one at the same time, and issues the imperative to think Good and Evil simultaneously, and as inseparable and inextricable dimensions of the same present of time. This is then a more productive way of transcending Good and Evil than the cynicism and lawlessness which so many readers attribute to the Nietzschean program.

Can we not then draw the conclusion that side-taking constitutes the sign of the necessary investment of the subject in narrative? In that case, it is the mark of that "I" which as Kant puts it is always added on to whatever I think. The contemporary analogy might then be found in Althusser's theory of ideology, which expresses the relationship of the subject to the representation of its conditions of existence, as opposed to science, as a discourse without a subject.[59] But, surely, any representation of my relationship

---

[59] Louis Althusser, "Ideology and Ideological State Apparatuses," in *Lenin and Philosophy*, trans. Ben Brewster, New York: Monthly Review Press, 2001.

to that vaster historical and social reality (which I map to myself in the form of a multilayered situation) is already a narrative, whether implicit or explicit, whether virtual or already a form of discourse. It would indeed be possible to reverse Althusser's priorities and grasp science as the attempt to de-narrativize my positionality as a subject and to remove the subjectivity from it, that is to say, to divest it of the little phrase "I think" that always seems to accompany it. But if narrative is the form through which I necessarily grasp history, if consciousness of history is always an emplotment (Ricoeur's *mise en intrigue*), then the taking of sides which is the sign and symptom of my subjective investment in it would also seem to be inevitable (however disguised or repressed it may be).

2. Peripeteia

Now indeed we can turn to our second line of inquiry, which has to do with the appropriateness of narrative categories—and particularly the three Aristotelian narrative categories: peripeteia, anagnorisis, and pathos; or, if you prefer, destiny, the Other, and the Absolute—to the structure of the historical text itself, or of historiography: and to the way in which—as in Ricoeur's analysis of his three exemplary modernist novels "about time"— such narrative structures can be said to "produce" History as such or rather to make appear the very transcendental experience of historical Time.

We have already registered a certain asymmetry between these three structural principles: peripeteia clearly describes a general plot dynamic, a reversal about which it would be worth speculating whether it is a universal one: whether, in other words, it is abstract enough to be a plausible category for a generalized theory of historical narrative.

Recognition, however, seems to be a good deal more specific, and, while a very interesting candidate for the attention of narrative theory, not at all universal in the preceding sense.[60] It is obvious enough that not all narratives involve recognition scenes, even though the attempt to universalize this particular empirical form could be interesting in other ways, for example in associating narrative with the family as such (insofar as recognition would always seem to presuppose at least a figurative family connection if not a literal one).

Finally, suffering, as a spectacle, would seem to be of a different order of things: the name for a specific moment of the theatrical spectacle and not for the structure of a narrative. One might, indeed, speculate that we are poorly placed to grasp the full import of this narrative category, since we lack the

---

[60] It would seem important to differentiate the Aristotelian sense of the word from Hegelian recognition: we will return to this distinction below, in Section 4.

other half of Aristotle's treatise, namely the theory of comedy. For it seems possible that the latter proposed a jubilatory equivalent of what is here called suffering—or a spectacle of triumph over fate in opposition to what is here an undergoing or a "suffering" of it in another sense. In that case, pathos takes on a rather more central function than the merely occasional one, in which, as in the *Medea*, it designates something not unrelated to décor and a purely visual stagecraft, in that climactic moment in which the hideous fate of her children is displayed: an episode perhaps more related to the pleasure in horror movies (or vice versa) or the morbid fascination with physical torture (for example, evoked by the Laokoon statuary, which is the other canonical example in extant classical art).

But if the reading proposed here has any merit, then one could venture along its path a little further and suggest that pathos thereby becomes the driving force of the narrative altogether, and that what is here meant is simply the external seal and final exteriorization and confirmation of the secret thread of the story all along, namely to make visible to us the way in which people fall under the power of fate, in which they fail, in which they know the experience of defeat and of submission. No doubt, in one kind of comedy, that experience—if attributed to your enemies—can be pleasurable for the malicious spectator; in the other, however, it is the hero's triumph which records the other side of the coin, and allows us to know, even fleetingly, that other face of the human experience which is luck and good fortune, the success of our plans and projects, the achievement of that momentarily satisfied state Aristotle calls happiness, a state more dangerous than pathos insofar as it is manifestly a transitory one and doomed to pass, while suffering and failure may be supposed to be of a more permanent nature. The two states (and the two deeper functions of narrative) are thus not exactly symmetrical with each other, but they are certainly dialectical.

Yet it is precisely the establishment of some kind of dialectic of success and failure that constitutes the drama and the dynamic of peripeteia— returning to our first feature here. For in principle the reversal is possible in either direction: and the last-minute rescue, the emergence of the hero safe and sound from what looked like a complete defeat and crushing failure, a desperate trap and fatal outcome, given over to his enemies, and in despair —this salvational rescue is surely no less a dramatic turning or reversal, than the seemingly more moral one, in which the protagonist, at the height of success and good fortune, and sinfully exulting in his luck, is punished for that hubris and struck down beyond all hope of retrieval. The evaluation here—that tragedy is somehow nobler than comedy or romance—is both a literary and an ethical, that is to say a religious-ideological, one: for it is premised on the notion that suffering is good for us, while every success encourages the worst part of human nature: indeed, that human life is sinful and that good fortune is never really in the cards for human beings, so that drama would do better to accustom us to suffering and to its sacred rationalizations.

This is why a proper comedy will either be cautioned and motivated by nature as such—Frye's phallic comedy, the triumph of the young over the old and of sexuality over death—inasmuch as it cannot really last and is therefore less dangerous and a merely transitory experience. Thus, paradoxically, the other admissible form of such an outcome is the one clothed in and authorized by theology, namely the salvational form, in which the happy ending takes on religious overtones: here, as in George Eliot, the happy ending can seem acceptable insofar as it can be taken as an allegory of this or that religious process (it can also be taken without such ideological justification, as we have tried to show elsewhere[61]). None of this is to be grasped in terms of optimism or pessimism, although the variants certainly have their ideological roots in various worldviews: but it is not the ideology or the mood or temperament which is at issue here but rather the narrative form itself, the tale-type, if you prefer that expression, which in some deeper way expresses apparent mood, and is the source of the eudaimonic, that is to say, of the anthropomorphic character of narrative—a characterization which seems tautological but which we will find raising interesting problems when we come to history and collective narration.

None of this, however, touches as yet on what would make up the truly dialectical feature of peripeteia: that would consist in the unity of opposites, which is to say, a structure in which the two forms of peripeteia would be overlaid, or better still, profoundly identified with one another. For the dialectic is not to be understood merely as a success story, nor either as the experience of defeat: it consists in that difficult wisdom in which these two outcomes become one and the same, in which defeat becomes success, and success becomes defeat. It is a metaphysical twist conveyed in Sartre's paradoxical formulations, winner loses and loser wins. Yet this is a perception difficult enough to achieve in any situation and even more difficult to dramatize. People are willing enough to grant the element of failure inherent in any success, no doubt; but its opposite, and the way in which a success might be inherent in failure, is not so clear and certainly not so widespread a point of view (save, again, in certain forms of religion). The point of view must be an elevated and a distant, even a glacial one, in order for these all-too-human categories of success and failure to become indifferent in their own opposition.

Yet the simultaneity of these two things—success and failure all at once and combined together—is itself already incompatible with the *Bildungsroman*, which tends to separate them back out into the fruits of youth and age respectively, and which, even in its more religiously motivated forms,

---

[61] See above, note 48.

stubbornly insists on their rigorous differentiation. Rare are those strange and richly ascetic forms which, like *Peer Gynt* or Pontoppidan's *Lykke Per* (*Lucky Per*), hold the two together in a wondrous transparency.

The epic does not yet seem to pose the same problems, even though it remains subject to the lesson Lukács tirelessly reiterated, namely that of the mediation of genre. Indeed, in our present context, we may grasp the dynamics of genre at work in the most rudimentary forms of narrative, in what Ricouer calls emplotment. Yet no storytelling is neutral; narrative is always interpretation, not merely by virtue of the arrangement of its episodes, but above all by way of the narrative mode in which it is cast. For that particular generic mode also constitutes an interpretive choice, and as Claudio Guillén showed us long ago, genres are systems, and a text is always read against the background of its differential place in the generic constellation, situated among its generic relatives and opposite numbers.[62]

So it is that in *Epic and Empire*, which I here follow, a fundamental historical standpoint is established by virtue of the primal generic opposition between epic and romance.[63] This opposition is not merely traditional (and documented by interminable Renaissance theorizations), it is here given a kind of mythic status in the allegory of the two inaugural Homeric poems which mark not only the full-blown emergence of the two genres but also their inextricable dialectical interrelationship. But the two genres, or their mutual system if you prefer, do not only found a Western-oriented myth of literary history (analogous to Auerbach's initial dualism in *Mimesis*, but quite different in its implications); the dualistic system returns us to the existential and its phenomenology at the same time that it projects us outwards into political history.

Epic then becomes the genre *par excellence* of narrative time, of a project-oriented time which is diachronic and the raw material of beginnings, middles and endings. But romance would also seem to tell a story, albeit a different kind of story. Here, however, I want to go a little further than Quint does and to assert that what his analysis shows is that romance uses its narrative mechanisms to express a kind of non-narrative time (which can crudely be termed synchronic). Romance tells the story of "spots of time," of adventures in the sense of isolated and unrepeatable happenings and episodic events. At its outer limit, its organizational form—of which the journey is the archetypal category—threatens to break down into discontinuous encounters and experiences, non-narrative moments of the present which a different generic system would no doubt want to identify as lyrical. As the opposite of epic temporality, then, romance is always on the point of becoming non-narrative; or indeed, Quint's own analyses demonstrate that

---

[62]   Claudio Guillén, *Literature as System*, Princeton: Princeton University Press, 1971.

[63]   David Quint, *Epic and Empire*, Princeton: Princeton University Press, 1993.

romance always has to borrow what narrative logic it can muster from the antagonistic genre of the epic, in order to remain afloat as a storytelling vessel.

But when we inquire into the source of these temporal oppositions, between diachronic and synchronic, between narrative and proto-lyric, we find our attention turning not only to the groups of people living these distinct temporalities, but also to the different situations which govern their distinct experiences. At this point we reemerge back out into history and the political, and the two genres become the markers of two distinct historical experiences and destinies. The narrative time of epic is, we have said, the time of the project: it is in other words the time of the victors, and the temporality of their history and their worldview. Epic is therefore very precisely the generic expression of empire and of imperialism, understood as the intent and project of overcoming and subduing other groups and of achieving sovereignty over them. If the conquest and destruction of Troy is the paradigm, the triumphant expansion of Rome becomes the fullest realization of imperial fulfillment and the moment of its epic elaboration in Virgil, whose codification of the form will govern all later practitioners, even when they struggle against it. In that sense, Virgil's narrative is the only narrative as such (Petrarch famously said, "Quid est enim aliud omnis historia quam romana laus?"—"What is any history but the celebration of Rome?"). Virgil is thus the system which the various anti-systemic non- or anti-narratives must undermine and subvert, without having a narrative of their own to substitute for it.

But who are the subjects of those anti-narrative and anti-epic tendencies? They are, inevitably and virtually by definition, the losers in this imperial triumph: the subjugated Indians of the Spanish conquest, the Muslims defeated in Tasso's crusades, the Puritans whose revolution is repealed by the Restoration, and, not least, the Italic tribes conquered by Virgil's triumphant Trojans—a conquest which also expresses a different kind of victory and defeat, namely that of Augustus over his internal opposition and over the anti-imperialists within the empire itself (as, paradigmatically, in Lucan's *Pharsalia*).

Here, then, "romance" somehow expresses the experience of defeat, a shattering experience that annuls historical teleology: it is an end of history which is an end of narrative as well, and leads to the stubborn silence of the vanquished and the enslaved, the executed and the subjected, if not to some other kind of expression, one borrowed from the victors but subtly deformed and recast and recoded in order to convey the secret messages of the defeated, as in the Christianity of the slaves or Deleuze's "minor language." The happy ending of epic is then, if at all, transferred to heaven and salvation, or to some distant future; transformed into wish-fulfillment, it permits the reorganization of defeat and subjection into a new kind of narrative; and the *Odyssey* now rises into view as the story of Odysseus's unexpected defeats and failures, his oppression by the gods, offering the paradigm of the episodic journey, the wandering without a goal or a final landfall, the experience of exile and persecution, as a form which can express the truth of the defeated, when generically contrasted with the triumphalism of epic achieved.

Now, we may return to the matter of the dialectic and of the ambivalence of peripeteia and the unity of the opposites of success and failure. Traditional hesitations about the value of the derivative Latin epic (often allied to hesitations about the cultural authenticity of the Roman empire itself) mostly complain about its piety and its boredom as both are epitomized in the epic's rather bland hero, neither Achilles nor Hector, neither Odysseus nor Satan. Aeneas's piety is the mark of his submission to destiny, a particularly passive role for an epic hero. The destiny is the evocation of the imperial unification of the world, an end of history to which the fourth *Eclogue* and T. S. Eliot's ideology add the Rome of Christianity as well; and this offers an even more tiresome vision which can scarcely enflame our imaginations the way the conquest of a rival (and far more civilized) city can, or the return home (or even salvation). The truth is that success is itself boring, marking the end of a project and leaving us with nowhere to go and nothing to do. (We will explore the concept of authenticity as it emerges from capitalism and its commodifications: for nineteenth-century realism, success can never be as authentic as failure.)

As long as the *Aeneid* is read as a success story, in other words, it will remain as shallow as all self-congratulatory stories of triumph are, and all ideologies of empire that celebrate the victor, or in other words ourselves. What Quint has done in his aforementioned book is to make the *Aeneid* available again by uncovering the vein of silver that runs through its imperial gold, and to reveal the story of failure and the experience of defeat that secretly accompany all its victories.

It then becomes a double narrative, or one redoubled upon itself. From the traditional perspective, the *Aeneid* offers the story of the conquest of a new homeland, itself prophetic of the Roman Empire to come and of the age of Augustus. The story of the Trojans is then at best a heart-warming tale of the overcoming of adversity, and at worst the chronicle of the implantation of a settler colony, in which a people without land seizes the land of other "nations" or peoples and subjugates their hapless populations. It is a story one can tell with a clear conscience, inasmuch as the losers, the Italic tribes, are staged as the aggressors, having reacted with understandable anger and hostility to their new and unwanted neighbor: a reaction which endows them with unlovable personal traits (Turnus) and allows the imperializing Trojan propaganda machine to claim the right of self-defense.

Yet everything changes when we realize, not only that the Trojans were themselves the first victims of just such imperial aggression (on the part of the Greeks), but also, thanks to Quint's subtle and tireless detection of all the echoes and allusions embedded in Virgil's text—a play of repetitions and references too numerous and insistent to be an accident—that they are simultaneously to be read as the victors and the losers at one and the same time. The subtext then, the whispered reminders, not only of the first loss from which this ultimate victory emerges, but of the innumerable secondary identifications of the colonizing army with the tribes they are in the process of vanquishing, adds the experience of defeat to the complacencies of victory, and makes of this official state poem at one and the same time the secret expression of an opposition to empire and a consistent underground dissent. Virgil now becomes visible as a critic of the Augustan system and a political adversary of conquest and expansionism, at the same time that he remains a flatterer of the regime and a propagandist for Augustus's new order. Not unexpectedly, the new artificial epic becomes a far more complicated and interesting text, its beauties and harmonies now motivated by mixed feelings and themselves a kind of conquest and a music made from contradictions. It is rather as though we were suddenly able to see Raphael again for the first time in what Gertrude Stein called the "original ugliness" inherent in the struggle of his forms to come into being.[64] Quint puts it like this:

> T. S. Eliot's blandly reactionary appropriation of the *Aeneid* for Church and Empire ... is best countered by taking the poem's ideology seriously, by seeing the *Aeneid* questioning the Augustan regime and its party line *from the inside* and in its own terms. Playing these contradictory terms off against one another, the poem asks whether the new political foundation that the regime promises will be an escape from or merely a repetition of Rome's history of civil war. And in the process Virgil questions the therapeutic narrative of losers becoming winners—of "good" repetition replacing bad—that his epic presents as the founding model of Roman history.[65]

---

[64] Gertrude Stein, *Four in America*, New Haven: Yale University Press, 1947.

[65] Quint, *Epic and Empire*, 52–53. It may be worth pointing out the formal resemblance between this opposition and Michel Foucault's account of opposition between sovereignty and its decentralized opponent in his extraordinary seminar "Il faut défendre la société," Paris: Gallimard/Seuil, 1997 (something like the roundhouse at the very center of his work, from which virtually all his themes branch out). To be sure, on Foucault's historical reading, this second, decentralized term—whether it stands for bureaucracy or "bio-power," or in fact demonstrates that the two are one and the same—not only wins out in an interesting reversal of Quint's generic chronology here (in which in fact both forms destroy each other), but eventually refutes its initially non-narrative structure, by way of the narrative he himself provides. He himself associates the narrative of sovereignty with tragedy rather than with epic (155–157).

Indeed, we may descend for a moment from the lofty rather metaphysical level on which we have pitched this discussion—losers and winners, victory and defeat in general—to the more specific ideological contradictions which Augustus's new system faced and which are faithfully registered in Virgil.

For Augustus staged his new order as a restoration of the Republic, whose empty forms in the Senate and the various offices of the state are preserved, even as the supreme power of the *imperator* or *princeps* (not yet technical terms, save for avoiding the historically tainted designation of *rex* or king) divests them of their practical functions. The historical contradiction then takes two related forms: how to stage Augustus's triumph in the civil war in such a fashion as to cancel out civil wars as such and to disguise victory as reconciliation (a dilemma resolved practically by Octavian's personality, free from the egoism of conventional politicians). Meanwhile, on a more concrete historical level, this dilemma takes the form of the problem of Julius Caesar, whose memory is indissolubly bound up with the bloodiest and most vengeful and divisive of civil wars; but on whose divine status Augustus's legitimation rests. How to forget and remember Caesar at one and the same time? This is the sense in which the *Aeneid* (in which Caesar is mentioned only once, and as a god at that) can be said to constitute an imaginary resolution of real contradictions and a triumphant unity of opposites.

Still, that the poem's dominant appearance lies in the celebration of the victors and their empire is clear; this surface appearance now demands an investigation of those works that celebrate the losers, most notably (for Rome) Lucan's *Pharasalia*, or much later, in the wars of religion, d'Aubigné's *Les Tragiques*, or even Milton himself. The latter solves the problem by superimposing three distinct forms—epic, romance, and the providential—in a unique fashion we cannot now pursue further. In the case of Lucan and d'Aubigné, the saga of the opposition and of the losers tends to disintegrate into the episodic, without even taking on the consistency of romance. Quint is able to point out again and again how these poets can only rescue a narrative structure from this aimlessness by borrowing from the epic of the victors and in particular from the generic arch-enemy Virgil himself. The losers, then, have no unique narrative solution, no specific generic discourse of their own any longer; which is not to say that, for all kinds of historically specific and contextual reasons, the later epics of the victors (Camoens, Tasso) are any more successful. The latter tend to be monologic and to celebrate empire in monotonous tones, when not enlivened by romance interludes and in particular by journeys and adventures (generically, then, here too winner loses). It may thus be presumed that the narrative expression of opposition, of revolt, of defeat, only becomes possible by way of a wholly different generic system, namely in the emergence of the novel as such. Epic is now too thoroughly identified as a generic discourse with empire to be appropriated for a different political function.

All of which leaves romance itself in an interesting and highly ambiguous position, as the oppositional supplement of epic rather than its substantive opposite number. Still, it is the primal dualism of the Homeric poems that authorizes the interpretation of the *Aeneid* in the relatively allegorical terms of Quint's generic opposition of epic and romance. Thus romance—identified as the episodic journey—will dominate the first half of the *Aeneid*, taken as a series of insistent allusions to the *Odyssey*; while the second half, the conquest of Italy, will find its paradigm in the *Iliad*, in which, however, Aeneas is also a minor character: one ignominiously put to flight by Diomedes and then by Achilles himself:

> With astonishing artistry, Virgil combines the two Iliadic episodes almost simultaneously in the final duel between Aeneas and the stone-throwing Turnus ... In both [episodes of the *Iliad*] Aeneas is shown about to be defeated by the stronger Greek warriors, but rescued by favoring gods. At the end of the *Aeneid*, Aeneas is allowed to reverse both scenes and play the roles of Diomedes and Achilles, victorious over an Aeneas now played by Turnus.[66]

But this reading not only warns us that Quint's interpretations by way of literary allusions are allegorical as well as scholarly, and that allusion, rather than serving as an unconscious or conscious memory or imitation, actively collaborates in the production of the poem's dual meaning, as well as complicating the idea of narrative sequence or continuity. Thus the paradigms of *Iliad* and *Odyssey* not merely govern the two halves of the poem; they are also superimposed by a constant process of doubling and surcharge in which the victors of the *Iliad*, are also, at one and the same time, the losers of the *Odyssey*, and Aeneas is called upon to assume both roles simultaneously. This simultaneity of victory and defeat also complicates the purely sequential understanding of peripeteia: for if on the level of the Trojans' long voyage, the defeat in Troy turns around into the triumphant foundation of the Italian settlement which will eventually and providentially become Rome itself, the victory of the Trojans over the neighboring tribes recapitulates in a ghostly way their own grisly fate at the hand of the triumphant Greeks. We may also remember Auerbach's analysis of the perpetual present of epic, which we can now grasp as an epic opposite number to the non-narrative episodic structure of romance, so that both formally and in the content as well the transformation of negative into positive becomes an ambivalent simultaneity, turning from negative into positive and back accordingly as we rotate the episode in historical space.

---

[66] Quint, *Epic and Empire*, 72.

Peripeteia thereby becomes a dialectic wherein the deeper ambivalence of negative and positive is registered; wherein the triumph of the victors is undermined, and the more surely sapped and vitiated to the very degree to which it is overwhelming. In this transformation of peripeteia into dialectic (or its unveiling as dialectic) we may detect the emergence of historical time within the existential and its temporality, inasmuch as history (and the "longer view") corrects the very affect and the feeling tone of the individually lived. Victories are hollow; defeats are by contrast full of content. Is this to say that those ultimate defeats, of death and of torture, are also magically transformed, by a facile historicizing dialectic, into victories after the fashion of religious consolation? It is the very vocation of the existentialisms to deny this seemingly Hegelian consolation, and to insist on the irredeemability of loss and failure, which ought to put them beyond the reach of any such complacent history lessons. The extinction of any number of tribes in the course of imperial history, as well as the dizzying slaughters of the losers of battles, along with the holocaust of their families in the besieged cities, are sacred reminders that historical defeat is real; but they are reminders to the living, who are by definition not yet defeated.[67]

Hegel's lesson thus remains in force, both psychologically and politically: the Master's victory deprives him of the prize itself—namely, recognition by the Other, who has by virtue of his very defeat been transformed into a nonequal and a non-human, a Slave; and the leisure and consumption he has won has the effect of replacing the satisfactions of praxis itself by monotonous indulgence; the Slave, meanwhile, whose "truth is the Master" (unlike the latter, whose "truth is the Slave"), not only knows what recognition really means, but also what production brings, and the "labor and suffering of the negative." (We will shortly observe this new version of the dialectic to be recapitulated in modern literature and in particular in the history of the novel.)

But this then marks a momentous dialectical reversal for Quint's own epic narratives: the latter cease to be stories and fall to the level of the nonnarrative formerly occupied by the losers; while the losers' stories become the very center of the narrative dynamic as such, in this wholesale reversal of the generic system. But it was a reversal always faintly implicit on the traditional boredom of Virgilian panegyric and of Tasso's imperial celebration: what was absent was the possibility of any genuine narrative expression on the side of the losers, who had to be satisfied with romance if not with its complete breakdown into the magnificent yet episodic formlessness of a d'Aubigné.

---

[67] Kant's "enthusiasm" (see above, note 56) might thus also dialectically include commemoration.

Peripeteia, then, to return to our immediate topic, seems to have its possibility in the original dialectical identity of positive and negative. Capital, as Marx says in the *Manifesto*, being at one and the same time the most productive force in human history and the most destructive one, these simultaneous potentialities then get projected temporally into a succession whereby the victories of capital (securing a new market) turn into defeats (the market is saturated); while its defeats (stagnation, the rising costs of labor) turn into new victories (expansion of the field, production of new substitute technologies). Peripeteia is by way of being the narrative form or expression of this primal ambivalence of the dialectic as such.

Beginning with the *Grundrisse*, indeed, we can observe the emergence of a distinctive plot structure in which the very progress of a particular firm— in saturating the market with its product—at length brings about its stagnation as a business enterprise and its eventual collapse. Winner loses (and perhaps also loser wins)—the Sartrean version of this distinctive dialectical plot transforms the old bourgeois ideological categories of boom and bust, or prosperity and bankruptcy, beyond recognition (there is here also, no doubt, a relationship between this new narrative rhythm and the dialectical plot of the Hegelian period—the famous ruse of reason or history—in which a narrative logic is transferred from individuals to collective forces unbeknownst to the former).

Marx's analyses of the process (in the *Grundrisse*) tend to emphasize the destiny of the individual firm, which as it becomes successful in producing and marketing its product gradually saturates the market in such a way that it becomes stagnant. This is the point at which technology enters the picture, and invention stimulates a new expansion for a renewed product (often to replace the older one that everybody now possesses). Still, technology is not a foolproof solution, and for the moment I simply want to show how closely failure and success are dialectically intertwined in this particular mode of production.

In his pathbreaking history of capitalism,[68] Giovanni Arrighi generalizes this dialectic to the expansion of the system as a whole. We know how the development of capitalism has been discontinuous: beginning with the Italian city-states of the Renaissance (above all Genoa); then moving on briefly to Spain, until the influx of gold from the New World saps the vitality of Spain itself and passes the dynamic of the process on to Spain's extension and colony in the Low Countries. Thereafter, the leap to the more propitious framework of England, and from there, in modern times, to the United States, is only too familiar. What Arrighi wants to show however has very much to do with the matter of a propitious framework: for in each of

---

[68] Giovanni Arrighi, *The Long Twentieth Century: Money, Power and the Origins of Our Times*, London: Verso, 1994.

these instances, a flourishing onset of capitalist production quickly saturates its market; the business class then begins to shift its investments from production to finance capital and monetary speculation (this notion of a stage of finance capital is Arrighi's greatest theoretical innovation), until even that yields diminishing returns; finally, a leap to new and more profitable ground, an enlarged playing field, in which the process begins all over again. The virus, so to speak, is first carried by the Genoese bankers who finance the Spanish Empire, and then by the conversos and others who take the flourishing new territory of Holland and Flanders in hand. At any rate, this is still very much our paradigm of winner loses, where success itself blasts future development and unexpectedly turns into stagnation and failure like some classical doom.

Let me now give a more political example. We could for example follow Marx's *The Eighteenth Brumaire of Louis Bonaparte* in showing how the triumph of the bourgeoisie in the 1848 revolution leads dialectically to its defeat and submission to the first of the modern dictatorial or directorial systems. But that is a very complicated story indeed. So instead I pick a contemporary example from the work of the most prestigious historian of contemporary Italy: Paul Ginsborg makes an interesting point about the rise of Silvio Berlusconi, who first embodies the new world-historical assumption of power in a mediatic society by a media billionaire. Ginsborg's dialectical interpretation,[69] however, returns us to that older stage in which the excesses and self-indulgent violence of a younger *nouveau-riche* generation of Mafiosi led to universal revulsion and reaction all over Italy. We are all familiar with the heroic campaign called *Mani pulite* (clean hands), the struggle of heroic judges and martyrs to expose the extent of corruption in Italian political life and to convict the more notorious of the Mafia families. The success of this campaign, which really has no parallel in other advanced societies (even though the corruption itself has all kinds of parallels), is then the prototype of a winning and a successful force. It goes so far as to destroy the dominant bourgeois parties, the Christian Democrats, who ruled Italy since the end of World War II, and the Socialists, whose recent tenure was of briefer duration. This, it might be thought, could only give Italy a fresh start politically. On the contrary, according to Ginsborg, it was into this void left by the destruction of the parties that Berlusconi erupted, without a party (initially) and solely on the basis of money and media power. This is then very much the dialectic of winner loses and of the way in which success has an unexpected outcome, namely failure; or if you prefer a Hegelian version, the way in which the late capitalism of the media and communication and information comes historically to supplant an older stage of Mafia

---

[69] Paul Ginsborg, *Silvio Berlusconi: Television, Power and Patrimony*, London: Verso, 2004.

capitalism and even remnants of precapitalist forms of personal or clan domination.

Now, in conclusion, we may briefly return to the question of narrative form, as it expresses itself in the dialectic of the nineteenth-century novel. I take as my exhibit the centrality of the novel of adultery, which most fully exemplifies the power of the negative in nineteenth-century bourgeois society.[70] The novel of adultery is that negative or critical force that unmasks the emptiness of the social order and its institutions. The point is that the novel of adultery is first and foremost the drama of failure, and that it is failure that embodies the negative in a success-oriented society. I take as a counterproof the vacuousness of the novels of male success, particularly in the second half of the nineteenth century: the first half knows a few male successes, such as that of Rastignac, and its *Bildungsroman* is not necessarily a paradigm doomed to failure—*Wilhelm Meister* has a happy ending; but Stendhal's triumphs are the failures themselves, in Julien's self-chosen execution and Fabrice's ultimate choice of the clerical vocation as a kind of self-imposed withdrawal from life. Still, when we get to the first full-fledged business successes—I need mention only Zola's Octave, founder of the first great department store (in *Au Bonheur des dames*), or Maupassant's *Bel-Ami* —it becomes clear that these vacuous successes have nowhere to go except into the wish-fulfillments of mass culture.

This is then the sense in which the story of success is necessarily a literary failure: as the bourgeois or commercial age becomes established, success stories which are necessarily the success stories of business lose their content (money being itself without content, what Deleuze calls an axiomatic) and become degraded into the wish-fulfillments of the bestseller (taken as a genre). These are then the narratives of alienation and commodification; and as I will try to show elsewhere, the truth of such narratives—the symptoms of the omnipresence of the commodity form and of universal alienation, which is to say the truth of this society—can only be glimpsed

---

[70] I take the association of "failure" with women's novelistic destinies here, not in Tony Tanner's sense of transgression (and the Law), but rather according to some bitter-sweet Marcusian dialectic, where "the 'promesse du bonheur', although presented as destroyed and destroying, is, in the artistic presentation, fascinating enough to illuminate the prevailing order of life (which destroys the promise) rather than the future one (which fulfills it). The effect is an awakening of memory, of remembrance of things lost, consciousness of what was and what could have been. Sadness as well as happiness, terror as well as hope are thrown upon the reality in which all this occurred; the dream is arrested and returns to the past, and the future of freedom appears only as a disappearing light." Herbert Marcuse, "Some Remarks on Aragon," *Collected Papers*, Volume 1, ed. D. Kellner: *Technology, War and Fascism*, London: Routledge, 1998, p. 212–213.

from the vantage point of their dialectical opposite, which is to say from the standpoint of failure.

3. Anagnorisis

It thereby becomes clearer, I hope, how we can adapt the narratological category of the Aristotelian peripeteia to a modern and materialist historiography in such a way as to open up new perspectives on the narrative structure history shares with fiction. Now we need to reexamine the other two horizontal categories—of anagnorisis (or recognition) and pathos (or suffering)—from this perspective as well. Recognition in the most limited sense returned with a vengeance in nineteenth-century melodrama, where the identification of long-lost siblings or offspring became a popular form of narrative closure. I have already noted Gerald F. Else's observation that Aristotle's theorization of anagnorisis had much to do with the clan structure of archaic Greece and the political emphasis on great families.[71] Recognition would then be an essential component, in the *agon*, of disentangling the "us" from the "them." From a modern dialectical and materialist perspective, however, it would seem, in history, a matter of completeness or totalization: recognition would thereby mean the coming into view of those multitudinous others suppressed from the official story and field of vision.

So it is (returning to our earlier discussion of social class) that Livy's *Early History of Rome* has often been taken as the very prototype of class struggle, generating social and political categories that are still very much alive in modern political theory from Machiavelli and the French revolutionaries on. Indeed, nothing can become quite so tiresome, for any reader of Livy's first five books, as the perpetual return of the struggle between the Senate and the people, the great and wealthy aristocratic families and the "plebeians" or commoners—a struggle most vividly dramatized in Shakespeare's *Coriolanus*. This history is one of interminable cyclic alternations between the external wars between Rome and its Latin and Etruscan neighbors and the perpetual internal struggle between these two "classes."

> The peace was promptly followed by renewed political strife, the tribunes applying their old goad of agrarian reform until the commons were, as usual, completely out of hand.[72]

---

[71] See above, note 32.

[72] Livy, *The Early History of Rome: Books I–V of the History of Rome from Its Foundation*, London: Penguin, 1987, 168. Future references to this work are denoted *EHR*.

In the course of these events history was repeated and the successful conclusion of a war was once again immediately followed by political disturbances. (*EHR*, 192)

The campaign was no sooner over than the senatorial party had to face another—this time against the tribunes, who accused them of sharp practice in keeping the army in the field with the deliberate intention of stopping the passage of the law … (*EHR*, 210)

The hostility of the tribunes and the commons against the nobility was again on the increase … (*EHR*, 257)

In Rome meanwhile the leaders of the popular movement, continually disappointed of their hopes of political advancement so long as the country was not at war, began to arrange secret meetings in the tribunes' houses to discuss their plans. (*EHR*, 296)

In contrast to this campaign which was so much more easily settled than people feared it might be, a short period of political tranquility at home was unexpectedly broken by a number of serious disputes … (*EHR*, 316)

Throughout these two years there was peace abroad, though domestic politics were embittered by the old struggle for land reform. (*EHR*, 322)

In Rome meanwhile anti-government agitation reached a new intensity … The quarrel led to ugly scenes … and the only thing which restrained the mob from actual violence was the action of the leading senators … etc. (*EHR*, 369)

It is, to be sure, this eternity of class conflict which inspired Machiavelli to compose one of the fundamental works of political theory, and which governs our vision of the later history of Rome as it eventuates in failed revolution (the Gracchi), imperialism (the destruction of Carthage), and the ultimate triumph of a populist dictator (Julius Caesar): all categories we have projected back into the classical past from the experience of capitalism.

But in fact, this reading is based on a category mistake, and its correction will lead us to a reevaluation of the central role of anagnorisis in materialist history. This last can be instantiated by the powerful and elaborate demonstrations of Geoffrey de Ste. Croix in his book *The Class Struggle in the Ancient Greek World* (where Rome figures as a much more extensive and wealthy version of the Greek city-states). Ste. Croix tirelessly points out that the plebeians or commoners whom we have been casting in the role of the proletariat, or the laboring classes, were in fact free men, who were by no means the producers of surplus value in this social system. The ancient mode of production may well have had as its dominant the *polis* or the first genuinely political society (avoiding the word "democracy," which has a very different etymological meaning), but it was also a slave society whose wealth absolutely depended structurally on the labor of juridically unfree persons. (Wage labor and commerce were statistically insignificant.) "The single most important organizational difference between the ancient economy and that of the modern world is that in antiquity the propertied class derived its surplus mainly from unfree labour."[73] Ste. Croix's rich documentation of this proposition leaves no doubt as to the centrality of slavery and its accompanying ideologies and conceptualities in the ancient world. Indeed, the very brilliance of the ancient world in its heyday is inconceivable without the leisure made possible by the institution of slavery itself:

> The Greek propertied class, then, consisted essentially of those who were able to have themselves set *free* to live a civilised life by their command over the labour of others, who bore the burden of providing them with the necessities (and the luxuries) of the good life.[74]

> The most important single dividing line which we can draw between different groups of free men in the Greek world is, in my opinion, that which separated off from the common herd those I am calling "the propertied class," who could "live of their own" without having to spend more than a fraction of their time working for their living.[75]

Now slowly the Spartacus revolt begins to substitute itself for the political squabbles among the free (male) members of this society, and history is decisively transformed into that nightmare of the endless backbreaking labor of slaves over many centuries.

Technically or theoretically, of course, we may be tempted to renew a dispute over the nature of class, and whether, indeed, slaves as such can be understood as constituting one (just as clearly they are not a caste, and the emergence of what Ste. Croix terms serfs—indentured servants—further complicates the social-scientific discussion of the matter). But the advantage of our narratological perspective lies in cutting across these problems (whose value lies in demanding increasing specification and documentation) in a rather different way. For the sudden emergence, behind the struggles between the Senate and the commons, of a new collective character—one utterly divested of any voice or expression and indeed rendered virtually invisible by the noisy quarrels in the foreground of people who are in fact slave owners on both sides—this emergence of some ultimate subject of history bearing the full weight of all of human production and value on its back surely constitutes the strong form of historical anagnorisis or recognition as such. This is truly an actantial unmasking, in the theoretical sense of

---

[73] Geoffrey de Ste. Croix, *The Class Struggle in the Ancient Greek World*, Ithaca: Cornell University Press, 1981, 179.

[74] Ibid., 116.

[75] Ibid., 114.

the word, and also the stripping away of layers of ideological concealment and occultation, to offer a terrifying glimpse of the historically Real.

The question is not only a "scientific" one, in the Marxian sense of the appropriate categories to be used in this analysis (productive versus unproductive labor, and so forth). It is also a political question, one which involves the identification of the actors or agents of history, at the same time that it presupposes their recognition as just such "subjects of history."

But the word "recognition" is ambiguous; and Hegel's "struggle for recognition"—in context it is a kind of zero-sum game, only one of the parties to this struggle will achieve recognition—has also encouraged a tradition of liberal political thought in which recognition itself or *Anerkennung* becomes a stake in a multicultural settlement by which the various groups peaceably and electorally divide up the spoils. But at this point it is clear that the entities in question are no longer social classes—nor does it seem quite right to call the legalization of working-class political parties a recognition of the proletariat as a collective identity—so much as they are race, gender, and ethnic categories which thereby acquire legal rights. The struggle for this kind of recognition is therefore still an Enlightenment politics, one waged within the framework of a bourgeois civil society, and not yet a class politics whose stakes turn on the economic system or mode of production as such.

This is the point at which a different rendering of the Greek word *anagnorisis* may clarify the discussion, for rather than as "recognition" certain eminent editions (Bywater in the Barnes edition, Fyfe in the Loeb) translate this term as "discovery." Clearly, this puts a whole different face on the matter, and far more accurately describes the process by which the mass of Roman slaves are found to stand behind the visible political contests of the classical *polis*. In this form, then, it is a process we can also approximate in the age of capitalism, both on a national and on a world scale.

It is generally supposed, indeed, that Marx named and identified a working class already in the process of becoming visible in the first mode of production which was purely economic in structure, and which did not any longer in that sense need to be discovered. Meanwhile, it was precisely his account of the laboring body, the horror of the working day and of the factory itself as life imprisonment, that then retroactively illuminated the temporality of the *corvée* and of slavery ("a moderately patriarchal character as long as production was chiefly directed to the satisfaction of immediate local requirements"), and on back into the gold mines described by Diodorus Siculus, in which "all, forced by blows, must work on until death puts an end to their sufferings and their distress."[76]

---

[76] Karl Marx, *Capital*, Vol. 1, trans. Ben Fowkes, London: Penguin, 1976, 345. Future references to this work are denoted *Cap*.

Yet alongside the life sentence of labor, there lay the life sentence of idleness and the poor house: not the least astonishing and dialectical union of opposites discovered by Marx, and not the least terrible, is that indispensable function of capitalism to create what is blandly known as the "reserve army of labor," or in other words, the masses of the unemployed who are a requirement of the system and are produced in prosperity and crisis alike ("the overwork of the employed part of the working class swells the ranks of its reserve, while, conversely, the greater pressure that the reserve by its competition exerts on the employed workers forces them to submit to overwork …"[*Cap*, 789]). Not only are potential workers a truly "reserve" workforce thereby produced by the structure of capitalism as such, those unable to work are also "produced" in the form of what the period called pauperism, which also includes so-called lumpens (criminals, vagabonds, etc.), child workers, and "the demoralized, the ragged and those unable to work" [*Cap*, 797]). These unfortunates are not merely the personnel of the periodic visits to the lower depths of the modern great cities and the glimpses of London's poor or of the "mysteries of Paris"; they open a transcendent window onto human history itself, from which nostalgic glimpses of tribal Utopias are scarcely of much use as a relief and a remedy.

I have already cited the example of the increase in misery of industrializing areas:

> The economic paradox that the most powerful instrument for reducing labor-time suffers a dialectical inversion and becomes the most unfailing means for turning the whole lifetime of the worker and his family into labour-time at capital's disposal for its own valorization. (*Cap*, 532)[77]

But in the context of unemployment the crucial dialectic is that which Marx begins to deploy when he notes the peculiar fact that the increase in productivity of a given machine—that is, the reduction of labor time a new technology brings with it—is in fact accompanied by an increase in overtime, that is to say, a lengthening rather than a reduction of the working day itself (indeed, the struggle over obligatory overtime has been central to many modern American labor disputes and not merely in Marx's antique Victorian context). The dialectician resolves the contradiction in this way:

> The mechanism of the capitalist production process removes the very obstacles it temporarily creates. The price of labour falls again to a level corresponding with

---

[77] "Machinery in itself shortens the hours of labour, but when employed by capital it lengthens them" (*Cap*, 568). Or for a different example of such reversals (which are everywhere in *Capital*), see the remark on the piece-wages, which have "a tendency, while raising the wages of individuals above the average, to lower this average itself" (*Cap*, 697).

capital's requirements for self-valorization, whether this level is below, the same as, or above that which was normal before the rise of wages took place. We see therefore that in the first case it was not the diminished rate, either of the absolute or of the proportional increase in labour-power, or the working population, which caused the excess quantity of capital, but rather the converse; the increase in capital made the exploitable labour-power insufficient. In the second case it was not the increased rate, either of the absolute or of the proportional increase in labour-power, or the working population, that made the capital insufficient, but rather the converse; the relative reduction in the amount of capital caused the exploitable labour-power, or rather its price, to be in excess. (*Cap*, 770)

Such passages entitle us to characterize *Capital* itself as being in reality a book about unemployment; but they also raise theoretical and political questions about the relationship of the unemployed to class categories as such.

Indeed, in a famous and substantial article on Marx's concept of the lumpens (the "scum, offal, refuse of all cases"[78]) which help bring Louis Bonaparte to power in the great counterrevolution after 1848, Peter Stallybrass has argued[79] that this concept recapitulates all the respectable bourgeois distaste for society's Others and symbolically reenacts the social exclusion whereby all kinds of minorities are scapegoated and expelled from the social order itself. The very categories of Marx's class analysis (productive, unproductive) are thereby alleged to perpetuate what are properly bourgeois prejudices (and, by extension, Eurocentric ones). Marx is thus transformed into a social conservative, and the anti-Marxism of various forms of identity politics thereby richly confirmed.

I think that such passages need to be juxtaposed with the pages of *Capital* already cited above (from the chapter on "The General Law of Capitalist Accumulation"), in which the category of the lumpen reappears among the groups systematically excluded from productive society in the form of "pauperism." This passage, although far from confirming Marx's instinctive contempt for the excluded, does at least suggest that there is a hesitation here as to the classification of such people under the general rubric of the "reserve army of labor." Both are excluded categories, but the rubric of unemployment would seem to be distinguished from the other kinds of paupers, disabled, elderly, or indeed lumpens. It is as if able-bodied yet unemployed laborers nonetheless retain the dignity of the category of workers or working class, while the others fall outside that category altogether. Or perhaps, to

---

[78] Karl Marx, *The Eighteenth Brumaire of Louis Bonaparte*, New York: International Publishers, 1963, 199.

[79] Peter Stallybrass, "Marx and Heterogeneity: Thinking the Lumpenproletariat," in *Representations*, Vol. 31 Num. 1, Summer 1990, 69–95. But now, for the full historical context and political import of this term, see Michael Denning, "The Spectre of Wageless Life," forthcoming.

put this in more practical terms, we might observe that qua workers, the unemployed workers can still be politically organized, while the other category of individuals falls outside the realm of political action altogether: or in yet another language, the first can in a pinch still constitute "subjects of history," while the latter cannot in any way be conceived as subjects.

Yet as an historical matter, the latter are in fact gradually absorbed into those mass disturbances which develop into political revolutions, whose structure consists in a tendential yet absolute dichotomization of society into two great classes: those for and those against. This practical reabsorption and subsumption of lumpens and unemployed together under a revolutionary class rubric would seem precisely to reenact the process of discovery we are examining here, as an enlargement of historical knowledge which is then at one with practical political consequences.

The whole process and the debates surrounding it are then themselves recapitulated on a world scale by the theoretical development of Gramsci's term "subalternity" first in the work of the Indian historians of the so-called Subaltern Studies school, and then in a variety of other non-core areas (in particular Latin America), where it is in fact closely related to earlier arguments about the relevance of terms like "Third World" as a mode of "recognition" of post-colonial populations.

Gramsci's original usage seems to have been yet another example of a disguise of classical Marxist terminology designed to evade the attention of the fascist censorship: in that case, it simply means "proletarian". But such transcoding has often had the effect of a creative drift away from Marxian usage into a whole new semantic area which can be taken either critically to challenge a Marxian orthodoxy or to supplement and enrich it. In this case, the word has come to be invested with Gramsci's lifelong reflections on the Italian south and on the relationship between the peasantry and the urban (and northern) working class. "Subalternity" has in that context come to designate the habits of obedience and respect, the stubbornness and mutism, of a peasantry whose mode of resistance is utterly distinct from that of factory workers. But this is so far simply a designation of a caste mentality as it survives on into the world of class and demands a political strategy of its own, commensurate with its cultural and social specificity.

In the hands of Ranajit Guha and the Indian Subaltern Studies school, this notion of subalternity will be developed into a whole new analytic approach to the peasantry as such, and in particular a radical reconsideration of their historical uprisings, which have mostly been dismissed as forms of spontaneity to be replaced by organization and political analysis. Meanwhile, in the light of Maoism and the realities of Latin American politics, the whole notion of the peasantry as essentially "a sack of potatoes,"[80] as a

---

[80] Marx, *The Eighteenth Brumaire of Louis Bonaparte*, 124. See Ranajit Guha's preface in Guha and Spivak (eds.) *Selected Subaltern Studies*, New York: Oxford, 1985; and also

non-revolutionary, even often conservative class (if it is a class), has had to be revised.

Thus the Subaltern Studies group has been able to reconstitute that immemorial and equally stereotypical collective which is the peasantry into a genuine "subject of history," whose acts and interventions are not simply blind and spontaneous reflexes of *jacquerie* and irrational mob behavior, but rather know an intentionality of a kind not hitherto recognized or acknowledged.[81] Here too, then, a kind of anagnorisis has been achieved in which History can itself be glimpsed in a new and more energizing way.

But so-called subaltern theory, which comes into being in the era of the "new social movements," has also inflected this idea in a non-class direction, as a "recognition" of groups that are not technically social classes and whose collective consciousness is of a different type altogether. There here persists something of the original notion that these are classes beneath or behind classes, somehow hidden by them and inaccessible to political theory and, organization. These have taken a number of forms since Marx's ambiguous categorization of paupers and lumpens: Kristeva's notion of the abject, and more recently, Agamben's vision of "bare life," are only the most prominent theoretical attempts to inflect this ultimate rock bottom in the direction of the psychoanalytic or the existential. Still it may be objected that all such categories posit the theorist in an essentially aesthetic and contemplative position, and her object as the vehicle for what Alberto Moreiras has called "spectacular redemption."[82] As for subalternity itself as a more social and political category, in a famous essay, Gayatri Spivak decisively links the issue of the position of the subaltern to the problem of representation as such, and to the dilemma of naming, which other already named and represented groups seem to undertake to do in her place[83]; while Moreiras has speculated that the subaltern is a category of the residue or the excess, the unassimilable, such that each subaltern group will generate its own subalterns in turn, ad infinitum, the strategy of the lifting up and elimination of subalternity thereby becoming an impossible mirage.

Indeed, it would seem that we confront just such a phenomenon of infinite regress in the concept of a "Fourth World," which arose in the 1960s to challenge a then dominant and politically progressive Third-Worldism

---

Michael Denning, *Culture in the Age of Three Worlds*, London: Verso, 2004, 155–161.

[81] Ranajit Guha, *Elementary Aspects of Peasant Insurgency in Colonial India*, Delhi: Oxford University Press, 1983.

[82] Alberto Moreiras, *The Exhaustion of Difference*, Durham, NC: Duke University Press, 2001, 221.

[83] Gayatri Spivak, *A Critique of Postcolonial Reason*, Cambridge, MA: Harvard University Press, 1999.

which constituted something like a "recognition," in the age of wars of national liberation, of post-colonial identities by those already assimilated to First or Second World categories of class.

It is noteworthy that such a thinker as Manuel Castells should have recourse to this once doubtful ideological concept in his mapping of geopolitical space today. Castells generalizes the notion of an internal "social exclusion" (ghettos, unemployment, and the like) externally to the world of nation-states, in which exclusion takes the form of the "black holes" of history and globalization itself.[84] Whole regions and their populations simply drop out of history and development, they fall through the cracks and disappear into spaces comparable in international consciousness to those old blank spaces on the earlier maps of unexplored areas, areas unexplored and uncolonized by the West. And this is something that can happen to whole continents, as witness sub-Saharan Africa, given over to what Castells calls "predatory" regimes and to objects of international philanthropy. Such spaces are then grimly dialectical reversals of that positive process of delinking, a concept which Samir Amin invented in order to call for the withdrawal from capitalist globalization and the fostering of new modes of production.[85] But he was too optimistic about this possibility, in a global situation in which the international division of labor has already been imposed, destroying self-sufficiency and making it suicidal for even the potentially richest countries—Brazil, India—to escape the pervasive influence of the US free market and any longer to conceive of such a thing as "socialism in one country." Ironically, only the so-called failed states have succeeded in delinking, unwittingly and irrevocably, with the consequence of an irredeemable misery.

The free-market or neo-conservative economists simply write these states off, as one might liquidate a bad investment. On the other hand, a recoding of the situation in political terms offers a convenient way of shifting the blame and of concealing the underlying economic causes. The currently popular sociological term "failed state" provides useful cover for this operation. But already in 1993 Paul Johnson had bluntly observed:

> Some states are not yet fit to govern themselves. Their continued existence, and the violence and human degradation they breed, is a threat to their neighbors as

---

[84] Manuel Castells, *End of Millennium*, Vol. 3, *The Information Age*, Oxford: Oxford University Press, 1998, 70–75. But see in particular, for a critical enumeration of the various figures and stereotypes current in this field, what he terms "journalistic Malthusianism" and "apocalyptic temporalizations," (190–1) James Ferguson, *Global Shadows: Africa in the Neoliberal World Order*, Durham, NC: Duke University Press, 2006, 190–191.

[85] Samir Amin, *Delinking: Towards a Polycentric World*, London: Zed, 1985.

well as an affront to our consciousness. There is a moral issue here: the civilized world has a mission to go out to these desperate places and govern.[86]

This provides a rationale for First World intervention in which so-called US humanitarian responses (as in Darfur, for example) mask long-term military occupations of the US type. It is a classical example of that substitution of politics for economics which the Marxist critique of ideology traditionally denounces.

Meanwhile the work of Manuel Castells and others demonstrates the ways in which just such political stalemates—what he calls the emergence of "predatory" regimes in Africa along with the development of systems based on Western philanthropy and the dole—are to be explained economically in terms of globalization (he calls it informational capitalism): "the ascent of informational, global capitalism is indeed characterized by simultaneous economic development [in the First World] and underdevelopment [in the Third], by social inclusion and social exclusion."[87]

This is not simply an unfortunate combination of circumstances but rather a genuine dialectic, in which the positive and the negative are dependent on each other and evolve simultaneously and by interaction. Theories of this kind, coming in the wake of the free-market heyday of the 1980s and 1990s and on the ruins of the benefits promised by globalization (Castell's book is dated 1998), are increasingly characteristic, and mark an unexpected revival of the great 1960s invention of the slogan of the "development of underdevelopment," foreshadowed by Paul Baran, and then developed by theorists like Cardoso, Gunder Frank, and Walter Rodney (who invented the slogan)—a theory widely derided in the prosperous neoconservative era that followed, but now again back on the agenda.

In our time, however, it is Robert Kurz who has most powerfully drawn the ultimate conclusions from this dialectical situation in his stunning book, *Der Kollaps der Modernisierung*, which takes on the whole issue of global "development" from the standpoint of an implacable critique of ideologies of modernization: the latter, it will be remembered, were most memorably encapsulated in Walt Rostow's theories of the "take-off stage," in which world economics was imagined as a kind of airport, from which a number of jumbo jets were already in the air (the First World or advanced countries), while others waited on the runways, motors running, for the signal to move (he mentions Mexico and Turkey), while still others are still loading at the gates or undergoing repairs in the hangars. It is the immense merit of Kurz's disturbing work to argue that modernization is henceforth

---

[86] Paul Johnson, "Colonialism's Back and Not a Moment Too Soon," *New York Times Magazine*, April 18, 1993, 44.

[87] Castells, *End of Millennium*, 82.

impossible, that there is no longer any take-off stage, and that globalization itself is what secures this "death sentence of the world market" on the so-called underdeveloped countries.

> The analysis excludes political intervention: The problem consists in the fact that the abstract logic of profit inherent in the commodity form and thereby the world market which has been constituted by it does not have and cannot admit a politically induced strategy, one evolved by mere will and decision-making. The law of profitability—according to which only those goods are valuable and qualify for the market which correspond to the level of global productivity—must sooner or later implacably reassert itself.[88]

> Nor is so-called free-market shock therapy of any use here. Its "model" offers a merely abstract structure of economic competitivity; reality however requires this structure to function *within the world market itself*. Otherwise it is worthless. A country which is not competitive on the world market remains dirtpoor whether it has an internal market structure or not, that is, it will always be driven under by fearful economic competition. The simple opening of internal markets generates nothing but chaos or has already attained this "achievement." But the opening of such markets to the outside world can only lead to a situation in which the defenseless industries of the home country are wiped out by Western competitors and predatory business takeovers. (*KM*, 185)

It is ultimately a question of investments, the requirement for which radically distinguishes the situation of such Third World countries under current globalization from the classic stage of the "primitive accumulation of capital" in the West:

> The less the Third World is able to keep up in the competition for higher productivity, the less interesting does it become for the foreign direct investments of Western capital: investments necessary for its own development and the development of its own internal markets … (*KM*, 195)

> The basis of that powerful Western capital accumulation, from which development comes in the first place, can never be reached within the commodity logic that also governs other zones of the world. Every step forward in the development and increase in productivity of the "underdeveloped" countries is negatively overcompensated by two, three, and more steps up the ladder in the more developed ones. It is the race between rabbit and the tortoise, which can only be ended by the death of the rabbit. (*KM*, 197–198)

---

[88] Robert Kurz, *Der Kollaps der Modernisierung*, Frankfurt: Eichborn, 1991, 296. Future references to this work are denoted *KM*. It should be noted that much of Kurz's prophetic discussion in this early work concerns Eastern Europe.

As for Africa, here is Kurz's now predictable conclusion:

> The poorest countries—above all Africa, but also those of Asia and Latin America —from the outset never had a chance even to make a beginning in their own industrialization and social improvement. The constant deterioration of the "terms of trade" for their raw materials and foodstuffs has made them into hopeless world "invalids" who cannot even feed themselves on their own. The inner struggle over the remnants has led to bloody slaughters, ethnic and civil wars, famines and drought. (*KM*, 201n)

Such outcomes certainly seem to vindicate an historic shift in the ideology of human nature and of history: the enlargement of the pessimism about the Holocaust to include all manner of incomprehensible violence and cruelty in the Balkans and Africa, and indeed all over the world (not excluding Islam, now seen as a religion of fanaticism and violence). But there is no human nature, and the historical visions projected from this or that ideological (and aesthetic) affirmation of it are always better assessed in terms of their own hidden agenda and their own political programs.

We must therefore return again to those collectivities, those human individuals, who have "fallen out of history"—not in order to be in conformance with Ricoeur's narrative humanism, which dictates the discovery of anthropomorphic characters behind a system that may transcend them— that is essentially the task of anagnorisis, as we have already seen—but rather precisely to achieve some representation of the relationship of such collectivities to the dialectical system we have already been outlining here—the structural necessity for capitalism to create a reserve army of the unemployed and to exclude whole sections of society (or here, in globalization, whole sections of the world population).

This passage from system to agents or actors will then involve a translation from time to space: and indeed we may anticipate that the vision of history we seek—that very emergence of relationship as such—will constitute precisely that image of the transition point of the translation, of time into space, or of space into time. Such an image will in fact project that spatial dialectic we have been seeking here: but it will also require some final detour through the unity of positive and negative in the world system, before we conclude with a speculative account of the possibility of appearance of History itself.

In fact, we have already staged this alternation of positive to negative and back in a previous discussion of globalization[89]; it must now be restaged in terms of an older Marxian debate about imperialism. Nothing has indeed been quite so scandalous, in Marx's legacy, as those texts (particularly the

---

[89] See above, chapters 17 and 18.

writings on India[90]) in which the father of communism seems to appreciate the role of capitalism in bringing its colonies up into the light of its modernity, thus making them available for socialist revolution and consigning their village past, if not to the "ashcan of history," then at least to the scrapbook of nostalgic images of worlds before money and history.

Africa is preeminently the space which has, in the contemporary world Imaginary, fallen out of History itself. It can serve as an object lesson in the way in which natural catastrophes—famine, ecological disaster, questions of population and so-called bio-power—express and at the same time mask that other, more fundamental reality, which is the falling out of capitalism itself.

Unfortunately, it is not so easy to fall out of a now globalized capitalism or world system. In the 1960s there were many idyllic images of the possibilities of a different kind of life that would be made available if capitalism passed you by, if you lived beneath its radar-detection system, or were simply not worth the effort of appropriation or assimilation. This was then the Utopian image of the village as a precapitalist enclave within the frantic momentum of a larger system, a place of calm within that momentum, a refuge in which precapitalist social relations (which might well be oppressive in different precapitalist senses—hierarchies of gender and age, the struggle between clans, the oppression of religious taboo) could survive. This possibility of Utopian imagination—encouraged by a historically momentary stalling of the process of capitalist expansion by wars of national liberation and the like—was theorized in various ways by Lévi-Strauss's recovery of Rousseau, by anthropological theory like those of Sahlins and Baudrillard, and by the ethnography of Colin Turnbull[91]; and it was given content and representation by the African writers themselves.

But today those peaceful village enclaves have becomes places of famine and ecological disaster, and the closure of the village itself has been transmuted into the desperate limits of the refugee camp, when the populations have not, as with Turnbull's forest people, been forcibly transported away and settled firmly within the system. There are, as we have implied, two forms the negation of the negation can take (and these also wear the valences of positive and negative respectively). On the one hand, the negation of capitalism no longer leads back to the Utopian but simply destroys the preexisting form itself; on the other, it constitutes a progression within the system itself towards greater and greater complexity and "modernity," and

---

[90] Iqbal Husain, ed., *Karl Marx on India*, New Delhi: Tulika, 2006.

[91] Claude Lévi-Strauss, *Tristes tropiques*; Marshall Sahlins, *Stone Age Economics*; Jean Baudrillard, *The Mirror of Production*; Pierre Clastres, *La Société contre l'état*; Colin Turnbull, *The Forest People*.

this is the negative power of the imaginary which promises the break in the system and the imaging of a new one. The regression to the enclave is thereby distinguished from the transformation of the system itself, its replacement by a wholly different system. At best the enclave can be allegorical of the new system (that is, it can function as a Utopia); at worst, that is to say, in reality, it is simply destroyed, leaving rubble and ruin behind it, detritus which is however the life of the human individuals themselves, who have "fallen out" of the system and are henceforth part of nothing, a remainder or excess of what Agamben might call naked life, biological survivors denuded of any possibility of working or acting, simply living on in camps, at the mercy of international philanthropy.

It is indeed these camps themselves which serve as the strong form of our current images of social exclusion on a world scale: those enclosed settlements in which people have lived out their lives for some sixty years; and beyond them the provisional settlements of refugees in which, the object of philanthropic attention from the United Nations and the NGOs, individuals unlikely ever to be welcomed back into homes destroyed by civil war or fled in famine pass their lives in enforced idleness, in the agonizing inactivity and powerlessness of populations excluded from history. The changing of the valences on such black holes, such descriptions of exclusion, involves nothing less than their incorporation into the world system, and the completion of a global commodification which has not yet reached them. At this point, then, the lost populations of the earth would cease to be some new and unimaginable category of lumpen or bare life, they would then rejoin the universal reserve army of the unemployed which even a now global capitalism must perpetuate in order to continue its existence.

We need at this point to return to the abstract categories in terms of which the discussion has thus far been conducted; and we also need to disentangle the conflation of ideology and economics into which—particularly from a social-scientific perspective—this whole exploration of anagnorisis will have seemed to have led us. Indeed, the language of black holes and failed states, of a fall out of history and as it were a baleful curse laid upon the undevelopable countries of the former Third World, is ideological through and through; but its deficiencies are not to be remedied by the replacement of ideology by science, or even by a better and more progressive ideology. It would be improbable indeed if the various ideologies of fate were to be adequately corrected by developmental statistics, when "development" is itself yet another ideology and a mutation of the old ideologeme of modernization. As in individual or existential life, Ideology is always with us in the realm of historical analysis (and in the questions the economists seek to solve); and our analyses of objective conditions and their possibilities are always organized by a certain social Imaginary (or by what I have called cognitive mapping).

What the emphasis on anagnorisis reveals is that the structure of ideology is an actantial process, and that its evaluation is not to be based on the optimism or pessimism it expresses, nor on its quotient of prejudice or stereotypes, but rather on the collective characters and actants in terms of which it organizes a given historical situation or event. In the case of Africa, it seems clear that the fundamental ideological struggle has to do with the assignment of blame: is it to be assigned to the Africans themselves, their culture and traditions (or national character), or to their predatory elites and post-colonial governments; or, on the other hand, to the IMF and to the policies of essentially US globalization; or indeed to geography, to colonial history, or simply to bad luck and maledictions of fate itself (yet another actant in some of these systems)? It seems equally clear that it would be impossible to analyze the African situation without organizing it in terms of such actants or collective actors, whatever conclusions are to be drawn, and however much it is possible to neutralize the question of blame. The more pertinent issue is the way in which the situation is to be distinguished from the agents themselves (who might on other readings themselves constitute the situation to be faced and corrected). The act or operation of anagnorisis, then—recognition but also discovery, the identification of agents not yet fully visible, the reorganization and redistribution of the actantial field—is an indispensable preliminary moment in the process of analysis, and demonstrates that the narrative perspective is one in which the distinction between ideology and science (in this case the scientific approaches of economics) is impossible and undesirable.

Let us therefore return for a moment to the question of Marx on unemployment, for the consignment of Africa to the ashcan of history presents an eerie semblance to the troubling issue of Marx and the category of the lumpens. There seems to be a contamination here in which the much-debated opposition between productive and unproductive work crosses wires with the whole questions of the reserve army of labor (that is, workers currently unemployed). What is illicitly transferred from one of these circuits to the other is what is misunderstood to be the moralizing content of the productive/unproductive distinction. But Marx never meant the term "unproductive" to carry a moral judgment on the type of work in question; and the distinction was a purely descriptive one which separated labor that produces capital (productive) from labor which produces wages which are used up in immediate consumption. Something deep in the Western, or perhaps in the Weberian, psyche seems unable to grasp "unproductivity" as anything but a reproach and a judgment, despite the fact that it characterizes whole areas of the labor of the historical past: such listerners are therefore likely to be stunned by Marx's dry remark "To be a productive worker is therefore not a piece of luck but a misfortune" (*Cap*, 644). This is, however, scarcely a countercultural celebration of idleness (except in the sense of his son-in-law's famous pamphlet on the subject), but rather a reminder of what "productive labor" entails, in this strict sense of incorporation into the infernal machine of the capitalist system.

When we turn to that different opposition in which work is opposed to unemployment, we confront a situation in which the positive term seems to have two opposites (or if you prefer a more technical language, a contrary as well as a contradictory): these are the unemployed and the unemployable respectively, or on Marx's analysis, the reserve army of the unemployed and those—aged, infirm, as well as the famous lumpens—who are not available even for the seasonal or boom-condition employment for which the reserve army is destined to be drawn upon. A schematic graph of these oppositions, however, reveals a missing term:

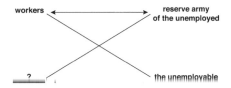

This empty slot is already implicitly identified in *Capital*, which presciently includes a withering attack on pious notions of retraining in its epic account of whole industries driven out of business: but it remained for globalization to dramatize this category far more visibly by projecting it out into visible geographical space. For the new category can be none other than the *formerly employed*: that is to say, the working populations once active in vital industries which have now ceased to function, and around whose idle factories the veterans of dead labor live on with their families in enclaves not much more hopeful than the camps themselves, particularly when it comes to dwellings and foreclosures.

But now this actantial system can be mapped onto the space of globalization itself, where alongside the working populations and the disabled, groups of unemployed First and Second World workers hesitate between the status of a reserve army (should new industries and possibilities start up in their immediate vicinities) and that of the formerly and now permanently unemployed situation of people whom "development" has permanently passed over. Globalization has then immensely and tangibly accelerated this process in its tireless quest for ever cheaper labor: abandoning the former workers of the Mexican *maquiladoras* who assumed the tasks of former US factory workers, and moving to a China, where already recently built factories are being closed in view of even lower-paid labor elsewhere in Southeast Asia. Marx's vision of the world market, or the stage of universal commodification (wage labor), is therefore not to be understood as some immense, fully filled and packed space in which everyone is working for wages and "productively" producing capital; but rather a space in which everyone has once been a productive laborer, and in which labor has everywhere begun to price itself out of the system: a situation he anticipated to be an explosive one.

We may now return to the question of the "recognition" or "discovery" of Africa in this light. In a remarkable comparative analysis, Giovanni Arrighi has pinpointed the historical moment in which the former Third World began to separate into the industrial "miracles" of the Asian tigers (Korea, Taiwan, Singapore, and now China itself) and regions once no less "under-developed" than they were, such as Africa, but which have now, particularly in their light, come to seem essentially undevelopable.[92] This moment is of course the moment of the full-blown emergence of late capitalism (or glob-alization, or postmodernity), namely the Thatcher/Reagan moment of the early 1980s, in which "the United States, which in the 1950s and 1960s had been the major source of world liquidity and of direct investment, in the 1980s became the world's main debtor nation and by far the largest recipi-ent of foreign capital."[93] This periodization, essential for cultural as well as socioeconomic understanding of our current situation, constitutes one of the two basic causes proposed by Arrighi for what he calls the African crisis, namely the reversal in capital investment, which now begins to stream away from the Third World to the First. The second cause, fundamental in the new bifurcation in the destiny of the former Third World countries, has to do with the colonial histories and policies which made West and Southeast Asia preeminently serviceable sources of cheap labor, while depopulating Africa. In terms of our present discussion, then, these factors explain why the developing or (Asian) "former Third World" comes to be identified as a fundamental reserve army of labor, while the "undevelopable" and under-developing former Third World (and in particular Africa) comes to fill that third actantial space which we have termed that of the "unemployable." At this point, then, Arrighi, like the other scholars of Africa's socioeconomic (and even cultural) situation, offers some practical suggestions for future policy, without much optimism.

Here, however, where our interest is, for good or ill, purely theoretical, it is rather a question of the shifting of this "actant" from one semiotic cate-gory or space to another—the transfer of the imaginary entity "Africa" from the "contradictory" of employed work (the "unemployable" slot) to that of its "contrary," namely the "employable" or Marx's reserve army. Such a reidentification is the constitutive operation of anagnorisis, but at the same time would in historical reality correspond to an immense transformation of African socioeconomic reality in the emergent world market of late

---

[92] Giovanni Arrighi, "The African Crisis," *New Left Review* Vol. 2, Num. 15, May–June 2002, 5–36.

[93] Ibid., 21.

capitalism. That such a displacement is preeminently conceivable can be justified by the vision of a discontinuous expansion of globalization from one site of cheap labor to another one where the development of the first site has raised workers' wages and living conditions beyond what is profitable for the production in question: this picture of capitalism's uneven expansion is already present in *Capital*, but can today be worked out on a much larger canvas, as so many recent studies testify. Meanwhile, the false picture that tends to accompany Marx's fragmentary allusions to some eventual world market or universal commodification is corrected by our fourth category of the "formerly employed," or in other words those areas now abandoned by capital in its *fuite en avant*: now fully commodified at the same time that they are blighted and devastated. The closure of the world market is therefore not to be understood as the filling up of an empty container but rather as the progress of an epidemic.

Both are, however, figures, each one with its own specific disadvantages and constitutive distortions, which can only be corrected by the distortions of yet another figure. The argument I have outlined here is meant to demonstrate the inseparability of the figurative process from any more properly cognitive mapping as such. But it is to be sure on the order of a thought experiment with which we may usefully compare historical debates such as the discussion of "wages for housework": this was probably not a practical political program, but its philosophical emphasis on the rethinking of the category of commodification (wage labor) in feminist analyses of the condition of women placed the whole issue on a contemporary political agenda, an anti-capitalist one, rather than on some historical study of the survival of precapitalist forms. (Meanwhile the industrialization of food and to a certain degree the automation of housework, cleaning, and the like, began to show the degree to which such spaces were indeed subject to the colonization by modern capitalism as such—a colonization only fully completed when we add to it the possibility of "wages for housework.")

So now in the same way the unlikely possibility of the industrialization of the abandoned populations of the postmodern world nonetheless allows us to reconceptualize, and cognitively remap, their structural positions within the world system, and to re-create actants, agents, narrative characters, in a far more inclusive narrative about late capitalism or globalization, than the ones in which this whole range of debates has hitherto moved. Here, in other words, we grasp anagnorisis as an act of theoretical production, in which new characters are produced for our collective and political discovery and recognition.

4. Pathos

i. The Temptation of the Visual

From the Aristotelian categories of peripeteia or reversal, and anagnorisis or discovery/recognition, we now move on to the final term of the triad Ricoeur has found to be at work in the *Poetics*. To be sure, this final term— pathos—is not only subject to philological correction, it also risks misleading us as to the structural nature and function of the thing itself. It may well, in other words, be argued that in the *Poetics*, pathos is not at all the same kind of narratological category as peripeteia or recognition. Indeed, his fundamental commentator agrees, saying, "It is clear that Aristotle thought the pathos the basic, indispensable 'part' of the tragic plot, since peripety and recognition are limited to complex plots while pathos is not."[94] This is not the place to argue the interpretation of Aristotle any further, nor even to debate Ricoeur's intent in constructing his triad,[95] which has merely served us as a point of departure.

Yet the Aristotelian reference will help us to clarify our own argument in two further ways. Else, indeed, insists strongly on the non-subjective nature of Aristotelian pathos, which has to do (according to him) with events rather than emotions. This is then the moment to say our discussion here will not commit us to any of the rich explorations of melancholy or trauma theory in recent years, nor to the psychoanalytic hypotheses about the construction of subjectivity to which they are related. The only issue which has any psychological resonance in what follows will be the eudaimonic one, whose dialectical ambiguity (the union of opposites) will support an alternating vision of history in either nightmarish or salvational terms.

The word "vision" then suggests a further comment touching the nature of the representation of pathos Aristotle had in mind, which is generally taken to mean a bloody concluding tableau: we have already evoked the suicide of Ajax, Medea surrounded by her dead children, Oedipus blinded, or, perhaps even more paradigmatic for the traditional understanding of pathos, the Laokoon statuary—Laokoon and his sons struggling desperately in the fatal grip of the enormous sea-serpent, which gave rise to Lessing's famous discussion of succession and simultaneity, time and space, in the arts. Else concludes

> "On stage" is not Aristotle's meaning … Aristotle is contrasting the *pathos* with
> peripety and recognition. For it is in the nature of peripety and recognition that
> they are invisible events, transactions which take place in the realm of the mind,
> though they may be accompanied by visible tokens. Death, pain, wounds, on the

---

[94] Else, *Aristotle's Poetics: The Argument*, 229.
[95] See above, Ricoeur, note 27.

other hand are physical events in their own nature; they belong to the visible realm. But that does not mean that they have to appear as physical events in the course of a tragedy. What is required is that they be there as the postulated physical correlate of the moral or mental events which transpire as peripety and recognition.[96]

For the moment, this discussion can serve to alert us to the temptation of visual reification in our theorization of pathos. The very fact of the identification of pathos with some kind of concluding tableau—Lessing's *Nebeneinander* following on the *Nacheinander* of events and history—is bound to strengthen this temptation, at the same time that it gives us a way of evaluating any new formulation of the problem, which must be articulated so as to exclude the visual as such.

But pathos here will commit us to the attempt to transform Ricoeur's project of coming face to face with Time into an effort to confront History itself. The overtones of visuality and visualization were already inescapable in Ricoeur's model, namely Heidegger's phenomenological project of an approach to Being itself. This project was organized around the Greek verb *phainesthai*,[97] which, at the root of the noun "phenomenon," he takes to mean a showing or appearing (*scheinen*) or, better still, the way in which a given reality shows itself or is made to appear. The temptation of visuality is still there, but more faintly, and Heidegger tries to deal with it even more energetically by insisting that the appearance of the reality in question—in this case, it is nothing less than Being itself, as opposed to the innumerable empirical beings all around us in the world—is at one and the same time its disappearance or waning, its withdrawal at the very moment of its emergence. Heidegger's ontology then posits a receptivity to this fleeting sense of Being which is difficult to distinguish from an active provocation of its emergence. In his later, more religious language, this deconcealment of Being is related to the mission of philosophy, which, if it cannot intervene in the world to summon a sense of Being, can at least attend to its silence and its absence; can induce a state of waiting and expectation and at best offer "a preparation of the readiness, of keeping oneself open for the arrival of or the absence of the god."[98]

Ricoeur's modification—to make Time appear—is (despite Heidegger's famous title) at once an interpretation of the *phainesthai* of *Sein und Zeit* and an implicit critique: since for Ricoeur Time is something which, in philosophy but more particularly in literature, can actively be made to appear as

---

[96] Else, *Aristotle's Poetics: The Argument*, 357–358.

[97] Heidegger, *Sein und Zeit*, par. 7A, 28–31.

[98] Martin Heidegger, "Only a God Can Save Us Now," in *The Heidegger Controversy*, ed. Richard Wolin, New York: Columbia University Press, 1991, 108.

such by way of those multiple and overlapping levels of temporality we have examined above.

Meanwhile our own modification of Ricoeur—to make History appear —will then return us to Heidegger in a rather different way, which might be characterized as the demonstration that Marxism is itself an ontology. Heidegger himself grudgingly admits as much, when in the postwar "Letter on Humanism" he identifies the ontological elements of the theory of alienation in the 1844 manuscripts[99]: but it might be argued that this concession was his way of hedging his bets, in a Europe in which the Red Army was but an hour or two away. Heidegger's student Herbert Marcuse had previously offered a stimulating argument for the fundamental historicity of Hegel's climactic notion of Life[100]; but did not prolong the story to the crucial issue of capital itself. The contemporary "capitalogicians" were more suggestive when they provocatively deduced the identity of Absolute Spirit to be capital itself,[101] thereby making a link between Hegel and Marx's "world market," and opening up a perspective in which the only meaningful totality today lies in globalization itself. But this perspective depends on an identification of History with capitalism on the one hand, and of capitalism with the Absolute on the other, which certainly both remain to be shown. Is it so then, as E. P. Thompson put it, that "sometimes the 'lonely hour of the last instance' really does come"?[102]

A few preliminaries will be necessary before we can make so audacious a claim. We may for example want to recall Else's reminder about complex and simple plots in the Aristotelian scheme of things. In complex plots, peripeteia and anagnorisis are part and parcel of pathos, and the experience of the latter is truly dialectical, insofar as it involves an articulation of these three categories which also unites them in a single reality, that of pathos itself, which, from being a word for one part of the process, comes to stand for the whole of the process itself as appearance (a dialectic not unlike the one Marx outlines in the 1857 introduction to the *Grundrisse*[103]). Thus a

---

[99] Martin Heidegger, "Brief über den Humanismus," Bern: A. Francke, 1947.

[100] Herbert Marcuse, *Hegel's Ontology and the Theory of Historicity*, trans. Seyla Benhabib, Cambridge, MA: MIT Press, 1987.

[101] *Kapitallogik*: see Hans-Georg Backhaus, *Dialektik der Wertform*, Freiburg: Ça ira, Freiburg: 1997; Helmut Reichelt, *Zur logischen Struktur des Kapitalbegriffes bei Karl Marx*, Ça ira: and most recently, Christopher J. Arthur, *The New Dialectic and Marx's Capital*, Leiden, Brill, 2004.

[102] E. P. Thompson, *The Poverty of Theory and Other Essays*, New York, Monthly Review Press, 1978, p. 98.

[103] The analogy would be Marx's deployment of the three fundamental categories of production, distribution, and consumption, where one of the three (production) is then elevated to govern that class of which it is itself a part. It is also worth adding

perception of the unity of opposites in Fate or Destiny (peripeteia) is achieved through the very recognition of historical agency (in anagnorisis), in their explosive unification with each other resulting in the first tragic tableau of pathos.

Yet Aristotle's simple plot, which eschews anagnorisis and peripeteia alike, would seem to offer the model of a single disaster or catastrophe in which history cataclysmically intervenes in individual life and takes the simple, overwhelming form of the irrevocable, whether in natural disaster, war, drought, depression, plague, atomic accident, or other events of the type we are tempted to call acts of God. It is ironic that we so often date History in terms of these "simple" catastrophes, and that it is in terms of nature or the natural that we should grasp History as what breaks into the continuity of daily life and the seemingly natural reproduction of the social routine. We will then want to wonder whether that daily life is itself to be considered unhistorical, as well as how History's complex plots are then to be imagined and read. Yet the inevitable expression of these "acts of God" in catastrophic terms will also require a different kind of reminder about Aristotle's *Poetics*.

For as is well known, these categories belong to a fragmentary treatise whose other (lost) half defined comedy. Comedy no doubt also knows its moments of pathos, in particular the exemplary punishments of its various misers and tyrants (in Molière and Shakespeare alike): whose defeats are however less the consequence of their moral defects (for the most part ludicrous rather than frightening) than they are the penalty of old age. The comic villains, insofar as they represent society and order, are all necessarily associated with that elder generation called upon to pass away. Comedy is the triumph of the young, or, as with Azdak, of those associated with their revolt or renewal, and with a new age coming into being. As such, it would seem obligatory to hypothesize this moment of triumph in a somewhat different fashion than is dictated by the tragic function of pathos, yet in a form or structure suitable to accommodate either outcome, as well as to specify either as just such a moment of the *phainesthai*, the coming to appearance, which we here seek but for which we will continue to use the original Aristotelian word "pathos" which was our starting point; we will return later on to the form some positive or Utopian version of pathos might take.

In any case, this prospect of a changing of the valences of pathos from negative to positive also complicates the opposition just posited, between a daily life where "nothing appears" and a discontinuous History which is

---

that there is a political advantage in distinguishing recognition from pathos (or the vision of history as a totality): serious mistakes have often been made when the discovery of a new historical agent has triumphalistically been celebrated as being the same as revolution, as the *phainesthai* (appearing) of History itself.

little more than a series of punctual breaks and catastrophes. Is it inconceivable that History might also be made to appear in those longer and seemingly uneventful continuities which the Annales School, with its multiple temporalities, sought to foreground in the place of the great historical personages and the great historical events (the slower changes in the geography and the institutions of the Mediterranean in place of the Battle of Lepanto and the decisions and temperament of Philip II)? Yet this possibility would seem to require more microscopic registering and recording instruments, capable of detecting the tremors of History in the existential itself, in the individual experience of biological subjects whose life span is disproportionate to the great, well-nigh geological rhythms of history itself. Ricoeur's work centers on the construction and calibration of such instruments in literature; and there is much to suggest that history, and allied disciplines such as ethnology, biography, and psychoanalysis, have here and there undertaken to conduct similar experiments. The question then arises whether postmodernity any longer wishes to honor these essentially modernist efforts and ambitions.

ii. Tableau and Temporality

We may now rewrite these themes and problems in terms of the concept of pathos as such, where the danger of visualization and reification must be balanced against the possibility of appearance as an event. This concept or category attempted indeed to square the circle and to combine the possibility of a tableau with the temporality of a destiny or a fate. But it is easier to observe this combination in the world of ancient tragedy, where history itself was limited by the dimensions of the city-state, and temporality by the seasonal campaigns, in which a given community sallies forth to destroy the crops of a neighbor, as well as by the shortness of individual life itself. It would seem quite another matter to inquire into the forms in which some modern sense of History makes itself felt. Still, for the dialectic, such tensions as that between tableau and temporality are not antinomies that bring us to a standstill, but rather contradictions that hold the promise of development as such.

The representational advantage of the notion of pathos in fact lay precisely in its capacity at least momentarily to reify history, to make it visible by forcing it to appear as an entity with a force of its own. This momentary arresting of the multiple and seemingly unrelated tendencies and currents of history may be thought of as their provisional (or even ephemeral) unification, and it is with this process that we must begin.

Sartre once observed, to those who like Lévi-Strauss challenged the very idea of history as a single entity of some kind, that this entity is itself historical, that History must itself gradually come into being in the course of history.[104] In the beginning, he tells us, there was no history, or rather there were many: the local histories of innumerable tribes, the vanishing histories of the peoples without writing or stable collective memories, the autonomous dynamics of states as isolated in space as so many galaxies. A single history begins to come into view only with the destruction of these multiple collective temporalities, with their unification into a single world system. That unification (or totalization) is what we call capitalism, and it is not yet complete in current globalization (the system's third stage), but will only be completed by universal commodification, by the world market as such.

Making history "appear" is then dependent on this process of unification, whose vicissitudes alone can generate the discontinuous situations in which such a glimpse is possible: which is to say that the "appearance" of History is dependent on the objective historical situations themselves. There is here a unity of theory and practice (or Foucault might call it an ambivalence of power and knowledge) according to which the cognitive (or representational) possibility of grasping the unity of history is at one with situations of praxis as well. Just as it is in revolutionary situations that the dichotomous classes are so radically simplified as to allow us to glimpse class struggle as such in a virtually pure form, so also only privileged historical crises allow us to "see" history as a process—and it is also in those crises that "history" is most vulnerable. The possibility of representation is then necessarily a political and a social possibility as well; and it is only by insisting on this objectivity that we can rescue the notion of pathos from aesthetic trivialization or, if you prefer, can endow the aesthetic with its appropriate political and practical dimension as well.

This way of staging the problem of the appearance of History then raises the stakes well beyond Ricoeur's humanism at the same time that it reifies all the elements in a different way. Braudel's Mediterranean is "unified" by the emergence and emergent conflict of the two great world empires at either end, but its historical destiny—epitomized by the Battle of Lepanto on the one hand, and the death of Philip II on the other—only becomes visible when the Mediterranean world begins to come apart and the center of gravity of world history shifts to the Atlantic. But neither the "pathos" of this decline nor our own identification of revolution with representation above is a satisfactory way of coming to terms with the problem adequately. For here the place of the visual (in this higher-level temptation) is taken by the old notion of an entity or substance, a unified object of some kind, which could finally be the object of "representation" in much the same spirit as the ideological error denounced by Heidegger, in his attack on "worldviews."[105]

---

104 See Lévi-Strauss, *La Pensée sauvage*, and Jean-Paul Sartre, *Critique de la raison dialectique*, Paris: Gallimard, 1960.

105 Martin Heidegger, "Die Zeit des Weltbildes" in *Holzwege*, Frankfurt: Klostermann, 1980, 73–110.

For Heidegger, indeed, the reification of the worldview is one of the consequences of the modern split between subject and object, the triumph of epistemology over ontology, or even—as with the passage from the Greek experience of being to Roman or Latin abstraction[106]—the will to dominate and possess a world which has itself become a kind of thing, a realm of gray Cartesian extension, a geography from which the great primal tension between Earth and World[107] has been eliminated. This now familiar diagnosis of modernity should not obscure the immensely influential and still potent critique of representation Heidegger deduced from it, even though we are here using the term "representation" in a more general and more neutral sense.

Indeed, the insistence of the Heideggerian critique and the Marxian diagnosis of reification that preceded it both require us to correct our attempt to think History through the category of pathos by specifying that the object of such representation is not an entity but rather a contradiction, and that a contradiction is not a thing and cannot be pictured or imagined as a kind of static object. What is here to be represented can also be described as a totality, provided the latter is identified with contradiction as such: and at one and the same time specified as a non-thing, a non-object. Yet if it is not spatial or visual, it is not to be thematized as temporal either (although that temptation is certainly stronger for historical chronology and even for Hegelian dialectical contradictions than the spatial one). The commitment of contemporary philosophy to a kind of absolute present is helpful in resisting this temptation, but not in keeping faith with those pasts and futures, that collective experience, with which a dialectical conception of historical necessity seeks to enlarge the existential and the private or personal.

But here the dialectic must part company with tragedy, or at least with that fragment of Aristotle's treatise that deals exclusively with pathos in its modern sense of the contemplation of suffering and misery. To be sure, it must necessarily deal primarily with that: and any glimpse of History today must necessarily constitute a long, dizzying look into the nightmare of history. Such a vision can in the very nature of things not last, it cannot be long endured ("to see how much I can bear," was Max Weber's suggestive account of his own essentially historical vocation). Meanwhile, like all such encounters with the totality, the event stages an intersection between the singular and the universal, taking a specific historical moment and situation as the seldom opened door to an unimaginably interminable flight backwards towards the very beginnings of human history. Nor, save for pity and terror, is the content of such an experience at all stable: for the ancients, the

---

[106] Heidegger, "Der Ursprung des Kunstwerkes" in *Holzwege*, 7–9.
[107] Ibid., 26–35.

brevity of life; for the Christian centuries, the omnipresence of sin and an incorrigibly corrupt human nature—can we really assume that these obsessive themes are anything more than the scarecrows with which dominant classes tried to keep their subordinates in line? At any rate, they have left records and traces of revulsion and horror in the surviving literature, about which we can only assume that it was a hegemonic and not a popular expression. But as we approach, in the eighteenth century, that more democratic age that capitalism began to open in the West, a new preoccupation with imprisonment, tyranny and despotism, arbitrary punishment, fanaticism, and superstition begins to inflect political passion, and to prepare the overthrow of the old regimes. Yet the installation of parliamentary systems and a relative political equality only serves to shift the horror and to disclose the deeper perspective of labor as such, of the factory as prison, as a lifelong toil, which then retroactively illuminates the time of the laboring body in a new and perhaps more salvational perspective.

These are all so many historical totalizations of History, and as such they have their absolute truth as well as their historical and theoretical relativity. Thucydides' unification of the interminable Peloponnesian War under the tragic concept of Fate (along with the moralizing religious notions of hubris that accompanied it)[108] still has the deeper truth for us of identifying a necessity at work beneath the contingencies of the empirical events, implacably expressing itself through their ephemeral victories as well as their local defeats. This conception of historicity as necessity must still be ours, however much it must be grasped in terms of oppositions not yet available to the Greek historian, such as the potential or exhaustion of modes of production. But it would be wrong to assume that our own relationship to such oppositions—yesterday the contradiction between determinism and freedom, tomorrow that between conspiracy and Utopia—is any less mired in ideology than those of earlier moments of human history. The only advantage we have over the historians of the past is that of the comparative enlargement of our own history as it approaches a truly global one.

iii. Two Totalities

But now we need to return to the processes of unification and totalization in order to have a clearer idea of what is at stake. I will propose two exhibits of such moments, in which a stream of events suddenly seems to be interrupted by the chance for a glimpse of the entire historical system, which can however itself be alternately characterized as system or as event. After that, I want to formulate our possible relationships to such phenomena, which are best conceptualized, not in the current language of universalization (as

---

[108] Francis Cornford, *Thucydides Myth-historicus*, London: E. Arnold, 1907.

opposed to singularities), but perhaps more satisfactorily in terms of an older religious language of the Absolute: after which it will be possible to make an approach to the fateful question of the valences of historical pathos, and its twin negative and positive faces.

The first exhibit will be a moment in Sartre's eve-of-war novel, *Le Sursis* (*The Reprieve*), in which, à la Dos Passos, multiple destinies intertwine on the way to a climactic fusion, its title only provisionally confirmed by the postponement of the Munich Pact. The following reflection, in indirect discourse, is not the philosophical climax of this work (which famously takes place in Mathieu's discovery, on the Pont Neuf, of the nature of freedom); but it is in many ways the novel's central experience, the auto-referentiality of its cross-cutting technique, and the demonstration of that non-freedom or dependency-against which alone the thesis of freedom can be judged and evaluated:

> A vast entity, a planet, in a space of a hundred million dimensions; three-dimensional beings could not so much as imagine it. And yet each dimension was an autonomous consciousness. Try to look directly at that planet, it would disintegrate into tiny fragments, and nothing but consciousnesses would be left. A hundred million free consciousnesses, each aware of walls, the glowing stump of a cigar, familiar faces, and each constructing its destiny on its own responsibility. And yet each of those consciousnesses, by imperceptible contacts and insensible changes, realizes its existence as a cell in a gigantic and invisible coral. War: everyone is free, and yet the die is cast. It is there, it is everywhere, it is the totality of all my thoughts, of all Hitler's words, of all Gomez's acts; but no one is there to add it up. It exists solely for God. But God does not exist. And yet war exists.[109]

In such an experience, History is truly registered as a nightmare; but it is not the dizzying nightmare of immemorial slaughter and carnage, and of an

---

[109] *The Reprieve*, trans. Eric Sutton, New York: Knopf, 1947, 326; in French: "Un corps énorme, une planète, dans un espace à cent millions de dimensions; les êtres à trois dimensions ne pouvaient même pas l'imaginer. Et pourtant chaque dimension était une conscience autonome. Si on essayait de regarder la planète en face, elle s'effondrait en miettes, il ne restait plus que des consciences. Cent millions de consciences libres, dont chacune voyait des murs, un bout de cigare rougeoyant, des visages familiers, et construisait sa destinée sous sa propre responsabilité. Et pourtant, si l'on *était* une de ces consciences on s'apercevait à d'imperceptibles effleurements, à d'insensibles changements, qu'on était solidaire d'un gigantesque et invisible polypier. La guerre: chacun est libre et pourtant les jeux sont faits. Elle est là, elle est partout, c'est la totalité de toutes mes pensées, de toutes les paroles d'Hitler, de tous les actes de Gomez: mais personne n'est là pour faire le total. Elle n'existe que pour Dieu. Mais Dieu n'existe pas. Et pourtant la guerre existe." *Le Sursis*, in *Oeuvres romanesques*, Paris: Gallimard, 1981, 1,024–1,025.

inveterate human malice that no religion or political system has ever been able to wipe out. (The characters of *Le Sursis* are all in *mauvaise foi*, no doubt, but far from being uniformly malignant.) Rather, this nightmare is one of helpless interdependence, of a population growing aware of its collective nature by way of helplessness and passivity as such. A Sartrean rhetoric of the imperceptible theft of my freedom by other people is here parlayed into a kind of vision of the Absolute, an absolute of bodies packed together in a cattle car in motion towards an unknown fate. But "vision" is the wrong word, as we have learned already: for this is not an achieved representation, it is a representation of Mathieu forcing himself to philosophize about something he can neither think nor represent, and turning this failure into an improbably cognitive achievement. The achievement bears the philosophical name of totality, and it will be at once clear that attacks on this "concept" in the name of its omniscience or its pretense of intellectual mastery are utterly misplaced. At best, it can be said to constitute the individual or existential attempt to grasp the collective dimension of individual existence; and, to rehearse a now familiar Sartrean dialectic, it can only succeed by failing.

Yet we must also note the way in which this revelation, itself a kind of event, is dependent on the Event as such: it is only on the occasion of certain of its events that History can be grasped as an Event in its own right: the great convulsive crises, of which war is clearly paradigmatic, are here presumed to be radically different from the everyday, the routines of peacetime, the world of repetition in which nothing in particular happens. Sartre's "aesthetic of extreme situations" is thus at the antipodes of the Annales School and their program, to downgrade events in historiography and foreground longer and longer *durées*: whether they could achieve historical narrative is as interesting a question as whether Sartre could ever do justice to everyday life (*La nausée* being itself a crisis of a well-nigh physical type).

At any rate, with Sartre and war we touch a moment in which History undoubtedly appears, as an absent totality and as an experience of anxiety, if not of horror. Let us now examine another comparable moment in which the glimpse of History brings with it a kind of giddy exultation. This is Immanuel Kant's characterization of the French Revolution, in which History is experienced as the very incarnation of that freedom as whose absence Mathieu lived it:

> The revolution of a gifted people which we have seen unfolding in our day may succeed or miscarry; it may be filled with misery and atrocities to the point that a sensible man, were he boldly to hope to execute it successfully the second time, would never resolve to make the experiment at such cost—this revolution, I say, nonetheless finds in the hearts of all spectators (who are not engaged in this game themselves) a wishful participation that borders closely on enthusiasm, the very

expression of which is fraught with danger; this sympathy, therefore, can have no other cause than a moral predisposition in the human race.[110]

This celebration of an event as momentous to its contemporaries as World War II seems to lie at the opposite end of the affective spectrum from Sartre's characteristically energetic pessimism: to an historical situation in which people feel absolutely powerless is here juxtaposed a revolutionary moment in which freedom and collective self-determination are triumphantly exhibited and rehearsed. For the philosopher of enlightenment, the French Revolution is truly a moment in which a whole people passes from the status of collective minor or ward of despotic authorities and comes of age, above all "by providing itself with a civil constitution."

And yet both passages record encounters with History and memorialize moments in which truly History can be said to have appeared. I want to argue for what both experiences have in common, beginning with their charge of affect as such: distinct in that from the heterogeneous catalogue of empirical emotions and feelings, affect can be described as one immense mood swing from high to low, from moments of exaltation to bad trips and comprehensive depressions. What Kant characterizes as "enthusiasm" is thus intimately related to what is today analyzed as melancholy, and indeed the two states are dialectically related in a kind of affective union of opposites. In both, then, the intensity of affect signals the transformation of empirical experiences into transcendental ones, the looming sense of the proximity of totalities beyond the immediate particulars.

In fact, both accounts register this process: Sartre does so negatively, by bringing the whole weight of the contemporary crisis of representation to bear on the word—in this case, "revolution"—which is indispensable and yet incapable of naming so immense and overwhelming a phenomenon. Kant, meanwhile, characteristically describes his version of the experience in terms of the Idea that shines through the news and current events of empirical history: "the pure concept of right" as it resists self-interest either of a "monetary reward" or in the vested class interest of "the old martial nobility."

We must take seriously the objection that both these passages are cognitive and contemplative rather than narrative and that they are didactic as well, aiming to convey ideas rather than concrete mimeses of actions. Sartre explicitly shows us Mathieu in the act of thinking (and of thinking Sartre's own thoughts); while Kant explicitly underscores the historicality of the experience he describes: it takes an historical event as its occasion ("such a phenomenon in human history is not to be forgotten"[111]), but isolates it from its immediate historical or narrative context and brackets it as a

---

[110] Kant, *The Conflict of the Faculties*, 153.
[111] Ibid., 159.

possible cause of anything ("even if the end viewed in connection with this event should not now be attained, even if the revolution or reform of a national constitution should finally miscarry"). He thereby transforms a unique historical event into a permanent possibility or potentiality of human collectivities.

In effect, such objections are tantamount to converting an encounter with history into a thought about history; and they are to be juxtaposed with those other kinds of objections which see in both passages a merely subjective expression of feelings about the objects they are contemplating. Both objections therefore reduce us to a world of purely empirical experiences, a world on its way to a thoroughgoing nominalism. They fly in the face of the phenomenological force of modern philosophy (and even of the phenomenological tendencies in Kant) for which knowing (with its purely epistemological problems) is not to be radically separated from other intentionalities and other relationships to the objective world, such as the affective: or, if you prefer, for which affect is also a form of knowing and a consciousness of what used to be called objectivity. Like the dialectic, phenomenology also underscores the "preponderance of the object" (Adorno). All the more must this be the case when that object is of a transcendental type, something that immensely exceeds our own individual capacities for perception and for cognition. This is the sense in which both experiences and their descriptions are expressions of the "sublime" in Kant's sense, and suggests, indeed, that the sublime is itself always the sign or symptom (*Geschichtszeichen*, says Kant) of an approach to History as such (or of its approach to us).

Yet for Kant the sublime was specified as a mode of aesthetic judgment, and we must also take into account Jean-François Lyotard's suggestion, fraught with ideological consequences, that what Kant here describes is precisely an aesthetic experience, and that such enthusiasms for revolutionary politics are always the reactions of spectators to the political scene rather than participants.[112] Indeed, does not Kant himself insist on the relatively disinterested spirit of his enthusiasts? It is not only that their positive feelings for events in another country are not to be taken as threats to their own monarchy, but above all that they are an "uninvolved public looking on ... without the least intention of assisting."[113] They are not thereby tempted to execute such a revolution for the second time, given its miscarriages and its "misery and atrocities"[114]; in any case, Kant adds, revolution "is always unjust."[115]

---

[112] Jean-François Lyotard, *Le différend*, Paris: Minuit, 1983, 238–240.

[113] Kant, *The Conflict of the Faculties*, 157.

[114] Ibid., 153.

[115] Ibid., 157.

I would be inclined to respond that this view of the aesthetic as a bracketing of reality is the depoliticizing ideology of a current aestheticism which does not even do justice to the high-modernist practice to which it appeals or to the German idealism (very much including Kant) which it purports to enlist. It is, however, enough to note that very different views of the relationship of the aesthetic to reality are available, very much including Heidegger's that art is one of the essential ways in which truth "sets itself into work."[116]

Yet the very notion that aesthetic spectatorship is a passive-contemplative distance from reality may also be addressed in a different way, one opened up for us by our contemporary experience of globalization. Even in the modern (or imperialist) period the outside world was never simply an object of disinterested thought or aesthetic consumption: but rather a symbolic experience of that part of our own extended reality which was repressed and occulted by virtue of our privileged position in the world system. Our participation in the radically different situations of other populations greatly transcends the origins of the breakfast food we consume or the gas we use in our automobiles. It is wrong to imagine such relationships in an unmediated way, as we do when we think of them in terms of a pseudo-concept like "influence." There is here an action at distance, which may be mimetic or may even involve an inversion of structures. What can only be posited in advance is the way in which a distant (and absent) space within an international or globalized system opens up possibilities for me which are different from anything in my own situation. What is called influence is then simply the sense that something hitherto unsuspected is possible, which I can then reinvent by way of an imaginary reproduction or indeed by revulsion and flight.

War is, to be sure, the potentiation and becoming-actual of all those occulted virtualities: the presence of those absent enemies which peacetime and daily life confined to newspaper or television news when their existence intersected at all with my own. (And to be sure, the media are also dimensions of our inextricable and unconscious involvements in the world system —more on the order of Kant's *Geschichtszeichen* than of any direct representational channels.)

This is the sense in which Kant's enthusiasm in the kingdom of Prussia for the revolution in Paris is far from being a purely contemplative one: this new space of political and economic possibility opening up in what it would be anachronistic to call a First World country has profound consequences for the life world of the German principalities, then certainly Third World entities. Nor is this a one-way street; and it is not only in our own time that

---

[116] Heidegger, "Der Ursprung des Kunstwerkes," 49.

movement in peripheral or semi-peripheral spaces has impacted the experience and the concrete perspectives of the states of the core—witness the impact of the Haitian Revolution on Hegel himself, as Susan Buck-Morss has revealed it to us.[117] Indeed, if History is a totality, or better still a process of totalization, one which is an ongoing incorporation of ever more extensive parts of the globe, then its experience will necessarily include a new and original relationship of absence to presence, of the far to the near and the external to the internal: it will not only be a "sign" of the historical as Kant thought but a mode of grasping these new and hitherto unsuspected relationships and of bringing them to consciousness.

But now we must return to that union of opposites as which we have characterized these two historical testimonies: for it is time to explore the dialectical nature of the encounter with History and to affirm that it can be lived in the two distinct valences of horror and of enthusiasm. The approach to History, its ephemeral encounter as an Event, can be shattering or energizing, the experience of defeat or on the contrary the awakening of immense possibilities and the sense that *tout est possible*. For the opposite of defeat or of searing impotence is not the cheap and self-congratulatory gloating satisfaction of victory but rather precisely the initiation of new activity and the animation of new forces and unsuspected potentialities. Marx can give us a sense of this dialectical ambivalence when, at the very center and as it were narrative climax of *Capital*, Volume I, he suddenly transports us to a new dialectical level and introduces the dimension of the collective.

This is the chapter on "cooperation" in which Marx, controlling his "enthusiasm," outlines the ways in which the new social division of labor (not discussed until this point) constitutes "the creation of a new productive power, which is intrinsically a collective one" (*Cap*, 443). References to Aristotle's famous metaphysical definition (man as a political animal, which Marx rightly translates as meaning "the citizen of a town") and to Franklin's dictum that man is a "tool-making animal" (*Cap*, 444, n. 7) suggest a swirling of the waters from which Marx's own metaphysic—man as a "social animal," the human distinctiveness of the collective—will abruptly surface. Cooperation is then very precisely that lifting of human life to a new dialectical level: the worker's labor time does not increase, but his productivity immediately rises—"a free gift to capital," Marx exults (*Cap*, 451). Meanwhile the first references to Darwin hint at the temporal perspective of the new dimension and its originary function ("capitalist production really only begins," he tells us, with just such multiplicity and collectivite labor [*Cap*, 432]). The thematics of collectivity thereby wins its right to be a

---

[117] Susan Buck-Morss, "Hegel and Haiti," in *Critical Inquiry*, Vol. 26, Num. 4, Summer 2000, 821–865.

candidate for some properly Marxist philosophy as such, alongside notions of alienation and of productivity.

But the story does not conclude there, for in the very next chapter it is pursued in far more somber tones, reflecting the way in which "cooperation" or the collective assignment of tasks and social division of labor is historically objectified in the machine itself, the vehicle for an industrial capitalism Marx sharply distinguishes from the latter's "manufacturing" stage. Now, in a prophetic anticipation of Taylorization, Marx rewrites Hegel's "geistiges Tierreich" ("zoological kingdom of the spirit") as a teratology and, the Whitmanesque enthusiasms of the enumeration of various parts of the machine (the watch mechanisms and their production [*Cap*, 451–452]), denounces the machine's conversion of "the worker into a crippled monstrosity by furthering his particular skill as in a forcing-house, through the suppression of a whole world of productive drives and inclinations, just as in the states of La Plata they butcher a whole beast for the sake of his hide or his tallow" (*Cap*, 481).

Now slowly the moment of historical totalization looms into view. Marx unmasks, in passing, the celebratory rhetoric of the apologists of industrial capitalism, who (like those of globalization later on) transfer their admiration of the productivity of the individual factory's division of labor to the "anarchy" of production in the market system as a whole (*Cap*, 477, 635). It is not in that "market freedom" that History is glimpsed, however, but in the materiality of the machine itself:

> an organized system of machines to which motion is communicated by the transmitting mechanism from an automatic centre is the most developed form of production by machinery. Here we have, in place of the isolated machine, a mechanical monster whose body fills whole factories, and whose demonic power, at first hidden by the slow and measured motions of its gigantic members, finally bursts forth in the fast and feverish whirl of its countless working organs. (*Cap*, 503; and see also 544)

So it is that even in Marx the very same process can know a dual, antithetical expression: first in the enthusiasm for the collective which will finally touch a Utopian future by way of a modest invocation of that "association of free men" (*Cap*, 171) and which gives us a glimpse of "the organization of the labor of society in accordance with an approved and authoritative plan" (*Cap*, 477); and then the dystopia of machinery which yields in nothing to the nightmare of futuristic anxieties.

Marx thereby confirms the impression that the identification of historical tendencies obeys that dialectical rhythm called the unity of opposites, in which a given phenomenon can be marked alternately as positive or negative without falling under the law of noncontradiction or requiring any definitive choice of one or the other of the apparent alternatives. Not only does such a phenomenon challenge the static habit of conventional ethical logic—the exclusivity of good and bad, of the negative and positive valences —it also incites us to probe more deeply into the structure of the phenomenon itself in order to touch the dialectic at its core.

iv. History as System

In the phenomenon that interests us here, the sudden flash of a sense of history, we must somehow account for the evidence that History in that sense can be experienced either as a nightmare or as a sudden opening and possibility that is lived in enthusiasm. It is an alternation which suggests the existence of some deeper duality in the thing itself: the way in which, for example, the appearing of History, its *phainesthai*, entails a new opening up of past and future alike, which can conceivably be marked antithetically: a somber past of violence and slaughter giving way to a new sense of collective production, or on the contrary a glimpse of promise in the past which is shut down by a closing of horizons in universal catastrophe. Better still, both these dimensions can be experienced at one and the same time, in an undecideable situation in which the reemergence of History is unrelated to its content and dependent above all on that form in which after a long reduction to the lowered visibility of the present, past and future once again open up in the full transparency of their distances.

But this opposition between the blindness of the present and the deep breath of the deployment of the temporal ek-stases still gives us little more than a formal account, which we need to trace back to its conditions of possibility, that is to say, to recode in this or that language of content. I want to suggest that—leaving the negative and positive valences out of it for the moment—we reread this alternation as one between the figures of the total system, on the one hand, and of the Event on the other, provided "Event" is here understood itself as being of a systemic nature, namely a convulsion capable of transforming an older system as such and reaching through all the layers of the social totality. Space and time, then, or better still, synchronic and diachronic, or even, perhaps, Spinoza versus Hegel, an all-encompassing totality versus a rushing stream of temporalities, a total flow of experience. Either one of these poles can then be articulated into an opposition between individual and collective, or even subject and object, insofar as either space or time can be reduced to individual experience, or on the other hand grasped as an unimaginable multiplicity. This alternation then no doubt also constitutes the distinction between Kant's two forms of the sublime, the mathematical and the dynamic, that of scale and that of sheer power. In all these possibilities, however, what counts is not the weighing of one pole against the other, their evaluation in terms of good and evil—about which our point has been that there seems to be a ceaseless transformation of the one back and forth into the other—so much as the fact and experience of opposition itself. Whether this duality is a permanent characteristic of history, extending back into a so-called prehistory, where it remains latent and as yet imperceptible, only to be called forth by capitalism and globalization itself, or whether the oppositional structure is itself a new historical phenomenon developing in correlation with the emergence of the world market, is a question that cannot be answered deductively, but which it is also productive to place on the agenda.

But it is obvious that from a current perspective the notion of system (and, along with it, of totality) will tend to be experienced negatively, as an omnipresent nightmarish constraint; while that of the Event tends (as in Kant, above) to be read as an expression of freedom and possibility. We will therefore for the moment respect this eudaimonic form however ideological, and disregard the fact that both poles of this opposition are organized around figures of unification, rather than of difference and diversity.

The category of the system has known a rich contemporary elaboration beginning with the rediscovery of structural linguistics; and it is not necessary to recapitulate all of its familiar features, such as its organization by binary oppositions along with a theory of synchronic understanding which relegates diachronic thought to the merely mechanical or additive. What it may be more useful to emphasize in the sketch we propose of an experience of History as all-encompassing system, will be Michael Mann's conception of encagement, of the way in which a system keeps itself in being by mechanisms which exclude its dissolution and prevent it either from reverting to an earlier form or being assimilated and transformed by a later or more advanced one.[118]

This was already implicit in Marx's relatively untheorized conception of system as "mode of production," where historical examples underscore the necessary destruction of the older mode of production by the newer one which seeks to supplant it. Enclosure is a classical example of this process and not limited to Marxian accounts of the emergence of capitalism and the displacement of agricultural societies by money economies. Marx's discussions of the destruction of the older relatively self-sufficient village communities in India are complemented by his description of the static or changeless structures of such societies (also called the Asiatic mode of production), which know only a ceaseless replacement of dynasties and tributary rulers at the top, and a ceaseless reproduction of peasant economies at their base. Marx then sometimes characterizes these reproductive mechanisms more explicitly, as in this account of the way in which the older guilds

---

[118] Michael Mann, *The Sources of Social Power*, Vol. 1, Cambridge: Cambridge University Press, 1986, 124–127.

resist transformation into the new manufacturing system as this last expands in the direction of industrial capitalism: "the rules of the guilds ... deliberately hindered the transformation of the single master into a capitalist, by placing very strict limits on the number of apprentices and journeymen he could employ" (*Cap*, 479). Manufacture, whose own transformation into industrial capitalism turns on the new division of labor of the machine, knows only a relative period of dominance owing precisely to the lack of such mechanisms.

At its most dramatic, this struggle between systems must display the system as possessing a kind of conatus, in that it keeps itself in being, and it knows an innate drive to persevere and to flourish at all costs; and also that it must necessarily destroy and eliminate any other systems (residual or emergent) that threaten to take its place and occupy its space.

The first of these demonstrations may find its analogy in the work of Pierre Clastres on tribal society, or more specifically on hunters-and-gatherers, about which he found himself able to identify the principle whereby such a system (or mode of production) was able to prevent itself from becoming a society organized around power, in this case around the emergence of the so-called big men. State power in general, and big men in particular, can only emerge as a result of surplus, which enables the support and the perpetuation of non-productive members, of army or bodyguards (or of ideologists in the case of priests). Surplus is in any case more widely possible only with agriculture and granaries: but in the societies with which he was working Clastres identified a possible instantiation of power in the superfluity of meat returned by successful or talented, or physically more powerful hunters. This threat to the mode of production of the hunters-and-gatherers is then forestalled by a simple rule, itself the very mechanism of its survival and reproduction, namely that the hunter is forbidden to eat his own kill.[119] He is thus automatically dependent on the game brought back by others, while his own bounty serves the purpose of collective redistribution and communal sustenance.

Michael Mann's contribution to this development of the idea of system will lie in the positing of a mechanism whereby the new system triumphantly wards off any breakdown and regression into the older ones: a state of dominance it presumably does not reach until its drive towards expansion has been defeated numerous times by the defense mechanisms of the older forms of society and production, that is to say, by the reversion (devolution) of new and emergent social forms to earlier and simpler ones.

> Civilization was an abnormal phenomenon. It involved the state and social stratification, both of which human beings have spent most of their existence avoiding.

---

[119] Pierre Clastres, *La Société contre l'état*, Paris: Minuit, 1974, 99.

The conditions under which, on a very few occasions, civilization did develop, therefore, are those that made avoidance no longer possible. The ultimate significance of alluvial agriculture, present in all "pristine" civilizations, was the territorial constraint it offered in a package with a large economic surplus. When it became irrigation agriculture, as it usually did, it also increased social constraint. The population was caged into particular authority relations.

But that was not all. Alluvial and irrigation agriculture also caged surrounding populations, again inseparably from economic opportunity. Trading relations also caged (though usually to a lesser extent) pastoralists, rain-watered agriculturalists, fishermen, miners, and foresters over the whole region ... It was now relatively difficult for the population caged there to turn their backs on emerging authority and inequality, as they had done on countless occasions in prehistory.[120]

Mann's theory of encagement has unique resonance for us today, when older national unities are in the process of being assimilated into that new and more comprehensive system called globalization, their former self-sufficiencies eliminated in the name of the emergence of a new kind of international division of labor and interdependence of production.

That the new system is often experienced in a relatively nightmarish mode may be illustrated by Stephanie Black's excellent documentary on Jamaica entitled *Life and Debt* (2001), in which we witness the systematic destruction of Jamaica's chicken industry by American corporations, which drive the locals out of business by flooding the home market with cheap chicken products whose prices they cannot match. At length, when the home competition no longer exists, the foreign producers, secure in their monopolies, raise the prices again. This practice, in all the relative fields of production, secures Jamaica, an immensely rich and fertile land, as a satellite in the new global system, utterly dependent on imported food and on an international division of labor imposed from the outside. In such a system the new and unwilling member is generally assigned a specific mono-culture or export crop as its contribution. In this case, besides sugar and tobacco, the function assigned to Jamaica in the system would seem to be tourism, which is indeed one of the fundamental new industries developed under globalization, and ensuring as it were the Disneyfication and the transformation into spectacles and simulacra of the older historical and social realities.

This new form of Mann's encagement will also strengthen the impression not only that the system is dystopian, but that it is also a conspiracy. "What kind of a crime is the robbing of a bank," asked Brecht, "compared to the founding of a bank?" And the same question may be posed to the new global monopolies. But if the ideology of conspiracy is a prevalent one today in full

---

[120] Mann, *The Sources of Social Power*, 124.

postmodernity, serving indeed a kind of political and pedagogical function, it must not be forgotten that it also—as human intention and act—begins to swing the characterization back away from system and towards Event as such. This is the spirit in which the great business conspiracies—those of the neo-conservative or free-market ideologists, or of the oligarchs in post-Soviet Russia—may also be greeted as immensely creative and world-historical acts, on the order of other innovative strategic interventions in earlier recorded history (including Heidegger's *staatsgründende Tat*).

v. History as Event

We must now therefore turn away from that face of History which is the increasing constriction of a given historical unification, perceived as a totality, towards that other code and interpretive possibility which is that of the Event and indeed the Act as such. Here it seems to me most fitting to recall the classic Althusserian conception of structural causality, now read as an account of the Event as such.[121] It should be remembered that like the experience of totality or system just evoked, structural causality also designates a unification of multiplicity (or in Ricoeur's language, a discordant concordance), but in a kind of perceptual inversion of the first form. There what was foregrounded in the phenomenon—that is to say, what comes first in the cognitive perception—was the nightmarish unification itself, the sense that everything is linked together in some properly monstrous encagement; along with the temporality of the perception of this glimpse of History itself, as pathos and spectacle, a temporality which demands that we first glimpse the One and only then begin to discern the Many—that it is the conspiracy itself which is foregrounded, only subsequently enabling an analytic inventory of its components, features, factors, and items. An immense thing like totality precedes the dawning horror of everything swept and swallowed up in its network.

On the Althusserian conception, on the contrary, it is the variety of the factors and participants that comes first: historical agents, "pre-given" situations, contingencies and accidents from other series (natural as well as man-made), spatial concentrations, the temporalities of multiple cultural and national traditions (in the case of war), or of multiple groups, classes and class-fractions (in the case of internal crises), and so forth. Here it is the incomprehensible fact of an inexhaustible multiplicity that confers a retroactive power of unification on the event itself: what Althusser calls overdetermination is then a reconsideration and an enumeration of this multiplicity after the fact of its unification as a single event we name (and ritually date). Perhaps an older Sartrean language can usefully disentangle

---

[121] Louis Althusser, "Contradiction and Overdetermination" and "On the Materialist Dialectic," in *For Marx*, trans. Ben Brewster, London: New Left Books, 1969.

the two experiences: if system is apprehended as a totality, then the Event is grasped in its totalization, as a process.

From another thematic perspective, it may then be said that system relentlessly transforms all its "human" elements into something like a natural and inhuman determinism; while the logic of the Event draws everything non-human into its recoding as will and as act. The prototype of this process might then be that geological substratum which the strategist transforms into a landscape that becomes a scene for military confrontation and the elaboration of strategy: the geographical markets and accidents transformed into a battlefield (real or potential), which gradually acquires its own name and enters history as a deed either successful or abortive.

Put this way, it becomes clear that the perspectives can also be reversed, and that our account of a system as a conspiracy then reconverts a seemingly "natural" process into an intentional act; while the unpredictability of outcomes tends to turn the history of actors and agents back into something like chemical interaction or a seismographic accident. Still, the opposition between these two modes of encountering History will be useful only on condition of maintaining their differences; and in that spirit one might take War as the paradigm of the first or systemic mode, while Revolution becomes that of the second one and of History as event and as collective act.

However this opposition is positioned, it unites phenomena which share a dual existence as One and as Many, as a multiplicity which corresponds to our empirical experience of history as a time of succession and a space of random and optional perception, suddenly and sharply transformed by a conviction of profound unity and interdependence, of an irreversible dimension of relationality that cannot be apprehended directly as an object, but which rises behind this multiplicity as a transcendence on the order of Heideggerian Being. The experience of History is impossible without this dual perspective of system and event. Each without the other falls short of History and into another category altogether: the isolated sense of unity becoming philosophy and metaphysics, the experience of merely empirical events becoming at best existential narrative and at worst a kind of inert or positivistic knowledge.

vi. History as Absolute

The word "Absolute" has been pronounced in connection with this phenomenon, along with the even less timely philosophical term "transcendence". In conclusion, it will be necessary to specify the nature of the relationship to either of these things which defines the experience of History; and in particular to disentangle it from religious stereotypes as well as from the static aesthetic-contemplative spectatorship implied by Aristotle's theatrical pathos as well as Kant's seemingly purely receptive enthusiasm.

The notion of a relationship to the Absolute can apparently not be shorn of its overtones of authenticity or of truth, however much we may wish to secularize it or even to endow it with a possibility of praxis. But at this point a conventional distinction between modernism and the postmodern seems to impose itself: the former insisting on a radical distinction between a life in the Absolute and the fallen behavior of a repetitive daily life and a degraded culture; while the problematic of postmodernity always seems to regenerate the interminable quarrels over relativism by recalling the inevitable multiplicity of absolutes that confront each other in a postmodern age.

The example of Heidegger remains a useful space in which to discuss these problems, but another, now equally untimely and disgraced, writer from the modern period will be helpful in dramatizing the argument. For the language of the Absolute was indeed borrowed from a writer for whom none of Heidegger's modes of truth (see below) was alien, and whose life and work can for that very reason sometimes come to seem an implacable posturing and a repertoire of portentous lies and gestures, of metaphysical affectations no less suspicious than the Heideggerian solemnities, although of a wholly different style and range. But perhaps it is only by way of such excess that the Absolute can be made visible and inescapable at all. It is not only in the transcendences of art—human and inhuman—as André Malraux evokes them in *The Voices of Silence*, but even in the very passions of the characters of *La Condition humaine* that one finds a relativity of absolutes that may be helpful to us here (this is old Gisors, something like the omniscient sage at the very center of that labyrinth which is *La Condition humaine*, reflecting on the destiny of the various characters who surround him):

> "Red or Blue," said Ferral, "the coolies will continue to be coolies just the same; unless they have been killed off. Don't you consider it a stupidity characteristic of the human race that a man who has only one life should be willing to lose it for an idea?"
>
> "It is very rare for a man to be able to endure—how shall I say it?—his condition, his fate as a man ..."
>
> Gisors thought of one of Kyo's ideas: all that men are willing to die for, beyond self-interest, tends more or less obscurely to justify that fate by giving it a foundation in dignity: Christianity for the slave, the nation for the citizen, Communism for the worker. But he had no desire to discuss Kyo's ideas with Ferral. He came back to the latter:
>
> "There is always a need for intoxication: this country has opium, Islam has hashish, the West has women ... Perhaps love is above all the means which the Occidental uses to free himself from man's fate ..."
>
> Under his words flowed an obscure and hidden counter-current of figures: Ch'en and murder, Clappique and his madness, Katov and the Revolution, May and love, himself and opium ... Kyo alone, in his eyes, resisted these categories.[122]

But, like Heidegger, Malraux will anchor his observations of these various life-passions in human finitude ("sa condition d'homme"), which is to say in the fact of death: something which then immediately transfers the center of gravity of the analysis from object to subject, from the objective nature of the commitment to the subjective need of individual *Dasein*. However, when Sartrean existentialism boldly jettisons this metaphysical remnant and abandons the death anxiety as some ultimate motive (substituting for it freedom as such), we descend into a true relativity of life-passions or authentic commitments and originary choices from which a Kantian ethics of respect for freedom cannot rescue the ethical thinker. Here the burning question (confronted in their own situation in a different way by Deleuze and Guattari, but not necessarily more successfully resolved, as the opposition between the paranoid and the schizo, or the Nomads and the State) remains the distinction between humanism and fascism, between a human and an inhuman ethics—a distinction which the aesthetic metaphysician Malraux later became did not have to respect, in his even-handed appreciation of the arts which celebrate life and those which meditate with fascination on what crushes it ("une extase vers le bas ..."—"il y a aussi quelque chose de ... satisfaisant dans l'écrasement de la vie ...”[123]).

In fact, it does not seem exaggerated to argue that in both Malraux and Heidegger, death and finitude play a crucial role in demarking the authentic

---

[122] André Malraux, *Man's Fate*, trans. Haakon Chevalier, New York: Modern Library, 1961, 227; in French:

> —Rouges ou bleus, disait Ferral, les coolies n'en seront pas moins coolies; à moins qu'ils n'en soient morts. Ne trouvez-vous pas d'une stupidité caractéristique de l'espèce humaine qu'un homme qui n'a qu'une vie puisse la perdre pour une idée?
> —Il est très rare qu'un homme puisse supporter, comment dirais-je? sa condition d'homme ...
> —Il pensa à l'une des idées de Kyo: tout ce pour quoi les hommes acceptent de se faire tuer, au-delà de l'intérêt, tend plus ou moins confusément à justifier cette condition en la fondant en dignité: christianisme pour l'esclavage, nation pour le citoyen, communisme pour l'ouvrier. Mais il n'avait pas envie de discuter des idées de Kyo avec Ferral. Il revint à celui-ci:
> —Il faut toujours s'intoxiquer: ce pays a l'opium, l'Islam le haschisch, l'Occident la femme ... Peut-être l'amour est-il surtout le moyen qu'emploie l'Occidental pour s'affranchir de sa condition d'homme ...
> Sous ses paroles, un contre-courant confus et caché de figures glissait: Tchen et le meurtre, Clappique et sa folie, Katow et la révolution, May et l'amour. lui-même et l'opium ... Kyo seul, pour lui, résistait à ces domaines. (*La Condition humaine*, in *Oeuvres complètes*, tome I, Paris: Gallimard, 1989, 678–679.)

[123] Ibid., *La voie royale*, op. cit., 449.

from the inauthentic: the encounter with death and the death anxiety alone seem to qualify a given choice or experience as an encounter with the Absolute, which is then reduced to this or that way the individual comes to terms with his or her mortality, but not necessarily a mode of access to totality, nor even to the collective. (I hasten to add that the Sartrean version—the encounter with freedom and anxiety—does not necessarily do this either.)

Characteristically, old Gisors excepts the most "committed" of Malraux's characters, his son Kyo, from this relativizing list of absolutes ("Kyo seul, pour lui, résistait à ces domaines") while including Kyo's comrade-in-arms Katow in what looks like a restriction of the political Absolute to a mere passion for "revolution." We may then conjecture that Kyo's relationship to the Absolute and his political practice take a form that transcends mere individualism and its individual passions: a dimension of the collective is at stake here which displaces the experience of human finitude in some way distinct from the anxiety of solitary death (the final scene of the novel, in which Katow sacrifices his cyanide pill, also conveys something of this combination of passions).

Still, is it a question of "values" which are somehow absolute or taken to be such, or is it not rather a relationship to the Absolute which is at stake here (not to speak of a possible resistance to the Absolute, in this case the Absolute of death)? And to what degree does that relationship not insensibly slip from an active or passional set of choices back in the direction of a kind of cognitive or contemplative knowledge, in which somehow knowing the Absolute as totality, glimpsing it in rare moments of its visibility, takes priority over any acts its viewers might perform? Even if death were the Absolute, according to this alternative it would be something only glimpsed in ephemeral moments of lucidity and anxiety. It is not some relativity of absolutes which is in question here: for the contemplative relationship to the Absolute as truth knows its variations fully as much as the passionate or obsessional acting out of a hopeless situation. It is indeed this variety of relations with the Absolute that Heidegger underscores in a decisive and climactic moment of his meditation on art:

> One essential way in which truth establishes itself in the entity opened up or disclosed by it is the setting-itself-into-work of truth [where *Werk* designates the work of art]. Another way in which truth exercises its being is the deed that grounds the state. Still another way in which truth comes to shine forth is the nearness of that which is not simply an entity, but the entity that *is* most of all. Still another way in which truth grounds itself is essential sacrifice. Still another way in which truth becomes, is the thinker's questioning which, as thinking of being, names the latter in its question-worthiness ...[124]

---

[124] I here excerpt "Origin of the Work of Art," in *Philosophies of Art and Beauty*, eds. Albert Hofstadter and Richard Kuhns, Chicago: University of Chicago Press, 1964,

The passage is equally useful in dispelling the religious overtones of the terminology we have been using (absolute, transcendence), insofar as religion is only one of the "ways" Heidegger envisions; and the same may be said for death itself ("essential sacrifice," a euphemism for death in war). Political praxis, however, here regains its rights, in the form of the *staatsgründende Tat*: and it is not superfluous to observe that the very term "praxis" itself (reinvented in its modern form by Count Ciezkowski in 1838) designates a relation to empirical events which includes its own philosophical transcendence within itself.

But despite this (and despite the revolutionary setting of Malraux's great metaphysical novel), nothing seems to guarantee that the Absolute invoked in such meditations should be identified as History.

The phenomenological term "horizon" first deployed by Heidegger and then used by Sartre in his argument about historical unification, offers perhaps the most effective way of ensuring this proposition, which takes as its starting point the conviction that the worldwide triumph of capitalism at one and the same time secures the priority of Marxism as the ultimate horizon of thought in our time. As something like the philosophy of capitalism, then, it is necessary for other thought modes to find their positions and develop their possibilities within Marxism as such. This was not yet the case with modernist passions and absolutes which still disposed of other lines of flight in a global situation which did not yet seem definitively sealed and secured by the logic of capital. Postmodernity, no doubt, has absolutes of its own—as witness the recrudescence of those postmodern religions which are the so-called fundamentalisms—but they are of an altogether different type, governed by a new kind of relativity which may be termed a relativism of the codes, a kind of absolute transcoding.

685; in German: "Eine wesentliche Weise, wie die Wahrheit sich in dem durch sie eröffneten Seienden einrichtet, ist das Sich-insWerk-setzen der Wahrheit. Eine andere Weise, wie Wahrheit west, ist die staatsgründende Tat. Wieder eine andere Weise, wie Wahrheit zum Leuchten kommt, ist die Nähe dessen, was schlechthin nicht ein Seiendes ist, sondern das Seiendste des Seienden. Wieder eine andere Weise, wie Wahrheit sich gründet, ist das wesentliche Opfer. Wieder eine andere Weise, wie Wahrheit wird, ist das Fragen des Denkers, das als Denken des Seins dieses in seiner Frag-würdigkeit nennt." [Ironically, Heidegger goes on to exclude science from these privileged modes of access: "Dagegen ist die Wissenschaft kein ursprüngliches Geschehen der Wahrheit, sondern jeweils der Ausbau eines schon offenen Wahrheitsbereiches, und zwar durch das Auffassen und Begründen dessen, was in seinem Umkreis sich an möglichem und notwendigem Richtigen zeigt. Wenn und sofern eine Wissenschaft über das Richtige hinaus zu einer Wahrheit und d. h. zur wesentlichen Enthüllung des Seienden als solchen kommt, ist sie Philosophie."] *Holzwege*, op. cit., 48.

This is then the horizon within which the Absolute is to be sought today. If one wants to characterize it as secular, then the various religions take their new locations as already relativized and postmodern reinventions of tradition and contemporary passions and life-choices. If one wishes to think this immense domination of History in terms of the sublime, then one must recall those passages in which Edmund Burke (the first great modern theoretician of the sublime) confronts the excesses of the French Revolution with that dizzying nausea which is indeed an *extase vers le bas*; as well as those grim speculations of some of Hegel's most interesting contemporary interpreters (already mentioned) that in fact Absolute Spirit is capital itself. Meanwhile, if one thinks of the sublime as a unification of multiplicities (or at least of one type of such unification), then Sartre's observation that history, which once was multiple, is now ever more unified into a single History, then one must mentally add that the tendential unification of history in globalization transforms it into the History of capitalism as such.

We have indeed secreted a human age out of ourselves as spiders secrete their webs: an immense, all-encompassing ceiling of secularity which shuts down visibility on all sides even as it absorbs all the formerly natural elements in its habitat, transmuting them into its own man-made substance. Yet within this horizon of immanence we wander as alien as tribal people, or as visitors from outer space, admiring its unimaginably complex and fragile filigree and recoiling from its bottomless potholes, lounging against a rainwall of exotic and artificial plants or else agonizing among poisonous colors and lethal stems we were not taught to avoid. The world of the human age is an aesthetic pretext for grinding terror or pathological ecstasy, and in its cosmos, all of it drawn from the very fibers of our own being and at one with us in every post-natural cell more alien to us than nature itself, we continue murmuring Kant's old questions—what can I know? What should I do? What may I hope?—under a starry heaven no more responsive than a mirror or a space ship, not understanding that they require the adjunct of an ugly and bureaucratic representational qualification: what can I know *in this system*? What should I do in this new world *completely invented by me*? What can I hope for *alone in an altogether human age*? And failing to replace them by the only meaningful one, namely how can I recognize this forbiddingly foreign totality as my own doing, how may I appropriate it and make it my own handiwork and acknowledge its laws as my own projection and my own praxis?

As only Marx theorized this historically original secular totality, which is henceforth the horizon of our being, all the absolutes invented within it are at one and the same time an acknowledgement of that ceiling itself, a recognition of our ultimate Being as History. Our individual or existential absolutes must therefore all carry within themselves as their very structure a relationship explicit or implicit to that ultimate Absolute which is History as such: even the transcendental ones are secretly secularized by this vaster existential commitment, so all-encompassing that it is often invisible and like Heidegger's older concept of Being only becomes visible ephemerally, only appears on the mode of disappearing, only emerges on the mode of withdrawal.

For we may also use the code or language of Deleuze and Guattari to evoke a triumph of the axiomatic so complete that only local and ephemeral deterritorializations are henceforth possible, local hobbies and passions, private religions, fantasized ethnicities, gated communities of professional strata, lunchrooms of power, boardrooms of jet-set culture, fortunes that are numerals on a screen, sacrificial deaths which are little more than statistics … These must clearly also include the various radical fantasies to which the name of Marx is sometimes attached: that the old problems—such as party and organization—are still relevant and unsolved does not mean that their literal reinvention in a wholly different geopolitical situation is anything more than yet another reterritorialization.

Anti-globalization perhaps offers a more authentic glimpse of History as a totality and an absolute than any of the older motifs, despite the fact that no satisfactory praxis has yet been invented to come to terms with this horizon of being. The form of the experience is no doubt a negative one and most often richly justifies the characterization of paranoia that has been attributed to it. For it is as a conspiracy that this immense totality of a globalized capitalism is apprehended: and that whether it is conceived as an impersonal system, a kind of unimaginably vast encagement; or whether, on the contrary, it is an act of the combined wills and intentions of an elite (as has palpably been the case with the numerous neo-conservative programs initiated around the world in the 1990s). These alternatives do not reflect factual differences but rather historiographic decisions. They are choices based on a narrative strategy which is essentially ideological in nature (provided that term is understood to include and encompass the philosophical and the metaphysical within itself).

vii. History as Emancipation

So far these options—which correspond to the modes in which History can be perceived, however fleetingly—correspond to the binary structure of a dialectic which, both positive and negative simultaneously, can be inflected or staged either way. But they must also be positioned within a larger opposition in which both versions of conspiracy—as system and as human agency—are united as a single essentially negative term over against a positive one, which now remains to be considered.

Pathos, as the culmination of a properly tragic spectacle, can indeed be expected to have been only the negative counterpart of a quite different celebration in the joyous comic outcome. We do not particularly need to think this in terms of success or failure, although those all-too-human words have occasionally seemed to be useful reminders of what is at stake in this opposition. Yet surely what Kant still terms enthusiasm is not a bad suggestion for the general jubilation one would expect to witness at the end of the comic transformation of the world. Comedy has so often been theorized in terms of the phallic triumph of the young over the old that it should be clear such a triumph is scarcely to be thought of in any of the possible senses of an "end of history"; while myths of renewal and cosmic sunrise, of genesis and the birth of new worlds, are there to add archaic figuration to this great collective sense of History, which may be distant enough from us today, but which is scarcely absent from recorded history as such. Kant's reminder is thus a timely one:

> Such a phenomenon in human history *is not to be forgotten*, because it has revealed a tendency and faculty in human nature for improvement such that no politician, affecting wisdom, might have conjured out of the course of things hitherto existing, and one which nature and freedom alone, united in the human race in conformity with inner principles of right, could have promised.[125]

Such moments, in which History is glimpsed with euphoria, range from the deliverance from unexpected cataclysms all the way to revolution itself. Luck or national good fortune would seem to diminish the teleological overtones of the notion of the providential, inasmuch as the latter still carries within itself something of the more negative baggage of intention or conspiracy (for is not the whole Christian vision of history that of a conspiracy of God to save the descendents of Adam?).

Perhaps indeed the spirit of comedy is better fulfilled by images of breakdown and release, of the suspension of the law or even the dissolution of society itself and the end of encagement. Such images, in the epoch of bourgeois revolutions, expressed salvation as the opening of the prisons, the fall of the Bastille and the great trumpet-call of *Fidelio* that signals the prisoner's liberation from the dungeon. Yet for an established bourgeois society the jubilation of universal freedom is perhaps better rendered by the ending of Dickens's *Bleak House*, in which, to the merriment of the street crowds, the innumerable dossiers of Jarndyce versus Jarndyce are thrown out and the interminable generational trial ends with the exhaustion of the heritage and the discharge of all parties concerned: a true popular festival and one echoed by Marx himself, in the second grand climax of *Capital*, Volume 1 (after the Beethoven-like triumphalism of the prediction of the expropriation of the expropriators).

---

[125] Kant, *The Conflict of the Faculties*, trans. Mary J. Gregor, Lincoln, University of Nebraska Press, 1979, p. 159.

Here, indeed, Marx evokes that sorry expiration of the accumulation process in the settler colonies (and in particular Australia), when no precaution has been taken to bind or indenture the future workers to their appointed tasks. So it is that we witness the sad spectacle of Mr. Peel, who, having shipped to Swan River not only a rich provision of his means of production but also thousands of workers and their families, " 'was left without a servant to make his bed or to fetch him water from the river.' Unhappy Mr. Peel, who provided for everything except the export of English relations of production to Swan River" (*Cap*, 933).

Marx adds that it would have been more prudent in advance to secure these future wage workers by slavery, than to have deposited them, thus unbound, on free soil. And indeed the most magnificent image of the liberation from the constraints of an all-subsuming social order is that of emancipation itself:

> Blacks relished opportunities to flaunt their liberation from the innumerable regulations, significant and trivial, associated with slavery. Freedmen held mass meetings and religious services unrestrained by white surveillance, acquired dogs, guns, and liquor (all barred to them under slavery), and refused to yield the sidewalks to whites. They dressed as they pleased, black women sometimes wearing gaudy finery, carrying parasols, and replacing the slave kerchief with colorful hats and veils. In the summer of 1865, Charleston saw freedmen occupying "some of the best residences," and promenading on King Street "arrayed in silks and satins of all the colors of the rainbow," while black schoolchildren sang " 'John Brown's Body' within ear-shot of Calhoun's tomb." Rural whites complained of "insolence" and "insubordination" among the freedmen, by which they meant any departure from the deference and obedience expected under slavery.
>
> Among the most resented of slavery's restrictions were the rule that no black could travel without a pass and the patrols that enforced the pass system. With emancipation, it seemed that half the South's black population took to the roads. "Right off colored folks started on the move," a Texas slave later recalled. "They seemed to want to get closer to freedom, so they'd know what it was—like it was a place or a city." Blacks' previous treatment as slaves seemed to have little to do with the movement. "Every one of A. M. Dorman's negroes quit him," an Alabama planter reported. "They have always been as free and as much indulged as his children." The ability to come and go as they pleased would long remain a source of pride and excitement for former slaves. "The Negroes are literally crazy about traveling," wrote a white observer in 1877. "The railway officials are continually importuned by them to run extra trains, excursion trains, and so on, on all sorts of occasions: holidays, picnics, Sunday-school celebrations, church dedications."[126]

---

[126] Eric Foner, *Reconstruction: America's Unfinished Revolution, 1863–1877*, New York: Harper and Row, 1988, 79–81.

This is truly jubilee: not simply the remission of debts but the very lifting of the constraints of the social itself in all its forms. It is the true historical analogue of Bakhtin's seasonal carnival, and the comic pendant to those dystopian visions of the breakdown of society in the archetypal "time of troubles," the violence and anarchy of those innumerable apocalyptic visions from Ballard to *Road Warrior* that haunt a middle-class imagination shadowed by thoughts of vengeful underclasses and the undermining of law-and-order. But such a glimpse of History as a happy end is perhaps as rare as Kant's unexpected confrontation with the realization of a transcendental freedom.

It would therefore be prudent, in conclusion, to distinguish such providential outcomes as History affords us from Utopia itself as the absolute opposite of our history as a whole. Returning to earlier speculations about a spatial dialectic, we may argue that in that sense Utopia is no longer in time, just as with the end of the voyages of discovery and the exploration of the globe it disappeared from geographical space as such. Utopia as the absolute negation of that fully realized Absolute which our own system has attained cannot now be imagined as lying ahead of us in historical time as an evolutionary or even a revolutionary possibility. Indeed, it cannot be imagined at all; and one needs the languages and figurations of physics—the conceptions of closed worlds and a multiplicity of unconnected yet simultaneous universes—in order to convey what might be the ontology of this now so seemingly empty and abstract idea. Yet it is not to be grasped in the logic of religious transcendence either, as some other world after or before this one, or beyond it. It would be best, perhaps, to think of an alternate world— better to say the alternate world, our alternate world—as one contiguous with ours but without any connection or access to it. Then, from time to time, like a diseased eyeball in which disturbing flashes of light are perceived or like those baroque sunbursts in which rays from another world suddenly break into this one, we are reminded that Utopia exists and that other systems, other spaces, are still possible.

Acknowledgments

The following chapters are reprinted, in revised form, with permission from the publications in which they first appeared.

The first part of Chapter 3 appeared in *Critical Quarterly*'s fiftieth anniversary issue, 50: 3, 2009, 33–42.

Chapter 4 appeared in *New Left Review* 1: 209, 86–120.

Chapter 5 was first published in the *South Atlantic Quarterly* 96: 3, 1997, 393–416.

Chapter 6 appeared in *Rethinking Marxism* 1: 1, 1998, 49–72.

Chapters 7 and 8 were introductions to volumes 1 and 2 of Jean-Paul Sartre's *Critique of Dialectical Reason* (London: Verso, 2004 and 2006).

Chapter 11 appeared in *Science and Society* 62: 3, 1993, 358–372.

Chapter 12 appeared in *Lenin Reloaded* (Durham, NC: Duke University Press, 2007).

Chapter 13 appeared in the *South Atlantic Quarterly* 104: 4, 2005, 693–706.

Chapter 14 was written for Deakin University, Geelong, Australia.

Chapter 15 appeared in *Polygraph* 6–7, 1993, 170–95.

Chapter 16 will appear under the title "Walmart as Utopia" in *Utopia-Dystopia: Conditions of Historical Possibility* (Princeton, NJ: Princeton University Press, forthcoming 2009).

Chapter 17 appeared in *Cultures of Globalization*, Fredric Jameson and Misao Miyoshi (Durham, NC: Duke University Press, 1998), 54–77.

Chapter 18 appeared as "Globalization and Strategy" in *New Left Review* 2: 49–68.

Index